THE
FIFTY-YEAR
MISSION

FIFTY-YEAR MISSION

THE COMPLETE, UNCENSORED, UNAUTHORIZED
ORAL HISTORY OF *STAR TREK*

The First 25 Years

EDWARD GROSS
& MARK A. ALTMAN

THOMAS DUNNE BOOKS

ST. MARTIN'S PRESS NEW YORK

THOMAS DUNNE BOOKS.
An imprint of St. Martin's Press.

This book was not prepared, approved, licensed, or endorsed by Paramount Pictures, CBS Television, or any other entity involved in creating or producing *Star Trek*.

THE FIFTY-YEAR MISSION: THE COMPLETE, UNCENSORED, UNAUTHORIZED ORAL HISTORY OF *STAR TREK*: THE FIRST 25 YEARS. Copyright © 2016 by Edward Gross and Mark A. Altman. Foreword copyright © 2016 by Seth MacFarlane. All rights reserved. Printed in the United States of America. For information, address St. Martin's Press, 175 Fifth Avenue, New York, N.Y. 10010.

www.thomasdunnebooks.com
www.stmartins.com

The Library of Congress Cataloging-in-Publication Data is available upon request.

ISBN 978-1-250-06584-1 (hardcover)
ISBN 978-1-4668-7285-1 (e-book)

Our books may be purchased in bulk for promotional, educational, or business use. Please contact your local bookseller or the Macmillan Corporate and Premium Sales Department at 1-800-221-7945, extension 5442, or by e-mail at MacmillanSpecialMarkets@macmillan.com.

First Edition: June 2016

10 9 8 7 6 5 4 3 2 1

FROM MARK A. ALTMAN

To my magnificent mom, Gail, for taking me to see *Star Trek: The Motion Picture* when she'd rather have been anywhere else in the galaxy. At least you got to have *The Mommies'* Marilyn Kentz play you in a movie.

To my unforgettable dad, Michael . . . for everything—and even occasionally turning off the baseball, football, hockey, and basketball games to let me watch *Star Trek.*

To my sensational grandfather, Seymour, for stopping and taking me to a *Star Trek* convention in New Jersey when he really just wanted to get home to watch the Jets game.

To my brotastic brother, Ira, for caring about sports and not *Star Trek* so we never competed with each other, Decker.

To my wonderful wife, Naomi, for being the most enterprising woman I know.

And my amazing kids, Ella and Isaac, who helped me get over my aversion to children after watching "And the Children Shall Lead." It's okay that you love the Ewoks . . . really.

And, of course, Frederick S. Clarke; a mentor, a friend, and the man who made this book possible. You showed us all how it's done. Remember.

Finally, Ed Gross. Thanks for being such a nudge. I would have never written this book with you if you hadn't kept bugging me for years about it. I can't imagine doing it with anyone else.

Also special thanks to our editor extraordinaire, Brendan Deneen, for being a *Deep Space Nine* fan, among many other things that make him awesome.

FROM EDWARD GROSS

To my wife and best friend, Eileen. Over thirty years on and we're still boldly going! There's no one I'd rather be on this voyage with. Sorry this book turned you into a *Star Trek* widow.

To my sons, Teddy, Dennis, and Kevin. I am so proud of all three of you, and thrilled beyond words that we share a love for all things geek.

To my mom, dad, sister, and brother. Thanks for all the years of nodding and smiling politely no matter how strange my obsessions seemed.

To my father, who took me to the first *Star Trek* convention ever in 1972. Sorry we didn't connect on much, but that was one moment when we did.

To all of the editors—among them *Starlog*'s David McDonnell, *Cinefantastique*'s Frederick S. Clarke, *Cinescape*'s Douglas Perry, *SFX*'s Dave Golder, *Long Island Nightlife*'s Bill Ervolino, *Movie Magic*'s Karen Williams, *SciFiNow*'s Aaron Asadi, and *Geek*'s David Williams—who saw something in me and my writing and helped keep the dream going for all of these years.

To my friends who have shared my love for *Star Trek* over the years, including John Garry, Kevin Oldham, Tom Sanders, Dexter Frank, Linda Miracco, Scott Milner, Jay Starr, Allen Lane, and Leon McKenzie.

To all of the people connected with *Star Trek* that I've interviewed over the decades. So many of you made it easy to once again talk *Trek* for this book, and it's genuinely appreciated.

To Laurie Fox and Brendan Deneen, respectively agent and editor extraordinaire, for believing in this project as much as we do.

And to Mark A. Altman. Throughout the process of writing this book, I could not imagine a better collaborator or cheerleader. It was such a joy to take this trip back to the Final Frontier with you.

DATABASE

Sam Cogley asked me to give you something special. It's not a first edition or anything, just a book. Sam says that makes it special, though.
—Ariel Shaw, *Star Trek* episode "Court Martial"

Space may be the final frontier. But it's made in a Hollywood basement.
—Red Hot Chili Peppers, "Californication"

There are three sides to every story: your side, my side, and the truth. And no one is lying. Memories shared serve each differently.
—Robert Evans, *The Kid Stays in the Picture*

FOREWORD

BY **Seth MacFarlane**

A llow me to introduce myself. I'm Ensign Rivers.

Even if you're a huge *Star Trek* fan, you may not know who that is. He was an assistant engineer on the first starship *Enterprise*, and although he's hardly the most memorable character I've played, he's one I'm very proud of. It's because he allowed me to be a small part of *Star Trek*, a franchise that has literally changed the world.

No, I'm not exaggerating.

When *Star Trek* creator Gene Roddenberry sold that legendary pilot so many years ago, he was, of course, doing what lots of television writers do: He was creating a series in the hope of a steady paycheck. But that wasn't all he was doing. Because Gene was also a man of passion. He was angry about the suffering and injustice he saw in the world around him. And like other great television writers, such as Rod Serling and Norman Lear, Gene saw the medium as a powerful tool to comment on those injustices. To him, television was more than just a way to tell stories. He saw it as a platform to address things like politics, bigotry, religion, and sex. To him, such usage did not constitute preachiness. On the contrary, he felt it was his responsibility as a thoughtful writer to make a statement; to express a point of view, rather than simply to crank out filmed pablum with which to entertain the masses.

With *Star Trek*, Gene conceived a vision of the future that was unashamedly optimistic: effectively a blueprint for what humanity could become should it eventually succeed in evolving beyond its superstitious, xenophobic adolescence. The show celebrated and glorified the virtues of human ingenuity, scientific advancement, and moral progress. It's a vision that, to me, is sorely lacking in today's entertainment landscape. In our era of *Hunger Games*–flavored dystopian science fiction, there is a conspicuous absence of such worthy models for the future. This should be cause for some concern. Carl Sagan once said, "The visions we offer our children shape the future. It matters what those visions are. Often, they become self-fulfilling prophecies. Dreams are maps. I do not think it is irresponsible to portray even the direst futures. If we are to avoid them we must understand that they are possible. But where are the alternatives? The dreams to motivate and inspire?" Indeed, when I watched *Star Trek* as a child, the moral guidelines it advocated were not lost on me. It *meant* something that those phasers were almost always set on stun, and that the crew never killed unless they had no other choice. Life was presented as precious. And while I loved the shoot-'em-up action of *Star Wars* as much as the rest of my generation, it's *Star Trek* I thank for the fact that, when I find a spider in my house, I am morally obliged to put it outside rather than dispose of it. *All* life is precious. Message received, Gene.

So there is no question that *Star Trek* makes a fine "dream map." It's a world we'd all like to live in. And Gene truly believed we'd get there. He felt that the better, more civilized side of human nature was ultimately the stronger side, and would only grow more dominant as our species evolves. In that belief, he shares some philosophical ground with Martin Luther King, who said, "The moral arc of the universe is long, but it bends toward justice." If this is true, and humanity naturally and inevitably evolves toward ethical maturity (as Michael Shermer powerfully and effectively argues in his book *The Moral Arc*), then there can be no more ideal vision of the future in popular fiction than *Star Trek*.

The teams of artists and artisans who've brought *Star Trek* to life over the last five decades (many of whom have shared their stories with Mark and Ed for their amazing book), have given body and voice to that vision, and in doing so have not only captivated audiences, but also inspired people around the globe to pursue careers in science, engineering, and medicine, to explore outer space, and to work toward finding solutions to many of our problems here on Earth.

In that sense, *Star Trek* has already helped shape our present. When asked about the appeal of the show, Roddenberry said it best in a shining example of his wonderful distaste for mysticism of superstition in favor of respect and regard for human achievement: "*Star Trek* speaks to some basic human needs: that there is a tomorrow—it's not all going to be over with a big flash and a bomb; that the human race is improving; that we have things to be proud of as humans. No, ancient astronauts did not build the pyramids—human beings built them, because they're clever and they work hard."

Unfortunately, I think we still have a ways to go, since there are still plenty of folks who think aliens built the pyramids, and that one of them is Barack Obama (look it up; people really believe that), but we're moving in the right direction.

In this book, Mark and Ed tell the fascinating story of that rare Hollywood product that actually means something to mankind. And though it can sometimes be difficult to maintain hope for our prospects as a species, I'm optimistic that, by the twenty-third century, things will be better than they are now. Maybe that's because *Star Trek* has inspired me so much in my work and in my life. Or maybe it's because I'm already living there.

Remember, I'm Ensign Rivers.

Seth MacFarlane is an animator, voice actor, screenwriter, producer, and filmmaker. He is the creator of the TV series *Family Guy*, cocreator of the TV series *American Dad!* and *The Cleveland Show*, and writer-director of the films *Ted*, its sequel *Ted 2*, and *A Million Ways to Die in the West*. He is an acclaimed singer and pianist as well.

MacFarlane also served as executive producer of the Emmy Award–winning *Cosmos: A Spacetime Odyssey*, an update of the Carl Sagan–hosted *Cosmos* series, hosted by Neil deGrasse Tyson.

WHAT A LONG STRANGE TREK IT'S BEEN

Mark A. Altman

HOLLYWOOD IS THE ONLY BUSINESS WHERE
YOU GET TO SHAKE HANDS WITH YOUR DREAMS
—writer/director NICHOLAS MEYER

Sitting across from me at a small table in a cluttered room in a Miami cemetery was the bearded rabbi with a small yarmulke resting atop his mop of thick gray hair, who was about to conduct my grandmother Edna's graveside funeral. As we all sat around in a melancholy haze as the fateful time approached to bury Edna, I'll never forget the words he shared with me when he found out what I did for a living at the time. "I love *Star Trek*," he stammered excitedly. "You know why I think that show is so significant? Every story had a moral; it was a parable for the same ethical issues we grapple with in religion every day. I think it's a very meaningful and important show. The original, at least. The others were crap."

Now, I wouldn't necessarily say "amen" to that (although admittedly some of the series are *way* better than others), but the reality is the original *Star Trek* was the center of the Big Bang that gave birth to a universe that is still expanding to this day. From the voyages of the original starship *Enterprise* (no bloody *A, B, C,* or *D*) as well as their animated adventures, to the *Next Generation* of twenty-fourth-century explorers, the gallant crew of the wildly underrated *Deep Space Nine*, the *Voyager* ensemble lost in space, Captain Archer and the crew members of *Enterprise* and, of course, J. J. Abrams's latest reinvention of one of pop culture's most beloved and lucrative franchises.

One can't escape the inexorable gravitational pull of *Star Trek*, much like the Beta Nairobi nova. I know I haven't. Ever since September 8, 1966, I've always had a very special connection to the *Star Trek* universe. It might have something to do with the fact we both made our respective debuts on this planet the same year. I'm not sure exactly when I first discovered *Star Trek*, but I do have vivid recollections of obsessively watching the series every weeknight at six o'clock back on WPIX in New York City ("Oh no, not 'The Way to Eden' *again*!") and lashing out at the television when a self-professed Trekspert on *The $100,000 Pyramid* responded dumbfoundedly to a question about the name of the ship that was destroyed in "The Doomsday Machine" ("The *Constellation*, you moron!"). Yes, I loved *Star Trek* . . . a lot.

It was shortly thereafter that I waited on line for several hours to get the late Leonard Nimoy's autograph at Macy's inside the Kings Plaza Mall in Brooklyn, New York (probably the first—and last—time I ever cared about such things). But knowing this was the man who had called his first autobiography *I Am Not Spock*, I decided I would cleverly avoid asking anything about Spock and instead inquire about *In Search Of* . . . . Because in my sadly deluded mind, I was just the coolest nine-year-old on my block. (And in case you were wondering, he didn't go to any of the exciting locales they visited in that series; Nimoy just did the voice-overs. Seems obvious now, but back then it was less than readily apparent.) It was an exciting time to be a *Trek* fan. Rumors of a new series or movie, the release of Franz Joseph's brilliant *Star Trek Blueprints,* followed by the the even more sensational *Star Fleet Technical Manual*, Susan Sackett's *Letters to Star Trek*; as well as Jacqueline Lichtenberg, Sondra Marshak, and Joan Winston's *Star Trek Lives!,* the birth of *Starlog,* and a litany of novels, poster books, and Mego action figures (I went on that mission to Gamma VI *a lot* as a kid).

In the years ahead, I continued to passionately follow *Trek*. As anyone who's familiar with my first feature film, *Free Enterprise,* may recall, my junior-high-school friends and I went to see *Star Trek: The Motion Picture* excitedly on the day it debuted, December 7, 1979, *another* day that shall live in infamy. After we were turned away from the box office by an overearnest ticket taker who refused to allow children under sixteen into a G-rated movie due to some recent unruly theatregoers, I was forced to boldly seek out my mother at a nearby bank as she was depositing her paycheck with a teller (this was *way* before ATMs, you know) and prevailed on her desperately to accompany us to the film since they wouldn't let us in otherwise. She did—and she's never forgiven me since.

Many years later, I was visiting Los Angeles for the first time and found myself on the Paramount lot, where I got a giddy thrill from seeing Starfleet uniform–clad extras for the first time milling around during a break at the studio commissary as production commenced on "Encounter at Farpoint," the premiere of the then-new series, *Star Trek: The Next Generation*. It's hard to understand now—it was almost impossible to believe at the time—but *Star Trek* was finally coming back to television two decades after its inauspicious cancellation on NBC. It was with an all-new cast, but with much of the same creative team in place that had stewarded the original seventy-nine episodes, spearheaded by the so-called Great Bird of the Galaxy himself, Gene Roddenberry. At least, for the time being.

A few months later, as editor in chief of my college newspaper, *The Justice,* I received a query letter from Paramount publicity as part of their first-season press kit for the series that suggested ways news outlets could cover their new show. They were desperate for some good press (*any* press, actually) and success was in no way assured. Buried amongst all the hyperbole about this exciting new program was the suggestion of a set visit. Sounded good to me. I proceeded to hastily arrange for myself and my two best friends (my college roommate and the copublisher of a mimeographed fanzine I had produced since I was ten, *Galactic Journal*) to make the trek out to Hollywood to visit the set. We arrived in sunny Los Angeles ready to beam down to Paramount Pictures Stage 8 where the first-season episode "Too Short a Season" was filming, and we proceeded to spend the day interviewing the new cast and crew. Mitchell Rubinstein, my college roommate, still waxes nostalgic about the lobster he shared with "the very visual Rob Legato" that day in the studio commissary. For me, it would be the first of many visits.

Shortly thereafter, a professor of mine at Brandeis, who contributed many thoughtful analyses to the preeminent genre magazine of its time, *Cinefantas-tique,* introduced me to its publisher and enfant terrible, the late, great Frederick S. Clarke. Fred was J. Jonah Jameson incarnate. A man who did not suffer fools gladly and unlike others in the field was not a cheerleader for every schlocky sci-fi film or TV series that came down the pike, but a hardheaded, even harder to please arbiter of taste. I could never watch Jason Robards in *All the President's Men* as Ben Bradlee without thinking of Fred . . . and still can't. He offered me a chance to write about the series' revolving door for writers during that turbulent first year in space. And I did. Fred was happy . . . and I was ebullient. And it was the beginning of a beautiful professional friendship as I contributed numerous feature stories to the magazine over the next several years (prompting a deluge of mail from readers to beg him to *stop* covering *Star Trek* every issue, but they sold so well that he kept printing them incessantly) in which I used to joke I spoke to everyone associated with *The Next Generation* with the possible excep-tion of the gaffer and the craft service PA . . . mostly because I got paid by the word. In the heady days before the Internet decimated print journalism, not to mention quality entertainment journalism in general, this gave me unprece-dented access to the show for its seven-year run and its savvy creative team.

It was about this time that another writer, who was a frequent contributor to *Starlog, Cinefantastique*'s less erudite but equally essential periodical, contacted me, the jocular Edward Gross. Ed, who had spent years interviewing virtually every living member of the original *TOS* production team and has an insatiable and buoyant enthusiasm for the subject matter, suggested we might make good collaborators, and we subsequently worked together on a number of projects culminating with this—I suspect, and hope—definitive accounting of the past, present, and future of the *Star Trek* franchise.

Covering *Star Trek* for those many years for *CFQ* proved a film school of a sort as I learned about the minutiae of television production, inside and out. When offered my own genre magazine to launch by none other than the infamous Larry Flynt, I jumped at the opportunity, with Fred's blessing, and *Sci-Fi Universe*, the self-proclaimed magazine for sci-fi fans with a life, was born. Snarky and smart, *Sci-Fi Universe* was a great and beloved magazine that also undermined my relationship with the *Trek* brain trust when our honesty proved a little too, well, honest. After that magazine was sold, I was done with genre journalism forever . . . or so I thought.

My days at *Sci-Fi Universe* proved to be the basis for my first feature film, originally called *Trekkers*, later *Free Enterprise*. If they say "write what you know," then *Free Enterprise* certainly validated that axiom. The film, about two die-hard and dysfunctional *Star Trek* fans who meet their idol, William Shatner, and find out that he's more screwed up than they are, was the opportunity of a lifetime. Not only did I get to write and produce my first movie, but it starred William Shatner, a man I had admired and idolized since I was in utero. And still do.

Prior to the film's premiere—it opened in theaters in 1999, propitiously on June 4, the same date that *The Wrath of Khan* was released in 1982—director Robert Burnett and I traveled to the Cannes Film Festival with Mr. Shatner . . . or Bill, as he preferred to be called. Although he was on the Concorde and we were flying coach on Delta, it was a wonderful week of screenings and walking (more often staggering) along the Croisette as Bill admired the view of the beach and winked with a sly grin as he muttered in his legendary staccato fashion, "Topless . . . topless is good." A few hours later he was giving away a bomber jacket to Planet Hollywood Cannes that he had worn in the film, telling the assembled throngs of press that he unearthed it in a secondhand thrift store in Los Angeles and that it had once belonged to the famous World War I flying ace Eddie Rickenbacker. He added that he was now returning it to the beaches of France.

I was stunned. How come he had never told *us* this? What an incredible find. "I made it up" was his simple and elegant reply. And I learned something that day about the art of great storytelling and a great storyteller.

Because in the end, the magic that had always endeared *Star Trek* to me wasn't necessarily its optimistic (some would say, Pollyannaish) view of the future, the gee-whiz and prescient peek at the technology of tomorrow (although I did dig those sliding doors and Automat-like replicators), the cutting edge of visual-effects technology or even the great writing, directing, and scores. It was its anchor: William Shatner as Kirk. A man who, I've often said, had the respect of his crew, the loyalty of his friends, and a green girl on every planet. What more could you ask for in life? But perhaps that's too frivolous an answer. Maybe the rabbi was right, maybe there's more to this *Star Trek* stuff than just some cool spaceships and crazy alien characters. The thing about Kirk that makes him a great leader is that while he is open and inviting of the opinions of others, he's ultimately decisive, smart, and insatiably curious. And willing to disregard rules and regulations when necessary. He is a leader in the best sense of the word. John F. Kennedy by way of Bill Clinton. With the debut of *The Next Generation*, Captain Picard proved a different type of leader for a different era. Not the twenty-fourth century, mind you, but the early 1990s. He was a consensus builder, and thoughtful and deliberate; George H. W. Bush meets Barack Obama. These two templates would color the captains that would follow and forever define what *Star Trek* was for a generation of viewers.

While *Star Wars* is wonderfully elevated pulp, *Star Trek* is something else entirely. At its heart have always been characters who are a family, united by friendship, loyalty, and an insatiable curiosity about the unknown. In a culture in which cynicism and fatalism are the currency of the day—whether it be because of political gridlock, economic depression, famine, or the horror of disease—in which all our best contemporary television series from *Breaking Bad* to *The Walking Dead* plumb the darkness of man, what makes *Star Trek* so unique is that even when it goes into the heart of darkness, it still manages to come out the other side extolling the human adventure with a palpable sense of optimism and hope for the future. It's a progressive, liberal vision that is to be lauded and not deconstructed or replaced with the fashionable pessimism that permeates the zeitgeist of today. I don't think optimism needs to be old-fashioned, but it needs to be earned. In the end, it's harder to write characters that aspire and situations that inspire without being hokey and, dare I say, passé. It doesn't mean there can't be conflict—there must be both interpersonal and interstellar conflict in order for *Star Trek* to be good drama—but humanity united has always been at the very heart of *Star Trek* rather than humanity divided. At its best it's space opera writ large with something profound to say about the human condition.

Since *Free Enterprise*, I've produced many films and worked on a number of popular TV series, but *Star Trek* has continued to remain a source of continued fascination for me. After Fred Clarke's death, I was involved with the acquisition of *Cinefantastique* and published it for several years with Mark Gottwald until selling it, and even launched the fictional *Geek Magazine* featured in, you guessed it, *Free Enterprise* as a real publication.

But I never suspected that one day I would find myself once again going back to the future. So when Ed Gross approached me with the suggestion that we create the definitive history of the *Star Trek* franchise for the show's fiftieth anniversary, I didn't exactly jump at the chance at first. Frankly, I didn't know if there was anything left to say. But I was embarrassingly wrong. It was shortly after reading a lively and lacerating oral history of MTV, as well as Tom Shales's magnificent *Live From New York* about *Saturday Night Live,* that I realized that Ed and I were in a unique position to tell the *Star Trek* story in a new, fresh, and, most important, uncensored way that no one had before . . . and no one else could. And while it would mean reaching out to hundreds of actors, writers, craftsmen, sociologists, executives, and fans again for new insights on the dawn of its fifth decade in space, it would also allow us to honor the many richly gifted and all too deserving talents whom we have spoken to over the last thirty years who are no longer with us to tell their stories: Gene Roddenberry, Gene L. Coon, DeForest Kelley, James Doohan, John Meredyth Lucas, Ricardo Montalban, Michael Piller, Harve Bennett, and the remarkable Leonard Nimoy . . . the list is sadly all too long to recount here.

So our mission was clear. Our mantra: learn all that is learnable, know all that is knowable . . . and print not the legend but the real story. The whole truth and nothing but the truth. And that's what you now hold in your hands. I am immensely proud of this volume and, if I hadn't written it, you could bet credits to navy beans, I would be reading it.

It is my sincere hope this isn't a book cherished by just Trekkies, Trekkers, and Trekophiles, but rather anyone who's interested in the truly Shakespearean drama behind the scenes of the making of an iconic television series. You don't need to love *Star Trek*—or even have seen *Star Trek*—to appreciate the Herculean (some would say Sisyphean) task of creating and re-creating this franchise, but as Groucho Marx might add, it couldn't hurt.

In the end, I don't think this is necessarily a traditional work of scholarship or even an artifact of a pop-culture phenomena. After all, the original *Star Trek* series easily ranks alongside *The Twilight Zone, Hill Street Blues, Crime Story, Twin Peaks, The Sopranos, The Wire, Arrested Development, Breaking Bad,* and *Mad Men* as one of the greatest television series ever made. This book is a love letter. It's a love letter to a show that has given us so much . . . and, hopefully, will continue to do so until the twenty-third century and beyond. And if you don't get it already, maybe you will after reading this volume.

Live long and prosper,
Mark A. Altman
September 8, 2015

REFLECTIONS ON THE TREK OF A LIFETIME

Edward Gross

My three sons' most passionate involvement with *Star Trek* has been the Abramsverse film efforts, so I found it particularly interesting when my middle son, Dennis, and I were watching 1991's *Star Trek VI: The Undiscovered Country*. As William Shatner's Kirk offered commentary on what the adventure we'd just watched was all about, Dennis turned to me with a thoughtful expression on his face and mused, "*Star Trek*'s supposed to be *about* something, isn't it?"

If I'd had any Romulan ale in the house, I'd have offered the lad a toast.

Of course, when I first discovered *Star Trek* sometime during its 1966–69 run, I wasn't *really* aware that it was supposed to be about something either. After all, I was somewhere between the ages of six and nine, and my greatest memories of those days were "playing" *Star Trek* with my friends. John Garry was Captain Kirk, Raymond Ciccolella was Spock, and I was "Bones" McCoy, armed with a toy binocular case as my tricorder and a Tiger water gun as a phaser. Together, we secured Brooklyn, New York, in general and Schenectady Avenue in particular for the Federation!

Flash-forward to January 1972 and New York City's Statler Hilton Hotel. The first *Star Trek* convention, and *I* was there. Not that I have many clear memories of that day, beyond the fact that there was a long line of people waiting for . . . something. My eleven-year-old self looked up at a nearby adult and asked what the line was for. When he replied, "Gene Roddenberry's autograph," and I said,

"Who's Gene Roddenberry?," he just shook his head sadly and offered, "You're on the wrong line, kid."

Maybe. But I'd eventually find my way.

Throughout the seventies, as I watched *Star Trek* five nights a week at six on New York's WPIX, my love for the show grew to the point of near obsession. It was during this time that I, too, came to realize that *Star Trek* was *about* something; that the relationship between Kirk, Spock, and McCoy had a life to it that seemed to transcend ordinary television and sparked my imagination, making me conscious of true character interaction and giving me new personal heroes to add to a pantheon that included Superman, James Bond, and Caesar (not Julius, but the chimp from the original *Planet of the Apes* films).

Reruns, additional conventions, novels, and poster books devoted to the show, gleaning any information on possible revivals in the pages of *Starlog* magazine, excitement over *Star Trek: Phase II* (the series that was never to be), and anticipation for *Star Trek: The Motion Picture* made up much of that decade for me. I remember on the morning of December 7, 1979, that the entire newspaper staff of Suffolk County Community College joined me on a trip to Sunrise Mall in Nassau County and the only multiplex on Long Island, New York, showing a morning performance of *Star Trek: The Motion Picture*. We watched the film and then headed back to the newspaper office, where I pounded out a review, giving it three and a half stars and proclaiming in the headline, "*Star Trek: The Motion Picture*: Worth the Wait!" I headed back to theatres on December 8 to be transported to the twenty-third century once again and wondered where the film I'd seen the day before had gone. Obviously I'd gotten caught in some sort of transporter malfunction involving the space-time continuum.

I still remember the press screening, in the first week of June 1982, of the sequel, *The Wrath of Khan*. We watched the trailer that played on a loop at an outside kiosk at the Manhattan theatre and couldn't believe how incredible it looked. A few hours later it was obvious that *this* film had lived up to its hype. *Star Trek* was back!

A year later, my career in entertainment journalism began as I sold a story on the James Bond film *Octopussy* to *Daredevils* magazine and received my first-ever payment for writing: fifteen dollars! In 1985, I began writing for *Starlog* magazine, for which—among many other subjects—I interviewed a wide-ranging number of writers and directors from the original *Star Trek,* discovering in years to come that I had probably covered that show more than just about anyone else.

As time went on, my love for *Trek* dovetailed perfectly with my journalistic ambitions, resulting in a number of career highlights:

- Endlessly fascinated by *Phase II* and the *Star Trek* that could have been but wasn't, I began researching that proposed show, conducting many interviews and piecing together the story that had never been told.

- Sitting with Leonard Nimoy—the man from Vulcan himself—in his New York Paramount office in November 1986 to discuss *Star Trek IV: The Voyage Home.* My twenty-six-year-old brain couldn't comprehend how it was possible that I could actually have been sitting there talking to *him.*

- A year after the 1987 launch of *Star Trek: The Next Generation,* I found myself in California and uncovering the *true* behind-the-scenes story of the tumultuous start-up period for that show, meeting with the likes of the late Herb Wright, David Gerrold, and Dorothy Fontana, and obtaining a wide variety of resource material—much of the results of which are being revealed for the first time in the pages of Volume Two of this book

- Becoming the *Star Trek* "go-to" guy for magazines like *Cinescape, SFX,* and *SciFiNow,* interviewing cast and crew of the various series and films.

- Meeting William Shatner and Patrick Stewart at the *Generations* junket, and having Patrick Stewart remember me two years later when I was on the set of *First Contact.* And in terms of the latter, being shocked when director Jonathan Frakes started referring to Sir Patrick as Butt-Head—*until* I saw the Beavis and Butt-Head T-shirt the good captain was wearing.

- With the arrival of *Deep Space Nine*—the only one of the spin-off series that came *this* close to rivaling the original in my heart—connecting with the various producers who, each year, took the time to discuss that season's episodes with me.

- Visiting the set of *Voyager* and sitting down to chat with Captain Janeway's real-life alter ego, Kate Mulgrew, and, in one of her first interviews after being signed to the show as Seven of Nine, Jeri Ryan.

- Being among the first to interview the entire cast of *Enterprise* to preview the last *Star Trek* series to date.

- Continuing my tradition of *Star Trek* coverage by interviewing J. J. Abrams, Chris Pine, and various cast and crew members making the 2009 and 2013 rebooted universe, *Star Trek* and *Star Trek Into Darkness,* for *Movie Magic* and *SciFiNow* magazines.

In between all of this, I became aware of Mark A. Altman through his own magazine, *Galactic Journal,* and his in-depth coverage of *Star Trek: The Next Generation* in *Cinefantastique.* After giving him a call, we instantly connected and established a professional and personal friendship that's lasted for nearly three decades, no doubt fueled by our mutual love for *Star Trek,* James Bond, and *Wiseguy* (and if you don't know what that is, go stream it as soon as you're finished with this book!).

In the years since, a number of things changed, among them the diminishing of interest in *Star Trek* as a whole, many believing that it was at least partially due to oversaturation between television series and feature films. Then there was the rise of the Internet, which in turn played havoc with the publishing industry, the belief being that anything people would want on a particular pop-culture subject, they could find online.

We disagree.

For starters, on the eve of its fiftieth anniversary, *Star Trek* is very much back, the success of the Abrams films serving as a reminder to the media and the public of what *Star Trek* was all about, reinvigorating the franchise—particularly the original series—in the process.

And as far as the Internet is concerned, you simply cannot get *everything* online that you could get from a book. Especially *this* book.

When Mark and I agreed to collaborate on *The Fifty-Year Mission,* we believed that, given our decades of research, and the hundreds of new interviews we would be conducting, we could tell the real history of *Star Trek* in a way that no one else would be able to. That we could take this thing that has meant so much to us for almost our entire lives—and to millions of people around the world—and serve as its caretakers, crafting a telling of its history unlike any that has been presented before.

The writing of *The Fifty-Year Mission* has been a genuine labor of love. Our way of giving something back to a universe that has given us *so* much, and promises to do so for the rest of our lives.

Edward Gross
August 2015

DRAMATIS PERSONAE

STAR TREK ABBREVIATIONS

Star Trek: The Original Series: TOS
Star Trek: The Animated Series: TAS
Star Trek: Phase II: Phase II
Star Trek: The Next Generation: TNG
Star Trek: Deep Space Nine: DS9
Star Trek: Voyager: VOY
Star Trek: Enterprise: ENT
Star Trek: The Motion Picture: TMP
Star Trek II: The Wrath of Khan: STII
Star Trek III: The Search for Spock: STIII
Star Trek IV: The Voyage Home: STIV
Star Trek V: The Final Frontier: STV
Star Trek VI: The Undiscovered Country: STVI
Star Trek: Generations: Generations
Star Trek: First Contact: First Contact
Star Trek: Insurrection: Insurrection
Star Trek: Nemesis: Nemesis
Star Trek (2009): Star Trek
Star Trek Into Darkness: Star Trek Into Darkness

J. J. ABRAMS is a director, producer, and writer best known for his work directing *Star Trek, Star Trek Into Darkness, Super 8,* and *Star Wars: The Force Awakens.* He is also the cocreator of the hit TV series *Lost, Alias,* and *Felicity.*

MARTIN ABRAMS is the cofounder of Abrams Gentile Entertainment (AGE). Previously he had been president of the Mego Corporation, which was the original manufacturer of *Star Trek* action figures in the mid-1970s.

LARRY ALEXANDER is a television writer who has written episodes for such series as *The Streets of San Francisco, MacGyver, The Six Million Dollar Man,* and *Phase II.*

HOWARD A. ANDERSON was a cinematographer who worked in special effects and was president of the special-effects house The Howard Anderson Company, which produced the visual effects for *TOS*.

MICHAEL ANSARA was a stage, screen, and voice actor. He is known for his portrayals of Cochise in the series *Broken Arrow* and Commander Kang—who needs no "urging to hate humans"—on three different *Star Trek* series.

DEBORAH ARAKELIAN is an Emmy-nominated television writer who wrote episodes of *Cagney & Lacey* and *Quantum Leap*. She also worked as a production assistant to Harve Bennett on *STII* and *STIII*.

MARGARET ARMEN is a television writer who wrote episodes for *Wonder Woman*, *TOS*, *TAS*, and *Phase II*.

RICHARD ARNOLD is a former research consultant on *TNG*, holding the position of official "*Star Trek* archivist."

RENE AUBERJONOIS is a screen and stage actor. He is known for his role as Father Mulcahy in the feature film *M*A*S*H*, Clayton Endicott III on *Benson*, and Odo on *DS9*.

JEFF AYERS is the author of *Voyages of Imagination: The Star Trek Fiction Companion*.

SCOTT BAKULA is an actor known for his roles on *Quantum Leap, Men of a Certain Age,* and *NCIS: New Orleans,* and as Captain Jonathan Archer on *ENT*.

IRA STEVEN BEHR is a television writer and producer best known as an executive producer and showrunner on *DS9*. He is currently a writer and executive producer on *Outlander* and has previously worked on such series as *Fame, Alphas,* the TV version of *Crash,* and *TNG*.

HANS BEIMLER is a television writer known for his work on *TNG* and *DS9*.

HARVE BENNETT was a television and film producer as well as a screenwriter. He was an Emmy Award–winning producer and occasional writer, and produced *STII* through *STV*. Among the TV series he produced were *The Mod Squad, The Six Million Dollar Man, The Bionic Woman*, and the miniseries *A Woman Called Golda*.

RICK BERMAN is a former documentarian and producer of *The Big Blue Marble* for PBS and studio executive who went on to executive produce *TNG*, later cocreating and producing *DS9, VOY,* and *ENT*. He was also a producer on all of the *TNG* feature films.

JEROME BIXBY was an author, editor, and television writer. He is known for writing the short story "It's a Good Life" (adapted into an episode of *The Twilight Zone*) and writing several episodes of *TOS*.

CHRIS BLACK is a television writer and producer. He has worked on such series as *Desperate Housewives, Ugly Betty, Reaper, Sliders, Mad Men, Outcast,* and *ENT*.

JOHN D. F. BLACK is a television writer, producer, and director who is known for his work on such series as *The Mary Tyler Moore Show* and as story editor on *TOS*.

MARY BLACK is the former assistant to John D. F. Black, whom she later married, on *TOS*.

ROBERT BLACKMAN is a television and film costume designer. He is known for his work on *TNG, DS9, VOY, ENT, Pushing Daisies, Rizzoli & Isles,* and *GCB*.

ROBERT BLOCH was the legendary sci-fi, crime, and horror writer who is best known as the author of the novel *Psycho*, on which the classic Hitchcock film was based. He also wrote several episodes of *TOS* as well as episodes of *Alfred Hitchcock Presents* and *Thriller*.

RICHARD BLOCK is the former vice president and general manager of Kaiser Broadcasting Corporation who made the original television syndication deal for *TOS*.

MARGARET WANDER BONANNO is an author best known for her bestselling *Star Trek* novels, which include *Dwellers in the Crucible* and *Strangers from the Sky*.

ANDRE BORMANIS is the former science consultant to several *Star Trek* series and has written for *VOY* and *ENT*. He was also technical consultant on *Insurrection*.

BRANNON BRAGA is a television writer, producer, and director. He is known for his work on such shows as *Threshold, Terra Nova, Flash Forward, 24, Salem, Cosmos: A Spacetime Odyssey, TNG,* and *VOY*. He was executive producer and cocreator of *ENT*. He also cowrote the screenplays for *Generations* and *First Contact* as well as the story for *Mission: Impossible II*.

LARRY BRODY is a television writer who has worked on shows that include *The Six Million Dollar Man, Manimal, The Fall Guy, The New Mike Hammer* (which he cocreated), and *TAS*.

FRED BRONSON is a journalist, author, television writer, and former network publicity executive at NBC. He is known for his Chart Beat column in *Billboard* magazine and wrote episodes for *TAS* and *TNG*.

ROLLAND "BUD" BROOKS was an art director on *TOS*, beginning with the second pilot, "Where No Man Has Gone Before." He also worked on the TV series *Hogan's Heroes, The Untouchables,* and *Mission: Impossible*.

JUDY BURNS is a television writer who has written episodes for such shows as *Knight Rider, The Bionic Woman,* and *TOS*.

ROBERT BUTLER is a prolific television and film director. He is best known for directing the pilots for *TOS, Hill Street Blues, Batman, Remington Steele, Lois & Clark: The New Adventures of Superman,* and *Moonlighting*.

WILLIAM CAMPBELL was an actor who had a long career appearing in such shows as *Bonanza, Gunsmoke, TOS,* and *DS9*.

STEVEN W. CARABATSOS is a television writer who has written episodes for such shows as *Kojak, The Fugitive,* and *TOS*, for which he served as script consultant.

ROGER C. CARMEL was the actor who played the lovable rogue Harcourt Fenton Mudd on *Star Trek* (and provided his voice for the animated series' "Mudd's Passion"). He was a frequent guest star in such series as *Banacek, Voyage to the Bottom of the Sea, Hawaii Five-O* and played the villainous Colonel Gumm on *Batman*. He was being considered to reprise his role of Harry Mudd for *Star Trek: The Next Generation* in 1986 when he died.

KIM CATTRALL is a film and television actress. She starred as Samantha Jones in the HBO series *Sex and the City* and portrayed Valeris in *STVI*.

DENNIS LYNTON CLARK is a writer for television and film. He wrote the book as well as the screenplay adaptation of *Comes a Horseman* and worked on *TMP*.

RICHARD COLLA was a television and film director. He directed the three-hour premiere episode of *Battlestar Galactica* (1978) as well as episodes of *Miami Vice* and *TNG*.

ROBERT L. COLLINS directed numerous TV movies and series including episodes of *The Bold Ones, Police Story,* and *Marcus Welby, M.D.* He was the director of the unproduced *Phase II* pilot and for a time was the original director for what would become *TMP*.

STEPHEN COLLINS is an actor, writer, director, and musician. He is known for his role as Eric Camden on *7th Heaven* and Captain Will Decker in *TMP*.

LESTER COLODNY was a friend of Gene L. Coon's and a producer, writer, and theatrical literary agent who represented such clients as Neil Simon, Mel Brooks, and Jerry Lewis

JEFFREY COMBS is a television and film actor. He has portrayed various roles on *DS9, VOY,* and *ENT,* and memorably starred as Dr. Herbert West in *Re-Animator*.

JAMES L. CONWAY is a film and television director whose work includes *Supernatural, Charmed, Burke's Law,* and Sunn Classic Pictures' *Hangar 18* and *In Search of Noah's Ark,* as well as episodes of *TNG, DS9, VOY,* and the two-hour premiere of *ENT*.

CHARLES CORRELL was a cinematographer and television director. He was the director of photography on *STIII*.

MANNY COTO is a writer, director, and producer for film and television. He is best known as the executive producer and showrunner for *24, Dexter,* and *ENT,* as well as cocreator of *Odyssey Five* for Showtime.

ALEXANDER COURAGE was an orchestrator, composer, and arranger of music. He is best known for composing the theme music for *TOS*.

YVONNE CRAIG was a ballet dancer and actress. She is best known for her legendary role as Batgirl in the television series *Batman* as well as the green Orion slave girl Marta in *TOS*.

OLIVER CRAWFORD was a screenwriter and author. He worked on a variety of television series including *Bonanza, Perry Mason,* and *TOS.*

JOSHUA CULP is the former assistant to uncredited *TMP* screenwriter Dennis Lynton Clark and brother of *ENT* actor Steven Culp.

ROBIN CURTIS is a film actress who is best known for her role as Lieutenant Saavik in *STIII* and *STIV.* She also appeared in the *TNG* episode "Gambit."

MARC CUSHMAN is best known as the author of *These Are the Voyages,* a series of in-depth books devoted to the making of *TOS.*

MARC DANIELS was a television director who worked on a variety of series, including *I Love Lucy, Gunsmoke,* and *TOS.*

ROXANN DAWSON is a television actress and director. She is best known for portraying the role of B'Elanna Torres in *VOY.*

FRED DEKKER is a television director and writer. His films include *Night of the Creeps, The Monster Squad,* and *Robocop III,* and he worked as a consulting producer on *ENT.* He is currently writing a remake of *Predator* for 20th Century–Fox.

DEAN DEVLIN is the executive producer of such TV series as *Leverage* and *The Librarians.* He was a cowriter and producer on such hit films as *Stargate, Independence Day,* and *The Patriot.* He recently directed his first film, *Geostorm,* for Warner Bros.

DAREN DOCHTERMAN is a film illustrator and conceptual designer. He has worked on such films as *Get Smart, TRON: Legacy,* and *Monster House* and was the visual-effects supervisor on the director's edition of *TMP.*

THOMAS DOHERTY is a professor of American studies at Brandeis University and author of such books as *Pre-Code Hollywood: Sex, Immorality, and Insurrection in American Cinema; Hollywood and Hitler: 1933–1939; Teenagers and Teenpics: Juvenilization of American Movies in the 1950s;* and *Cold War, Cool Medium: Television, McCarthyism, and American Culture.*

JAMES DOOHAN was a television and film actor and veteran of the invasion of Normandy as part of the Royal Regiment of Canadian Artillery. He is best known for his role of Chief Engineer Montgomery Scott in *TOS, TAS,* and the films based on the series, as well as such shows as *Jason of Star Command* and *Homeboys from Outer Space.* His son, Chris Doohan, plays Scotty in the fan film series *Star Trek Continues.*

DOUG DREXLER is as visual-effects artist, designer, sculptor, illustrator, and makeup artist. He worked as a makeup artist on *Dick Tracy,* for which he won an Oscar, and *TNG.* He went on to work as a designer, digital artist, and effects artist on *DS9, VOY,* and *ENT.*

RENE ECHEVARRIA is a television writer and producer. He has worked on a variety of shows including *The 4400, Terra Nova, Castle,* and *TNG,* and as supervising producer on *DS9.*

EDDIE EGAN is a veteran publicist/marketer with nearly four decades of experience in the motion picture industry. He was on the Paramount publicity team for *TMP* and served as unit publicist on *STII–IV.*

CLIFF EIDELMAN is a film composer who scored *Star Trek VI: The Undiscovered Country.*

HARLAN ELLISON is a legendary award-winning author, screenwriter, and raconteur. He has written for *The Twilight Zone, Babylon 5,* and *TOS.*

JOEL ENGEL is a journalist and author of the book *Gene Roddenberry: The Myth and the Man Behind Star Trek.*

DAVID FEIN is a producer who oversaw the director's edition DVD release of *TMP* for Robert Wise Productions.

JACKIE COON FERNANDEZ was married to *Star Trek* writer Gene L. Coon.

BRAN FERREN is the founder of Associates & Ferren, which created the visual effects for *STV.* He is the former president of research and development at Walt Disney Imagineering.

GERALD FINNERMAN was a cinematographer who worked on a variety of television shows including *Moonlighting* and *TOS.*

ROBERT FLETCHER was a costume designer who worked on *TMP, STII, STIII,* and *STIV.*

DENNY MARTIN FLINN was an author and screenwriter. He is known for co-writing *STVI* with Nicholas Meyer.

DOROTHY "D. C." FONTANA is a television writer who is best known for writing for *TOS, TAS*, and *TNG*. She also worked on such series as *The Streets of San Francisco, Fantastic Journey, Logan's Run*, and *Buck Rogers in the 25th Century*.

ALAN DEAN FOSTER is an author known for his works of science fiction and fantasy. He has written novelizations of myriad motion pictures and adapted the *Star Trek Log* series based on *TAS*. He also has a story credit on *TMP*.

JONATHAN FRAKES is an actor and director. He is best known for his role of Commander William T. Riker in *TNG*. He also directed the films *First Contact* and *Insurrection* as well as episodes of *Castle, Leverage*, and *The Librarians*.

FRED FREIBERGER was a television and film writer. He produced such shows as *The Wild Wild West*, the second season of *Space: 1999*, and the third season of *TOS*.

MICHAEL JAN FRIEDMAN is a television, radio, and comic-book writer as well as an author. He is the author of many *Star Trek* novels and has written for *VOY*.

BRYAN FULLER is a television writer and producer. In addition to creating and executive producing the popular series *Pushing Daisies, Dead Like Me, Wonderfalls, Hannibal*, and *American Gods*, he was a writer for *DS9* and coproducer on *VOY*.

JOHN FURIA JR. was a television writer known for working on *Bonanza, Hawaii Five-O*, and *The Twilight Zone*. He was a former president of the Writers Guild of America.

DAVID GAUTREAUX is a television and film actor who was originally cast as Xon in *Phase II*. He is also known for playing Commander Branch in *TMP*.

DAVID GERROLD is a television and film writer as well as an author. He has written for *Land of the Lost, TOS*, and *TAS* and wrote numerous popular sci-fi novels including the novelette *The Martian Child*, which was adapted into a feature film starring John Cusack. He was heavily involved in the development phase of *TNG*.

VINCE GILLIGAN is an Emmy Award–winning film and television writer, producer, and director. He is best known for creating the TV series *Breaking Bad* and *Better Call Saul* and working as a coexecutive producer on *The X-Files*.

JERRY GOLDSMITH was a legendary composer and conductor best known for scoring television and film. He won an Academy Award for his score to *The Omen*. Among his hundreds of classic movie scores are *Planet of the Apes, Patton, Total Recall, TMP, STV,* and *First Contact*.

JAMES GOLDSTONE was a television and film director. He directed the pilot to *Ironside* as well as "Where No Man Has Gone Before," the second pilot for *TOS*.

DAVID A. GOODMAN is a television writer and producer. He is an executive producer of *Family Guy* and wrote the beloved *Futurama* homage to *Trek*, "Where No Fan Has Gone Before." He was also a consulting producer on *ENT* and is author of *The Autobiography of James T. Kirk* for Titan Books.

ROBERT GOODWIN is a producer who worked on *Phase II*.

CHRIS GORE is a comedian and writer who was a regular on G4TV's *Attack of the Show*. He is the founder of *Film Threat* magazine.

PETER GOULD is a television writer and producer known for his work on *Breaking Bad* and as cocreator of its spin-off, *Better Call Saul*.

RICH HANDLEY is a *Star Trek* comic book historian and contributor to IDW's *Star Trek* newspaper strip reprint hardcovers as well as an editor at Hasslein Books.

DORRIS HALSEY was the founder of the Reece Halsey Agency, which represented Gene L. Coon as well as Henry Miller, Upton Sinclair, and Aldous Huxley, author of *Brave New World*. Born Dorris Vilmos in Budapest, Hungary, Halsey joined the French Resistance in 1940 and was a German prisoner of war after she was caught and imprisoned, sharing a cell with thirty-eight other women.

DAVID P. HARMON was a television writer and author. He worked on a variety of shows including *The Brady Bunch, TOS,* and *TAS*.

RUSS HEATH is a legendary comic-book artist who has worked for DC, Marvel, and Peter Pan Records, where he worked on illustrations for their *Star Trek* record album inserts.

ARTHUR HEINEMANN is a television and film screenwriter and artist. He worked as a writer on *TOS*.

CATHERINE HICKS is a television and film actress. She played the roles of Annie Camden on *7th Heaven* and Dr. Gillian Taylor in *STIV*.

JAMES HORNER was an Oscar-winning conductor, composer, and orchestrator. He has worked on a wide range of films including *Titanic, Gorky Park, Aliens, Battle Beyond the Stars, Avatar, STII,* and *STIII*.

GENNIFER HUTCHISON is a former assistant to John Shiban on *The X-Files* and *ENT,* producer for *Breaking Bad* and *The Strain,* and supervising producer on *Better Call Saul*.

GERALD ISENBERG is a longtime film and television producer and former partner of Jerry Abrams, J. J. Abrams's father. He was hired to produce *Star Trek: Planet of the Titans* by Paramount in the mid seventies.

ANDRE JACQUEMETTON is a television writer and producer. He has written for such shows as *Baywatch Hawaii, Mad Men,* and *ENT*.

MARIE JACQUEMETTON is a television writer and producer. She has written for a variety of shows including *Baywatch Hawaii, Mad Men,* and *ENT*.

STEVEN-CHARLES JAFFE is a writer, producer, and director. He has been a producer on a variety of films including *Ghost, Motel Hell, Strange Days,* and *STVI*.

WALTER "MATT" JEFFRIES was an aviation and mechanical artist, set designer, and writer. He is the designer of the original starship *Enterprise*.

JOSEPH R. JENNINGS is an art director and production designer. He worked on various *Star Trek* projects including *Phase II, TMP,* and *STII*.

GEORGE CLAYTON JOHNSON is an author and television writer. He is the coauthor of the novel *Logan's Run*. He also wrote episodes of *The Twilight Zone* and *TOS*.

ROBERT H. JUSTMAN was a producer and assistant director on such series as *The Outer Limits*. He was one of the original producers on *TOS* and also worked as a supervising producer on *TNG*.

STEPHEN KANDEL is a television writer who has written for numerous shows including *Wonder Woman, The Six Million Dollar Man, MacGyver, TOS,* and *TAS*.

OSCAR KATZ was a television producer and executive who was the head of production at Desilu, Lucille Ball and Desi Arnaz's production company, which produced the first two years of *TOS*.

PHILIP KAUFMAN is a director and screenwriter. He is best known for directing such films as *The Wanderers, Invasion of the Body Snatchers, The Unbearable Lightness of Being*, and *The Right Stuff*. He was attached to direct the aborted film project *Star Trek: Planet of the Titans*.

SALLY KELLERMAN is an actress, author, producer, and singer. She has appeared in the movies *M*A*S*H* and *Pret-a-Porter* as well as a variety of television programs including *The Outer Limits, Last of the Red Hot Lovers*, and *TOS*.

DeFOREST KELLEY was an actor, screenwriter, and poet. He is best known for his roles in *Gunfight at the O.K. Corral* and as Dr. Leonard McCoy in *TOS, TAS*, and the spin-off films.

LUKAS KENDALL is a prolific producer of soundtrack albums as well as the editor of *Film Score Monthly*. He also cowrote and produced the film *Lucky Bastard*.

PERSIS KHAMBATTA was a model, actress, and author. She is best known for her role in *Megaforce* and as Lieutenant Ilia in *TMP*.

RICHARD H. KLINE is the Oscar-nominated director of photography whose films include *The Andromeda Strain, Soylent Green, The Fury, Body Heat*, and *TMP*.

CHRISTOPHER KNOPF is a longtime television writer and friend of Gene Roddenberry.

WALTER KOENIG is an actor, writer, and director. He is best known for his roles as Alfred Bester in *Babylon 5* and Pavel Chekov in *TOS* and the six films based on it. He also wrote an episode of *TAS*, "The Infinite Vulcan."

JAMES KOMACK was a television director, producer, actor, and writer. He worked on a variety of television shows including *Get Smart, Chico and the Man*, and *TOS*.

JOE KRAEMER is a composer who worked on such films and television series as *Jack Reacher, Femme Fatales, The Way of the Gun*, and *Mission: Impossible—Rogue Nation*.

PETER KRIKES is a screenwriter who contributed to the script for *STIV*.

DAVID LANGHAUS is a longtime *Star Trek* fan who attended many early conventions in New York City.

DEVRA LANGSAM is the former publisher of *Spockanalia,* the first *Star Trek* fanzine. She is also one of the first *Star Trek* convention organizers.

JONATHAN LARSEN is a former producer for such news outlets as ABC News, CNN, and MSNBC, where he was executive producer of *Up with Chris Hayes* and *Up Late with Alec Baldwin.*

GLEN A. LARSON was a prolific television writer and producer. He is best known as the creator of the original *Battlestar Galactica; Magnum, P.I.; Quincy M.E., Buck Rogers in the 25th Century,* and *Knight Rider,* among many others, and worked with Gene L. Coon on *It Takes a Thief.*

ANDREW LASZLO is a cinematographer who worked on such films as *First Blood, The Warriors,* and *STV.*

ROBERT LEWIN was a television writer and producer who worked on such shows as *The Streets of San Francisco, Hawaii Five-O, The Man from Atlantis, The Paper Chase,* and *TNG.*

JACQUELINE LICHTENBERG is an author who has written a variety of novels, short stories, and nonfiction material including the seminal *Star Trek Lives!*

HAROLD LIVINGSTON is a longtime writer, producer, and novelist and the sole credited screenwriter of *TMP.*

GARY LOCKWOOD is an actor who is known for his roles as Dr. Frank Poole in *2001: A Space Odyssey* and as Commander Gary Mitchell in *TOS.*

DAVID LOUGHERY is a screenwriter and producer. He has written a variety of films including *Lakeview Terrace, Dreamscape,* and *STV.*

JOHN MEREDYTH LUCAS was a television writer, producer, and director who worked on such shows as *Kojak, The Six Million Dollar Man, TOS,* and *Phase II.*

ADAM MALIN is the cofounder of Creation Entertainment, which specializes in producing conventions for fans of comic books, television series, and films.

SCOTT MANTZ is a film critic and producer who has appeared on such programs as *Access Hollywood* and *The Today Show*.

VINCENT McEVEETY is a director and producer who has worked on a variety of programs including *Gunsmoke*; *Murder, She Wrote*; and *TOS*.

STEVE MEERSON is a screenwriter who contributed to the screenplay for *STIV*.

NICHOLAS MEYER is a screenwriter, producer, director, and author. He is the writer of the bestselling novel *The Seven-Per-Cent Solution*, which was adapted into a feature film. In addition to writing and directing *Time After Time*, *STII*, and *STVI*, he cowrote *STIV* with Harve Bennett.

HAROLD MICHELSON was a production designer who worked as the head of the art department on *TMP*.

MICHAEL MINOR was a conceptual and production illustrator who worked on *Phase II*, *TMP*, and *STII*.

LAWRENCE MONTAIGNE is an actor who appeared in such series as *The Streets of San Francisco*, *Batman*, and *TOS*.

RICARDO MONTALBAN was an actor whose career spanned seven decades during which he portrayed various roles including most famously Mr. Roarke on *Fantasy Island* and Khan Noonien Singh in *TOS* and *STII*.

RONALD D. MOORE is a television and film writer and producer, whose credits include *TNG*, *DS9*, *Carnivale*, *Roswell*, the critically acclaimed remake of *Battlestar Galactica*, *Caprica*, and *Outlander*. He is also the coscreenwriter for *Generations* and *First Contact*.

DIANA MULDAUR is a film and television actress whose credits include *L.A. Law*, *Born Free*, *TOS*, and *TNG* on which she played Dr. Katherine Pulaski during the show's second season.

KATE MULGREW is a film and television actress. She is known for her Emmy-nominated role as Red on *Orange Is the New Black* and as Captain Kathryn Janeway on *VOY*.

EDDIE MURPHY is an actor, writer, comedian, and former cast member on *Saturday Night Live*. He is also known for his comedy film classics *48 Hrs.*, *Beverly Hills Cop*, and *Shrek* as well as his Oscar-nominated role in *Dreamgirls*.

KENNY MYERS has been a makeup artist and designer on myriad feature films, including *STV* and *STVI*.

ED NAHA is an author, journalist, screenwriter, and producer. He has written for the magazine *Starlog*, produced the spoken-word album *Inside Star Trek*, and wrote the popular film *Honey, I Shrunk the Kids*.

GARY NARDINO was president of production at Paramount Pictures and executive producer of *STIII*. He also produced the TV series *Time Trax* with Harve Bennett.

NICHELLE NICHOLS is an actress, singer, and performer. She is best known for her role as Lieutenant Uhura on *TOS*, *TAS*, and in the *Star Trek* feature films.

LEONARD NIMOY was a prominent actor, director, poet, and producer. While he is best known for his legendary portrayal of Mr. Spock in the *Star Trek* series, he also directed numerous films including *Three Men and a Baby*, *The Good Mother*, *STIII*, and *STIV*. In addition to appearing (and disappearing) as Paris in the *Mission: Impossible* TV series, Nimoy starred in the TV movies *A Woman Called Golda* and *Never Forget* as well as in *Fiddler on the Roof* and *Equus* on Broadway.

MIKE OKUDA is a scenic artist whose credits include *STV*, *STVI*, *TNG*, *Generations*, *First Contact*, *Insurrection*, *DS9*, *VOY*, *Nemesis*, and *ENT*.

KERRY O'QUINN is the creator and former publisher of *Starlog*, *Fangoria*, *Cinemagic*, and *Future Life* magazines.

GLEN C. OLIVER is a film and television critic for the popular Web site *Ain't It Cool News*.

ROBERTO ORCI is a prolific film and television writer and producer. He is the cocreator of *Fringe* as well as the cowriter on *Star Trek* and *Star Trek Into Darkness*.

GEORGE PAPPY is director of the documentary *The Green Girl*, a film about the late *Star Trek* actress Susan Oliver.

SAMUEL A. PEEPLES was a television writer and author. He published several novels and wrote the second pilot episode of *TOS*.

JOYCE PERRY is a television writer whose credits include *Land of the Lost, The Waltons,* and *TAS*.

DON PETERMAN was a cinematographer whose credits include *Flashdance, Men in Black,* and *STIV*.

JOSEPH PEVNEY was a television and film director. He directed episodes of such shows as *Bonanza, The Paper Chase,* and *TOS*.

DAVID V. PICKER is the former president of three major film studios including Paramount, where he oversaw the development of *Star Trek* as a feature film property as well as shepherding such iconic films as *Tom Jones*, the James Bond series, *A Hard Day's Night, Midnight Cowboy, Last Tango in Paris,* and *The Jerk* to the screen.

MICHAEL PILLER was a journalist, television writer, and producer who is best known for his work on *TNG* and for cocreating *DS9* and *VOY*. He also developed and executive produced *The Dead Zone* TV series as well as *Legend,* starring John de Lancie. In addition, Piller wrote the screenplay for *Insurrection*.

JON POVILL is a screenwriter who was story editor for *Phase II,* his teleplay for which "The Child" was adapted as an episode of *TNG*. He served as associate producer of *TMP*.

CHRIS PRATT is a television and film actor. He is best known for his roles as Andy Dwyer in *Parks and Recreation,* Peter Quill in *Guardians of the Galaxy,* and Owen Grady in *Jurassic World*.

ANDREW PROBERT is a conceptual artist who helped design the *Enterprise* for *TMP* and the *Enterprise-D* for *TNG*.

KEN RALSTON is a visual-effects supervisor for Industrial Light & Magic who has worked on myriad films in both the *Star Trek* and *Star Wars* series.

ANDE RICHARDSON worked at Desilu and was secretary to Gene L. Coon on *TOS*.

HANK RIEGER was a publicist and journalist. He was the West Coast director of press and publicity for NBC from 1965 to 1979 and promoted such shows as *Laugh-In, I Spy,* and *TOS.*

GENE RODDENBERRY was a television and film writer, producer, and futurist. He is famous for being the creator and executive producer of the original *Star Trek* series that inspired the *Star Trek* franchise as well as the creator of *TNG.* He also executive produced *TMP* as well as numerous TV pilots including *The Questor Tapes* and *Genesis II.*

MAJEL BARRETT RODDENBERRY was an actress and producer. She is known for her roles as Nurse Christine Chapel on *TOS* and Lwaxana Troi on *TNG* and *DS9.* She was also the wife of Gene Roddenberry.

ROD RODDENBERRY is CEO of Roddenberry Entertainment and a respected philanthropist. He is the son of Gene and Majel Roddenberry.

MARK ROSENTHAL is a screenwriter who is the cowriter of the film *STVI.* His other credits include *Mona Lisa Smile* and *Flicka.*

ELYSE ROSENSTEIN is one of the earliest members of *Star Trek* fandom who helped organize the first *Star Trek* conventions.

STEVEN JAY RUBIN is a unit publicist, journalist, and author who has worked on such films as *Pretty in Pink*; *Honey, I Blew Up the Kids*; and *Silent Night.* He also wrote *The James Bond Companion.*

JIM RUGG was an Emmy Award–nominated special effects artist who was responsible for most of the on-set practical effects work for the original *Star Trek.*

SUSAN SACKETT is a former executive assistant to Gene Roddenberry, a position she held for more than seventeen years. She also cowrote two episodes of *TNG.*

ROBERT SALLIN is a television commercial director and producer. He was the producer of *STII.*

LOU SCHEIMER was a producer and one of the original founders of Filmation, creators of such cartoons as *He-Man, The Secret of the Sword,* and *TAS.*

PAUL SCHNEIDER was a television writer who worked on such programs as *Bonanza, Ironside, TOS,* and *TAS.*

BARRY SCHULMAN is the former vice president of programming at the Sci-Fi Channel. He was involved in the channel's airing of remastered episodes of *TOS* as well as the creation of bonus material for their debut.

ALLAN SCOTT is a screenwriter for such films as *Don't Look Now,* who was attached to cowrite the aborted film *Star Trek: Planet of the Titans.*

RALPH SENENSKY is a television director and writer who directed episodes of such series as *The Waltons, The Partridge Family, Dynasty,* and *TOS.*

NAREN SHANKAR is a television writer, producer, and director. In addition to being a science consultant for *TNG*, Shankar went on to executive produce *CSI: Crime Scene Investigation.* He also wrote for *Farscape, Grimm, VOY,* and *DS9.* He developed and executive produced *The Expanse* for SyFy.

WILLIAM SHATNER is the legendary actor, writer, singer, and director who portrayed the iconic Captain James T. Kirk in *Star Trek.* In addition, he won an Emmy for his work as Denny Crane in *Boston Legal,* also starred as the titular *T.J. Hooker* in the hit ABC series, and served as the host of *Rescue 911.* In addition to directing *STV,* Shatner has also starred in such films as *Judgment at Nuremberg, The Intruder,* and *Kingdom of the Spiders,* and played an unhinged version of himself in the comedy *Free Enterprise.*

FELIX SILLA is an actor whose credits include *The Addams Family, Spaceballs, Star Wars, Buck Rogers in the 25th Century* as Twiki, and a Talosian in the original pilot for *Star Trek.*

ROBERT SILVERBERG is a well-known science fiction novelist and editor. He contributed story ideas for the first *Star Trek* film.

JERRY SOHL was a screenwriter whose credits include *The Twilight Zone, The Outer Limits,* and *TOS.*

HERBERT F. SOLOW is a former executive in charge of production for Desilu and vice president of worldwide motion picture and television production for MGM. His credits include *Mission: Impossible, Then Came Bronson, Mannix, The Man from Atlantis,* and *TOS.*

JACK B. SOWARDS was a screenwriter who is known for being credited for writing *STII* as well as an episode of *TNG.*

ADRIAN SPIES was a writer who worked on a variety of television shows including *Dr. Kildare, Hawaii Five-O,* and *TOS.*

NORMAN SPINRAD is an author, essayist, and critic. He has written a variety of novels and wrote an episode for *TOS* and *Phase II.*

FRANK SPOTNITZ is a former journalist and television writer-producer who has worked on such series as *The X-Files, Millennium,* and *Hunted.* He is currently the executive producer of Amazon's *Man in the High Castle.*

JOSEPH STEFANO was a screenwriter and producer known for writing the screenplay of the film *Psycho* as well as creating the original *The Outer Limits* for ABC. He wrote "Skin of Evil" for the first season of *TNG.*

DAVID STERN is a former editor for Pocket Books' *Star Trek* book line as well as a writer for DC Comics.

PATRICK STEWART is a television, film, and stage actor. He is best known for his roles as Professor Charles Xavier in the X-Men film series and Captain Jean-Luc Picard in *TNG* and its subsequent films.

MIKE SUSSMAN is a former journalist and television writer and producer who has worked on such series as *VOY* and as a producer on *ENT.* He is cocreator of the series *Perception*, which starred Eric McCormack.

HAL SUTHERLAND was a painter and animator. He worked on a vast array of animated projects including *Sleeping Beauty* and *Peter Pan.* He was a director on *TAS.*

GEORGE TAKEI is an actor, author, and activist. He is best known for his role as Hikaru Sulu in *TOS, TAS,* and the subsequent films.

MICHAEL TAYLOR is a television writer and musician who has worked on both *DS9* and *VOY* as well as on such series as *The Dead Zone, Battlestar Galactica* (2004), *Defiance,* and *Turn: Washington's Spies.*

RICHARD WINN TAYLOR II is a director, graphic artist, and designer. While working for Robert Abel and Associates, he supervised the storyboarding of *TMP* and designed and supervised the building of the miniatures including the *Enterprise.* Taylor has received four Clio awards for his advertising efforts and has worked on such films as *TRON* and *Looker.*

TRACY TORME is a screenwriter and television producer. He is best known for his work on *Saturday Night Live* and *TNG,* for which he won a Peabody Award for "The Big Goodbye." He also wrote the film *Fire in the* Sky and created the TV series *Sliders.*

JOSE TREVINO is a television director whose credits include *Babylon 5, DS9,* and *VOY.*

BJO & JOHN TRIMBLE are longtime fans as well as organizers of various *Star Trek* and sci-fi events. Bjo is credited with creating and popularizing the "Save *Star Trek*" campaign that convinced NBC to renew the series for a third season. Bjo is also the author of the beloved *Star Trek Concordance,* the original episode guide to the series, and *On the Good Ship Enterprise.*

JAMES VAN HISE is an author and editor who writes about film, television, and comic-book history. He created and edited the seminal *Star Trek* fan magazine *Enterprise Incidents.*

DAVID WEDDLE is a television writer and producer who has worked on such shows as *Battlestar Galactica* (2004), *Falling Skies, The Strain,* and *DS9.* He is also author of the biography of *Wild Bunch* director Sam Peckinpah, *If They Move . . . Kill 'Em.*

LEN WEIN is a prolific writer and editor for comic books and the creator of such iconic characters as Swamp Thing and Wolverine. He also contributed as a writer to Gold Key's original *Star Trek* comics.

HOWARD WEINSTEIN is a television writer and author who is known for being the youngest person ever to write a script for *Star Trek,* having written the teleplay for "The Pirates of Orion," an episode of *TAS,* at age nineteen.

GRACE LEE WHITNEY was an actress best known for her role as Janice Rand on *TOS* and in the subsequent film series, as well as for appearing in Billy Wilder's classic comedy *Some Like It Hot.*

RALPH WINTER is a producer whose credits include *X-Men* and *STIII* through *STVI.*

ROBERT WISE was a film director, producer, and editor. He is best known for his work as a director on *The Day the Earth Stood Still, The Sound of Music, West*

Side Story, and *TMP.* He was also the editor of Orson Welles's masterpiece, *Citizen Kane.*

MORT ZARCOFF is a producer and writer who worked on such shows as *It Takes a Thief, The Lawbreakers,* and *The Misadventures of Sherriff Lobo* and was a longtime friend of Gene L. Coon.

BIRTH OF A [TREK] NATION

"LET'S MAKE SURE THAT HISTORY NEVER FORGETS . . .
THE NAME . . . *ENTERPRISE.*"

*S*tar Trek is a unique pop-culture phenomena that is unlikely to ever be repeated. It represents the improbable story of a television series that—given the era in which it was birthed—should never have existed, let alone survived *or* ultimately flourished

The brainchild of World War II veteran and former police speechwriter Gene Roddenberry, the original incarnation of *Star Trek* was an expensive NBC television pilot called "The Cage." Produced by Lucille Ball's Desilu Studios, it was rejected by the network. However, intrigued enough by the show's unique sci-fi premise that Roddenberry once dubbed "*Wagon Train* to the stars," they took the unprecedented step of ordering a second pilot with an emphasis on action-adventure. This time NBC *was* interested, but the order was almost rejected by Desilu's board of directors as being fiscally untenable. Then, giving us another reason why we love Lucy, Lucille Ball *personally* stepped in and greenlit the show. The resulting series, sold to the network as a sci-fi action-adventure drama, was also used by its creator as a soapbox to comment on the issues of the day by using metaphor and allegory . . . while selling, well, soap.

Battling network executives and censors whom he frequently antagonized, Gene Roddenberry had to deal with the fact that *Star Trek* was struggling in the ratings to the point where, in its second year, the show was on the verge of cancellation. Its voyage would have ended there if not for a massive letter-writing campaign initiated by the fans themselves. So impressive was this campaign that NBC changed its corporate mind and renewed *Star Trek* for a third—and ultimately final—year.

And that, as they say, should have been that.

Only it wasn't.

Star Trek lived thanks to the fledgling business of television syndication, which introduced the show to an entirely new audience that had missed it the first time around. Many of those viewers—young and affluent—watched the sacred seventy-nine classic episodes over and over again, eventually passing them on to *their* children.

In 1973, Filmation produced two seasons of an Emmy Award–winning animated series based on the show for NBC. Unlike other kidvid of its time, it included the involvement of the series' original creators and cast and dealt with surprisingly adult and heady themes for a Saturday-morning cartoon series.

But ultimately *Star Trek*, its blockbuster movie series, and the myriad spin-offs it later inspired—including its highly rated successor series, *Star Trek: The Next Generation,* which blasted off in 1987—have had a seismic cultural impact that extends and endures far beyond their television airings. Not only did the series inspire fervent fan conventions that continue to flourish decades after its original airing, but the show itself inspired numerous fans to become doctors, engineers, inventors, and showrunners. Its influence can be seen in the most cutting-edge of today's technological gadgets, ranging from mobile phones to tablet computers and virtual reality.

The series also was one of the first to feature a multicultural and multiracial cast, and whose fans range from such legendary figures as Martin Luther King Jr. to Barack Obama, Tom Hanks to Ben Stiller, Angelina Jolie to Eddie Murphy, and Bill Gates to Steve Jobs.

In addition, the series lexicon of Treknology is well known and often invoked in contemporary journalism, whether it be "beam me up, Scotty," "warp speed," or "resistance is futile."

Today, *Star Trek* continues to live long and prosper after five decades of boldly going. Some are obsessed by it, others perplexed. For decades, critics and fans have attempted to dissect the unique alchemy that has ensured the franchise's ongoing popularity as well as understand the man who created it, Gene Roddenberry. Here are a few more reasons why it still endures.

GENE RODDENBERRY (creator, executive producer, *Star Trek*)

"Trek" means walking, voyaging. And the name *Star Trek* really means voyaging from star to star. I knew it was the right title because when I first mentioned it to the network executives, they said, "We don't like it."

IRA STEVEN BEHR (executive producer, *Star Trek: Deep Space Nine*)

The theory I've always heard says that when the western died, science fiction filled the gap. We could not dream in the past anymore, so we started to dream in the future.

THOMAS DOHERTY (professor of American studies, Brandeis University)

The Frederick Jackson Turner notions of what defines Americans is the frontier; it's not our Puritan past, but how the frontier is always rehabilitating and nurturing and reestablishing the American traits of individualism and freedom. It's the frontier which makes us Americans, and we have to have initiative and inventiveness and youth and strength and canniness to survive on the frontier— and also we also have to kill the Indians. "Space, the final frontier" is really manifest destiny.

DAVID A. GOODMAN (consulting producer, *Star Trek: Enterprise*)

Star Trek wasn't a big hit in the sixties when it came out, but it hit in the seventies when there was this malaise and lack of trust in government and you had this iconic American hero at the center of it, and he's surrounded by an international group. It really spoke to America as this great thing. For the British, James Bond is sort of patriotic. The British are still at the center of the world, even though historically they're not. There's a way in which *Star Trek* is the same thing for America.

THOMAS DOHERTY

The show is sort of both modest enough to respect the indigenous aliens of off-worlds, but at the same time, we know in the end we have to show them how to do things and our values are better. It has the arrogance of American exceptionalism, even though we say we have the noninterference prime directive, but basically we're going into these places and showing them "how to live right," which is very American, too.

JONATHAN LARSEN (executive producer, MSNBC)

The image we have of *Star Trek*'s politics changes with our own politics. It can be tricky trying to divine the political ideology of *Trek*'s creators and writers from the plotlines and story resolutions and the tics and arcs of individual characters. Yes, "James Tiberius Kirk" reads an awful lot like an analogue of "John Fitzgerald Kennedy."

MICHAEL PILLER (executive producer, *Star Trek: The Next Generation*)

The early *Star Trek* original recipe was a very Kennedy-esque sort of mission to save the universe. Let's get these guys out there and show them what democracy is and educate . . . and if they don't do it the way we want to, we'll hit a few and line them up and get them the way we want them.

JONATHAN LARSEN

Kennedy saw the exploration of space as an obligation, not necessarily in pursuit of a goal, but because he recognized space exploration as the inevitable next step if our society was to remain forward-looking and forward-moving. Similarly, Kennedy had little interest in looking back, in honoring old grudges and historical enmity.

BRANNON BRAGA (executive producer, cocreator, *Star Trek: Enterprise*)

There was something ineffable running through them all, which was Gene Roddenberry's philosophy. And whether or not people were aware of *Star Trek*'s appeal because it presented a utopian future, what I think was critical to its appeal is that it's a universe where everyone has a place. No matter how weird or perhaps even disabled you are, even if you're blind, you have a role, and that's attracted a lot of people.

JONATHAN LARSEN

Consider how jaw-droppingly radical and likely unacceptable the resolution of "The Devil in the Dark" would be today. The rock-like monster slaughters miners relentlessly. What is its punishment? A business deal. A contract to work with those miners it did not kill. There is no retribution. There is no vengeance. More-over, denying the emotional need for retribution is portrayed not as weakness, but as manly maturity. It's virtually impossible to imagine mainstream fiction in the post-Reagan, let alone post–9/11, era forswearing a violently punitive ending to a story such as this. But that was what mature, realistic, clearheaded, albeit ideal-ized, government looked like back then. Mature leadership meant becoming the generation that finally severed the self-regenerating legacies of violence.

ROD RODDENBERRY (son of Gene Roddenberry)

It's based on the idea of IDIC, which was one of the backbones of the original series. It's the philosophy that's always really kind of resonated with me. I did not grow up watching *Star Trek*. I liked *Knight Rider* and *The Dukes of Hazzard*. It wasn't until later in life, through the fans, that I got a different perspective of what *Star Trek* was, and then I went back and I'd start to get it. We all know the term "IDIC," which means "infinite diversity in infinite combinations." It's the idea that it's universal acceptance.

JONATHAN LARSEN

The same astonishing quality of mercy, or maturity, drives "Balance of Terror." Kirk admonishes a crewman whose descendants were killed by Romulans that it was "their war . . . not yours." Try to imagine a modern epic with the kind of in-the-moment self-reflection we see in "Arena." "We could be in the wrong." What political leader would ever dare utter publicly the words "that is something best decided by diplomats"? It's an acknowledgment of and respect for nuance and expertise—and a rejection of essentialism and exceptionalism—that's virtually unimaginable today.

BRYAN FULLER (coproducer, *Star Trek: Voyager*)

The Munsters and *Star Trek* were the shows I would watch when I got home from school. They both had a lot to do with creatures and also being inclusive worlds, in a way. Because the Munster family was very much an inclusive world. They allowed any kind of freak flag to fly. And we learned that in *Star Trek* there is an entire universe out there of different varieties of people—and all of them are okay. It was an early lesson in inclusivity. I was living in a household where my dad didn't want me to watch *The Jeffersons* because it had black people in it. It was that level of small-town seventies suburban racism.

SCOTT MANTZ (film critic, *Access Hollywood*)

Star Trek was at its finest when it was a morality play. It took decades for me to draw the correlation between "This Side of Paradise" and the Summer of Love. But of course, even as a kid, I knew that "Mudd's Women" was about space hookers.

DAVID A. GOODMAN

I think that the multiculturalism was great because of the time; you had an African-American, an Asian, and this fake Russian on the bridge of the *Enterprise*.

ROD RODDENBERRY

There was a great quote that D. C. Fontana said about Nichelle Nichols and having a black officer on the bridge and what my father said to that. Apparently, he would get letters from the TV stations in the South saying they won't show *Star Trek* because there is a black officer, and he'd say, "Fuck off, then."

CHRIS PRATT (actor, *Guardians of the Galaxy, Jurassic World*)

It had all kinds of different races and various male and female characters from different alien races all around in power, in relationships with each other at a time when that wasn't cool, you know? It was very progressive.

JONATHAN LARSEN

It's interesting that no matter how sophisticated or advanced we imagine some work of fiction to be, the years almost always seem to reveal some element that was awkwardly, embarrassingly backward. Many early cartoons had their moments of racism—in both the depiction of people of color and the lack thereof. And *Star Trek* had its moments in that regard, too.

But its worst, most well-documented flaw can be found embodied in the output of the wardrobe department, courtesy of Mr. Roddenberry: the skirts. Maybe the creators of *Star Trek* believed that a true portrayal of an utterly gender-equal, let alone non-ageist, future would not fly on commercial television in the 1960s and so did as much as they could—giving women, albeit short in years and hemlines, "real" jobs and occasionally real authority. One would hope this was the case, given that the creators themselves were not all men.

Either way, the extent of gender equality that *Star Trek* did muster paved the way for public acceptance, not just of future female Federation captains . . . but actual, real-life female astronauts, too. As in so many other regards, even when it came to elements of our politics and our culture, in imagining our future, *Star Trek* made it possible.

SCOTT MANTZ

I will never forget in "Turnabout Intruder" when Kirk goes, "It's better to be dead than to be alone in the body of a woman." That makes the episode so dated, but there are others that are the absolute opposite. In "Metamorphosis," Commissioner Hedford is going to stop a war. Commissioner Hedford is a woman. An attractive woman.

DAVID A. GOODMAN

There are plenty of roles for women in *Star Trek*; doctors, lawyers . . . and they all seem to have been somehow involved with Kirk. But at least they had their own careers.

GENE RODDENBERRY

Star Trek will always work as long as you have imagination. We have never had anyone in *Trek* who wasn't into growth. During my first *Trek,* for instance, I didn't pay any attention to women.

LEONARD NIMOY (actor, "Mr. Spock")

His attitude toward women on *Trek* were miniskirted, big-boobed sex objects— toys for guys. He cleaned up that act gradually only because people pointed it out to him. He was a funny guy. At least, I find him funny.

ROD RODDENBERRY

First of all, he loved women. I love women. Women are the most beautiful creatures on the planet. And so that came out very clearly in all the *Star Trek*s, but I think he was also of the belief that by women wearing short skirts and a woman choosing to do that, then she was empowering herself. Use your beauty, use your mind, use everything you have.

GENE RODDENBERRY

In the years I have grown into something of a strong feminist. I was the product of a Southern family background. My parents never spoke of any race with contempt. They encouraged me to try strange ideas and philosophies.

ROBERT H. JUSTMAN (associate producer, *Star Trek*)

Working with Gene Roddenberry, very often it was a lot of fun. He had great intellect. This was someone who came from a very poor background and made himself what he was.

FRED BRONSON (publicist, NBC Television)

I went to Cal State Northridge and the paper was the *Daily Sundial* and I walked in as a freshman and they started giving me stories to write. A lot of my stories were for the entertainment section. And one day I said I'd like to interview Gene Roddenberry and so I called his office and arranged an interview. I went over to Paramount in early 1967 and I'm sitting outside Gene's office with the secretary. I hear this noise like a jackhammer and I seriously realized it was my heart pounding. It was a combination of nerves and excitement. When I went in and did the interview, the main thing he told me, which probably shouldn't have been that big a revelation, was that the only purpose of TV was to sell toothpaste.

ED NAHA (producer, *Inside Star Trek* LP)

The *Star Trek* approach to life is all-inclusive and positive. When the TV show first was aired, the politics of America was anything but. It was a time of war, protests, race riots, and brutality—but also a time when a counterculture was emerging. The original show was sort of an intellectual and emotional refuge for people who believed in positive change. And cleavage.

GENE RODDENBERRY

I used to speak at colleges a lot because it was what kept me alive and paid the mortgage in the days when *Star Trek* was considered a gigantic failure. I have met some of these people. I remember one night someone called me over and said, "Can you possibly talk to this man?" And here was a fellow with some kind of nerve disorder who had an electronic box. He couldn't speak, and by hitting the box he could make halfway intelligible sounds. He could only make grunting-like noises.

And finally I began to understand what he was saying, and he was asking me why I did a certain thing in a certain show, and why I had invented somebody who had something of his disorder. I said to him, "Someday when we become wise, we won't look at those things. We will look at communication and knowledge, etc." And I saw his hand rise up with great determination and he said loudly and clearly, "Yes!" Those are the high moments in my life.

LEONARD NIMOY

One of the large questions we have been asked time and time again is what is giving this thing its longevity? Why does it continue to survive, to touch people, to intrigue? I think one of the major reasons is that the whole structure of *Trek* is a moral one—it's a moral society that people are attracted to. It really is a meritocracy.

If you do well, you advance. If you are good at what you do, you can have the job. It doesn't matter who you are or what you are, what your origins are, your color or race. None of that matters. We need to get jobs done here, and if we have someone who can do the job, they have the job. Audiences recognize that. There's a rightness about that. There's a correctness, not a political correctness, about a meritocracy where performance is valued, where the reality of the truth is recognized and valued. Where things are right because they are right, because we need them to be right.

We had our flaws. We had certain political flaws, a certain kind of righteousness, to a degree that come from the humans that were making these shows. But given that, there is still a moral structure within *Star Trek* that makes sense.

MARIE JACQUEMETTON (story editor, *Star Trek: Enterprise*)

The fact that it was conceivable that man could go to another planet or even moonwalk was incredible. I had a scrapbook, like all kids from my generation do, of every astronaut and what they were doing. To our kids, James Cameron is what space is; *Alien* and *Battlestar Galactica*. It's almost like a movie, it's not even a real thing. They would not think of becoming an astronaut and going into space. It's not even part of their concept of what the future is. Everything's turned into the Internet. It's all about being famous for a second and how can I get noticed. There's no awareness of what's out there beyond our little bubble. And when we were kids I think what was so exciting about *Star Trek* was the "what if" possibilities.

HANS BEIMLER (coexecutive producer, *Star Trek: Deep Space Nine*)

The best definition of science fiction I'd heard is this, that in 1900, at the turn of the century, pretty much anybody could tell you that the car was going to revolutionize the transportation industry. That's not science fiction. But if you could predict in 1903 that it was going to change the sex lives of Americans by all the fucking that was going to be happening in the backseats of cars, that's science fiction. In the sixties, the new technology was CB radios and being able to talk to people on the other side of the world. But my mother would say to me, "Yeah, but they don't have anything to say to each other." So it didn't really matter.

RONALD D. MOORE
(coexecutive producer, *Star Trek: Deep Space Nine*)

I discovered *Trek* because I was into the Apollo space program as a kid. I had seen the original moon landing and I was really taken with the space program, and that led me to *Star Trek*. *Lost in Space* was the first space show that I fell in love with, and then I started seeing *Star Trek* and that became the show for me. It was on five days a week at four in the afternoon, and after I got home from school I could watch *Star Trek* every day. I saw it as where NASA was going someday and where we could all go someday. I read it as a prophetic show, that this was what was going to happen. I remember thinking, "When are we going to have one world government and start building starships?"

DEAN DEVLIN (writer, producer, *Independence Day, Stargate*)

My mother played a role in the "Wolf in the Fold" episode of *Star Trek*. It's a terrific episode with murder, intrigue, and spirits! But what I most remember about it was that they gave my mother a phaser to take home. I was a little boy at the time and my mom brought me an actual phaser from the TV show to play with. This was my "crack" that started my addiction to science fiction.

RENE ECHEVARRIA
(supervising producer, *Star Trek: Deep Space Nine*)

My first memory of *Star Trek* is it being on the air . . . and being sent to bed. I remember hearing the theme song and seeing a spaceship unlike anything I had ever seen before. And it was nine o'clock on a Friday night and I was being told it was bedtime. I was six years old or something. Space was happening. Man was going to the moon. So, for me *Star Trek* is just woven right into that part of American history.

BRANNON BRAGA

When I was in middle school, there were cliques that I remember very specifically. There were the horror guys who were into *Fangoria,* which was me and my group. There were the fantasy *Dungeons & Dragons,* the *Lord of the Rings* dudes. And there were the *Trek* guys who were sitting reading *Spock Must Die!* And each group thought the others were nerds.

JONATHAN LARSEN

I wanted a show that I could watch with my seven-year-old son, Jeremy, that would be fun and exciting but also open doors for us to have conversations about ethics and big ideas. Important ideas. So we decided to watch the entire original series, in order. I went with unremastered, in part because I didn't want spiffy special effects to take center stage. If special effects weren't the main appeal, I thought Jeremy would focus more on the characters and their motivations and the underlying dynamics of each story. That said, Jeremy loved the aliens and the monsters and the spaceships.

But more than that, he came to know the characters—we argued over which were coolest—and when I'd pause the shows to explain some of the more subtle story elements, we often found ourselves in those big-idea conversations I had hoped for. Jeremy knows at least a bit about World War II and the Cold War, and mutually assured destruction, and Vietnam and the domino theory and on and on, primarily because of our conversations about what elements from our history *Star Trek* was addressing in individual episodes. We've watched lots of other movies and shows—none has opened the door so powerfully or insistently to that kind of exegesis about cultural and historical relevance. I don't think it's a coincidence that none has stayed with him as deeply as *Star Trek* has.

ALAN DEAN FOSTER (author, story, *Star Trek: The Motion Picture*)

It's fairly obvious that it represented, more than anything else, a sensible future. A future where people worked together and utilized science and reason and logic to try and solve problems, instead of just blowing things up.

BRANNON BRAGA

Star Trek isn't just a shoot-'em-up laser show. There's a certain expectation that you're going to explore some aspect of humanity in an interesting way, which distinguishes this show from most sci-fi series. The different series seem to reflect the time in which they were created to some degree, but there's always a humanistic philosophical core that seems unchanged, and I would hope that *Star Trek* would retain its essence going forward.

ROBERT LEWIN (coproducer, *Star Trek: The Next Generation*)

The old series endured because it is basically rooted in two elements. The first element is that the shows have ideas. Some are good, some are not so good. There is philosophy, extravagantly designed ideas with other planets that you can't express in any other show. Some of the ideas are wild, but they're always grounded in science-fiction reality. The other reason is that the affection the characters felt for each other was, in a sense, the same kind of affection you got in all the long-running series.

THOMAS DOHERTY

The show is also about the Freudian triad: the id, the ego, and the superego. That's the core of the series.

FRANK SPOTNITZ (executive producer, *The Man in the High Castle*)

The original *Star Trek* and *The Twilight Zone* were the key things to my childhood. The good episodes of *Star Trek*—and most of them were really good—were *about* something. They were about ideas. To me, the genius of it was that Kirk was the character of action, Spock was the character of the mind, and McCoy was the character of emotion. You had mind and emotion, logic and conscience, arguing, and Kirk had to meditate and take action. It was a beautiful prism for storytelling, and it drove those episodes week after week. *That's* what made that show so great. That and *Twilight Zone* were by far the most thought-provoking things on television in the 1960s and the 1970s. There was *nothing* else remotely as good.

SCOTT MANTZ

My love for *Star Trek* was fueled because of the characters. When I was a kid, I wanted to be James T. Kirk . . . and I still do.

DAVID A. GOODMAN

He could kick anybody's ass.

SCOTT MANTZ

He *was* the James Bond of outer space.

RENE ECHEVARRIA

There are certain actors who just grab a role with such gusto that you can feel it. And he did. He believed. They all did remarkably when you think about the fact they were standing on these sets made of cardboard, practically, wearing these costumes and makeup, and how outlandish it all was. The way they committed to it was extraordinary. The perceived wisdom is that the show was this quirky show that was canceled that nobody watched, but Leonard Nimoy was nominated for an Emmy.

DAVID A. GOODMAN

There is a way in which Kirk is wish fulfillment for a lot of guys, in that he's obviously an action hero, but he's also smart. And then his best friend is the supernerd, Spock, and the supernerd can actually beat up the Kirk character, which is also is a bit of wish fulfillment. And that's true going forward as well, Picard is the intellectual leader who leads by the weight of his intellect.

MARIE JACQUEMETTON

I remember lying on my living-room floor with my brothers and watching it, and it was just the excitement that they were in space, and there would always be a moment in every episode where their life was in jeopardy and "oh my God, are they gonna make it back?" And also, Captain Kirk was pretty cute.

HARVE BENNETT (executive producer, *Star Trek II: The Wrath of Khan*)

Leonard was to *Star Trek* what David McCallum was to *The Man from U.N.C.L.E.* Bill is the centerpiece, but the thing that makes it work is this extraordinary oddball who makes the show unpredictable. I've always thought that. The fans validated that in Leonard's first two years on the old series.

ADAM MALIN (cofounder, Creation Entertainment)

Mr. Spock was part of the cultural zeitgeist at the time. Spock was the biggest character in *Star Trek*, with all apologies to Captain Kirk. I don't think you can top Spock for being the most intriguing, beloved *Star Trek* character of all time. He was Roddenberry's and Leonard's perfect creation. Leonard Nimoy really created that character—the writers did wonderful things to help define him, but it was Leonard who created this amazing multifaceted being, and it doesn't surprise me that Leonard amassed worldwide fame and attention just off of that character.

KIM CATTRALL (actress, *Star Trek VI: The Undiscovered Country*)

I loved the sixties show. When I was growing up I just thought Spock was the most amazing character. He was so smart and sexy. He was just the perfect man to me, maybe a little lacking in passion but underneath all that *was* this incredible passion.

RENE ECHEVARRIA

For any kid who was into *Star Trek*, it was, "Did you identify with Kirk or were you a Spock guy?" I was a Spock guy. There's an age when you're twelve or thirteen where logic seems like the answer to all the world's problems. You're like, "I can logic my way to anything." The idea of logic appeals to the adolescent brain.

ROD RODDENBERRY

It's interesting because I do have a unique perspective on it. I met the fans first and then watched *Star Trek*. I didn't watch *Star Trek* as a kid. I didn't watch *Star Trek* as a teenager except *The Next Generation*—barely—because I was a PA [production assistant] on the show. I still didn't get it.

It wasn't until after going to the conventions and talking to the fans after my father passed away that I pulled my head out of my ass long enough to start listening and asking questions like "Why do all you nutjobs dress up in these costumes and praise this show?" And they started telling their stories and it just fucking blew me away.

DOUG DREXLER (scenic artist, *Star Trek: Deep Space Nine*)

We had Rod [Roddenberry] as a PA in the art department for a couple of years. You know how cool it is to work and be able to yell, "Roddenberry, get in here!" Just by Rod, you knew that the parents were good people to raise a good kid like that.

ROD RODDENBERRY

It's not like I hated it, but I just didn't get it. I didn't really consider something on television being so deep, and I was also a teenager. Things like Mötley Crüe were what spoke to me. I wasn't thinking about the future. So it was going to the conventions and just hearing story after story about how it touched people or what their views on it were or how it made humanity a better humanity that interested me.

JESUS TREVINO (director, *Star Trek: Voyager*)

I went to Occidental College and every Friday night when it was broadcast the whole dorm would amass in the common room. In those days it was the boys' dorms and the girls' dorms. And in the boys' dorms every Friday night, everybody would storm down and watch the episode. We were just huge fans of the series. I remember one of the fraternities made a huge replica of the *Enterprise* twenty-five or thirty feet long out of kegs and beer cans.

JOHN D. F. BLACK
(executive story consultant, associate producer, *Star Trek*)

It's very easy to look back now and say Gene Roddenberry knew what he was doing. He didn't know, but the collective knew. Robert Justman, myself, and other people who were involved with the pieces as they came out. We were a collective "one." And that one turned out to be in quotes "Gene Roddenberry." We were all in that mix. It was a wonderful thing to be involved with—except when you were there and then it was terrible.

ED NAHA

I loved working with Gene. He was one of the smartest, most gracious and optimistic people I've ever met. Having said that, I also would not have wanted to get on his bad side. He had things he wanted to accomplish, and accomplish them he would.

Gene *knew* people. He'd been a civilian pilot who'd survived a nasty crash and helped save the crew, and he'd been an L.A. cop. He'd seen a lot of crap. Yet his vision for the near and distant future was one of optimism. For instance, he believed in equal rights. That was just a given with him. As someone who started marching for civil rights at the age of fourteen, I couldn't believe a "grown-up" would just assume that it was the right thing to believe in.

ADAM MALIN

I'll never forget his kindness, his mentorship, his positive outlook toward society and the future of society, considering what a screwed-up world it is in so many ways. His humanism and his optimism still remain inspiring. I think Gene's optimism for the future of the human condition is a message that is just as vital today as it was fifty years ago; it's part of what inspires new generations of *Star Trek* fans, and whatever Gene may have been as a business associate, a writer, a showrunner, a producer, he was a man with a very noble vision for society, and that has come through the spirit of *Star Trek* through all these years, and for me remains his greatest achievement. Simply saying to the world that in the future our society will be better, that's a beautiful message, and I think it's Gene's greatest legacy.

FRED BRONSON

I found him funny; he loved to laugh. I don't mean this as a pun, he was down-to-earth. He loved women, he loved many women, and somehow that was part of his charm, but he was generous and kind, and he would pick up the bill always.

ED NAHA

Gene also had a great sense of humor. I went over to his house for dinner one night, and I said I had to check in with my then girlfriend back in New York. He let me dial the number and then he got on the phone, identifying himself as an L.A. cop who had me in custody. My girlfriend gave him hell, saying that *that* was impossible. There must be some mistake. I was not the kind of guy who'd do anything illegal. "What if I told you he was caught exposing himself?" he said, grinning at me. My girlfriend hesitated. Gene laughed his ass off, identified himself to my girlfriend, and handed me the phone. She was *not* amused.

A few months later, Gene was in Manhattan and we invited him over to our apartment for dinner. He showed up and we opened the door. He hesitated before entering, looking above his head, expecting some booby trap. There was none. Later on, however, he discovered that his salad was filled with rubber and plastic toy insects. He got a kick out of that.

THOMAS DOHERTY

In the golden age of television, writers lived life. Today's writers live television.

CHRIS GORE (founder, *Film Threat* magazine)

For me, *Star Trek* was always about Kirk, Spock, McCoy, the starship *Enterprise*, and a galaxy to explore. All the spin-offs just made me miss the adventures of the characters I loved originally.

BARRY SCHULMAN
(vice-president of programming, Sci-Fi Channel)

No matter how successful *The Next Generation* was, this was still the grand-daddy of them all. I think viewers today would be hard-pressed to think of any talent on *Star Trek* other than Shatner and Nimoy. *Next Generation* was a great-looking show and a great series, but you can't ignore the fact that it's much like with the original *Star Wars*. No matter how major all of these others are, and how spectacular the techniques and the effects are today, and the casting is brilliant, you'll never forget the original, Mark Hamill, Harrison Ford and Carrie Fisher.

ED NAHA

It's funny, because I was the A&R guy on both *Inside Star Trek* . . . and *Born to Run*. It's very hard to summarize what was going on in the seventies. It's almost an "it was the best of times, it was the worst of times" scenario. With the end of the Vietnam debacle, a lot of young people felt, rightly so, that they had played a pivotal role. There was a very optimistic attitude around. In a small way, this dovetailed into the *Trek* philosophy. But by the mid seventies, everything began to get co-opted and commercialized. It wasn't obvious but it was happening. I think people who were aware, people who valued creativity sensed it coming.

Ironically, *Born to Run* was released during a time when live music was being delivered a body blow by disco, a genre of sound where the producer took precedence over the performer. Soon, it became as calculating and craven as any other assembly-line product. And, again, those with a creative nature smelled the decay. It's no accident that Springsteen went from *Born to Run* to *Darkness on the Edge of Town* by 1978. He followed that up with *The River* and *Nebraska* before launching *Born in the USA* in '84. Ironically, the song was about Vietnam, lost friends, and dreams either destroyed or deferred. A lot of the public embraced it as a nationalistic arena rock anthem. This, I think, shows that not only was optimism on the fast fade but intelligence as well.

It's no mystery as to why Gene was shunted aside once the *Star Trek* movie series began. His brand of optimism couldn't be packaged and sold in bulk. It had to be felt.

DAVID A. GOODMAN

Breaking Bad is dark, but it's also light, it's also really funny, and that's also what *Star Trek* did really well. It walked that line, creatively, of always being dramatic, but also having a sense of humor about its characters.

VINCE GILLIGAN (creator, executive producer, *Breaking Bad*)

There probably is something to that. To be fair, as much as I love *Star Trek, Star Trek* was not the first dramatic story to levy its drama with humor. I can think of *The Thing from Another World*, which did that. A bunch of military guys in an installation at the North Pole in a very life-or-death situation and yet cracking wise whenever they had the chance.

Having said that, *Star Trek* did it very well indeed, and it's a good lesson to any writer to not take your drama too seriously. In other words, the most dramatic moments in real life oftentimes have a bit of absurdity or humor contained within them. Gene Roddenberry and the writers of the original *Star Trek* knew that lesson and used little dollops of humor very well. We later learned that lesson on *The X-Files,* another show that was very dramatic but had a couple of outright hilarious episodes—which shows how elastic that dramatic form can be.

DAVID A. GOODMAN

J. J. Abrams kind of proves that despite all the changes and all the iterations, the Kirk–Spock dynamic is something people like to see. I watched a lot of TV from the sixties; the production value of TV, the writing—nothing approaches *Star Trek*. That's what gets lost in the discussion of the *Star Trek* phenomenon. People talk about how it represents hope for the future and the stories are exciting and it was so far ahead of its time. But as a TV producer, I look at it and think about what else was being produced at that time, the endless westerns and the endless cop shows shot on the Universal backlot. Here you have this drama where you can't get all the costumes at a rental house, they had to be handmade. You're creating aliens and makeup, but also the writers are creating societies, they're creating the Federation, they're creating Vulcans, they're creating the Andorians. They're creating societies that live on their own, and it all works and it all comes together.

You can create these sequel series that can harken back without it feeling stupid, they connect because the work of those artisans, the writers, the producers, the actors was so far ahead of its time.

In a certain way, *Next Generation*, as big a fan as I am of it, pales in comparison to the original series, because it builds on something that someone had already created. By then TV had done plenty of things that were like it, very well-written shows, great casts, but in terms of the accomplishments of the original series, that's what is lost in the discussion of *Star Trek*. The reason it's a success is because it's amazing.

VINCE GILLIGAN

There's a lot of admirable writing and directing and acting in the subsequent *Star Trek* series, but the original series just has the most meaning for me emotionally.

PETER GOULD (cocreator, executive producer, *Better Call Saul*)

Nothing will ever replace the original sixties *Star Trek*. There was just something a little bit special about that one in terms of the storytelling and the cast, even the way it looked, that I always found very fascinating. The later incarnations in a lot of ways are more sophisticated and you might even say deeper science fiction, but I have to say my heart belongs to Kirk, Spock, and McCoy.

RICHARD ARNOLD (*Star Trek* archivist)

It's been said time and again, but it's worth repeating: Gene gave us a future where we survived our current immaturity and did so with dignity. We're not out there empire-building, we're out there exploring and learning. His vision has changed so many people's lives, and will continue to do so for a long time.

NICHELLE NICHOLS (actress, "Nyota Uhura")

The success of the show and the genius of Gene Roddenberry was in taking a message—as did Shakespeare so cleverly—and making it dramatically sound while adhering to the first law of show business—to entertain.

WILLIAM SHATNER (actor, "James Tiberius Kirk")

I'm often asked why *Star Trek* has had such longevity and why people continue to be interested in the original series and who knows how many more manifestations of *Star Trek*. I think it has to do with mythology. *Star Trek* with its hearty band of followers, its heroes, its villains, and its tales of good and evil, provide modern culture with a mythology and also bespeaks of a future and the certainty that the future will exist.

ROXANN DAWSON
(actress, "B'Elanna Torres," *Star Trek: Voyager*)

I thought of *Star Trek* as more of a cartoon before I got involved, and then I realized, "My God, it's almost like these are the myths of our times." I realized there was all this depth here. It was really shocking to me.

IRA STEVEN BEHR

It was a quintessential sixties show, and the other thing that was great about it—which, unfortunately, has more or less disappeared off of the cultural landscape—is the fact that as far as we were concerned, it was *our* show, my sister and I. We found it, no one told us to watch it, no one said it was good, no one said it was must-see TV. There was no hype, there was no mass culture telling you that if you wanted to be a card-carrying member of the hip mass culture you have to watch it. So, that made it so special. It's sad to have that kind of disappear. It's much harder nowadays to own pop culture, because that ground has been covered by the hype machine.

JEROME BIXBY (writer, *Star Trek*)

Star Trek was a great vehicle for advancing social critique via paraphrase and allegory. You showed how the world sucks by showing another world so occupied. Also, for playing with serious scientific possibilities. No other show has come so close to the elbow room of literary science fiction. Those were the days.

GENE RODDENBERRY

I think that all serious writing is valuable. It is the duty of the writer to speculate on things of importance to us, and to give us new insights into ourselves, who we are, what our society is, what its pitfalls are—what its joys truly should be. In that sense I think *Star Trek* was valuable, and that all serious and entertaining writing is valuable.

HERBERT F. SOLOW (executive in charge of production, *Star Trek*)

I maintain all along that if it wasn't for Gene being a genius at self-promotion and having a massive ego about his work and about *Star Trek*, it would have died. It would never have come back to life in syndication, it never would have made other series, other movies. It would have faded away.

DAVID WEDDLE (producer, *Star Trek: Deep Space Nine*)

It's now the same amount of time talking to someone about the original *Star Trek* as it was somebody in the sixties talking to Buster Keaton about making silent movies and working with Fatty Arbuckle.

J. J. ABRAMS (producer, *Star Trek Beyond*)

I'm honored to have been the temporary captain of the show that Roddenberry built. I only hope that my involvement helped bring more people into this universe, so lovingly and wonderfully drawn by its creator.

DIANA MULDAUR (actress, *Star Trek,* "Return to Tomorrow")

I just wish we could be around forever and ever, so we can see how long it lasts.

UNCAGED

"IT'S LIKE NOTHING WE'VE ENCOUNTERED BEFORE."

The year is 1966. Fans at the World Science Fiction Convention, Tricon, in Cleveland, Ohio, are about to get their first glimpse of "Where No Man Has Gone Before," the second pilot for the new NBC science-fiction series *Star Trek*. Introduced by its creator, Gene Roddenberry, who had already given attendees a taste of the show via elaborate costumes modeled at the convention, the episode unspooled alongside the pilot for Irwin Allen's *The Time Tunnel*. Whereas Allen's was derided, Roddenberry's was greeted by thunderous applause from the 850 assembled fans.

Much like rock fans demanding an encore at a concert, Roddenberry dutifully complied and screened the first pilot, "The Cage," as well that weekend to an equally rapturous response. It would be a first look at the television series that would entrance, delight, and obsess fans for the next fifty years.

GENE RODDENBERRY (creator, executive producer, *Star Trek*)

I was nervous, particularly when I saw the Tricon audience watching other films that were shown before, and booing, and stomping, and laughing at things. I walked out there thinking, "They're finally going to show this one." Then I watched how they accepted this show. I said to myself, "Yes, there *are* people, if we go this way and try these things, who are going to appreciate them." I realized then that we would have fans of some sort, and of course, where that went is insanity.

JERRY SOHL (writer, "The Corbomite Maneuver")

There was what felt like three thousand people watching a new Irwin Allen show, and as soon as they saw his name they started booing. They just *booed* his name. Then when Gene Roddenberry showed *Star Trek*, they really loved that. I was really surprised. When Gene and I sat up at the podium answering questions, I was introduced as the "head writer" of *Star Trek*, which I wasn't. I just went along with it, because I thought it would be good politics. And it was. It was fun.

This would be the first, but far from the last, taste Gene Roddenberry would get of fan adulation for his groundbreaking series. Born Eugene Wesley Roddenberry on August 19, 1921, the tall but often shabbily dressed Texan had already lived a remarkable life by the time he arrived in Los Angeles with his then wife, Eileen Anita Rexroat, with whom he would have two daughters and on whom he would have an extramarital affair with Majel Barrett before they would eventually be married.

CHRISTOPHER KNOPF (writer, producer)

Eileen Roddenberry was a very quiet woman, totally different from Majel Barrett. She was very happy being a cop's wife. Hollywood was very hard for her to handle; he had a lot of social commitments, and she wasn't very comfortable with that at all. He had these two daughters, and when they broke up it was very bitter. She went after him financially and won big-time. The two daughters took their mother's side, and I think Gene had virtually no relationship with them. Then Majel and Gene had a son, they called him Rod, who is a really nice guy.

ROD RODDENBERRY (son of Gene Roddenberry)

I have very fond memories of Christmas and dinners with the whole family there. Both my grandfathers had passed before I was born, so both grandmothers, my father's sister, my half sisters, and their two children all having Christmas dinners and stuff like that. None of the history was there, so I got introduced to it after my father passed away because the ex-wife came around. One of my father's daughters sued the family alongside the ex-wife and I was very upset with that.

The other daughter didn't, she sided with us and I was kind of confused and distraught. I have sympathy for them, because they were around during the original series. My father even said in one of his interviews that he was focused so much on the original series, he was never there, so I could see why they felt wronged by him. And he had an affair with my mother for ten years before they got married. So, I can't say I feel what they feel, but I can understand how they would feel betrayed.

ANDE RICHARDSON (Desilu secretary, assistant to Gene L. Coon)

I met Eileen. She wasn't all that friendly. She wasn't warm and open to other people. She was quite elitist. People were beneath her, especially after Gene was really doing well. So that was the impression. That wasn't Gene Roddenberry. Gene was still a pretty cool guy. I remember I came back from Mexico with a whole bunch of joints ready-rolled and he was thrilled. [An assistant] used to sit there at the desk and empty all the tobacco out of the cigarettes and then stuff the pot into the empty cigarette.

A former pilot and second lieutenant in the United States Army Air Corps and copilot of a B-17 Flying Fortress during World War II, Roddenberry had made the move from military to civilian aviator and narrowly survived the crash of Pan Am Flight 121 in the Syrian desert that he was flying from Calcutta. Joining the Los Angeles Police Department in February 1949, Roddenberry found himself writing speeches for Chief William H. Parker as well as articles for the LAPD newsletter, *The Beat*.

GENE RODDENBERRY

I was a policeman and learned to write as a speechwriter for Parker. I learned to write long before that, though, with the idea that if you write eight hundred words a day, soon you will be a writer. It took me eight years or so. Once I quit Pan American as a pilot, it seemed to me that, yes, I'm a writer, whether people believe that or not.

Although I suppose you could have called me a science-fiction fan, this certainly was not the alpha-omega of my reading. I think all writers are omnivorous in their reading. I know few writers that I respect that read only science fiction. As a result, when I decided to become a writer, I decided to become a *writer*, not just a science-fiction writer. But I've loved science fiction since I was a child, and I suppose most of the ideas were a combination of things I had read and heard about, although I have a smattering of knowledge in the scientific field. I had been an airline pilot, so I suppose that helped.

Not content to remain a policeman the rest of his life, Roddenberry began to contribute ideas to *Dragnet* producer and star Jack Webb, who became a fast friend as well as a rival for the affections of actress Majel Lee Hudec, later Majel Barrett Roddenberry.

FRED BRONSON (publicist, NBC Television)

Jack Webb, who was a great guy, dated Majel Barrett at the same time as Gene. Gene, who was friends with Webb since he had been a cop—and Webb played a cop—told me years later that Majel was on a date with Jack when Gene sent flowers to the table with a card.

YVONNE CRAIG (actress, "Whom Gods Destroy")

Majel and I lived at The Studio Club because when I first came out to Hollywood I didn't have a place to live. It was like the Y for show-business people. I hadn't seen her for years, and when I saw her at a party for the twentieth anniversary of *Star Trek*, I said, "Majel Barrett, how are you?" And she said it was "Majel *Roddenberry*," and I said, "Oh, I didn't know that, I don't keep up with Hollywood gossip." I didn't know that she was having an affair with him while he was still married to his wife. And she said, "It is *not* gossip!" And I thought, "God, what a crab she turned out to be."

Hired as a consultant to *Mr. District Attorney,* Roddenberry sold his first script in 1954. Subsequently, he had scripts produced for such series as *Goodyear Theatre, The Kaiser Aluminum Hour, Four Star Playhouse, Highway Patrol, Dr. Kildare,* and *Naked City,* among others.

GENE RODDENBERRY

I remember myself as an asthmatic child, having great difficulties at seven, eight, and nine years old, falling totally in love with *Tarzan, Lord of the Jungle* and dreaming of being him and having his strength to leap into trees and throw mighty lions to the ground. It was a part of my growing up. It was a lovely dream. It carried me through many a hacking and coughing and sneezing attack.

Then there was a boy in my class who life had treated badly. He limped, he wheezed. I don't know all the things that were wrong with him, but he was a charming, lovely, intelligent person. He, because of being unable to get on the athletic fields and do many of the things that others were able to do, had sort of gone into his own world of fantasy and science fiction. He had been collecting the wonderful old *Amazing* and *Astounding* magazines from those great old days, and he introduced me to science fiction. I started to read them and then discovered in our neighborhood, living above a garage, was an ex-con who had come into science fiction when he was in prison. He introduced me to John Carter and those wonderful Burroughs things. By the time I was twelve or thirteen I had been very much into the whole science-fiction field.

Resigning from the police force in 1956, Roddenberry continued to write for television and sold several pilots as well. Later, he provided a number of scripts to a man who would become a good friend, Sam Rolfe, for *Have Gun–Will Travel,* the brilliant and groundbreaking TV western starring Richard Boone. In that show several familiar *Star Trek*-ian tropes would be introduced, including a character named Robert April. Roddenberry also won a Writers Guild of America Award for his episode "Helen of Abajinian." It's impossible to overstate the importance of *Have Gun–Will Travel* in the formative, progressive thoughts of Gene Roddenberry.

CHRISTOPHER KNOPF

Sam Rolfe is really the one who gave him his big shot, on *Have Gun—Will Travel.* That's what put him up and made people say "Whoa, this guy can do something."

In the series, Boone plays Paladin, an erudite bon vivant in San Francisco who supports himself from bounty-hunter work, usually by Paladin discovering their plight through the daily newspaper with the help of his valet, Hey Boy, and sending them his iconic business card by mail or telegraph. Once on his way, the man in black is as skilled with a gun or in a brawl as he is at quoting Shakespeare or Dickens. More important, *Have Gun* was a morality play in which nothing was usually as it appeared (a rare western that depicted Native Americans sympathetically and not as outright villains), and Paladin often took the side of the underdog, even if it turned out they were not the ones paying his rather exorbitant fee. Paladin had the passion of Kirk, the intelligence of Spock, and the beating, bleeding heart of McCoy.

DOUG DREXLER (scenic artist, *Star Trek: Deep Space Nine*)

Paladin is Kirk, Spock, and McCoy fused into one. Gene split Paladin up to make those three guys. Look at Paladin, he's got all the elements of Spock, he knows about everything. He's a bon vivant, he's a humanitarian, and he's a man of action—he's all that stuff.

Two of my all-time favorite *Have Guns* were Roddenberry episodes. One was called "The Great Mojave Chase." Paladin is at the hotel and he's sitting reading the newspaper with a friend of his who's a cavalry colonel, and this guy is stinking drunk. He's going on and on about how he just got off this awful assignment and he's glad it's over with. The army decided to try out camels instead of horses. Now, this is true. Roddenberry, I'm sure, looked at the books and said, "Ah, how can I get Paladin on a camel?" And while he's going on and on about how bad they smell and they have a bad attitude and stuff, Paladin's reading the newspaper and there's the voice-over of him reading about the great Mojave chase. And he gets the idea right then and there to get into the race, but with a camel. He knows he can kick everybody's butt. And just as he is making this realization, the cavalry colonel says, "Who the hell would want one of those stinking things anyway?" And he goes, "I don't know. Could be your best friend." And he goes out and he gets the camel. It is so unique and unusual. It has that gimmick that makes it so special.

And then there was another one that was Roddenberry exercising his love of men romancing women. It was called "Maggie O'Bannion." He ends up getting robbed by some highwaymen. They take his clothes, they take his horse, they take everything. He comes across this house where there is a woman who has a farm. She'll help him, but he has to do chores around the house like cook and clean. She falls in love with him because he knows how to make amazing dishes and stuff like that. She is very smart, though. She takes his gun hand and goes, "How did you get a callus like this on your thumb?" There's this wonderful scene where he brings her food and she wants to have nothing to do with him. And he gets into a conversation about Shelley and Shakespeare and he picks up a book and quotes from it. It's so wonderful.

Later on, there's a scene that's right out of "The Cage." Paladin goes out riding on the horse and she is following him. He stops and waits for her. They argue and she goes to smack him and he grabs her hand and before you know it, they're not making out like Kirk would with someone, but they basically sit down under the tree together and she's leaning against him. It's the sweetest moment. It's so *Star Trek.*

At the very end of the show two women are saying good-bye to him and it's just like it was almost "I'll watch the stars." And instead of beaming out, he rides off as the two girls are looking at him and she says, "I'll never find help like that again." And the other one goes, "Never find help like that again. Cook, clean, fight. I get chills just thinking about it." It's perfect Roddenberry.

GENE RODDENBERRY

Paladin was as close to being SF as you could get. Richard Boone was a marvelous person as actors go.

DEBORAH ARAKELIAN
(assistant to Harve Bennett and Robert Sallin)

I always suspected he had a thing about Armenian girls because when I met him he said, "When I was a cop and I was working in Hollywood, I got called out on a loud party call." And so he and his partner show up and it's a full-out *kef.* Big Armenian party; belly dancers, hookahs, the whole nine yards. These guys say, "Hey, come on in. Join us." His partner says, "No." Gene says, "I'm down." Gene stayed and partied with them all night long. He went home and, according to Gene, he wrote the very first thing he'd ever written, "Helen of Abajinian," which he later sold to *Have Gun—Will Travel.* I think he had a general like of little dark swarthy women. He would have loved the Kardashians.

GENE RODDENBERRY

I can remember at the beginning of television when many of us were working as screenwriters on even the bad shows that we started with, like *Mr. District Attorney,* we would always insert in our scripts that to be of a different color or a different creed does not make you bad. Lessons of tolerance and things like that. You had to do it very carefully, the network didn't want any preaching in it, but I think these things had an effect. I don't think these things could play every night in Mississippi and places like that around the country and not have an effect on the society and on the people growing up. I think TV has done some good. I just think it's a damn shame that we've had to do it as saboteurs and not with the support of the studios and the networks.

JOSEPH STEFANO (creator/producer, *The Outer Limits*)

Dealing with the television network is like dealing with a two-headed monster. On one hand, they want high ratings, and on the other, there are people who want to safeguard the hearts and minds of viewers, and they come from the same source. So one half of the network is telling you to cut this or that out, and the other half tells you to give them more. I don't think it's as big a problem as it was, because they've determined a time when sex and violence should be on TV. We had very little sex in *The Outer Limits,* and very little violence except in the scary sense, not violence as in shooting eight people.

ROBERT H. JUSTMAN
(associate producer, *The Outer Limits, Star Trek*)

In doing *The Outer Limits*, what the network wanted was not necessarily an intelligent science fiction show. What they wanted was a science fiction show that would return a lot of numbers. Their theory was that to do that you had to have a monster in every show. If you're an intelligent person and you like monsters, no, it wasn't a problem keeping science fiction on the air. But if you're an intelligent person and you *don't* think it should be monsters to do an intelligent show, yes, it was difficult.

Somewhat of the same attitude was found in the early days of *Star Trek* when the network suggested they wanted to open with an episode called "The Man Trap," because it had a monster. We felt that it wasn't a very good show compared to some of the others we had already made. We lost the battle, they won the battle, and "Man Trap" was aired first.

GENE RODDENBERRY

Our plan all along was to present drama. Due to postproduction difficulties, our opening show, including a "monster," was the only one available for air. Our entire concept is and has always been to demonstrate that science fiction is a much broader and more dramatic field of literature than is generally recognized by the public.

JERRY SOHL

There was a lack of *true* science fiction on television at the time. Theodore Sturgeon, Richard Matheson, George Clayton Johnson, and myself got together and formed what we called The Green Hand. We were going to knock television dead by doing really *responsible* science fiction. Certainly the medium could stand better material. We wanted script and quality control. We wanted to breathe something new into the shows, bring the medium up to date and in step with what was happening in SF at the time. We thought at least half of prime time should be devoted to SF and fantasy. We offered a number of scenarios and met with the different networks who said they loved the concepts.

In the end, though, they didn't buy *any* of the series we offered. It was too bad for the networks, too bad for The Green Hand, and too bad for the viewing public. The corporation was dissolved and the four of us went our separate ways. But the ironic thing is that *all* of our series premises eventually became TV shows in one form or another.

In 1963, Roddenberry had his first pilot produced by MGM for NBC, the short-lived series *The Lieutenant.* Many faces familiar to *Star Trek* fans would appear in *The Lieutenant,* ranging from lead actor Gary Lockwood, playing Marine Corps Second Lieutenant William Tiberius Rice; to Majel Barrett, Nichelle Nichols, Walter Koenig, and, most memorably, Leonard Nimoy. All of them had been cast by Joe D'Agosta, who would rejoin Roddenberry for *Star Trek.* The character of Robert April (designated as the first captain of the *Enterprise* in Roddenberry's original concept description of the series) would also once again make an appearance in the final episode of the *Star Trek* animated series.

The Lieutenant was a Marine Corps drama set and shot at Camp Pendleton near San Diego, thanks to the cooperation of the military. Until they pulled their support late in the run, when Roddenberry butted heads with both the military and the network, insisting on producing an episode about racial prejudice in the military, "To Set It Right," which featured a young Dennis Hopper.

MARC CUSHMAN (author, *These Are the Voyages*)

NBC didn't want to air it; the Marines, who had been cooperating with the show, didn't want them to air it; and the Pentagon even said, "If you air this episode, we're not going to let you film down on our bases anymore. We're not going to give you free tanks and trucks and soldiers and uniforms," and all of the things that made *The Lieutenant* work. Yet he was determined to put it through; he went to the NAACP and forced them to put the heat on the network to air that episode. The week after that episode aired, NBC canceled *The Lieutenant.* So his relationship with NBC was bad at the get-go.

JOHN D. F. BLACK
(executive story consultant/associate producer, *Star Trek*)

The network didn't like him, nobody liked him, and the writers, in particular, didn't like him because when he had done *The Lieutenant* he had rewritten everyone on that show just like he had done with us on *Star Trek.* GR would sit in his chair and look *through* a writer. I don't know if you've ever had anyone look through you. It's very disconcerting and a great many of the writers had that feeling.

GENE RODDENBERRY

Writers for the television audience do the same thing as the great sculptors and painters and composers do. When you do say to the world, "Hey, these are things as I see it! These are my comments. This is how I see the world," you do this with utter selfishness—which is what an artist should *always* do. All writers should be selfish and say, "This is the way I see it," and under the voice should say, "Screw you! If you want yours, you can do it, too."

After *The Lieutenant*'s cancellation at the conclusion of its first and only season, Roddenberry's studio on that series, MGM, turned down his pitch for a new series called *Star Trek*. However, his agents at Ashley-Famous quickly set it up at Desilu Studios, which was looking to produce more provocative television dramas after years of unprecedented success in comedy. Headed up by former CBS executive Oscar Katz, Desilu signed Roddenberry to a three-year development deal. After being rebuffed by CBS, which already had *Lost in Space* in development, Roddenberry and the Desilu team set up their pilot at NBC, and "The Cage" (originally entitled "The Menagerie," which would become the title of the two-part first season episode that would reuse footage from this first pilot) was born.

OSCAR KATZ (vice-president of programs, Desilu)

If I had to pick the three people who had the most to do with getting *Star Trek* into reality, they would be Gene Roddenberry, myself, and an agent at Ashley named Alden Schwimmer. I had problems signing creative people, getting them to pitch projects. Schwimmer said, "Let's get a couple of guys and make overall deals with them. Let's not say, 'I like this property, I don't like this property.' Let's approach them and say, 'We'd like you to come to Desilu and would like you to make Desilu your home. The way we'd like to do it, don't tell us your properties. We'll make a deal for three properties to be determined.'" Roddenberry is the guy he recommended.

I started working for Desilu in April of '64 and began to develop programs. The first year I did three or four pilots, which means that I might have had fifteen or twenty projects in earlier stages of development, from which the four were selected. They had to be sold to a network in order to get financing. I think all four sailed, but it was hard to attract creative people. Desilu had a reputation for heavy overhead charges, etc. The second year, I did five pilots and of the five, three got sold, which is a pretty good batting average. Especially when you consider that two of them were *Mission: Impossible* and *Star Trek*.

GENE RODDENBERRY

Before *Star Trek* I had written pilots that were produced by other people, and none of them sold. I began to see that to create a program idea and write a script simply wasn't enough. The story is not "told" until it's on celluloid. Telling that final story involved sound, music, casting, costumes, sets, and all the things that a producer is responsible for. Therefore it became apparent to me that if you want the film to reflect accurately what you felt when you wrote the script, then you have to produce it, too. This is why television writers tend to become producers.

OSCAR KATZ

The studio [Desilu] made money two ways. One, by shows which they owned, such as *I Love Lucy* and *The Untouchables*. The second way was as a rental studio. For instance, Bing Crosby Productions shot all their stuff there, as did Danny Thomas and Sheldon Leonard. Desilu owned three lots, and the studio probably made money just by having real estate, which was going up in value while they were sitting there. But at the time, the number of shows they owned was declining. Desi Arnaz was a ballsy guy who at one time had seven or eight series on the air that Desilu owned. But now it had declined and they were down to practically Lucy's show and fourteen or fifteen rentals.

GENE RODDENBERRY

Producing in television is like storytelling. The choice of the actor, picking the right costumes, getting the right flavor, the right pace—these are as much a part of storytelling as writing out that same description of a character in a novel. Although the director plays an important role in this, the director in television comes on a show to prepare for a week, shoots for a week, and then goes on to another show. Unlike the producer, he is neither there at the beginning of the script, nor rarely there for long after you end up with some twenty-five thousand feet of film, which now has to be cut and pasted into something unified. There are immense creative challenges and pleasure in taking all of these things and putting them together into something that works.

DOROTHY FONTANA (writer; *Star Trek* story editor)

One of the things about *Star Trek* is that so many of us came to it with no prior knowledge or experience with science fiction. Aside from some of the noted writers who did do scripts, most of us were virgin-fresh as far as science fiction went, and I believe it was one of the things that made *Star Trek* so good. We weren't trying to do the hardware, we weren't trying to do the science-fiction gimmicks, the flash. We were trying to do people stories.

GENE RODDENBERRY

Star Trek came about very slowly, as everyone who was with me at the time can testify. I was so tired of writing about what I considered nothing. I was tired of writing for shows where there was always a shoot-out in the last act and somebody was killed. I do not consider that the "ending" of anything. I would watch a whole show in those early days and, at the end, would feel like I had wasted time on nonsense. *Star Trek* was formulated to change that.

DOROTHY FONTANA

Most of the villains on *Star Trek* had personalities. They weren't necessarily evil, they had goals of their own. Those goals were good for them. On many other shows, they were just villains and they were evil because they were evil. I think the audience responded to that, that you could feel that Kirk and Spock and the others had worthy opponents, people who thought, who had feelings and who had visions and goals in addition to our heroes. Now, we always knew our heroes would win, with the exception of a few red-shirted fellows who lost a lot of blood. But the villains were awfully unique and different persons.

GENE RODDENBERRY

At the time, I had said, "Gee, too much of science fiction is about gadgetry and not about people. And drama is people. If I ever get the chance to write science fiction, I'm going to try to make it scientifically accurate as possible and write them the way they wrote the old *Playhouse 90*s." And it worked. I applied the rules of drama to science-fiction writing. There was a great deal of room for drama in science fiction in the time that *Star Trek* appeared. The stories are about people. And if they aren't people, they must have some characteristic that is human. When you do a story, you imbue the characters with personality qualities with which you can identify.

CHRISTOPHER KNOPF

Sam Rolfe, who created *Have Gun—Will Travel,* Gene, and I and a few others had become very good friends in the early 1960s. One day Gene called me up and said, "I have a couple of tickets on first base for a Dodgers day game." So we went out there, and during that game he told me he had an idea for a series about a blimp. A blimp that goes around the world in the late 1800s and stops in various exotic places, and that there would be a mixed crew. So that was the beginning of *Star Trek.* While we were talking, one of the Dodgers stole home and neither one of us saw it. Well, the next thing I knew, Gene was developing *Star Trek,* which was the same basic premise he had told me about, but he put it in the future.

RICHARD ARNOLD (*Star Trek* archivist)

Gene had been a big fan of 1961's *Master of the World.* But less known is that five years earlier, in 1956, Gene had pitched an idea for a new series called *Hawaii Passage,* which followed the adventures of a cruise ship, her captain, and senior officers. What was different here was that Gene referred to the ship as one of the characters, unheard of at the time.

GENE RODDENBERRY

I had been a freelance writer for about a dozen years and was chafing increasingly at the commercial censorship on television, which was very strong in those days. You really couldn't talk about anything you cared to talk about, and I decided I was going to leave TV unless I could find some way to write what I wanted to. I recalled that when Jonathan Swift was writing *Gulliver's Travels,* he wanted to write satire on his time and went to Lilliput in his story to do just that, and then he could talk about insane prime ministers and crooked kings and all of that. It was sort of this wonderful thing.

Children could read it as a fairy tale, an adventure, and as they got older they'd recognize it for what it really is. It seemed to me that perhaps if I wanted to talk about sex, religion, politics, make some comments against Vietnam, and so on, that if I had similar situations involving these subjects happening on other planets to little green people, indeed it might get by, and it did. It apparently went right over the censors' heads, but all the fourteen-year-olds in our audience knew exactly what we were talking about. The power you have is in a show like *Star Trek,* which is considered by many people to be a frothy little action-adventure; unimportant, unbelievable, and yet watched by a lot of people. You just slip ideas into it.

JONATHAN LARSEN (executive producer, MSNBC)

Even without introducing us to a single crew member, *Star Trek* tells us everything we need to know about its core politics. If you accept the premise that Democrats are big government and Republicans are small government, you should also acknowledge that the United Federation of Planets is about as big a government as you can imagine. Where in *Star Trek* is the free market? Ask Harry Mudd. Ask Cyrano Jones whether he considers himself overregulated in the Tribbles trade.

DOROTHY FONTANA

Gene asked me to read the first bible for *Star Trek* in 1964. This was the very first proposal; the series presentation. I read it and said, "I have only one question: who's going to play Mr. Spock?" He pushed a picture of Leonard Nimoy across the table, and I, of course, knew Leonard because he had appeared in my first [script sale], *The Tall Man.* I thought the proposal had a lot of possibilities and was certainly exciting. Of course you could never tell if it would sell and if somebody else would believe in it, but I certainly did. The captain at the time was Robert April [later James Winter], who eventually became Christopher Pike and the ship was the *Yorktown.* Mr. Spock was pretty much like the Mr. Spock that appeared in [the first pilot] "The Cage," and the doctor was Dr. Boyce. The other characters weren't as settled. Nobody was doing anything like it on television.

GENE RODDENBERRY

Leonard Nimoy was the one actor I definitely had in mind—we had worked together several years previously when I was producing *The Lieutenant.* Leonard had been a guest star and I was struck at the time with his high Slavic cheekbones and interesting face, and I said to myself, "If I ever do this science fiction thing I want to do, he would make a great alien. And with those cheekbones some sort of pointed ear might go well." And then I forgot entirely about it until I was laying out the *Star Trek* characters, and then to cast Mr. Spock I simply made a phone call to Leonard and he came in. That was it.

SAMUEL A. PEEPLES (writer, "Where No Man Has Gone Before")

In the beginning, Mr. Spock as we know him now didn't exist. He was a red-tailed devil who didn't eat. He absorbed energy through a red plate in his stomach. This is the way he was laid out in the original concept. I argued with Gene that it should be a humanized character, because I was adamant that it should be straight science fiction without fantasy.

GENE RODDENBERRY

Series are a process of refining ideas. I'd like to say that all the ideas that I get are bright and eternal and right for all time, but they're not. You do evolve things.

With Spock, originally, I also thought that there were such few choices in doing someone who was of average height. You can do a little with the ears and fake eyes and so on, but actors tend to come in roughly the same size. So I was thinking of making Spock a "little person," which would at least break some of those things, and make him stand out. Then, it also fit into the feelings I had that size should not be that important.

SAMUEL A. PEEPLES

I was one of the first people to see the *Star Trek* series proposal. Gene Roddenberry and I had known each other from writing *Have Gun—Will Travel*. He was trying to start a science-fiction series and he knew that I had one of the largest science-fiction collections in the world. At first, I remember he borrowed a copy of *Odd John* by Olaf Stapledon. Then, to research the show, he asked if he could go through my magazines and get some ideas for the *Enterprise*. Gene went through all the covers, and that's really how the *Enterprise* was born.

GENE RODDENBERRY

With the name *Enterprise,* I'd been an army bomber pilot in World War II. I'd been fascinated by the navy and particularly fascinated by the story of the *Enterprise* in World War II, which at Midway really turned the tide in the whole war in our favor. I'd always been proud of that ship and wanted to use the name.

SAMUEL A. PEEPLES

Gene and I went through all of my magazines and photographed some of the covers. We discussed every element of what he was doing. I thought it was fascinating and fun, because he was going to try to do what I considered to be science fiction, which was not often done in Hollywood. Most so-called science-fiction movies were horror plays, and similar stuff that dates back to the silent days. Gene actually had an idea, a plan, a dream of making a genuine science-fiction series that would be very much like the better science-fiction magazines.

GEORGE CLAYTON JOHNSON (writer, "The Man Trap")

One influence on the creation of *Star Trek* was *Captain Future,* which was a pulp magazine which ran for indeterminable damned issues, and was about this guy called Captain Future who was in this spaceship. [He] had this android named Otho, a robot named Grag, and a brain in a glass cage called Simon Wright, and Simon was the Mr. Spock character, and these other characters interchangeably played the other aspects of what was a four-man ship, which then became the great starship *Enterprise.* Basically any single *Captain Future* is *Star Trek.* Read one, read the other, and you can see that one is the direct linear descendant of the other, and merely rethought into a wide screen or video kind of format as opposed [to] a pulp format, but the act of creation is minimal.

STEVEN JAY RUBIN (author/journalist)

I don't think you can talk about [1956's] *Forbidden Planet*'s influence without also talking about the concept of the U.S. Navy in outer space, and I think that obviously *Star Trek* is a military picture, because even though we're on a peaceful voyage, this is an armored ship with firepower. *Forbidden Planet* introduced a crew of spacemen who were essentially a military operation. These guys were armed and they had the ability to fight back, so they were an armed navy cruiser in the twenty-third century.

GENNIFER HUTCHISON (supervising producer, *Better Call Saul*)

That movie is also very dramatic and shouty, which is sort of the first season of the original. Especially the original pilot. I can see the influence in the idea of exploration and the danger of interfering with other cultures as well as this headstrong captain who knows what's right—and is a total ladies' man at the same time.

DAVID GERROLD (author; writer, "The Trouble with Tribbles")

I have this hunch, which I will never be able to prove, that Gene Roddenberry was sitting and watching *Forbidden Planet,* and he said, "Let's do that as a TV series." Somebody probably said, "Let's have a disc-shaped spaceship," and he probably said, "No, that's too obviously *Forbidden Planet.*" But if you look at the film, there's a doctor, a captain, and so on, which I don't have a problem with.

STEVEN JAY RUBIN

Forbidden Planet gives kind of a military hierarchy to the crew: there's a captain, there's a second-in-command, a medic, there are essentially the "blaster" men. The whole concept of a naval ship applied to outer space begins heavily with *Forbidden Planet* and, to me, is a direct influence on *Star Trek.* Then there was the use of the uniforms in the film. Of course uniforms for spacemen wasn't that novel, but I think there was this kind of military aura among the *Forbidden Planet* crew that, of course, exists in *Star Trek* as well. Add to that Cruiser *C-57D* was part of the United Planets, which is similar to the United Federation of Planets in *Star Trek.*

MANNY COTO (executive producer, *Star Trek: Enterprise*)

What to me makes the original *Star Trek* so eye-opening was here is a world, a science-fiction world, as opposed to *Lost in Space,* which was made so you would actually believe it. Just the naval terminology makes you believe it's real. It made it grounded by injecting that little simple thing, the naval hierarchy, and the names of the ships and everything, that touched on reality and made you accept it.

DOUG DREXLER

The other interesting thing is that [*Have Gun—Will Travel*'s] Sam Rolfe went and did *The Man From U.N.C.L.E.* and there are so many elements from *The Man From U.N.C.L.E* in *Star Trek*. For instance, Roddenberry was impressed by the U.N.C.L.E. Special, the pistol that goes together and makes a rifle. It was a huge hit on the show and the gun used to get its own fan mail. Gene hired the guy who built that gun to make the laser rifle from "The Cage." The Kirk–Spock thing is also very much like Illya and Napoleon Solo. In the mid sixties, the idea of teaming up with a Russian was pretty out there.

JOSE TREVINO (director, *Star Trek: Voyager*)

When I first saw *Star Trek*, I thought it was like A. E. van Vogt's *The Voyage of the Space Beagle*. The similarities were so strong between the two because basically the *Space Beagle* is a ship traveling through space to find different races. Even the captain is very similar. It was a series of short stories put together in novel form told from different points of view. So the narrative voice keeps changing from one chapter to another. I don't know if Gene Roddenberry ever acknowledged that or not.

GENE RODDENBERRY

I cannot remember a single time during the planning of *Star Trek* that I looked at another show and said, "I will borrow this." On the other hand, of course, you have this marvelous thing called a brain that all of your life is storing away information, and sometimes you pull it out and say, "This is Heinlein, this is such and such." Or even probably what happens more often is your brain, being the marvelous thing it is, will take bits and pieces from three or four things and then meld them together in something you need for a particular show. Most writers who are good writers, or at least *care*, very seldom borrow things specifically.

Hacks do that. On the other hand, most good writers do write things where people can go to them and say, "Ah, this is a bit of this from this and this is a bit of that from that," but they don't write it that way.

THOMAS DOHERTY

At the core of the show is something profound, which is teamwork and adventure and tolerance, and that's why it's a World War II motif in the space age. It has all those World War II values that are projected into a different era. Even though Kirk and some of the others are privileged, it really is a team, and that was the great message of the World War II film, that you're making a heroic contribution by doing your bit; the communications officer, the navigator—they celebrate these different roles, and *Star Trek* is more hierarchical than the air force, whereas in the air force it really is everybody's equal.

GENE RODDENBERRY

The ship was *paramilitary*. There were no systems of punishment. No one was ever sent to the brig. A paramilitary system existed for efficiency, especially in times of emergency. It was a system that worked on respect. It was a well-defined system of command.

HERBERT F. SOLOW (executive in charge of production, *Star Trek*)

Gene was just a young, eager writer who had an idea, who needed help developing that idea and taking it to a network and getting it sold. The story about me refusing to leave [NBC's Grant] Tinker's office until he gave us a script commitment is absolutely correct. And then I had to work with Gene on the script, because there was no way that a relatively inexperienced pilot writer could sit down and write "The Cage," which was the ninety-minute script that Gene wrote. He needed what I refer to as a "script producer," which is the function that I fulfilled. I oversaw the production of the pilot, acting as executive producer, and Gene produced it. He was an eager, hardworking guy, who for whatever I did for him, he did likewise for me.

GENE RODDENBERRY

Desilu was the only studio that would take it. The reason Desilu took it was because they had gone five years without selling a pilot and they were desperate. They said, "We'll even try Roddenberry's crazy idea!" I think we would have had an easier time with it if we'd been at a bigger studio with more special-effects departments and so on, but it probably wouldn't have ended up much different.

MARC CUSHMAN

Desilu came into existence because Lucille Ball and Desi Arnaz owned *I Love Lucy*. It was the first time someone owned the rerun rights to a show. CBS wanted to shoot it live out of New York; they didn't want to move to Los Angeles, so they said, "We'll pay the difference to shoot it in L.A. on film." Nobody had ever shot a sitcom on film before, and that's why it still looks so good to this day. It looks like it could have been a movie; it's clean whereas if you look at *The Honeymooners,* the faces are kind of stretched because it's from kinescope, whereas *I Love Lucy* looks really good for its time period.

So they said they would pay the difference and what Desilu wanted was the rerun rights. CBS said okay; no one had ever rerun anything before. Seems like a no-brainer today, but back then no one had done it. Eventually CBS bought the rerun rights back from Lucy and Desi for a million dollars, which was a lot of money back then. Lucy and Desi take that money and buy RKO and turn it into Desilu Studios and everyone is coming to them and asking them to film their sitcoms the same way they did their own. The company grows, but then the marriage falls apart and Lucy ends up running the studio and by this point they don't have many shows. Lucy says, "We need to get more shows on the air," and *Star Trek* was the one she took on, because she thought it was different.

HERBERT F. SOLOW

I tend to be an optimist about everything. If someone tells us we have to build a bridge from here to Liverpool, I'll say we can do it, and I'll find out why we can't and we'll do our best to change it. For this little, tiny, dinky studio to go ahead and try to do this kind of show, if I had expressed any doubts or even consciously thought I had any doubts, I don't think we would have ever done it. I had so many people at the studio, so many old-timers trying to talk me out of it. "You're going to bankrupt us, you can't do this. NBC doesn't want us anyway, who cares about guys flying around in outer space?" The optical guy said it was impossible to do. Everyone said there wasn't enough time or money, and from the physical production point of view, we can't attract the talent needed. If you don't listen to that and stubbornly go into it, that's the only way we could have got it done.

MARC CUSHMAN

Lucy was trying to do things the way Desi taught her. It was his idea to do *I Love Lucy* in the way they did. He set up the formula, he created the template. But he wasn't there anymore. He was drinking at that point; he was not leaving his house and was basically just burned out. So she is asking herself, "What would Desi do?" because she really loved and respected him. "Desi would get more shows on the air that we own, not just that we're producing for other companies." So that was her reasoning to do *Star Trek*—and she felt that this show could, if it caught on, rerun for years like *I Love Lucy*. And guess what? Those two shows—*I Love Lucy* and *Star Trek*—are two shows that have been rerunning ever since they originally aired. The problem was, her pockets weren't deep enough.

OSCAR KATZ

When we brought the show to the networks, we told them there were four kinds of stories that would represent the *Star Trek* concept. First, you have to remember that the spaceship is five stories high, it has five hundred people on it. One of the girls, who's a female yeoman in the crew, it turns out has signed on because she's having trouble back at home in Boston with either her boyfriend or her parents. She's getting away from them and she has an emotional relationship problem. Our two leads, unspecified, are the catalytic agents who help her face her problem and solve it. You never see her again, because she's just one of the crew people. I said, "In that respect, what you have is *Wagon Train*." *Wagon Train* had two leads, the wagon train traveled through the West, although it never got where it was going, and a guest star who was in wagon number twenty-three had an emotional problem which the two leads had to help solve.

The second kind of story is you have to remember that they're out for five years at a clip. They get a message from Earth that there's a planet on which there are Earth people doing mining, and there is claim jumping. They have to go to the planet and do a police action. In that respect, it's *Gunsmoke*.

The third thing that happens is they go to a planet where everything is pretty much like Earth, and subsequently the people on this planet look and have developed very much like us, except that their Chicago, their Al Capone, is in the future; or their Civil War is about to break out. They're either ahead of us or behind us. So it's people that look like us that are going through what we went through or what we will go through.

The fourth type is where they go to a planet where the atmospheric conditions are different than on Earth. Everything is different. The people don't look like us, they don't behave like us. They're fierce-looking animals or whatever.

When we went to NBC, we brought those four story types and they picked number four. They did so because it was the hardest to do. With the Desilu reputation, they wanted to make it as hard as possible, so we could prove ourselves. I tried to talk them out of it, because I knew it was going to be expensive and, even more, I felt that it might not be representative of the series. But they couldn't be talked out of it. That's how the first pilot, "The Cage," came into being.

In "The Cage," the starship *Enterprise* arrives at Talos IV to answer a distress signal. Captain Christopher Pike is taken prisoner by the telepathic Talosians, who want him to mate with another human named Vina so that they can repopulate their nearly lifeless world. To accomplish this goal, they use their abilities to plunge Pike from one fantasy into another, attempting to blur his hold on reality. Number One, Mr. Spock, and other crew members work together to free him and stop the Talosians' seemingly sinister plans.

ROBERT BUTLER (director, "The Cage")

Gene had finished writing "The Cage" and he asked me to read it, which I did. I remember thinking it was a terrific yarn, but that it was somewhat obscured because it was such a showcase script. "The Cage" showcased solid, good, and fascinating science-fiction disciplines, examples and events, that it was, I thought, a little obscure. The story was somewhat remote, and I discussed whether or not people would get it. I could tell at that point that Gene was a little consumed with it and that he couldn't have heard any objections.

ROBERT H. JUSTMAN

Robert Butler was worried about the pacing of "The Cage," which he thought moved slowly, so he added exclamation points to everything. I wasn't aware of it, because I was so damned busy just getting stuff ready for him, but that's very true—television is an exclamation point–type medium. You don't have that enormous screen, so you have to go a little bit overboard, dramatically speaking, so that by the time it reaches your famished eyes on the television set, there's something there to react to. That probably did happen on the first *Star Trek* pilot, and Bob was wise to recognize it.

ROBERT BUTLER

I thought *Star Trek* as a title was heavy. I tried to get Gene to change the title to *Star Track*. That seemed lighter and freer. It's not my business to be able to do that, and yet I was trying to convince him. I believed in it and, you know, water off a duck's back, which is okay.

GENE RODDENBERRY

When it came to the role of Captain Christopher Pike in "The Cage," we considered a number of actors, including [*Sea Hunt*'s] Lloyd Bridges. I remember Lloyd was very much under consideration, except when I approached him with it, he said, "Gene, I like you, I've worked with you before in the past, but I've seen science fiction and I don't want to be within a hundred miles of it." I understood what he meant then, because science fiction was usually the monster of the week. I tried to convince him that I could do it differently, but at the time I wasn't sure that I *would* treat it differently.

> Among those being considered for the lead role at the time, then still named Captain Robert April, were Paul Mantee, Rod Taylor (*The Time Machine*), Robert Loggia, Sterling Hayden (*The Killing*), Warren Stevens (*Forbidden Planet*), Rhodes Reason, Leslie Nielsen, and Jack Lord (*Dr. No*), the latter of whom wanted too big a piece of the show in terms of profit participation to make him a viable candidate, but who would eventually go on to big success (and a lucrative financial cut) in *Hawaii Five-O*.

ROBERT BUTLER

Whether Jeff Hunter was a compromise candidate or whether everyone believed in him at the time, I don't know. When the eleventh hour approaches, you finally have to take your money and bet it. That's always the case. Generally he was an extremely pleasant, centered guy, and maybe decent and nice to a fault. A gentle guy. I did not know Jeff, except professionally from a distance, not personally at all. I thought he was a good, chiseled hero for that kind of part. I remember thinking, "God, he's handsome," and this was, sadly, the opinion of him at the time. When one is trying to bring reality into an unreal situation, that usually isn't a wise thing to do, to hire a somewhat perfect-looking actor. You should find someone who seems to be more natural and more "real." I don't remember saying those things, but that continues to be my view.

Jeffrey Hunter, who was eventually cast as Captain Pike, described the pilot to the Los Angeles *Citizen News* at the time: "The idea for *Star Trek* is that we run into prehistoric worlds, contemporary societies, and civilizations far more developed than our own. It's a great format, because writers have a free hand—they can have us land on a monster-infested planet, or deal in human relations involving the large number of people who live in this gigantic ship. It has a regular cast of a half dozen or so and an important guest star each week. The thing that intrigues me the most is that it is actually based on the RAND Corporation's projection of things to come. Except for the fictional characters, it will be like getting a look into the future, and some of the predictions will surely come true in our lifetime. With all the weird surroundings of outer space, the basic underlying theme of the show is a philosophical approach to man's relationship to woman. There are both sexes in the crew. In fact, the first officer is a woman."

MAJEL BARRETT (actress, "Number One," "Nurse Christine Chapel")

Gene decided he would write something for me and he did. He wrote a part called Number One in "The Cage," the lady who was the ship's second-in-command. Well, they thought we were strange with this *Star Trek* and this space talk, so they sent us out to Culver Studios, which is an old, deserted place; there wasn't another thing shooting on the soundstage.

LEONARD NIMOY (actor, "Mr. Spock")

When I was done with *The Lieutenant,* Gene called my agent, my agent called me, and they asked for a meeting. I went in to see Gene at what was then Desilu Studios and he told me that he was preparing a pilot for a science-fiction series to be called *Star Trek,* that he had in mind for me to play an alien character. As the talk continued, Gene showed me around the studio; he showed me the sets that were being developed and the wardrobe that had been designed, the prop department and so forth. I began to realize that he was selling me on the idea of being in this series, unusual for an actor.

I figured all I had to do was keep my mouth shut and I might end up with a good job here. Gene told me that he was determined to have at least one extra-terrestrial prominent on his starship. He'd like to have more but making human actors into other life-forms was too expensive for television in those days. Pointed ears, skin color, plus some changes in eyebrows and hair style were all he felt he could afford, but he was certain that his Mr. Spock idea, properly handled and properly acted, could establish that we were in the twenty-third century and that interplanetary travel was an established fact.

MAJEL BARRETT

You'll notice when you watch "The Cage" that Leonard as Spock *does* smile, or has a little grin from time to time. My character was the one who was supposed to be very austere.

ROBERT BUTLER

Spock was an extremely attractive character right off the bat. And I would like to think that he was foreign but still not so foreign that he was inaccessible and un-comfortable for the audience. We could make the jump to his planet without it causing us any emotional discomfort. I think that's where the success of his char-acter lies. Leonard was always thought to be a very fine character actor, really.

GENE RODDENBERRY

One thing I wanted to do was make Spock half human and half Vulcan. I wanted to have an interesting personality. I wanted part of him to be at war with the other, the human part and the alien part. And half-breeds traditionally on dra-mas have always been highly interesting characters.

ROBERT BUTLER

John Hoyt was cast as the ship's doctor, Philip Boyce, in "The Cage." I'm not really proud of this, but as I was casting the doctor, I was against DeForest Kelley being cast, who was the person Gene Roddenberry wanted. As a younger guy I guess I felt that he was somewhat more of a heavy. At the time, I remember thinking that he was somewhat earthbound. Maybe I thought his youth at the time defied reality somewhat, whereas if we got a seasoned veteran in there, that might bring us a great spread of reality in your main people. I remember Gene stood up for DeForest to the end, but ultimately he backed me and went with John Hoyt.

MAJEL BARRETT

Susan Oliver was playing a green-skinned Orion slave girl, but I had to test her makeup because she was too expensive and I was under contract already; I was cheap, they had to pay me anyway. The makeup they put on me was green as green can be, but they kept on sending out the rushes and we would get it back for the next day, and there I was just as pink and rosy as could possibly be. This went on for three days until they finally called the lab and said, "What do we do? We're trying to get it *green*." And they said, "You *want* that? We've been color-correcting."

GEORGE PAPPY (director, *The Green Girl*)

Susan [Oliver] wrote in her autobiography that "it was not easy to be green." It took two hours in the morning to have the makeup applied, and she couldn't even sit down or handle anything for fear of rubbing off the green or losing a fake fingernail. And she noted a definite change of demeanor in the men on the set when she came out as the green Orion slave girl—they either "stood back and stared" or else averted their eyes entirely. She wrote that "Gene had touched on something dark in man's unconscious" with the green girl. Susan's outfit, makeup, and very demeanor as the Orion girl was really pushing the boundaries of acceptability or propriety—and the men on the set reacted!

MAJEL BARRETT

While this makeup was on, we were really removed from everything, way out in Culver City, and suddenly we were through with one of the tests and somebody yelled, "Lunch!" We looked around and there was nothing there, no restaurant, no commissary, nothing. You had to walk out to the sidewalk, down the street, and over to Washington Boulevard to go into a restaurant. Needless to say, Leonard, who was made up as Spock, and I arm-and-armed it down the street. The cars honked, of course, the tooting, the stopping, the screeching, and so forth. You expect that, because even according to Hollywood standards, we looked strange. When we entered the restaurant, the waitress automatically did a double take, the cast went into hysterical fits of laughter.

GEORGE PAPPY

Gene Roddenberry first approached Susan at the Culver City Studios sometime in 1964 and really sold her on the role of Vina. She indicated that she'd known of him previously because he'd written scripts on other shows she'd been in, and he really drove home the fact that this was an opportunity to play five different women in one role, and on a very high-profile new TV pilot. It's been indicated that Gene had a fairly long list of potential actresses to play the role, including Barbara Eden and Yvonne Craig, but it's my suspicion that he was simply keeping this list to make the network and studio executives happy—he really wanted Susan, which makes perfect sense because it's no exaggeration to say that she was the "go-to" female guest star in 1964 television; a huge name at the time. So who better to play Vina? Also, Gene's list misrepresented Susan's dancing abilities—she really was not a trained dancer at all and had to work with a choreographer [Peggy Romans] for a few weeks to learn the Orion slave-girl dance which, obviously, she did successfully.

Other actresses being considered in a casting memo from Gene Roddenberry on October 14, 1964, included Yvette Mimieux (*The Time Machine*), Jill St. John (*Diamonds Are Forever*), Ann-Margret, and Carol Lawrence. Of interest is the fact that he also had Lee Meriwether as a suggestion for Number One, eventually played by Majel Barrett, and Jill Ireland for the role of Ensign Colt. Dialogue from the script such as "Don't let me hurt you. Take the whip . . . tame me" were deleted at the insistence of NBC's Standards and Practices Department which also admonished Roddenberry that "the movement of dancers shall be kept within the bounds of decency."

The late Susan Oliver, who was originally conceived as a red, not green, Orion slave girl, related to *Starlog* magazine that "there were many experiments in makeup. Fred Phillips, head of the makeup department, couldn't find any green makeup that would stick to skin, so they tried many, many things on me until they finally got help from New York, where they found out what they wanted. One of the unique things about this job was I wasn't really a dancer. They had a choreographer work with me a solid week, every day, before I began filming. There were different faces in this role, and the green girl was the most challenging."

GEORGE PAPPY

For her, this was just another of her many, many guest star roles in what must have been a nameless sea of constant one- to two-week TV acting gigs during those years. I was blown away to find out what an accomplished pilot she was, that at one time she was engaged to Hall of Fame baseball pitcher Sandy Koufax, and yet sadly died alone at just fifty-eight years old due to cancer. I was very saddened to see that such an amazing life had been so forgotten or, perhaps a better term would be "completely unnoticed" since so many, including myself, never even knew about her in the first place.

She attended at least one *Star Trek* convention, in New York back in 1976. One of her fans, Hank Shiffman, said that she seemed somewhat amused and surprised by the burgeoning *Star Trek* fan phenomenon at the time, quite possibly her first concrete evidence that this two-week commitment in late 1964 was going to be her cultural legacy, and quite a memorable one at that.

For her part, Oliver told the assembled crowds at the Bi-Centennial-10 convention in New York in one of her rare public appearances, "I think *Star Trek* has become the success that it has because it is about hopes, dreams, magic, make-believe and love. It was a very happy experience. None of the cast, including myself, ever realized what history *Star Trek* would become."

FELIX SILLA (actor, Talosian in "The Cage,")

I came out to Hollywood in 1962 and I shot "The Cage" in 1964. I was brand-new in the business. As Talosians, we wore these really big heads with the veins sticking out. The problem was, every time we went to lunch—a friend of mine and I—we couldn't even talk to each other because we couldn't hear each other, because of the muffled head. So we had to do sign language, even though I didn't really know how to do it. We were kind of playing around as we tried to understand each other. I did meet Gene Roddenberry; he used to come to the set. We never really had a big conversation; you don't really want to bother these people. They're very busy, they've got business to take care of. Fifty years ago I never thought that all these years later I would still be talking about it or people would care about it.

The opening establishing shot of "The Cage" is described in very visual detail by Roddenberry in his teleplay, which would make the starship *Enterprise* unique in the annals of science-fiction history. "Obviously not a primitive 'rocket ship' but rather a true space vessel, suggesting unique arrangements and exciting capabilities. As CAMERA ZOOMS IN we first see tiny lettering 'NCC 1701–U.S.S. ENTERPRISE.' Aiming for the surprise of the ship's actual dimensions, the lettering looms larger and larger until it fills the screen. Then, surpassing even the previous illusion of size, we see a tiny opening above the huge letters and realize this is actually a large observation port. CAMERA CONTINUES IN, MATCH DISSOLVING THROUGH OBSERVATION PORT TO REVEAL the bridge, command station of the U.S.S. *Enterprise*. And as we see crewmen at the controls inside, the gigantic scale of the vessel is finally apparent."

ROBERT BUTLER

When the first shot kind of goes into the flight deck and we see the crew sitting there in control, and then there's that subsequent Doctor–Pike scene that's so good. We've seen that scene thirty, sixty, a thousand times, the enervated hero needs a lift confessing to his mentor, whomever, and yet that beckon was in there. Those legs were playing, and in spite of the directorial superiority, the damned thing works! It's okay.

Roddenberry's amazing attention to detail even extended to prescient thoughts regarding the ship's computer at a time when computers were punch card-operated behemoths that filled entire rooms. In a memo on July 24, 1964, to production designer Pato Guzman, Roddenberry suggested, "More and more I see the need for some sort of interesting electronic computing machine designed into the U.S.S. *Enterprise*, perhaps on the bridge itself. It will be an information device out of which April and the crew can quickly and interestingly extract information on the registry of other space vessels, space flight plans for other ships, information on individuals and planets and civilizations. This should not only speed up our storytelling but could be visually interesting."

It's a subject that would continue to fascinate Roddenberry. In May of 1967 he wrote, "We've lost some of the wonder of how a giant computer brain operates the *Enterprise*. Suggest we look for ways of getting back to it, getting more use out of it."

Roddenberry's interest in realistic technology led to him hiring his cousin, Harvey Lynn, who worked for the RAND company as an administrative physicist, as a consultant for which he was paid fifty dollars a week.

WALTER "MATT" JEFFRIES (production designer, *Star Trek*)

Since I was a member of the Aviation Writers Association, I had collected a huge amount of design material from NASA and the defense industry which was used as an example of designs to avoid. We pinned all that material up on the wall and said, "*That* we will not do." And also everything we could find on *Buck Rogers* and *Flash Gordon* and said, "*That* we will not do." Through a process of elimination we came to the final design of the *Enterprise*. Lynn's suggestions included MASER for a microwave weapon, which eventually became phasers.

HOWARD A. ANDERSON (president, Howard A. Anderson Company)

Our work on *Star Trek* began a full year before the first pilot was made. Gene Roddenberry outlined the concept of the series for us and asked us, aided by the *Star Trek* art designer Walter "Matt" Jeffries, to design a model of the *Enterprise*. One of our most difficult assignments for the series was to create the impression that the *Enterprise* was racing through space at an incredible speed—faster than the speed of light. Other space shows have shown spacecraft more or less "drifting" through space. We wanted to avoid that cliché. The solution did not come easily or quickly. We experimented with dozens of ideas before we hit on an effective solution.

ROLLAND "BUD" BROOKS (supervising art director, *Star Trek*)

Matt [Jeffries] had worked for me as a set designer and Matt was an airplane nut. His interest in airplanes went beyond all bounds. I was sitting there thinking, "We gotta come up with a lot of stuff here" and I thought of Matt. I can't think of anybody better to design the original flagship.

HOWARD A. ANDERSON

The spaceship as imagined was larger than a battleship, had eight separate levels or decks and carried a crew over four hundred. The first step was a series of art renderings by Jeffries. When Roddenberry approved his final design, we moved to the next step: translating the renderings into a four-inch scale model constructed of wood. Our next step was the construction of a three-foot model, which, again, was constructed of solid wood. The second model, of course, had far more detail than the first.

WALTER "MATT" JEFFRIES

The first time we had a review, I probably had a hundred different sketches. There were certain elements of some that we liked and certain elements of others that we liked, and we kinda tossed the rest aside and began to assemble things with the elements that had some appeal to us.

HOWARD A. ANDERSON

Once it had been approved by Roddenberry, we were ready to proceed with the large, detailed model. This was an elaborate fourteen-foot model which was made mostly of sheet plastic and required hundreds of man-hours of work. The diameter of the dome—or main body—of the ship was ten feet. The pods were hand-tooled from hardwood. The principal elements in our solution are a space sky and the use of an Oxberry optical printer to make the space sky. We painted black stars on a white background about two and a half feet by three feet, arriving at a suitable design. We then made a series of blackout mattes that we could use later with the sky in the optical printer.

DOUG DREXLER

Star Trek premiered a year after the World's Fair in Flushing Meadows, New York. It was about the world of tomorrow and was kind of like a world's fair. Look at all the technology we have today that we take for granted, that we first saw on *Star Trek* or the World's Fair. I always used to tell [*Star Trek* graphic designer] Mike Okuda that ground zero for *Star Trek* design ethic was the 1964 New York World's Fair, and I think he was always like, "Yeah, sure." And then one night we went to dinner with Matt [Jeffries] and I brought up the World's Fair and he said, "Oh yeah! Me and [my wife] Marianne went and we just had a ball and walked our legs off. And when I got home there was a message from a guy named Roddenberry." And I kicked Mike under the table. You can see the World's Fair influence on *Star Trek*. I mean, Starbase 11, really?

RENE ECHEVARRIA

There's an extraordinary level of creativity. Who would have thought that's what a spaceship looks like? It was so original and smart and unique. It just grabbed your attention. In my mind, it was almost like the same way you watched the moon launch, which was all grainy and hard to see.

DOUG DREXLER

Have you heard what Neil deGrasse Tyson said about the *Enterprise* during the Starship Smackdown at Comic-Con? "What did that spaceship look like at the time it came out compared with anything that had been imagined before, like the flying saucer from *The Day the Earth Stood Still* and its weaponry was the guy in the silver underwear? When you consider that, the *Enterprise* is the most astonishing, awesome, beautiful, seductive *space*ship that has ever graced the screen." The man speaks the truth. A lot of shows like *The Twilight Zone* used footage of an old V-2 rocket taking off and have it going backwards and disappearing behind a mountain range. I was mesmerized by the show. It just blew me away.

Equally pleased with Walter "Matt" Jeffries's work was Gene Roddenberry, who expressed his admiration of Jeffries in an August 9, 1965, memo: "I have already told you personally of my appreciation for your hard work . . . More than that, I was enormously pleased by your unusual creativity and flexibility in meeting constantly changing problems in time, budget, and dramatic needs of the show." It was also Roddenberry who suggested that turbo elevators on the ship "go up, down, and sideways."

Upon completing work on "The Cage," Roddenberry wrote to his science consultant and cousin, Harvey Lynn at RAND, while filming his next pilot, *Police Story*: "The *Star Trek* pilot looks good to me in the present rough cut and those others who have seen it seem elated. They feel it is an excellent job and much more commercial without any sacrifice of quality. And the hallway scenes plus the elevator ride up to the bridge did as I hoped, i.e. gives the feeling of a huge and complex vessel. With our eleven-foot model now improved to be lit from within, with greater detail added, etc., the two should combine to make the U.S.S. *Enterprise* a real thing. In short, we're highly optimistic." Lynn, who had suggested the diagnostic beds in sickbay, also pointed out that "the more information and data I acquire on interstellar flight, the more I keep coming back to the one basic point which you may wish to include in the basic script as well as in the vehicle design. This is the point that flights are likely to be of long duration (years), unless we find a new dimension or something."

GENE RODDENBERRY

The ship's transporters—which let the crew "beam" from place to place—really came out of a production need. I realized with this huge spaceship we'd come up with, which is practically the size of an aircraft carrier, that, number one, I would blow the whole budget of the show just in landing the thing on a planet. And second, it would take a long time to get into our stories, so the transporter idea was conceived so we could get our people down to the planet fast and easy, and get our story going by page two.

HOWARD A. ANDERSON

For the transporter effect, we added another element: a glitter effect in the dematerialization and rematerialization. To obtain the glitter effect, we used aluminum dust falling through a beam of high-intensity light. This was photographed on one of our stages at our Fairfax Avenue plant. In addition to making a matte of the figure to be transported, we also made an identically shaped matte of the falling particles of aluminum. Then, using the two mattes, we slowly dissolve the person, leaving only the glitter effect, then slowly dissolve the glitter effect to leave nothing but the empty chamber.

ROBERT BUTLER

Subsequently, after doing the pilot and executing it in the way we thought it should be done, I'd heard that NBC had said, "We believe this. We think there's a show here, but we don't understand it." Apparently the network, at its level, was feeling exactly as I did.

In fact, a July 31, 1964, memo from the network to production prior to filming on the pilot expressed the following concerns that the pilot might already be too erudite for the average TV viewer. "Be certain there are enough explanations on the planet, the people, their ways and abilities so that even someone who is not a science-fiction aficionado can clearly understand and follow the story." And second, "Can we do a little more to establish the spaceship in the beginning, possibly something which also helps establish the secondary characters a little better, too."

GENE RODDENBERRY

The reason they turned it down was that it was too cerebral and there wasn't enough action and adventure. "The Cage" didn't end with a chase and a right cross to the jaw, the way all manly films were supposed to end. There were no female leads then—women in those days were just set dressing. So, another thing they felt was wrong with our film was that we had Majel as a female second-in-command of the vessel. It's nice now, I'm sure, for the ladies to say, "Well, the men did it," but in the test reports, the women in the audience were saying, "Who does she think she is?" They *hated* her. It is hard to believe that we have gone from a totally sexist society to where we are today—where all intelligent people certainly accept sexual equality. We've made progress.

MAJEL BARRETT

NBC wanted some changes after they saw "The Cage." They felt that my position as Number One would have to be cut because no one would believe that a woman could hold the position of second-in-command.

GENE RODDENBERRY

Number One was originally the one with the cold, calculating, computerlike mind. Spock, at the start, was not quite the character he became. He was the science officer on the *Enterprise,* but he was sort of satanic. He even smiled and got mad. He had a catlike curiosity. When we had to eliminate a feminine Number One—I was told you could cast a woman in a secretary's role or that of a housewife, but not in a position of command over men on even a twenty-third-century spaceship—I combined the two roles into one. Spock became the second-in-command, still the science officer but also the computerlike, logical mind never displaying emotion.

LEONARD NIMOY

Gene felt the format badly needed the alien Spock, even if the price was the acceptance of 1960s-style sexual inequality.

GENE RODDENBERRY

The idea of dropping Spock became a *major* issue. I felt that was the one fight I *had* to win, so I wouldn't do the show unless we left him in. They said, "Fine, leave him in, but keep him in the background, will you?" And then when they put out the sales brochure when we eventually went to series, they carefully rounded Spock's ears and made him look human so he wouldn't scare off potential advertisers. Once the show had been on the air for six to eight weeks, of course, the audience reaction to Spock was very strong, and a new NBC vice president came to the West Coast and he called me in and said, "What's the matter with you? You have this great character and you're keeping him in the background?" And we pointed out the sales brochure and told him what NBC was going to do, and his only answer was, "I think I'm going to throw up."

LEONARD NIMOY

A new pilot was written and Mr. Spock was in Number One's place as second-in-command as well as having some of the woman's computer-mind qualities. Vulcan unemotionalism and logic came into being.

GENE RODDENBERRY

When they initially wanted Spock dropped, it was one of those cases where you go home at night and pound your head against a wall and say, "How come I am the only one in the world that believes in it?" But I said I would not do a second pilot without Spock because I felt we had to have him for many reasons. I felt we couldn't do a space show without at least one person on board who constantly reminded you that you were out in space and in a world of the future.

TRACY TORME (creative consultant, *Star Trek: The Next Generation*)

Gene told me how NBC wanted Spock off the original show, until he came up with the idea of a space cigarette that had green smoke and the network loved that. He hoped they would just forget about it, which they did, so he never used it, but he felt that had saved Spock from being taken off the show.

GENE RODDENBERRY

We had what they called a "childish concept"—an alien with pointy ears from another planet. People in those days were not talking about life-forms on other worlds. It was generally assumed by most sensible people that this is the place where life occurred and probably nowhere else. It would have been all right if this alien with pointy ears, this "silly creature," had the biggest zap gun in existence, or the strength of a hundred men, *that* could be exciting. But his only difference from the others was he had an alien perspective on emotion and logic. And that didn't make television executives jump up and yell "Yippee."

MARGARET BONANNO (author, *Star Trek: Burning Dreams*)

The idea for *Burning Dreams* came from Simon & Schuster editor Marco Palmieri, who called me out of the blue and made the offer for me to write the definitive novel about Christopher Pike. I took that to mean a biography, from beginning to end, and that was exactly what Marco wanted. We knocked some ideas around and at some point—whether during that initial conversation or after I'd submitted a first-draft outline—he suggested an environmental theme. Really what he said was *"Mosquito Coast,"* and it clicked, so that was the frame to hang Pike's childhood on, as well as what becomes of him once he returns to Talos IV [in the episode "The Menagerie"]. In between, I tried to pick moments in Pike's career as a young officer that would show why he became, at the time, the youngest starship captain in the fleet, and weave in a personal life that shaped him as a human being.

GENE RODDENBERRY

The Talosian planet's "ridiculous" premise of mind control annoyed a great many people, and the objection, of course, overlooks the fact that the most serious threat we face today in our world is mind control—such as not too long ago by Hitler, and what's now exercised by fanatical religions all over the world and even here in our own country. Mind control is a dangerous subject for TV to discuss, because the yuppies may wake up someday and be discussing it and say, "Well, wait a minute, television may be the most powerful mind control force of all" and may begin taking a very close look at television. Most executives would like to avoid *that* possibility.

MARGARET BONANNO

Watching "The Cage" and "Menagerie" [the season one two-parter that incorporated footage from the former] over and over again, I realized how much of the character's story was below the surface. I started digging. It seemed as if almost every line of dialogue could be a hook to something in his backstory. There was also something heady about taking a character that Gene Roddenberry had created more or less by the seat of his pants and probably never gave a second thought to once he had created Kirk, and whom other writers had used effectively in several novels and comics, but always in the action-adventure mold, and being able to really get inside his head and ask, "What makes this man what he is?" What was really interesting was what I saw as Pike's drive for perfection, as well as him distancing himself from his crew, unlike Kirk, who goes way beyond the bounds of any real-life commanding officer, which is part of his charm, but also a bit of weakness in terms of credibility.

I had the same attitude toward Pike that I think a lot of original series fans have: interesting character, interesting performance by Jeffrey Hunter, but good or bad, he's nothing like Kirk. There's been a lot written about how Pike was an "intellectual," as opposed to Kirk, who was a "man of action," but it didn't seem quite that simple. Yes, Pike is more apt to think things through than to charge headlong into a situation, but you don't get to be a starship captain if you're brooding like Hamlet all the time. There's also a haunted quality to Pike, a suggestion of something in his past that the Talosians—like all good interrogators— would try to exploit in an attempt to control him initially.

OSCAR KATZ

When they rejected "The Cage," I asked NBC, "Why are you turning it down?" and I was told, "We can't sell it from this show, it's too atypical." I said, "But *you guys* picked this one, I gave you four choices." NBC said, "I know we did and because of that, right now we're going to give you an order for a second pilot next season."

HERBERT F. SOLOW

Getting a second pilot was enormously rare. If a pilot didn't work the first time, the networks said, "Oh, forget it; it's over." Television is unlike any other business in that way. But we got the second pilot.

STEPHEN KANDEL (writer, "Mudd's Women")

NBC's attitude was to forget it and to abandon it. So, after much argument and discussion, Gene got the money to write three additional pilot scripts. "The Cage" had been a sample of what the series would be like and that frightened the network. They thought the audience wouldn't understand it.

ROBERT BUTLER

Gene asked me to direct the second pilot, but I told him I had been there and done it already, and didn't wish to repeat myself. Another reason I didn't wish to do it is that science fiction, directorially, is a bit of a chore, because you have to share the reins with graphics, special visual effects, and all the other people who supply the tricks. It's very much direction by committee, and I was a little impatient with that. I like working on pilots because you're in on the formulation, and you're handed fewer givens, so, as a result you direct more. The more control and freedom I have to direct, the more I enjoy it. I will say that we were all praying and doing our best on "The Cage." The eventual phenomenon was bigger than I expected, not that I really measured it at the time. That wasn't in the equation. You just roll up your sleeves and decide what the hell it is you're trying to do. Then you jump in and never look back.

GENE RODDENBERRY

Jeffrey Hunter decided he did not want to come back and play Pike again. I thought highly of him and he would have made a grand captain, except his family convinced him that science fiction was really beneath him.

OSCAR KATZ

When you make a pilot deal with an actor, you can't tie him up forever. You usually have a hold on him for the following season, so we had no hold on Jeffrey Hunter. And either he or his wife didn't like "The Cage" and he didn't want to do the second pilot. I already had the set built—I think it was the largest set in the history of Hollywood, that planet in "The Cage"—we had the interior of the spaceship, the miniature of the outside of the spaceship, etc. We had everything and all we had to do was write a new script. But we didn't have a leading man.

Business affairs negotiated with Jeffrey Hunter, and we all thought it was the usual actor-network situation. They don't want to do it for reason XYZ, and it's a device for getting the price up. We kept increasing the price and he kept saying no. One day I said, "What's with Jeffrey Hunter?" and I was told he just won't do it at any price. Finally I said, "Tell Jeffrey Hunter to get lost. Tell him we're going to do the pilot without him." And that's how William Shatner got into it, because Hunter wouldn't do it.

RICHARD ARNOLD

Gene would not have agreed with me here, but I thought that Jeffrey Hunter seemed a little wooden in the role, as though he couldn't quite get a grip on the character. I've read things since that would seem to disprove that, but he just wasn't captain material, in my opinion. His turning the series down was probably the best thing for *Star Trek*. No one could have known how well Bill and Leonard would work together, nor how De Kelley would fit into the picture, but it all turned out, even if by chance, to be just what the show needed.

> At the time, Jeffrey Hunter confessed to the *Milwaukee Journal,* "I was asked to do it, but had I accepted I would have been tied up much longer than I care to be. I have several things brewing now and they should be coming to a head. I love doing motion pictures and expect to be as busy as I want to be in them."
>
> Ironically, it was only a few years later that Hunter and his agents were lobbying hard for him to play Mike Brady, the paterfamilias of the Brady clan in Paramount's *The Brady Bunch,* a part that was instead offered to Gene Hackman (which he turned down), eventually going to Robert Reed, making him a television icon in a role that the actor absolutely loathed.

GENE RODDENBERRY

At that time we were putting *Star Trek* on, TV was full of antiheroes, and I had a feeling that the public likes heroes. People with goals in mind, people with honesty and dedication, so I decided to go with the straight heroic roles, and it paid off. My model for Kirk was Horatio Hornblower from the C. S. Forester sea story that I always enjoyed. We had a great deal of trouble casting it, many actors turned us down, and later on, of course, wished they hadn't. But science fiction at that time had a very bad name and many serious actors had made up their minds because what they had seen on TV was so bad they didn't want their name associated with it. Shatner was available, he needed a show, was open-minded about science fiction, and a marvelous choice because he did great things for our show. I was happy to get him. I'd seen some work he did, and I thought he was an excellent choice, no question of it at all.

JAMES GOLDSTONE (director, "Where No Man Has Gone Before")

I think Shatner was the choice partly of the network, partly of Desilu, and partly of Gene. I don't know whether I had approval within contract, though I was a creative partner as the director. I thought he could play it marvelously. I liked him very much and thought he was a marvelous balance for the Spock character.

WILLIAM SHATNER (actor, "James Tiberius Kirk")

They showed me the first pilot and said, "Would you like to play the part? Here are some of the story lines that we plan to go with; you can see the kind of production we have in mind. Would you care to play it?" And I thought it was an interesting gamble for myself as an actor to take, because I've always been fascinated by science fiction. I liked the production; I like the people involved with the production, and so I decided to do it.

But it was under these peculiar circumstances of having a first pilot made that I did it. I then talked to Gene Roddenberry about the objectives we hoped to achieve, and one of those objectives was serious drama as well as science fiction. His reputation and ability, which I knew firsthand, was such that I did not think he would do *Lost in Space*. And I was too expensive an actor, with what special or particular abilities I have, to warrant being put in something that somebody else could walk through. So I felt confident that *Star Trek* would keep those serious objectives for the most part, and it did.

ROBERT H. JUSTMAN

Gene was very happy that he was able to get Bill Shatner, who was highly thought of in the industry. I had worked with Bill on *Outer Limits* and he had a good reputation in the television and entertainment industries even at that time, well before the second pilot of *Star Trek*. He was someone to be reckoned with, and we certainly understood that he was a more accomplished actor than Jeff Hunter was, and he gave us more dimension.

> Shatner was hired for $10,000 an episode, as opposed to Jeffrey Hunter who was getting $5,000 for the original pilot. Alongside Shatner was Leonard Nimoy at $2,500 an episode, Paul Fix as Dr. Piper for $1,250, with James Doohan's Scotty getting $750, and George Takei, a meager $375. Legendary stuntman Hal Needham doubled for Gary Lockwood, who was getting $5,000 for his efforts.

SCOTT MANTZ (film critic, *Access Hollywood*)

When you go back and you watch "The Cage," Pike and Kirk were so different. Let's say you're watching "The Cage" and you're part of a focus group. Which captain would you follow? You watch the scene where your captain, your hero, is telling his doctor, "I don't want to be the captain. I want to raise a horse or be a slave trader, whatever. I don't want to be the captain anymore." And then you see this captain joking around, charming, and you know he looks like he *likes* being the captain. I'd follow Kirk in a second.

Pike was a stiff captain. He didn't want to be the captain. He was more like Picard than Kirk. He had more of Picard's traits than Kirk's. They lucked out with Shatner. Shatner's performance as Kirk is the reason I became a *Trek* fan.

ROBERT H. JUSTMAN

The network seemed to feel that Jeff Hunter was rather wooden. He was a nice person, everyone liked him, but he didn't run the gamut of emotions that Bill Shatner could do. Shatner was classically trained. He had enormous technical abilities to do different things and he gave the captain a terrific personality. He embodied what Gene had in mind, which was the flawed hero. Or the hero who considers himself to be flawed. Captain Horatio Hornblower. That was who he was modeled on.

SCOTT MANTZ

Jeffrey Hunter was a dashing guy. He looked a little bit like Elvis. He had a clean, WASPy, Christian look to him. He was a commanding figure but he wasn't a passionate one.

IRA STEVEN BEHR (executive producer, *Star Trek: Deep Space Nine*)

Jeffrey Hunter in "The Cage" was a terrific captain. I remember thinking that Bill was a little too actory as the captain. And I kind of liked the more stoic Jeffrey Hunter. The other thing I will say about Hunter, which was different than Shatner, was I had seen Hunter in *The Searchers* [with John Wayne], I'd seen him in Disney's *The Great Locomotive Chase* with him chasing after Fess Parker, and he was in *The Longest Day*. So he was kind of like "the movie star" and he had a command to him.

MARGARET BONNANO

Like a lot of people, I asked myself how *Star Trek* would have been different if the series had focused on Pike rather than Kirk. Not an original thought, but as a less . . . precipitous leader than Kirk, Pike would have interacted differently with his crew, particularly Spock, and we might have ended with fewer fistfights and more clever dialogue—more or less what we got in the films starring the original series cast. Not necessarily a bad thing, but something, given sixties TV, that might have killed the show in fewer than three seasons.

GEORGE PAPPY

There's no doubt that the casting of Kirk, the reimagining of Nimoy's role, and all the other new actors made the crucial difference and guaranteed that *Star Trek* would become the everlasting phenomenon it is today. Honestly, can you see people watching decade after decade of *Star Trek* reruns featuring the cast of "The Cage?" I can't.

LEONARD NIMOY

Bill Shatner's broader acting style created a new chemistry between the captain and Spock, and now it was quite different from that of the first pilot.

DAVID GERROLD

All of the movies and all of the episodes hold together because Shatner holds it together. Spock is only good when he has someone to play off of. The scenes where

Spock doesn't have Shatner to play off of are not interesting. If you look at Spock with his mom or dad, it's very ponderous. But Spock working with Kirk has the magic and it plays very well, and people give all of the credit to Nimoy, not to Shatner.

IRA STEVEN BEHR

It's funny because I actually remember my sister saying to me one night, "Watch Spock. Watch how much he does with so little." She actually said, "The actor on the show *is* Spock." She was my older sister, so everything she said was like the voice of God.

LEONARD NIMOY

During the series we had a failure—I experienced it as a failure—in an episode called "The Galileo Seven." The Spock character had been so successful that somebody said, "Let's do a show where Spock takes command of a vessel." We had this shuttlecraft mission where Spock was in charge. I had a tough time with it. I really appreciated the loss of the Kirk character for me to play against, to comment on. The Bill Shatner Kirk performance was the energetic, driving performance, and Spock could kind of slipstream along and make comments and offer advice, give another point of view. Put into the position of being the driving force, the central character, was very tough for me, and I perceived it as a failure.

SCOTT MANTZ

Starting with the first regular episode they shot, "The Corbomite Maneuver," so much changed; the uniforms, Spock's makeup, some of the set designs. All except for one thing. Act one, scene one, the second pilot, Shatner had Kirk down. He was Kirk from the beginning. You watch the first half of the first season you can tell that Nimoy is trying to find Spock. He is kind of a wiseass and loves women. And at the end of "The Enemy Within," where he is saying, "Oh, the imposter had some very interesting qualities. Huh-huh?" Would mid–first season Spock do that? I don't think so. But Kirk was Kirk from that first scene in the briefing room in the rec room playing three-dimensional chess. Until he went off the rails a little bit in the third season because he was trying to make up for the shitty scripts.

JOHN D. F. BLACK

There was such a natural balance between William Shatner and Leonard Nimoy. There was no way to tell, really, whether they got along or not, because they had an easy relationship off camera, and on camera there was an absolute difference that was writable. You had the advantage in any scene between Shatner and Nimoy where Shatner could take one side and be correct, and Nimoy could take the purely logical side of the situation and also be correct. The scene carried out the conflict which could spark anything along the lines of what was upcoming. I don't mean to sound like a professor of a screenplay class discussing a script's structure, but that's the reality. We know that conflict is the heart of any scene, and the more conflict you have between the characters, the better it is. And it was just built in.

GEORGE TAKEI (actor, "Hikaru Sulu")

The first time I talked to Gene about *Star Trek*, it was for the second pilot and it was an exhilarating prospect, because almost every other opportunity was either inconsequential or defamatory, and here was something that was not only a positive opportunity but also a breakthrough for a Japanese-American actor. I was really excited about it, but then reality sets in, the whole struggle for survival of the series itself, and then the struggle for your character to find his spot in the limelight. The initial entry into the project and what happened during the course of its life were two different stories.

JAMES DOOHAN (actor, "Montgomery 'Scotty' Scott")

Two weeks before they were actually going to shoot the second *Star Trek* pilot, my agent sent me to read for the part of a Scotland Yard inspector for a show called *Burke's Law* with Gene Barry. I did three British accents for them, and they smiled and said, "That's very good, Jimmy, but we think you look a little too much like Gene Barry and it would look like nepotism." I said, "Well, I'm much better looking than he is," but I said it smilingly and walked out the door. Ten days later, the director, Jim Goldstone, called me and said, "Jimmy, would you come in and do some of your accents for these *Star Trek* people?" I had no idea who they were, but I did that on a Saturday morning. They handed me a piece of paper—there was no part there for an engineer, it was just some lines, but every three lines or so I changed my accent and ended up doing eight or nine accents for that reading. At the end, Gene Roddenberry said, "Which one do you like?" I said, "To me, if you want an engineer, he'd better be a Scotsman," because those were the only engineers I had read anything about—all the ships they had built and so forth. Gene said, "Well, we rather like that, too."

GENE RODDENBERRY

I had never worked with him, but director James Goldstone brought James Doohan in and asked him if he could do a Scottish accent. He did like an hour and a half of accents and had us falling on the floor laughing, so there was never any doubt that he had the job.

JAMES DOOHAN

When I did that pilot, to me it was just another job. You have to understand that I had already done 120 stage plays, 4,000 radio shows, 450 live television shows, and I was what you called a working actor. My instructor, Sanford Meisner, who I give all the credit in the world to, plus my ability to work hard, told me, "Jimmy, in the long run, it's still going to take you twenty years to be an actor," and after nineteen years, I started to feel what he was talking about, because it got to the point where I started looking at myself saying, "Wow, there isn't anything I can't do." Besides that, there was my ability to do different accents and different sounds; my vocal cords can do just about anything I ask them to do. To me, it's fascinating, and my friend Leslie Nielsen said to me while we were coming up, "You lucky bastard, you're just a natural!" And of course I wasn't before. I maybe had the talent hidden somewhere, but it took hard work to get it out.

JAMES GOLDSTONE

My vague memory is that there had been several problems with "The Cage." One of them was that it cost so much money, and the other was that it took so long to shoot. NBC was skeptical that a series could be manufactured, so to speak, on a weekly basis. One of the requisites put on the second pilot was to shoot it in, as I recall, eight days, which would then prove to them that a weekly series could be done in six or seven days. We needed the extra day because we were doing the prototype. The other requisite, I would guess, it being television, is that NBC very much wanted something that could be "commercial" against the police shows and all the other action things that were then on television. The concept of our show was not so much a pilot as it was an example of how we could go on a weekly level.

SAMUEL A. PEEPLES

The first pilot Gene did for NBC, "The Cage," was more fantasy than science fiction. NBC was apparently unhappy with it, so they told him they would commission a second pilot, and they wanted a story. Gene asked me to do it and I did, guessing it would be more of a challenge to me because it's easy to open up your mouth and criticize somebody else's concept. Then if somebody says, "Okay, let's see you do it your way," you've got to prove that you know what you're talking about.

Gene and I were trying to avoid the space-cadet cliché. We were both very concerned about it being an adult show.

JAMES GOLDSTONE

Gene's whole concept was of doing the sort of classic storytelling form in which you can tell the same kind of stories that were told in the Elizabethan theater, told in the nineteenth century, that were told in classic novels. The convention with westerns is if you take it out of today and put it in a western setting, people accept these conventions. We would create conventions which people would accept, and you could therefore tell dramatic stories which people would accept because it was not on the streets they lived on, but were projected forward a little. On the same level, the characters and the dramatic conflicts, albeit space fiction, were really human conflicts.

SAMUEL A. PEEPLES

One thing, as later episodes proved, was the problem which never should have existed: the bug-eyed monsters. We both discouraged the idea, believing that we should keep things as realistic as possible. If a person was different physically, then explain the reason for that difference. In a particular atmosphere he might have a larger lung. If it were a planet with an extraordinarily bright sun, he would have different eyes. We were actually trying to project reality against an unfamiliar background. In other words, we would deal with reality according to the environmental background we encountered.

> The three scripts under consideration for the second pilot were Stephen Kandel's "Mudd's Women," Gene Roddenberry's "The Omega Glory," and Samuel Peeples "Where No Man Has Gone Before." In discussions between NBC and Desilu's Herb Solow, it was decided to go with the last, because, as Solow noted in a June 10, 1965, memo, as a finished film it would "better complement the first pilot, and would also show the two different ranges in which the series can go."
>
> In Peeples's script, the *Enterprise* comes across a charred metallic "black box" from a long-lost space vessel. Captain James R. Kirk (the middle initial eventually changed to *T* once the pilot went to series) has the distress beacon beamed aboard. As the starship approaches an energy barrier at the edge of the galaxy, Gary Mitchell and psychologist Elizabeth Dehner are injured while entering the barrier and slowly transformed into godlike beings with powerful esper abilities. Kirk is left with the unenviable choice of killing his best friend or allowing him to destroy the *Enterprise*.

JAMES GOLDSTONE

Three scripts were written for the second pilot. A combination of NBC, Gene, perhaps other executives at Desilu, and I read all three scripts, discussed them in length, decided on what became "Where No Man Has Gone Before," and then embarked on a great deal of polishing and rewriting on a conceptual and physical level, so that we could make it in eight days. This one just seemed to have the potential to establish those characters on a human level. The only gimmick is the mutation forward, the silvering of Gary Mitchell's eyes as he becomes more godlike, and it works because it's simple, as opposed to the growing of horns or something. Ours was a human science-fiction concept, perhaps cerebral, certainly emotional.

> It was a theme that Gene Roddenberry embraced immediately in a memo he sent to writer Samuel Peeples: "This story line seems to have the potential of being direct and excitingly dramatic, a straight-line growth of powerful peril and danger to our lead and his ship, leading to head-to-head conflict between the captain and the guest star, and yet containing meaningful themes and points of view which should lift it far out of the ordinary. A tale of absolute power corrupting absolutely, even played as melodrama action, certainly offers splendid opportunities."

SAMUEL A. PEEPLES

We were intrigued with the corruption-of-power theme manifesting over the ordinary individual. That was the basic premise, and we had to put in extrapolations of known scientific principles. At that time, the radiation belt had been discovered around the Earth and my premise was that galaxies themselves might be separated by this type of barrier.

GARY LOCKWOOD (actor, "Gary Mitchell")

To tell you the truth, I thought it was a little bizarre and I thought it was kind of embarrassing and I hoped it worked out, because everybody was excited about it. It was a very hard job to do. I'd rehearse and get everything all ready, but I couldn't see the actors because of the contact lenses that changed my eyes.

They didn't blind me for the first few days, but after a few days the eyes swelled up and got sore. Then to have them on for just two or three minutes was agonizing. Scenes were rehearsed without them. The other thing about it, people always thought I was kind of egotistical, so when I got to play that part, a lot of people laughed and said, "He's finally found his niche." That's been a joke among my friends.

JAMES GOLDSTONE

My proposal was that from the time Gary suffers the first realization—once he begins to give in to it, to enjoy it even—he moves from his human status toward the status of a god within all and any of the criteria we place on such deities in our Christian-Judaic culture. Specifically, I proposed that he become oracular in the sense of Moses or even Cotton Mather.

I proposed he do this in his stature, his way of using his hands and arms and eyes, silver or normal, his attitude as it applies to the script, aside from specific stage directions, perhaps physical actions that pertain to the dialogue. I didn't mean to suggest that it become so stylized as to become a symbol rather than a human being. I suggested it happen on a more symbolic level. This could be done by starting him more on the flip, swinging level of articulation so that we wouldn't even notice at one moment that this drops, but it does, on its way to becoming more formal, then more laden with import, more self-declarative, and, finally, downright miraculous.

GARY LOCKWOOD

That character was tough to reach, because there's no prototype character to look at. So you create a mental image and try to fill that slot. All I tried to do was downplay the mechanics and not be too dramatic. It's the same thing I did in *2001*. Try to play the part very quietly and very realistically, and later on people don't think you're pushing. That's the way to sustain it. There was a natural progression to the character. In order to do that, you have to think it out. Let me say one thing to you that I can say about American actors I don't like and who don't like me. You have to apply a certain amount of intelligence to your role first, and then you can apply the emotion after you've made an intellectual decision. With Gary Mitchell, the idea was trying to go to the character and not make the character comfortable to me. I'm *not* Gary Mitchell.

SALLY KELLERMAN (actress, "Dr. Elizabeth Dehner")

I knew nothing about science fiction. I didn't read any of the famous science-fiction writers like Ray Bradbury, and I'd been guest starring on every show in the sixties. I'd just finished *Kraft Theatre* with Gary Lockwood, and the one time we were shooting our scene and he didn't know his lines, I thought, "Oh, what an amateur." Next thing I know, I'm cast in the pilot of *Star Trek* with Gary Lockwood, The Amateur. When I saw him stage all the fight scenes, I got over that amateur stuff! I was swooning offstage. But, anyway, we had no idea what it was and that awful outfit, with the pants that didn't quite fit.

I was always playing the hard-bitten drunk or beaten up, and now I'm in this outfit and wondering what the heck it was all about. Of course, Bill Shatner has a great sense of humor, so it was a lot of fun around him. Leonard Nimoy had directed me in a play before this, for which I came late probably more than once to rehearsal. The last time I came there he said, "Please step outside," and so we went outside and he said, "Why is it that all you talented people are always the ones who come late?" Of course, I didn't hear anything about being late, I just heard the word *talented*.

Last year someone came up to me and said, "You are the reason the pilot sold," and I said, "I always felt that was true. Of course it was me!"

ROBERT H. JUSTMAN

As an assistant director in television, you know how long it takes to get a setup shot and the seat of your pants tells you how long it will take. The amount of work you have left to do will just fill up the amount of time you have left to do it in, so we worked as hard as we could on the second pilot, which James Goldstone directed, and on the last day of production, when we were a day over, we did two days' work in one day.

That's the day that [Lucille Ball] came on the stage, because we were supposed to have an end-of-picture party and we were still shooting, so in between setups she helped Herb Solow and me sweep out the stage. I think she just did that for effect, because she wanted to get the party started, but we worked hard, and we wouldn't have done the second pilot in that short a time if Jimmy Goldstone and I hadn't worked so well together before on *The Outer Limits*.

JAMES GOLDSTONE

I was very happy with it. From a director's point of view—or *this* director's point of view—you have certain targets and certain problems which have to be overcome in any picture, whether it's a twenty-million-dollar feature or a television show. A director measures his success in two ways. Obviously, like everybody else, you measure it by whether or not it's a critical and commercial success, but you also measure it in terms of overcoming obstacles. The obstacles were temporal, budgetary, but they were also conceptual. I was very proud of the work we were able to do. When I say "we," I don't mean it in a generous sense. I mean that it was a very collaborative effort, as are all pilots. We, being Gene, especially; Bobby Justman, and the main actors who later became the main stars. Everything was planned in detail, and Bobby and I knew if we didn't move from one set to another or one scene to another by a certain hour, we were in trouble.

ROBERT H. JUSTMAN

We had a method in our madness. I always knew what setups Jimmy had planned to cover the work we had to do that day, and he'd give me the list of setups and I'd arranged them so that no time would be lost. So if we'd point the camera in one direction and lit in that direction for the most part, we would shoot everything that needed to be shot that day in that direction before we turned around and shot the opposite angle.

On day one of principal photography, Gene Roddenberry received a telegram from Robert Butler, director of the original pilot. "Good luck today. Once again I hope all goes well and it sells." Oscar Katz and Herb Solow were more to the point in their telegram that arrived at Stage 15 of the Desilu Studios in Culver City that day: "Do us a favor and make it good this time."

GEORGE TAKEI

That first day of production, and that was at the Desilu Culver studios, not the Desilu Studios in Hollywood, has the same kind of memory of the first day of the first film, *Star Trek: The Motion Picture.* Shooting the pilot was exciting, participatory, and a little scary, because so much hope was vested in it.

And as an actor, you have the responsibility for creating this new world, and make it seem as though it's a normal part of that character's existence. It was really quite different from, say, getting cast in a detective show where all of the settings are familiar and understood and you're able to move right into the character. In this case, it's an entire environment that you have to create, so it was both exciting and a little scary.

I knew when I got cast as Sulu that it was a breakthrough opportunity for me. I never thought he would become a role model, but it was a pioneering effort in that until then any regular series roles for an Asian or an Asian-American character were either servants, buffoons, or villains, so it was a breakthrough.

GARY LOCKWOOD

I guess "Where No Man Has Gone Before" is effective because it sold the series. You've got to keep in mind that the *Star Trek* pilot was made in those days on a very tight budget. I think there was a big fight between the network and Roddenberry over making the second pilot, so there was a lot of pressure on him. They came up with this idea of two characters getting ESP, which I liked. I think they made up for not having an opportunity do a lot of effects by just creating a couple of interesting characters, and that helped sell the show. It was a good creative decision on the part of Roddenberry.

GENE RODDENBERRY

When you get into SF, you're lucky if 75 percent of your pilot is believable, because you're creating, in space science fiction, everything new. It was very helpful to be able to do one pilot, take a look at it, and then do a second. The second pilot was really better in many ways because we had a chance to look at the costume work, how the gadgets worked, and all that. And the second pilot seemed to have great concepts; humans turning into gods. But they were nice, safe gods, gods who go, "Zap! You're punished!" Kind of like the guys you see on those Sunday morning shows. The biggest factor in selling the second pilot was that it ended up in a hell of a fistfight with the villain suffering a painful death. Then, once we got *Star Trek* on the air, we began infiltrating a few of our ideas, the ideas the fans have all celebrated.

LUKAS KENDALL (editor, *Film Score Monthly*)

Gene Roddenberry told his composers not to give him "beeps and boops" space music à la *Forbidden Planet*. He wanted the scoring to emphasize the timeless human drama, not the strange future environment. This was a conceptual leap in sci-fi music—to let the setting take care of itself and score the storytelling. His producers, particularly Bob Justman, did a great job picking the right composers, who were genuinely inspired by what they saw. A lot of 1960s television music is drab and repetitive even some by the same composers—but *Star Trek*'s music stands out for its quality.

ALEXANDER COURAGE (composer, *Star Trek*)

Wilbur Hatch was doing music for the original Lucy radio show which was called *My Favorite Husband*. When that became *I Love Lucy*, he continued to do it. When Lucille Ball bought Desilu, he came in as head of music. So when *Star Trek* came on the scene, Wilbur suggested me to Roddenberry and I turned out a theme. Roddenberry liked it and that was it. He said, "I don't want any space music. I want adventure music."

LUKAS KENDALL

The *Star Trek* theme is in two parts. The opening "space, the final frontier" fanfare sums up the entire franchise in just eight notes—the questing nobility of the *Star Trek* mission. It is recognized worldwide, an extraordinary achievement. Only a handful of TV themes reach that level of awareness—maybe *Twilight Zone, Mission: Impossible, The Simpsons*. The second part, the wordless female vocal over the jazzy groove, is kind of like what the title *Peanuts* is for Charlie Brown. Today, everybody knows what *Peanuts* is, but it has nothing to do with the strip. (It was foisted upon Charles Schulz, who hated it, by the syndicator.) That to me is the second half of the *Star Trek* theme: it's kind of lame and doesn't work, yet it's forever *Star Trek*.

On March 6, 1966, Gene Roddenberry dispatched a Western Union telegram to star Bill Shatner at the Hotel Richmond in Madrid, Spain. It read simply "Dear Bill. Good news. Official pickup today. Our Five Year Mission. Best Regards, Gene Roddenberry."

THESE WERE THE VOYAGES

"SOMETIMES PAIN CAN DRIVE A MAN HARDER THAN PLEASURE."

In reflection, 1966 was a time of unprecedented pop-culture phenomena dominating the media, planting seeds that would still be flourishing many decades later. There was The Beatles, winding down their time as the Fab Four and preparing to become something more . . . substantial. James Bond had single-handedly launched the spy craze that dominated that decade (and continues to this one). The ABC gothic soap opera *Dark Shadows* had launched and was about to revolutionize the genre with the introduction of vampire Barnabas Collins. In prime time, Adam West and Burt Ward became the Dynamic Duo, Batman and Robin. And on September 8, 1966, *Star Trek* made its debut "in living color" on NBC.

At the time, it was a show that, even as it coalesced in terms of its cast and on a creative level, spent its lifetime struggling. Struggling to meet its budget, struggling for production time, struggling to create visual effects unlike anything that had been attempted in the medium before, struggling in a never-ending battle between Gene Roddenberry and the network, both of which were united in their goal to create a first-rate series, but divided in their views on how that could be achieved. And most of all, it struggled to find an audience.

But all of that paled in comparison to the primary struggle: to provide the high-quality scripts that held the key to *Star Trek*'s potential by offering up episodes that differed from anything that television had ever presented. It was a challenge that plagued the show right through the end of its network run.

OSCAR KATZ (vice-president of programs, Desilu)

The secret of its success was its attention to detail. Up until that point, science fiction on television was all Irwin Allen–type shows, whereas Gene's concept was science fiction in the true sense of those words. It was like what things might be about in the future, not only in the size of the concept and the ship and the problems they face, but in the smallest details. And Gene was a stickler for details.

One of the earliest decisions Roddenberry made to avoid the show seeming dated was the cut of the men's sideburns, which were to be shaved in a point, including extras, rather than reflect the fashions of the mid sixties. It was a source of consternation to many of the series leads, who tried to avoid having their sideburns groomed for the twenty-third century. On June 10, 1966, Roddenberry shot out a memo to Shatner. "Dear Bill. You're cheating. See Freddie." Of course, Freddie was Freddie Phillips, the head of makeup and hair who was waiting in the makeup trailer with razor in hand to shear the squared sideburns on Shatner. As Roddenberry asserted in a memo of May 20, 1966, "This is mandatory for all actors appearing in our show."

Roddenberry's attention to detail extended to each and every square foot of the starship *Enterprise*. He wrote in a May 24, 1966, memo to Walter "Matt" Jeffries, "Much pleased with our *Enterprise* sets, Matt. However we will shortly be getting two scripts which call for other *Enterprise* sets. Referring now specifically to the need for 'Engineering Deck' or 'Engine Room,' we should definitely think in terms of creating an illusion of a room of considerable size. We've got a huge ship and I definitely feel the audience will ultimately be disappointed if they are not taken occasionally into a set or sets with some feeling of vastness. Perhaps some of this can be done in cohort with Anderson Company, letting them create the extra space with some form of optical matte."

In another memo, Roddenberry told Jeffries, "I'm sure you've already thought of this, but I think we should be medically accurate on which instruments we decide to show on the bed, and then very carefully label each of them so the audience can easily read it and know exactly what these gizmos are doing."

Roddenberry even weighed in on the appearance of Kirk's quarters. "Suggest interesting set dressing in captain's quarters, possibly in some other places too. Might be barbaric odd-shaped shields, lances, maces, etc. collected on various planet expeditions, used as colorful wall dressing. Also would it be possible to make use of what appear to be animal pelts taken from strange creatures?"

GENE RODDENBERRY (creator, executive producer, *Star Trek*)

I didn't want only science-fiction writers, because many of the science-fiction writers available to me then talked about objects, about science, rather than about people. Over half the writers we used are just good, regular writers, because I wanted my show to be about people, not objects, and if you think back, the things you remember are the characters.

JOHN D. F. BLACK
(executive story editor, associate producer, *Star Trek*)

I joined the show about two months before we shot anything. Harlan Ellison and I had [each] won an award at a Writers Guild ceremony and we were cheering each other and racing toward each other to exchange congratulations. As I neared Harlan, Gene Roddenberry—who neither one of us knew from a bar of soap—was standing there. Harlan and I had both talked to him once, separately, in regards to his upcoming show *Star Trek*. Gene said, "We're having a party at my house for the winners, so come on over."

So we went to Roddenberry's house for a rather laid-back, dull party, but there were many people there and a lot of Scotch. At the party, I found out, because my agent just happened to be there, that I had an assignment on *Star Trek*. GR took me into the den and asked me if I would like to come onto the show as executive story consultant and associate producer. It was the first offer of its kind that I had ever gotten, so I said, "What have you got?" And he said, "I've got six assignments out, and your job would be to work with the writers and learn whatever production you want to learn." I went away, discussed it with my agent, and took the gig.

I can't remember specifically which writers were on line, but I went in with an ultimate respect for writers. I insisted, as any credible writer would, that I get the opportunity to give shots to young writers who had a great story. Here I was talking with Theodore Sturgeon, Ray Bradbury, and those kinds of heavy-weights. And it was an awesome thing to confront. I was not talking to anybody like Edgar Allen Poe, but at that moment in time, I was already aware that Theodore Sturgeon was the most anthologized writer in the history of the English language, which is pretty spooky. And now I'm "Johnny the Black Space Bear" in Theodore Sturgeon's books. I was also in one of Harlan Ellison's books as John D. F. Black. So *that* was my introduction to *Star Trek*.

JOSEPH SARGENT (director, "The Corbomite Maneuver")

My episode was the first one they shot, and during it Leonard Nimoy was unhappy because his character was without emotion. He said, "How can I play a character *without* emotion? I don't know how to do that. I'm going to be on one note throughout the entire series." I agreed with him and we worked like hell to give him some emotional context, but Gene said, "No way, the very nature of this character's contribution is that he *isn't* an earthling. As a Vulcan, he is intellect over emotion." Leonard was ready to quit because he didn't know how he was going to do it.

LEONARD NIMOY (actor, "Mr. Spock")

Spock is *not* a character without emotions; Spock is a Vulcan who has learned to *control* his emotions, and in his particular case it's even more difficult because he is half human and he has that side to control as well. Believe me, twelve hours a day, five days a week of controlling your emotions can have some strange effects on you. I remember one time in a meeting room having a conference with a couple of writers and suddenly finding myself crying for no reason at all. The emotions just had to come out somewhere, sometime. So I welcomed opportunities to do scenes or episodes where Spock had some kind of emotional release.

> Although it has been suggested elsewhere that NBC was reluctant to embrace the multicultural aspect of the *Enterprise* crew, that could hardly be farther from the truth. In fact, NBC encouraged the casting of non-Caucasian actors. In a letter to Gene Roddenberry sent by network VP Mort Werner on August 17, 1966, Werner points out NBC's interest in championing diversity and presenting "a reasonable reflection of contemporary society," noting that "NBC's pursuit of this policy is preeminent in the broadcasting industry," citing such shows as *I Spy*, *The Man from U.N.C.L.E.*, and *Run for Your Life* as being indicative of their progressive casting. "While we have made noticeable progress we can do better, and I ask for your cooperation and help."

NICHELLE NICHOLS (actress, "Nyota Uhura")

I tried to put into Uhura the qualities that I admire and demand of myself. Discipline, a forward attitude toward life, and high demands. She's head of all communications on that ship, so she's not just sitting there pushing buttons. For her or anyone to be entrusted with that kind of responsibility I felt she had to have a strength and dignity and a command of authority very much like Spock has.

JOHN D. F. BLACK

In some ways, Uhura was a difficult character to deal with. Nichelle was breathtakingly gorgeous, a skilled actress, and limited to "I'm hailing them, Captain." We could open it up a little, but not much. George Takei, when he came in and became the helmsman, had that marvelous stentorious deep voice that very few people are even aware that he has, although they heard it over and over again. That voice really gave strength to that chair, so that when the captain said whatever to George, and he said, "Aye, Captain," the audience knew he was going to do his best and that it was going to be enough. Scotty . . . if he got an awful lot of repetition because the engines had to go out a number of times, Jimmy Doohan never lost that characterization that he walked in with on the first day. The dialect stayed in place, as did the amount of smile he permitted. He was a very gifted actor.

GRACE LEE WHITNEY (actress, "Yeoman Janice Rand")

Rand had a lot of strength and a lot of guts. I think her character could have been further developed. Rand was on the same card of credits as McCoy in the beginning. She was to be the major female character. All the early publicity shots were with Bill, Leonard, and me in the middle. The thing about this business is that you have to survive no matter what they do to you. Taking her out of the show has made Rand somewhat of an underdog and the fans have always rallied behind her all this time. I feel cheated.

I was supposed to do thirteen episodes of *Star Trek*. I was not in all thirteen, but I was contracted to do thirteen. I did seven where I had a major part and then there were two or three where I did walk-ons to fulfill the contract. I actually did nine out of thirteen. They did use me in some of those, though. I remember one time in the episode "Conscience of the King," I just walked across and handed Bill Shatner a clipboard and winked and walked away. But there was no dialogue. I knew at that time that I had been let go. I was let go because of several reasons. The main reason was that they told me they wanted Captain Kirk to have more female friends. They felt Rand and Kirk were getting too close and they didn't want that. They were going to write Scotty out, too, but decided to keep him. They even had a clause in Leonard's contract that said if his ears didn't go over they could get rid of him.

GENE RODDENBERRY

The mistake I made with Rand, and I've regretted it many times, was the network said to me, "We've been meeting on this and we think what you should do is get a different, exciting young lady every week, rather than the same one." And I had said no so many times to the network that I thought I maybe should give them a yes this time. But looking back now, I would've kept Rand on the show and I'm sorry I didn't. I know what a disappointment it was to Grace Lee Whitney as it was to Majel to be the number two in line and then be gone. But producing is not a science and sometimes we make mistakes.

JOHN D. F. BLACK

DeForest Kelley was as experienced an actor as you could ask for. He had gone from juvenile to character juvenile to young leading man to leading man and there he was on *Star Trek* with an enormous amount of training. He had his character in hand, although it changed *slightly* during the first five or six episodes, where he became a tad more earnest. The conflict built in between Spock and him was electric. Even the extras who would run in and out with their little zap guns were into their characters and into the show. I think that was relevant to the audience. It triggered their emotional responses.

DeFOREST KELLEY (actor, "Dr. Leonard 'Bones' McCoy")

The character was laid out by Roddenberry, of course, and there was a guide that went into a good deal of detail about each character. But I remember having long discussions with Gene about McCoy. One thing we had both arrived at, and which was indicated in the breakdown, was that McCoy was supposed to be something of a future-style H. L. Mencken. So I went to the library and read about him and tried to work some of the more personal writings about Mencken into the characterization of McCoy.

The character began to really take shape after about six or seven of the episodes. It's always difficult to step onto a set and fall immediately into a character—with the exception of the captain, of course. His attitude is not as complicated as Spock's or McCoy's, but that's how the character actually began. As it was originally written, McCoy was even to be dressed differently. He would often be seen, for example, in an oversized-type sweater or something of that nature. He was to be the least military of all; he was described that way in the guide. But we never got to that part about the dress.

That was the beginning of him. In addition to that sardonic-type wit, I tried to inject as much warmth as I could give to him at the proper times, and also a sense of great caring. Bill and Leonard being the fine actors they are, there seemed to be a certain chemistry that fell into place among us. It all came together, and each of us had in the beginning of *Trek* this feeling of unity, of trying to make it as fine a show as possible. We were generous with each other in the discussions of the characters, among ourselves. I might say to Bill, "I don't think that line is mine. I think it's yours. It sounds like a captain's line." Or we might suggest some other line that seemed more appropriate than what was in the script, and then, with the producer's permission, of course, they might put it in. It was kind of a team effort.

NICHELLE NICHOLS

I had a car accident on the way to the set on the first day. I went to the hospital and the doctor put stitches in my lip and in my knee. He gave me a shot and some pills and it kept the swelling down and I didn't feel the pain. He told me the medicine would wear off about three or four in the afternoon. Later, I was doing my last scene of the day and we were moving right along. I was standing up by my communications panel and Captain Kirk is standing down by his chair, and the director, Joe Sargent, said, "Well, we're going to get this shot and we can call it a day. We've done really well." While I'm standing there by the railing, I remember somebody saying, "You know what I mean, Nichelle? Nichelle? Oh my God!" And all I remember was Bill Shatner leaping across to catch me, because I had passed out and was falling straight for him. I fell over the railing and he caught me. Captain Kirk to the rescue! My first day was almost my undoing.

DeFOREST KELLEY

We all made suggestions concerning our characters all the way through. The longer you live with it, the more comfortable you become with the role. Every bit of input that you give to the creator he will buy. He knows that you're beginning to get with it. The Spock–McCoy situation is a thing that started with a very small moment. It was just a line that he threw at me and I, in turn, threw the line back in a certain manner. Nobody thought much about it at the time. But when it hit the screen, it created an uproar. So they started to build on it and put more of that in. We all gave a great deal of input to our characters, but Gene Roddenberry laid them out for us in the beginning and tried to keep us on track.

JOSEPH PEVNEY (director, "The City on the Edge of Forever")

I loved the characters. Gene was constantly trying to give it a universal aspect, because that's what's going to be in the theory regarding the future when we go to other worlds. There will be all kinds of things out there. Some will not be completely humanoid, but that was okay. He was quite convincing about that. So he wanted some more nationalities in the show. He had an Oriental, a black, eventually a Russian. . . . The sixties were boiling over with this out here. At that time we had all kinds of college things going on. The beginning of the ERA and so on. Civil rights were tumbling all over the place. In the second season, Gene was saying, "Let's put a Russian in there." Wow, what a shockeroo that was!

STEVEN JAY RUBIN
(author, *The James Bond Films: A Behind-the-Scenes History*)

Whatever influence *Forbidden Planet* had on it, *Star Trek* was very much a series of the 1960s in that there was a certain diversity in the cast. You had the Russian; Mr. Sulu, who was Japanese; and the African communications officer. Very much an international element. *Forbidden Planet* was very white bread, but that was typical of the fifties, so probably was very typical of the navy. As the navy integrated, so did the space operas.

THOMAS DOHERTY
(professor of American studies, Brandeis University)

I think the multiculturalism in World War II is there: the Italian, the Jewish guy, the guy from Texas, and the guy from the farm, and later on it gets more open with the Asian guy and the Hispanic guy. That kind of works like the *Enterprise* being a B-17 in space.

JAMES GOLDSTONE (director, "Where No Man Has Gone Before")

Right back from when we did the second pilot, we had the idea that it would be a multiracial crew. We were doing this at a time when racial violence in the United States was rampant, and we were saying that in the future that it will not be a pressing problem, that we will have transcended that.

MARC DANIELS (director, "The Man Trap")

Right from the beginning it was easy to see that the characters were extremely well drawn. There was some trial and error with the peripheral characters, but the main ones—Kirk, Spock, and McCoy—were excellent. With that many characters, it was difficult to give each of them their due. There was a very good contrast between them, because you didn't have the same thing going on between any two of them.

ROBERT H. JUSTMAN (associate producer, *Star Trek*)

They all added to their characters. For instance, as Nimoy added to the character of Mr. Spock, we saw certain things in the portrayal that Gene thought could be taken advantage of and expanded, which we did. You have to learn in making film to deal with the film and not necessarily with what the original conception was. Film has a life of its own, and if you try to bend it toward what you originally intended and it didn't turn out that way, it's going to turn out to be quite awkward. You have to learn to take advantage of what's there, to perhaps give it a new shape. It's an interesting problem. You have to have a good concept for a character to begin with to enable the actors to do something with it.

GENE RODDENBERRY

The three-star billing between Kirk, Spock, and McCoy was the one that you would see a lot of. Plus science fiction wasn't "in" in those days, and we were going to do a lot of things we knew people might not understand. I wouldn't have stream of consciousness. In novels, stream of consciousness goes inside the hero's head and you can read what he's thinking. You don't have that in television, and so I thought that if I took a perfect person and divided him into three parts, I could have the administrative, courageous part that would be the captain, the logical part who is the science officer, and the humanistic part with the doctor. Then, when something comes up, the captain could say, "I don't know, fellas. We must do it," and Spock would say, "However, the logical thing is," and the doctor would say, "Yes, but the humanity of it," and I could have them talk about it without having stream of consciousness, and it worked.

DOROTHY FONTANA (story editor, *Star Trek*)

There was a very good team feeling. Gene had put together an extremely good team, between the cast, crew, and staff, who were united in the feeling that this is a good show, we're doing a fine show and let's keep it up. In fact, I don't think I've ever encountered such a great team spirit on any other show I've ever worked on, although I've had good working relationships with other crews. But that whole unity of everybody, from the top to the least important production person, was right there.

JOHN D. F. BLACK

The show was meaningful for many people. Bill Shatner had just done the TV pilot *Alexander the Great*. He was good, but it was not a hit. On the night of the first shoot, I left the office and found him leaning against my car. He had a look of enormous innocence on his face. I said, "How's it going, Billy?" and he said, "Fine." I figured there was something going on. And he just looked at me and said, "It's just so damned important to us." And I said, "Yeah, we've got a hit." That's what you say to everybody when it's in the fan and you don't know what's going to happen next, particularly to actors who are so vulnerable. And he said, "I hope so," and walked away. The sense I had was that we were all doing the best we could and we were giving it everything we had.

On May 4, 1965, Gene Roddenberry wrote to Shatner to express how happy he was so far with the way the show was progressing while also foreshadowing future difficulties with the star. "You must know how delighted I am that our arrangement together on *Star Trek* seems to be working out. Recalling our conversation and aiming in that direction, I already have three scripts at work which emphasize the captain in the dominant central role with powerful personality spiced with personal warmth. These three stories, each against an entirely different background and situation, are designed to combine believability with great personal jeopardy to firmly establish the man. Although I can make a number of guesses from your many performances I have seen, it would really be valuable at this early stage to have your comments, suggestions, and points of view. Can we get together for lunch soon? I'm enthused and pleased at the prospect of working together, particularly on a project with this much potential and challenge."

JERRY SOHL (writer, "The Paradise Syndrome")

Gene Roddenberry knew that I was a science-fiction writer from people evidently telling him I was. So he called me up one day and asked me if I would like to go down to the studio. I met him there in, like, 1965, and he said, "I have this idea for a science-fiction TV show, which I think the networks are going to buy, and wanted to talk to you about the possibilities of stories. Would you be available? I'm meeting with other science fiction writers like A. E. van Vogt, Ray Bradbury, Fredric Brown." He would meet with them down there and really sort of drained them by lunch of any ideas. We all did the best that we could, suggesting what to do. We hoped that it wouldn't be like Truman Bradley's *Science Fiction Theatre*. We wanted something more than that. He told us that it would be a good thing, but nobody believed that it would be.

I spoke to some writers afterward and they said, "Well, what did he do? Gene Roddenberry has only done *The Lieutenant* series and he was a police officer. What the hell does know about science fiction? It's just going to be a pile of shit."

So we all agreed that, yes, it would be a pile of shit, but we would all work for it anyway. But it didn't turn out to be that way and we wound up being very friendly with him.

HARLAN ELLISON (author; writer, "The City on the Edge of Forever")

In the beginning, I was very optimistic about *Star Trek*. I was vice president of the Science Fiction Writers of America, and I was the one who set up the West Coast banquet. I showed the pilot the first time it was shown to the science-fiction community. I said, "This is our chance to get good science fiction on the tube. It's being run by people who seem to know what they're doing and they want us." That was how Roddenberry came to hire Ted Sturgeon and the others, because of *my* intercession. Everybody else takes credit for it, but all of these people were friends of mine, and *I* got them to go in on the show.

JOHN D. F. BLACK

What *Star Trek* always strived to do, from my perspective, is to take things people can relate to now because it's real in our own lives, and *move* them. What happens if somebody burns down your building? It's the same thing as a monster showing up in your building. So they used the monster. The parallel was clean. The way television was, there was a hell of a lot that you *couldn't* do, but there was also a hell of a lot that you *could* do then, but nobody was noticing. So when a show like *Star Trek* came along, it was a marvelous advantage. There was no writer I knew who didn't want to work on that show. We were looking for the most acute science-fiction minds it was possible to acquire, because we were doing something new. But our dilemma was, first of all, that every plant that we showed had to be made. Every weapon or device had to be invented. What the hell did a plant look like on Rigel 9? Dilithium crystals were a rock which one of my kids brought home. It had a beautiful crystal-like shine, and I really fell in love with the look of it and took it into the office. Somebody asked me what it was and I said, "It's a Dilithium crystal." I didn't know what the hell it was, but it became the power source of the *Enterprise*.

We were creating *everything*. Conceiving an idea was one thing, getting it on film was another. Cost is relative in doing any series. *And* I wasn't that familiar with science fiction. I had read a great deal of it, but science fiction is playing tennis without a net. You could do anything you wanted, and if you look at the one segment I wrote, "The Naked Time," you'll see what I did, purely and simply, was take drunkenness and remove the slurs and staggers from it.

ADRIAN SPIES (writer, "Miri")

In those days, Gene told the writers he called that this was "really an anthology. This is a chance to write about anything you want." I didn't know what he was talking about. But we were two professionals and we worked out the story for "Miri" together. He had good ideas. I had gone to Gene and offered him the idea of a bunch of kids in this place where they are permanently young, but are really very old. I do remember that he said, "You have to develop a language for these people." I said, "What the hell are you talking about?" He said, "The kids would talk differently." In that conversation he made up the word *grups* for grown-ups. I immediately liked it. That's an example of a creative producer at work.

JOHN D. F. BLACK

There was no limit to what we could do. We could have villains that you could see and villains you couldn't see. You could have any character do a complete turnaround simply because there was a difference in oxygen somewhere. We jumped right in there without one single solitary thing in terms of theatricalism that we couldn't do. We could have done Oedipus or anything, although the censors wouldn't allow us to do the Oedipus story. Nor would they allow it anytime you got into those overtly sexually driven stories at that point in time. One exception was the episode "Mudd's Women," which was basically prostitution at large, which was in the papers every day. We were not promoting it or coming out against it. All we were saying is that it happens here and it happens in outer space, and the censors let us go.

NORMAN SPINRAD (author; writer, "The Doomsday Machine")

I thought it was a genius thing Roddenberry did. The anthology was dead on television as a doornail, and he devised a format in which you could do a self-contained anthology story every week. All you had were these people on a spaceship who could go to any damned planet they felt like. It was a genius concept, because it literally left them open to do anything at all.

JOHN D. F. BLACK

The *Star Trek* offices at the Desilu Studio were directly below those of *Mission: Impossible,* which was gearing up for production at the same time. At the end of the day, we would gather together and talk. Everybody was going crazy. You know, how the hell do you do a science-fiction series? How the hell do you do *Mission: Impossible*? We would bat the day's story problems back and forth, so there's no way to tell who came up with what about what at what time. It was all madness. It was a great deal of work, more work than I had ever done in so compacted a time. It was twelve to eighteen hours a day. I can remember many nights wandering around the sets at midnight, trying to figure out story logistics.

ROBERT H. JUSTMAN

To mount an episode of *Star Trek,* just imagine the most incredibly difficult process you can imagine and double it. The gestation is very, very difficult. We had to satisfy *many* masters. I can't begin to tell you. Add to that the time constraints—you *never* had enough time to write the episodes properly, much less produce them properly. The world of series television is an arcane sort of work, an arcane art. In essence, you really can't do anything in a way that's true. You can only do the best that you can do. You have a finite amount of time and you need to sleep at least a few hours every night, so you accomplish what you can accomplish within those constraints. That's it. It's not easy. The reward every now and then is perhaps turning out a show that affects people, causes them to think, and perhaps changes their lives. There was a feeling that we were all together, doing something that was different. Not only different, but worthwhile. *That* was the feeling.

HERBERT F. SOLOW (executive in charge of production for Desilu)

There were more freedoms on television, and there was more of a challenge by a lot of the aggressive young writers to challenge the authority of the network censors; to see how far they could push the envelope. *That* was Gene.

ROBERT H. JUSTMAN

It was all we could do just to do the show. Forget about worrying about anything else. It was a new show, and because of that, the network programming department was understandably nervous about what we could show and what we couldn't show, and what subjects we could deal with. Luckily, the fact that the show was allegorical in nature, sometimes the content escaped the network's notice. They took the content of the show for what the content *purported* to be. Allegory oftentimes is not about what's there, but what's *not* there. You see, when you're doing a show for a network, you not only have to deal with programming departments and development, but also with what in NBC's case was called the Broadcast Standards Department, which was the censors. Programming might accept a story that Broadcast Standards might find objectionable. It was quite difficult to satisfy three masters, two of them being the network and one of them being ourselves.

MARC CUSHMAN (author, *These Are the Voyages*)

It was a bad relationship between NBC and Roddenberry. It's like a bad marriage—two people who don't belong together, who are just not going to make a go of it. Neither one of them is a bad guy, it's just that Gene Roddenberry couldn't live within the network system. His relationship with NBC went sour with *The Lieutenant,* before *Star Trek* ever went on the air. The only reason they did *Star Trek* was because of Herb Solow, who was a former NBC man. And the fact was that they wanted to do business with Lucille Ball, who was CBS's golden girl. They needed a science-fiction show (they'd never had one) and ABC was doing well with *Voyage to the Bottom of the Sea*. CBS was doing well with *Lost in Space*, both of which had debuted the year before.

So NBC took the show for three reasons: to change their look, to be in business with Lucille Ball, and because they liked Herb Solow. They just didn't want to do business with Roddenberry, and then once the show came on, the relationship got worse and worse. The stories were making commentary on Vietnam, on racism, sex, hookers in space, guys that were half white and half black, and things like that. The network is saying, "We're getting too many letters; we're getting too many people who are offended."

HERBERT F. SOLOW

For years, Gene had painted NBC as the diabolical, evil-spirited, evil rich people who were always fighting against him, and that just wasn't so. NBC put up a lot of money, had a lot of patience, and put up with a lot of crap from Gene and a lot of other people, and were always there, ready to help us put it on the air. They did two pilots, and for all those years, no one ever mentioned NBC in any decent light.

MARC CUSHMAN

In the speeches he would make during the time *Star Trek* was on the air, Gene would get in front of audiences all the time, or give interviews to the press, and he was constantly rapping the network. You can't do that unless you're number one, but even the *Smothers Brothers,* which was a top-ten show, got canceled by CBS because they were constantly giving the network a hard time in the press. Back then you did *not* do that.

GENE RODDENBERRY

I remember once when I was a freelance writer and I was sent out to a place and they said, "We've got a show called *Riverboat.* Would you like to write it?" And the price was right and it was an adventure thing, so I went out and it was Mississippi 1850s and I talked a story and they said, "Fine. You've got an assignment. Oh, uh, just one thing: No Negroes." Mississippi, 1860? We got into an argument and I lost the assignment on that one. That is patently false. That is lying to both children and adults, and I think things like that are immoral. It's those immoralities that are my principal fight with the networks.

Within the limits of their commercial system, where television exists only to sell products, they probably do the best they can. I, for one, am waiting for the whole system to be changed so that when we make a show, that our appeal is directly to the audience. If the audience doesn't watch it, then fine, I goofed and I'm willing to admit my blame; it is this present strange system when you never get an appeal to the audience, you go through so many committees and agencies and vice-presidents that make the decisions that most of us, most dramatists, object to so strongly.

ROBERT H. JUSTMAN

NBC wanted as many "planet" shows that they could get. Of course that was very difficult for us to achieve. They, as anybody does, wanted more for their buck. The more things you could cram in a show, the more action you could cram into a show, the happier they were. Their need was to achieve good numbers. In a way,

I guess that was our need, too, but we were more concerned with the content of the shows. The network was concerned with content, too, but it was their kind of content and the kind that would, in their mind, attract viewers.

TRACY TORME (creative consultant, *Star Trek: The Next Generation*)

Gene and I had many golf-cart rides across the Paramount lot. We would go from one end of the studio to the other, taking these long meandering drives. He would wave at people he knew, saying hi to the security guards, and he used these times to talk to me about a number of things; personal things, professional things, great stories about the old *Trek,* stories about Shatner, stories about Majel, stories about his ex-wife, his divorce, his relationships with women.

He told me he thought I would be running my own show one day and things I needed to know about how to work with the network executives, how sometimes they will give you the stupidest notes in the world and you would have to choose when to nod your head and say, "That's kind of interesting"—and then hope that it never comes up again.

JERRY SOHL

Right from when the show got going in September 1966, it was obvious that Gene Roddenberry had done a good thing in having little moral lessons in most of the episodes, and it seemed to be that pointed kids in the right direction. Not only that, it made the show entertaining. I don't think it was sugarcoated particularly, because some of those episodes had some pretty racy things in them. On a whole, I think it was, in its time, about the best thing that existed as far as science fiction on-screen was concerned. Just the idea of going where no man has gone before is very good.

JOHN D. F. BLACK

As far as the scripts for the show were concerned, Gene was working from the position that he had created the show so it was *his.* GR's approach was that he was in control of the show and he approached the scripts in that way. My deal going in was that if I was going to get really good heavyweight writers, I know that they don't want anybody to screw with their material. They want it to be their concept. The only reason they're going to take television money, which is short and it was shorter than short-story money at that time, and the only way that I will talk to them about it, is if they can rewrite their own material without interference. We could give them all the input we want, but we can't put pencil to paper on their material. Gene said okay, and the head of the studio said yes, and that's the way I took the deal.

This is the reality. When stories came in on Thursday or Friday, I would read them, make my notes, copies would be made, and GR would take them home on the weekend. And instead of notes, he would come in on Monday with a rewrite. He would have rewritten everything. God knows how much. And it would never, in my judgment, have been that much for the better. In some cases he got closer to the pattern that the show was becoming, because it was evolving while I was there. But GR has never been the writer that Harlan Ellison, Jerry Sohl, or Teddy Sturgeon were. He isn't it. That's no knock. Very few people are up to that standing, but Gene couldn't keep his hands off a script. God knows what he would have done with "to be or not to be, that is the question," but there's one thing that's absolutely certain: what would have been in the script and what was shot would *not* have been "to be or not to be, that is the question."

ROBERT H. JUSTMAN

When we were doing the original show, the well-known science-fiction writers came up with all kinds of marvelous concepts, marvelous premises. But just because you have marvelous premises when you deliver a teleplay doesn't mean that you've written a proper drama. They didn't write anything that could actually be photographed or made. Whereas you might accept it in the world of prose, you're not necessarily going to accept it in TV drama.

GENE RODDENBERRY

During the first year, I wrote or rewrote everybody, even my best friends, because I had this idea in my mind of something that hadn't been done and I wanted to be really there. Once we had enough episodes, then the writers could see where we were going, but it was really building people to write the way I wanted them to write. I lost a lot of friends, writer friends, because writers don't like to be rewritten, but the whole thing was in my head and I couldn't say, "Mr. Spock, write him like you would write so-and-so," because there'd never been anyone like that around. So I rewrote them and lost friendships.

JOHN D. F. BLACK

After Gene would do his rewriting, I'd get the script back, try to satisfy him and get it back to as close a shape to the writer's work as I possibly could. The writer would come in, we would have a story conference, we would discuss changes, the writer would go away, and, generally, I would get the writer to do the polish . . . *if* there was time. The dilemma with *Star Trek* was that what seemed to a writer to be something that could be done easily inside the context of the starship, became impossible. So alterations were made in a lot of things. They were slight, but necessary.

The writers, I think, deserve credit for everything good in everything they did . . . while I was there, anyway. Any faults you could find in any material can be blamed on me and GR. The stuff we got was, by and large, brilliant. I cannot remember one instance where I sat across a table from a writer and said, "Why is this happening?" and they couldn't explain it to me. There was always a reason.

ROBERT H. JUSTMAN

A lot of the writers suffered from bruised egos, and I can't say that I blame them. Nobody wants to be rewritten, because you put a lot of thought and emotion into what you're writing. You believe it's correct or you wouldn't have written it that way. But Harry Truman used to say, "If you can't take the heat, stay out of the kitchen." No use determining that you're going to work in a certain medium if you're not willing to accept the rules that go with it, the restrictions that apply. This may surprise you, but people don't like to rewrite because it's hard work. You'd much rather get in a script that you can put right to work, but that's not necessarily the way things happen.

JOHN D. F. BLACK

When I wrote "The Naked Time," I delivered my first draft and gave a copy to GR. I figured, "Here I am, I'm working on the show, and if anybody knows the show besides GR, it's me." And GR brought back a rewritten script. I couldn't cope with it. That was not something I could suck up. The question in my mind, and I put it to GR, was what the hell am I doing here if I don't know the show? And I asked him what his problem was with it. He told me and I said, "Okay, I will rewrite it." And I rewrote it from my original—*then* he rewrote my second draft. So *nobody* got their show on the air.

ROBERT H. JUSTMAN

I guess I'm prejudiced. I think Gene Roddenberry is a genius. Not only in creating *Star Trek.* I *know* him and have known him for years when he has said and done some amazing things. He's an original thinker. His background was very humble, but he's a man who educated himself and he's found that his mind is fertile ground. It's an astonishing mind. You don't jump into a pool and swim without making waves.

DIANA MULDAUR (actress, "Return to Tomorrow")

A lot of people try to diminish his genius in order to put themselves up there, and I have said to them, don't ever forget his genius, because none of us would be here without him, period. That's just the way it is whether you like it or you don't like it. He created this. There is no question in my mind that Roddenberry is a genius.

JOHN D. F. BLACK

GR had a view that nobody liked him. When Gene would come up with an idea, I would say there was an 80 percent chance he was right; he was right about the characters, the crossover between outer space and inner space, he was right about a lot of things. And I don't like to say that. I was one of the ones who didn't like him.

ROD RODDENBERRY (son of Gene Roddenberry)

My father does get all the credit and others are often overlooked. Not Nimoy and Shatner, but the significance of others' contributions sometimes are overlooked, and I think that hurts them. It was a collaborative effort. A lot of people make *Star Trek* what it is. Yes, my father brought it to the table, he built the team and made mistakes along the way. He deserves plenty of credit, but I do feel for all the ones that feel wronged or don't feel like they've been listened to or recognized. I think they should be . . . but they should also stop bashing my fucking father.

JOHN D. F. BLACK

It's always mattered to me that my word was good, and if I told somebody that they would be permitted to rewrite their own work, that nobody would touch it, and then I would get it back already diddled with, that was not going to move us into a very happy state of mind. I was there because I could talk to those writers. Those writers respected me and I respected them. Integrity mattered, and I couldn't bear to see quality work changed to the point where the dialogue did not have the sharp edge that it had, and GR would use the word "fast" at least once a page as in, "We've got to get there . . . fast." I was watching too much good material getting screwed up, and I couldn't take it. I confronted an executive at the studio and I said, "I can't really continue if my word does not remain good," and he said, "It's GR's show." So I said, "Would you like my resignation or would you like to fire me?" And he said it could be one or the other. There was *no* alternative, so I left the show.

STEVEN W. CARABATSOS (story consultant, *Star Trek*)

I came in as story consultant for about fifteen weeks after John Black left. The show hadn't been on the air yet. By the time I came on, there were about six episodes in the can. I'm sure today it's even more frantic, because the stakes are higher, but at the time, on the shakedown year of a show, everyone was trying new things and was concerned about it being a success, as well as being the kind of show they wanted it to be.

ROBERT H. JUSTMAN

While this was going on, Gene was very fatigued and so was I. We both nearly didn't make it through the first season because of overwork. We were at our wits' end. I was so tired that first season that I came unglued one night at home. My wife called Gene and said, "That's it, I'm taking him away." You try working for about six months, seven days a week, and averaging three or four hours of sleep a night, with enormous pressure. Eventually something's going to give. It happened to be me that night, and Gene was next. We were both basket cases. As a result of that, that's how Gene Coon came to be on the show. Gene Roddenberry just couldn't do it by himself. He was excellent, Gene Roddenberry wrote wonderful scenes, but it took its toll.

As Gene Roddenberry left on a desperately needed shore leave of his own, he dashed off a memo along with his completed pages to "The Menagerie," which repurposed the original "Cage" pilot as part of an inspired two-part episode. Wrote Roddenberry playfully to Bob Justman, "As indication of my vast and sincere regard for you, I leave behind while I am on vacation in the High Desert, some fifty or sixty pages of sheer genius. Read and weep as did Alexander when he beheld the glories of Egypt."

On August 8, 1966, one month before the series would make its network debut, *Star Trek* underwent something of a seismic shift, when Gene L. Coon was brought on to the show as producer. To a large degree, it would be Coon who would ultimately define the show creatively in the coming months.

Born Eugene Lee Coon on January 7, 1924, in Beatrice, Nebraska, he was educated within the public school system in both Nebraska and California. In 1942 he enlisted in the United States Marine Corps, where he spent four years. During that time he was stationed in the Pacific and the Far East. Taking part in the initial occupation of Japan, he was ultimately sent to China, ostensibly to help repatriate the Japanese, but he ended up editing and publishing a small newspaper. For eight months he remained in northern China, and then went stateside, where he became a radio newsman, member of the National Association of Radio News Editors, and a freelance writer.

He wrote the novels *Meanwhile Back at the Front* and *The Short End,* both of which dealt with the Korean War. Writing for film and television came next, beginning in 1957 when he wrote the screenplays for *The Girl in the Kremlin* and *Man in the Shadow,* and, then, in 1964 he wrote Don Siegel's remake of *The Killers,* which starred Lee Marvin and Ronald Reagan, in his last on-screen role. Meanwhile, on television he wrote scripts for shows such as *Wagon Train, Bonanza, Have Gun— Will Travel, Rawhide, Alcoa Premiere, The Eleventh Hour, Hotel de Paree, Riverboat, Suspense, General Electric Theater, Mr. Lucky, Peter Gunn,* and many others.

MORT ZARCOFF (producer, writer)

At Universal we had a charge to come up with new projects. We would develop new concepts, new ideas, bring them on to script form, and hopefully we would create little units that would then produce the shows. The spark to it all in terms of sheer energy and ability to turn out work was Gene.

LESTER COLODNY (writer, producer)

They had a series on the boards called *McHale's Navy* and Jennings Lang, who was the VP of television, loved the idea, but the script didn't work. The original version was a one-hour drama and it was terrible. Jennings said, "How do we make this work?" I brought Gene in and made a deal for him to write two pilots. Gene took a dramatic series and made it into a half-hour comedy, and they started making the pilot.

MORT ZARCOFF

He was an incredible source of creative energy. We would all work and write scripts, but it was a question of degree. Most of us could turn out so many pages a day, but Gene would lock himself in the office and the pages would just pour out. We reworked a little bit of it, but he would get into that fourteen-cylinder typewriter of his and whip the pages out. They were, without a doubt, some of the cleverest, most craftsmanlike work that I'd seen in a long time.

LESTER COLODNY

Jennings Lang said to me, "We own all these Frankenstein movies. How do we make a series out of this?" Gene and I started watching the Frankenstein movies, and the more we watched them, the more we were falling on the floor screaming. We were laughing and I turned to him and said, "Wouldn't this make the funniest series in the whole world?" We put our heads together and between the two of us we came up with the concept of *The Munsters*. We took the idea back to Jennings Lang and he said, "You're out of your mind." Later, the head of the studio, Lew Wasserman, said, "We sold your crazy, goddamned series. We don't understand it, but we sold it."

They gave it to other people and they made it into a kid's show. Our version was very funny and very hip. We were doing a satire of *The Donna Reed Show* with monsters, because we wanted to do something very adult. The first two scripts were a very sly, tongue-in-cheek, and arch takeoff on *The Donna Reed Show*, but *The Munsters* never became that.

MORT ZARCOFF

During this time, they would get Gene to fix everything. Whenever there was something going wrong, they would call Gene Coon. He would fix scripts, he would fix pilots. He was a jack-of-all-trades. *That* is what he brought to *Star Trek*.

Gene L. Coon was a progressive in many ways, ranging from his general attitude toward life to hiring Ande Richardson—a young African-American woman who counted among her friends Malcolm X, Martin Luther King Jr., and Maulana Karenga—as his secretary and assistant. She had been hired a couple of years earlier to serve as a "floor secretary" at Desilu before she began working for Coon at *Star Trek*.

ANDE RICHARDSON (assistant to Gene L. Coon)

Desilu, after Watts exploded, realized that they had no black staff. Just the black actors who would come in, but they had nobody working on the lot that was black other than the janitors. So they called the Urban League and asked them to send over a couple of people. I went over and interviewed as a secretary, which I was not and never was. Anyhow, I worked in all the different departments all over the lot, including the desk on the Gower Street entrance.

Then Gene Coon came along and he had me come in and work with him. Then one day he asked me if I'd like to work *for* him and give up the other job. It took a little bit for me to decide that, because I had come from working with Malcolm and Karenga and all those people, and to work for a white dude named Coon was not exactly what I planning. But we worked it out and Gene became my heart.

DAVID GERROLD (writer, "The Trouble with Tribbles")

If you look at the episodes that Roddenberry was responsible for in the beginning, which was pretty much the first ten episodes, there's not a lot of *Star Trek*'s noble purpose there. There's a bumbling around trying to find out what the show is about, yet at the same time they did some great episodes. Because no one knew what *Star Trek* was, they were continually inventing it. You see stuff like "Charlie X," "The Enemy Within," and they also did a lot of rip-offs—"The Galileo Seven" was *Flight of the Phoenix*, "Balance of Terror" was *The Enemy Below*—and so they didn't really know what they could do with the show yet.

When Gene L. Coon first came on board in the second half of the first season, you start getting things like the Prime Directive and a lot of the stuff that was later identified as the noble parts of *Star Trek*. Gene L. Coon created the noble image that everyone gives Roddenberry the most credit for.

JACKIE COON FERNANDEZ (Gene L. Coon's widow)

Science fiction per se was not a particular choice for him. It was a genre he did, but he didn't think of himself as a science-fiction writer at all. If you hadn't had that name on it, it was just another drama which Gene was interested in. Another thought, another quest, another way to look at a situation from a different angle. It just happened to fall into that category.

GENE RODDENBERRY

I had no choice. The only way I could get people like Gene Coon to come in and produce—and I needed a producer, more helping hands—was to become executive producer. Actually a supervising producer. Today it would be different. No one would object to a very complex show having two, three, or even four line producers with a supervising producer over them. In those days, it was unheard of, but I just had to get some extra people in any way I could. I had found myself working twelve or fourteen hours a day, and I could no longer do it. Everyone on our staff was in the hospital at least once during those three years just from total exhaustion. We were doing half a science-fiction movie every week. Imagine what a burden that is. Science-fiction movies usually take twenty weeks to do. We were doing one every week.

LESTER COLODNY

Gene Coon could work on many projects at the same time because he taught himself something called "automatic writing." He had this crazy thing in which he hypnotized himself, and he was convinced that he could put himself in a state of almost disembodiment in which once he was ready to write, after having thought out the story and worked out what he was about to write, he would go into a room, put on some jazz music, and sit down at his typewriter. His fingers flew like you never saw in your life. He would be in a state of self-hypnosis, which he called automatic writing. His mind was only focused on one single thing: that script. The most astonishing thing you've ever seen in your life.

ANDE RICHARDSON

I used to go to the most unethical doctor you could find. I could buy jars of amphetamines from him. Then I'd take them back and give them to Gene. He'd give me some and off he'd go to write, and at night I'd go dancing.

JACKIE COON FERNANDEZ

His way of writing was going to bed with the thought in his head of what he had to come up with, and then it was there when he got up. It was just there. He went from sleeping soundly to getting up feeling fresh, and it just came out of his fingers onto the typewriter and he just never had to think about it.

JOHN FURIA JR.
(writer/producer/former president of the Writers Guild of America)

Gene was an extremely prolific writer. He wrote novels and lots of television in lots of genres. A lot of prolific writers tend to be sloppy, facile, and not very good. Gene was not that. He just happened to be a writer who wrote fast. He cared a great deal about writing. I think there were a lot of things he cared about. He loved to talk, he loved writing. A lot of writers kind of write defensively and hate the process. I sometimes say I have a love-hate relationship with writing. I hate to be doing it, but I love it when I'm finished. But Gene really relished the process of writing itself.

JACKIE COON FERNANDEZ

I never once heard him complain about writing. It would have been unthinkable for him to be anything else *but* a writer.

DOROTHY FONTANA

He had a delicacy of writing that was really remarkable. A subtlety of relationships that showed in the writing. His secretary was a young black woman who had very much gotten into Malcolm X's philosophy, and she was telling Gene about it. Gene said, "Well, I don't know. Is he going to be speaking? I'll go down and listen to him talk." And they had these discussions on the black movement and all that involves, the philosophy of life that involves, the determination of the black people to be more equal. Gene was always an open-minded and fair man. I always liked that about him, because it showed up in his writing and I think it made him a good writer.

ANDE RICHARDSON

Gene wanted to go to the mosque and I said, "Sorry, mate, you can't come to the mosque. No white folks allowed." Gene came from a background where his dad was a Klansman, and Gene was the opposite of that. Remember, he was a war correspondent. He had to go back again to World War II and then back to Korea. He was no lover of war, and he was open to all opinions. He was just a *good* man.

While we were working together, Gene didn't really share his feelings about *Star Trek*. I'd get a script and he'd come in and say, "Oh, how is it?" And I'd say, "Second act needs work," or whatever. I'd gotten so used to reading them and analyzing them, and then he would take it, look at it, and put it all together. So it wasn't so much that we would talk about *Star Trek* as we would talk more about the world. About politics, what was going on. And then I would see all of that in *Star Trek*. Look, I had been working with Martin Luther King Jr. and Malcolm X, and working with Gene was as normal as being with them.

LESTER COLODNY

Gene was always a commentator in everything he wrote. Everything had a message. He was very tuned in to things. You know how many years ago you're talking about? Gene was so aware of the ozone layer or forests being decimated. If you go over the episodes he did, so many of them have an underlying message that were very apropos to our culture. Whatever he wrote—he could write the funniest comedy—there was *always* a sociological point of view that had to do with the betterment of mankind. He was very dedicated in that way. Of all the people that I've met in my life, I would say he was one of the most guileless people I've known. There were no hidden agendas. No bullshit.

JACKIE COON FERNANDEZ

Gene was kind of like a grown-up Huckleberry Finn. It was a great quality, because everybody knew where they stood and didn't have to do any tap dancing. Gene Roddenberry's personality, even though he was a very soft-spoken man, was a very expansive, huge personality, bigger than life, so to speak. That ran true to form when it came to the show. Gene Coon's personality was quite the opposite. He was introspective, he was quite content to let others shine— Roddenberry, me, or anyone else who wanted to shine. He would let them and just be there.

DAVID GERROLD

There was no *performance*. I have to contrast him with Gene Roddenberry on this. Gene Roddenberry was always doing the performance of a great man, and people were awed because they would go into his office wanting to see the great man, and of course he would do the performance. Gene L. Coon just did Gene L. Coon. He was very accessible, very straightforward, and very unpretentious. He had a very nuts-and-bolts attitude about the fact that we were doing a television show. That was very refreshing, because what we've got now is that *Star Trek* has become this whole religion. People argue about this, that, and the other thing; there's a significance about it. With Gene Coon there was an understanding, first, that what we're doing is television. Good television. We're not on a mission from God, we're here to entertain the audience.

ANDE RICHARDSON

There were certain people who had my respect, and Gene Roddenberry didn't really get in that group. I mean, he came to my wedding and I went to his and Majel's wedding party after they'd gotten married in Japan. We were all friendly, but Gene Coon was my heart. I always say it was Malcolm, Martin, and Gene Coon. Those were the people I valued, admired, and I had respect for their integrity. But Gene Roddenberry was a sexist, manipulative person who disregarded women. I didn't value and respect him. He was funny in his own way, but he was a man of no substance. No integrity . . . well, I can't say no integrity, but he was paper-thin. He wasn't substantial. Having hung out with those three men, I have no hesitation putting them together and saying that Roddenberry came nowhere near them. Sure, he may have been the Great Bird, but he wasn't a great person.

He would have women walking from Bill Theiss's fitting rooms through to his office in the skimpiest outfits so he could perv them. He was really *such* a sexist. I remember him telling me something and I thought, "Why is he telling me this?"

Just personal kind of stuff I couldn't really care to know about him. Disregarding people's private space. I remember seeing him with Nichelle in his office, which is when I realized, "Oh, he's been banging Nichelle." But he moved Majel into an apartment just down the street so he could go for nooners. I don't know why he had to be lecherous, looking after every woman. He came back from Japan with Majel and he said to me, "You know, Ande, you can go from the front to the back but you can't go from the back to the front. Majel's got a heck of an infection." Again, *why* are you telling me this? But that was him: freaky-deaky dude.

ROBERT H. JUSTMAN

Gene Coon shaped a lot of the individual shows, but he didn't shape the concept. It was Gene's concept and it was never changed. Gene Coon rewrote the episodes while he was there. He wrote some originals and he was a workaholic. He would push himself to the limit and was marvelous. But the concept of the show had been established early in the first season. It was always Gene's concept. He shaped the show the way he wanted it to be. Then Gene Coon did his best— and his best was really very high—to make the show live up to that concept.

WILLIAM SHATNER (actor, "James Tiberius Kirk")

In my opinion, Gene Coon had more to do with the infusion of life into *Star Trek* than any other single person. Gene Roddenberry's instincts for creating the original package is unparalleled. You can't even discuss it. He put it together, hired the people, and the concept was his and set in motion by him. But after thirteen shows, other people took over. Gene Coon spent a year and set the tenor of the show. Gene Roddenberry was more in the background as other people actively took over.

ROBERT H. JUSTMAN

Gene Coon was almost totally involved with story and script. He did some casting, but he had nothing really to do with the editing of the show or the scoring. I did all of that, as well as the props, the set dressing, and all the other garbage. Honestly, Gene Roddenberry would have died if he didn't have Gene Coon or someone to do this. Gene Coon was a brilliant find; you couldn't find anyone better. The problem is that we wore him out, which is why he ultimately left in the middle of the second season.

HARVE BENNETT
(executive producer, *Star Trek II: The Wrath of Khan*)

Gene Roddenberry was the Douglas MacArthur of this particular campaign, the George Patton. And guys like Gene Coon were the Omar Bradleys.

GLEN A. LARSON
(producer, *It Takes a Thief, Battlestar Galactica, Buck Rogers in the 25th Century*)

My whole introduction to television came through working with Gene Coon. I think he was the spirit and soul of the show. I don't think the show would have gone in the direction that it did nor had its enormous credibility if not for Coon. Gene had a good sense of drama in addition to strong concepts.

DAVID GERROLD

When Gene L. Coon came in, one of the things that happened is that by then they knew what they could do, and he would concentrate on those areas. The episodes he did were more sure of themselves, but they weren't as adventurous in the same way as the early shows. The characters by then were more established, so Coon let the characters have the relationships with each other. The advantages were that when he took over, the characters locked into place very tightly and crisply. And it became Kirk, Spock, and McCoy. Before that time, there was a vagueness because Roddenberry didn't know who or what the show was about. After Gene Coon took over, he decided it was about Kirk, Spock, and McCoy, and the other characters were ancillary. That became kind of the formula, which was successful.

DOROTHY FONTANA

Gene Coon's writing influenced the writers who came in, who were structuring their stories. You could see this kind of flow happening. Another thing that happened is that the humor between the characters began to become more and more developed, particularly the Spock and McCoy relationship became a lot more fun. It evolved into what it ultimately became, which was a basic friendship. It was a friendship conducted with little insults and jabs, but the verbal fencing matches were always fun. It was fun to create those conversations once we started getting into that. I think Gene Coon led the way on that.

STEVEN W. CARABATSOS

Gene Roddenberry worked very hard. I've got to give the man a lot of credit, he busted his butt. But he had taken on executive-producer responsibilities and the line producer was Gene L. Coon, who was actually making sure the scripts got into the right form for shooting, and physically produced the show. He's the one I reported to once I came to work.

DAVID GERROLD

Roddenberry always took the show too seriously and everybody preached. I think Roddenberry wanted to be a preacher and couldn't make it or something. Everybody preached and Gene said, "No, in the future our people work together," but what he would write would be sermons.

ROBERT H. JUSTMAN

It didn't take long for Gene Coon's personality to almost overwhelm me because after a few days, and especially after I read the first thing he wrote for us, I was thrilled, because, number one, no one else of the writers that we had been using up until that time had the concept of *Star Trek* within his grasp, but Gene Coon did. It didn't take him long, and I knew how good he was, because I read the work and realized as I was writing my notes to him on his script or a story that he had just turned in that I was highly entertained. He understood the characters that the actors were playing, and it went on like that. The more I worked with him, the better I liked him, both personally as someone that was after the same things that Gene Roddenberry and I were after, and also because he was a very likable fellow.

DAVID GERROLD

In Gene L. Coon's scripts, people interacted with each other in a whole different way and didn't preach, although it was mandatory to do a little preaching at the end of the script where the captain explains—the captain being the father fig-ure. Gene L. Coon's characters joked with each other. I think that's why the fans loved the show so much. While our people were having an adventure, they were never too busy to snipe at each other, which was the way they showed their af-fection. There was never a question of how much Spock and McCoy loved each other, and that was shown by how vicious they would get when they would start sniping at each other. I think a lot of that was Gene L. Coon.

ANDE RICHARDSON

Gene would make comments in his scripts, and then he put in a joke so that you can laugh. And it keeps the balance. He keeps you laughing and learning. If they're laughing, they're breathing and they're learning. They can listen, hear, and take stuff in. That was Gene. He mixed it up so beautifully.

ROBERT H. JUSTMAN

One day I was almost stunned by the sight of him writing a script, and I watched him. He was pounding the keys for all they were worth and churning out what seemed to me to be reams of material. To my knowledge, he was the only person who ever wrote for *Star Trek* who gave you more than you were looking for. His scenes were highly playable, and he had lots and lots of ideas. He was like some-one who comes in scattering happiness wherever he goes, because his work was so superb.

STEVEN W. CARABATSOS

Like I said, some scripts could be put before the cameras quickly, but others re-quired substantial rewriting, which Gene Coon and I handled. It was an exciting time for me, because I was really just a kid, and this was a big opportunity. I also remember being impressed by the fact that Roddenberry was enlisting a writing corps of experienced science-fiction writers. All of them came to their assign-ments with great enthusiasm and a sense of excitement to do *their* kinds of sto-ries done in the way they wanted them done. My problem is that I didn't share that background; I didn't feel that I had the same preparation for it.

ROBERT H. JUSTMAN

With both Gene Coon and Gene Roddenberry, their major function was not necessarily to write originals, although they both did. Their job was to ride herd on the writers that we had corralled and get something wondrous out of them, which seldom happened, because it was a difficult show to write. You had to have an interest and a knowledge not only of the world of SF but also the way Gene predicted the future. That's a tough call. He was so skilled and enthusiastic that he would sit there typing with a cigarette between his lips, the smoke curling in front of his nose and just jamming out ideas, the richness of which never ceased to make me happy.

JAMES DOOHAN

The gorgeous thing about Gene Roddenberry was that he recognized Gene Coon. I worked with Jackie Gleason before he became famous and what's amazing to me is how he recognized the genius in Art Carney. He knew real talent when he saw it, because he was a real talent himself. That was also Gene's talent in picking people like that.

DOROTHY FONTANA

After Steven, I became script consultant. I had dealt with the scripts all the time and had my own opinions about them. I just never put them down on paper, although I spoke to Gene and Gene Coon secretly about the shows they were doing. I got involved with the show first as a writer, so I had my own story conferences with them about it. I felt I could do that same job [of script consultant] and so did Gene, so he let me have it.

Under the sure hands of *Star Trek*'s fab four of the time—Coon, Roddenberry, Fontana, and Justman—the scripts for the show began to rapidly improve as the first season went on, focusing heavily on the interaction of the characters, increasingly addressing social commentary, and laying the groundwork for what would become the most memorable aspects of the concept such as the non-interference Prime Directive and the introduction of the Klingons as our heroes' primary antagonists. At the same time, the ratings, although initially fairly strong, were not consistent or high enough to guarantee a continuation of production. There were rumors that NBC was considering cancellation and, in desperation, Roddenberry turned to Harlan Ellison for help.

In a time before things turned acrimonious between them as a result of the extensive rewrites on Ellison's script for "The City on the Edge of Forever," the legendary author wrote a letter on December 1, 1966, to the Science Fiction Writers of America saying, in part, "*Star Trek*'s cancellation would be tragic, seeming to demonstrate that real science fiction cannot attract a mass audience. We need letters! Yours and ours, plus every science fiction fan and TV viewer we can reach through our publications and personal contacts."

The word got out, helped in no small way by a science-fiction fandom that had been waiting for genuine science-fiction television series and finding it in *Star Trek*. As noted above, it was never a certainty that cancellation was possible, but it was already becoming obvious that the show had touched a chord with many—even if they *weren't* Nielsen families.

BJO & JOHN TRIMBLE (authors, *On the Good Ship Enterprise*)

When the first hint of cancellation wafted through Desilu, Harlan Ellison went into action with a plea to science-fiction writers to help save the show. For the most part, Harlan went to the people whose main interests in *Star Trek* were in potential sales of scripts. The fans got wind of the plan and sent letters also. It was enough of a flurry to convince NBC that *someone* out there in the Vast Wasteland actually watched *Star Trek*. The network renewed the TV series and everyone breathed easier.

DEVRA LANGSAM
(writer; publisher of *Spockanalia*, the first *Star Trek* fanzine)

During that first season, my cousin, Debra Langsam, picketed NBC and walked around passing out "Save *Star Trek*" flyers in Manhattan, and had people telling her that that "Dr." Spock was a commie. They were a little confused. So we were definitely handing out flyers and buttons, and NBC kept sending secretaries down, and they'd report, "They're still there; there's four of them, they're still picketing us." It was only a very small number of people, but we kept handing out those flyers and buttons and writing them letters, not petitions. A petition isn't as good; it's a lot less effort, but writing them letters is stronger. They sent what we called "Thank you very much and please drop dead" letters. You know, "Your opinion has been noted and logged." But it really did surprise them that there was so much interest in the show, and eventually they said, "All right, we'll do it again," but it was a lot of effort. I don't know in the end if we really made that much difference, or whether it was that they decided it would make them money, but we were in there digging.

I will say that Roddenberry encouraged them and sent out little presents from the show in support. They were sending out cutting-room clippings, actual pieces of film. You know, "Here it is, it's pictures of Mr. Spock and it's the real film!" He was sending them out as presents to say thank you, and then there was the fact that the network was sort of reacting to the protests. People started to find each other and get together more.

JACQUELINE LICHTENBERG (founder, *Star Trek* Welcommittee)

At the time, the attitude of the general public in the U.S.A. prior to *Star Trek* was total rejection of science fiction as just for people who were completely out of touch with reality. Being *in* touch with reality was the litmus test for being trustworthy. Science-fiction readers were not respected, and the literature was viewed by English teachers as toxic to a student's development of good taste. The same was true on TV (and radio, for that matter). The writers, producers, and audience all agreed "that" is nonsense. Of course detective series, westerns, and others were admired even though they contained more fantasy than any science-fiction story.

The first real break in this attitude came at the time when the TV series *My Favorite Martian* hit its peak. There is an underlying truth behind this that still works today. Comedy can make serious, deep philosophical points that drama cannot. Put the popularity of *I Love Lucy* against the feminist movement, and you will see the connection. Lucy struck a blow against the tyranny of "the husband" by using slapstick comedy. It may have become popular because it made fun of the subconscious bitter resentment of a generation of women. Likewise, *My Favorite Martian* introduced to prime time the Saturday-morning kiddie-show idea of "a visitor from another planet," only more like the Doctor [*Doctor Who*], a kid comedy in prime time.

So *My Favorite Martian* let the kids who had grown up on *Johnny Jupiter* laugh in prime time, and *Star Trek* brought the concepts to the level of adults who watched *Wagon Train*.

ELYSE ROSENSTEIN (organizer of early *Star Trek* conventions)

Science-fiction fandom has been around since about 1939. It was quiet, unpublicized. You only knew of a gathering if you knew someone else was going. It was all word of mouth. Science-fiction fans by their nature are intelligent, often involved in or at least very interested in science. They're loners by nature, they're not generally joiners, they are vocal when it's appropriate, they're very devoted to their genres. There were fan magazines out there in which people debated small stuff ad infinitum, but they did it intelligently. It wasn't just, "Well, I think it should have been *this!*" or "Why didn't they do *that*?" The thing about *Star Trek* is it was intelligent and hopeful. It wasn't your typical "let's see if we can kill the aliens" kind of thing. And that appealed to a lot of people. Roddenberry was very upbeat, and it really came across as making sense. Why would we necessarily kill every alien we saw?

DEVRA LANGSAM

From the very beginning science fiction was very male-focused or male-controlled. There were a few women involved, but an awful lot of them were just the wives of the fans. So when *Star Trek* started, it had a very large female component, which I think the networks never really understood. They had these three sexy guys as heroes and they didn't expect that women would say "Oh, wow!"? But they persisted in feeling that all *Star Trek* fans were sixteen-year-old guys with acne who wore eighty-seven buttons on their shirts. I mean, we tried to tell them, but they never listened. A lot of people were drawn into fandom because of *Star Trek,* many of them women, and the old-line fans started to feel like they were losing their grip on their own hobby. Look, I'm sure it must have felt like an invasion, just as when *Star Wars* came out and lots of people switched over from *Trek* to *Star Wars.*

Then there was the added problem that many of the old-line science-fiction fans were . . . less than perfect in regards to socialization. So if they saw a girl and they came up to you, they had a little difficulty perhaps socializing, and that annoyed the hell out of them because they thought, "Well, she's here and she's a girl, she must be interested in science fiction and me." I'm not being very polite about this, but, again, it was just a question of "I want to talk about Asimov and you've never even heard of Asimov, so why are you trying to take over? There are so many of you!" I mean, we had about four thousand attending the Worldcon in 1967, and then when Elyse Rosenstein and I decided to do our convention, it was so many more people. So the science-fiction fans sort of felt overwhelmed, and there was a certain amount of hostility.

BJO TRIMBLE

A close friend, Luise Petty, had volunteered to put together a "Futuristic Fashion Show" for Tricon 2, the 1966 World Science Fiction Convention in Cleveland. Luise involved me, and we contacted fans from all over the country for science-fictional costume designs. After a nice selection of those costumes was chosen, we contacted other fans to construct and model the outfits at a special fashion show during Tricon.

Seems a new science-fiction TV show was to be introduced and some SF writers suggested to the producer that it would be nifty to show this series pilot to a bunch of SF fans. What better place than a convention? Aha! Even better idea: why not take some of the costumes from some of the episodes already "in the can" and put them on models? Contact was made with the convention committee in Cleveland, and someone else came up with an even niftier idea: put those costumes in the Futuristic Fashion Show! Plans were made to do so. Gene Roddenberry hired some Cleveland models and brought the costumes to the convention. There was one serious problem: nobody told me that a carefully coordinated, even more carefully timed fashion show was being enlarged by three costumes neither Luise nor I had ever seen! One member of the convention committee thought of asking the producer to reason with me. And that's how I met Gene Roddenberry.

After meeting him, I said I'd have to see the costumes. I didn't even know what show he was talking about—something to be introduced on that season's schedule called *Star Trek,* which he *claimed* was good science fiction. We'd had several seasons of other shows that were *supposed* to be good SF and weren't, so I was dubious, and rather resentful that my fashion show was turning into nothing but an advertising stunt for a stupid new TV show. But Roddenberry had the models parade them for my reaction. I agreed to put them in the fashion show and, with a little subtle urging from GR, even to make a specific mention of *Star Trek.* There's a type of Irish charm that can, as they say, charm the birds out of the trees. GR had that. Everyone liked the *Star Trek* costumes, and it certainly—as it was intended to do—stirred up great curiosity about the show itself.

YVONNE CRAIG (actress, "Whom Gods Destroy")

I've never stolen anything from a set ever, but I'm so sorry that I didn't say, "Could I have my costume?" from *Star Trek,* because it was done by a woman who made costumes for the Folies Bergère and it had one hook and an eye that held it up. She designed it like a bridge and it never moved. It was really comfortable and wonderful. There were a lot of women who want to dress up as Marta [season three's "Whom Gods Destroy"]. I saw someone on the dance floor who was in that costume once, and I went down to meet her and *she* was a *he*. A hairdresser who did a beautiful job. The wig was there and he had made the costume and it was just gorgeous and he was wonderful.

JACQUELINE LICHTENBERG

The first time I heard of *Star Trek* was way before the debut at Worldcon, because I knew people in fandom. I knew this show would be *real science fiction*. But I still didn't "get" the whole Spock thing. I just did my write-in letter begging them to keep it on the air until I could see it. In those days, canceled shows became inaccessible. No Netflix or Amazon Prime.

In its first season, *Star Trek* had a remarkably successful run of episodes as the writers continued to try and discover the show and mine the richness of its characters. Among those episodes that would eventually define the series as a television classic were "The Enemy Within," in which Kirk is split into "good" and "evil" versions of himself, with the discovery that one cannot survive without the other; "Space Seed," which served as the introduction of the genetic superman Khan Noonien Singh, a character that would return in the feature films *Star Trek II: The Wrath of Khan* (1982) and *Star Trek Into Darkness* (2013); "A Taste of Armageddon," one of TV's first true allegories for the Vietnam War; "This Side of Paradise," which gave viewers one of its earliest insights into the human side of the Spock character; "The Devil in the Dark," and its not-as-obvious-as-it-seems-on-the-surface tale of not judging by appearances; and "The City on the Edge of Forever," the poignant and heartbreaking time-travel story in which Kirk must decide whether or not to sacrifice the universe for the love of a woman.

RICARDO MONTALBAN (actor, "Khan Noonien Singh")

As an actor, I thought it would be great fun to do it. Khan was not the run-of-the-mill sort of portrayal. It had to have a different dimension. That attracted me very much. When they sent me the script, I thought it was a fascinating character and I loved doing it.

Khan was a character that was bigger than life. He had to be played that way.

He was extremely powerful both mentally and physically, with an enormous amount of pride, but he was not totally villainous. He had some good qualities. I saw a nobility in the man that, unfortunately, was overridden by ambition and a thirst for power. I saw that in the character and played it accordingly. It was very well received at the time and I was delighted. Then I forgot about it and went on to the next thing . . . until the second *Star Trek* film.

DOROTHY FONTANA

Gene Coon did a rewrite on "A Taste of Armageddon." Some of the things he added really had a lot to do with the character of Kirk. It was Gene who wrote the speech at the end that man has a reputation as a killer, but you get up every morning and say, "I'm not going to kill today." It was one of those things that began to identify Kirk far more solidly than we had before.

DAVID GERROLD

I would have to point to "Devil in the Dark" as being the best episode Gene L. Coon ever wrote, because it really gets to the heart of what *Star Trek* was. Here you had this menace, but once you understood what the creature is and why it's doing what it's doing, it's not really a menace at all. We end up learning more about appropriate behavior for ourselves out of learning to be compassionate, tolerant, and understanding.

HARLAN ELLISON

The idea of "City" came from the image of the City on the Edge of Forever, and it was an image of two cities, which is what it says in the script. The City on the Edge of Forever is the city on this planet. It was *not* a big donut in my script; it was a city. That was a city that was on the edge of time, and it was where all of the winds of time met. That was my original idea. All the winds of time coalesce, and when you go through to the other side, here is this *other* city which is also on the edge of forever, which is New York City during the Depression. They're the mirror image of each other. In that time, all I was concerned about was telling a love story. I made the point that there are some loves that are so great that you would sacrifice your ship, your crew, your friends, your mother, all of time, and everything in defense of this great love.

That's what the story was all about. All of the additional stuff that Gene Roddenberry kept trying to get me to put in, kept taking away from that. The script does not end the way the episode does. Kirk goes for her to save her. At the final moment, by his actions, he says, "Fuck it. I don't care what happens to the ship, the future, and everything else. I can't let her die. I love her," and he starts for her. Spock, who is cold and logical, grabs him and holds him back and she's hit by the truck.

The TV ending, where he closes his eyes and lets her get hit by the truck, is absolutely bullshit. It destroyed the core of what I tried to do. It destroyed the art; it destroyed the drama; it destroyed the extra human tragedy of it.

JOSEPH PEVNEY

"City on the Edge of Forever" was toward the end of the first season. Harlan was very happy to get his story on *Star Trek*. He was down on the set thanking me. It's great that Gene rewrote it though, because Harlan had no sense of theater. He had a great sense of truth, which was very nicely placed in there—all of the 1930s stuff was well documented. It was a well-conceived and well-written show, but in the original script's dramatic moments, it missed badly.

HERBERT F. SOLOW

We got a lot from Theodore Sturgeon and George Johnson and Harlan Ellison and Gene Coon, who without a doubt was the one who masterminded most of what *Star Trek* is today, not only inventing and developing the Klingons and their culture, but Gene produced and was in charge of writing all the shows, I think from number seven on until the middle of the second year. It was Gene [Roddenberry] who agreed to bring in some of these science-fiction writers, as opposed to the usual available television writers, who were very good but were not versed in science fiction, fantasy, or fascinating alien characters.

We could have brought in people who wrote horror shows, but I think we would have gone off the air in the first year. In the first season we built into it a fascinating subculture, if you will, of alien life. We used writers who did a lot of work for Rod Serling on *Twilight Zone*, because we wanted to get that feeling, and we did, and the audience picked up on it, and that what makes *Star Trek* today.

We did not do monster shows per se, we didn't have blatant heavies on the show. I think what we did was very introspective stories. We did people stories. I think we dealt with alien life on a very fair basis—just because you were an alien doesn't mean you're bad. We dealt with benevolent dictators, we took various sides on issues, and I think that's what the audience picked up and has liked all these years, but I must tell you, that wasn't what we had in mind when we first started. It was an action-adventure series in outer space, and NBC felt it could be a very successful adventure show, RCA felt it could sell color television sets, and we felt it would make Desilu important again as a supplier of quality television.

JIM RUGG (special-effects chief, *Star Trek*)

The first year on *Star Trek* was the most exciting year I've ever spent in the business. It was all new and we were all experimenting and nobody knew where we were going. We fumbled our way through and sometimes lost and sometimes won . . . it was the only show, before or since, where the effects men got fan mail.

SCOTT MANTZ (film critic, *Access Hollywood*)

Think about it: back in the sixties nobody knew what *Star Trek* was. It was an expensive show. It's easy for us to lose sight of this now. Every time they were doing something with regards to a visual effect, it had never been done. Compare the look of the first season of *Star Trek* to *Lost in Space*. [Director of photography] Jerry Finnerman was a genius. That is art. I love how in "Charlie X," after Charlie makes the crewman disappear for laughing, Kirk steps into the shot, the light is on his eyes, and he goes, "Go to your quarters before I pick you up and carry you there." It's brilliant. You look at an episode like [season two's] "Metamorphosis" with a purple sky and the way when they went to Cochrane's home you see the clouds above. They never really did that before. And they turned off all the fans and said, "Nobody move." So that the clouds would look stationary. The cinematography of that episode with the purples and pinks is beautiful. By the time [Director of Photography] Al Francis took over halfway through the third season, it was too light and bright.

GERALD FINNERMAN (director of photography, *Star Trek*)

I felt the pilot looked a little too lush. We had discussed a look on the show that they wanted but didn't get. It was a ratio of lighting. We didn't want it to look like just people and no background, of course we wanted to see the background, but they didn't want everything so full, musical-looking. The pilots were rather full. I brought my camera crew over from Warner Bros. and we started *Star Trek* and it was very ambitious. I took a look at the sets and they were tremendous. There were these big cycloramas, and I talked to the producers and said, "Wouldn't it be nice for each planet to have a different atmosphere? Who's to say that Planet 17 isn't purple or orange or magenta?" And they really liked that idea.

DOUG DREXLER (scenic artist, *Star Trek: Deep Space Nine*)

I watched the entire first season in black-and-white, which I tell people all the time. Try watching the original series shows with the color off and you'll be really impressed. And then watch an episode of *Enterprise* with the color off. It's mud. In those days, most people had black-and-white television sets. The DP shot for black-and-white and color. He had to know it was going to look good in both. So the use of shadows and contrast and the graphic quality of it was all very important. If you watch the original series of *Star Trek,* the episodes look great in color *and* black-and-white. No one ever looks at them in black-and-white anymore. I can't imagine why anybody would, but if you're interested in film or television, you should.

GERALD FINNERMAN

The network would say, "Don't use color on the people." We had a sequence, I believe it was on the first show, where they go into a red alert, and it was wonderful. It gave me the opportunity to try something different. There we were on the bridge of the *Enterprise* and they're being attacked, and I went to this red alert and took out all of the white light and came on with the red. I had a little crosslight of white for a source for the lab, and I would have the red around for backlighting and process. It was very effective, and everybody loved it. Then that got me into using more and more colors. I may have gone overboard on it possibly, but it was so much fun. I look at the episodes today, and they're terrific.

GENE RODDENBERRY

Star Trek was considered a silly fantasy, because man had not yet landed on the moon. My own father went out and apologized to the neighbors. He said, "I know the boy's up to something silly, but he'll come back and write a good American western."

At the end of the season, *Star Trek* won the Hugo Award for Best Dramatic Series. Gene Roddenberry quickly dispatched a telegram to Mort Werner at NBC: "Hugo Award was given to *Star Trek* for the Pilot #1 combined two-parter (referred to internally as 'The Envelope'). 'The Menagerie' won over *Fantastic Voyage* and Ray Bradbury's *Fahrenheit 451*. Hope you are pleased too. Is it too late to make use of voice announcement on *Star Trek* promotional spots over the next few days?" Apparently it was, as such promos were never created.

GERALD FINNERMAN

I was only thirty-two years old, and it was my first job as a cinematographer. I made a lot of artistic decisions without sharing too much information in advance. Otherwise, I'd have ended up playing it safe. On a show like *Star Trek*, you have to push the envelope. The result of playing it safe is a diet of pabulum. I was always pushing the directors to go a little further. I'd say, "On this two-shot, when Kirk walks away from McCoy, we can dolly over and take him over to the bridge." They weren't comfortable with that. I liked to see a scene flow for three or four pages rather than shoot a straight master and then break it into close-ups.

I think much of the look also came from the placement of lights and the use of colored gels. We also saved the company a lot of money, since they didn't have to paint sets to make them look different. We painted them with light. We changed walls from gray to blue to green, depending on the mood and what we wanted to say about the planet. One day we created a purple sky. Another day, the same set looked like a hot desert in March. A third day, it was deep blue. We did it with filters and lights.

FAMILY FEUD

"ONE DAY OUR MINDS BECAME SO POWERFUL WE DARED THINK OF OURSELVES AS GODS."

The addition of Gene L. Coon in the midst of *Star Trek*'s first season set the show on a fairly steady course creatively, with some of the series' best episodes yet to come in the sophomore year. At the same time, the seeds of discontent that had been planted in that first year began to take root. As production commenced on year two, the shock waves were truly beginning to reverberate.

When *Star Trek* was launched, the concept was that William Shatner would be the series' star as Captain James T. Kirk. Indeed, the show's "bible" offers, "The stories, certainly for a series, certainly for all the early ones, must be built strongly around the central lead character. The basic problem must be his and he must dominate the events and work out his solution. Considerable attention must be given to establishing and constantly examining his full character, giving him an interesting range of mixed strengths, weaknesses, and idiosyncrasies—and the net sum must result, must attract the audience and invite audience-identification."

The intent seems pretty clear, but once episodes began to air the audience very quickly embraced Leonard Nimoy's Spock, with the media following in lockstep. As this so-called second banana rose in popularity, the stoic Vulcan science officer threatened to eclipse the captain. Now, whether this was ego or an actor recognizing his position and attempting to maximize the potential for himself, Nimoy and his talent agency representatives came up with a list of demands—both creative and fiscal—that resulted in the very real possibility that the character would be replaced. Indeed, actor Lawrence Montaigne, who had played a Romulan officer in season one's "Balance of Terror" and the Vulcan Stonn in season two's "Amok Time," was put under contract in early April 1967.

LAWRENCE MONTAIGNE (actor, "Amok Time")

Leonard wanted more money and they negotiated with my agent for me to replace him as another character, not Spock, but with the same background. Then Leonard came back and my agent called me and said, "You're out." But I was working so much at the time that it didn't really matter to me. The idea of joining the show *was* interesting. They made a very attractive deal. Not as much as Leonard was getting, but it was steady work and I wouldn't have to go out and audition for roles. I'm one of those actors where I had three shots at series, but none of them worked out, for better or for worse. So I was not very upset or anything.

MARC CUSHMAN (author, *These Are the Voyages*)

They almost didn't have Spock for the second season of *Star Trek*. The fan mail got so intense during the first year, sacks and sacks of mail every day. His agent said, "He's only getting twelve hundred and fifty dollars a week and he needs a raise," but Desilu is losing money on the show and the board of directors was thinking of canceling it even if NBC wanted to continue because it was bankrupting the studio. So they said, "We can't give you a raise," and they replied, "He's not reporting to work." Gene Coon returns from vacation on April 1 and has a memo from Gene Roddenberry that says "Dear Gene: This is not an April fool's joke. It looks like we'll be going forward without Mr. Spock. We've hired another actor and he'll be playing a different Vulcan character on the show." It really came down to the wire, and the one that broke the stalemate was the one that didn't want Spock in the first place: NBC. "You are not doing the show without that guy. Pay him whatever you need to pay him to keep him on the show."

LAWRENCE MONTAIGNE

Shortly thereafter they called me and said they wanted me to play the character of Stonn in "Amok Time." They sent the script to my agent and he called me and said, "I think we'd better discuss this." So I went to the office and all of the character's dialogue was on one page. It didn't explain that he was a focus all the way through, that he was *the guy*. But I looked at the five lines and said, "I ain't doing this." My agent said, "Don't worry, we'll ask for some ridiculous amount of money and star billing, and they won't consider it." So he calls me back and says, "I've got good news and bad news. They accepted the deal." And I was stuck. I went ahead and did it, it was an easy job. I just had to stand there and look menacing. But the funny part about it is that almost fifty years later I returned as the same character in the [fan] film *Star Trek: Of Gods and Men*. And Arlene Martel, who played the girl I was supposed to marry in "Amok Time," performed the marriage ceremony between my character and Nichelle Nichols as Uhura. *Star Trek* is a small world.

While Roddenberry and Desilu were united in the notion of recasting Spock, NBC ultimately rejected the idea, recognizing the importance of Nimoy's presence and not willing to alienate the fan base for a show that was, to use the parlance of today's television-speak, "on the bubble." In the end, Nimoy's demands were met and instead of Kirk or Spock being the lead, the scripts began focusing on them as a team. Problem solved? Not exactly. The sense of competition continued, and it impacted the production of the series—as did the actors' attempts to exert more control on the show creatively.

JOSEPH PEVNEY (director, "Amok Time")

In the beginning, there was the word and the word was "cooperation." But then they started reading the fan mail. This was the first year and they were on tenterhooks. Every time the phone would ring it was, "Are we canceled? Are we canceled?" Everybody was lovely in the beginning. The relationships were exciting and good and then Gene Roddenberry let things get out of hand. I have to blame the producer on this, because the director is a lover and father image and all that, and he's in love with his people and must treat them very carefully so as not to offend or hurt. But the producer's function is to be the stern father who punishes for misbehavior and so on. Gene could never play that role. Gene Coon could a little, but they didn't pay too much attention to him because Roddenberry was the top boss. So they would give lip service to Gene Coon, and then Roddenberry would come down and love everything he saw.

MARC CUSHMAN

Most of the people didn't get a sense of the feud. They came back for that second season, and the Emmy nominations came out, and Leonard Nimoy was nominated for an Emmy, and William Shatner wasn't. Here your costar, your second banana, just got a raise, a record deal, and script approval, and is up for an Emmy and getting more fan mail than you, but other than that they were friends. But as the star you have to protect your position. And William Shatner was a star.

JOSEPH PEVNEY

Right after the second season pickup, things started to occur. The actors wanted to make a bigger contribution in the writing, so they wanted a rehearsal table thrown on the stage. The motivator of all this was, I think, Bill Shatner. Leonard could make his contributions in a quiet way by going into the office and talking to Coon or Roddenberry, and they were all very receptive. But all of a sudden things started to move away from the producer and director and to the actors. So like a producer himself, Bill would arrange the table and seats and he would talk to the property man to move things over to the side. Well, when you're doing television in five or six days, or whatever the schedule was back then, there's no time for this constant rehearsal, a reading rehearsal, offstage, with pencils in hand and making changes. Because once you start making changes on the set, they have to be approved by the producer.

The propensity of the leads to make changes, particularly Shatner, prompted a memo from Roddenberry which he copied to Nimoy as well as Gene Coon and Robert Justman. "Due to our production staff being deeply involved in postproduction problems, it was necessary to make a number of script dialogue and action changes on set. And we appreciate the hard work you and others did in accomplishing this. However, obviously none of us want this to become a habit since it is precisely this type of thing which has destroyed the format and continuity of more than one television series . . . where one person makes a change, others who may be less capable are encouraged to stick in their oar too, the director is encouraged to toss in some ideas of his . . ."

ROBERT H. JUSTMAN (associate producer, *Star Trek*)

Bill was the instigator of the rehearsal table. He wanted to be able to rehearse and I said, "Okay, I'll tell you what. In between takes we'll set up a table, we'll grab everyone and go over the next scene." Bill had wanted to do that and we made it possible. It was useful. It certainly helped an awful lot.

JOSEPH PEVNEY

It's time-consuming. It destroys the most important thing of all, the disciplinary control of the director on the set. It's a very critical and tentative thing, which the television industry has gone away from completely. The director on a television set is nothing anymore. He doesn't mean a goddamned thing. He's an errand boy. I'm an angry guy when it comes to this kind of shit. I come from a disciplined school where everything is in the script. Nothing else counts. What is the story? And *that* is your function. Your responsibility is to tell the story as the writer intended it. That is my definition of a director. Once that's interfered with, he loses all control. So anyway, every time you would have a "Cut. Print," you'd have these guys rushing over under Bill's command to the table to work on the next scene.

ROBERT H. JUSTMAN

I don't think Leonard or Bill ever gave up wanting to make the show better. Especially Leonard. He always wanted to make it better, make his character more believable, and not take the easy way out. The problem is, of course, that the actors get the script a few days before they start the shooting, and then it's a little late to try and effect changes. We did try to accommodate them as much as we possibly could, even though it made our lives hell. There wasn't any time.

I initiated a policy in the second season that may have had something to do with that feeling. We alternated directors rather than in the first season where we had scattergunned. For the most part we had Marc Daniels and Joe Pevney alternate, because they knew the show, they seemed to know what to do with the show first season very well and the film was generally very, very good. So I said, speaking from a cost factor, we'd be able to get as many shows as we could possibly get with the time and money we had to spend.

These two guys were very, very good, but at the same time we found out—I found out—familiarity breeds contempt. I shouldn't say that. It tends to relax a little bit too much when it's the same guy every time and you lose a little bit of that excitement you wanted to maintain. You should understand that Joe was extremely well liked on the set. The cast really liked him, the crew really liked him. He was very likable and motivated. Marc, on the other hand, was a different kettle of fish. Marc, in my opinion, turned out better shows, but he was a more difficult personality. He was truly well versed in all forms of drama and comedy. His experience was unlimited, because he had been a successful movie director, stage director, television director, and he had a very good eye for compositions. He was a very all-around kind of director, but he was more demanding than most. He ran a tougher set.

JOSEPH PEVNEY

While Marc and I went off to other shows, they brought in new directors, and the new directors had ideas. But the actors were already ingrained in behavior patterns which did not permit new inventiveness which was, as they felt, opposed to their character. That was the real beginning of the problem. Bill would not do certain things because Kirk wouldn't do that. Leonard certainly felt that way, very strongly, because his character was so deeply ingrained that he knew precisely how Spock would behave in a certain setting.

VINCENT MCEVEETY (director, "Balance of Terror")

I think it's true of many series. Look at how locked *Gunsmoke* was. Take Jim Arness, for example. How much did he vary from his basic portrayal? Any time there was a stretch, they'd pull back. The traditional words on *Star Trek* were "Well, Spock wouldn't do this; Kirk wouldn't do that." All of a sudden they're entities in and of themselves, when they were nothing two years prior when no one knew what they would do in a situation. By saying this, I'm not necessarily being critical, but as Joe Pevney said, it *is* extremely limiting and that's all. I have worked on too many series where the attitude has been similar, if not more vocal, and they've been extremely successful.

JOSEPH PEVNEY

It was right in certain respects with the actors protecting themselves, and it was wrong in the fact that their minds were closed to new inventiveness. There were good and bad things involved, but then when we would come back, there would be a whole different attitude by the actor. Now the actor had become coproducer, codirector, and cowriter. A whole different attitude toward me or Marc Daniels.

RALPH SENENSKY (director, "Metamorphosis")

Doing episodic television is like jumping on a freight train that's in movement. As a director what you have to do is jump on it and not break your legs. Once you've boarded it, you have to climb on top of the train, run across, and get in the engine and take over running it. What happens is that before you can bring anything personal to the story, you have to get acquainted with who the people are. Not in terms of who you want them to be but in terms of who they really are already. These are already established characters. You do that, and *then* you can start to find the warts and things to do, outlets to extend and expand. As a result, what would happen is that you have to rely on the cast to help you out. You'd say, "Would your character do this?"

WILLIAM SHATNER (actor, "James T. Kirk")

Somewhere along the line, Captain Kirk and I melded. It may have been only out of the technical necessity; the thrust of doing a television show every week is such that you can't hide behind too many disguises. You're so tired that you can't stop to try other interpretations of a line, you can only hope that this take is good because you've got five more pages to shoot. Lacking that pretense, you have to rely on the hope that what you're doing as yourself will be acceptable. Captain Kirk is me. I don't know about the other way around.

DeFOREST KELLEY (actor, "Dr. Leonard 'Bones' McCoy")

I think perhaps all of us have some of the traits of our characters. I think that really comes about in casting. Roddenberry sat down and probably said, "Gee, this guy has a quality I want for the doctor." That's what he's looking for, that particular quality. When he looked at Leonard Nimoy, he probably thought, "Gee, this guy is what I want in Spock." We all, however small it might have been, have some of these behavior patterns within us. You find yourself more or less building on that. You know, it's a building block. Bill is like Captain Kirk in many ways. He loves to ride horses and motorcycles and he is very athletic. Leonard in his way is not unlike Spock. I guess we all have a bit of it.

WILLIAM SHATNER

I played Kirk the way I would like to be. Given his battles with a monster, or his decisions to go to war or whatever, I played him as I'd like to have behaved in that situation.

VINCENT McEVEETY

They call it protecting the character. The character first, before story, before stretch, before anything, because they claim in their vision that that is the key to the success of the series, and I think in many instances they're right. What you have to do is write *for* the character. Sometimes writers get very lazy and just write a script, but these actors are very concerned about being put in a weak position. That's okay in acting class, but they're depreciating their character. If anything was lacking in later years on the show, even more than not accepting growth of the characters or even more conflict, it was lack of writing. I think it became more cliché writing, if you will. They came up with a story, went in there, and put the actors in that story. They bring in writers who aren't terribly familiar with the series who say, "Wouldn't it be fun if Spock did this?" Then you get on the stage and you find out that Spock just doesn't do those kinds of things, so it *isn't* much fun. It's not writing with total intelligence.

HARLAN ELLISON (author; writer, "The City on the Edge of Forever")

They operated off the philosophy that exists in the television industry, which is "Our characters wouldn't act like that," meaning that there is utter inflexibility. That's the death of drama. It's bad enough that you have the rigors of a weekly series where the characters have to reappear every week and you can't kill anyone, but people don't act that way. They don't act in a uniform way. They act bizarrely. That's why they're people, for Christ's sake.

GEORGE TAKEI (actor, "Hikaru Sulu")

There was one director—and directors go from show to show, they don't know about the conventions that have been established—who wanted me to hit a button near the top of the panel, just for the camera effect, and that's not where warp three was supposed to be. I had to get into a very involved discussion and he kept saying, "This is science fiction, I just need it for the shot." So to persuade him away from that, I told him that was the button we used just last week to implode the engines, so that wasn't the thing to do. Another argument I used, in a contemporary show, if I was driving a car and wanted to stop it, I wouldn't make a hand gesture to where the horn is; it would be a foot gesture to stop the car, and this was the same thing. There were certain conventions and you can't break them. It wasn't until I threatened him with implosion that he was finally persuaded.

JOSEPH PEVNEY

If I had come in with the script for "The Trouble with Tribbles" during the third season, I would have been laughed off the set. They'd say, "You can't do this piece of shit," and that would be the end of it. The hero of the show was a little fuzzy animal, and they don't want that. They want to constantly be the heroes, and this is the mark of a spoiled actor. This is a guy who reads his mail and is no longer aware of the need for teamwork.

RALPH SENENSKY

Sometimes actors come in for the first season and get a job that they're thrilled to get, but by the second season they know more about writing, directing, producing . . . whatever else, than anyone. There is a taking advantage of that position, too. There's a very fine line that I certainly appreciate, because actors do help. Through the years I've found myself many times using the actor as a way to get a script changed when we've both agreed that it should be. I would go through the actor, because the producer will be more apt to relent if the actor goes to him than if a new director comes in and says, "I don't like your script."

I remember on the third-season episode "Is There in Truth No Beauty?," it was the first day of shooting and the cast literally refused to shoot it. Gene Roddenberry, who wasn't very involved in the third year, came down, they had a meeting, and we lost half a day. We literally sat around talking, and then I went off to shoot something with the guest stars. I shot a scene with them in the afternoon while Gene was rewriting the other sequence to try and mollify the objections. That's not only *Star Trek,* that's an ongoing battle. That doesn't mean that I'm more lenient about it than Joe or Marc, but I've had it in so many other places, too, that people shouldn't think that it only happened on *Star Trek.*

As for the so-called Shatner–Nimoy feud, in an interview on the *Inside Star Trek* record album from 1976, Shatner addressed the situation directly, noting, "I would put it in a way that two children from the same family might squabble over something. Loving each other, but squabbling. Any member of a family would know what I mean, and that means all of us. You can say, 'No, I don't think that's right' in that querulous tone and be angry at the moment, and then forget it the following moment because you care about that person."

For his part, Nimoy added in the pages of David Gerrold's *The World of Star Trek,* "Bill and I are both very committed to and concerned with the work that we do, and we both tend to have strong personalities . . . and we both have strong feelings about what's right and what's wrong. So yes, there were times when we had differences of opinion about how a thing should be done or whether it should be done at all. But we are very good friends; we're very close."

DAVID GERROLD (writer, "The Trouble with Tribbles")

The problems with Shatner and Nimoy really began during the first season when *Saturday Review* did this article about *Trek* which stated that Spock was much more interesting than Kirk, and that Spock should be captain. Well, *nobody* was near Shatner for days. He was *furious*. You've got to look at it from his point of view. He had been hired to be the star of the show. It was "starring William Shatner, *with* DeForest Kelley and Leonard Nimoy." All of a sudden, all the writers are writing all this great stuff for Spock, and Spock, who's supposed to be a subordinate character, suddenly starts becoming the equal of Kirk.

The show that started out about Kirk is now about Kirk and Spock. Bill definitely feels that he was lessened by that. On the other hand, Leonard is a very shrewd businessman, a very smart actor, and recognized that this Spock business was a way to be more important than an also-ran, and he pushed.

NORMAN SPINRAD (writer, "The Doomsday Machine")

I had had a long unpublished novella that took place entirely on a spaceship, which was kind of a variation on *Moby-Dick,* so that became "The Doomsday Machine" on *Star Trek*. I was also told to write a part for Robert Ryan, who they wanted to give a good role to. So I developed the idea of Robert Ryan playing an Ahab-type character. And then when they didn't get Ryan and they got William Windom, things had to be adjusted. I had to make him a little softer, and I think it might have taken some of the edge off of the story. In the original version, Commodore Decker was much stronger. They don't find him slumped over in the ruined ship as they do in the episode. Instead, they find him staring out the viewscreen and in a *very* bad mood.

There was also the feeling that a guest star with that kind of presence would overshadow Captain Kirk, and therefore his character had to be toned down and his lines reduced. Also, some of Spock's lines had to be given to Kirk.

ANDE RICHARDSON (assistant to Gene L. Coon)

Shatner would take every line that wasn't nailed down. "This should be the captain's line!" He was very insecure. Shatner was the one who had to have the apple crate on set. He's the one that insisted that when William Marshall [as Richard Daystrom] appeared on the show, that Marshall should be sitting down so Shatner could be as tall as him. He had to be at least eyeline or taller than the other person. I remember seeing him standing on it. I can't say he did it for a lot of people, but maybe because William Marshall was one of my favorites, so I tended to be around a bit more when there was somebody like him or Ricardo Montalban on the set. Like I said, William Marshall is a very tall guy . . . so tall that out would come the apple crate.

JOSEPH PEVNEY

If there are rumors about a rivalry, they're probably true. Now, Leonard and Bill are both good actors. They enjoy working with each other. If the script is equally good to both characters, there's no problem. It's when one becomes a straight man for the other that you have rivalry. That they resent and probably for good reason. Sometimes, storywise, it's impossible to have both people answer the question, but a good writer can solve that in two seconds. All he's got to have is a straight man who's a third character, and let both of the heroes be heroes. It's not *too* difficult to do. Roddenberry was always conscious of it, but he lost control of the show because of Bill and Leonard. I'm sure of that.

NORMAN SPINRAD

Yes, Shatner counted lines. I was on the set during the making of "The Doomsday Machine." Marc Daniels was directing and they couldn't get it to work. The reason for this is that it was a dialogue sequence set up as Kirk, Spock, Kirk, but the intervening Spock line had been taken out in the line count, so there was no reaction line for the next line to work. I took Marc aside and said, "Have him grunt or something," and I explained that there was a missing line there. But things like that did happen. Observing it depended on how close you were to the production. Here I was watching the director struggle. But not too many people were able to hang around the set. The point is that they have to give their lead characters prominence.

WALTER KOENIG (actor, "Pavel Chekov")

I was off in somewhat of a cloud. I heard Leonard arguing one day on the phone so I knew there was a problem with the front office on occasion. I saw Bill blow up on the set and I knew there was jockeying between these two gentleman as to their roles, but I really knew nothing concrete about what was going on. My recollection was a general sense of well-being for the second season, a growing ennui in the third season. I asked to leave for a month for a play, which they gave me permission to do. It was a happy set with Shatner being the leader and cracking jokes, laughing a lot. Not a lot of tension in terms of our involvement. Whatever tension was between those guys and the executives. On the set, it was always great fun. Always the sense, on the other hand, that he was the star, but not in a negative way. It was just a pleasant time.

TRACY TORME (creative consultant, *Star Trek: The Next Generation*)

Gene used to say that it was very difficult dealing with Bill's ego, that you always had to factor his ego into whatever he was doing or complaining about or not wanting to do. It all had to do with [Gene's perception] that he was very insecure, and because he was so insecure his ego was kind of off the charts.

ROBERT H. JUSTMAN

I don't think the rivalry began to arise until later, when Leonard started getting all this fan mail. To both of their credit, it never got in their way. They were professionals, they came in prepared, they knew what they had to do that day, they were never late, they knew their lines, and they worked their asses off. They couldn't have been more professional, so it came out in other ways. They both had to work together, and I'm sure that there must have been, at first at least, some liking between them, but at least outwardly they were professional, and we never had to come down onstage and smooth things over because one of them was in a snit.

The rivalry further heated up in the summer of 1967 when Charles Witbeck, in the *Los Angeles Herald-Examiner,* claimed that Mr. Spock "saved *Star Trek* from oblivion," while numerous articles asserted that Nimoy was receiving the most fan mail on the show, prompting a full-court press by Roddenberry to protect the fragile détente between his stars.

Frank Liberman, William Shatner's publicist at the time, wrote to Roddenberry after Rona Barrett, a prominent gossip columnist, reported Shatner was going to be replaced on the show—a rumor debunked by Gene Coon—and he noted, "I'm sure that you're aware of the fact that Bill Shatner has always said only complimentary things about Leonard Nimoy and his fellow cast members. Needless to say, he will continue this policy—not only for his own good but for that of the series." He closed his letter by acknowledging, "This sort of thing went on with Robert Vaughn and David McCallum [on *The Man from U.N.C.L.E.*] and I guess it will always happen when two men are involved in a series."

Roddenberry also wrote Nimoy's publicist, Joe Sutton, on August 16, 1967, to put the kibosh on comparisons regarding fan mail. "We're all riding in the same boat, perhaps in this case the same starship, and comparisons of this type in any area, true or not, damage morale as nothing else can. I'm equally sure you understand and approve my strong feelings that we simply won't have it and would cease to cooperate in publicity with any actor who gave out such information. They must boost each other!"

Attempting to further douse the flames of the growing antagonism between Shatner and Nimoy, Roddenberry wrote to Charles Witbeck on August 22, 1967, at the *Herald-Examiner,* to dispel him of the notion that it was Nimoy who saved *Star Trek.* "We agree that Leonard Nimoy has done an excellent job in portraying the character, but in all fairness must point out that Mr. Spock was conceived at the same time as the rest of the format and is being played today almost exactly as conceived over five years ago. We believed Mr. Spock would 'catch on' and are delighted to have this belief and plan proved right," further pointing out that "his ability helped us stay on the air but to credit him with a 'save' overlooks the contributions by Bill Shatner and the other extraordinarily talented actors on the show, the fine writers we had, the excellent directors, the whole *Star Trek* production 'family.'"

JOSEPH PEVNEY

When we started the show, "teamwork" was the key word. Nobody was more important than anybody else. The captain was the captain of the ship, but the actor was no more important than anybody. When Gene Coon left the show, a lot of the discipline had gone out of it. From the time I made "Arena" to the time I did my last show, there was a hell of a difference.

If you run both of them, there was a difference in performance quality, changes which give you a sense of the overbearing captain and Spock. And a kind of challenging between the two of them on-screen, which is okay in life and rehearsal, but shouldn't be there on-screen. Then Leonard would say, "I'm the second in command, when can I do a story where I'm commanding the ship?" Well, those stories came to be and, after a while, Bill would say, "Wait a second, I'm the captain!" There you've got problems originating from, I would say, actor to producer, because when they were through with their shows, Leonard, primarily, and Bill would be up in Gene's fanny, making suggestions as to how the show should go, some good and some horrible. All of them, I think very selfishly instigated.

Even producer Bob Justman was concerned about the way the characters were being developed. In a memo of March 21, 1968, Justman says, "I am struck by the fact that Captain Kirk seems to be getting even more of the lion's share of the action and content of our stories. I know Captain Kirk is the star of our show . . . as presently written, the parts of Mr. Spock and Dr. McCoy are nothing more than a little flavoring added to the stew to make it more palatable. My feeling is that if Kirk is the meat, then Spock and McCoy are the potatoes and gravy and should be considered vital ingredients."

HERBERT F. SOLOW (executive in charge of production, *Star Trek*)

The last thing we wanted was to have the network, the sponsors, or the television audience feel that it was not a wonderful, marvelous family on *Star Trek*. We didn't want anybody to see a crack in this dam that we built; we wanted everybody to see that everyone loved each other and got along, and that Bill was the star and Leonard was the second, but it happened on the stages, in the offices, and we knew there was friction. If you know actors, they count their fan mail, and if one has ten and the other has eight, and the one who has ten happens to slip it into the conversation, that's the way it works. Actors are very competitive people, and when you get a man who is the star of the show and he's contracted, paid, and billed as the star of the show, and then you get a second guy who gets a quarter of his money, who doesn't get star billing but becomes the most popular actor on the show, there's always going to be friction. Happily, the guys kept it under control, so internally there was some friction but as far as the outside world was concerned, we all did our best, including the actors, to play the game and not upset NBC, the sponsors, or the fans.

WALTER KOENIG

Shatner was a lot of fun. You'd blow a line and he'd laugh. There was a lot of joy and enthusiasm and ebullience on the set, but I did notice that every shot was ultimately set up so everyone who was in a scene with Bill was behind him. But he was fun. I really didn't know about all this acrimony and the counting of the pages, which I had validated by Harlan when Bill came up to his house and showed him a script and how in "City" Spock had more lines than he did. I shudder at that. That's something that actors don't do.

GENE RODDENBERRY

Bill was very upset when Leonard came on particularly strong at the beginning [of the series] because he said, "Am I not the captain? How come [the writers] don't appreciate that?" It was a very natural reaction. I said to Shatner, "If we had an Eskimo as a second character, you could be sure the Eskimo would get the most delightful lines because of what he is." I advised him not to worry about Spock because all that reflected on Shatner. Particularly if Shatner continued to treat Spock properly in the show. I suggested they should show each other a lot of friendship in the show and it would eventually right itself.

NORMAN SPINRAD

Bill Shatner's problem is that he just wasn't given as interesting a character to play as Nimoy was. He was the lead character—supposedly the most important—but he couldn't be most interesting. It was not a reflection on him as an actor, because I remember him as a very good actor before that, but he didn't have the part even though the contract said he did. That led to all the line stealing and all that kind of crazy lunatic stuff in any number of scripts where the captain went crazy, because somebody was trying to take away his ship. In a funny kind of way, this gave the character of Kirk more depth. It gave Kirk a little edge somewhere that was really Shatner, which is a good way to use it. Another thing to consider is that if this cast has been together for this long, then the actors have got to become a part of the character which can give them more depth . . . *if* people know what they're doing.

GEORGE TAKEI

There is a difference between working with Leonard and working with Bill. Leonard has an iron core, that determination to get what he wants, but at the same time you get from Leonard a principled position, and there is sincerity in what he says. With Bill, you always suspect a second agenda; that he's got his reason for wanting whatever he wants. If you don't agree with Leonard, you can have an honest, straightforward discussion of issues, whereas Bill would try to cover it up with a jokey camaraderie, an anecdote, or some flattery, but you don't trust Bill. With Leonard, I usually see what he's driving at, and if you don't he will sincerely be open to listening to you, taking what you see and either accepting it on its merits, or if he has differences, you discuss them until you arrive at a genuinely mutual position, whereas Bill has a more vivaciously suspect attitude.

WALTER KOENIG

Bill had an enormous sense of responsibility for the show. He was the star, he was going to make it work, and he was the guy who was getting paid the big bucks, so he wanted to make sure the vision that he saw that represented the show's success was consistently there in every episode. But he was also very self-involved and was concerned primarily about his character, but he was fun and charming.

YVONNE CRAIG (actress, "Whom Gods Destroy")

I didn't want him to touch me, he's an awful man. Part of it is the fact that he just has no social skills. As long as I was painted green, he was trying to grab me behind flats on the sets. He invited me to his dressing room to have lunch the first day and it was the strangest lunch I ever had. We didn't talk, we ate lunch, and he told me that he raised Doberman pinschers. He didn't grab me or anything, it was just weird, and after that, when he wasn't after me he's giving me all this background about my character and telling me where he wants me to stand so that his best side is showing. It was just horrible.

ROGER C. CARMEL (actor, "Harry Mudd")

Bill Shatner, that very dignified captain, is really at heart a very crazy kind of comic. He's a giggler and loves to laugh. A couple of years after *Star Trek* folded, I was doing a charade game show called *Stump the Stars*. It was all charades. We laughed so much on that show. I was on the home team and we would challenge all the newcomers. Bill Shatner was a guest and we always wanted him to come back because he had such a good time. He couldn't really let out that comic spirit on *Star Trek*, he had to be the responsible leader so he didn't have much of a chance to let out on-screen that comic devil inside him. He sure did let it out on the *Star Trek* set, though! We had a hell of a good time!

WALTER KOENIG

Leonard was so Spock that I truly never got to meet him. "This is a wrap for today, do you want to have a beer?" Nothing like that, never happened. Never got to know who this man was. He was Spock always. It certainly enhanced the character. There are thousands of actors that could have played the roles that we played, but there was only one actor who could've played Spock.

The gentleman who plays it in the new *Star Trek* movies is great, but he's acting. Leonard *was* Spock. He was always the character. I didn't get to know him or any sense of him until *Star Trek VI* and I came off camera and Leonard and Bill are talking about familial problems that Leonard was having, but that was a guy I never met. That was the difference between the two guys.

DIANA MULDAUR (actress, "Return to Tomorrow")

Leonard was a very dear guy, he was the one I'd go out and have a drink with afterward, and we would talk about the old days. He had a wife and then he changed wives, but he couldn't have been a sweeter guy, but I felt no tension of any kind. It was a very different show, we were learning our lines on the set because they were being written overnight, and I just noticed the genius of the people around; the cameraman was brilliant and the directors were terrific, everyone was an "old pro."

YVONNE CRAIG

I adored Leonard Nimoy, he just had the most droll sense of humor. The first time I went into makeup I had my eyes closed, and when I got home I realized they had shaved my eyebrows. They could just as easily covered them with mortician's wax and I was furious. I said, "If my eyebrows don't grow back, I swear to God I will sue them," so Leonard said, "Yvonne, I couldn't help but overhear what you were saying and I just wanted to say when I started the show I went to a dermatologist and he assured me that anyone who can grow a beard can grow their eyebrows back" and with that he turned and left. So I'm standing there saying, "Grow a beard?" He was so funny. He has a great sense of humor.

NICHELLE NICHOLS (actress, "Nyota Uhura")

Initially, *Star Trek* the series and *Star Trek* the films were designed for an ensemble of stars who would each be given equal time. But at some point, the decision was made to separate Bill and Leonard from the rest of us, and I'm not happy with that situation. I don't mind Bill and Leonard being the stars, but in light of the fact that we were totally typecast through *Star Trek*, I felt the least they could have done was not totally defuse our characters.

WILLIAM SHATNER

If the original concept of the show was still in effect and the series was still going today, the situation would be exactly the same. There are people whose names and parts are above the title and people who aren't. That's the nature of the business and that's the way these stories are told.

JAMES DOOHAN (actor, "Montgomery 'Scotty' Scott")

Bill has a big, fat head. Bill thinks of Bill, whereas Leonard thinks of the show first and thinks of himself second. Bill doesn't like anyone to do good acting around him. I can remember De [DeForest Kelley] complaining about that when we were doing the series. The scripts would come in with De having major parts and somebody talked them out of it. And there were parts where I was favored during the second year that were all cut out. I'd end up with six lines.

WILLIAM SHATNER

Certain people and certain characters lose sight of the overall larger issues and are totally involved in their own world. That's good for an actor because he takes care of his own business. Traditionally actors are totally self-involved. There's no reason for them to see "Where does this scene fit in?" and "Where does the character fit in?" Take the actor who comes in during the last five minutes of Tennessee Williams's play *A Streetcar Named Desire,* who plays the doctor, who has the last five lines of the play. When asked what the play was about, he answered, "It's a play about a doctor who comes in." That's okay. That syndrome has always been part of an actor's makeup. I can't fault Jimmy Doohan for thinking what he does.

WALTER KOENIG

I was more aware about cast members losing lines and close-ups to Bill on the features. I was pretty much grateful for whatever I got in the TV show, because I was the new kid on the block and it was such a novelty to be getting a paycheck every week. Yes, I was aware of it, but it's old news. It's interesting, because I think appearing on the TV series *Babylon 5* gave me an insight into Bill Shatner, because there was a point when I was trying to reconcile how somebody could be diametrically opposite in terms of his behavior from one situation to another, and the immediate solution that you grab for is one behavior is false; that he's pretending when he's being charming or funny, that it's all a ruse.

That seems to be the only way to justify such contradictory behavior. But while exploring the character of Bester on *Babylon 5,* I realized from appearance to appearance, there are very specific changes or the introduction of new elements to the character, and I had to justify on the one hand killing people with my mind, and on the other hand feeling great passion for a love that I had.

In exploring the character, I began to realize a very obvious truth about Bill, which is that we're all complex beings. It's not a matter of hypocrisy or chicanery, that Shatner, like everybody else, is capable of a vast variety of attitudes and emotions. It's just that he's in the spotlight and his behavior is so magnified that he's given certain license to express all of this. Whereas the rest of us learn to restrain ourselves on behalf of socialization and a sensitivity toward our fellow beings, Bill being the star and constantly heralded as the star, how do you *not* get seduced by all that? He thought that he had license to behave exactly how he felt. Not to say that we don't feel the same way, it's just that we don't have that same license.

WILLIAM SHATNER

It's coming from a couple of people. I don't understand that. I'm not even aware of it, quite frankly. Occasionally, I'll hear something from an ardent fan of mine who'll say, "So and so said this about you" and it bewilders me because I have had no trouble with them. Nothing certainly bad, nothing particularly good either. We have done our job and gone on and I have never had bad words with anyone. I don't know what vitriol is spilling out.

HERBERT F. SOLOW

When you're dealing with a film editor, you turn out one show a week, and back then we didn't have the advantage of working with computer-generated editing machines. You worked on a Moviola and cut each piece separately, and therefore there wasn't that much time to properly finish each show. When there was any confusion, the famous line in the movie business is "Cut to the star." The star is the money, and even though there is a big difference between what Bill did and what Leonard did, the bottom line is, the star of the show was always Bill. The action stemmed from Bill. He drove the action, he was the one who was there at beginning saying, "Start the engines," and at the end saying, "Close down the engines."

It was always Bill who was the stereotypical captain of the ship. What happened with Leonard is that he was such a different character, and he handled his role so well—*and* became a pain in the neck after a while, demanding certain things for his character, but those demands were not for Leonard, his only interest was making sure that his character was properly portrayed week after week. Although I think Leonard was brilliant at what he did, he was never the star of the show. However, if push came to shove, and we had to recast both characters, it would have been easier to recast Bill's part than Leonard's, so you tell me: Who's the star of the show?

ROBERT H. JUSTMAN

I don't think Bill has any mean bones in him. I just think he didn't realize that perhaps he was trampling on other people's prerogatives. It just never occurred to him in his determination to do as good a job as he could do, and his knowledge that he was the star. Well, we sometimes—and I've been guilty of it, too—bruise other people's egos in our quest for excellence, and we don't realize that we've done that. We would probably be horrified to discover that we had done it and feel very guilty, so I don't think Bill was ever aware of it. Bill is Bill, and he's a particular kind of person.

DIANA MULDAUR

Bill could be a pain, he would ruin a take deliberately, just for fun. He did it to DeForest one day, and we had to shut down shooting because DeForest had one of the nine-hundred-page speeches to make and by the time he got through two-thirds of it and was interrupted, as a joke, he couldn't remember anything any-more. He was totally in the zone and lost it, and we went home. We went back in the morning and he started with that and he knocked it off right away. I felt so sorry for DeForest, it's not what you want to watch happen to someone who is totally capable and wonderful. It was always practical-joke time.

WALTER KOENIG

I think Bill's difficult. He's the epitome of the star in many of the negative ways. He's totally preoccupied with himself and his career and his work on the show. I want it understood that I respond to the working relationship, not the man. He can be congenial and enormously seductive. It's very difficult to dislike him if he decides he wants you to like him. He has incredible charm. In fact, I have to keep slapping myself.

Problems with the cast—particularly Shatner and Nimoy—finally came to a head insofar as Gene Roddenberry was concerned on August 17, 1967, when he issued an ultimatum written to the two of them, with DeForest Kelley thrown in for good measure.

Of this famed letter, David Gerrold wrote in *The World of Star Trek*, "There was a deterioration of morale. And Gene Roddenberry felt that much of the grumbling was unwarranted. He was very aware of the problems and was working to solve some of them. So he wrote *the* letter. It was a very confidential piece, sent only to the cast, only the regulars. No one, not even Gene Coon, saw copies of it. In this letter, Gene Roddenberry—the silver-tongued bird of the galaxy himself—took his actors to task and gave them all a proper bawling out. What was said to each is unimportant—what is important is that it worked. Afterward, things settled down. Somewhat.

"Toss these pages in the air if you like, stomp off and be angry, it doesn't mean that much since you've driven me to the edge of not giving a damn," Roddenberry wrote in part in that letter, which is excerpted for the first time in this volume. "Gene Coon is ill and leaving, due to emotional fatigue for which you bear some share of the blame; Robert Justman came by last night asking to get out; I'm discussing with my agent now the pros and cons of turning the series over to the tender mercies of Paramount and their Gulf [&] Western accountants."

"No, William," Roddenberry stated, "I'm not really writing this to Leonard and just including you as a matter of psychology. I'm talking to you directly and with an angry honesty you haven't heard before. And Leonard, you'd be very wrong if you think I'm really teeing off at Shatner and only pretending to include you. The same letter to both; you've pretty well divided up the market on selfishness and egocentricity. Of the three, it goes to DeForest to a lesser extent, but even you have shown signs lately of wanting to join our Child Star Club. I want you to know exactly where you're all taking yourselves, your professional reputation, the show, and the investment you've all made in it.

"... *Star Trek* began as one of the TV productions in town where actors, as fellow professionals, were not only listened to but actually invited to bring their script and series comments to the production office. When small problems and pettiness begins to happen, as it happens on all shows, I instructed our people that it should be overlooked where possible because we should all understand the enormous physical and emotional task of your job. Think back, Gentlemen, on the staggering list of efforts made to understand, to fix, to set right. You and I agreed that a company of mature professionals should be treated as mature professionals, thus we'd have no insoluble problems. Well, it hasn't worked. . . . The result of Gene Roddenberry's policy of happy partnership? *Star Trek* is going down the drain."

Roddenberry compared the three of them to a trio of "fishwives trying to divide the day's catch" noting that, in his opinion, each was "weighing, counting, craftily trying to con others and each other with smiles or tantrums, depending on which seems to work best at the moment. Then departing bitter that God in His wisdom did not provide a Solomon who would have understood that your true worth deserved more. Well, God didn't have a Solomon to spare for *Star Trek*." This, he clarified, was due to the fact that they felt that one script or another didn't put their character in strong enough light, or that they wanted a line that had been written for another, or even which one of them a scene would end on. Added Roddenberry, "If the show should go on, under whatever leadership, or if you manage to kill the show and go on to some other, you're still going to get shit on now and then. And I doubt that your continued cries of surprised indignation are going to change the hard realities of life and the television business.

"Now, to specifics. William, yes, when discussing the Spock character you say all the right things—'Wonderful character for the show; highly valuable; a large factor in our success; Nimoy handles it with skill.' Nice sentiments, very 'pro.' Except that your actions make it painfully obvious to everyone that you don't believe it for a minute. Your constant frantic concern, not only over Spock's lines, but lately McCoy's, Scott's, and most recently even Chekov's small part, is almost embarrassingly apparent and is a key factor in the sabotage and breakdown of whatever stage morale is left.

"You said to me the other day, and more lately to others, that you're going to show us what a star is really like. If that is meant as a threat, I'll be forced into the only possible answer—I'll show you what a producer is really like. Let each of you be aware that as long as I'm on this show, I'll run it and I'll damned well keep running it until the day I leave. You've been saying lately that you were told you'd be completely dominant as the star of the show, that you've been misled, and the stories had better start being exclusively about you or else! Bullshit! You saw the first pilot, you read the format, you played some twenty or more episodes without any such comment or complaint. The name of this show is *Star Trek*; it's not about to be changed to *The Adventures of Captain Kirk*. The concept stays as we've played it for a year and a half and that concept will not be changed.

". . . I want you to realize fully where your fight for absolute screen dominance is taking you. It's already affecting the image of Captain Kirk on the screen. We're heading for an arrogant, loud, half-assed Queeg character who is so blatantly insecure upon that screen that he can't afford to let anyone else have an idea, give an order, or solve a problem. You can't hide things like that from an audience, the camera is there day after day, and like it or not it'll show through.

"And now, Leonard. I must say that if I were Shatner, I'd be nervous and edgy about you by now, too. For a man who makes no secret of his own sensitivity, you show a strange lack of understanding of it in your fellow actors. And an appalling lack of gratitude for the good fortune which has swept you almost overnight into a prominence."

Roddenberry drove home the point that he wasn't actually expecting anything in return, except perhaps that, given his rising popularity, Nimoy could have for a moment taken Shatner's feelings into consideration, to recognize the personal pain it would cause his costar to see all of the media attention focusing on Spock.

"Let me tell you what people you respect are saying . . . A growing opinion is that Leonard feels that he has now broken the anonymity barrier via the Spock character. And thus with the world waiting, certain there can be cruel disappointments such as has happened to a long list of others who charged on at the first blush of popularity, he has no real need now to inconvenience himself in order to protect our joint enterprise or fulfill express or implied or even moral obligations. . . . There is no reason to not apply pressure in any way that makes the Spock role stronger or more pleasant for him to play, and nothing lost if this rocks the boat to the point where it sinks.

"True? Any portion true? We know this—whereas Shatner, for all his incredible mistakes, will sometimes blow and get it out of his system, sometimes even apologize and try to make up to people, any wrongs or inequities to Leonard Nimoy, real or fancied, seems to result in an image of unshakeable, surly, and eternal unforgiveness. Not true again? Let's repeat what you said at one time or another . . . 'I've got so much personal integrity I'll leave if the role isn't what I think it should be, if it fouls up the future of my fellows who invested in this, if they starve, too, that's tough.' According to my dictionary, Leonard, that describes selfishness.

"Although I've blasted Shatner on his foolish and self-destructive insecurities, let's take a look at what he faces in you. This not Shatner's description but one by a former studio fan of yours—'I see a growing image of a shrewd, ambition-dominated man, probing, waiting with emotions and feelings masked, ready to leap at the right moment and send others broken and reeling when Nimoy thinks he can finally take what he's been waiting to take.' Wrong? Unfair? That's how it looks to some.

"A paradox in this—the above seems to be your very image of Shatner. And others wonder, too, whether under his more jovial exterior, the same beast doesn't lurk. Funny if it turned out you're both right. Now, I've told Shatner that Spock won't become *Star Trek*'s lead. I've also made clear to Shatner that although Kirk is the lead of the show, he will be my concept of the lead, not his. I've also made it clear that you are and will remain a strong, effective, and integral second lead. Perhaps he believes despite that that you have secret agreements or strange devilish plans that will make you the star despite all I do. Forget the wisdom of such doubts, forget even common decency. It would still seem to me that a man of intelligence and sensitivity would have by now found ways to make it abundantly clear that this simply isn't so.

"Yes, it's affected your image on the screen, too. No actor under TV's week-to-week pressure can totally hide from camera his real feelings about a fellow he works closely with. The audience will ultimately realize that Spock's great 'loyalty' is a facade; the viewers will begin to say that maybe this isn't a warm love-oriented Earthman trying to break out of a Vulcan body but maybe instead there is alien Vulcan in there and maybe that Vulcan wouldn't be so pleasant if he got out."

At that point he more or less removed DeForest Kelley as an addressee—deciding the letter should more or less serve as a cautionary warning for him—and concluded, "For as long as I stay with the show, starting Monday, there will be no more line switches from one to another. The directors will be instructed all such changes they wish must be made during their preparation week. No more of the long discussions about scenes which lose us approximately a half day of production a show—the director will permit it only when there is a valid dramatic story or interpretation point at stake which he believes makes it necessary. The director will be told he is also replaceable and failure to stay on top and in charge of the set will be grounds for his dismissal."

Roddenberry concludes by saying, "All right, my three former friends and 'unique professionals,' that's it. In straight talk, not just my opinions but a summation of feelings held by almost all your fellows. Maybe everybody's wrong and you three are right. Nothing I've seen yet leads me to believe that won't be your opinion. Again, I don't want to talk about it. If I'm wrong, show me!"

The Great Bird of the Galaxy had spoken. Whether his message would be heard remained to be seen. . . .

BOLDLY GOING

"IN EVERY REVOLUTION, THERE IS ONE MAN WITH A VISION."

At the beginning of the second season, several noticeable changes greeted viewers. Not only was DeForest Kelley's name now added to the opening credits, there was a new face at the helm: Navigator Pavel Andreievich Chekov, played by Walter Koenig. The addition of a new cast member who would potentially lure in a younger audience was eagerly embraced by both NBC and Gene Roddenberry.

In a September 22, 1966, memo, Roddenberry alerts casting director Joe D'Agosta to the casting. "Keeping our teenage audience in mind, also keeping aware of current trends, let's watch for a young, irreverent, English-accent 'Beatle' type to try on the show, possibly with an eye to his reoccurring. Like the smallish fellow who looks to be a hit on *The Monkees*. Personally I find this type spirited and refreshing and I think our episodes could use that kind of 'lift.' Let's discuss."

It was only later that Roddenberry reconceived the character as Russian, in deference to the success of the Soviet space program at the time. He attributed this, in a story that may very well be apocryphal, to an article that allegedly appeared in the Soviet daily newspaper *Pravda,* in which they took the show to task for not featuring any Russian characters.

GENE RODDENBERRY (creator, executive producer, *Star Trek*)

The Russians were responsible for the Chekov character. They put in *Pravda* that "Ah, the ugly Americans are at it again. They do a space show, and they forget to include the people who were in space first." And I said, "My God, they're right."

JOSEPH PEVNEY (director, "Amok Time")

When Roddenberry said he wanted to put a Russian on the show, I said, "I just used a kid in a television show at Universal named Walter Koenig, who I think I heard do a little Russian. Why don't we have him in and have him read?" He looks Russian; his face has a Slavic look to it. He looked right and was not a typi-cal Russian cliché.

WALTER KOENIG (actor, "Pavel Chekov")

They were looking for somebody who would appeal to the bubblegum set. They had somebody in mind like Davey Jones of The Monkees. All that stuff about *Pravda*—you know, the complaining—that's all nonsense. That was all just publicity. But it was a very practical decision. They wanted somebody who would appeal to eight- to fourteen-year-olds and the decision was to make him Russian. My fan mail came from eight- to fourteen-year-olds who weren't that aware of the Cold War and what was going on anyway. At the time the whole thing of getting fan mail was so novel to me that I read every single letter I got. I was literally getting about seven hundred letters a week, so that took up a lot of my spare time.

I had become involved because I had done the part of a Russian on another show [*Mr. Novak*] and the casting director was the same man. I had also worked with Gene Roddenberry in a leading guest starring role on *The Lieutenant* and worked with Joseph Pevney on *The Alfred Hitchcock Hour* he directed, so my name was already known, and it was a relatively painless situation. There was only one other actor who was brought into read, and I was told I had the part before I left that day.

Joe [D'Agosta] called me in and I read the lines, and his name was Jones, not Chekov, because Davy Jones was who they had in mind for somebody to play this role. I went in and there were all the executives and Gene Roddenberry and Bob Justman and I read. When I was done, there was dead silence. Either I had knocked them into a stupor or I really fucked up. So they said to me, "Yeah, Walt, can you make it funnier." Make it funny? How do I make it funny? So my read-ing was something like, *"Keptin, guess what, the ship is about to blow up."* They asked me to wait in the outer lobby and there was one other actor there. an actor I had worked with on a series and we had played French Resistance fighters to-gether. He went in and read and he didn't come out. I waited and waited and after a while, literally, the sun started to go down and I'm still waiting. What I found out was there was another exit out of Gene's office which bypasses where I was. So I'm waiting and waiting and waiting and another fellow comes in and says, "Are you Walter Koenig?" And he drops to his knees, puts his hand between my legs, and I said, "What are you doing?" And then I see a tape measure. He says, "I'm measuring you for your pants." That's the ignominious way I found out I had been cast in *Star Trek*.

GEORGE TAKEI (actor, "Hikaru Sulu")

I had lobbied in season one and Gene had written some wonderful things for Sulu into the second season's scripts. But I had taken off for *The Green Berets*, which went over, and because of the delay, Walter was brought in and he got those lines.

WALTER KOENIG

I had no idea how momentous this casting was in my career. I was told that the character might recur, but there was no guarantee. One of the things that happened, fortuitously, was that George Takei was shooting on *The Green Berets* and was late reporting for the second season, so they brought me back mainly to fill that seat for some sense of continuity, because at that point we had not had an audience reaction. I guess I was lucky that George was unavailable.

Unbeknownst to Koenig at the time, George Takei, as he admitted in his autobiography, *To the Stars*, was jealous of the newcomer with whom he now needed to share the spotlight, who was also getting featured in some of the series' most popular episodes, all originally intended for Sulu.

WALTER KOENIG

It never came to my attention. I was never aware of his animosity. He was always cordial, and it wasn't until years later that he said how he felt about me. I should have been more aware that these parts were being lost because of my presence. But on the other hand, he was doing a movie with John Wayne, so I didn't feel guilty. George is the consummate professional. He was disappointed and treated badly on several occasions and always bore it with enormous dignity and professionalism. And I admire him for that.

DOROTHY FONTANA (story editor, *Star Trek*)

In the first and second season I think we went from strength to strength, because, basically, we knew our direction by the sixth show in terms of the actors who filled out the characters. We had begun to know them as the characters and began writing for their strengths. I think the stories just got better, although you always have a clinker or two. On the whole, I think our batting average was awfully good during the first two seasons.

ROBERT H. JUSTMAN (associate producer, *Star Trek*)

One of the problems we *did* have in the second season is that once you solve anything, the thrill is gone. The thing that's motivated me in working in the television business was getting the challenge of a new show and finding out if you could do it. My feeling was once you knew you could do it, I wanted to try something new. So, yes, the original magic, the original excitement, tends to pass on once you solve the mysteries of it. But there was still the camaraderie.

We had another problem in the second season that was highly intensified during the third. In the second season we were cut down on how much we could spend per show by a sizeable amount of money. Despite the fact that there had been cast escalations, so our cast costs were higher. This in turn had an effect on the kind of shows we could do. It was even worse the third season when we got cut down again despite more cast escalations.

RALPH SENENSKY (director, "Metamorphosis")

There wasn't any money. If you saw the soundstage we shot on, you'd be amazed. One of them was the starship interiors, which filled the entire stage, and it wasn't that big a stage to begin with. The other one was the stage where we built everything else we needed. For example, on "Metamorphosis" we had the *Enterprise* shuttle, the *Galileo,* on the soundstage. We were supposed to have a spacecraft and sell the idea of a huge, huge planet. If you remember the wide shots we did, the spacecraft looks so small that you would think it was a model.

This was achieved by our cinematographer, Jerry Finnerman. We literally had the spacecraft at one end of the stage and the camera's as far back as it could go on the other end of the stage. Jerry shot it with a nine-millimeter lens just to give it that scope. You see it today, I think it's marvelous. But you couldn't use the nine-millimeter with actors because it distorts. That's an example of the budgetary limitations. Rather than fight it, you try and find a way to use the imagination and rise above it.

Unfortunately for Lucille Ball, the crushing deficits incurred by *Star Trek* and *Mission: Impossible,* both shows that would go on to enduring legacies and prove immensely profitable for Paramount, forced her to reluctantly sell the studio she and ex-husband Desi had built on the back of her wildly successful sitcom to Paramount, her studio's neighbor at Gower and Melrose. At the time, Paramount was actually more interested in the real estate Lucy owned than the television series the studio was producing.

MARC CUSHMAN (author, *These Are the Voyages*)

Paramount took over at the halfway point of the second season and started tightening the budget. Paramount's attitude to *Star Trek* was "You're not going to ruin us like you ruined Desilu." Lucille Ball lost her studio because of *Star Trek*. She had gambled on the show, and you can read the memos where her board of directors is saying, "Don't do this show, it's going to kill us." But she believed in it. She moved forward with it, and halfway into the second season she had to sell Desilu to Paramount Pictures. And once Paramount Pictures came in they said, "We're going to run this like a business. You're not going to go over budget anymore." Lucille Ball gave up the studio that she and her husband built, it's all she had left of her marriage, and she sacrificed that for *Star Trek*.

RALPH SENENSKY

Desilu was like a family. Herb Solow, who was the head of the studio, used to come down and talk with you on the soundstage. He didn't seem like the other studio heads who never seemed to talk to you. Herb went out of his way to help you. Can you imagine a studio working like that?

When Paramount bought it, a kind of corporate mentality took over. In a way I think that's why I resent Paramount having such a hit in *Star Trek,* because if they had their way, they would have killed it off. It survived in *spite* of them, and now they have this bonanza making them all of this money.

MARC CUSHMAN

Lucy's instincts were right about *Star Trek*, that it would become one of the biggest shows in syndication ever. The problem was that her pockets weren't deep enough. They were losing fifteen thousand dollars an episode, which would be like five hundred thousand dollars per episode today. The board was saying, "We're not a big studio. We can't afford this, it will break us," and she kept thinking, "No, somehow we'll get through it, we'll get them to live within their budget, somehow it's going to work out." You know, if she could have hung on just six months longer, it *would* have worked out, because by the end of the second season, once they had enough episodes, *Star Trek* was playing in, I believe, sixty different countries around the world. And all of that money is flowing in. It's just that she couldn't last those extra six months.

She was several million dollars shy of being able to hang on, and you couldn't go out and get bank loans like you can today. And you can't keep going on credit cards, so she had no choice but to sell. She actually took off and went to Miami. She ran away because it was so heartbreaking to sign the contract. They had to track her down to get her to do it. There's a picture of her cutting the ribbon after they've torn down the wall between Paramount and Desilu, and she's standing next to the CEO of Gulf and Western, which owns both studios now, and the frozen expression on her face is she's trying to put on a brave face for the photographer, and trying to fake this smile for the camera, and you know it's just killing her. But she was right. One hundred percent. The two most rerun shows in the history of TV are *I Love Lucy* and *Star Trek*.

The turmoil of the second season continued with the announcement that Gene L. Coon would be leaving the series in the middle of the production year, which, as it turned out, would deal the series a very serious and potentially crippling creative blow from which it never really recovered.

GLEN A. LARSON
(creator, executive producer, *Battlestar Galactica* [1978])

In the second season, Gene Coon decided to leave *Star Trek*. He had two scripts on his desk in front of him which he had to rewrite. He suddenly put his pencil down and finally said, "This is it," and he got up and walked out. It had been an around-the-clock, very draining experience.

WILLIAM CAMPBELL (actor, Trelene in "The Squire of Gothos," Kor in "The Trouble with Tribbles"; friend of Gene L. Coon)

It was starting to become a tremendous chore for the show to come up with anything new. Don't forget, they were using writers from the outside, and it was becoming more difficult to get them. You've got to remember that we're talking about a period when the great writers no longer were doing anything. When television was making its first inroads, you had some of these great people doing television shows.

MARC CUSHMAN

Why did Gene Coon leave *Star Trek*? Roddenberry was off doing a Robin Hood script, a Robin Hood TV pilot, which never got made, but he was being paid to do it, so he took off at the halfway point of the second season to go do the script assignment for four weeks. He comes back, and a couple of scripts he'd assigned while he was still there are now being filmed, and he walks onto Stage 9 and he hears all this laughter, which was not unusual because Shatner was always making jokes and there was always laughter. But this is more so than usual, and the lights are on so he knows they're filming, so why is everyone laughing while they're filming? And he walks over and it's the scene from "The Trouble with Tribbles" where Shatner is opening the storage compartments and all the Tribbles are falling on him and he's buried in Tribbles.

Roddenberry is standing there watching this scene being filmed and he's *not* laughing. This isn't *his Star Trek*, this is *Lost in Space* stuff. And so he turned and walked away and he went to the screening room and he said, "Show me the last episode that's now being edited," and the previous episode was "I, Mudd." Roddenberry had given that assignment, the story was his idea, he's the one who did the story for "Mudd's Women" the year before and it was supposed to be more serious, a flamboyant character but still serious, and he's watching this thing that is total comedy.

Then he watches more footage from "Tribbles" and *then* he takes a look at the next episode to be filmed, and it's "Bread and Circuses," which was also his idea, and it's been turned into a bit of a comedy. So he starts rewriting it and he starts taking a lot of the comedy out, and he and Gene Coon have a powwow. Gene Coon comes out of that meeting and types up his resignation. That day, the day after Roddenberry returned, Gene Coon turns in his resignation.

ANDE RICHARDSON

If Gene Roddenberry said anything to him about what he was doing with the humor and everything, then why stay there and take that? He was doing fine.

I will say that after Gene was brought in, the Great Bird would do a disappearing act, sneaking in and out of the back door. Everything fell on Gene Coon, and I don't think that's what he signed on for. I think he thought that Roddenberry was going to be there carrying his load as well. I can't say he dumped everything on Gene, but I got the feeling that Gene was more burdened once there was no Bird around. He never complained about anything, but you can only do that many uppers for so long and then you've got to wear out. And Gene was wearing out.

HARVE BENNETT (executive producer, *Star Trek II: The Wrath of Khan*)

The loss of Gene Coon was critical. Credit for the success of the show of course goes to Gene Roddenberry. There's no disputing his genius. But it also goes to Gene Coon, the hardheaded rewriter who made a lot of things work. I think of myself as the Gene Coon of the feature movies. Fandom never understood the contribution that Coon made to that which they loved in the movies, notwithstanding Roddenberry's genius. It's my gut feeling, knowing all the players and the material, that whenever the name Gene Coon is on the episode as producer, they are generally the best shows.

MARC CUSHMAN

Coon wanted out so quickly at that point, he looked out his window and saw John Meredyth Lucas coming to his car, because John was working over at *Mannix,* and he said, "Can you get out of *Mannix*? I want you to take over for me." And it was done that fast. Roddenberry had to approve Lucas so Roddenberry had him come to his house, talked, and he thought, "Okay, John is going to dial down the comedy, he's going to make the show more like what I wanted, he's going to make Kirk more driven."

One of the first episodes John did was "Obsession." It had more of the tone Gene Roddenberry wanted it to be, and so he approved him. Now, they still had all these scripts that Gene Coon had been rewriting, and even though Coon's name doesn't appear on the screen for the second half of the second season, almost all those scripts were started by him, he got memos from him on all the scripts, but then John Meredyth Lucas and Gene Roddenberry started rewriting them and taking the humor out, and making it more of the show Roddenberry wanted it to be. And it wasn't quite as good as the first half of the second season. It lost a little steam there.

JOHN MEREDYTH LUCAS (producer, writer, director, *Star Trek*)

I was on the lot shooting *Mannix*, and I wrote a script for Gene Coon. Gene was going to retire and suggested that I take over because I had produced *Ben Casey*. We talked for a while and that was it. At that time, Bob Justman was handling the production end of things. When I came in, I got into production, too, and was also directing. Gene had said, "When they hired me, they knew I was writing and that was it." That was *not* the way that I produced.

DAVID GERROLD

The last six episodes were finished up by John Meredyth Lucas, who was something of a caretaker just to make sure that things moved in the right way. A very nice man, but probably someone very much under the thumb of Roddenberry. Grateful for the job, and Roddenberry said, "We're going to do it my way," and the last six episodes of the second season were . . . adequate.

ANDE RICHARDSON

When Gene left—and he didn't tell me exactly why he did leave—he said, "I'm going to go, and when I find someplace, I'll let you know and you can come and join me." So I worked with John Meredyth Lucas. He was a nice guy, he did the job, but I don't think he really sparked anything. For me, the whole situation became *bleh*. I just came in, did my job, collected my paycheck. The joy was gone. I had such freedom with Gene. I could read the scripts, I could tell him honestly what I thought about things, and we would talk about the scripts. In the sense of what was going on, I felt like I was contributing. That was gone after Gene left. I was glad to get the heck away from there after he was gone.

JOHN MEREDYTH LUCAS

When I came on, I remember a great deal of tension between the actors. Not civil war, but a great deal of tension among the cast and the company. As a matter of fact, Gene took me out to location to introduce me as producer. We came up to the company. When they'd gotten a particular shot, we walked over and Shatner walked away from us. He would not speak to Gene or to me. They were feuding over something, though I've no idea what the problem was.

There was also tension among Shatner and Nimoy and Gene that had built up. It happens on every show, but it was particularly noticeable on *Star Trek* when I first came on. I won't say I solved it, but I simply ignored it, went on and was on the set a great deal. I tend to be hands-on with everything. It was just a different kind of approach. Whatever had caused the tension, I'm not quite sure. Actors tend to feel that if you're not there all the time and petting them a little bit, or at least there to hear their screams of anguish, that they're abandoned. Eventually we all became very friendly. That doesn't mean there weren't complaints about someone's part not being meaningful, but we developed a mechanism to talk them out.

DORRIS HALSEY (manager of Gene L. Coon)

Gene was happy on *Star Trek* for quite a while. Then both personal and professional things started weighing on him. He was having personality problems with Shatner and Nimoy. He had a very low respect for actors, except his friends. Gene also had a low threshold for boredom.

WILLIAM CAMPBELL

I don't know anything about the relationship between the two guys, but I can tell you this: What happens to actors when they've acquired a position on a television show after a short period of time—they can't help it—they become precious. And recognize that in some ways they can tell producers off, can make their presence felt. They all have ideas.

JACKIE COON FERNANDEZ (widow of Gene L. Coon)

Gene wasn't crazy about actors. They were just too needful and too egocentric. He wasn't. He didn't get along with Robert Wagner either when he went over to *It Takes a Thief.* I would take his feelings about these actors he didn't get along with with a grain of salt, because he didn't care for actors in general.

WILLIAM CAMPBELL

I don't remember a situation where Gene Coon would tell either Shatner or Nimoy how to act, nor did he suggest that he was a director, but he did have an inner sense and he might have held the line on certain things that they would have changed. Or areas where they would have liked another direction be taken, and Gene Coon perhaps debated them on occasion and they didn't like it. But I never heard him say one bad word against anybody.

JACKIE COON FERNANDEZ

I don't think there was a personal falling-out between Gene and Gene Roddenberry. Roddenberry liked the glory more than Gene wanted in the show. He wanted more guts and less glory. Less razzmatazz. Less show business and more thought. Roddenberry wanted more flash into the quirky trappings of science fiction. Gene [Coon] was a philosopher in his feelings. There probably was a certain difference there, but not enough to disturb a friendship because they remained friends for as long as he lived.

ANDE RICHARDSON

When Gene Coon was there, we were in a groove. We were changing the world. When I would answer his phone "Coon's Coon," it was okay because we were going to where no one had gone before. We were making a difference. I felt that way with Malcolm [X], I felt that way with Martin [Luther King], and I had it with Gene Coon. We were making a difference. My friends were, like, "I want to be a film producer," but I wanted to be a television producer because I wanted to do what Gene Coon had done. I wanted to put things out there for people so that they could see a different way of thinking and being. I wanted to do "The Devil in the Dark," because we are made out of the same material; we can't dismiss one life-form over another. We were doing something. We were doing something good. And Gene just did what he did. He didn't do it for people to say, "Wow, that was great." He just did his best and he did it with his heart.

JOHN MEREDYTH LUCAS

If there was one element that I brought back to the show when I was producer, because it had been a little bit lost, it was Gene Roddenberry's inspiration for the series Horatio Hornblower. That's the thing that I kept trying to bring back. The constant warfare—frontier warfare—to make Kirk Captain Hornblower again. A lot of that stuff had gotten lost into the areas of fantasy, which is fine. But as the season progressed there'd been less and less of the Hornblower elements, which appealed to me as exemplified in "The Ultimate Computer" and things like that.

A creative problem on the show was that we loved doing pieces which had some kind of concept. That's a terrible word to use when you're talking to the network. You would think that high-concept would mean a lofty purpose, but to them it simply means something you can tell in one word. The network tended to want green space monsters that ate the ship each week, and we tended to want to do shows which had, what seemed to us, some kind of concept, saying something and being different. But God knows we did our share of the green monsters eating the ship.

Despite all of the behind-the-scenes turmoil *and* a notable change in quality once Gene Coon had departed, season two of the original *Star Trek* is considered perhaps the best season of the show produced. Among the now-classic episodes: "Amok Time," in which Spock is internally driven to return to Vulcan to mate or die—and finds himself in a battle to the death with Kirk; "Mirror, Mirror," which found Kirk, McCoy, Scotty, and Uhura in a savage parallel universe aboard a very different *Enterprise,* where rank is achieved through assassination; "Metamorphosis," a genuinely moving exploration of the nature of love; "Journey to Babel," in which *Enterprise* serves as host for a number of aliens en route to a diplomatic conference, which also explored the estranged relationship between Spock and his father, Sarek; "The Trouble with Tribbles," *Star Trek*'s first comedic episode, which pits Kirk and company against the Klingons and thousands of purring fur balls; and semisuccessful visits to a number of Earthlike planets with a society mirroring old-time Chicago ("A Piece of the Action") and modern-day parallels to Nazi Germany ("Patterns of Force") and the Roman Empire ("Bread and Circuses").

JOSEPH PEVNEY

The fight in "Amok Time" was absolutely excellent and one of the best we ever did. What made it dramatically interesting is that it took place between Kirk and Spock. During this episode, Leonard Nimoy and I also worked out the Vulcan salute and the statement "live long and prosper" together.

GENE RODDENBERRY

Leonard Nimoy came in with the "live long and prosper" sign—the split fingered salute. He came into my office and said, "I feel the need for a Vulcan salutation,

Gene," and he showed it to me. Then he told me a story about when he was a kid in synagogue. The rabbis said, "Don't look or you'll be struck dead or blind," but Leonard looked and, of course, the rabbis were making that Vulcan sign. The idea of my Southern kinfolk walking around giving each other a Jewish blessing so pleased me that I said, "Go!"

DOROTHY FONTANA

On "Amok Time" I don't remember if it was Gene Roddenberry, Gene Coon, or [writer] Ted Sturgeon who came up with the idea of the Vulcan seven-year mating cycle, but the way we have established it, Vulcans mate normally anytime they want to. However, every seven years you do the ritual, the ceremony, the whole thing. It's a biological urge. This every-seven-years business was taken literally by too many people who aren't stopping and understanding. I mean, every seven years would be a little bad, and it would not explain the Vulcans of many different ages, which are not seven years apart.

When Ted was writing the episode, there were some places where we, as I recall, said to him, "Well, you know McCoy has this role in relationship to Spock, and Kirk has this role," and Ted just put them together in a really nice blend of relationships, which is, again, what *Star Trek* is about. Relationships. The stories that didn't go well were stories that were against objects without human relationships involved somewhere in the story.

JEROME BIXBY (writer, "Mirror, Mirror")

I had already done a fiction story called "One Way Street," which was a parallel-universe story, and I thought that would make a good *Star Trek*. The universe I created was a very savage counterpart, virtually a pirate ship, into which I could transpose a landing party. I submitted the outline, they loved it and I did the script.

DOROTHY FONTANA

"Metamorphosis" was a very delicate and touching love story. The idea that a man could accept a relationship with this alien, and the young woman, to save her life, accepted the alien into her body was a really lovely story and a very touching one. Gene Coon did it with great deftness and delicacy.

"Journey to Babel" came about because of the mention a couple of times of Spock's parents. I said to Gene, "We've talked about them, let's show them." So I sat down and created two characters, especially the relationship with Sarek and the rift between him and Spock, and Amanda positioned in the middle. She was a thoroughly human woman with an all-Vulcan husband and a half-caste son, which is bound to create a lot of character problems.

JOSEPH PEVNEY

"The Trouble with Tribbles" was a delightful show from beginning to end. I had a lot of fun with it, went out and shopped for the tribbles. It was the first effort of a writer named David Gerrold and I thought he made a hell of a contribution to the show. *My* biggest contribution was getting the show produced, because there was a feeling amongst the people involved that we shouldn't do it. It was a comedy and they felt we had no business doing an outright comedy. It turned out well, and Bill Shatner had the opportunity to do the little comic bits he loves to do. The premise was humorous as hell.

DAVID GERROLD

I have to be real honest here: It feels great to have written "The Trouble with Tribbles." I remember when I wrote it, I looked at it as an honor and responsibility, and I set out to write the very best episode of *Star Trek* ever made.

DAVID P. HARMON (writer, "A Piece of the Action")

I felt that our Western civilization is based on a Judeo-Christian ethic, so what I did in "A Piece of the Action" was say that suppose a ship crashed, and the people on the planet salvaged a book called *The Life of Al Capone*, which they treated as their version of the Bible, and from which they built their own society.

JAMES KOMACK (director, "A Piece of the Action")

The thing that always had to be kept in mind was that Kirk and Spock were from another time while we were trying to make a picture about the twenties. You constantly have to say that it's got to be the twenties from everyone else's point of view, but it's got to be future-time for Leonard Nimoy and Bill Shatner, and that gets a little bizarre. The joke going on around them was that they had never seen a machine gun before, they never saw pool tables or cars. We'd have to work out the jokes right there and then. You'd say, "Wait a minute, you've never seen that before. I've got to shoot something that shows you've never seen this before." Spock and Kirk came down with this great intellect and they were dealing with the equivalent of monkeys. These guys had an IQ of about room temperature, and it was funny to watch Kirk and Spock stare at them, because they were just ludicrous. They had a book, they were mobsters, they were taking over cities. Their brains just weren't working that well. That was great fun.

JOHN MEREDYTH LUCAS (director/writer, "Patterns of Force")

The totalitarian, particularly the Nazi, society had always fascinated me. How could this come about? I know the history, but how in the minds of people could this come about? I started off with the premise that I would try to explain it and explore how an entire country could get swept up in it. It's still difficult to comprehend. Thankfully there was very little problem in terms of covering such dramatic material. Gene Roddenberry tended to do no censorship on that basis. He would come in and, if anything, would encourage even *wilder* statements. He was a very adventurous guy, so there was no opposition in terms of, "My God, what *are* you writing about?"

RALPH SENENSKY

Gene Roddenberry is a very creative man. When we did "Bread and Circuses," I remember having a meeting with him about it, and he was going to do some writing. I went there the next morning at six o'clock to get the new material, because there were things about that script which weren't working. Both Gene Roddenberry and Gene Coon were writing on that show as we were shooting. I don't remember what the problem was, except that we were doing the Roman arena in modern times with television. I do remember that my concern was all of that talk about the "sun," which they talked about from early on, might not be a mystery when we got to the end. We didn't want to tip that we were doing a Christ story from the word go. That took some doing, because it wasn't really in the script, but they did it. They were sealing up the loose ends, because originally when they were talking about the sun, you knew right away that they were talking about the son of God.

DOROTHY FONTANA

Certainly there was a nice philosophy going on there with the worshipping of the "sun," and then the indication that it was the son of God, that Jesus or the concept had appeared on other planets. I thought that was a nice touch. There have been other stories written with the same theme as the main point, but just adding it at the end really seems quite nice.

Fontana remained concerned for much of the second season that the show was repeating itself. In a memo she wrote on June 19, 1967, she emphasized, "Even our devoted viewers will not stay with us if we do not vary our backgrounds, themes, and adventures. We've touted this series as one with creative imagination and daring. Where is it?"

One of the more controversial episodes in the second season, spearheaded by Roddenberry, was "A Private Little War," in which the Klingons are providing weapons to a primitive planet, prompting Kirk to do the same to maintain the "balance of power" on both sides, an analogue for the ongoing conflict in Vietnam.

WALTER KOENIG

That was the one episode that I thought digressed from a rather liberal, political posture. I had a very strong feeling about it. I thought that in maintaining this balance of power we were justifying the building of armaments.

In so many ways Star Trek was a standout compared to the rest of the shows being broadcast by the networks, but insofar as NBC was concerned, the show was more trouble than it was worth. Not only was there a continuing series of battles with Gene Roddenberry regarding content, but the series was not a ratings powerhouse. Indeed, it seemed that season two could very well be the show's last. The only hope would be if the word could somehow get out to the fans, a challenge made more difficult by the fact that Harlan Ellison, who by this time had had a major falling-out with Roddenberry over his script for "The City on the Edge of Forever," would not throw his support behind such a campaign. The show's future was strictly in the hands of the fans.

HARLAN ELLISON (author; writer, "The City on the Edge of Forever")

I was very optimistic about the show in the beginning, but within a couple of years that changed and everybody was laughing at me. When these people said, "*Star Trek* is going to be the new horizon for us; we're going to sell more science fiction than ever before and it's going to be the Golden Age," I said, "No, it's not, you fools. You're not going to sell one more of your novels. What they're going to sell are *Star Trek* books," and this was before there ever was a *Star Trek* novel.

Everybody looked at me and laughed and told me not to be ridiculous. Well, there it is. *Star Trek* books and that idiom, that space-opera crap, pushed everything off the bestseller list. I don't like being right, but it was obvious to me that that's the way things were going to go. This was a series that had the *potential* of being truly great. There are few series that really transcend the medium. All the rest of it was just television. That's what, to me, *Star Trek* was mostly: just television.

BJO & JOHN TRIMBLE (authors, *On the Good Ship Enterprise*)

By the middle of the second season *Star Trek* was once again in danger, and hints of possible cancellation kept disturbing the set. We were visiting the shooting of "The Deadly Years" when cancellation was certain at the end of the second season. This episode being shot was one of the last *Star Trek* episodes to be aired before cancellation. But there was something *we* could do. Fans could play the largest game of "uproar" in the world and if nothing else, make certain that NBC and everyone connected with *Star Trek* knew that fans were unhappy about the cancellation.

JACQUELINE LICHTENBERG (founder, *Star Trek Welcommittee*)

The reaction to news about the cancellation among Trekkers was based on knowledge of the television business model: If we didn't have a full three seasons of a show, there would be no syndication reruns. This was pre-video recorders in every home. Without a third season, we would lose it all *forever.* The reaction was *panic.* This was material to be passed down to grandchildren, not left to rot in some vault. This was *historic breakthrough,* not a trivial bit of failed entertainment. So the reaction went from "You just don't understand!!!!" to "*You and what army???"* There was even a movement to try to buy enough Paramount stock to control the company.

BJO & JOHN TRIMBLE

We wrote up a preliminary contact letter, ran it off on our ancient little mimeograph machine, and mailed it out to about a hundred and fifty science-fiction fans. These fans had been especially selected because they had some further contacts, either as fanzine editors, club members, or for some such reason. We even had addresses of some *Star Trek* fan mail that Gene helped us obtain from the fan-mail service that Paramount contracted with. We didn't have enough money to have a letter printed, so we had to fly on the strength of the message and its urgency to get people's attention. We used the Rule of Ten: ask ten people to write a letter and they ask ten people to write a letter, and each of those ten asks ten people to write a letter. And so on and so on.

JACQUELINE LICHTENBERG

Bjo put out directions for how to write such letters, and the directions were mostly followed. The audience was educated adults more than gaga kids with no buying power.

BJO & JOHN TRIMBLE

NBC was convinced that *Star Trek* was watched only by drooling idiot twelve-year-olds. They managed to ignore the fact that people such as Isaac Asimov, a multiple Ph.D., and a multitude of other intellectuals enjoyed the show. So, of course, the suits were always looking for reasons to cancel shows they didn't trust to be a raging success.

JACQUELINE LICHTENBERG

This was before Nielsen got demographic analysis down to where sponsors could use that data. The bulk of the *Trek* audience was college students, grad students, and recent grads. People with potential earning power that sponsors wanted, but the sponsors had no way to know that until that letter campaign produced a flood of original letters formatted as business letters.

BJO & JOHN TRIMBLE

NBC began to get a wave of letters that rocked them off their fat complacency. Fans were not to know this for some time, so we just kept sending in letters on faith that something was happening. The first intimation our plan was working was a party where a computer systems analyst heard someone call Bjo's name. "Are you Bjo Trimble?" he asked with a grin. Bjo asked how he knew her name. "Everyone at NBC knows your name," he said. "You've cost NBC a lot of money. They had to hire extra help to keep opening that mail, sorting it, and trying to find out what the average *Star Trek* fan is like. Labels are everything in the TV biz. They keep running everything through our computers to see if they can come up with the *definitive Star Trek* fan. You know, how old, what income bracket, and so on. So far it cost them a lot of money to find out nothing at all. You guys can't be nailed down to any one label, and it's driving NBC crazy. Also, it rattled cages to find that someone managed to put *Star Trek* Lives! bumper stickers on all the limousines in the very private executive parking lot."

ELYSE ROSENSTEIN (organizer of early *Star Trek* conventions)

Do you realize how many pieces of mail NBC eventually received on *Star Trek*? They usually got about fifty thousand for the year on *everything*, but the *Star Trek* campaign generated one million letters. They were handling the mail with shovels—they didn't know what to do with it. Their policy was to answer everything, even if it was a form letter, and a million pieces of mail is *a lot* of money. So they made an unprecedented on-air announcement that they were not cancelling the show and that it would be back in the fall.

BJO & JOHN TRIMBLE

Well into cancellation and/or pickup time for all the TV series, NBC had been so flooded with mail that they were ready to throw in the towel. Naturally they weren't about to give GR and the *Star Trek* crew any relief from their worries, so everything still hung in the air until NBC made their momentous, unprecedented announcement at the end of the spring 1968 season.

No one had ever come on during prime time, even with a voice-over announcement, and told the watching public that a TV show had been renewed. So a major triumph of the consumer public over the network and over the stupid Nielsen ratings was accomplished through advocacy letter-writing. At the end of the Save *ST* campaign, we were told unofficially that one million letters had crossed their desks. We have no way of knowing how true this statement really was.

ANDE RICHARDSON

A guy named Thom Beck had a radio show in Pasadena called *The Credibility Gap*. It was a really popular show and it was all about antiwar and things like that. When I told them we were having problems with getting the show renewed, they did a whole segment on *Star Trek*. It got a lot of comments and a lot of press, and it helped with the renewal. It's something that's never mentioned, but *Star Trek* had definitely gotten help from a local radio station.

RICHARD ARNOLD (*Star Trek* archivist)

I knew nothing about possible cancellation at the end of season one. I don't think very many fans did know about it. But when the write-in campaign started during season two, I became very active, along with my friend Alan. We signed up as many people in my junior high school as we could, not knowing yet that a petition would only count as one letter, and wrote letters ourselves to the addresses that Bjo and John Trimble were supplying to fans everywhere.

GENE RODDENBERRY

The letter-writing campaign surprised me and, of course, it was personally gratifying. What particularly gratified me was not the fact that there was a large number of people who did that, but I got to meet and know *Star Trek* fans, and they range from children to presidents of universities. One of my greatest enjoyments from the show was meeting the people we attracted and some of the relationships we formed with them.

BJO & JOHN TRIMBLE

Gene wanted very badly to be completely involved, but we said it would only make NBC say it was a put-up job. Gene did do things like send over platters of food and drink when we were doing a collating of a mailing. He also paid for postage when we'd run out of funds, but for the most part fans paid for the Save *Star Trek* campaign, or it came out of our own pocket.

ROBERT H. JUSTMAN

Gene absolutely encouraged the campaign. Without his encouragement, I don't think those campaigns would have gotten as far as they did. They were successful campaigns and they kept the show on the air. There was just an enormous amount of pressure exerted on the network by people who wrote in and demonstrated. It was wonderful. It was no fluke, as proved in later years when this same three seasons' worth of episodes just kept on playing and playing and playing. There was something there.

JOHN MEREDYTH LUCAS

It sounds like the usual publicity trick a company would pull, but the company had absolutely nothing to do with it. This was a spontaneous thing. Some of the most fanatic support came from Caltech, which was heaven. It was nice to know. Unfortunately, the numbers on the show were never really spectacular. They were much, much better in reruns. At the time, the people that loved it were mad about it, but there just wasn't enough of them with Nielsen boxes.

The letter-writing campaign, which was rumored to have inspired anywhere from twelve thousand to a million letters, depending on who you believe (more likely the two hundred thousand number that NBC's Mort Werner asserted in *TV Guide* at the time), culminated in a massive march on the network's Burbank headquarters, where protestors from Caltech and elsewhere picketed on January 8, 1968, in the hopes of forcing a renewal of the series.

FRED BRONSON (publicist, NBC Television)

I met Bjo and I knew about her march on NBC, so I got my friends together and we made signs, and went to the park in Burbank where we were all congregating, and we marched on NBC. Stan Robertson from programming was there and Hank Rieger from publicity, the irony being that two or three years later, I was in college and I got an internship at NBC and Hank became my boss. I worked for him for years.

HANK RIEGER (publicist, NBC Television)

Unfortunately, I was one of the people designated by Herb Schlosser to go out and talk to the big demonstration they had in front of the studio in Burbank. They weren't really in the mood to be talked to, but they listened, and Stanley [Robertson] said his words and I said my words, and essentially it was that we appreciated them, we heard them, we would take a look at it, and they saved the show for another year.

We had all the extra Burbank police around and a few county deputy sheriffs there in case anything happened, but it wasn't that type of crowd where they were going to storm the place. I'm a Trekkie, too, so I was just as sorry as they were to see it go off the air. I thought that *Star Trek* would do better initially than it did. I was one of the many disappointed ones when NBC announced they were going to take it off the air.

FRED BRONSON

Hank and Stan came out and, of course, they accepted our petitions. They said they would be taken seriously and, as you know, it was saved, and we felt like we did it ourselves. I remember them making the announcement on the air one night, over the closing credits basically, and said please stop writing and calling.

JACQUELINE LICHTENBERG

The concession from NBC was grudging, and despite Roddenberry's best efforts, the third season bombed. But thanks to that letter-writing campaign, *Star Trek* went to syndication and then . . . and only then . . . the audience exploded.

GENE RODDENBERRY

We won the fight when the show got picked up for a third season. NBC was certain I was behind every fan, paying them off. And there was a group from MIT picketing the building, and a group in New York. Bless MIT, bless Caltech, bless them all. The network had a coterie of junior executives down there buttonholing all of the people, saying, "Listen, did Gene Roddenberry send you?" And they finally called me up and said, "Listen, we know you're behind it." And I said, "That's very flattering, because if I could start demonstrations around the country from this desk, I'd get the hell out of science fiction and into politics."

THE END OF THE BEGINNING

"TO SURVIVE IS NOT ENOUGH . . . TO SIMPLY EXIST
IS NOT ENOUGH."

Star Trek concluded its second season on an incredible, and unprecedented, high
note, with NBC essentially acknowledging the success of the fans' letter-writing
campaign by announcing that the series would be returning for a third season.
On the surface, it would have seemed that with season three, *Star Trek* could
begin to soar, but nothing would be further from the truth as the struggles that
plagued it for the first two years only intensified in year three, resulting in the
Enterprise's final year in space . . . on NBC in live action, at least.

GENE RODDENBERRY (creator, executive producer, *Star Trek*)

At that time I told NBC that if they would put us on the air as they were
promising—on a weeknight at a decent time slot, seven-thirty or eight o'clock—I
would commit myself to produce *Star Trek* for the third year. Personally produce the show as I had done at the beginning. This was my effort to use what
muscle I had. In fighting a network, you must use what muscle you have. They
are monolithic, multibillion-dollar corporations whose interests are not necessarily in the quality of the drama.

It is one of the unfortunate curses of television that you can have as high as
eleven or twelve million devoted fans, more people than have seen Shakespeare
since the beginning, and be a failure, because at a certain time on a certain night
you have to pass the magic number of fourteen million. At any rate, the fans
scared the hell out of the network and they decided to keep the show on.

About ten days or two weeks later I received a phone call at breakfast, and the
network executive said, "Hello, Gene baby . . ." Well, I knew I was in trouble right
then. He said, "We have had a group of statistical experts researching your audience, researching youth and youth-oriented people, and we don't want you on a
weeknight at an early time. We have picked the best youth spot that there is. All
our research confirms this and it's great for the kids and that time is ten o'clock
on Friday nights." I said, "No doubt this is why you had the great kiddie show
The Bell Telephone Hour on there last year." As a result, the only gun I then had
was to stand by my original commitment, that I would not personally produce

the show unless they returned us to the weeknight time they promised. I wasn't particularly anxious to put in a third year of fourteen hours a day, six days a week, but *Star Trek* was my baby and I was willing to risk it if I could have a reasonable shot at a reasonable time. And we talked it over and held fast.

We almost swayed them and ultimately they said, "No, we will not do it." And then I had no option. I could not then say, "Well, I'll produce it anyway," because from then on with the network any threat or promise or anything I made, once you back down you become the coward and your muscle from then on in any subsequent projects will never mean anything.

GEORGE TAKEI (actor, "Hikaru Sulu")

Gene was aware that even if he had stayed with *Star Trek*, NBC intended to cancel the show after its third year. From another vantage point, maybe it should have been a matter of personal integrity on Roddenberry's part. *Star Trek* was Gene's creation, and the third season would be identified with him whether he liked it or not.

If the quality of the show was in some way to erode, it couldn't help but reflect on Roddenberry. Inevitably, it would be Gene's reputation that was at stake. Now, Gene Roddenberry's a human being, so I can certainly understand his position. At the same time, giving myself distance and perspective, I can't help but wish that Gene had looked at the entire picture and realized how *Star Trek*'s third season might finally affect his professionalism and artistic integrity.

DAVID GERROLD (writer, "The Cloud Minders")

Roddenberry, rather than try and do the very best show possible, walked away and picked Fred Freiberger. If he *was* there, there would have been some of that stuff that was there in the beginning. When the show first started, there was a lot of really nice stuff there that you always wanted to see developed. I wish Roddenberry had been there in the third season to take care of his baby.

Roddenberry later addressed his departure and reflected, "I think there was a little rationalization in my decision. I think also what was affecting me at that time was enormous fatigue; I think maybe I was looking for an excuse to get out from under the fight that I had just been having for two years, but really for four. I think fatigue just caught up with me . . . I think I would come back and produce it the third year myself if I had it to do over. I'm not taking a backhanded slap at the people who did produce it the third year, line-produced it. Obviously when you bring a producer in and you're going to let him produce it, you've got to let him do it his way. I think his way, or their way, was somewhat different than our way the first two, so it did look different. As long as the original creator stays with the show, it gives it a certain unity. When other minds become involved, it's not that they're lesser minds or not as clever writers, but you lose the unity of that one driving force."

DAVID GERROLD

The fact of the matter is that you have to work with other people, and Gene's pattern is that he doesn't work well with anyone. If he can't be the boss, he doesn't want to work. Gene does not have a track record of working as a writer with other producers, so he doesn't know how to bend. There's no working with other people's considerations on a story. He never learned that trick, because he's always been the boss. He's never, ever been an Indian; he's always been a chief. You know what you get when you get people who have always been chiefs? You get spoiled brats.

DEVRA LANGSHAM (editor, *Spockanalia*)

We all felt very annoyed about Gene leaving. I mean, it's his show and truly he loves it as much as we do. On the other hand, he's saying, "I put myself on the line, I said if you do that I'm not going to work on the show, and if I don't follow my word I will have no credibility." So you can understand it . . . sort of. But people were definitely annoyed.

MARC CUSHMAN (author, *These Are the Voyages*)

NBC didn't like Gene Roddenberry, and they didn't like the type of shows that *Star Trek* was airing. It was too controversial and too sexy, and they couldn't get Roddenberry to tone it down. He was disrespectful to them, and it got worse, so it was just a matter of "we don't want to do business with this guy; we don't quite like how the show is going, so let's maybe not pick it up." And there's another factor, too, back then. They weren't getting the top sponsors for the hour, so the feeling may have been that they weren't making as much profit off of *Star Trek* as another show. So they move it to Friday night—and they didn't even want to pick it up, but there was the letter-writing campaign that made them cry uncle on the air and announce that they *were* picking it up, but they put it in the death slot. And they knew when they picked it up that they were determined that season three would be the last year.

SCOTT MANTZ (film critic, *Access Hollywood*)

Roddenberry abandoned the show, but it's interesting that he still had a lot to do with it. A lot of people don't realize that he was still sending memos and notes and watching screenings. But a lot of times he would watch the screening, and it would be too late to change any of the problems. You watch an episode like "Balance of Terror," where Kirk hunches over the briefing room table and goes, "I hope we won't need your services, Bones." And McCoy goes, "Amen to that. You're taking an awful gamble, Jim." And he walks out, the doors close, and he and Sulu are just walking down the hall and all the people are running by, it's a busy ship. Or you look at the "The Corbomite Maneuver," when Kirk is going from the sick bay to his quarters and you hear "All decks alert, all decks alert." That is a busy ship that looks like there's 428 people on board. In the third season it looked like there were four people on the ship.

GENE RODDENBERRY

I found a producer, Fred Freiberger, who had produced *Slattery's People* and *Ben Casey,* and has impeccable credits and an honest love of science fiction since boyhood. He was backed up by our regular staff of Bob Justman and the directors; the cameramen; Bill Theiss, costumer; Walter "Matt" Jeffries, art; so backed up by the regular staff. They were producing *Star Trek* while my function in it was judiciary, policy administration.

MARC CUSHMAN

Everyone says Fred Freiberger was a show killer, when, in fact, he had a wonderful track record in Hollywood. He was the guy who got *Wild Wild West* up and running. I've read in books and I've read in articles that Fred produced the *last* season of the show, but he actually produced the first season. *He* was the producer who got that whole show and somehow did the magic act of taking a western show, a spy show, elements of sci-fi, and blended it into a hit. He did very well with *Ben Casey* and a couple of different shows.

FRED FREIBERGER (producer, *Star Trek*)

I was familiar with *Star Trek* only in that I had seen the first pilot they had done. I had met Gene Roddenberry at the beginning to talk to him about producing the show at the start, but I was going to Europe on a vacation that I had planned. I mentioned to Gene that the pilot was terrific, and if the job was still available when I got back, I was interested. By the time I came back he had gotten Gene Coon and I was off doing other shows. Then, when third season came along, my agent brought me into Gene's office and he said he would like me to produce the show. Gene Coon had done the first season, John Meredyth Lucas did the second, and I assumed he wanted to change producers every year.

My first meeting with him was uncomfortable. Something like thirty people from the network came in, and I was amazed at the contempt with which Roddenberry treated them, and I could see they didn't like him at all. I'd thought to myself, "Holy shit, what have I gotten myself into?"

ROBERT H. JUSTMAN (associate producer, *Star Trek*)

Because of the budget cut in the third season, we were reduced to what I call a radio show. We couldn't go on location any longer because we couldn't afford it. We had to do shows that we could afford to do. It was quite difficult, and that did affect what the concept was. Certain concepts just couldn't be handled. We didn't have the money.

Forget about what the actual numbers are, but in those days, in the first season each show cost $193,500. That was good money in those days. The second season was $187,500. The third season was $178,500. So that was an enormous drop. The studio had deficit financing situations, and every time you shot a show you lost more money. In those days, they didn't think they had a chance of syndication, especially since everybody knew the third season was it.

FRED FREIBERGER

Joining the show wasn't a daunting situation, it was a question of going in on a show that was being successfully produced with a lot of people involved who were very loyal to the show. You can walk into another show and it can be daunting for you. You get into a situation where everybody knows each other and

they've been together for some time. I was more concerned with improving ratings, because the show had about a twenty or twenty-four share. Today that
would be a hit. In those days, even if you had a thirty share, you were very iffy. It
was the loyalty of the fans that kept it on when NBC threatened to cancel it. And
they *did* keep it on—it was impressive for NBC to succumb to that.

In all three years, the ratings remained the same no matter what went on. It
kept the same fans. Our hope was to improve the ratings, and we tried different
kinds of stories. But the ratings always stayed the same. Always. It's always all
about ratings. And the situation wasn't helped by the cutting of the budget. That
hurt us badly.

GENE RODDENBERRY

If demographics had come in a year earlier, we would have had a twelve-year-run.

ROBERT H. JUSTMAN

They just cut it down to the bone to cut their losses. And we were on Friday nights
at ten. If your audience is high-school kids and college-age people and young
married people, they're not home Friday nights. They're out, and the old folks
weren't watching. So our audience was gone.

SCOTT MANTZ

You went from $193,500 per episode to $178,000, so you lose $15,000 dollars per
episode, but you lost more than that because some of the stars got raises. And
that came out of that budget. So if you think about it, the fact that they got maybe
half of a good season is lucky.

FRED FREIBERGER

We had to do at least four of the shows completely on the *Enterprise*. There were
a lot of restrictions, but that's no excuse if the stories aren't very good. It's a question of judgment and you have to go with what you think. That's the way television works. I think, on balance, we did some pretty nice stories and some that

didn't come out so good. Some shows you're happy with, some you're disappointed with, and others you're ashamed of. That's the way it goes, but you're a pro, you accept those things, you understand them, and all you can do is make sure that everybody does their best.

MARC DANIELS (director, "Spock's Brain")

Fred Freiberger and I didn't agree on what the director's role was. There are many writer-producers who don't consider the director a partner. They consider him, shall we say, an employee. This is particularly true in episodic TV. They just want you to do the work, get the shots, and forget the rest of it. I didn't particularly care for that kind of thinking.

MARGARET ARMEN (writer, "The Paradise Syndrome")

I wrote *Star Trek* for Gene Roddenberry and Fred Freiberger, and I suppose they were looking for two different types of stories. Working with Gene was marvelous, because he *was Star Trek* and he related to the writers. Fred came in and to him *Star Trek* was "tits in space." And that's a direct quote. Fred had been signed to produce and was being briefed. He watched an episode with me, smoking a big cigar, and said, "Oh, I get it. Tits in space."

You can imagine how a real *Star Trek* buff like myself reacted to *that*. It didn't sit well with me at all. But I got along well with Fred and with him I did "The Paradise Syndrome." Of course, Gene was the executive producer in an advisory capacity and he really had the last say on okaying story ideas. So I think it was actually Gene that accepted that one, because I feel "The Paradise Syndrome" was one that Fred would have let gone by.

In "The Paradise Syndrome," a lushly photographed episode shot primarily on location, Kirk loses his memory and is mistaken for a Native American deity by the planet's indigenous population, while the *Enterprise* attempts to prevent an asteroid from colliding with the planet.

MARGARET ARMEN

It turned out well, and Gene insisted that it be done. Fred thought the sponsors wouldn't like it at all, but it happened that it was the only one that they *did* like of the first group he presented. I didn't really know if Fred ever realized that *Star Trek* was a series about people. Fred was looking for all action pieces. That's why he wasn't crazy about the script for "The Paradise Syndrome," because there wasn't enough violent and terrifying action in it. He didn't realize that the suspense would come from the characters, their relationships and so forth. There was some action in it, but there were no monsters and that sort of thing. So Fred was looking primarily for action pieces, whereas Gene was looking for that subtlety that is *Star Trek*. Action, but with people carrying the story.

FRED FREIBERGER

Star Trek had to change just by the nature that there was a different producer in place. This is the nature of this business. If people come in to produce a show—Gene Roddenberry, Gene Coon—that show has to be shaped in terms of what they think. Writers have fragile egos. They come in and submit something. You generally know your show better. You change that show. You rewrite that show. You make suggestions. The professional writer who has been in the business and knows what it is, changes it. Some of them will accept the fact that some good suggestions are made. They have to if they want to stay with the show.

That is the nature of television. That's the nature of Broadway in spite of the Dramatists Guild contract which says they can't change any words. They just say to you, "We can't change a line, I think our backers will pull out of this," and so they get their way. Who's kidding who? With a novel, if you won't do what the editor says, unless you have a fantastic, powerful name, you just will not get that thing published. That is the essence of the procedure between staff on a show and writers.

DAVID GERROLD

I understand Freddy Freiberger's problems a lot better now than I did then. Oddly enough, I have a respect for the man that I don't think he realizes. He's able to do something that not a lot of people can do: He can bring in a show on time and under budget. He can do the job. There are people who crumble under that kind of pressure. As a *producer*, I'm sure his decisions were correct for what he was doing. I think his biggest weakness is that he doesn't have a sense of humor. He doesn't allow the shows he's working for to have fun.

FRED FREIBERGER

Our problem was to broaden the viewer base. To do a science-fiction show, but get enough additional viewers to keep the series on the air. I decided to do what I would hope was a broad canvas of shows, but I tried to make them more dramatic and to do stories that had a more conventional story line within the science-fiction frame. The first show was "Spock's Brain," the second one was a more conventional kind of show, almost a fairy tale, "Elaan of Troyius." I tried to do something a little different there.

I also tried to do shows like the one I personally loved, "Spectre of the Gun." I thought that came out pretty well. Those are the kind of things I tried to do: good stories with different kinds of elements, such as romance or surrealism. I did one in which Kirk fell in love with an android. I wanted to do good stories with interesting twists to them. When you come into a series, you try to do shows which won't diminish a series, but will help a little. In some cases it doesn't work out.

"Elaan of Troyius" was an example of the new approach. The crew seemed happy with the idea. You assume these things, though you never know who's saying what behind your back. With that episode we were trying to do a variation of *Taming of the Shrew,* and added the element of her teardrops being an aphrodisiac.

It was fun, but part of the reason we did that one was because the network had told us that they had done a survey and discovered that although there were a lot of female science-fiction fans, women generally are terrified of space. They needed stability, they needed surroundings; they'd rather be in valleys than on tops of mountains. So we tried to get the women, which is why we did a romantic story. We tried to reach that audience we couldn't reach otherwise, but we didn't succeed.

MARC CUSHMAN

People would be surprised to know that Gene gave out the first sixteen script assignments for the third season, and he gave a lot of memos as they were being developed. He would come in for screenings and give Fred memos on the episodes, things to change and so forth. So he was definitely involved, but as the season progressed his involvement became less and less because he was off making the film *Pretty Maids All in a Row* for MGM.

FRED FREIBERGER

When Gene Coon left, he left with three assignments from Gene Roddenberry, which I honored.

GLEN A. LARSON (creator, executive producer, *Knight Rider*)

The reason he had assignments for the third season was that at first Gene Roddenberry wouldn't let him leave because he had a contract. The only way they'd let Gene out is if he continued to write for the show, and he did so under a pseudonym. He would be in there typing away while we were supposed to be doing *It Takes a Thief*, but that was great because more of it fell on me and I became an instant producer. Roddenberry knew they needed Gene, and didn't feel they could function without him, so he had to promise to make script commitments.

FRED FREIBERGER

Gene Coon was a lovely, talented guy who came up with certain stories and said do what you want with them, because he couldn't get involved. He worked as much as he could with us and he was a complete gentleman and completely professional about the whole thing.

The first of Coon's commitments, writing under the nom de plume Lee Cronin, was "Spock's Brain," considered by many to be one of the worst *Star Trek* episodes ever filmed. In it, a race of beautiful, short-skirted, buxom alien women steal Spock's brain, and it's up to Kirk and a zombielike Spock to retrieve it. What audiences fail to appreciate today is the fact that organ transplantation was very much in the zeitgeist when the series was being produced, with the first successful heart transplant taking place in 1967. This still can't explain—or excuse—such execrable and laughable dialogue as "Brain and brain, what is brain?"

DAVID GERROLD

I suspect that "Spock's Brain" was Gene L. Coon's way of thumbing his nose at Roddenberry or something. If not Roddenberry, he was thumbing his nose at how seriously the show was taking itself. I suspect what had happened is that they were a little panic-stricken because there weren't a lot of scripts to shoot.

The history of *Star Trek* is management by crisis. I think somebody called up Gene L. Coon and said, "We need a script in a hurry, can you do it?" and he did it under a pen name. I don't think he deliberately set out to write that show seriously. I don't think there's any way you can take that episode seriously. You've got to take it as an in-joke. What's the stupidest science-fiction idea to do? What if somebody stole Spock's brain? Gene L. Coon had that kind of sense of humor to do that kind of impish stuff. He had an irreverent sense of humor, and I think he wanted to poke *Star Trek* because someone was taking it too seriously. Maybe it was his way of not buying into it.

DOROTHY FONTANA (story editor, *Star Trek*)

Gene Coon was under enormous time pressure and forced to write these *Star Trek* scripts between other assignments. It wasn't like being on a series where you could devote all your time to that series. The writing suffers because of that.

GLEN A. LARSON

If you're not producing, somebody else takes it and does the rewriting. Knowing Gene's attention to detail and his work ethic, I would imagine that somebody rewrote him. It would be interesting to be able to see his first-draft scripts.

FRED FREIBERGER

Besides Coon, Dorothy Fontana had two assignments, and David Gerrold had none. I gave him one ["Castles in the Sky," later renamed "The Cloud Minders"] on the strength of "Tribbles," but it's one of those things that happened that didn't work out too well. We tried it, and if it doesn't work, you bring in other people. Any pro accepts that and understands it. Nobody enjoys it, but that happens when you're doing a show. It doesn't mean it diminishes their talent, it just happens. That's the nature of television. Some people don't understand that and it's too bad, but if you're a pro, you do.

DAVID GERROLD

I went in to meet Fred Freiberger with the attitude that I had to prove myself to the new producer. I said, "I know how well 'Tribbles' turned out. I know I can do it, I've got my credential, everyone who saw 'Tribbles' loved it, the episode turned out well, I don't have anything to be embarrassed about." I walk in, Freddy Freiberger is looking at me, and his very first words are, "I saw 'Tribbles' this morning," because he was having episodes screened for him. The polite thing to say is, "Not bad," or "Well done," or "Good job." His words were, "I didn't like it. *Star Trek* is not a comedy." From that point on, our relationship never recovered.

So he tells me *Star Trek* is not a comedy, and I'm thinking, "It's not? The two scripts I worked on, 'I, Mudd' and 'Tribbles,' the reason I had specifically been asked to work on 'I, Mudd' is that they wanted it to be funny." Gene L. Coon said to me, "You know, 'Tribbles' has given us a new insight into our characters. Our characters can be funny, but we can still have things at stake." Joe Pevney said, "I've been arguing that *Star Trek* could do funny stuff, and I was right."

MARC CUSHMAN

Fred was left alone in the second half of the season, but during the first half he was making the show that Roddenberry wanted it to be. It was Roddenberry's mandate to get rid of the humor, and to have Kirk instead of referring to Scotty as Scotty, like he was in the second season, he would say, "Engineer." Instead of calling Mr. Spock Mr. Spock, he would say, "Science Officer." He wanted more formality. Not every line, but usually in the teaser and the beginning of act one. Roddenberry sent out a memo to Fred Freiberger saying that they were in a new time slot and there would be people who had never seen the show before, so they had to establish who these characters were, their rank, their position.

So in the teaser instead of Kirk saying "Mr. Spock" he wanted him to say, "Science Officer, what's your opinion?" and things of that nature. Well, we fans who had been watching it for two years are suddenly asking, "Why is he talking to them like this?" And we're *not* getting episodes like "Tribbles" and things of that nature, so we're blaming Fred Freiberger.

But these are all memos from Gene telling Fred that he wanted to get back to the way it was when it was first on the air. "I want it more military, I want it more serious, they're professional astronauts, they're military in outer space, and they should talk that way." It was getting too chummy for his taste. Kirk shouldn't be friendly with his crew; he's the captain and things like this, because Roddenberry had been in the military and captains don't get chummy with their men. He always had a problem with Gene Coon for doing that.

ROBERT H. JUSTMAN

As far as I could tell, the atmosphere on the show behind the scenes was still the same in the third season. I got on fine with everyone, as always. I got on fine with Fred Freiberger, as always. He was a nice man. I think he did what he did as best he could do it. I never had any harsh words. I don't think I ever had an argument the entire three seasons with anyone. I would disagree with Gene Roddenberry at times and fight with him on certain things that I thought we ought to do or should not be doing, but in the end if Gene said it was yes, it was yes. If he said no, it was no. Whether I felt he was right or wrong, if that's what he wanted to do, that's what I would do. After all, it was his show. I had wonderful feelings working with those people. It just wasn't the same without Gene in a hands-on position that third season.

MARC CUSHMAN

Things *did* change behind the scenes. Gene Roddenberry had thrown up his hands in the middle of the third season, Dorothy Fontana left, and Bob Justman left. So you had some of the most talented people from *Star Trek* that were leaving. The concepts were still interesting, but you didn't have Gene Coon, Gene Roddenberry, or Dorothy Fontana finessing the scripts. And they didn't have the money to really put into them. They were all vital elements of *Star Trek*. And when you take them out of the mix, it's like having The Beatles and taking away John Lennon and Paul McCartney. "Okay, we still have George and Ringo. We're still The Beatles." No, you're not. You're still good, but not *as* good, and that's what you have with the third season.

SCOTT MANTZ

The director of "The Empath," John Erman, brought the episode in on time and budget, and the cast tells him, "Well, you'll be back." And the director said,

"Nope, I'm never working with you guys again." Ouch! *That's* what season three was like.

DOROTHY FONTANA

I was becoming too associated with *Star Trek* and wanted to prove that I was able to write other shows. In fact, when I left I did several westerns, dramatic contemporary shows, and so on. I had to prove to other producers that *Star Trek* wasn't all I could do.

ROBERT H. JUSTMAN

I felt I was in prison and I had to get out. I just didn't want to take it anymore, because I was so unhappy with what was happening with the show. We couldn't make the kind of shows that we wanted to make because we couldn't afford them, and I felt that the content of the shows was going downhill. I finally asked for my release and left. I left a lot of bruised feelings at Paramount. They pleaded with me not to go. I said, "Fine, I won't go. Just take me off the show, and I won't take any other jobs, and I'll come back to you on anything else you want me to do in the spring." They didn't want that, and I said, "I'm leaving. I just don't want to stay anymore." I went to work at MGM.

It was my feeling that the show wasn't what it ought to be. There was also the feeling of disappointment over the fact that I was made coproducer instead of producer. I know that doesn't mean anything to people not in the industry, but in effect I had been line-producing the show since the beginning, even though my title was associate producer. When the third season came around, instead of producing the show, Freddy was brought in with the title of producer and I was made coproducer to him. The studio felt, as all studios do and I can't blame them, they wanted a writer to be there to do the work of story and script.

On the other hand, I felt that I could produce the show with someone there to do the writing. Of course there's a lot of ego in that. I was much younger and ambitious. I can't blame the studio, but in the meantime I was unhappy about that and I didn't like the way the scripts were turning out. There was no excitement, or there wasn't enough excitement. And when they had good concepts, they kind of got whittled down and weren't as magical as they ought to be.

RALPH SENENSKY (director, "Is There in Truth No Beauty?")

I always felt that with the production staff of the last year, the tenor had changed. In "Is There in Truth No Beauty?" there were some cuts made in postproduction that, for my money, were schlock, horror cuts. They hadn't been in the script, were not in the concept, and were thrown in by Fred Freiberger. He kept cutting back to this box, or container, with lights flashing. You didn't need it. That's underestimating the intelligence of the audience. Because they weren't planned cuts, they became arbitrary and rather like jump cuts, which I've *always* resented. That was the third season's problem. The real tightening of the budget was the first thing, and then, probably having to do with those budgetary cuts, the caliber of the writing went down.

Early in the season, Robert Justman had already anticipated issues with the cast responding to their new boss and sent a memo on May 8, 1968, to Roddenberry to try and address these concerns. He emphasized the importance of pointing out to William Shatner the way that Roddenberry expected the actor to work with Fred Freiberger and, more important, that Roddenberry himself was still serving as "great bird" of the series. Wrote Justman, "Bill is as rapacious an animal as any other leading man in a series, and I think it would help Freddie enormously in his relationships with Bill if you let Bill understand how much confidence you have in Fred and how much respect that you, Gene Roddenberry, have for Freddie's creative talents and executive abilities. It also might be a good way to get a fairly close look at Bill and see what sort of physical shape he is in at the present time. Come to think of it, perhaps it would be a good idea to have this get-together before the end of this week, so that if Bill is on the pudgy side, it can be suggested that he start slimming down right away."

Justman added, "Now that DeForest Kelley has been firmed for this season, all our cast have been locked in. Would you want to send a personal letter to each one of our seven regulars, in which you express your personal gratification at the fact that his, or her, particular talents and abilities will be once more enhancing the value and prestige of *Star Trek*?"

Unfortunately, unlike Shatner—who *did* enjoy a good relationship with Freiberger, and who in turn considered Kirk the sole star of the show—Nimoy felt slighted by him, as did many of the other cast members who were vying for screen time and were less than fond of the new producer.

JAMES DOOHAN (actor, "Montgomery 'Scotty' Scott")

Fred Freiberger was just a producer. He had no inventiveness in him at all. He was a no-talent businessman. There were so many episodes third season that were so wordy, and Gene Coon would have knocked that up, but Gene Rodden-berry wasn't paying attention either. He was unhappy that his series was going to be canceled. We had done some forty shows at Desilu, and then Paramount bought Desilu and here was this damn space show as part of the package and they couldn't care less about it.

WALTER KOENIG (actor, "Pavel Chekov")

One day during the second season I asked Gene to have a meeting between sea-sons when it looked like we were going to be on eight o'clock Mondays and asked him about how my character would evolve based on his popularity. I went to his house, and he proceeded to show me some memos he had written the guys at NBC, and memos from Paramount, and all the memos were very positive, say-ing "Let's involve Chekov more, he has appeal. Let's bring him down to the planets more, involve him with members of the opposite sex."

And it looked enormously promising. "Spectre of the Gun" was the first epi-sode written with that in mind for third season, and it reflected what my antici-pation was going to be. Immediately thereafter, our time slot was changed and everybody sort of threw up their hands and gave up on the show. They brought in Freiberger, who had no particular style, as far as I could tell, or empathy for the character. I don't think he had any antipathy either, but he didn't see it as being important.

FRED FREIBERGER

They wouldn't be actors if they didn't want more. You're doing an ensemble show and what's selling the show, hopefully, is the personality of the stars, the relation-ship between the three most important ones, Shatner, Nimoy, and Kelley. You would try to give all the others something. I gave Scotty a love affair in one show. It's very difficult, because when you have many format characters, to try and keep them going in a limited time is hard. I certainly sympathize with any of them who wanted more to do.

In one of the third year's most infamous installments, the *Enterprise* comes across a band of space hippies searching for a mythical Eden. Originally pitched by D. C. Fontana as "Joanna," about McCoy's estranged daughter arriving aboard the *Enterprise,* Fontana took her name off the episode, which shared few similari-ties with her original pitch. One has to wonder, though, if it was Freiberger who rejected the idea or Roddenberry, who had actually dismissed the pitch as early as 1967. In a memo to John Meredyth Lucas, Roddenberry had written, "While Dorothy has come up with an interesting character in McCoy's long-lost daughter . . . there is really not sufficient story in the premise. I recommend we give this one a pass while leaving the way open to Dorothy to submit a new story using this character and situation." The script would eventually be written for Chekov and a former girlfriend and would be retitled "The Way to Eden."

WALTER KOENIG

I read "The Way to Eden" and I thought it was all wrong. First of all, it wasn't even my character. Chekov became very uptight and very establishment, saying, "No, no, no" and "Don't do this." I don't think that was the way he would have responded. What happened was "The Way to Eden" was really written for McCoy's daughter rather than Chekov's former girlfriend.

As a matter of fact, prior to that I had submitted a four-page statement of how I felt Chekov could be improved and made more multidimensional without subverting the story. Freiberger's comment was, "I read it, forget it." I knew the character was always going to be subordinate, but instead of spending the time pushing buttons, we could have spent that same thirty seconds on Chekov in a more fruitful way.

Even though he said, "I read it, forget it," the episode was his way of giving me something and making Chekov a featured player. But I knew it just wasn't any good when I read it, and then the casting was terrible. They were all good actors, like Victor Brandt, but they were totally miscast. They're supposed to be playing thirty-year-old flower children, hippie types, and they looked much rougher and much tougher than that.

DAVID GERROLD

There's a way to say no to an actor other than "Read your memo. Forget it." You know, "I read your memo, thank you for taking the time to let us know so much about what you want to do. It's not quite going to fit into our plans, but I'm certainly going to keep your comments on the top of my mind when we talk about Chekov." The actor goes out saying, "Well, he said no, but he let me down gently," and he feels good toward the producer.

FRED FREIBERGER

When you have a second banana, like Spock, who's probably getting more fan mail than the lead, it gets twice as murderous. They want the last line, they want this, they want that. They're measuring each other's dressing room. Even this kid, Walter Koenig, was always asking for more. I told the writers to put him in more. So I read Shatner's book [*Star Trek Memories*], and Koenig is complaining that he's supposed to be representing progressive youth of the decade and the producer finally gave him more to do and it was establishment shit.

So I wrote to Bill and said every time I start to feel good about *Star Trek,* something like this shows up. I wish somebody would whisper into that little schmuck's ear that the producer was trying to meet what he asked for. If I disappointed him, the least he could do is understand that an attempt was made to satisfy him and not take a cheap shot. It's that kind of stupid little stuff that drives me crazy.

WILLIAM SHATNER (actor, "James T. Kirk")

I thought Fred Freiberger did a yeoman's job. There was a feeling that a number of his shows weren't as good as the first and second season, and maybe that's true, but he did have some wonderfully brilliant shows and his contribution has never been acknowledged.

FRED FREIBERGER

Shatner's a pretty creative guy. When I say creative, I mean he's willing to try *anything.* He loved "Turnabout Intruder." I was, frankly, a little concerned when Gene Roddenberry came up with a story where Kirk changes places with a woman, but Shatner absolutely loved the idea. When I originally read it, I had said to Gene Roddenberry, "I wonder what Shatner is going to say about this." Gene said he wouldn't have a problem at all, and he was correct. When I mentioned it to Shatner, he just loved the idea. He was a Shakespearean actor and I have great admiration for him.

SCOTT MANTZ

"Turnabout Intruder" is a bad episode. I mean, right after the opening credits Kirk goes, "Believe me, it's better to be dead than to be alone in the body of a woman." Who would get away with saying something like that today? *Nobody.* It is such a dated and sexist episode. But as bad as it is, and as much of a travesty as it was to end *Star Trek* with that episode, Shatner's performance is pretty incredible.

WALTER KOENIG

To me, the most heinous violation Freiberger perpetuated was casting Melvin Belli in "And the Children Shall Lead." That infuriated me, because Melvin was a friend of his evidently, and it's one thing to cast friends who are actors and another to cast friends who are not actors. He was a lawyer! Not only did it dilute the impact, whatever there was to begin with, but it took an acting job away from an actor. I was really upset after that. It was very unfair.

FRED FREIBERGER

To boost the ratings we tried to get something unusual in there, and in this case unusual in terms of casting. So we brought Melvin Belli in. It could have been a better show. I thought the idea was good, but it just wasn't as strong as it could have been. I don't think it boosted our ratings.

DAVID GERROLD

Everybody disliked Freiberger intensely. Leonard and Bill didn't like him, nobody else on the staff liked him. Nobody knew what to make of him. It was a very difficult situation for everyone.

FRED FREIBERGER

The truth is, I've been the target of vicious and unfair attacks even to this day. The fact that at the end of the second season *Star Trek*'s ratings had slipped, it was losing adult fans and was in disarray, carries no weight with the attackers. The dumping was all done on me and the third season. It seemed it was now *Star Trek* law to lay everything on Freiberger. Every disgruntled actor, writer, and director also found an easy dumping ground on which to blame their own shortcomings. Whenever one of my episodes was mentioned favorably, Gene Roddenberry's name was attached to it. When one of my episodes was attacked, Roddenberry's name mysteriously disappeared and only then did the name Freiberger surface.

As an example, I read an article, which I think was in the L.A. *Times,* praising the episode "Plato's Stepchildren" as the first television show to allow an interracial kiss. A breakthrough. Roddenberry was lauded for this, when in fact Roddenberry wasn't within a hundred miles of that episode.

ARTHUR HEINEMANN (writer, "The Savage Curtain")

My feeling was that when Gene Coon left, much of the quality of the original show was lost. When Freddy Freiberger took over, I felt the show was being cheapened. The ideas during the third year weren't as good, and it seemed as though he didn't care as much. I don't want to say anything against him, because he's a nice guy, but he always seemed frantic and I couldn't tell why. My feeling was that when he was in his frantic moments, he would make decisions that might be wrong.

DAVID GERROLD

There's a difference between doing *Star Trek* and going through the motions of doing *Star Trek*. It was very much true on the first show. There are ten people down on the soundstage doing *Star Trek*, and eight of them are there to collect paychecks; they're going through the motions of doing the show. It's just a job to them. There are other people, like set decorator Johnny Dwyer, to whom *Star Trek* is a special job. Where *Star Trek* is a privilege and your life, it's just this wonderful, marvelous thing to do.

With the third season, the reason that it was the way it was, is that the guy at the center, the guy who represented the vision of what the show was supposed to be, was going through the motions. He *wasn't* doing *Star Trek*. You try and explain that to the fans, and they think you're disloyal to the show. Where that comes from is a loyalty to what the show represents.

FRED FREIBERGER

I have no quarrel to make with the right of critics, self-styled or otherwise, to dislike my episodes and to state that dislike. What angers me is when they choose to attack my character, sometimes labeling me as indifferent or uncaring. None of that could be farther from the truth, and I'm thankful that on occasion people like Bob Justman have gone out of their way to publicly stand up for me.

MARC CUSHMAN

Roddenberry's adversarial relationship with NBC played a large role in why there was no fourth season. There were legitimate business reasons in that they perhaps weren't getting as much as they could have for commercial time, but mostly it was political and it was personality. And so the folklore begins, because why is a network trying to cancel a show? Well, it must be because it had bad ratings.

No, there are other reasons why networks cancel a show. They didn't want to renew it for the third season, but the write-in campaign forced them to. In second season they put it on Friday night, which is not a good night for *Star Trek*, but it was *still* their highest-rated Friday night show. It was their centerpiece show for the entire night. The show before it, *Tarzan*, wasn't doing that well, and the show after it was a disaster. People would switch over and catch the movie on ABC at the halfway point, so even though the rating came down a bit on Friday nights and it wasn't really standing up to *Gomer Pyle* too well, it was beating ABC and it was, again, NBC's highest-rated show of the night.

So normally you *don't* cancel that. But at that point they just didn't want to do business with Roddenberry. So after the write-in campaign they put it in the death slot, the single worst time of the week, Friday night from ten to eleven p.m. They were determined that season three would be the last year.

JACQUELINE LICHTENBERG (coauthor, *Star Trek Lives*)

Nobody wanted more third season, but everyone wanted more first season. But having *syndication* was what mattered most, because of the lack of any other distribution channel. Today we see webisodes made by fans. George Takei was in one. Major Kickstarter funding is being raised for webisodes. But back then there simply was no recourse, no alternate channel for fan creativity.

BJO & JOHN TRIMBLE (authors, *Star Trek Concordance*)

The third season ground down, show after show being worse than the last, until even the authors of the scripts were having their names removed or using pseudonyms in place of their real names. To be fair, there were a few good scripts in the third season, but in the main those few seemed to be almost mistakes that slipped by.

RICHARD ARNOLD (*Star Trek* archivist)

At the time, it was great just to have new episodes to watch, but even at the age of fourteen and fifteen, I knew that the show wasn't as good as it used to be. When season three ended, I don't remember feeling the need to start writing letters again, nor do I recall any hue and cry from my friends to do so. And looking back now, I have very little fondness for any of the season three episodes.

FRED FREIBERGER

Despite everything, morale on the show for the most part seemed okay. When they cut the budget down, you know that's not a good sign. The last couple of shows the morale went down a little, but prior to that I hadn't noticed. Despite that, if you're a pro, you do the best you can right up until the last minute. Listen, three years for a show—any show—isn't bad, especially when the ratings are so low.

While the third year of *Star Trek* has largely been dismissed as a creative failure by many, there are still a number of notable and beloved (or at least groundbreaking) episodes that were produced that season—no easy task, given the budget crunch and the departure of so many of the show's previous key players. "Spectre of the Gun," the first draft of which was written by Gene L. Coon, was a surrealistic western in which Kirk, Spock, and McCoy find themselves reliving the shootout at the O.K. Corral. In "The Paradise Syndrome," an accident gives Kirk amnesia and has him becoming Indian god Kirok. He takes a bride in Miramanee, and ultimately becomes the victim of the people who realize he is *not* a deity—culminating in her tragic death and that of Kirk's unborn child.

Then there was "Day of the Dove" which has an energy force that feeds on anger, hatred, and hostility, arming both the Klingons and Kirk's crew with swords and setting them at one another's throats on the *Enterprise* for what is intended to be an eternal battle, as none of the opponents actually die; "The Tholian Web," in which Kirk is presumed dead but is actually trapped between dimensions; "Plato's Stepchildren," a disturbing episode in which aliens with telekinetic abilities torture *Enterprise* crewmen for their amusement—and during which Kirk and Uhura share television's first interracial kiss; "Let That Be Your Last Battlefield," a treatise on racial intolerance that focused on two survivors of a warring civilization, the source of hatred for which is derived from which side of their face is white and which side is black; "All Our Yesterdays," which presented a very different Spock as he and McCoy are projected backward in time to a period before Vulcans embraced logic and he finds himself driven by primitive impulses, including love; and the series swan song, "Turnabout Intruder," which has Kirk switch bodies with former lover Dr. Janice Lester.

FRED FREIBERGER

When Gene Coon wrote the original script for "Spectre of the Gun," it took place in an actual western town. Bobby Justman and I thought about how we could help it some, and therefore we did this surrealistic kind of town to try and give it an otherworldly approach. Vincent McEveety was a hell of a creative director. I thought he did some wonderful things with it. I thought the show came out well, and that was satisfying, considering that was my first episode on *Star Trek*, though it aired later in the season.

VINCENT McEVEETY (director, "Spectre of the Gun")

Even though "Spectre of the Gun" is not one of my favorites by a long shot, the effects, the wind, the stylized sets—the fragmented sets—all make it feel like a stage play. It was the kind of thing that takes a lot of imagination to relate to. However, it's interesting that what little fan mail I get in my life usually pertains to that show. People love it, which I can't believe, because I don't.

MARGARET ARMEN

My thinking in writing "The Paradise Syndrome" is that these people on a spaceship for years and years have to get awfully sour, and have a special longing for their home planet and the simplicity of Earthlike nature. So I wondered what would happen if they were just hungry for R & R on an Earthlike planet, and they suddenly and unexpectedly came upon a planet which has a primitive Earth sort of idyllic civilization. I thought it was a good story, which kind of touched on man's longing to go back to very simple things. To love in a simple, open way, and to be loved in a simple, open way. I think if Gene Roddenberry had been producing, it would have come out better, but who's to say?

JEROME BIXBY (writer, "Day of the Dove")

"Day of the Dove" was kind of my response to the Vietnam thing at that time. Throw down the swords! My original story was very late-sixties, and I ended it with a peace march which, thank God, came out. By the way, I first wrote Kang as Kor, the splendid Klingon commander in "Errand of Mercy." John Colicos was in Italy at the time shooting a film. They wouldn't give him a week off to come back and reprise Kor. He was furious. He could taste the role. So Kor became Kang, played by Michael Ansara, and he chewed the scenery. He also has referred to it as one of his favorites. Even his tousled rug was perfect, an almost boyish Klingon, tough as a ten-minute egg but genuinely likable.

MICHAEL ANSARA (actor, "Day of the Dove")

This was the only *Star Trek* I had done at the time. I loved the part of Kang. I loved doing it, even though you never know how good a role is going to turn out until you see the final product. In this episode, it seemed to be the first time the Klingons were not purely "bad guys" but beings with a sense of honor and purpose. Everything I have done, even the bad guys, I try to give the character a sense of honor and believability.

FRED FREIBERGER

A shipboard show, which we needed. Considering our restrictions, I thought it came out well. It was more of a derring-do kind of show, and Michael Ansara was wonderful as the Klingon Kang.

JUDY BURNS (writer, "The Tholian Web")

I met a student who was a physicist and told him that I wanted to write a *Star Trek* script which would be a ghost story based on fact. He said, "Why don't you use the theory of infinite dimensions?" What came out was "In Essence Nothing," which became "The Tholian Web." At the time, if I remember correctly, the very first draft of the story had Spock as the one who disappeared. Eventually I received a classic memo from Bob Justman, who summed up by saying, "I think we can use it, but it should be Kirk out there. He would be schmuckishly heroic to stay behind on this other ship." Besides that, there was another episode called

"Spock's Brain" in which Spock was out of it for a period of time, and they didn't want to have him incapacitated for two scripts.

Some of the things I was a little disappointed in were caused by technical problems. Originally there were no space suits when Kirk and the others beamed over to the other ship. There were force-field belts which kept them encapsulated in a kind of mini force field, which included an oxygen bank. It kept them secure as long as the batteries held, but if the batteries ran out, which was the greatest threat to Kirk, then they die. Therefore, Kirk would have wandered around the ship looking like he looks, except for a little force-field belt. I think it would have made a better ghost story. He looks silly constantly making brief appearances on the *Enterprise* in that space suit. I really had a lot of qualms about that. From a story point of view it would have been better. They felt strongly that if they started something like a force-field belt, it might have ramifications down the line on other stories.

DIANA MULDAUR (actress, "Is There in Truth No Beauty?")

For "Is There in Truth No Beauty?," we read the script and it all got thrown out. It was out of order when we shot it. I came in from Broadway and I thought, "My god, is this what film is all about?" You had no idea what you did before that scene or after that scene. But it was one of the most wonderful shows I think they made. We shot it all out of sequence and we learned our lines when we got on the set that morning as they were writing it.

FRED FREIBERGER

The big thing about "Plato's Stepchildren" was who was going to kiss Uhura, a black girl. We had quite a few conversations on that one, because someone said, "Let's have Spock do it," and I said, "No, if we have Spock do it, we're going to have all these people screaming that we didn't have the guts to have a white man kiss her." We went through a whole thing, but it all worked out, and Shatner said to her as he fought against the aliens' control, "It's not that I don't want to, but I don't want to humiliate you." That's a show I'm very proud of.

OLIVER CRAWFORD (writer, "Let That Be Your Last Battlefield")

This was originally a Gene Coon story that was brought to me. It dealt with racial intolerance, and I thought it was a marvelous visual and cinematic effect. The whole point of the story was that color is only skin deep. How could any writer not respond to that? That fit right into the times and I was very pleased to write the episode.

FRED FREIBERGER

Gene originally had a devil with a tail chasing an angel. We thought, "What an idea it would be to do black on one side and white on the other, and the other guy has it the opposite way." *That's* the stupidity of prejudice. There's a wonderful moment when Kirk says, "What's different about him?" and he says, "He's white on the *other* side!" That was a big morality show and I liked the idea of it.

YVONNE CRAIG (actress, "Whom Gods Destroy")

People come up to me and say, "Do you remember the fourth episode?" and I say to them I only saw two episodes of *Star Trek*, one was "The Trouble with Tribbles" because I just love them, and I saw mine once ["Whom Gods Destroy"]. When I was doing the scene where I was blown up, we couldn't keep that green paint on me. It was just a nightmare, and so when I raised my arms I had what looked like Spanish moss in my pits. It was just dangling so I said to the cameraman, "Does this bother you?" And he said, "No, it's too far away, they'll never see it." Years later, I thought "Oh my God, I wonder if with Blu-ray you see it all." Well, you didn't because they cleaned it up. I was just so grateful. But it was hard to keep the paint on, it was a mess.

When they had to audition me they said, "Can you do a three-minute dance?" and I said, "Unless you're doing *The Red Shoes*, three minutes is a long time," but I said, "Yes, I can do a three-minute dance if you want it, but you'll probably just have to cut it to pieces, because that's crazy." It's nuts, but it was fun to do.

FRED FREIBERGER

With "All Our Yesterdays," I remember that when Leonard Nimoy read that script he came to me and said, "I'm a Vulcan, how can I be passionately in love with a woman with emotion involved?" So I said, "This is way back in time, before the Vulcans had evolved into a nonemotional society." He accepted that, for which I was very grateful. One of my favorite episodes.

RONALD D. MOORE
(coexecutive producer, *Star Trek: Deep Space Nine*)

As a fan, whenever I watched the third-season episodes in syndication, I was always like, "Here we go. I've got to watch 'Way to Eden' and 'Spock's Brain' and 'And the Children Shall Lead,'" which was my least favorite of the entire run. Worse than "Spock's Brain." "Spock's Brain" is goofy and it's almost absurdist. I just hated those kids and wanted them all to die. It's too bad, too, because the third season is the best-looking of the show. The lighting is really good, the special effects were as good as they were ever going to be. It was a much more handsome show. It really found its footing. There was much more texture in the photography. Everything looked good but the stories were just crap. They weren't quite on the *Lost in Space* level, but they had definitely fallen from where they were.

FRED BRONSON (publicist, NBC Television)

Back when the original series was in production, you could call a number and they'd arrange a set visit. So I called the office. You didn't have to be anyone special, they just did it, and I got an appointment to visit the set. My appointment was four p.m. on December 31, 1968, and I was told I could bring a guest. I had a fourteen-year-old friend named Marc Zicree who was a huge fan, so I made it his Christmas present. I drive us over to Paramount, we go to the office, and they walk us over to the set. The guy says, "Stay about a half an hour and then go," and he leaves! Would never happen today. Unchaperoned, we were basically two kids watching. They were filming a scene in sick bay, the only regulars were Shatner and DeForest Kelley.

I couldn't tell from the little bit we saw what the story was, but it turned out to be "Turnabout Intruder." We stayed longer than a half hour because no one was chasing us out. It was also the stage where the bridge was, and all the corridors, so we walked around, and the two things that I remember distinctly were the assistant director saying, "Come on, people, it's New Year's Eve, last episode of the season. Let's get this done." And Majel Barrett, who I did not know yet, walked by me and said under her breath, "Last episode, period." Inside I said, "No!" because they hadn't announced it even though we all knew it was on the brink. That was how I found out the show was officially canceled.

BJO & JOHN TRIMBLE

Unfortunately the very last third-season episode, "Turnabout Intruder," was very good and it might have won an Emmy for William Shatner, but all TV shows got rescheduled for President Eisenhower's funeral coverage. So the episode missed the Emmy-nomination deadline, because "Turnabout Intruder" was shown in the first rerun season, which made it ineligible for an Emmy.

SCOTT MANTZ

That's how production ended. You've got to think about what Shatner went through during the original run of the series; his father passed away, which was something that really affected him. And then after the second season he and his wife separated. You can easily forgive Shatner if he chose to not have fond memories of *Star Trek,* because he went through two traumatic moments during the making of that show. One of them was sudden, the other one was probably caused by his workload and the fact that he was never around.

But as bad as "Turnabout Intruder" was, there is something somewhat apropos about the last words of the episode, "If only. She could have had anything she wanted. If only." And then he walks off. If only . . . If only Paramount and NBC realized what they had. . . . If only Roddenberry had got his wish to have a better time slot in the third season. . . . Can you imagine how great those third-season episodes would have turned out with him being the day-to-day line producer like he was for the first half of the first season? If only. If only indeed.

RICHARD ARNOLD

When I was putting together the guest list for the Hollywood Walk of Fame party at the studio for Gene, I was going over the list of who was invited with Gene in his office. I asked him if there was anyone missing from my list, and he gave me a couple of names of behind-the-scenes people I had omitted. I remember [original *Star Trek* editor] Fabien Tordjmann being one of them. As I was about to leave, I asked him, half in jest, if there was anyone who should *not* be on the list. He responded, "If Herb Solow or Fred Freiberger are there, I will not be!" It was the one and only time that I ever heard him mention either of their names, and I was somewhat surprised by his response, as he was quite adamant.

FRED FREIBERGER

I have read that the fans didn't like any of the episodes of the third season. If true, that hurts me, but there is another truth. In my travels throughout the United States, Canada, and Europe, I have run into many *Star Trek* fans and not one of them has ever treated me with anything less than courtesy and respect. For that I thank them.

But I have to be honest. I thought the worst experience of my life was when I was shot down over Nazi Germany. A Jewish boy from the Bronx parachuted into the middle of eighty million Nazis. Then I joined *Star Trek*. I was only in a prison camp for two years, but my travail with *Star Trek* lasted decades.

LIFE AFTER DEATH

"WE'VE BEEN THROUGH DEATH . . . AND LIFE TOGETHER."

The seeds of *Star Trek*'s rebirth were actually planted while the original series was still in production, fighting for its very existence. NBC may not have recognized it right away, but the show had most definitely struck a chord with viewers, who developed a passionate interest in *Star Trek* very early in its run.

It was that early fervor that would ultimately spawn the first fanzines devoted to a television series—mimeographed amateur fan-created magazines filled with illustrations, short stories, analysis, and interviews. Later, the record-breaking success of the show in syndication would inspire a plethora of merchandise and full-fledged *Star Trek* conventions, as well as the hope that the *Enterprise* would someday fly again, a dream that would eventually be realized with the release of 1979's *Star Trek: The Motion Picture*.

Without the fans keeping *Star Trek* alive in the late 1960s and throughout the 1970s, it's very unlikely it would have ever survived into the twenty-first century.

DAVID GERROLD (author, *The World of Star Trek*)

In retrospect, I would have to say that *Star Trek* was overrated; that its survival, the phenomenon, is based more on what we *imagine* than what's really there. This is true about all television. Television is imitation movies, so what we do in television is hint at and suggest what we really can't show, because people don't want it in their living room. So you go back and look at the original *Star Trek*, and there's about a dozen episodes that are quite good as either television or science fiction. Not much more than that.

ALAN DEAN FOSTER (author, the Star Trek Log series)

It's fairly obvious that *Star Trek* represented, more than anything else, a sensible future. A future where people worked together and utilized science and reason and logic to try and solve problems, instead of just blowing things up. It was the idea we go out into space and even if we meet hostile aliens, we can manage to get along; and everyone on the *Enterprise* gets along. The whole tribal issue of humanity has disappeared, and we have a sensible world. Just that we go forward and the world isn't destroyed by climate change or some other environmental disaster, and we're not fighting each other. That's the message of all hopeful science fiction. I believe that's what the fans latched on to.

DAVID GERROLD

The strength of the show is the format and the characters, not the episodes. Because the characters and the format suggest a possibility, and it is the *possibilities* that *Star Trek* suggests that I think are responsible for the phenomenon of the TV series. We would go to *Star Trek* conventions—and this would be about 1972—and people would say, "Why is *Star Trek* so popular?" I'd say, "I think it's because *Star Trek* represents a world that works for everyone; that we could solve problems. It represented an opportunity to say that the human race is going to outlive its troubles and survive and succeed, and truly will learn to live together." This was in the middle of the Vietnam War, race riots, famine, and Watergate, and here's *Star Trek* saying, "No sweat, we'll be okay." That's *real* valuable. When I started saying that to other people, and I said it in my book *The World of Star Trek,* which was published in 1973, other people started picking up on it and repeating it.

I did an analysis in *The World of Star Trek* that said that there are really three worlds of *Star Trek*. There's the show itself, what gets transmitted; behind the scenes; and the fans.

JACQUELINE LICHTENBERG (author, *Star Trek Lives!*)

Fanfic has been the main artistic outlet for writer-type people since the dawn of time. However, the *fanzine* was invented by science-fiction fandom circa the commercialization of the spirit duplicator . . . purple ink on a gel. Science-fiction fanzines did not usually publish fan-written fiction. One simply did not infringe copyright by writing in another person's professionally published universe except for short humor. And fan-written original fiction was just too awful and nobody wanted it. So fanzines were discussions and reviews, personal life events, news of forthcoming books, etc.

DEVRA LANGSHAM (editor, *Spockanalia*)

A lot of the time they were letterzines—you wrote to someone about something and they wrote back—or there were con reports. You know, "I went to this con and I saw Isaac Asimov and it was neat." Or there were book reviews, but there wasn't fiction. There were three or four professional magazines that were buying fiction at the time. If your story is good enough to be published, why haven't you submitted it to one of *them*? So nobody had thought of publishing fiction. I don't know if people wrote stories related to other shows and other books. It didn't occur to me that I should look for a fanzine with fiction in it, not that I think there were any. And if there were, there was no Internet, so it was a question of people finding each other.

JACQUELINE LICHTENBERG

Devra Langsham in New York did the first fanzine, *Spockanalia,* as a one-shot with the attitude, "Let's just publish these *Star Trek* stories in a fanzine." There were only a few stories, but there were too many people who wanted them to distribute this by carbon copy (the usual method was carbon paper before Xerox). Meanwhile, Ruth Berman called for stories for a fanzine she named *T-Negative.* I'm not sure, but I think the first ones were mimeo and only later when circulation broke five hundred or a thousand did they go offset press. It's all circulation size versus production cost and storage space in someone's basement.

DEVRA LANGSHAM

My friend Sherna Comerford and I talked about *Star Trek* stories a lot. Then we met someone at a science-fiction convention in Newark and she said, "Here, you should talk to this lady; she's got a magazine she's published with book reviews and letters, and she's written a couple of articles on *Star Trek* saying things like, 'Hey, isn't this neat: you can tell the service these people are in by the color of their shirts.'" Which, of course, we *didn't* know, because we didn't have a color TV. She put us in touch with Ruth Berman, a longtime science-fiction fan who had written a story and may have printed up a few copies for her friends. Then we met [writer] Eleanor Arnason and Kathy Bushman, who was an artist, and it just kind of went from there.

JACQUELINE LICHTENBERG

Note the Vulcan connection of each fanzine title. It was *Spock* that woke up female science-fiction fans and produced a torrent of stories. Then the Kirk fans

and everybody else wrote stories about their favorite characters. Zines prolifer-
ated and differentiated, re-creating genres from scratch.

One such "re-creation" of fan fiction was so-called Kirk/Spock (or K/S fiction, also
known as slash fiction), which brought the relationship between the two characters from close friends to something far more . . . intimate.

JACQUELINE LICHTENBERG

Gene Roddenberry explained it this way. When he created the bridge crew,
he created the Kirk-Spock-McCoy triumvirate from fragments of his own mind.
He could identify with each character, they were components of his own creative view of the world. So when Trekkers studied the TV series, they saw Kirk
and Spock as a *unit*. As one entity, as needing to "get together," as two poles of a
magnet, because GR created them to be two halves of a whole.

DEVRA LANGSHAM

Spockanalia was introduced in 1967 while the show was in its infancy. We were
really careful and didn't want to look like fools, so we said, "Don't introduce
things that aren't on the show—if it's in an episode, that's great, but don't suddenly
decide that Kirk has golden nipples or anything like that." We were writing and
publishing this zine as though *Star Trek* is the real world, so we're not going to
publish articles on "I got to go on the set and I saw the actors," because that was
already being published by other people.

JACQUELINE LICHTENBERG

Human nature being what it is, sexuality is the expression of that "get together"
and "irresistible attraction." The *soul mate* hypothesis runs deep in romance literature. Many of the women drawn to *Star Trek* fandom, who wrote fanfic, were
not science-fiction readers or fans nearly as much as they were romance readers
and fans. The *other* factions of *Star Trek*'s female fandom were scientists, often
working in science labs. Many others were librarians and teachers whose educa-
tion and professions include sociology as a science. Given that Kirk and Spock
belong together—"well, then . . . maybe . . . uh, no, but . . ."—one fan wrote a
story where that hypothesis was brought to the fore, played with, and suggested.

That story circulated on carbon copies, then got printed—today we'd say it "went viral"—and all of a sudden people everywhere were arguing the hypothesis by writing stories.

Simultaneously, the gay community was in the process of coming out of the closet, so while many *Trek* stories were fem-lib based, others were gay-lib based. My thesis is that popular fiction follows and reflects social trends but does not cause them. Popular fiction can and does help people who are not part of a particular social trend to understand the people who *are* part of that social trend.

DEVRA LANGSHAM

When *Spockanalia* was published, that was the year that the World Science Fiction Convention was held in Manhattan. We printed up our magazine and walked around the convention holding a picture of the front cover so people would see it was *Star Trek*. And either they said, "Blech, that stupid show" or they said, "Whoooooooa!" We developed what is commonly known as "unsold fanzine shoulder," which is the way you get after you've been carrying ten magazines around. After that, we got a table, but this was the very first time and we just walked around and held it out to people.

JACQUELINE LICHTENBERG

As far as fans connected to established science-fiction fandom were concerned, character distortions as the show went on were no problem. That's what fanfic is for. You just *fix it yourself.* People generally liked the show because it was real science fiction or hated it because it was television and pretty much distorted or ignored the real-science ingredients. But they watched every episode, memorized them or recorded the soundtrack on sound recorders before video recorders, and discussed every error and development with vast differences of opinion.

BJO & JOHN TRIMBLE (authors, *Star Trek Concordance*)

By the time *Star Trek* fandom emerged as a force to be reckoned with, the quick-print shops were common and offset prices were down so everyone could afford them. One of the first things science-fiction fans noticed was that *Star Trek* fans began turning out beautifully reproduced fanzines all over the place. This rubbed some of the science-fiction old-timers the wrong way, as they remembered all too well the frustration of trying to produce a letter-perfect fanzine using outdated methods of reproduction.

JACQUELINE LICHTENBERG

There are two types of science-fiction fans: "fandom is a way of life" folks and "fandom is just a goddamned hobby" folks. *Star Trek* added another division: those who follow canon and those who embroider it with their own original material, and thus write "alternate universe" stories. My *Star Trek* fanfic series *Kraith* is "alternate universe" and was published first in *T-Negative*. I wrote a nonfiction article for *Spockanalia*, the fanzine that held strictly to canon.

BJO & JOHN TRIMBLE

Star Trek fans also thought they should make a profit off their endeavors. As one of the all-hallowed and totally illogical early ideas of science-fiction fandom, the unspoken "rule" that it was immoral to make a profit off fellow fans is probably one of the most stupid. *Star Trek* fans, without any of this "tradition" behind them, hit fandom broadside with expensive fanzines and conventions that were openly designed to make money for someone.

JACQUELINE LICHTENBERG

Fandom was composed of *readers*—other media just didn't connect. Thus at conventions, "Trekkies" were socially shunned, and eventually *Trek* items were prohibited from being on the program schedule. The year *Kraith* was nominated for a Hugo, the anti-*Trek* movement in fandom reached vitriolic levels.

BJO & JOHN TRIMBLE

Science-fiction fandom, established since the 1940s, viewed the sudden invasion of *Star Trek* fans with alarm. Until the popularity of the show, most fans discovered SF via books and magazines. This was long before Internet communication, so fans joined fandom as individuals or small groups. This made it easier to absorb the "WOWEE! More people like me!" enthusiasm of newcomers, as SF fandom seldom got rocked by the gentle intrusion. SF fans had muddled along nicely until *Star Trek* burst on the scene. Then everyone got a rude awakening to modern times.

JACQUELINE LICHTENBERG

We coined a new vocabulary. *Trekkies* were gaga media fans, celebrity groupies who couldn't tell the difference between an actor and a character; people who didn't read books—maybe a *Trek* novel, but not real books—and didn't even know who Hal Clement was. We, however, were Trekkers, not Trekkies. We understood actor and character difference, and knew all the differences between real science and *Trek* science, the gap of which has closed recently, and criticized *Trek* for literary flaws while admiring it for incorporating Shakespeare and many classics just as science-fiction novels do.

BJO & JOHN TRIMBLE

The World Science Fiction Convention was held on Labor Day weekend in 1967, about two weeks before *Star Trek*'s second season debut, "Amok Time." There was a benefit auction to bring a Japanese science-fiction fan named Takumi Shibano to the United States for a visit and tour. We were head of the auction committee and had asked Gene to donate some *Star Trek* memorabilia to include in the auction. Those items made the auction the biggest draw at the convention outside of the Hugo Awards. We packed the room. The needed five thousand dollars was raised in two and a half hours. That auction also became a galvanizing moment in *Star Trek* history. It was when *Star Trek* fandom first came together and became a force in and of itself. People who met each other at the convention went off and started producing fanzines and formed clubs.

GENE RODDENBERRY (creator, executive producer *Star Trek*)

We had Paramount pretty well convinced that fanzines are the lifeblood of the movement, and they always have been. I said, "The day we start sending cops in to arrest a junior-high-school student because he's using *Star Trek* on a mimeographed thing he circulates to fifty friends, that's the day I walk out of the studio."

A primary reason that many of the show's fans supported the letter-writing campaign to save *Star Trek* for a third season was that they were cognizant of the fact that without enough episodes, the show would quite simply disappear forever. The elusive goal of syndication—a situation where independent stations would air reruns of a network show—would never materialize, and *Star Trek* would be little more than a minor footnote in television history.

But they weren't the only ones who recognized the significance of *Star Trek*. Richard Block, vice president and general manager of Kaiser Broadcasting Corp., a company that owned and operated broadcast television and radio stations in the United States from 1958 to 1977, saw the potential of the series early on and presciently secured the syndication rights during the show's third season. This unsung hero in *Trek* lore may truly be the man who saved *Star Trek*.

RICHARD BLOCK
(vice president, general manager, Kaiser Broadcasting Corp.)

At that time we were developing independent stations, and UHF was viewed negatively, with the preference being VHF, and it wasn't helped by the fact that, at the time, there wasn't much cable. The FCC limit in terms of owning stations at the time was seven, and we owned six.

Back then network affiliates couldn't air reruns. It was outrageous that the government was involved like that and telling people what they could air from seven to eight p.m. at night, but the thought was to develop more diversity and more producers. Of course, this was to our advantage, because the network affiliates in the top fifty markets were struggling. That's tantamount to 80 percent of television households.

So we bought a lot of syndicated programming, and Bob Newgard, who was VP and sales manager of worldwide television at Paramount, knew that I had an interest in *Star Trek*, but he kept telling me that the company wanted to quit doing the show. It cost too much money, Gene Roddenberry was tough to deal with, and so on. I do have to say that Gene was great with me. I taught at Stanford at the time and I'd invite Gene to talk to the kids. One time he couldn't do it, and one of my students asked, "Could I design costumes?" He was working on a new episode. I asked him and he said, "Yes, tell her to design them and come down and watch it being shot." I thought that was pretty amazing.

Anyway, NBC was kind of doddering over the whole thing and stopped production after seventy-nine episodes.

I kept pushing Bob, saying, "I want to buy *Star Trek*," and he would say, "We don't even know if we're going to syndicate it." I still pushed, and eventually we scribbled the deal out on a napkin or menu for us to play the show in Boston,

Detroit, Cleveland, and Philadelphia. From there he went back to Paramount and said, "Why don't we launch it?" There was also interest from San Francisco's KTVU and, afterward, WPIX in New York entered the situation.

SCOTT MANTZ (film critic, *Access Hollywood*)

I believe Philly was the first city to broadcast *Trek* reruns as early as 1969. I was barely a year old when that happened, so I don't remember which station it was on. But when I started watching *Trek* in 1974, I was six years old. The episode that popped my *Trek* cherry was "Mirror Mirror," and I was instantly hooked! Interesting how that was the episode that did it, since it was such an atypical episode (it was set in the evil universe most of the time).

But of course *Trek* made a *huge* impact on my life, because A) it was on *five nights a week,* B) it was on early enough so I could watch it before my bedtime, and C) I caught it while they were running it in its production order (not the broadcast order)—and I was watching so many classic episodes from the first half of the second season ("Amok Time," "Doomsday Machine," "Metamorphosis"), when *Star Trek* really hit its stride.

Also worth mentioning is that they showed *Trek* complete and uncut! *No* edits were made, so I saw all fifty minutes of each and every episode! I didn't realize that *Trek* was edited for syndication until a few years later, when I was visiting relatives in New York and caught a few edited *Trek*s on Channel 11.

RICHARD BLOCK

Star Trek did great on independent stations at eleven o'clock at night, because it ran against the news. The news skews old, and *Star Trek* got younger viewers. I remember the guy from the Cleveland station was really angry at me—as angry as you can be with your boss—saying, "Why are you cramming that down our throat?" But that's how it started. Then we ran it from six to seven and *killed* CBS News in Philadelphia.

We had to run the show five nights a week. The network could do one night a week, but we didn't have the circulation to get that to work. Stripping, as far as we were concerned from a marketing standpoint, was the only way to go so that people would know six o'clock to seven o'clock was the time for *Star Trek*.

We were *so* successful with *Star Trek*, and many other independent stations started airing the show the same way.

DAREN DOCHTERMAN
(visual-effects supervisor, *Star Trek: The Motion Picture–Director's Edition*)

When I was a kid, the first *Star Trek* I saw was a 1973 animated show. That first episode, "Beyond the Farthest Star," with the creepy alien message and the strange bug-like ship with the exploded pods, was creepy as hell and scared me to death. And *that* is what drew me to it, because I wanted to know *why*. I watched the whole show and then I started watching the live-action show on WPIX. It seemed funny to watch the opening titles and hear different music, because I was used to the Saturday-morning show. But of course immediately I started loving the live-action show and started tape-recording them off of TV.

BRYAN FULLER (executive producer, *Hannibal*)

My first discovery of *Star Trek* came when I was very small. I wasn't in school yet and I wasn't old enough to go to church. So I would be left alone sometimes with my older brother when everybody went out to church. I remember one time he had built a Klingon battleship and had rigged it with lights. He turned off all the lights in the house and he was flying it around. I was, like, "What is this ship? What does it belong to?" So my first exposure to *Star Trek* was through a Klingon battle cruiser.

It was probably the mid seventies that I was exposed to the animated series and rerun after rerun of the original show. I was always dazzled by the brightness of the world that we were transported to, and as I got older I really started appreciating the level of the storytelling. I was old enough to know that there were adventures that they were having in space with aliens. That was very exciting in a way that westerns were a little dusty for me. It took science fiction for me to appreciate western storytelling.

ANDRE BORMANIS
(science consultant, *Star Trek: The Next Generation*)

I was too young to really comprehend it, but when I was in high school in the seventies, I began watching the reruns in syndication and I became fairly addicted, as my mother would say.

RICHARD BLOCK

Our success with *Star Trek* legitimatized the stations. Initially we were dismissed; the feeling was that UHF was for kids' programming. There was also a feeling that airing *Star Trek* five nights a week—because there were only seventy-nine episodes—would wear it out quickly. That didn't happen.

In 1966, AMT/Aurora released a model kit of the *Enterprise,* which would be the first of several such kits, including the "Galileo Seven" shuttlecraft. The deal came about originally when AMT agreed to build a miniature model of the starship, as well as a full-size shuttlecraft mock-up that could be used for filming in exchange for the license to sell the model.

The following year saw the start of Western Publishing's Gold Key comic-book series; Bantam's twelve-volume series of episode adaptations by James Blish, beginning in January 1967 (which culminated with the 1970 original, *Spock Must Die!*); Bjo and John Trimble's creation (with the help of Gene Roddenberry) of Lincoln Enterprises, a mail-order business that was part of Roddenberry's Norway Productions and sold episodic film clips from the cutting-room floor mounted as slides, copies of the show's scripts, and other forms of merchandise. (Today that company still exists in the form of Roddenberry.com.) And September 1968 marked the publication date of Stephen E. Whitfield and Gene Roddenberry's seminal *The Making of Star Trek,* the first-ever behind-the-scenes account on the making of a television series.

GENE RODDENBERRY

Merchandising was a very big part of our concern. It's become a big business since those early days, when we used to send out five-by-seven black-and-whites of the stars in the days when Lincoln [Enterprises] slowly got into it. I don't have a great deal of control over it, except the control of the fact that they kind of feel like they have to listen to me, because I might get mad and say nasty things to people. I've tried to use that without being an ass about it as best I can. I've said to them a number of times that whatever we do, we must see that the fans get a square deal for their money. I would not stand for putting out toys, as they did once, with box labels of Mr. Spock killing some monster with a zap gun, because it happened to look ugly.

LEN WEIN (writer, *Star Trek* Gold Key Comics)

I started writing for Gold Key on a regular basis early in my career, doing stories for the various anthology books like *Twilight Zone, Boris Karloff Tales of*

Mystery, and *Grimm's Ghost Stories,* and quickly graduated to series books like *Mod Wheels* and *Microbots.*

I had been annoyed for a while by the inaccuracies and flat-out mistakes I was seeing in the *Star Trek* book, so one day I mustered up my courage; went to see my editor, the wonderful Wally Green, and said, "Your *Star Trek* comic is a mess. I don't think your writer has ever even watched an episode of the series." Wally replied, "Probably not." I said, "Well, you know, I've watched every episode of the series so far. I know it front to back. Maybe you should let me take a crack at it." Wally mused for a moment, then said, "Y'know, maybe I should." And that's how I got the gig.

First thing I did when I got the book was to send a letter to the brilliant Alberto Gioletti, who was drawing the book, to bring him up to speed on what had to be fixed in the art. First, those long tubes at the rear of the *Enterprise* were *not* rocket engines; they were impulse engines, so there should *not* be fiery exhaust coming from the engines. Second, our heroes did *not* carry backpacks. They transported down to the planets they visited and had anything they needed transported down to them.

> The first *Star Trek* novel was a hardcover novel for kids, *Mission To Horatius,* by Mack Reynolds, a popular pulp sci-fi author of the time. While fans at the time loved it, the producers were less sanguine."Mack Reynolds' novelization of *Star Trek* is not technically in bad taste," noted producer John Meredyth Lucas in a memo in November of 1967, "but it is extremely dull and badly written."
>
> Even at the time, Lucas was deeply concerned about violations of *Trek* canon including the fact that "the Romulans have nothing to do with the Organian Peace Treaty." He was even more concerned, however, with the fact that Sulu is described as "a bland faced, small Oriental; to Uhura as a Negress and compounds this by having her break into a spiritual chant. We run a totally integrated crew and it would seem we should avoid these particular stereotypes for a juvenile market."
>
> More successful were the James Blish episodic adaptations, which also had their fair share of inaccuracies, however.

JEFF AYERS
(author, *Voyages of Imagination: The Star Trek Fiction Companion*)

The short-story adaptations by James Blish were extremely popular. The editor at Bantam, the publisher that owned the *Trek* license at that time, was Frederik Pohl, and while nobody can remember how Blish was asked to write the stories, he had the dubious task of writing the stories based on the scripts sent to him by the studio. That's why you see all of the various discrepancies and attempts to write logical explanations for some of the wilder stuff. His wife, Judith Lawrence, ended up helping him with the later books, and when he passed away, she finished the series. Blish wrote almost all of the stories without actually seeing the episodes first.

The first novel, *Spock Must Die!*, came about due to Pohl asking Blish to write one. According to Judy, James was fascinated by Spock's character, and wanted to delve deeper into his psyche. Fans were clamoring for more and more stories at this point, so Pohl arranged for the two anthologies, *Star Trek: New Voyages* and its sequel almost two years later. More novels followed, but Pohl admitted he didn't pay much attention to *Star Trek*.

BJO & JOHN TRIMBLE

Lincoln Enterprises was very innovative and unprecedented for the time, especially in Hollywood. We didn't *help* build Lincoln Enterprises; we built it entirely from the ground up. I know that revisionist history says that LE sprang full-blown from Gene's brow, and that several others had a great deal to do with setting the business up, but the realities are that not one person ever had the mail-order experience that we Trimbles had. We'd run several small but successful mail-order companies. We talked GR into the idea, and put LE together entirely on our own. We eventually hired a fan to help sort mail, and found out later she was claiming that she'd originated LE and we were actually working for her! She was fired later by Gene.

Once we had a going concern, Majel wanted to run the business, which was Gene's idea all along. So we were fired on trumped-up charges. This broke our hearts, because we saw it as a long-term business that would benefit Gene and us, too. But then, nobody in Hollywood has ever been accused of gratitude, have they? Oh well!

ROD RODDENBERRY (son of Gene Roddenberry)

The Making of Star Trek was actually a great book, and that's where I learned a great deal about how my father and the other people on the production staff would contact JPL and Caltech. And I think one story that's in there is simply about the phaser, where my father sort of said, "We need a weapon." The response was, "Well, right now we're working on lasers." My father said, "So what's the next step?" And it was the phasing laser, which is where the phaser came from. So the believability was a very important part. In fact, in the show bible, the writing document for the original series, there's a whole paragraph on believability, where my father talks about how important it is to make things believable.

BRANNON BRAGA
(executive producer, cocreator, *Star Trek: Enterprise*)

That may be the most groundbreaking behind-the-scenes book ever written.

DAVID A. GOODMAN (executive producer, *Family Guy*)

I became a TV writer because of that book. Before that book, I didn't even know the job existed. Like, you're watching television and you don't stop to think about the fact that somebody wrote every word that's coming out of Hawkeye Pierce's mouth, and it's not just Kirk—it's somebody sitting down and writing. That book opened my mind. "Oh my God, this is a job . . . I can do this as a job."

MANNY COTO (executive producer, *Star Trek: Enterprise*)

It led me to the decision that this was what I wanted to do, because I realized that people could actually do this for a living. I had a dog-eared copy, and it was actually a really good book. I look at it every once in a while; it was really detailed with memos and was very sophisticated. It was *The Making of Star Trek* and *The Making of 2001*, the Kubrick movie, which was a great favorite. Also *The Jaws Log*, which I devoured as well.

PETER GOULD (cocreator, executive producer, *Better Call Saul*)

It was the first behind-the-scenes book that I ever read, and I just consumed it. I didn't just want to watch *Star Trek*, I wanted to be involved in the production of *Star Trek*. So that's something that was always fascinating to me, and it certainly was one of the things that sparked my interest in television.

ANDRE BORMANIS

I was in high school and some friends of mine and I discovered the book *The Making of Star Trek*. It was like my bible, you know? I just thought it was the coolest thing, because I knew nothing about making a TV show. Nobody did if you didn't work in the business back then. I found it fascinating. The set layouts, the tech memos, the development of the characters, the story ideas, the production schedule, the budgets, and so on. I just thought, "Wow, this is the coolest thing ever."

Aside from the comic books themselves published by Gold Key (and later Marvel, DC, and IDW), there were also two distinct eras of *Star Trek* comic strips that ran in newspapers in the United States and across the Atlantic. There was a weekly U.K. strip that ran from January 1969 to December 1973. The second ran a decade later in the United States as a daily newspaper strip, from December 1979 to December 1983, following the release of *Star Trek: The Motion Picture*.

RICH HANDLEY (*Star Trek* comics historian)

Concurrent with the Gold Key series, British readers were treated to weekly *Star Trek* comic strips that were not reproduced for American audiences. In 1969, six months prior to the TV series airing in the United Kingdom, the strips debuted in the pages of *Joe 90: Top Secret*, a British comic magazine featuring serialized strips based on Gerry Anderson's Supermarionation puppet TV series and other adventure titles. *Joe 90* lasted for thirty-four issues, with *Star Trek* featured throughout as a two-page spread.

Joe 90 merged with another British comic magazine called *TV21*, and *Trek* became *TV21*'s most popular title, expanding from two pages per issue to three—despite the TV show's cancelation that same year. Another title change took place in 1971, following *TV21* issue 105, when the comic merged with yet another magazine, *Valiant*, to become *Valiant and TV21*. *Star Trek* survived the merger, inhabiting the center two-page spread for another 118 issues until being dropped in 1973 (though *Valiant* continued publication for another three years, sans *Trek*). In total, the British *Trek* strips ran for five years, which is amazing when you consider that the TV show hadn't even aired in Britain when the strips began.

Ten years later, U.S. fans received their own *Star Trek* comic strips. Distributed by the L.A. Times Syndicate, the daily newspaper strip chronicled the *Enterprise*'s post–*The Motion Picture* adventures and depicted a new five-year mission. The syndicate retained the immensely talented Thomas Warkentin as the inaugural writer and artist. The series was well received—at least, by the small handful of readers who even knew it existed, since most newspapers unfortunately declined to run it.

The British strips are actually pretty well drawn, sometimes beautifully so, even though they are wildly inaccurate. The American strips, on the other hand, are mostly well written, though the artwork ranges from excellent to . . . well, something a good deal less than excellent. The British strips ran almost entirely in color, while the American series was in black-and-white for all but the Sunday strips, which were in color.

As with the early Gold Key comics, the writers and artists for the *Joe 90* and *TV21* iterations had little knowledge of the TV series, and thus based their scripts and artwork on whatever limited reference materials they were provided by Paramount. As a result, the *Enterprise*'s interiors look nothing like those on the TV show, the uniform colors are frequently wrong, the weaponry and spaceships look like something out of *Lost in Space* or pulp sci-fi novel covers, the Klingons and Romulans look nothing at all like Klingons or Romulans, and the cast—including Spock—constantly utter melodramatic and space-y phrases like "G-g-great suffering galaxies!" Also, adherence to the TV show's concepts is practically nonexistent, with Kirk (called "Captain Kurt" in early issues) and company acting and speaking wildly out of character. Some of the tales are actually pretty engaging, featuring stunning artwork that helps to make up for most of the plots being B-movie clichés. If nothing else, there's a great *MST3K* enjoyment one can take from making fun of them.

The U.S. strips, however, are a different story. Warkentin was not only an immensely talented writer and artist, but also clearly a *Star Trek* fan. He brought back Harry Mudd, introduced McCoy's ex-wife, created Klingon characters with great depth, and showcased a number of aliens and concepts from the TV show as well as from *The Motion Picture* and even *The Animated Series.* His successors, writer Sharman DiVono and artist Ron Harris, continued this trend, contributing a Kzinti story cowritten by Kzinti creator Larry Niven, introducing Admiral Nogura's grandson, and crafting a wonderful adventure about a hivemind machine species called the Omnimind that predated the Borg by half a decade.

The series' final writer and illustrator, Gerry Conway and Dick Kulpa, also turned in a number of solid tales, particularly one in which Kirk and McCoy resign from Starfleet to become privateers, and another in which the *Enterprise* crew enters a parallel universe in which *Star Trek* is just a twentieth-century TV show. The U.S. strips are a gem, both in terms of writing and artwork, and anyone who hasn't read them is missing out on some genuinely good *Star Trek.*

The perfect storm of events in the world of *Star Trek* continued in its third season, when, on March 1, 1969 (just a couple of weeks before the show would all but finish its network run; the final show, "Turnabout Intruder" wouldn't air until June 3 because of an earlier preemption due to the death of President Eisenhower), the first "convention" devoted to the show was held at the Newark, New Jersey, Public Library. Hosted by Sherna Comerford and Devra Langsham, there were reportedly three hundred people in attendance (consider the notion of three hundred people descending on a library at once), and programming included a fan discussion on the *Star Trek* phenomenon, a slide show featuring images of the *Enterprise* sets and some of the aliens showcased on the show, *Star Trek*-inspired folk singing, and a talk by author Hal Clement on *Star Trek* and science. It all concluded with a skit by Sherna Comerford called "Spock Shock."

ELYSE ROSENSTEIN (organizer of early *Star Trek* conventions)

I wanted to go, but my mother didn't want me to, although I did send one or two things over there. Here's the problem I have with it, though: people call it the first *Star Trek* convention, but it *wasn't* a convention. It was an afternoon at the library. It was a very nice afternoon, which had some local publicity. There were a couple of panels of *Star Trek* fans and it had a display of some items Sherna borrowed.

DEVRA LANGSHAM (organizer of early *Star Trek* conventions)

That was just a little group of us in Newark, because my friend Sherna lived there and we were able to get the library auditorium. We went, talked about *Star Trek*, and showed some pictures. The library people thought we were crazy. "This is a TV show. . . . You're having a meeting to talk about a TV show?" There was a bit of that. Of course the hotel didn't care as long as we paid the bills.

The hotel she references is the former Statler Hilton, currently the Hotel Pennsylvania, located across the street from New York City's Penn Station. From January 21 to 23, 1972, it was the site where the first *actual Star Trek* convention—pulled together by a group of fans known as the Committee—was held, featuring such guest speakers as Gene Roddenberry, Majel Barrett, Dorothy Fontana, David Gerrold, and Isaac Asimov. It was the first of what would eventually be thousands of *Star Trek* conventions to be held all over the world throughout the next several decades.

ELYSE ROSENSTEIN

The resurgence of *Star Trek* actually started with myself and a friend of mine, Devra Langsham. She was a children's librarian, and we both had a pretty vast collection of thirty-five-millimeter *Star Trek* slides, which were stuff off the cutting-room floor. She used to put together slide shows for the library that she worked in; it was something she would do for the kids. While we had a large overlap, we each had a good selection of slides that the other didn't have. So we were looking at the slides, and she had a couple of narratives that were fan-written that she was putting to them. After doing this for seven hours, you get a little loopy.

We were both members of the Lunarians, which was a fiction society, and they ran Lunacon, a fan-based science-fiction convention, once a year. I turned to her and said something like, "We ought to have a science-fiction convention for *Star Trek*," and she replied, "Yeah, we can get five hundred of our closest friends"—which was just the kind of thing she used to say.

DEVRA LANGSHAM

Following a Lunacon, Elyse had come over to my house to help me with a slide project, and one of us said, "Wouldn't it be nice if we had a convention that was only for *Star Trek* people?" and three days later she called me and said, "We've got a hotel—the Statler Hilton—and a printer." It was sort of, like, *"What?"* The printer, of course, would be for flyers. We had other people that we asked to help us, like setting up an art show. The whole thing was modeled very much on the standard science-fiction convention with panels and art shows and costume presentations.

ELYSE ROSENSTEIN

Our original idea wasn't a *Star Trek* convention, but a science-fiction convention with a major emphasis on *Star Trek*. We also had science-fiction panels, mostly on Sunday because the emphasis was on *Star Trek*.

JACQUELINE LICHTENBERG

How did the concept of this convention "go viral" before Twitter and Facebook? It was Joan Winston, mostly. She worked in television management of contracts in New York and knew *everyone* in the media. And she could handle the media folks while not wasting their time. So she got the word out, and the fans who couldn't get to New York read about what happened and wanted to make their own—which they did.

Understand, the core groups here were mostly people who had run science-fiction conventions, so they knew how to put together a small event. It's a whole profession, founding a small business, and then shutting down that small business and paying all the bills. Takes lawyers, accountants, logistics managers . . . in other words, it takes fans.

DEVRA LANGSHAM

We talked to people and said, "We'd love to have your artwork exhibited," and we had a dealers room which Phil Seuling ran. Nobody was worried at that point about whether Paramount had licensed them or not. They were fan-made things and Joan, through her contacts with the networks, invited the guests to come, and they came even though we didn't pay them anything.

ELYSE ROSENSTEIN

One of the major differences in the conventions—and this is relevant—is that science-fiction fandom never advertised. Nobody ever put an ad out or flyer, except at other conventions. The only way you heard about conventions was through word-of-mouth. The World Science Fiction Convention that was held immediately prior to the first *Star Trek* convention had about a thousand to fifteen hundred people attending, which is a nice number.

We, on the other hand, *did* publicize it. We didn't take an ad in the paper or anything, but we did call the networks, and we had two camera crews down there. ABC and CBS came down. NBC claimed they had too much news to cover to spare the crew. The long and short of it is that those networks, at least in local coverage, had stories about it. Not only did we get science-fiction fans who are *Star Trek* fans, but the public became aware of this event and they showed up.

DEVRA LANGSHAM

We had people that we knew in the New York community help us, and Joan Winston, who worked at one of the networks as a secretary, got in touch with NASA and got us an exhibit, including a real space suit.

ELYSE ROSENSTEIN

Joanie at the time knew *everybody*. She contacted NASA and asked if we could get some sort of exhibit, because this was 1972 and the space program was still going strong. They said yes and that the exhibit would be arriving in seven cartons to the hotel. Unfortunately, those cartons were actually crates. They fit into the freight elevator with about half an inch to spare. There was a mock-up of a space capsule and, among other things, a mannequin in a space suit, which she assumed was also a mock-up.

DEVRA LANGSHAM

That space suit was *real*, which over the course of the convention someone stole the arm off of. That was just dreadful.

ELYSE ROSENSTEIN

Joanie apologized to someone at NASA, and that's when we learned that it was real. We were mortified that it actually happened—there was a rope around it, but no glass barrier at that point. She had told them about the fun we had getting the crates in and out of the freight elevator, and they actually apologized to *us*.

DEVRA LANGSHAM

By the time we arrived ahead of the convention, we had between eight hundred and nine hundred preregistered people. We thought that was great; usually your preregistration doubled for the convention itself.

ELYSE ROSENSTEIN

We thought maybe fifteen hundred or sixteen hundred people would show up altogether. We had two thousand badges and two thousand program books. Apparently, as we discovered, when you advertise, you get more people. We ended up with about thirty-five hundred people showing up. Not all at once, thank goodness.

DEVRA LANGSHAM

We ran out of *everything.* We ran out of name tags, we ran out of program books, we ran out of trivia contest sheets. I was printing them in my house on a mimeograph, and you don't realize how long it takes to print two thousand things.

ELYSE ROSENSTEIN

We had the facility from eight a.m. Friday morning, but the convention didn't start at eight a.m.—it started at two p.m. However, the hotel posted it in the lobby as eight a.m., which we didn't realize because most of us came in Thursday night and stayed over. We weren't in the lobby, and we were on the top floor of the Statler Hilton, where the convention was held. By ten a.m. we had no choice but to open registration, because the dealers were still setting up. It was a crazy day. It was a Friday, Saturday, and Sunday convention. By Sunday you were pretty much just letting people in, because there was no point. You're going to charge them for coming in for two or three hours on a Sunday afternoon?

We had gotten a number of episodes of the show in thirty-five millimeter from Paramount, which were loaned to us for the duration of the convention. We had gotten waivers from the Screen Actors Guild that we didn't have to pay royalties as long as nobody made any money on it. So what we had to do there was allow people to come in and watch the episodes without paying for membership into the convention. The films were run Friday and Saturday night and they were free. It was posted down in the lobby that if you wanted to come and watch it, you could.

We had a dinner on Saturday night for the Committee and our guests, and among them was Majel Barrett. The hallway was pretty quiet because everybody was in the main ballroom watching, I think, "The Trouble with Tribbles." We were outside the ballroom, and you could hear virtually the entire audience quoting the lines along with the screen. She was astonished, because this was 1972 and the show had gone off the air in 1969. It was in reruns, but that was about it. They didn't really appreciate how much of a loyal fan following they still had.

HOWARD WEINSTEIN (author; writer, *Star Trek: The Animated Series*)

When the first *Star Trek* convention happened in 1972, I was in college. I was a freshman at the University of Connecticut. Our winter-break vacation didn't coincide with a lot of other schools, so most of my friends had gone back to college when the convention took place. I was still home, and I said, "Dammit, I'm not missing this *Star Trek* convention, I'm going to go by myself if I have to— there may not be another one."

I went on Sunday, but they had run out of badges. I didn't get a badge. I did get to see the big speakers, like Isaac Asimov and Gene and Majel. And I wandered through the dealers room, which was not big enough for the crowd. It was really wall-to-wall humanity. There was a relatively small ballroom area and a relatively small cordoned-off dealers area. It was *packed.* There was really no room to move without bumping somebody with your elbows. But it was great fun and just an amazing experience for everyone who was there. I feel really lucky that I went to the first convention.

ADAM MALIN (cofounder, Creation Entertainment)

I went to that 1972 show and it was amazing. Seeing Gene Roddenberry at that show was just unbelievable, and I remember sitting in the Penn Top Room, the eighteenth floor of the Statler Hilton. The room was packed with fans watching the classic blooper reels. I just could not believe it—I mean, to this day I think they were hysterical, but to see them then, in 1972, and to be surrounded by *Star Trek* fans was so amazing.

I realized that there was a *Star Trek* fan community just like there was for comic-book fans. I slowly began to realize that fandom was a growing, living thing. My peers in grade school and junior high school and high school, particularly the girls, really looked upon me as very dweebish for my interest in the genre. I was so excited about it and drawing pictures all the time and talking about monsters and aliens, and really quite a few of them saw me as eccentric and socially backward for my love of that.

DAVID A. GOODMAN

What separated *Star Trek* fans from other TV fans is that we really wanted to watch those things over and over. You would always rewatch the episodes, looking for more details and trying to fill in the blanks of this world they created, and that's what led to people wearing costumes and really just participating.

It's similar to Sherlock Holmes fans who do the same. Michael Chabon wrote a great essay about this, that popular fiction does this thing where it creates this world, and it doesn't fill in the blanks, and that means that the fans want to. And that leads to, like when we were kids, self-published stories in fanzines or, today, Web sites. We wanted to participate. And there was some way in which *Star Trek* really was the first television show to do that.

ELYSE ROSENSTEIN

These people were just happy to be there, which was true of science-fiction fans in general. People at the time who were real science-fiction fans, and who were aware of science fiction, but even people who weren't, a lot of them were kind of outsiders to the mainstream. Most people were reading romance novels, most teenagers were reading about rock and all this other stuff. How many wanted to read about a speculative future? You don't get that.

People who were interested in it were kind of outsiders, myself included. I always had a book in my hand. Still do. At that *Star Trek* convention, there was an acceptance of people, taking them at face value without dismissing them. It was a different frame of mind. That's why that first convention had no trouble. Despite the number of people that were there, we didn't have any fights. We didn't have the kind of problems that would normally be associated in an overcrowding bunch of people.

> The crowds would only get larger. In 1973, the Committee would move the convention to the Commodore, a much larger New York hotel, and invited guests James Doohan and George Takei, with Leonard Nimoy making a surprise appearance, much to the thrill of the sixty-two hundred attendees.

DAVID LANGHAUS (*Star Trek* fan)

I remember being really annoyed that *Star Trek* was canceled, despite sending letters to NBC each season, telling them how much I loved the show and my friends felt the same way. One of my friends told me there was going to be a *Star Trek* convention at the Commodore Hotel in NYC and did I want to go. I immediately said yes and got really excited. He said there would be some of the actors, but didn't know which. It seemed fun and interesting to get all the fans together and find out what it would be like. Not many people knew what to expect. Naturally my folks felt I was wasting my time and money to go spend time with fans of a canceled TV show. Boy, were they wrong! It was very exciting from the moment we got there. A lot of the fans were wearing homemade uniforms, both *Star Trek* and sci-fi in general. I was sorry I was only in the period-traditional outfit of jeans and T-shirt.

What initially excited me was all the pictures, movies, and TV clips being shown. We now take four thousand cable channels and the Internet for granted.

In 1974, the party moved to the Americana Hotel, with the crowd swelling to over fifteen thousand, with an additional six thousand reportedly being turned away. The 1975 convention, back at the Commodore, limited registration to six thousand, which was the case in 1976 as well. Also in 1975, one of the Committee members, Al Schuster, splintered off and launched his own competing convention, which was also successful.

DEVRA LANGSHAM

The fact that the conventions grew bigger and bigger was shocking. We had about fifteen people working on the Committee, of whom only five actually did most of the work. That's the way that goes—we had help from a friend who had access to a real computer, so we were able to computerize our mailing list long before anybody besides big companies ever dreamed of that, and we sent out a progress report, which is what the Worldcons do, saying, "Hey, look at this. We've invited this person to come, and he says he's going to come." We didn't say how much we had to pay him. The first convention was such a success, in terms of reaching people, that when we started to do the second one, we got a lot of people coming back. So it was like you had three weeks off and then you started all over again for the following year's convention.

DAVID LANGHAUS

The important thing for me was Gene Roddenberry said how happy he was to see us and how this may help to bring the show back. At the time, I felt he was just saying what we wanted to hear, but it was still great. Later, I went to the art auction and then the room where they sold fan memorabilia. I remember being unhappy that I couldn't buy all the things I wanted, but I was able to get an original *Enterprise* engineering manual, a bust of Spock, and a *Star Trek* T-shirt, which I still have. The highlight of the convention was the original pilot and very first *Star Trek* blooper reel. Over the weekend, I had lots of discussions with other fans about how excited we were and how glad we were that we came. I was so excited to see Bill Shatner, Leonard Nimoy, DeForest Kelley, James Doohan, and

Nichelle Nichols in person. I remember in the later conventions how excited we all were when told about the animated *Star Trek* show and, later, the first movie.

But *Star Trek* conventions were not limited to New York at the time, with Bjo and John Trimble running Equicon in Los Angeles, which went from a sci-fi, fantasy, and film convention in 1971 to a *Trek* convention in 1973. Conventions would, of course, start spreading to other states as well and, later, other countries.

BJO & JOHN TRIMBLE

It started with a conversation at San Diego Comic-Con and continued at the 1972 Westercon (the West Coast Science Fantasy Convention). "Gee, wouldn't it be nifty to have a large *Star Trek* con in California like the guys throw in New York?" So the idea grew into a reality with author William Tuning forming a committee, including us, to run the first Equicon in 1973. The name came from the time of the year, the vernal equinox (Easter weekend), hence, Equicon.

The first con was so large the fire marshal closed down registration. The local newspapers wrote up the convention as having "ten thousand screaming Trekkies"; the fire marshal said we had eight thousand people, about three thousand more than the hotel could handle.

The Equicons were a huge success for the attendees; in those early years, most of the *Star Trek* stars were not "audience-shy," nor did they charge large fees as they did in later years. Most of them attended an Equicon or two. There were also many activities to keep everyone busy. The first Equicon gave two thousand dollars to the Sophia Salvin school for handicapped children, helping to start the tradition of *Star Trek* fans supporting worthy causes.

SUSAN SACKETT (assistant to Gene Roddenberry)

They were fan-run. Bjo always had an interest in fandom, so she had been to many of them and then she decided to run this thing which was called Equicon. I was put on the public-relations committee, and I had to contact a number of people. Then I was there at the reception table when people checked in for their talks. It was all done by volunteers; no one got paid. They barely managed to cover expenses. I was at the table when Gene arrived, and I looked up, and he had the blooper reel with him, and I said, "Follow me," although I had no idea where it had to go. When I applied for a job with him, he did not remember that encounter at all, which was probably a good thing or I might not have gotten the job.

GERALD ISENBERG (producer, *Star Trek: Planet of the Titans*)

The conventions were really bizarre. I went to one with Gene and his wife, and I brought my kid with me, and I had become a judge for the costume contest. So we had Scotty on one side and I don't remember who was on the other side, and this girl comes up with this weird costume and she was right in front of my face. She lifts up her skirt and flashes her crotch at me. My mouth dropped open and I turned to Scotty and I said, "Did you see that?" And he said that it happens all the time.

Like its East Coast counterpart, Equicon ran until 1976 and drew many thousands of fans who gathered to celebrate the show and listen to cast and crew speak. And although other conventions would spring up to replace them, it wouldn't be long before these conventions would move away from being fan-run to being for-profit, licensed by Paramount to organizations such as Creation Entertainment, whose long association with *Star Trek* continues to this day.

ELYSE ROSENSTEIN

Things reached a point where we had to stop. First of all, it got expensive to mount these conventions, because they were big, which meant that we needed a major venue of some kind, usually at a hotel because people wanted to come in and stay for the weekend. We were there when nobody else was. The people on the show, the actors in particular, had a soft spot for us, because if it wasn't for us there wouldn't have been the other conventions for them to go to. And we did pay the guests toward the end, but nothing like the money they were getting from other conventions.

DEVRA LANGSHAM

The attitude from the guests about getting paid changed fairly quickly. They would say, "I'm giving you my time where I could be off someplace else getting paid." We were distressed by this, but it's quite true: there's only so much time an actor has and this *is* his livelihood. He has to earn money while he can. Of course, some people were more difficult to deal with than others, but we managed.

BJO & JOHN TRIMBLE

Equicons were true fan-run conventions, not a commercial enterprise, so in spite of what some cynics say, we never made any profit. With luck, we made just enough from one convention to organize another Equicon for next year. We still meet fans who fondly remember those cons, some of whom met their spouses there, many of whom made film-industry contacts that led to entertainment-world careers.

ELYSE ROSENSTEIN

The conventions were not about being a business, though there were some people who thought it *could* be a business. There were certainly enough people attending, but things were becoming prohibitively expensive. But the bottom line is that—Al Schuster notwithstanding—no one who worked on the Committee *ever* did it for money. I figured out in the last year that if I'd gotten paid, I would have been paid the rate of about ten cents an hour for the time I put in. After five years, when we split up what was left, it came down to about eleven hundred dollars a person, because the money we brought in went right back into the convention. We clearly didn't do it for the money.

DAVID GERROLD

I knew it was time for me to stop going to conventions when I showed up at one and there were thirty people selling Tribbles. You say to them, "You don't have the right," and they'd say, "Fuck you, you made enough money off *Star Trek*. Now it's my turn." This was the shift. In '72 or '73, you'd meet the fans, and they were grateful for the opportunity to meet the people who worked on *Star Trek*. By '75 or '76, the attitude was "We own *Star Trek* now. The studio doesn't care. We do."

> The impact of these early conventions on the history of *Star Trek* cannot be under-estimated, primarily because it united fans around the country, serving notice to the world that the series and its fans weren't going anywhere; that this was no flash in the pan.
>
> Playing key roles in uniting the fandom were Jacqueline Lichtenberg, who created the *Star Trek* Welcommittee (which would eventually lead her along with Sondra Marshak and Joan Winston to write the 1975 book *Star Trek Lives!*); and David Gerrold's 1973 nonfiction book *The World of Star Trek*.

JACQUELINE LICHTENBERG

I grew up in a professional news-business family. I learned to spot a *news* story before sixth grade. When I first heard Devra Langsham's call for stories for the *Spockanalia* one-shot, I identified the news story that *Trek* had become. But newspapers just weren't covering it. News magazines? Nope. Radio? Nope. TV news? No way. "What's the matter with these people?" Well, if they wouldn't, I *would*.

So I set out to write a short article and tried to peddle it to my local newspaper and put out a few letters. There were more zines and subscribers and readers and contributors than I thought, and the number kept growing as I tried to count them. There were people I actually didn't know personally. Wow. That's news!

So I put out a questionnaire and asked all the zine publishers to publish it. That's how fandom worked before Twitter and Facebook. That's when I realized that this was a book, not a newspaper article. To get all the zines, I put out a round-robin letter and asked each zine publisher to sign it with name and address and to pass it on to another zine publisher. Eventually, there were hundreds of zine publishers on my list when it got back to me. Trying to be sure that everyone knew everyone, I published the *Directory of Fanzines*. But I still needed the same information for a nonfiction book. In the end I got back enough questionnaires to fill a thirty-gallon garbage can, where I stored them for years until I had to throw them away.

It took five years to write that book. It took taking on two coauthors to get the job done. Once I had the contract, I went sort of white-faced as I realized the sheer *volume* of incoming mail, all wanting that *Directory of Fanzines*. So at a *Trek* con in New York, I called a meeting in my room and appointed one of the volunteers to head a *Star Trek* Welcommittee to introduce people to each other the way that the National Fantasy Fan Federation Welcommittee had welcomed me to science-fiction fandom when I was in seventh grade. I put a POB number in the back of *Star Trek Lives!* as the direct contact to the *Star Trek* Welcommittee, and the hundreds of volunteers answering thousands of pieces of mail kept the *Directory of Fanzines* current for decades. The Welcommittee grew as *Star Trek Lives!* went through eight printings and attracted new people into what was the prototype organized structure.

DAVID GERROLD

The first convention had been the only hint that something was happening. Then they were going to do one in '73, which I went to, and six thousand people showed up. The following month in Los Angeles, people showed up there, too. That was the first real hint that this thing was *not* dead. But the studio said, "Three thousand people is no big thing." You really needed to demonstrate a continuing phenomenon, which had not been demonstrated at that time. So my book was out there, and here were all these fans who did not know that other fans existed. But every fan who got the book got a list of fan clubs and things like that, and every fan found out about other fans. We kept the fan club and convention list updated, so that by the time the conventions started to peter out, we noticed that an incredible network of fans had been created. I don't take credit for all of it, but I claim credit for triggering a large part of it, because I also helped the other conventions build up their lists. Once the process was initiated, it became a chain reaction, and toward the end of '74 or '75, we began to notice that the phenomenon had developed into something really big.

If attending a *Star Trek* convention and trolling the dealers room for *Star Trek* swag was not enough, fans could walk down East 53rd Street in New York to The Federation Trading Post, managed by Ron Barlow and Doug Drexler. A press release announced the New York store (once located at 210 East 53rd Street in Manhattan, now a towering office building): "The Federation Trading Post, the only retail store ever devoted to a television series, will open its New York branch . . . [It] will feature over three hundred different items from the highly popular science-fiction series *Star Trek*. In addition to the large assortment of unusual *Star Trek* posters, buttons, bumper stickers, magazines, books, model kits, etc., the avid *Star Trek* fan can lay claim to his own personal 'Tribble,' don a pair of pointed Vulcan (Spock) ears, dress up in an authentic Starfleet uniform complete with hand phaser, or just absorb the 'sounds of *Star Trek*' from the unique sound system running constantly."

Ron Barlow related to *All About Star Trek Fan Clubs* magazine at the time, "Everyone that comes into the store realizes that the store is not just set up to make money, but it's set up to encourage fandom. It's set up to give them whatever hope they have in the show. We have a bulletin board which is a public-access board for any *Star Trek* fan to use. From time to time, we put up newspaper clippings, information that we've come up with for them to read. It saves us the time of explaining it, and all of the personnel working at the store are hard-core *Star Trek* fans, so if we don't have the information, chances are very few people would."

DOUG DREXLER (CG supervisor, *Defiance*)

Ron Barlow and I were huge *Star Trek* geeks, and I had a big collection of stuff. We used to print our own slides, which came from our personal collections. We started a museum in the back room and we put all kinds of props back there. We found a couple of guys in New Jersey who had a six-foot Klingon ship they made that was beautiful. We had a model of the bridge.

The thing is that for the first month and a half there was no business; it was *dead*. And we were getting worried. The local merchants were laughing at us, and I'm not kidding. There was one day when I was walking back to the place, and one of the merchants made a snide remark and giggled. I got in his face. I can't believe I did that, because I'm not that kind of guy. "It's *Star Trek*. You're not just insulting me, you're insulting *Star Trek*!" We managed to save enough money so that we could buy a thirty-second commercial on WPIX during *Star Trek* or *Outer Limits*. It was a thirty-second slide of Spock and us proclaiming, "It's the only *Star Trek* store in the galaxy," blah, blah, blah. That ran on TV and the next day there was a line around the block, and it stayed there for months and months. We would let in two people and let out two people.

When there would be a convention, we would take fanzines on consignment— we had a wall of fanzines. We had posters printed and slides made. The uniforms on *Saturday Night Live* that John Belushi and the others wore in a skit, those were from us. We became the center of *Star Trek* in New York. If someone had DeForest Kelley on a show, they would send over a PA and say, "We need props," and we would loan them to them. *But* we'd get to go and meet these people.

DAREN DOCHTERMAN (conceptual artist)

None of the other kids in school knew about *Star Trek* or talked about it, so I thought I was the only one who liked it. Then when I found out about The Federation Trading Post in New York in 1976 or early '77, my dad took me there one time saying, "There's a place I think I should take you to that I think you might like." I went in there and my head exploded. It was a store that was *only Star Trek,* and I'd never seen anything like that. I'd seen a couple of action figures in the Two Guys store when Mego put out the *Star Trek* action figures, and I had all of those, of course. But this was a whole world, and everyone in the store loved *Star Trek*. It was just an amazing thing to realize I *wasn't* alone; there was this thing that I thought was all mine that I found out a lot of people loved. It's a wonderful day when you learn that you're a part of something bigger.

DOUG DREXLER

There was one night I'll never forget. It was one of those steamy, rainy nights in New York and I ran out to get a cup of coffee. When I came back, my glasses were fogged over and I couldn't see anything. My friend Mitch was working behind the counter and says, "Doug, you should come over here, there's someone that I think you should meet." I walk over and I'm looking into somebody's chest. I look up through my foggy glasses—and it's Gene Roddenberry. He had heard about the store and wanted to come by and see it. He was really nice. He said, "The important thing is that you guys are doing a good job. You take care of everybody and you're treating it well." He was happy about the store.

The success of The Federation Trading Post led Doug Drexler—along with Allan Asherman and Geoffrey Mandel—to Paradise Press to produce *The Star Trek Giant Poster Book,* a magazine that totaled eight pages and featured articles on various *Star Trek*-related subjects. When unfolded, the magazine would become a 34-inch by 22.5-inch poster.

Additional merchandise that helped play a significant role in keeping the show alive in the minds of the public were action figures from the Mego Corporation; a series of eight Power Records albums featuring scripted audio adventures (and accompanying comic books) that served as a perfect entry point for children and featured new *Star Trek* stories to delight older fans; the publication of Susan Sackett's 1977 book *Letters to Star Trek,* which is an intriguing look at the kind of exchanges taking place between fans and Gene Roddenberry; Bantam's official publication of Bjo Trimble's previously self-published *Star Trek Concordance* with its iconic episode cover wheel; the creation of one of the most famous sci-fi media magazines ever, *Starlog*; and the Columbia Records LP *Inside Star Trek*, featuring Gene Roddenberry and several cast members, which was the brainchild of Ed Naha, at the time the A&R rep on Bruce Springsteen's classic *Born to Run* album, who would later go on to write *The Science Fictionary* as well as numerous films and television shows.

MARTIN ABRAMS (president, Mego Corporation)

We had been in the superhero business; we had done all of Marvel and DC. The next thing that became available was *Planet of the Apes*, so we took that license. From there it was real easy to roll into *Star Trek*, because we already had the top three key brands in the male action line. Paramount was the next target and they were doing *Star Trek*, although, interestingly enough, they didn't have an internal licensing department. They used an outside agent [The Licensing Corporation of

America]. Back then the companies with their own licensing department were Disney and Universal, and Universal's was very, very tiny.

When we got the *Star Trek* license, we started with the basic characters like Kirk, Spock, McCoy, Scotty, and Uhura, and a couple of aliens. We had such success with *Star Trek* that we expanded the action figure line to include different aliens, then there were playsets; a *Star Trek* calculator that looked like the pads they had on the show. We even had walkie-talkies that were modeled on the communicators.

DOUG DREXLER

We spoke to Paradise Press and said to them, "Look, we know everything about the show. We've got slides, we've got photos, we can write articles." And they gave us the poster book.

Some of the articles are actually, I think, considered classic. I did one called "The Smithsonian Report," for which I went to the Air and Space Museum and they let me in before they opened. They gave me a ladder and I went up and laid hands on the *Enterprise* model. I took pictures. I met Fred Durant, who was the head of the museum, and he was a real nice guy. And when I was in his office, Michael Collins walked in. And I was, like, "Oh my God! Michael Collins!" He was my favorite astronaut. It was just so amazing to meet him. But you know, we did some really good stuff in that poster magazine that people still refer to.

ALAN DEAN FOSTER

I had done a bunch of short radio scripts for an educational radio station out of Oregon on American history. They did eighty or ninety of them with sound effects and everything, but they were quite short. Under ten minutes. That was my only opportunity to do dialogue that would be spoken as opposed to read. And when Power Records came along, I essentially got the chance to write short *Star Trek* movies. That's what they were. I feel very comfortable that those could have been filmed, whether for television or anything else. Now *that's* a project for some fans—get the film rights to these ancient records and make short *Star Trek* episodes. I did seven episodes that were spread out over a number of albums. There hadn't been a *Star Trek* movie at this point, and I wrote them as filmable *Star Trek*.

RUSS HEATH (artist, *Star Trek* Power Records)

It came from Dick Giordano, Neal Adams's partner at Continuity Studios. He had the [illustration] job but couldn't do all of them, so I did two issues. I put [comic-book artist and *Man-Thing* creator] Gray Morrow's face as one of the crewmembers, in the background as a joke. I didn't like the show. It was just a job. I wasn't interested in any outer space stuff until *Star Wars*.

SUSAN SACKETT

It was 1974 and I was working with some mailbags from Lincoln Enterprises in Gene's living room, and one of the friends of the Roddenberrys who was there said these letters were so interesting that somebody should put them together in a book. At the time, they weren't saving the letters, just taking the orders and throwing the rest out. So I started saving the letters. Most were fan mail or high-level professionals who had written to Gene. I asked for permission to reprint them. Almost everyone agreed except for Carl Sagan. That book sold eighty-five thousand copies in the first year and then it went out of print.

KERRY O'QUINN (copublisher, *Starlog* magazine)

When we started *Starlog* in 1976, it was kind of an in-between period. *Star Trek* was only in reruns and it was before *Star Wars, Close Encounters,* or any of those things.

The way that *Starlog* came about is that we used to package magazines for other publishers on whatever subject they wanted to do. A publisher came to us and said, "We want one on *Star Trek*," which was great. We put together what was essentially the first issue of *Starlog,* with a complete episode guide and all of that. It was completely on *Star Trek*. We gave that to the publisher and a few weeks later he comes back and says, "We've discovered that Paramount owns the rights to *Star Trek* and they won't let us publish this because it would need to be a licensed product and we can't afford to do a magazine just on *Star Trek*. So we can't pay you and we have to give you back all of these materials."

They did, but it was such good stuff, so I said, "Instead of doing a magazine on just *Star Trek*, let's do a magazine that I've always wanted to do on science fiction, and we'll just use this material for a few issues. But we'll do it about the whole world of science fiction." *That's* how *Starlog* was born.

RONALD D. MOORE (supervising producer, *Star Trek: The Next Generation*)

In the pre-Internet era, and being from a little town in central California, I didn't have access to any of the stuff that was going on with *Star Trek,* so I had no idea what was happening out there in fandom. My knowledge of *Trek* in the seventies was fairly limited to *Starlog* magazine. I would always go to the drugstore and buy the latest issue, and that's where I realized there were *Star Trek* conventions. I remember the first issue of *Starlog* I saw. I was at the drugstore with my mom or something, and it was on the stand. On the cover they had this cartoon of the actors hanging from a chandelier, and inside I read this article about *Star Trek* conventions, which I'd never heard of and didn't know existed until that point. It was just this TV show that I loved, that I didn't even know anyone else liked but me. Then I read there were these conventions and these people out there who did love the show, and that the actors went. *Starlog* made me realize that there was this world of fandom.

KERRY O'QUINN

The first issue sold better than anyone *except* me expected, so the distributor let us go from quarterly to bimonthly, and then when *Star Wars* came out and made the cover of *Time* magazine and became the biggest thing in Hollywood, we went monthly. Suddenly science fiction was the hot item and just as suddenly we were the voice of science fiction.

ED NAHA (producer, *Inside Star Trek* LP)

I've read a few articles concerning the *Inside Star Trek* record, in which it was opined that this was Paramount's way of pumping up demand for a reconstituted *Trek* TV show. Nope. They gave us *no* cooperation. We couldn't even get a damned still or slide of the *Enterprise* for the cover. I should point out that Paramount Studios at the time was *not* enthused about anything *Star Trek* creatively. They didn't get it. Never did. As a result, Gene wasn't allowed to produce too much at the studio and basically bolstered his livelihood via his speaking engagements.

The finished album was released and promoted in college markets. The album served as a way to connect with *Trek* fans that were wondering what was going on with the show. Was it possible to bring it back to the small screen? Could *Trek* make it to the big screen? The album was recorded before the age of the Internet, where facts and rumors are now dispensed every ten seconds. Back in the seventies you had print, radio, and conventions to disseminate news, and that was tough sledding. There were no Hollywood backstage TV shows giving you scoops, either. The record was an attempt to give voice to the world of *Star Trek,* and that voice, of course, was Gene's.

The album was pretty much what it was intended to be. It was always sort of a "loose" project in that it was like herding cats trying to schedule recording sessions and the like. At the time, Gene was a hot commodity on the lecture circuit. He did a lot of colleges. We figured we'd record a couple of his presentations and then he'd write "sketches" with various cast members to be recorded in an actual studio on the West Coast, and we'd get a nice ebb and flow going through the two angles.

The origins of this record came about when *Crawdaddy!* magazine approached me about writing an article celebrating the tenth anniversary of the *Star Trek* TV series. So I began the dreaded freelance writer task of tracking down various publicists in order to contact the folks I wanted to interview. Gene Roddenberry, of course, was the big kahuna. Susan Sackett scheduled a hookup between Gene and me while Gene was attending a convention in New York. I met a very haggard Gene at his hotel room one morning. The previous night, when he and Majel were attending a convention function, a robber had broken into the room and ransacked the place, telling their son's nanny that he'd come for the jewels. Of course, there were no jewels. Gene had been up most of the night dealing with the police, jittery nerves, the whole nine yards. The first thing we did after we hit the lobby was hit the hotel bar, which was closed. A couple of rabid *Trek* fans made a real stink about Gene not getting served, he being the Great Bird of the Galaxy and all, and soon we were quietly drinking and philosophizing about life in the post-Nixon era. We hit it off.

We did the interview in a few meetings and the article made the cover of the magazine. At some point, Susan suggested that we do a spoken-word album for Columbia. I was all for it.

RONALD D. MOORE

I played that record over and over again. What was amazing about it was hearing Gene's voice directly. I think it was the only time I'd heard his voice—I'd never seen him on TV or heard him on the radio. It was the only time you heard Roddenberry speaking, and speaking at length. Unless you went to one of the conventions, you didn't have that opportunity, so it was fascinating to me. I remember him talking about his childhood; I think he said something about there being cardboard boxes he used as spaceships and he had a sickly childhood, as I recall. It was a very inspiring kind of talk, talking about the potential of humanity. I remember him saying something about people and sex objects and how he enjoyed being a sex object.

ED NAHA

The lecture material on the album was taken directly from Gene's prepared script. It varied a bit from school to school, but it was pretty much a set routine. It offered a lot of insight into *Star Trek,* but also of Gene and his creative process. The interviews he conducted were scripted . . . or started out that way. Susan Sackett contacted the actors and their representatives, and we booked time at a recording studio in Los Angeles. Mark Lenard was a total pro, reprising the role of Spock's father, Sarek, on the album. He never strayed from character and gave a great performance. DeForest Kelley and Gene tweaked their script during rehearsal. Isaac Asimov and Ray Bradbury riffed a lot more, with Gene gently nudging them back on topic.

Bill Shatner was, God bless him, Bill Shatner. He showed up over an hour late in tennis whites, straight off the courts. Mind you, this left Gene and me as well as the sound engineer, staring at the ceilings while the budget meter was ticking for studio rental. Bill sat down and the first thing he did was toss the script. He wanted to talk about something else. I think dolphins or something. Gene had this great, smiling face he put on when things were going south. But Gene also had this teacher-authoritarian aspect to him that he used to slowly get things back on topic. It was a hoot.

In terms of the content, Columbia Records couldn't have cared less about what was on it. My immediate boss had been left out of the loop initially and viewed the project as "Naha's Folly." We could've had the entire cast of *Star Trek* farting the Russian saber dance and he would've shrugged.

The power of the expanding *Star Trek* audience as a vocal movement became even more evident in 1976, when America's first space shuttle was the subject of a passionate letter-writing campaign that would result in the vessel—accompanied by a NASA ceremony that saw Roddenberry unite with most of the cast—being christened with the name *Enterprise.*

BJO & JOHN TRIMBLE

The project to get the space shuttle named *Enterprise* actually got started with two men in Washington, DC, and when they could not carry it, it got dropped on us Trimbles. We got a phone call asking if we could use our large mailing list to get the word out that the very first space shuttle should be named *Enterprise*. We were hesitant, because a mail-in campaign takes a lot of time and hassles, not to mention a great deal of printing and postage. But the idea seemed sound: the naming could generate thousands of letters to President Ford showing public support for our space program.

We gathered together many *Star Trek* fans and members of the Los Angeles Science Fantasy Society to put the mailing together by hand. We could not afford a mailing house, and we have never found one willing to donate its time, machinery, and people for such a project. Local fans helped to pay for this mailing, but the Trimbles paid for the bulk of it. The papers were folded, envelopes stuffed, and labels affixed, all by hand. The fans brought their own munchies, which accounted for more than one tortilla chip in, or a greasy thumbprint on, some envelopes.

We received every-other-day phone calls from Washington, DC, to tell us how the campaign seemed to be going. Then the day came for the president to hold a news conference on the shuttle and its future, and, only minutes before the conference, the world heard that President Ford had decided to name the shuttle *Enterprise*! NASA officials were stunned; the reporters had a field day about the "crazy Trekkies."

ELYSE ROSENSTEIN

It took a million letters to convince NBC to renew *Star Trek* for a third season, but it only took four hundred thousand to get the President of the United States to override NASA. What does that tell you about NBC? *Star Trek* was not there, but the conventions were, and science-fiction or *Star Trek* fans were absolutely determined that the first reusable spaceship this country—this world—ever saw was going to be named *Enterprise*. We won! The downside was that it turned out the second shuttle, named *Columbia*, was the one NASA picked that actually went into space.

JACQUELINE LICHTENBERG

That was the *main* argument, that *this* particular shuttle would never fly. It was a test vehicle, so we should go for one of the reusable ones to be named *Enterprise*. But that "energy" I keep talking about burst forth, and a huge explosion of sentiment carried the day. What we had been scorned for—the idea of going into space—was now a reality. We had been proven right. We *can* go into the stars, and the *Enterprise*'s successors will lead us there.

ED NAHA

The last project I worked on at Columbia was getting all the necessary clearances and publishing rights for the songs on the *Voyager* record that was shot into space. I worked with Carl Sagan and Ann Druyan. This was quite a challenge in that record companies were loath to have their "product" mixed with another label's "product." It didn't matter that it was being shot into space and wouldn't receive any Earthly radio time. Rules were rules and lawyers loved rules.

While this was going on, William Shatner rode to my rescue. He'd been impressed by my work on *Inside Star Trek*. He called and asked me if I'd publicize his new double album, *William Shatner Live*. The gig would last the summer. Bingo! I had rent money. I have to confess, I love Shatner. He's the most affable über-ego I've ever worked with. Being with him is almost like being included in an ongoing piece of performance art.

> In between all of this, the resurrection of *Star Trek* in terms of a new production had already taken its initial baby steps, the first having occurred during the 1972 New York convention.

JON POVILL (associate producer, *Star Trek: The Motion Picture*)

Gene had a big part in the conventions early on. Not just in terms of going and speaking there, but they were marketing ploys for him and Majel and Lincoln. It was all fostered to keep it alive and to take advantage, at least to some extent, of the syndication. So he was, I think, part and parcel of developing the phenomenon. He was terrific at marketing. He knew how to work his fans; he knew how to work that part of it. I would be very interested to see if he were in his forties now and had the Internet to work with and social media to work with . . . Jesus. I have a feeling he would be a *monster*. There was always the ego, but in terms of what he could do with a Facebook page, drumming up fandom to respond to things . . . I suspect he would have a huge empire. I think he would have been able to parlay *Star Trek* into a zillion other things, even starting a Web series or whatever. He would have been able to generate a whole lot more. Sort of in the way that Majel did with *Andromeda* and some of the other things from Roddenberry ideas, but to a much higher degree.

ELYSE ROSENSTEIN

When the convention first came up and Gene Roddenberry was given an invitation, apparently Oscar Katz had to encourage him to attend. They had been trying to set up a situation where Gene could talk to NBC about possibly bringing back *Star Trek*. On the one hand, if Gene was in New York it would be good to do that, but on the other he didn't want to seem too anxious.

The long and short of it was that Oscar encouraged Gene to come, because it would give him a reason to be in New York that wasn't directly associated with a meeting with NBC. So there was this going on in the background; it didn't have anything to do with our creating our convention or putting it together, but it had to do with some of the people who came. It did give Gene that opportunity. And the publicity generated reached California, where it really kind of lit a fire that maybe had been smoldering in the background. It was kind of saying, "You don't think anything is there, but look at what happened when the fans were given an opportunity." It showed there was a market out there and that people wanted more. In September 1973 we got it with the animated *Star Trek* series.

REANIMATED

"YOU CAN NO MORE DESTROY THIS SHIP THAN I CAN CHANGE COLOR."

Although Gene Roddenberry had floated the idea of a *Star Trek* motion picture as early as 1969 (while the original series was still in production), the first serious possibility of such a film actually being produced dates back to 1973, when Paramount began negotiations with Roddenberry and former Desilu exec Herbert F. Solow, who was then at MGM, on *The Cattlemen,* which was intended to be the first *Star Trek* movie.

Roddenberry's oddest notion to date was derived from an original pitch of his called "A Question of Cannibalism." In it, the *Enterprise* encounters a race of intelligent "cowlike creatures" being raised and slaughtered by ranchers for food. It wrestles with the moral quandary inherent in such a high-concept allegorical scenario. Despite Paramount and Solow's avowed enthusiasm for the project, Roddenberry ultimately balked at the comparatively modest writer's fees being offered by the studio and walked away from this strange little project with an aggrieved Roddenberry and Solow never talking again.

However, with the unprecedented success of *Star Trek* in syndication as well as the ever-growing runaway success of the conventions receiving increasing media attention, NBC was revisiting the possibility of bringing back *Star Trek.* The hitch: they wanted to repilot the show, but with the expensive sets long razed, Paramount wasn't interested in producing a new pilot and incurring the massive construction costs without a full season order.

As Roddenberry once put it, "They had seventy-nine pilots already." He elaborated on the situation to *Circus,* a popular music magazine at the time: "Right after the show was canceled by the network in America, Paramount, who owned the show fifty-fifty with me, decided they needed the studio space. So they tore down and broke up the sets. The costumes were sold or broken up! All that was left was seventy-nine cans of film . . . and memories . . . and fans . . . hundreds of thousands of them. There were rounds and rounds of meetings about reviving *Star Trek.* You would think that after laying an egg the size of Jupiter, the network would accept any offer . . . No! They wanted another pilot show. Paramount refused because the sets would cost seven hundred fifty thousand dollars to replace, too much of an investment for anything short of a whole season's worth of new episodes. That was the stalemate."

But *Star Trek* would, in fact, return to television, this time as an animated series produced by Filmation, the company responsible for such popular shows at the time as *Archie's Funhouse, Groovie Goolies, The Brady Kids,* and

Fat Albert and the Cosby Kids. Invoking a refrain that would become familiar in subsequent years, Roddenberry told *SHOW Magazine,* "I just didn't want space cadets running all over the *Enterprise* saying things like, 'Golly gee whiz, Captain Kirk!' You know, like Archie and Jughead going to the moon. There are enough limitations just being on Saturday morning."

As William Shatner observed in his book *Star Trek Movie Memories,* "Story editor Dorothy Fontana would assign scripts, shepherd them through a re-write or two, and pass the completed manuscripts along to Gene, who had assumed the title of executive consultant. Gene would then read each script, perhaps make a suggestion or two, and sign off. It was that simple. Rodden-berry had found the perfect vehicle. The animated *Star Trek* required almost none of his time, it kept his most durable brand name alive, and it served as a lightning rod, rallying the forces to cry, 'Bring back *Star Trek*!' In their minds, and this was carefully groomed by Gene at countless conventions, they won their first battle. The animated *Star Trek* should be seen not as a reward in and of itself, but as the first step back toward new and improved live-action *Trek*s, be they on television or the silver screen. Over and over again, fans were urged to keep fighting."

LOU SCHEIMER (president, Filmation)

It was 1972 or 1973 and I thought it would be a great time to do an animated *Star Trek*. Gene loved the idea, but there had been some problems between Rodden-berry, Paramount, and NBC, and basically they weren't speaking to each other. The root of the problem was creative control. In those days, it was difficult to deal with networks on Saturday-morning shows without them getting involved creatively.

HAL SUTHERLAND (director, Filmation)

Roddenberry was victorious and he was given carte blanche creative control.

GENE RODDENBERRY
(executive consultant, *Star Trek: The Animated Series*)

A number of production companies approached me about an animated series, but it was important to me that I have complete creative control so that we were sure the show was done properly. That was the reason I wanted control. We had to eliminate some of the violence we might have had on in the evening shows, and there was no sex element at all. But the idea was that it would be *Star Trek* and not a stereotypical kids' cartoon show.

DEFOREST KELLEY (actor, "Dr. Leonard 'Bones' McCoy")

I questioned it at the time when Gene said he was going to do it. I thought it was the death blow. Gene said, "No, I don't feel that way at all. I think it's important to keep some form of *Star Trek* alive and in the minds of people."

DOROTHY FONTANA
(associate producer, *Star Trek: The Animated Series*)

When Gene approached me to do the show, he asked me if I would like to come on as story editor and producer. Since I wasn't a part of another regular staff at the time, I decided to do it. I had not worked in animation, which I do enjoy, so I had a good time on the show. I left after the first season because I wanted to move on to something else and not get stuck in animation. The business is funny. If you stay too long in one thing, people start to buttonhole you there and say, "You can't do anything else," regardless of all your other credits.

FRED BRONSON (publicist, NBC Television)

We would announce the fall schedule in May, so I knew in September of 1973 we would debut the animated series. That whole summer I was in touch with Filmation and Lou Scheimer and [his partner] Norm Prescott. Dorothy had an office at Filmation. She was the showrunner. Gene would read the scripts, but she was running the show.

DOROTHY FONTANA

It takes three months to do an animated half hour, which is not a half hour, it's twenty-one minutes, and that's a lot of time. That is far more time than an active production company will be spending. If you're hurrying with live action, it would take—at minimum—six weeks. We'd like to have more time, but you can do it in six weeks. Three months is different. It's twice that, and it has to be done by hand. Everything was done by hand, except that they could Xerox the cells' backgrounds and some of the animated pieces. If allowed, we could draw any type of alien we wanted, because we didn't have to worry about whether the makeup looked right, just does it look right on a cell? We could have any kind of background we wanted, which was nice because we didn't have to worry about the cost of the set. You could say Rome burned and they could draw it.

HAL SUTHERLAND

Filmation was extremely busy and Roddenberry never knew when to quit. At one point on the first episode, we had just three days to start production and meet our deadline, and Gene kept pushing for improvements. I finally said, "Gene, we're locked into the deadline, we've got to do this!" To his credit, he stepped back and said, "Okay, we're done."

DOROTHY FONTANA

I had an office at Filmation, and I was in the same building where the animation was done. Unlike many companies, they didn't farm out their work to foreign countries. Everything was done in-house, and the artists and recording studio were all together.

FRED BRONSON

I went over to Filmation a lot. We would go and watch each episode, and Lou was just the best. I was a network publicist, but I was a kid. I was twenty-four years old. But he treated me like an equal, which I really appreciated. I set up interviews with him and Norm. They took great care of us when the Broadcast Standards guy, Ted Cortez, and I would go have lunch at Filmation and watch an episode.

I'll never forget, we were watching an episode and there's this scene with Mc-Coy with his back to camera, and you can see a yellow stream coming out of the lower part of his body. We're onto the next thing, and I said, "Wait, what did we just see?" And Ted says, "I don't know." I said, "I think we should go back." And, sure enough, McCoy's peeing. This is animated, this is not a blooper, this was put in on purpose. Then they all cracked up and said, "We just put it in for you to see if you would catch it." But Ted was really concerned it would end up on the air, so he made sure it did not. It was very funny.

LOU SCHEIMER

Dorothy and her writers wrote the scripts, Gene would offer his input, and then it was storyboarded.

DAVID GERROLD (writer, "More Tribbles, More Troubles," "Bem")

Roddenberry started out by saying he was going to be personally involved in every script, but as time wore on, he didn't have the strength to continue. Gene didn't write any of the scripts himself. The real problem was that Gene was having some difficulties at the time and he couldn't always remember what he'd previously said about a story; so from one draft to the next, he was always changing direction. His notes on "Bem" were very confusing, and he added elements that I felt pulled the story way off its original premise. When in doubt, Gene always had Kirk get into a fight with God.

HAL SUTHERLAND

After reading the scripts, I'd create instructions for the animators, working from storyboards. More often than not, I'd work well into the night, sometimes at my office, sometimes in my dining room at three a.m.

FRED BRONSON

I wrote a lot of press releases, I did a lot of interviews, I wrote feature stories that went out to the press. I gave this show a lot of attention, which obviously I thought it deserved.

DOROTHY FONTANA

We did not write our scripts as kiddie shows. We were writing for the *Star Trek* audience, and we did not think they were twelve-year-olds, so we tried to keep the quality of the show in the first year. Second year, I didn't have anything to do with it, so I don't know. I do know that they did most of the scripts we rejected in the first year, but, again, I had no say in this.

FRED BRONSON

I went to the first recording session where the cast showed up. I was there with an NBC photographer and wrote a story about it. I treated the animated *Star Trek* like it was a prime-time series.

LOU SCHEIMER

People are surprised that you record the actors' voices before you start animating. Everyone thinks the voices are added later, but the animator wouldn't know how to do it. He needs to hear the voices before he knows what the emotion is. So we'd record the voices from the storyboards, which are basically illustrated bibles. Then we'd do the full animation. And everything was done by hand. There were no computer graphics, and we did a lot of stock scenes of the characters walking and talking. We reutilized that material in different settings and different combinations.

> In her autobiography, *Beyond Uhura*, actress Nichelle Nichols said of the animated series, "Far from a 'kiddie' show, the animated series was quite good, with many of the scripts written by the same writers who had worked on the original series, all under the supervision of Gene and D. C. Fontana. The producers immediately signed up Bill and Leonard to voice their characters, but planned to hire other voice-over actors to provide everyone else's. This was not intended as a slight to any of us; it was just cheaper and made the most business sense. Bill saw nothing wrong with this plan and agreed to it. Leonard, however, asked, 'Where are George and Nichelle and the others?' When he was told that they did not have us, he replied, 'Well, then you don't get me.' It was only Leonard's deep sense of fairness that kept the classic crew together for that show. In June 1973 we reunited once again, and it was great to be working together as a team. I thought some of the scripts were quite good and in one—at last—Uhura got to take command of the ship."

LEONARD NIMOY (actor, "Mr. Spock")

We started to read through two or three scripts and I said, "Where are George and Nichelle?" You know, just out of curiosity. I thought, "Maybe they're out of town and they're doing what I was promised I could do later, if necessary, which was to record from out of town." I would go to a local recording studio in Boise or anyplace, wherever it was, and record my dialogue and send the tape back by mail. Then I found out they were not being hired. That's when I took my stand. Not only had they not been hired, but their characters were written in the show and were being played by other people. Their images would be on the screen and you would see an image of Nichelle and you would see an image of George Takei, but other people would be hired to play the voices. I was appalled. How could they do this?

FRED BRONSON

That's true. Leonard did come to their rescue. It's Saturday morning. It's a half-hour show and I don't think it was meant to be cruel or malicious. They had a budget. But he stood up and they got them.

WALTER KOENIG (writer, "The Infinite Vulcan")

I was upset with the way I found out that I wasn't a part of the show—at a convention. Everybody thought someone else had told me apparently. Dorothy thought Gene had, Gene thought Dorothy had. To save money, Filmation wanted Majel to do Uhura's voice also and Jimmy to do Sulu's voice since in cartoons at the time you got paid one check to do two characters' voices. To Leonard's credit, he said he would not do the series unless they hired George and Nichelle since they had been there from the beginning.

JAMES DOOHAN (actor, "Montgomery 'Scotty' Scott)

I think the show was ordinary. It was ordinarily drawn. It was kind of fun doing it because I did three characters and in ten of them I did four, and I pushed for that because once you did more than three, they had to double your pay. Strangely enough, I didn't use any accents. I just changed the tone of my voice. It was kind of like being back in radio again, and we made a little money. We certainly hadn't made any on the live-action series, because the residuals ran out in April 1971. The unions remedied it because of *Star Trek*, absolutely. They never thought any show would run like *Star Trek* has run.

LOU SCHEIMER

De Kelley was one of the sweetest human begins I ever met, and Jimmy Doohan was highly versatile. Jimmy worked with Filmation again on *Jason of Star Command*. On *Star Trek*, Jimmy and Majel Barrett did a lot of voices for us.

MAJEL BARRETT (actress, "Christine Chapel")

It's like seeing a caricature of yourself. I was the wind, the trees, a mountaintop, and anything that spoke. It was very imaginative. You almost couldn't give a bad performance.

LEONARD NIMOY

Frankly, I never really felt any sense of gratification doing it or a real sense of the communion that we had when we did the show in the flesh. For me, it was rather an exercise. Reporting to a recording studio during an occasional free moment in L.A., or in some Midwestern recording studio, doing your lines on tape and saying, "Thanks, fellow!" and walking out to the car was nowhere near as gratifying as acting in three dimensions. There were moments, but nothing spectacular.

One of the strengths of the series—which ran for only twenty-two episodes from 1973 to 1974—is the fact that the scripts were far more literate than anything else on Saturday morning, many of them having been created by writers from the live-action series. Helping in this area was the fact that there was a Writers Guild strike at the time, thus freeing many live-action writers to work on the animated show, which wasn't covered by a WGA contract. The series was honored with an Emmy in 1973 for Best Children's Program.

ROD RODDENBERRY (son of Gene Roddenberry)

I had never watched the animated series; I dismissed it as nonsense without ever seeing it. But the caliber of the stories was on par and even better than a number of *TOS* episodes. The animation, of course, was terrible. But storywise, for what they had to work with, it was phenomenal. I like to think of it as the fourth and fifth year of the voyage.

DOROTHY FONTANA (writer, "Yesteryear")

"Yesteryear" resulted from my looking back at the things we had done on the series and remembering the time portal from "The City on the Edge of Forever." I thought we could use that for a legitimate trip, but then have something happen so that Spock has to return to Vulcan to his childhood. We could probe into these characters and see the beginning of some of the trouble with Spock and Sarek, Amanda's problems back then, and part of what made Spock Spock. I had wanted to see Vulcan in "Journey to Babel" with a matte shot, but it got cut out. So with the script for "Yesteryear," I went back to the description from that script and said, "Let's do this now." I wanted to see a city with parkways and trees with growing things, and with unique spires. And we achieved that with animation.

LOU SCHEIMER

A pet's death had never been done on a children's program, but it was in "Yesteryear," and it was touching and provocative. Dorothy was instrumental in making it so creative.

DOROTHY FONTANA

I felt strongly about dealing with the death of a pet, in this case Spock's *sehlat* [a large teddy bear with fangs, as it was described in the show]. It was a very serious thing for kids. We were trying to put across a lesson to children, that when it comes time for an animal to die, if he must go, it should be with dignity.

MARC DANIELS (writer, "One of Our Planets Is Missing")

Gene Roddenberry encouraged me to write this episode of the animated series. I have to admit that it was fun to do some writing rather than just directing.

DAVID GERROLD

My two script ideas had been pitched to the third season of the original series. Surprisingly, nothing was cut. In fact, the animated scripts were almost as long as the live-action scripts, but they played faster as animation, which provided the chance to do the stories in depth. The only thing we didn't do was give Kirk a love affair in every episode. That gave us an extra twenty minutes per episode for more story and more action.

During third season of the original series, I went to Fred Freiberger and had been developing a thing called "Bem." When Freiberger said he didn't like "Tribbles," I said, "Well, Gene said he wanted a sequel," and he said that he had no interest in it. So I offered "Bem," which had to do with a practical joker, which he also didn't like. We did do the animated version of "Bem," but it was nowhere where we wanted it to be because, again, Gene kept rewriting it. He'd read something and say, "No, I don't think so," and he'd give Dorothy a memo saying, "Change it," because he wouldn't let you write the story you wanted to write. You had to write the story that *he* wanted you to write. Yet here's a guy who says, "I'm doing a show where you can write any story that you want to write." That's a great deal of frustration.

MARGARET ARMEN
(writer, "The Ambergris Element," "The Lorelei Signal")

I didn't see how the show could work, but they had marvelous artists over at Filmation. Dorothy Fontana was the story editor and she approached me. I thought it would be fun and she said, "The main difference, Margaret, is that for the artists' sake you have to describe every scene and every action in great detail so that the artists will know what to draw."

For "The Ambergris Element," I thought it would be interesting, since the artists were going to do it, to go to a water planet, with water covering ninetenths of the surface The only exception is an occasional little island not covered in water. I thought the artists could do interesting underwater scenes and so forth.

"The Lorelei Signal" is an idea I'd had about an Amazonian civilization where women were dominant and men were weaker. From that seed I came up with the idea of a planet which drained men of their youth and vitality very quickly, so that they aged within a month, yet the women were healthy and vivacious and beautiful. The key to it was that the women drew their vitality from the males. They were like black widows. They were always sending out the Lorelei Signal to space so that they could attract males to their planet. Both episodes were fun to write.

WALTER KOENIG

This was the one script I wrote for the show, and it was incredibly frustrating. Gene decided early on this is animation so we can do anything we want, so let's have talking plants. And I put in the talking plants and did ten drafts of the script and, at that time, I didn't know what writers were going through on *Star Trek*. I stuck with it and we finally got it done. They did, in fact, offer me another script and I said no; I passed. I couldn't go along with all the arbitrary decisions that didn't make the script any better, not that it was extraordinary to begin with. So to an extent it was an interesting learning experience, but it was painful. I was also still upset about not being part of the series.

DAVID GERROLD

We had very little troubles with "More Tribbles, More Troubles." When we did "Bem," Gene started to fuck around with the script, so it was like they had two scripts left over at the end of the season and they didn't shoot "Bem." When Filmation ordered six more episodes, Dorothy wasn't there, so they bought Howard Weinstein's episode, and they had "Bem" already there. "Bem" got made, but it was a silly script.

LARRY BRODY (writer, "The Magicks of Megas-Tu")

Taking my lead from the themes of the early *Star Trek* episodes, I figured that Dorothy and Gene would go for a story about the *Enterprise* encountering God in space. The "real" Christian God, not just one of the Greek myth gods. A couple of days after Dorothy and I talked about my God show, she called me back to say that Gene loved it and she was going to make a deal. I went back to her office the next week and, first, learned that NBC wouldn't approve the God idea, but that Gene had presented them with a counter they'd accepted—the Devil. As long as it wasn't the "real" Devil. So at that meeting Dorothy and I came up with an other-dimensional alien race that might have been the inspiration for devils and demons in ours. Then she took me into Gene's office so I could shake hands with the Great Bird of the Galaxy—yes, she called him that—and go home to write.

The show ends with Kirk defending the human race to a courtroom of devils and, of course, proving that humanity, and specifically the *Enterprise* crew, deserves to live. That particular idea had been part of my original pitch, because my favorite episodes of *Star Trek* had been the ones where Kirk had to do other variations of the same thing. Another thing I'd been sure that Roddenberry would love.

After the first draft was finished, I was done. A couple of weeks later I got the final draft and saw that although the story was the same, scene by scene, every line of dialogue had been changed. I called to ask her if I'd failed that badly, and Dorothy just laughed and said, "No, no, no. Gene loved what you wrote. He just made changes because that's what he does."

STEPHEN KANDEL (writer, "Mudd's Passion," "The Jihad")

"Mudd's Passion" was an opportunity to bring Harry Mudd back, which was great fun. Dorothy Fontana just called me for a script. It was as simple as that. Animation is great because you direct as well as write. You could go anywhere and do anything.

"The Jihad," in which Kirk and Spock are enlisted to prevent a holy war, was an idea I'd had for a long time. It was a message story and difficult to sell on network television. Network executives would have said, "My God, what are you doing? That's a message story!" I jumped at the opportunity to drop it into a *Star Trek* format and it worked very well. In fact, I won a humanitarian award for it.

PAUL SCHNEIDER (writer, "The Terratin Incident")

This was based on a one-paragraph story idea that Gene Roddenberry had. I took it from there with Dorothy Fontana. I just loved the concept of doing something related to *Gulliver's Travels*. I enjoyed that as well as watching the process of the animation develop.

SAMUEL A. PEEPLES (writer, "Beyond the Farthest Star")

Dorothy called me and said, "Gene suggested that since you had done the pilot for the original *Star Trek*, maybe you'd like to do the pilot for the animated *Star Trek*." That's what I did. It was the pilot, but it aired later. The *Variety* review was absolutely incredible. As far as inspiration for the story, I don't have the vaguest idea. It seems to me that I was trying to say that it would be interesting if there was a spaceship which was actually a living creature. It's alive, but it is used to going from one planet to another. They did great animated stories and they didn't write down to children, by and large. There were a couple that were, obviously, designed for the younger market, but most of them were quite mature.

JOYCE PERRY (writer, "The Time Trap")

I had this idea that a Klingon ship and the *Enterprise* would get trapped in a Sargasso Sea of space and be forced to cooperate to escape. I remember telling Gene this bizarre notion that two ships could combine engines and became more powerful as one than they were separately. I explained it with a straight face, but was afraid he might laugh me out of his office. Instead, he was quiet for about thirty seconds, then he said, "That's pretty good. Do it." And in the finest tradition, a story about cooperation was forged.

HOWARD WEINSTEIN (writer, "The Pirates of Orion")

I had an agent who submitted the script to Lou Scheimer at Filmation. When I was told they were buying it, I was supposed to call Filmation. Here I was, this nineteen-year-old college kid in my dorm room, and I was talking to Lou Scheimer on the phone. At one point he stops and asks, "What else have you written? Have you written a lot of stuff and we just don't know your name?" That's when I told him I was nineteen and a junior in college. They asked me to make a few changes and they bought the script, and that's how I became a professional writer at the age of nineteen.

FRED BRONSON (writer, "The Counter-Clock Incident")

There was literally one episode left to be produced, the sixth of six for the second season, so I came up with this story line. Filmation bought it and NBC approved it, but I didn't put my name on it. I went to my boss to get permission, and he said I couldn't write for an NBC show. So, since I grew up in Culver City, I became John Culver, who I didn't know was a senator from Iowa at the time. No Google. I found out later. So they bought it and they made it.

The idea that there was a captain of the *Enterprise* before Pike was my idea, and when I thought of it I looked in the *Making of Star Trek* book, and there's a list of names that Gene considered: Pike, Kirk, and one of the names was Robert April. I liked that name, so that's what I named the character in this script. I made up the wife, Sarah April, and that she was the first doctor on the *Enterprise* and that was that.

> While everyone had high aspirations for the new series, the real question was how the fans—who had proven vociferous in their opinions—would respond to *Star Trek* in cartoon form.

HAL SUTHERLAND

Lou took a hit from the fans. They had no concept of the agony or effort that went into that show.

LOU SCHEIMER

Let's just say the fans were very . . . concerned.

DAVID GERROLD

Originally there was a lot of skepticism, but the folks at Filmation were very serious about doing a good job, and when we saw their first artwork, we began to think that maybe there was a chance to do something special. And it was *Star Trek*, of course, so our enthusiasm began to grow as we got into the job. There were still lots of stories we wanted to tell.

DOROTHY FONTANA

I went to the World Science Fiction Convention in Toronto and I had a reel of the opening of the *Enterprise* flyby. There were skeptics, but when we ran the reel, the fans cheered. From that little clip, they realized it was really going to be *Star Trek*. It was a triumphant moment after months of hearing it wouldn't be any good.

HAL SUTHERLAND

Eventually we had Trekkie invaders at the studio all the time. Trekkies showed up pretending to be fire inspectors or janitors, and we'd discover them searching through our wastebaskets.

DOROTHY FONTANA

In animation, they order a set number to begin with, like sixteen, and that's your first year. If you're going to do more, it is in increments of six, and then they rerun the life out of the earlier episodes. That's because of the time lag. Animation takes longer than live action, and you have to write a year ahead.

FRED BRONSON

The series was set for a premiere date of, ironically, September 8, 1973—the anniversary of *Star Trek*'s debut. But since George Takei was running for city council in Los Angeles and there were equal-time provisions from the FCC, his opponent said, "If you put this episode on, I will want equal time." Now, what did that mean? That he was going to do a voice-over in another animated show? It was kind of ridiculous, but it had an impact enough that KNBC Channel 4 pulled the episode in L.A. only, because it was a local race. And so *Star Trek: The Animated Series* premiered in L.A. on September 15 with "Yesteryear," the second episode. I made a big deal out of that . . . anything I could do to get attention from the press.

LOU SCHEIMER

If it aired today with the same ratings, it would be considered a whopping hit. But little kids didn't watch it. They weren't our audiences. I always hoped it would air at night. But *Star Trek* was difficult because it had limited budgets, loads of story, and several characters to juggle in twenty-two minutes.

MAJEL BARRETT

We wanted characters on the order of Disney rather than what we got, but the show featured some of the best stories of any *Star Trek* series.

LARRY BRODY

It was a grown-up show that talked about important topics without compromise. I appreciate that, because I work in animation and it's not that way. Most kid shows are infomercials for toys.

HOWARD WEINSTEIN

Obviously it was a simplified version of *Star Trek*, because with twenty-two minutes of story there's only so much you can do. But at the same time it wasn't Saturday-morning kiddie television. I was impressed enough with it that I thought, "Who am I to sniff at this and say it's not live-action *Star Trek*?" At that time, for all I knew, it might be the only chance I ever got to write for *Star Trek*, and I was going to grab it.

DAVID GERROLD

Arguments about "canon" are silly. I always felt that *Star Trek* animated was part of *Star Trek* because Gene Roddenberry accepted the paycheck for it and put his name on the credits. And D. C. Fontana—and all the other writers involved—busted their butts to make it the best *Star Trek* they could.

"Bem" did establish that Kirk's middle name was Tiberius. We were at a *Star Trek* convention and somebody asked Dorothy and I what was Kirk's middle name. I had just finished a book on Roman history and was still thinking Tiberius, and so it popped out of my head, "Tiberius." And the audience loved it, so later on when we were doing the animated show, which was a few months later, we passed it in front of Gene and he said, "Okay." When I did my *Star Trek* novel *The Galactic Whirlpool*, I explained how Kirk got that middle name, which was more of a nickname than a real middle name. You do things for the fun of it sometimes.

JEFF AYERS (author, *Voyages of Imagination: The Star Trek Fiction Companion*)

The success of the James Blish book series, in which he novelized episodes from the original show, paved the way for something similar for the animated series. Alan Dean Foster was asked to adapt the episodes into book form—the *Star Trek Log* series—and like Blish, he worked from the scripts instead of watching the episodes. He quickly realized that a twenty-minute cartoon would not translate well to a novel, so he convinced his editor at Ballantine, Judy-Lynn del Rey, to let him pursue a similar route of putting three scripts into each volume.

ALAN DEAN FOSTER (author, *Star Trek Log* series)

Besides adapting three scripts in each book, I realized what I would have to do was expand each of them into novella length and link a couple of them together in some fashion to make it flow as a book as best I could.

JEFF AYERS

The sales skyrocketed, and the end result was that his editor wanted four books out of the last four scripts. That's why the last ones are full-length stories. One of the ones he added in utilized a screenplay he had written for the fourth season of the original series that never happened.

ALAN DEAN FOSTER

When Judy-Lynn said I needed to adapt one script into each of the last four *Log* books, I said, "Look, if I could have done it, I would have done that in the first place." She wrote back and said, "You don't understand. We're going through multiple printings of these as fast as we can print them." Judy-Lynn was very persuasive. The only thing I could do was adapt those scripts as I had been doing, and then make the last two-thirds of each of those last four books original material.

For *Log* six, I had actually done a two-hour screenplay for the original TV series and submitted it to Roddenberry at Norway Productions. I got a very nice letter back from someone saying, "Thank you very much for your submission. We really like your teleplay. Please resubmit for the fourth season." Of course, there was no fourth season. That story was basically *Run Silent, Run Deep* in space. There was a lot of mental stuff going on between the crew of the *Enterprise* and the crew of the other ship. That's one of the places you have to work hard as a novelizer. It's very easy to novelize battles in space or a chase in space or a confrontation with an alien. But when you're dealing with people's thought processes, to get that down in a way that involves the reader can be more difficult, and that requires more work on the part of the writer. There was a great deal of that in that particular book. But because it wasn't technologically heavy, I didn't have to worry about updating that from the original script I'd written.

So when Judy told me about the last four books, I had this 120-page screenplay sitting around and she wanted these things as fast as possible. I said, "What can I do for the first one where I have to adapt one teleplay for that book?" For the last two-thirds, I used that screenplay. That helped me get into the proper writing frame of mind, using one teleplay for two-thirds original material.

The only one I had any real concern about was the Larry Niven script, "The Slaver Weapon." The reason for that is that I view all of my novelizations as collaborations between myself and the original writers, and I'm very respectful of the original writing. This was different, because Larry had used some of his own characters from his own prose in the teleplay for *Star Trek*. So it wasn't just a case of adapting a Larry Niven teleplay, it was the case of adapting Larry Niven's actual original material and working with it myself. Kind of like with a "shared world" anthology, except that Larry, just like David Gerrold and D. C. Fontana and everybody else, didn't have a say in what I was going to do. I was very, very careful not to mess around with the original material.

It hit me at that point that if adaptations of the animated series were selling *that* well to prompt that kind of reaction from a New York publisher, that there was something going on here beyond mere casual spin-offs of an old TV show. That was kind of the realization point for me that there was a lot more happening here in terms of *Star Trek* than maybe was obvious to a lot of people.

DOROTHY FONTANA

There is this tendency to put down animated work as kids' stuff, but you have to consider the artistry that went into it; not just the writer but the actors who made themselves available. And the artists who drew the show were really good. Animation is a way to do the original series without worrying about how old the actors are, or what they look like.

GENE RODDENBERRY

I think one can always wish something was done better, but within the limits of how animation is done—the speed it's done, the dollars they're able to put into it, and so on—it was a fairly good job. I think the best proof of that is the Emmy it won. *Star Trek* has a spectacular record of getting awards and special attention either while it's on or after it's been canceled.

The animated series was *not* a compromise. NBC wanted a strong show in their morning cartoon time slot and they were willing to go along with my demand that it not be written down to the kiddie level. I believe children are much more intelligent than people give them credit for, so we used *Star Trek* writers and had standard stories. It wasn't a pacifier, it was just an effort to do something a little better on Saturday mornings.

ROD RODDENBERRY

I'd love to redo the animated episodes. I mean, not me, but it would be so easy to redo them because of the talent available to do the CG. I think the animated series needs to be reborn and brought back out. That's one of the last things that my dad *didn't* do.

LOU SCHEIMER

I called Gene a few months before his death and said, "Gene, it's time. How about another animated *Star Trek*?" He agreed it was time and was very enthusiastic. But that's as far as it went.

LOST IN SPACE

When looking back at the history of *Star Trek* from today's perspective, it's hard to believe that the cast and crew ever enjoyed anything less than immense prosperity due to their long-term association with the franchise. The reality, however, was dramatically different. When the series ended in 1969, over the next few years there was a genuine financial struggle for most of them. The show was booming in syndication, but due to the way residuals were structured at the time, Screen Actors Guild payments were made for only the first five reruns of each episode. So while *Star Trek* was providing a financial windfall to Paramount, which had scooped up the show as part of their acquisition of Desilu, few others benefited.

Prior to *Star Trek*, William Shatner had carved an impressive niche for himself as an actor, having scored quite successfully on stage, screen, and television. But his most difficult time came immediately after his three-year-stint as Captain Kirk, following a divorce which left him in a precarious financial position. First up was his ubiquitous work as a commercial spokesman for Promise margarine, a less than auspicious career segue from the command seat of a starship. He followed with episodic television guest appearances, a starring role in the short-lived ABC series *Barbary Coast,* and a number of forgettable low-budget films, including *The Devil's Rain* and Roger Corman's *Big Bad Mama*.

"There was a time, before *Star Trek*, when I wouldn't accept a role that I didn't think worthwhile enough to play. Then, because things are so cyclical in show business, I needed to take those roles," Shatner explained in his biography, *Shatner: Where No Man*. "There even came a point when I thought, 'I don't know whether I'm ever going to break through, to get those roles that I think I should be playing.' That was just before *Star Trek*. *Star Trek* hit. And after *Star Trek* I had the opportunity to play a few of those things that I thought should be coming my way. But I was in a financial bind and had to accept a lot of things that I wouldn't have done in an earlier day."

Leonard Nimoy, who would have seemingly been the most typecast from *Star Trek,* actually went on to the most successful career of all the cast members during the ten-year period between cancellation and revival. He immediately shifted from Spock to a costarring role in the hit series *Mission: Impossible,* on which he played makeup genius Paris. He quit the series after two seasons to pursue other roles. "Quitting the show was kind of a dangerous thing to do, but I felt confident," he admitted. "But '71 was the first year out of six years of TV series and it turned out to be a perfect year with a mix of all the things I wanted to do." Among them was the film *Catlow* and the lead in the national touring company of *Fiddler on the Roof.* Eventually his career led him to tackle another "logical" character, that of Sherlock Holmes, onstage.

In addition, he began directing episodic television, narrated the syndicated series *In Search Of . . .* (having been hired after the first choice, Rod Serling, passed away), and received acclaim for his one-man show, *Vincent,* based on the life of Vincent van Gogh, as well as for the books of poetry he wrote and his starring Broadway role in *Equus.*

LEONARD NIMOY (actor, "Mr. Spock")

One of the reasons I was rather excited when I first made the move from *Trek* to *Mission: Impossible* was because *Mission* was the opposite of a radio drama [like *Star Trek*]. You had to watch the show. I was intrigued by that. It wasn't about dialogue, it was about images. But I very quickly became bored and I left after two years because there was no substance. I had a four-year contract. At the end of two years I felt I had made as much of a contribution as I could to the series, and it was getting redundant for me. I asked the studio to let me out of my contract and they agreed.

HAROLD LIVINGSTON (writer, *Star Trek: The Motion Picture*)

I used to play golf with Bruce Geller, and one day we're on our way to the golf course on a Saturday morning and he tells me that he just sold this series, *Mission: Impossible.* But he said, "I want to tell you I'm not going to hire you, because your forte is character and this isn't a show about character."

CHRISTOPHER KNOPF (friend of Gene Roddenberry)

Bruce Geller and Gene had offices one floor on top of each other. And they each were very competitive, and they made their offices almost like a throne room— big long offices that you sort of had to march up to the throne to meet either one of them. I wouldn't be surprised if they compared notes on how to do an office. Both of them also loved the ladies. Gene was very much a devotee of a free flow of passion. I think that there was no woman he would say no to. I remember Bruce's wife told him, "Look, it's either them or me," and Bruce backed off. But then he got killed. He was flying with a guy from ABC, who was a former navy pilot, going to Santa Barbara, and they didn't realize they were on the east side of a mountain. They thought they were on the west side and they flew right into it.

DeForest Kelley, who had the most successful pre-*Star Trek* career, conversely had the shortest and most inauspicious post-*Trek* career of any of the cast: he did a feature film called *Night of the Lepus*, about giant killer bunnies, and retired, with the exception of future *Trek* projects.

DeFOREST KELLEY (actor, "Dr. Leonard 'Bones' McCoy")

The stuff offered to me after the series ended was crap, and I thought, "I've done so much crap I don't need to do that again." Fortunately I learned a long time ago in this business that when you make some money, you had better put a little bit of it aside. I'm not talking about living in Bel Air; I'm talking about living a nice normal life.

James Doohan earned a living for himself throughout the seventies via the *Star Trek* convention circuit, as well as roles in such films as *Pretty Maids All in a Row* (written and produced by Roddenberry) and as a regular on the CBS Saturday-morning series *Jason of Star Command,* which he left after one season. "They really didn't give me anything to do so I said good-bye," he explained of his decision.

George Takei certainly diversified following *Star Trek,* not only appearing on a variety of television series but writing a pair of science-fiction–swashbuckler novels and throwing his hat into the Los Angeles political arena. Nichelle Nichols parlayed her *Star Trek* success as Lieutenant Uhura into a singing career and a position with NASA and its astronaut recruitment drive. "When I began," she pointed out, "NASA had fifteen hundred applications. Six months later, they had eight thousand. I like to think some of those were encouraged by me." Walter Koenig, like his costars, did his fair share of episodic television work following his two seasons as Chekov, and even costarred in the Gene Roddenberry television pilot *The Questor Tapes*. Additionally, he served as an acting teacher, directed plays, wrote novels, and penned the scripts for such prime-time television fare as *Family* and *What Really Happened to the Class of '65?* It's unlikely that the ensemble could have known in 1969 that their lives would continue to be drawn together over the next several decades.

Faring the worst of everyone in those days was Gene Roddenberry. He wrote and produced the disastrous feature *Pretty Maids All in a Row* (1971), which more or less sealed his fate as a television producer-writer. Despite being lauded by the likes of Quentin Tarantino, this absurd sexploitation film stars Rock Hudson as a promiscuous high-school gym teacher who sleeps with many of his female students and may possibly be a serial murderer.

IRA STEVE BEHR (executive producer, *Star Trek: Deep Space Nine*)

Pretty Maids All in a Row was one hoot of a movie. That's an amazing film on a lot of levels. That's a movie that's almost beyond good and evil.

Shortly thereafter, he created a pair of pilots–*Genesis II* (1973) and *Planet Earth* (1974)–which postulated a future following a devastating global war in which twentieth-century scientist Dylan Hunt (Alex Cord in the former, John Saxon in the latter) works with a scientific organization, PAX, to rebuild society. "It's important to know that I wasn't saying that *Star Trek*'s future, which would oc-cur several hundred years after *Genesis II*, never happened," Roddenberry ex-plained. "I'm saying that humanity has always progressed by three steps forward and two steps back. The entire history of our civilization has been one society crumbling and a slightly better one, usually, being built on top of it. And on mankind's bumpy way to *Star Trek*'s era, we passed through this time, too." Al-though both came close to being picked up for series, the networks ultimately passed on them and, in the case of *Genesis II*, CBS ordered the short-lived *Planet of the Apes* as a TV series instead.

   The best of Roddenberry's seventies pilots was 1974's *The Questor Tapes*, written with Gene L. Coon shortly before his death, in which Roddenberry conceived of an alien race that had spent eons helping mankind's progress by placing humanlike androids within society to help guide the species. This tele-vision pilot presented Dr. Jerry Robinson (Mike Farrell), who ultimately teams up with an android named Questor (Robert Foxworth), who is on a quest to meet with his creator, Professor Vaslovic, and discover the truth about himself as well as his ultimate destiny. While NBC commissioned additional scripts, they ulti-mately decided to pass on taking the show to series, after the familiar creative differences with Roddenberry arose. Unfortunately, creative differences of an-other kind arose between Roddenberry and Leonard Nimoy after the *Star Trek* creator implied to Nimoy that he would star in the pilot. When he reneged on that promise, it contributed to the strained relationship that would typify their mutual dealings for the rest of their lives.

RICHARD COLLA (director, *The Questor Tapes*)

It was a wonderful experience for me. We were kind of reinterpreting Spock and Kirk, because that's really what it was, the emotional side of man and the intel-lectual side of man, and they come into conversation with each other. So what you really have is a character talking to himself, and that's delightful. I thought Questor's going off to find his creator was meant to be strong. It was meant to be moving. I'm sorry it never got made into a series.

Roddenberry's last attempt at creating a new TV series not connected to *Star Trek* was *Spectre* (1977), in which renowned criminologist and occult investigator William Sebastian (Robert Culp) and his old friend Dr. Hamilton (Gig Young) find themselves in England for a case involving the black arts. There was absolutely no talk of this pilot going to series.

Unfortunately, it would seem that Roddenberry's well-documented battles with—and disparaging remarks regarding—the networks during *Star Trek*'s run and in the years immediately following it, when appearing at conventions or earning a living by doing college lectures, didn't help in securing him any new long-term work.

DAVID GERROLD (story editor, *Land of the Lost*)

During the early seventies NBC was the villain, because they had canceled *Star Trek,* and Gene made sure that everybody knew that NBC was the villain. Gene was this man who wanted to change the world for the better, and NBC wouldn't let him.

JOEL ENGEL (author, *Gene Roddenberry: The Myth and the Man Behind Star Trek*)

Gene Roddenberry was, first and foremost, an ambitious salesman whose primary talent, I believe, was verbal. I admire that he flew during the war and afterward. That he made a good impression on [LAPD] Chief Parker [who he was a speechwriter for], I know from my last book, *L.A. '56*—which takes place during Parker's reign and makes him a fleshed-out secondary character—shouldn't be considered a small feat. He knew how to tell Parker everything he wanted to hear. And when he saw an opening to get into TV, where a lot of hustlers were doing well, he took it. Good for him.

He obviously had talent; those without it couldn't sell more than one script, and he sold a lot of them. And when he did, and saw guys like Sam Rolfe hitting it big, he wanted a piece of that, too. Good for him there, as well. It wasn't easy getting a series on the air, which he did with *The Lieutenant.* Then, good for him for trying to get *Star Trek* on the air. Terrific idea: *Wagon Train* to the stars. The problem was that he basically couldn't write well enough to carry it off. Lucky for him, and I do mean lucky, NBC broke protocol and allowed Desilu to shoot a second pilot, at which point Roddenberry knew enough not to argue that a bona fide writer needed to be brought in. Thus began his career as a producer rather than a writer-producer.

ROD RODDENBERRY (son of Gene Roddenberry)

I started reading my father's speeches and then I actually read a couple books about him, the good and the bad. Joel Engel did a book that kind of trashed my father and it was really good to get that perspective, too, since I knew my father as a real man. I knew his flaws, his weak points, but I knew he was a man. No matter how great someone is, they are flawed and fucked up in their own ways. So, it didn't bother me at all. I accept that of anyone. It bothers me now because I hear it so much.

JON POVILL (associate producer, *Star Trek: The Motion Picture*)

Gene's issue was that he was more of a producer than he was a writer. His skill set was better suited to that, mostly because he was desperate to prove that he was a writer. He was not secure at all about it. He would fall back on "I was the creator of *Star Trek,* I know what I'm doing," but like any writer, 80 percent of his ideas were crap. Eighty percent of *my* ideas are crap. But 20 percent of his ideas were really, really good. The issue was that he was sufficiently insecure to where he fought as hard for the 80 percent as he did the 20 percent. It wasn't a matter of quality control, it was a matter of *control.* It was a matter of exerting his will. It was a matter of being *the one.* Like George Bush: "I've got to be the decider." He needed to be in control of the script, of the idea, of the concept, to the greatest degree possible.

Gene's personality was all "It's got to be my way, because I'm right and I have to *prove* that I'm right." To some extent *Star Trek* proved that he was right, except to the extent that there were other people involved that may or may have had important roles. I heard that Gene Coon was essentially responsible for keeping the show on an even keel and maintaining the quality of it. If you look at the episodes Gene wrote, you start to get the picture of somebody who was very up and down. You can look at those scripts, and there are bits and pieces of scripts that are exactly what I said—20 percent of a script like "The Omega Glory" is good, but 80 percent isn't. He couldn't let go of anything, because it all had to be good because he had to *prove* it was good.

JOEL ENGEL

It's always worth remembering that the *Star Trek* universe we know today, with the Klingons and Romulans and Spock's family, etc., were introduced one element at a time by freelancers and Gene Coon and the great Dorothy Fontana. When the series went off the air, Gene had to reinvent himself again, which he tried to do by buying the talents of other writers—for instance, Jon Povill.

LARRY BRODY (cocreator, *The New Mike Hammer*)

I was a very successful working writer-producer in the seventies. I had a lot on my plate, so my first reaction to the growing *Star Trek* phenomenon was "Good for Gene." I felt invested in Roddenberry on a personal level, because whenever he had a deal somewhere, he would call me and talk to me about what the new shows were going to be and ask me to write for them. I felt flattered as hell by the attention, which was, I think, one of the big secrets of his success. He had so much energy and was so excited about whatever he was doing that the feeling transferred right into everyone around him.

RICHARD ARNOLD (*Star Trek* archivist)

He *was* the "Great Bird," a name Bob Justman had given him during the production of the original series. His generosity, sense of humor, and brilliance were all there for anyone to see. Yes, Gene was human, but I found him to be a better man to me than my own father had been, and he showed me more personal friendship than I could ever have asked for.

ED NAHA (producer, *Inside Star Trek* LP)

Gene had been treated very shabbily by Paramount all during the initial run of *Trek*, especially during the final season, and his TV movies were never viewed with a lot of enthusiasm by the "suits." Yet Gene kept plugging away. He had views he wanted to spread, dreams he wanted to share, and so he played the corporate game in order to keep those ideas in the spotlight.

JON POVILL

Shortly after I came out of school, I tried to get in to see Roddenberry about *Genesis II* and *Questor*, which he had going and were in their early stages. I had done a script for Ron Shusett. The first thing I did when I got out of school was write a script for him. It never got made, but that became a sample script. I gave it to Gene's assistant and it took about a year to get the fucking script read. When he finally *did* read it, it was because he had given it to D. C. Fontana. She liked it and recommended that he read it, which he did. By that time *Genesis II* was already gone, and *Questor* was still going, so I got to pitch episodes to *Questor*. I'd pitched to Larry Alexander, who was the story editor. He liked it and we were just getting ready to give it to the producer, Michael Rhodes, when *Questor* died.

LARRY BRODY

Gene was also a big user of the "we" word whenever he and I were together, including me in all his thoughts and plans and making me feel a part of whatever team he was putting together. During this time I was often invited to hang out with Gene and listen to his stories of how he was surviving—barely, he said—now that *Star Trek* was off the air. He'd kept the rights to all the paraphernalia used on the show, and a large part of his income, he told me, came from selling scripts, communicator pins, phasers, etc. All genuine and used in the production. It seemed to me that he was selling a lot more of that stuff than ever could've been made for the actual series, but I never said anything about that to him.

JON POVILL

I got a call some weeks later from Gene, who mentioned that he was moving off the Warner Bros. lot and back into his house, and he was going to do a book. He asked if I wanted to do research for him at some minimal, god-awful salary and I said, "Absolutely."

It was the period of time that I was closest to Gene in that year from about July of '74 to about May of '75. May of '75 is when he moved back into his Paramount offices to do the new *Star Trek* movie. It was a great period of time. The most personal. He was not doing well financially, but he was a real person. He did not see himself as the Great Bird of the Galaxy yet. He was running Lincoln, and he and Majel were making money from Lincoln Enterprises, and he was making money from *Star Trek* conventions, but there was less bullshit and more honesty. And despite the age difference and the obvious career difference, we were relating in many ways as equals. One of the more uncomfortable aspects of that is that he and Majel would fight constantly; they would drink and they would fight. The two of them would pull me into their arguments to try and mediate those. I was having dinner there practically every night. I would play with Rod.

JOEL ENGEL

What I can say with sincere admiration about Gene Roddenberry is that when the festival circuit reached critical mass, he knew enough to remake himself yet again as the Great Bird. It was a persona and, from what I could tell, until I took his words and boasts and compared them to the actual record, no one had publicly called him out on it. By then he'd become Machiavellian, sitting on a lucrative brand with millions of fans willing to do his bidding.

JON POVILL

Gene and I would sit around, we'd talk, bullshit, we'd speculate. We were pretty much just hanging out all of the time. We'd smoke pot. We'd swim. That was part of the most magical time to me. I really loved that period of time. He had all sorts of issues and was feeling insecure, but he was open about it. And he was *not* enthusiastic about *Star Trek* at the time. He really wanted to do something else. It was, again, the idea of trying to prove himself, not that he was aware he was proving himself. He was sort of desperate to show he could do something besides *Star Trek*. That came out as "I don't care about *Star Trek*, I want to move on."

Anyhow, while I was doing the research and while we were talking, he discovered that prior to this I was making my living doing part-time carpentry and contracting. Handyman stuff. At that point, when he decided he didn't want to write the novel anymore, he wanted me to baby-proof the house. I did that so that he wouldn't have to say no to Rod all of the time, and then there were other things that I did. I painted fences and repaired stuff on an ongoing basis.

Despite being busy on the convention and college-lecture circuit, Roddenberry had a family to support, and without a regular Hollywood income, it was becoming harder to sustain his lavish lifestyle. As a result, he was forced to leverage his fame as the creator of *Star Trek* into a succession of high-paying, albeit oddball, gigs that all eventually went nowhere.

One of them was *The Nine,* which came about in 1975 when Roddenberry was approached by a British former race-car driver named Sir John Whitmore. Whitmore claimed to be associated with a strange organization called Lab-9, dedicated to the research of paranormal phenomena that also claimed to be in contact with a group of extraterrestrials called the "Council of Nine," or simply "The Nine." Whitmore, along with channeler Phyllis Schlemmer, wanted to hire Roddenberry to write a screenplay based on the Council of Nine's imminent heralded return.

SUSAN SACKETT (assistant to Gene Roddenberry)

This was a time when he was broke and was sort of a writer for hire. A very eccentric Englishman had an idea for a project that aliens really had contacted us and that they were from the Pleiades. And he wanted Gene to write a fictional story about this based on what he called "facts." Gene said he will write what he finds. He had to do all of this research. Gene went around and talked to all these different people, and they were experimenting with plants and asking whether or not they had feelings, and things like that. Gene was trying to keep an open mind.

GENE RODDENBERRY (creator, executive producer, *Star Trek*)

I had been through harsh times. My dreams were going downhill, because I could not get work after the original series was canceled. I remember I was really devoted to the fans at colleges when they voted that they wanted me to come and lecture. One of my first speeches—I got all of six or seven hundred dollars, which included the cost of the trip. I felt lucky to net the four or five hundred that they paid for me. I was stereotyped as a science-fiction writer, and sometimes it was tough to pay the mortgage. They said, "You're a science-fiction type." I said, "Hey, wait a minute. I used to write westerns, I wrote police stories," and they said, "No, you're now science fiction." I don't feel bitter about that. That's the way Hollywood is and that's the way mediocre people think.

> Roddenberry handed in his first draft in December 1975, and the results were not what *anyone* expected. The story focused more on his fictionalized alter ego and his marital and financial worries than on the Nine themselves. Whitmore requested a rewrite and Roddenberry handed the task of doing so to Povill. In his revision, Povill posited that the hit sci-fi TV show that Roddenberry's alter ego had produced in the sixties was not actually his work but had been channeled through him by the Council of Nine.

HAROLD LIVINGSTON

This was a script that Roddenberry was very proud of. It dealt with a man who developed a television series for a big network. It had gone off the air and he was depressed. He had kind of gone insane. I read this script and the hair began to rise on the back of my neck, because that's *his* story. He was totally unaware of what he was writing. He was also writing his various sexual perversions, which I certainly don't hold a grudge against, because I've got my own problems. But there's something very, very amiss there.

JON POVILL

When I read Gene's first draft, I thought, "This is not what needs to be done here." I thought it was embarrassing, John Whitmore thought it was embarrassing. It certainly didn't suit what they needed, but it was very typical Roddenberry stuff. I changed it substantially in my second draft and continued to evolve it. I thought the last draft was eminently workable. We had a script that people would be interested in, and it served the purposes of fandom and commerciality and The Nine, from the Schlemmer-Whitmore perspective. They approached Gene because The Nine told them to.

> One of the more intriguing projects Roddenberry became involved with at the time was a collaboration with music legend Paul McCartney, who was not only a former Beatle but a major *Star Trek* fan.

SUSAN SACKETT

I have no idea whatever happened to that. It's probably stuck in a file, like the end of *Raiders of the Lost Ark*. Paul contacted him and was a *Star Trek* fan. He invited us to a concert, which was great, and we met him backstage, which was fun. Paul hired Gene to write a story about the band, which was Wings at the time, and it was a crazy story. Paul gave him an outline and Gene was supposed to do something with it. It was bands from outer space and they were having a competition. Gene was open to things at this point; *Star Trek* wasn't happening and he wasn't getting his scripts produced and he had a family to feed. It's kind of fun when Paul McCartney contacts you. Gene began working on it and it was about the time they started talking about bringing *Trek* back, so he never got to complete anything for Paul.

JON POVILL

In May of 1975, Paramount expressed interest in developing a *Star Trek* film, so Gene moved back into his old office on the lot. He brought me in to carry boxes down from the garage. All of the old crap from the original series he wanted back in the office. I brought boxes from his garage to Paramount. Interestingly, one of my friends came to help as well. Gene would diet from time to time and he had just lost a bunch of weight. He was hauling a box out of the garage and up into the house to go through them. My friend was carrying a box behind Gene, who was carrying a box, and Gene's pants fell down [*laughs*] and there he was, bare-assed.

Another idea for a *Star Trek* motion picture that was briefly announced and abandoned ironically presaged J. J. Abrams's 2009 film by several decades (as well as Harve Bennett's ill-fated *The Academy Years,* which had met with much derision from Roddenberry as well as the original cast), in which the show's iconic ensemble would be united for the first time.

Roddenberry, who had been talking about the idea in public since the 1968 World Science Fiction Convention, described his idea for the prequel to *Circus* magazine in 1975. "Most of it is in my head now," he offered. "People have been asking me for years how the whole thing came about. How did Spock meet Kirk and Scotty? How did the whole crew get together and reach the point where the television series began?"

WALTER KOENIG (actor, "Pavel Chekov")

In a conversation with George, Jimmy, or Nichelle they mentioned having received a letter from Gene saying, "Welcome aboard, we're going to go forward and do this new movie." I didn't receive a letter. I called up Susan Sackett, who said I was worrying unnecessarily and that even though Gene was out of town, she would speak to him by phone and he would reassure me. Well, he didn't call me until he got back to town, and he told me that this idea he had was going to take place three years before the five-year mission and since six years had transpired since the series and my character to begin with was already nine years younger than I was, they thought that I was too old to play myself. Then he said something that they would try to use me as Chekov's father, which would have been a kick. But, again, it was kind of a painful situation realizing that there were no concrete plans for using Chekov in that movie.

Abandoning the prequel idea, Roddenberry began work on a treatment for what would eventually be called *The God Thing,* in which *Admiral* Kirk would reassemble the crew to stop an entity on course for Earth that claims to be God. The ship turns out to be a living computer programmed by a race that was "cast out" of its own dimension and into ours. The story ends with the "God" entity miraculously granting our crew newfound youth and returning them back to the original five-year mission.

While many vestiges of *The God Thing* can be found in *Star Trek: The Motion Picture,* it's even more surprising to see how similar many elements are to William Shatner's *Star Trek V: The Final Frontier,* a film Roddenberry vociferously denounced throughout its production.

JON POVILL

The fact that *The God Thing* never got produced could have been the reason Gene hated the idea of *Star Trek V.*

SUSAN SACKETT

There was an entirely different story in which there was going to be some kind of creature that was going to claim to be God and turn out to be the Devil. It was a morality play. It was very esoteric and the studio turned it down. At one point it was going to be novelized, but it didn't come about.

WILLIAM SHATNER (actor, "James T. Kirk")

I was working on the series *Barbary Coast* at the time, which was done at Paramount. It was on one end of Paramount, and *Star Trek* had been filmed at the other end of Paramount. I had never, for the longest time, revisited the stage area where [we had] filmed. So one day I decided to go there, [and] as I'd been walking and remembering the times, I suddenly heard the sound of a typewriter! That was the strangest thing, because these offices were deserted. So I followed the sound, till I came to the entrance of this building. And the sound was getting louder as I went into the building. I went down a hallway, where the offices for *Star Trek* were . . . I opened the door and there was Gene Roddenberry!

He was sitting in a corner, typing. I hadn't seen him in five years. I said, "Gene, the series has been canceled!" He said, "I know, I know the series has been canceled. I'm writing the movie!" So I said, "There's gonna be a movie? What's it gonna be about?" He said, "First of all, we have to explain how you guys got older. So what we have to do is move everybody up in a rank. You become an admiral, and the rest of the cast become Starfleet commanders. One day a force comes toward Earth—might be God, might be the Devil—breaking everything in its path, except the minds of the starship commanders. So we gotta find all the original crewmen for the starship *Enterprise*, but first—where is Spock? He's back on

Vulcan, doing R & R; five-year mission, seven years of R & R. He swam back up-stream. So we gotta go get him." So we get Spock, do battle, and it was a great story, but the studio turned it down.

JON POVILL

The novel Gene had hired me to do research on was *The God Thing,* but it *wasn't* a *Star Trek* novel. I was researching stuff that would later appear in *Close Encounters:* How would the planet react? How would the military react? What would the interaction likely be at this stage in terms of if we discovered a ship and extraterrestrials in orbit around our planet? How would we deal with it? I was trying to ascertain that kind of stuff.

It was an original novel using all different characters, but the premise of it was that this big starship—shades of V'ger!—comes back to Earth and it hadn't been here since Christ's time, and it turns out that the starship interacts with planets by ascertaining the level society is at and providing a prophet that suits that level of development. Then it can interact and advance society in some way or another, contrary to the Prime Directive. But now this spaceship malfunctions and instead of ascertaining where we are now, it delivers us Christ again.

RICHARD COLLA

Gene showed me that script, which was much more daring than *Star Trek: The Motion Picture* would be. The *Enterprise* went off in search of that thing from outer space that was affecting everything. By the time they got into the alien's presence, it manifested itself and said, "Do you know me?" Kirk said, "No, I don't know who you are." It said, "Strange, how could you not know who I am?" So it shift-changed and became another image and said, "Do you know me?" Kirk said, "No, who are you?" It said, "Strange, how could you not know who I am?" So it shift-changed and came up in the form of Christ the carpenter, and says, "Do you know me?" and Kirk says, "Oh, *now* I know who you are."

JON POVILL

It probably would have brought *Star Trek* down, because the Christian Right, even though it wasn't then what it is now, would have just destroyed it. In fact, he started the script under one Paramount administration and handed it to another, to Barry Diller, who was a devout Catholic. There was no way on Earth that that script was going to fly for a devout Catholic.

RICHARD COLLA

Really, what Gene had written was that this "thing" was sent forth to lay down the law, to communicate the law of the universe, and that as time went on, the law was meant to be reinterpreted. And at that time two thousand years earlier, the law was interpreted by the carpenter image. As time went on, the law was meant to be reinterpreted and the Christ figure was meant to reappear in different forms. But this machine malfunctioned, and it was like a phonograph record that got caught in a groove and kept grooving back, grooving back, grooving back. It's important to understand the essence of all this and reinterpret it as time goes on. That was a little heavy for Paramount. It was meant to be strong and moving, and I'm sorry it never got made.

GENE RODDENBERRY

Actually, it wasn't God they were meeting, but someone who had been born here on Earth before, *claiming* to be God. I was going to say that this false thing claiming to be God had screwed up man's concept of the real infinity and beauty of what God is. Paramount was reluctant to put that up on the screen, and I can understand that position.

JON POVILL

He jumped at the chance to do this *Star Trek* film, because he needed the money. It was also always about proving something, so he was going to prove that it was no fluke. He was ambivalent about *Star Trek* at the time and grew to be enthusiastic, and became ambivalent when they threw it out. It was a love-hate relationship he had with the project, because it was his only big success.

Over the decades there were reportedly a number of attempts to novelize *The God Thing*, among the potential authors Susan Sackett and Fred Bronson, Roddenberry official biographer David Alexander, *Trek* star Walter Koenig, and in the version that came the closest to fruition, Michael Jan Friedman's adaptation for Pocket Books.

DAVID STERN (former *Star Trek* editor at Pocket Books)

We definitely wanted to make *The God Thing* part of the twenty-fifth-anniversary celebrations in 1991, and had been talking to Gene about doing that. My first memories of *The God Thing* really date to the period after Gene's death. Gene's lawyer, Leonard Maizlish, and I had several meetings, including a couple with Majel Barrett, regarding the manuscript.

The manuscript existed as a very long treatment, much more of a film treatment than a book. I had proposed Mike Friedman as the person to expand that treatment into a novel, because Mike was not only a good writer, but someone very, very used to the approvals process at that point. He could take a no and work with it. Which is what happened a couple times.

MICHAEL JAN FRIEDMAN (author)

Gene had written a script for the first *Star Trek* movie. Certain elements showed up in *Star Trek: The Motion Picture,* but most did not. So there was this mysterious script floating around that people talked about as if it were the Dead Sea Scrolls.

After I had written several successful *Trek* novels, *Trek* editor Dave Stern asked me to turn Gene's efforts into a novel called *The God Thing.* To the best of my recollection, I received both the script and a short narrative version of it. Naturally I jumped at the chance to translate and expand it. Gene was—and still is—one of my heroes, for God's sake, no pun intended. As he had already left the land of the living, this was a unique opportunity to collaborate with him. But when I read the material, I was *dismayed.* I hadn't seen other samples of Gene's unvarnished writing, but what I saw this time could not possibly have been his best work. It was disjointed—scenes didn't work together, didn't build toward anything meaningful. Kirk, Spock, and McCoy didn't seem anything like themselves. There was some mildly erotic, midlife crisis stuff in there that didn't serve any real purpose. In the climactic scene, Kirk had a fistfight with an alien who had assumed the image of Jesus Christ.

So Kirk was slugging it out on the bridge. With Jesus.

DAVID STERN

We worked up an outline, Leonard [Maizlish] and Majel looked at it, and said the things Friedman added here (subplots, etc., necessary to expand the treatment to novel length) are not reflective of what Gene intended. And that got frustrating, because we weren't getting specific enough feedback to know which direction to go in. And the manuscript—Gene's treatment—definitely needed more. There was the added complication—though I suspect this wasn't as much of a worry at the time—that a lot of themes in that treatment Gene had subsequently addressed in *Star Trek: The Motion Picture* and in his *TNG* work, and that *Star Trek V* had touched on some similar themes as well.

I believe what happened then—after a couple go-rounds—is that the project was simply allowed to die. I don't know for certain, though, because by that point I had left *Trek*.

MICHAEL JAN FRIEDMAN

Gene's feelings about organized religion had made their way into other *Trek* episodes and movies. In these other cases, his comments were more measured, more considered; they worked in the context of the story, making a point about our place in the universe. I don't think that happened in *The God Thing*. The best *Star Trek* is about ultimately embracing the alien and unfamiliar. This took the opposite tack. I discussed the problem with Dave Stern. Pocket had already invested in the project, even designed a dust jacket, so we decided I would come up with a coherent novel outline that incorporated as many elements of Gene's script as possible. I did this. However, Majel, Gene's widow, wasn't on board with what I had done. She insisted that Gene's script be expanded into a novel-length narrative, period. No changes, no substantive additions, no embellishments.

This was, of course, her prerogative. After all, she was Gene's widow. And I could have tried to do what she was asking—just stretch out the scenes to take up more pages. Certainly, it would have been a healthy payday for me. The print run was slated to be *enormous*. But public scrutiny of this story in anything approximating its original form would not have put Gene or his legacy in a good light. It would not have put me in a good light. And it would not have put Pocket in a good light. In the end, after discussions with Majel and after entertaining the possibility of using one other writer, Pocket agreed with my assessment and scrapped the project.

I wish it had turned out otherwise. But you know, all things considered, it's probably better this way.

JON POVILL

Gene went to work on *The God Thing* in May of 1975, and it was his first attempt at a *Star Trek* feature. By August it was shitcanned by Paramount president Barry Diller. Gene, who had gotten to know me pretty well by then, suggested that I take a crack at writing a treatment, which I did. Then he and I worked on a treatment together.

Treatment One was a spec story that I did after Gene told me that the studio had turned down *The God Thing*—which was *not* the actual title of his script, just what the script has come to be called since then. So, Gene told me it'd been rejected and told me that if I wanted to come up with a *Star Trek* movie story of my own, he'd be happy to look at it and to pass it along if he thought it was worthy. What I didn't know at the time was that about seven hundred thousand other writers had been told the same thing and that some of them (I think) were being paid to come up with their ideas. Amongst them . . . not sure, but I think there was Harlan Ellison, Norman Spinrad, John D. F. Black, Richard Matheson, and Ted Sturgeon. And probably others from outside the *Trek* universe.

In this story, planet Vulcan passes through an area of space in which they had previously released a "psychic cloud" that—they believed—would fill the enemy with distrust that would break down all military discipline and create chaos within the enemy ranks. They had done this in the final war that they'd fought, a war in which things were going so poorly that they were forced to release the cloud prematurely, without full testing that would have revealed the damn thing only worked on Vulcans. But as with most weapons, it's only a matter of time before whatever you came up with winds up being used against you—only in this case it was more a matter of the movement of star systems bringing Vulcan into this area of space. Interestingly, in order for Spock to be free of the influence of the cloud, he has to focus himself totally on the human half of his being—and he remains human and quirky for the majority of the story.

Ultimately, the *Enterprise* must go back in time to the final Vulcan war in an attempt to prevent the release of the cloud. When they fail to do so, Spock uses the equipment to send out a psychic cloud of his own—of logic, trust, restraint, and respect that effectively counteracts the effects of the initial cloud. And the *Enterprise* turns the tide in the war against the ancient foe so that Vulcan is not conquered or destroyed. I gave it to Gene sometime in late August or early September of 1975. He read it and said it would have made a swell episode, but that he didn't think it would work as a feature.

In December of 1975, he called me and said he had a new idea for a feature, would I like to work on it with him? I still remember standing in my kitchen and hanging up the phone after I said yes, and then whooping so loudly that my neighbors came running over to see what the hell was going on.

The result of that call was Treatment Two, which certainly seemed at the time to be my "big break." It was my first work for a studio—yes, I took over Gene Coon's old office (for the first time; I'd lose it and get it back again many times in the next four years)—and Paramount paid me for my efforts on it. The story has numerous elements in common with Treatment One, which at the time led me to believe that Gene's "new" idea had been inspired by my spec story, though he never said as much to me and so I have nothing to go on but my own presumption. In this one, rather than Spock being responsible for the change in Vulcan personality from hot-blooded warriors to peaceful beings ruled by logic, Scotty is responsible for wiping the Earth out of the Federation. The *Enterprise* and all aboard it had been destroyed by a black hole while Spock and Scotty, in smaller research vessels without the gravitational disrupting issues of warp engines, had managed to escape. Scotty, in a desperate attempt to go back in time and prevent his precious ship and crew from slipping into the event horizon, miscalculates, winds up in 1937, and triggers changes with a snowball effect.

His efforts to stop the snowball only make things worse for his original time period, though they do make things considerably better between 1937 and 1964. World War II is avoided, Kennedy is not assassinated, medical science advances substantially and a whole bunch of other boons make it impossible for world leaders to agree to help Kirk set things right for the future by plunging the twentieth century back into the horrors stored in the *Enterprise*'s history records. Kennedy, however, recognizes the greater good and helps Kirk destroy his world to create the better one. There's also a cool bit of stuff as Einstein along with Churchill, Kennedy, Hitler, and others tour the *Enterprise*.

As I read the two treatments, I felt like both of the concepts had merit. Treatment Two had a really great way of reintroducing most of the main characters—who are dead as the movie starts, but are literally resurrected by a mysterious process in some way related to the black hole. Both stories needed a lot of reworking, but there was potential there. If the studio had any real sense of what *Star Trek* was about and why it worked, they might have shown more patience, but the plug was quickly pulled and Treatment Two was rejected by the studio.

JOHN D. F. BLACK (story editor, *Star Trek*)

I came up with a story concept involving a black hole, and this was *before* Disney's film. The black hole had been used by several planets in a given constellation as a garbage dump. But with a black hole there's a point of equality. In other words, when enough positive matter comes into contact with an equal amount of negative matter, the damn thing blows up. Well, if that ever occurs with a black hole, it's the end of the universe. It will swallow *everything*. The *Enterprise* discovered what's happened with this particular black hole, and they try to stop these planets from unloading into it. The planets won't do it. It comes to war in some areas and as a result, the black hole comes to balance and blows up. At that point, it would continue to chew up matter. In 106 years Earth would be swallowed by this black hole, and the *Enterprise* is trying to beat the end of the world. There were at least twenty sequels in that story, because the jeopardy keeps growing more intense.

Paramount rejected the idea. They said it wasn't big enough.

JAMES VAN HISE (editor, *Enterprise Incidents*)

The story that Harlan came up with was never written down but presented verbally. The story did not begin with any of the *Enterprise* crew but started on Earth where strange phenomenon were inexplicably occurring. In India, a building where a family is having dinner just vanishes into dust. In the United States, one of the Great Lakes suddenly vanishes, wreaking havoc. In a public square, a woman suddenly screams and falls to the pavement where she transforms into some sort of reptilian creature.

The truth is suppressed, but the Federation realizes that someone or something is tampering with time and changing things on Earth in the far distant past. What is actually happening involves an alien race on the other end of the galaxy. Eons ago, Earth and this planet both developed races of humans and intelligent humanoid reptiles. On Earth, the humans destroyed the reptile men and flourished. In the time of the *Enterprise,* when the race learns what happened on Earth in the remote past, they decide to change things in the past so that they will have a kindred planet. For whatever reason, the Federation decides that only the *Enterprise* and her crew are qualified for this mission, so a mysterious cloaked figure goes about kidnapping the old central crew. The figure is finally revealed to be Kirk. After they are reunited, they prepare for the mission into the past to save Earth. And that would have been just the first half hour of the film!

In a tenth-anniversary article on *Star Trek* that appeared in *Crawdaddy!* magazine, Ellison elaborated: "My involvement with the film amounted to bullshit," he said. "It was the kind of bullshit you get from amateurs and independents but you don't expect from a major studio like Paramount. They don't know what they're doing over there. Gene may know, but the studio sure doesn't. They called me in on four separate occasions and they never paid me a nickel. I did one complete script that Gene liked. It was rejected. We worked on another idea together. We took it up to the executive who was in charge of the film, the head guy who, by the way, has never produced a film in his life. He's an ex-designer—right away you know where *he's* coming from.

"Now, the guy is a complete and utter moron. We're showing him the script and he's just read a von Däniken book about the Aztec calendar and how the Aztec gods were from outer space. He looks at us and says, 'Do you think you can put in something about the Aztecs?' Agghhh. And we're saying, 'Look. This story takes place at the dawn of time. There weren't any Aztecs then!' He doesn't flinch. 'How about one or two?' What can you do? These people are schmucks."

Author Robert Silverberg also wrote a treatment. Titled *The Billion-Year Voyage*, it was more of an intellectual foray as the *Enterprise* crew discovers the ruins of an ancient but far more advanced civilization, and must battle other aliens in order to take possession of the wondrous gifts left behind. Gifts which would surely benefit mankind some day in the future when they are ready to accept that responsibly.

ROBERT SILVERBERG (author, *Lord Valentine's Castle*)

My *Star Trek* involvement was minimal. I never wrote for the show, rarely watched it, and was quite surprised when Paramount unexpectedly asked me to take a shot at the screenplay for the first movie. I met with the Paramount executives, pitched an idea based on a book of mine called *Across a Billion Years,* was asked to write a treatment, wrote it, was paid quite generously for it, and then vanished from the scene when the project was canceled.

Perhaps the greatest "what if" in the history of the franchise is auteur Philip Kaufman's (*The Right Stuff, Invasion of the Body Snatchers*) proposed *Star Trek* feature film, *Planet of the Titans,* which featured a script from British screenwriters Chris Bryant and Allan Scott (whose credits included the acclaimed Nicolas Roeg film *Don't Look Now*), later rewritten by Kaufman himself. While the British screenwriters came to America, Gene Roddenberry was about to leave the country for Britain to shoot his supernatural *Spectre* pilot.

Despite not even having completed a script, the writing team was already being asked to attend *Star Trek* conventions, prompting the two writers to ask Roddenberry what to do. His response: "Forget it! Trekkie teenyboppers lurk outside your room at night yearning to meet you and talk about science. If you must go to one of these, our main concern is that you keep your fly zipped up while on platform."

Star Trek was viewed as a priority at Paramount, particularly after the first space shuttle, originally called the *Constitution,* was renamed the *Enterprise.* This prompted Paramount to take out a full-page ad in *The New York Times* proclaiming, "Starship *Enterprise* will be joining the space shuttle *Enterprise* in its space travels very soon. Early next year, Paramount Pictures begins filming an extraordinary motion picture adventure—*Star Trek*. Now we can look forward to two great space adventures." Ironically, neither would ever take off.

DAVID V. PICKER (president of motion pictures, Paramount Pictures)

Of all the films I developed, acquired, or green-lit while I was at Paramount, there was just one project that I was simply not interested in: [chairman of Gulf & Western, which then owned Paramount] Charlie Bludhorn's favorite—a movie based on *Star Trek*. Obviously, character and story are the main ingredients, and in this show the futuristic but accessible world that was portrayed played an important role. But I disliked sci-fi. I didn't like sci-fi books, movies, comic strips . . . none of it. Had George Lucas done *American Graffiti* for us at UA, I believe I would have passed on *Star Wars*. Jeffrey [Katzenberg] became Barry Diller's assistant after my departure, and I told Barry that as my parting gift to him, Jeffrey would get *Star Trek* made. Of course, he did.

RICHARD TAYLOR (art director, Robert Abel & Associates)

Charles Bludhorn's valet was Jeff Katzenberg. Somewhere along the way Jeff said, "You know I really want to be in movies." And he said, "All right, I'll send you to Hollywood." This was the first film that he produced and he was really green. He was this young guy and he wasn't unlikable, but he was learning as he went along and it was a much more complicated film than any traditional live-action film was where he should cut his teeth. Instead, he was thrown into this hydra, this Medusa with all the snakes.

GERALD ISENBERG (producer, *Star Trek: Planet of the Titans*)

I was brought into Paramount because I made a deal with Barry Diller, and that deal said that if a movie of *Star Trek* is made, I'm going to be the producer. David Picker, who was the head of the studio at the time, and I hired Phil Kaufman to direct and write. Phil was very taken with the Spock character and Leonard and thought that a lot of the other characters were past their usefulness. We began to develop a script that was a time-travel script that was really influenced by *Last and First Men* by Olaf Stapledon, which was a history of human evolution for a billion years going forward.

ALLAN SCOTT (writer, *Star Trek: Planet of the Titans*)

Jerry Isenberg, who was the producer at that time, brought us in. We came out and met with him and Gene. We talked about the project, and I think the only thing we agreed on at the time was that if we were going to make *Star Trek* as a motion picture, we should try and go forward, as it were, from the television series. Take it into another realm, if you like. Another dimension. To that end we were talking quite excitedly about a distinguished film director, and Phil Kaufman's name came up. We all thought that was a wonderful idea, and we met with him. Phil is a great enthusiast and very knowledgeable about science fiction.

PHILIP KAUFMAN (director, *The Right Stuff*)

I had done *White Dawn* for Paramount and it wasn't a big hit, but it was well regarded, so I got the call from my agent who thought I wouldn't be interested in doing it. But the minute I heard what it was, that they wanted to make a three-million-dollar movie of an old television series they thought would be worth reviving and there was a certain fan base, I knew I was interested. It wouldn't have ordinarily been something that would interest me if it didn't have all of these interesting situations, which I didn't feel were that well executed on the TV show, by necessity.

ALLAN SCOTT

We did a huge amount of reading. We must have read thirty science-fiction books of various kinds. At that time we also had that guy from NASA who was one of the advisors to the project, Jesco von Puttkamer. He was at some of the meetings, and Gene was at all of the meetings.

PHILIP KAUFMAN

I met with Gene and I looked at episodes with him and we talked about all sorts of things. Somehow through the whole process, I must say, Gene always wanted to go back to his script, that he always wanted to really just do another episode with a little more money. Paramount wasn't interested in that, because they'd already turned it down. But in the process of working with Jerry and Gene, we got them to commit to a ten-million-dollar movie, which was a good amount of money in those days.

GERALD ISENBERG

Phil was thinking *2001*. He wanted to make another great movie, like the way *2001* explored the future and alternate realities. That's where he was going.

PHILIP KAUFMAN

Whatever the requirements of sixties television were, they were really lacking in a visual quality and in all those things that a feature film in science fiction needed to have. I felt that those elements were in there, if properly thought out and expanded, and could be a fantastic event. We knew what the feature films in science fiction had been prior to this: *2001: A Space Odyssey, Planet of the Apes,* a few of these things that were wondrous adventures.

GERALD ISENBERG

David [Picker] believed Phil was a talented filmmaker and he is. He's made a couple of great movies and won Academy Awards. And a real thinker. We sat in a room and he basically talked to us about the *Star Trek* audience and who the characters are, who the most important characters are, and who is the center of *Star Trek* and it's Spock. You can take any other character out of that series and the series is the same. Even Kirk. You just replace him with another captain. But Spock is the center of that series. That character represents the essence of what that show is about.

PHILIP KAUFMAN

It was an adventure through a black hole into the future and the past, and there were more relationships really developed beyond just the crew relationships. Kirk was to have an important role but not the center. The center was Spock, a Klingon, a woman parapsychologist who was trying to treat Spock's insanity [he had gotten caught in his *pon farr* cycles], and there was going to be sex, which the sixties series never had, but we were here at the end of the seventies and we're in a world where great movies were being made and the times were really ripe for expanding your mind.

GERALD ISENBERG

Leonard's basic feeling was until he sees a finished script that he wants to do, whatever you want to do is fine. By that time in his life, *Star Trek* was a source of money for him through the appearances and everything else, but he was refusing to have that be his career and his image and his life. He was into writing. Leonard is a true Renaissance man, he's a writer and a photographer, a poet, he's an amazing human being. So with the Spock character, of course, he represents the great conflict between reason and emotion, inherent in that person, so the whole *Star Trek* cast was a nice add-on, but the central conflict existed completely within Spock.

PHILIP KAUFMAN

Don't forget, both Nimoy and Shatner were not going to participate in the feature when it first happened. There were some contractual problems they were having. I think I met Shatner briefly, but Leonard Nimoy and I got along great. I thought he was brilliant and after it was canceled I cast him in *Invasion of the Body Snatchers* and took some elements of Spock for the film. In the beginning, he is the shrink Dr. Kibner, who is warm and trying to heal people, the human side, and then he turns into a pod, which is the Vulcan side. Instead of pointy ears, I gave him Birkenstock sandals.

ALLAN SCOTT

Once we started working on the project with Phil, we were told that they had no deal with William Shatner, so in fact the first story draft we did eliminated

Captain Kirk. It was only a month or six weeks in that we were called and told that Kirk was now aboard and should be one of the leading characters. So all of that work was wasted. At that time Chris [Bryant] and I would sit in a room and talk about story ideas and notions, and talk them through with either Phil or Gene.

GERALD ISENBERG

We sent Gene the first draft and he was not happy at all, but neither were we. He thought we were making a mistake in dropping Kirk. He basically took the position that we were not helping this franchise.

ALLAN SCOTT

Without any ill feeling on any part, it became clear to us that there was a divergence of view of how the movie should be made between Gene and Phil. I think Gene was quite right in sticking by not so much the *specifics* of *Star Trek,* but the general ethics of it. I think Phil was more interested in exploring a wider range of science-fiction stories, and yet nonetheless staying faithful to *Star Trek.* There was definitely a tugging on the two sides between them.

One of the reasons it took us so long to come up with a story was because things like that would change. If we came up with some aspects that pleased Gene, they often didn't please Phil and vice versa. We were kind of piggies in the middle.

PHILIP KAUFMAN

Gene was a great guy, but it was a little bit of the Alec Guinness syndrome in *Bridge on the River Kwai.* He built a bridge and he didn't want to be rescued and he couldn't see anything other than what he wanted it to be. I thought science fiction should go forward and I thought that the order was to go boldly where no man has gone before, but Roddenberry wanted to go back.

ALLAN SCOTT

The difficulty was trying to make, as it were, an exploded episode of *Star Trek* that had its own justification in terms of the new scale that was available for it, because much of *Star Trek*'s charm was the fact that it dealt with big and bold ideas on a small budget. Of course the first thing that a movie would do, potentially, was match the budget and the scale of the production to the boldness and vigor of the ideas. We spent weeks looking at every single episode of *Star Trek* and I would guess that pretty much every cast member came by and met us.

Among those involved with preproduction on the film were visionary James Bond production designer Ken Adam and *Star Wars* and *Battlestar Galactica* conceptual guru Ralph McQuarrie. *Star Trek* continued to remain an obsession for the legendary Gulf & Western chairman, Charles Bludhorn, whose daughter, Dominique, was a devoted fan of the series.

PHILIP KAUFMAN

Ken Adam and I became good friends, and we had that sense of making *Star Trek* a big event with this sense of wonder and visuals. I got to know Ralph McQuarrie through George Lucas, and Ralph came aboard and started designing things.

I went to London scouting with Ken Adam, looking for locations. They were going to pull the plug on *Star Wars*. Fox and all the people in London were laughing at what a disaster it was. George and his producer, Gary Kurtz, had gone on with the last couple of days with cameras to hastily try and piece together what they knew they needed to finish the movie.

So there was this mood out there that *Star Wars* was going to be a disaster. I knew otherwise; I had seen what George was doing and had been to what became ILM in the Valley and had spoken to George about that when we were working on the story for the first *Raiders of the Lost Ark* together. It was a sense of storytelling of what science fiction could be that George was into. That was brilliant and excited me.

I'd been in touch with him while he was shooting *Star Wars*, and I think George possibly had tried to get the rights to *Star Trek* prior to his doing *Star Wars*. I knew there was something great there. Times were crying out for good science fiction. Spielberg was also developing *Close Encounters* at that time, but Paramount didn't really know what they had. It was to Roddenberry's credit that he and the fan base had convinced them that a movie could be made, albeit on the cheap, and I didn't want to do that, nor did Jerry.

Chris Bryant and Allan Scott turned in their first draft on March 1, 1977. It was Kaufman's hope to cast legendary Japanese actor Toshiro Mifune as the *Enter-*

prise's Klingon adversary, which could have been the greatest *Star Trek* villain in the franchise's history, exceeding even Khan.

PHILIP KAUFMAN

I had loved the power of those Kurosawa movies and *The Seven Samurai*. If any country other than America had a sense of science fiction, it was Japan. Toshiro Mifune up against Spock would have been a great piece of casting. There would have been a couple of scenes between the two of them, emotion versus Spock's logical mind shield, trying to close things off, and having humor play between them. Leonard is a funny guy and the idea was not to break the mold of *Star Trek,* but to introduce it to a bigger audience around the world.

GERALD ISENBERG

We weren't thinking, this is a franchise and we're going to do eight movies, we were thinking we would make one good movie. *Star Wars* launched as a franchise and nowadays you look back and think that everything is a franchise. What we would have ended up doing is a version that was essentially *Star Trek*, but not the *Star Trek* that was the series, because we would have focused on Spock and his conflict and being human and what being human is. And that's really what 80 percent of the *Star Trek* episodes are dealing with: being human. We were not trying to perpetuate the *Star Trek* franchise at that time. No one was.

In the script, the crew searches for Kirk and discovers him stranded on a planet where they must face off with both the Klingons and an alien race called the Cygnans, eventually being thrust back in time through a black hole to the dawn of humanity on Earth where the crew members themselves are revealed as the Titans of Greek mythology.

ALLAN SCOTT

I truly don't remember anything about the script, except the ending. The ending involved primitive man on Earth, and I guess Spock or the crew of the *Enterprise* inadvertently introduced primitive man to the concept of fire. As they accelerated away, we realize that *they* were therefore giving birth to civilization as we know it.

I also know that eventually we got to a stage where we more or less didn't have a story that everybody could agree on and we were in very short time of our delivery date. Chris and I decided that the best thing we could do was take all the information we had absorbed from everybody, sit down, and hammer something out. In fact, we first did a fifteen- or twenty-page story in a three-day time period. I guess amendments were made to that in light of Gene's and Phil's recommendations, but already we were at a stage by then that the situation was desperate if we were going to make the movie according to the schedule that was given to us. We made various amendments, wrote the script, went to the studio with it, and they turned it down.

PHILIP KAUFMAN

I still remember the night when I was getting very close, I was then writing and I stayed up all night, but I knew I had a great story. I remember how shaky I was trying to stand up from my writing table and I called Rose, my wife, and I said, "I've got it, I really know this story," and right then the phone rang. It was Jerry Isenberg saying the project's been canceled. I said, "What do you mean?" and he said, "They said there's no future in science fiction," which is the greatest line: there is no future in science fiction.

They just canceled it, they never saw my treatment, nobody read it. I still have it, but that was the end of the project. Barry Diller was going to start another network and go back to TV and said, "Let's just do what Gene Roddenberry was pushing for," which was that same stuff, which I found passé and kind of clunky. Now, people are coming back to TV, but back then everything was the world of features, which was the only way you could make a movie like *2001*.

On May 8, 1977, *Planet of the Titans* was officially shelved. With Bryant and Scott on their way back to England, their parting gift to those who remained behind was a memo wishing everyone well. "Giving birth takes nine months. We've only been gestating for seven. So there's no baby. But there's an embryo. Look after it."

SUSAN SACKETT

Robert Redford as Captain Kirk was one thing Gene used to joke about. The studio wanted to recast it with known names. He said this in his college lectures. There was some talk of that, but I don't think it was serious.

GERALD ISENBERG

Mike Eisner came into the studio and canceled the movie so that he could do *Star Trek* as a TV series again as part of a projected Paramount TV network. *Star Trek* was going to be the center of the network, and Gene became the executive producer in charge again, because he was not in charge of the movie. So they set out to do this TV series and about seven months later, after investing about two million dollars in sets, Paramount TV falls apart and they decide to do it again as a movie.

RICHARD ARNOLD (*Star Trek* archivist)

The studio never seemed to know exactly what it wanted, which was very exhausting for Gene. He went through so many attempts to get it restarted, and there were times where he was ready to just walk away from all of it. But once *Star Wars* proved that science fiction could be mainstream, there was no going back. The second attempt at a series, *Star Trek: Phase II*, ground to a halt and everyone and everything changed so that a major motion picture could be made.

PHILIP KAUFMAN

About two or three months after *Star Trek* was canceled, *Star Wars* was released and then shortly thereafter *Close Encounters* came out. It turned out there *was* a future in science fiction after all.

THE NEXT PHASE

With plans to develop a feature film now abandoned, preproduction began in earnest on the development of a new TV series, dubbed *Star Trek: Phase II*. Under the creative aegis of Gene Roddenberry, the new series—announced on June 10, 1977—was intended to serve as the cornerstone of a Paramount/Hughes TV network, which would launch with a two-hour premiere, to air on February 1, 1978. Among those joining the project were story editor Jon Povill; producer Bob Goodwin, who would oversee physical production; and Harold Livingston, who would handle the development of thirteen scripts for the first season.

Harold Antill Livingston, like Roddenberry, had lived a remarkable life prior to arriving in Hollywood, having served as a pilot in World War II, a commercial airline pilot for TWA, an advertising copywriter, a fighter pilot in the Israeli Air Force in 1948, and an acclaimed author of several novels.

HAROLD LIVINGSTON (writer, *Star Trek: The Motion Picture*)

I produced a show for ABC called *Future Cop*. He was a manufactured robot that couldn't be hurt and he had a mechanical computer brain. Ernie Borgnine was his mentor. It was a good show and I was very close to the head of production at Paramount Television, Arthur Fellows. As far as I know, they were very down on Roddenberry, and so Arthur brought me in when they decided to do this *Phase II* in which Paramount would launch their own network. I never saw *Star Trek* in my life, and my first meeting with Roddenberry was a total disaster. He said, "What do you know about *Star Trek*?" I said, "Nothing." Well, that went over very well.

ROBERT GOODWIN (producer, *Star Trek: Phase II*)

A guy named Gary Nardino came in and took over as president of Paramount Television, and made the decision to start a fourth network. The plan was that every Saturday night they were going to do one hour of *Star Trek* and then a two-hour movie.

HAROLD LIVINGSTON

The objective of the new series was very vague. All they knew was that the studio had some kind of arrangement with what was then going to be a fourth network. I suppose it would take the form of some kind of syndicated program. So thirteen episodes plus a pilot were ordered, and it was then my job to develop these stories, which I set upon doing.

JON POVILL (story editor, *Star Trek: Phase II*)

I think Gene was more comfortable doing *Star Trek* as a TV series than he had been when it was being developed as a film. He liked the idea of *Phase II*. Again, it was sort of "Fuck you, NBC, we're back!" And the control he wouldn't have had on the Jerry Isenberg–Phil Kaufman version, he would have on the TV series, so he was back in the driver's seat. That was to his liking. Keep in mind that *Star Trek* was one of the first TV shows to be remade as a feature. The previous attempts were shitcanned largely because nobody could figure out how to extend this to two hours and make it work. "What kind of story do we tell? It doesn't feel big enough." It seemed to lose its *Star Trek* flavor as soon as you got it that big. So I think Gene felt more comfortable with hour episodes. It also had to be something of an honor to be the flagship of the Paramount network, which was the intention. Of course, it happened ten years later with *The Next Generation*.

> Barry Diller, the chairman and CEO of Paramount Pictures, commented at the time: "We considered the project for years. We'd done a number of treatments, scripts, and every time we'd say, 'This isn't good enough.' If we had just gone forward and done it, we might have done it quite well. In the case of the Isenberg-Kaufman version, it was the script. We felt, frankly, that it was a little pretentious. We went to Gene Roddenberry and said, 'Look, you're the person who understands *Star Trek*. We don't. But what we should probably do is return to the original context, a television series.' If you force it as a big seventy-millimeter widescreen movie, you go directly against the concept. If you rip *Star Trek* off, you'll fail, because the people who like *Star Trek* don't just like it, they love it."
>
> In sharing his feelings with *Starlog* magazine, Roddenberry confessed, "The worst that can happen is someone would say that Roddenberry couldn't do it a second time. That doesn't bother me, as long as I did my damnedest to do it a second time."

ROBERT GOODWIN

My interest had always been more in the long form rather than the series side of television. Gary Nardino decided that he was going to put me in charge of all these two-hour movies, which was great for me. But then it turned out that they were looking for someone to come on as producer, and Gene Roddenberry had heard about me. To be perfectly honest, I wasn't anxious to do it. My real interest, as I said, was the long form, and I was supposed to supervise those movies. I was pretty much strong-armed to do it and not given too much of a choice. Paramount said, "Forget the two-hour movies, you're doing *Star Trek*."

So I went over to see Gene, and initially I got kicked out of his office. His assistant, Susan Sackett, thought I was an agent or something. She didn't know I had an appointment to see him and wouldn't let me in. I said, "Fine," and walked out. I was about a half a mile away at the other side of the studio when Gene Roddenberry came running after me. To make a long story short, he wanted me to go in as one of the two producers. They were going to hire a writing producer and a production producer. It was kind of a strange situation.

HAROLD LIVINGSTON

I had never met Roddenberry, but I think I was working at Paramount at the time. Bob Goodwin and I were both going to work under Gene. If I remember correctly, there were a lot of interviews and bullshit that went on, but Gene and I kind of hit it off. We had similar backgrounds. We had both been in the air force during the war and we both worked for civilian airlines after the war, so I think that's one of the reasons that Gene, in the beginning, liked me.

Roddenberry said, "You've got to read the *Star Trek* bible." So he gives me this unintelligible pamphlet, which I never read. I had to sit through seventy-nine episodes of *Star Trek*, at which point I decided that this was *Wagon Train* in space. So what am I going to do with it? I had no idea.

Star Trek: Phase II was intended to be set during the *Enterprise*'s second five-year mission. Led by Captain Kirk, the entire rest of the original crew was back . . . *except* for Spock. Gene Roddenberry has often said that Nimoy did not want to do television at that time. For his part, Nimoy claimed he had only been offered the pilot and the possibility of a recurring role, and had no interest in being a part-time Spock.

In addition, considerable acrimony remained over Nimoy's failure to receive a piece of the burgeoning Star Trek merchandise being sold as well as Roddenberry failing to cast him in the *Questor Tapes* pilot three years earlier, for which Nimoy had been told he would be starring. *Then*, through secondhand sources, he discovered that Robert Foxworth had actually been cast as Questor, and when he confronted Roddenberry about it, the Great Bird once again blamed the studio.

DAVID GERROLD (author, *The World of Star Trek*)

You have to ask yourself why Gene Roddenberry never got any other series on the air except for *Star Trek*. It's like he is the source of the problem. He was able to sell *Genesis II* and *Questor*, and Universal was actually willing to buy thirteen episodes of *Questor*, but Gene got angry and wouldn't do the series.

GENE RODDENBERRY (creator, executive producer, *Star Trek*)

At about the time the *Star Trek* movie was canceled by Paramount, I had a meeting with Leonard Nimoy in which we discussed *Star Trek* and television. At that time, he told me that he might consider long-form television specials, but "under no circumstances" would he return to play Mr. Spock again on a weekly hour television series basis. He explained that the pressures of weekly television would interfere with his career goal of stage, film, and other things. I still hoped he would change his mind, but could not ignore reports that he continued to reject any *Star Trek* television possibilities in newspaper columns and in television interviews.

Then when Nimoy finally became part of a successful play on Broadway, I had to accept that his rejection of *Star Trek* television was final. Convinced that no terms I could arrange would bring a willing and enthusiastic Leonard Nimoy into the role of Mr. Spock on television again, I had no choice but to get on with the difficult job of inventing a new science officer.

In the pages of his second autobiography, *I Am Spock*, Nimoy painted a slightly different version of the situation: "I'll confess that when I first heard about the new show, I had major reservations. I was still very concerned about being perceived as a one-character actor, and still war-weary from the unpleasant struggles from *Trek*'s third season. But I was at least willing to hear what Paramount and Gene Roddenberry had to offer. And here it was: a recurring role wherein Spock appeared in two of every eleven episodes. Quite honestly, the offer confused and startled me. Only *two* out of every eleven? I was being offered a part-time job. It made little sense for me to be technically tied up with a series and having to be unavailable for other challenging work, while at the same time making such a small contribution to the show. I passed."

JON POVILL

I don't think Gene was worried about Leonard not being on the show. Leonard is an example of someone he could demonstrate "revenge" on. You know, "I can show everyone that we didn't need Spock." Gene was pissed off at him. They were kind of feuding for most of that period. I don't know exactly what the bug up his ass was about Leonard. Leonard was complaining that he wasn't getting money from merchandising, including merchandising that was coming from Lincoln Enterprises, so there were arguments over things like that. Gene was just pissed off at him. I think there was more of a "Fuck him!" attitude. In retrospect, even though I didn't know Leonard really well, I have to say that in all of my dealings with him, I really liked the guy. He was very genuine.

HAROLD LIVINGSTON

I wanted Jon Povill to be my story editor and Gene wanted him to continue cleaning his garage or something, so we had a big thing about that. I eventually got my way.

JON POVILL

Harold was primarily responsible for getting me the story-editor job. Gene was reluctant to move me "that far, that fast," to use his words. Harold was adamant that I was doing the job of a story editor and, by God, I should be getting paid as one. Also, Harold had not been very familiar with the old series at all and kind of relied on me to be the monitor of whether something fit with *Star Trek* or not. Once everything got rolling, and we were in a lot of writers' meetings, I sort of took over as the person who pointed out where there were holes in the stories, and where they did not conform to what *Star Trek* was supposed to be.

One of the keys to me becoming story editor was that one of the stories we'd received, "The Child," had to be written in a week. I had Jaron Summers, who wrote the story, do a first draft. And then I had to do a pretty complete rewrite. It had to get into shape for shooting, and the way that script came out would determine whether or not I could be the story editor.

The staff put together a writers' and directors' bible for the series that was completed on July 15, 1977. The series bible was a guide for potential writers about how the ship would function, potential stories, and bios of the characters, emphasizing three new additions to the crew.

Lt. Xon is a full Vulcan, designed to take the place of Spock as ship science officer. The primary difference between the two is that Xon has virtually no knowledge of the human equation and realizes that the only way he will be able to equal Spock is by making an effort to touch his repressed emotions, thus allowing him to more fully relate to the crew. The bible notes that "we'll get some humor out of Xon trying to simulate laughter, anger, fear, and other human feelings." Interestingly, the Spock-McCoy feud would have carried over to Xon and the doctor, with the difference being that McCoy believes their "feud is a very private affair . . . and McCoy has been known to severely chastise in private those crewmen who have been unfair to the Vulcan in comparing his efforts to Spock's."

First officer Commander Will Decker was designed to be a younger version of Captain Kirk. He comes close to worshipping the captain and would "literally rather die than fail him." Essentially Decker is a captain in training, and the idea was that the audience would watch his gradual growth during the five-year mission. In many instances he would lead landing parties, thus alleviating the perpetual logistical flaw of the initial *Star Trek* TV series: a ship's captain would never beam into potential danger as often as Kirk did.

The final new addition to the crew was Lieutenant Ilia, the bald Deltan, whose race is marked by a heightened sexuality that pervades every aspect of their society. Additionally, Ilia has heightened intelligence, second perhaps only to Xon, and gifted with unique esper abilities. As noted in the bible, "Unlike the mind meld of Vulcans, it simply is the ability to sense images in other minds. Never words or emotions, only images . . . shape, sizes, textures. On her planet, sexual foreplay consists largely of lovers placing images in each other's minds."

HAROLD LIVINGSTON

The idea was to bring in a new generation. I think those characters would have developed well. Obviously you couldn't have a geriatric crew there; you have to have new people, and these were them. Gradually, Kirk would become an admiral and Decker would become captain. I thought on that basis we could develop some new directions with these people.

ALAN DEAN FOSTER (author, *Star Trek Log* series)

I loved the character of Lt. Xon. I loved the idea that there would be a full Vulcan on board. It was a change. It gives you different personal and interpersonal conflicts and relationships. I'm not saying they're better than a half Vulcan gives you, but they would have been *different*. Particularly Xon on board with Kirk, because Kirk would have been thinking—and this is in the original treatment—that Xon is fully aware that he is taking the place of the legendary Commander Spock, and even though he doesn't feel emotions, from a logical standpoint it presented all sorts of interesting dramatic possibilities. Kirk thinking, "This kid's good, but he isn't Spock." So a whole different relationship and all kinds of interesting and new interpersonal dynamics to explore there.

JON POVILL

We were helped out tremendously by the new characters. We wanted characters that could go in new directions, as well as the old crew. I particularly liked Xon. I thought there was something very fresh in having a nice young Vulcan to deal with, somebody who was trying to live up to a previous image. To me, that was a very nice gimmick for a TV show that was missing Spock. But we *never* wanted Xon to be a Spock retread. We wanted him to be somebody who definitely had his own direction to go in, and he had different failings than Spock. Xon's youth was also very important and he would have brought a freshness that people would have appreciated.

LARRY ALEXANDER
(writer, *Star Trek: Phase II*: "Tomorrow and the Stars")

Xon may not have been Spock, but I considered him Spock from a character point of view. I had a moment in the script where something has happened to Kirk, and the captain says, "Xon, what have you done to me?" So there was a little bit of resentment there that he *wasn't* Spock, which was fun to play with. It seemed like the "logical" thing to do.

ALAN DEAN FOSTER

When I wrote for the show, my idea with Xon was to have a lot of fun, because the old crew was back and they had this young squirt and everybody is looking over their shoulder, thinking, "This is the plebe we have to put up with instead of the great Mr. Spock," who was supposed to be off meditating someplace. Meanwhile, the Vulcan character has to think, "Talk about having burden dumped on your shoulders."

JON POVILL

Ilia was sort of an embodiment of warmth, sensuality, sensitivity, and a nice yin to Xon's yang.

ALAN DEAN FOSTER

One aspect of Ilia that didn't get utilized when she *did* show up in the first movie was the sexuality aspect of her. It barely got touched on. Deltans are sexually irresistible people and they cause a lot of trouble wherever they go. They unsettle guys.

JON POVILL

Decker, of course, was a young Kirk. He would have been the least distinct. He would have had to grow and the performance probably would have done that, bringing something to Decker that the writers would have ultimately latched on to for material.

ALAN DEAN FOSTER

The original idea was to have more conflict between Kirk and Decker. He's *supposed* to be equal to a younger Kirk, but he comes across as kind of a postgraduate nerd when the character eventually showed up in the movie. It's like everybody is sitting around wondering how this guy could get command. You weren't supposed to think that when the character was conceived.

JON POVILL

Xon and Ilia were concept characters. They would have developed, too, I'm sure, because characters grow when they're performed much more than they do from just the writing. In the early writing, you don't realize the full potential. You don't know who's going to play the character, how they're going to play it, and what the characteristics of their performance are going to be. If you look at "The Cage," for example, Spock laughs.

HAROLD LIVINGSTON

I wanted to make *Star Trek* more universal. I felt that success notwithstanding, the show had a restrictive audience. There was a greater audience for this. I felt that almost all of the stories seemed to be allegorical, and I wanted to make them a little harder and a little more realistic. My broad intention was to create a series that would attract a larger audience by offering more. We would still offer the same elements that *Star Trek* did—i.e., science fiction and hope for the future—and do realistic stories.

ALAN DEAN FOSTER

When they were thinking of reviving the TV series, a number of writers were called in to submit treatments for hour-long episodes. Roddenberry had gotten in touch with me, because of the *Star Trek Log* book series. He felt that I was comfortable with the *Star Trek* universe, and comfortable and familiar with the characters. So I submitted three story ideas. Then Roddenberry gave me a page-and-a-half outline, or notes, for "Robot's Return," a proposed episode of *Genesis II*. He thought that could be developed and wanted to see what I could do with it.

HAROLD LIVINGSTON

There was a young man named Alan Dean Foster brought in to me to write something. I wanted to see something he had written and he brought me two screenplays, which I thought were terrible. And I didn't want him to write, that's all. I didn't think he could do it, and this is obviously a subjective judgment. That's what they were paying me for, and it was my judgment that they should get someone else. In any case, we made a deal with Alan to do a treatment for the pilot, which was this business of the old machine coming back to Earth and assuming a kind of life-form. I don't think I knew this was similar to an episode of the original show. I thought I saw all seventy-nine episodes, some of which I liked and some I thought were just dreadful. Anyway, I made a deal with Alan's agent, Paul Kohner, that he would write a treatment and agree not to do the script.

ROBERT GOODWIN

The decision was made to do a two-hour premiere for the series, and I suggested to Gene that since it had never been done in the series before, that we should come up with a story in which Earth was threatened. In all the *Star Trek* episodes before, they never even came close to Earth. There was this guy named Alan Dean Foster who had this story that became "In Thy Image," which fit the bill perfectly.

ALAN DEAN FOSTER

After my treatment was turned in based on Roddenberry's page, it was decided to open the series with a two-hour movie for TV, which is fairly standard procedure when they can manage it. It was decided that of the treatments they had in hand, mine was the best suited to carry two hours. So I went home and developed what became an expanded thirty-two-page outline.

> In many ways, "In Thy Image" is *Star Trek: The Motion Picture* sans Spock. The newly refitted *Enterprise* sets out to combat the mysterious energy cloud that has been destroying vessels and is on a direct heading for Earth. Kirk and the rest of his crew, plus Xon, Ilia, and Decker, encounter the approaching object, discovering the truth behind it: it's actually an ancient Earth space probe en route to its home world in search of its creator.
>
> This story would prove highly significant to the next stage of *Star Trek*'s existence. In July 1977—a month after its announcement—the decision was made to cancel the fourth network, because projected advertising revenue would be insufficient to cover the anticipated production costs.

WALTER KOENIG (actor, "Pavel Chekov")

I'm already gun-shy because of the animated series, and I was more than a bit skeptical and concerned that I would not be involved with so many aborted starts from B-movie to a new series. Then incredibly, the series thing happened. I went in for a costume fitting of the old costume and came home and about an hour later they said the whole project was put on hold.

WILLIAM SHATNER (actor, "James T. Kirk")

I remember at one point giving a party at my home for the cast and production staff to celebrate the impending start of a new *Star Trek* TV series. Plans for it were canceled the day after my party.

After abandoning its plans for a fourth network, Paramount's initial idea was that "In Thy Image" would be filmed as a two-hour movie that would be shopped to the three networks as a backdoor pilot for a new series. Studio executives were concerned, however, that the networks would pass on the pilot in retaliation for Paramount attempting to launch their own network. As a result, the studio chose once again to mount a motion picture. Anxious to avoid another embarrassing failure to launch, work on *Phase II* would continue—set construction, scripts, etc.—until all the deals for a reconstituted feature film could be finalized.

ROBERT GOODWIN

At that point they had spent about four years trying to get a script for a feature, but they couldn't come up with anything that Michael Eisner liked. One day we went into a meeting in the conference room in the Paramount administration building. There was Michael Eisner, Jeff Katzenberg, Gary Nardino, me, and Gene. In the course of that meeting, I got up and pitched this two-hour story. Michael Eisner slammed his hands on the table and said, "We've been looking for four years for a feature script. This is it. Now let's make the movie." And that was basically it.

HAROLD LIVINGSTON

I began looking for someone to write the script based on "In Thy Image," but we were starting to come up against a production date. I couldn't find anybody I liked, and I just decided with five weeks to go I would have to write it myself.

While Livingston worked on the screenplay between September and October, director Robert L. Collins—whose previous credits included *Police Story, Medical Story,* and the TV version of *Serpico*—was brought on to helm "In Thy Image," and became part of the already turbulent and contentious creative process.

ROBERT L. COLLINS (director, *Star Trek: In Thy Image*)

They originally made me an offer to direct what was essentially a television movie to regenerate the *Star Trek* series. So we negotiated on that for a while, and then shortly after I came on board Paramount decided to make a feature of it instead. So it went the route of a feature, and we had a budget of about eight million dollars.

JON POVILL

As the summer of '77 wore on and the box office for *Star Wars* continued to build, Paramount brass became more and more convinced they wanted to do a feature. I think they were waiting, to some extent, to see the development of "In Thy Image," which, as a two-hour script, they felt showed promise but clearly wasn't ready yet. So, probably to hedge their bet, they continued to develop the series while being mostly interested in the "pilot." In the end I suspect greed took over and they decided to go all-in with the feature—even with Robert Collins—but then bringing in Robert Wise, who really made it happen.

HAROLD LIVINGSTON

I sat down and wrote this script. I delivered it and Gene said, "Great, you've done your job. Now just relax and I'll write the second draft." He wrote it in two days. Seriously, it was *that* fast. Then he brought it in, gave it to us in a bright orange cover, and there it is: *In Thy Image,* Screenplay by Gene Roddenberry and Harold Livingston. He took first position. We all read it and I was appalled, and so was everyone else. There was Povill, Bob Goodwin, myself, and Bob Collins, who was the director. We sat around looking at each other and somebody said, "Who's going to tell him it's a piece of shit?"

In Roddenberry's draft of the "In Thy Image" script, dated November 7, 1977, the film opens with Kirk and his girlfriend (an aide to Admiral Nogura), Alexandria, swimming nude. Notes Roddenberry in the scene description, "we limit to PG since we are using nudity to illustrate twenty-third-century natural attitudes." Hailed by Starfleet on his wrist communicator, Alexandria pulls him down underwater. When he pops back up, he tells Starfleet that "I was attacked by an underwater creature." San Francisco in the twenty-third century is a gorgeous and bucolic paradise with all industry and transportation now underground. With the *Enterprise* the only ship in the quadrant with an experienced captain and powerful shields, the vessel is dispatched to confront a mysterious probe that is on a heading for Earth. Alexandria is killed in the same transporter malfunction that would later be depicted in *Star Trek: The Motion Picture,* while, on the bridge, two "shapely female yeomans check out the young and inexperienced Xon, straight out of the Academy, and the new science officer, and ask him about *pon farr.*"

As in *Star Trek: The Motion Picture,* we are also introduced to the characters of Decker and Ilia—although in a far more clunky way. Decker acknowledges his lineage as the son of Commodore Will Decker from the original series episode "The Doomsday Machine," while Kirk assures Ilia, "I know that Deltan females are not wanton, hairless whores." Ilia laughs delightedly, prompting her retort, "On my world, existence *is* loving, pleasuring, sharing, caring," leading Kirk to ask Ilia, "Have you ever sexed with a human?"

Many familiar elements in *Star Trek: The Motion Picture* can already be seen in the *In Thy Image* script, although the V'ger probe is nicknamed Tasha by Chekov and the Ilia–Tasha probe takes a special interest in the irresistible Captain Kirk. "Kirk, let us make sex. In a few hours, Ve-jur will arrive. I will return to my original form."

Unlike *The Motion Picture,* however, both Decker and Ilia survive unharmed from their encounter with V'ger after Kirk screens a sixteen-millimeter print from NASA of the creator, which they uncover in San Francisco. In previous drafts the mysterious space probe was called N'Sa, which is discovered to be an abbreviation for NASA.

ROBERT L. COLLINS

After Gene gave us the script, Harold and I sat across from each other and asked which one was going to tell him that it wasn't quite right. I said, "Hell, I'm the director," and walked out [leaving the unenviable task to Livingston].

HAROLD LIVINGSTON

He kept the structure I'd created, but I don't know what he did to it. Just crazy shit. So I said, "I'll tell him." I went in and I said, "Gene, this doesn't work." Well, his face dropped to his ankles. Then I got myself wound up and I told him why it didn't work. I said, "Why'd you do it? When something works, you don't piss in it to make it better!" In any case, he was pretty stubborn about this. He thought it was good and said, "Well, we'll give it to the front office."

Well, about three days later we have a meeting in Michael Eisner's gigantic white office. We sat around this huge table. Michael had the two scripts. My version was in a brown folder and Gene's version was in an orange cover. Michael had one script in one hand and one in the other, balancing them in his palms. And he said, "Listen, this is the problem. This," Gene's orange script, "is television. This," the brown script, "is a movie. Frankly, it's a lot better." Well, holy shit! Everybody was clearing their throats. The great man had had his feathers ruffled. Anyway, after some heated discussion, it was decided to let Collins write a third version using the best elements of both.

ROBERT L. COLLINS

I did a couple of drafts and I had what I thought was a wonderful, spectacular idea for the end. Decker sacrificed himself at the end of the picture and unleashed a history of mankind. It would be a ten-minute sequence where we would flash images of mankind since the dawn of the apes up till the present. These flashes of images would be all over the ship and then, of course, all over the theater. All of this would be accompanied by a musical montage of Beethoven and Bach. It was a grand idea and very ambitious, and I think it would have set off the end of it in a very spectacular manner. I remember that I wrote something to that effect. Not particularly well, I imagine, but that was my thought on how the picture should end. I was trying to deal with what this animal known as man really is, and essentially I was saying that man was pretty good.

HAROLD LIVINGSTON

Collins's version was a total disaster. About that time, Roddenberry and I really began to get at each other's throats. I don't remember when I began to pierce the Roddenberry myth, but he and I suddenly started to have creative differences. I resented his interference and he, apparently, wanted someone to carry his lunch around, and that wasn't me. We became socially friendly for a while, but we started to have various difficulties.

ROBERT L. COLLINS

We eventually cast the part of Xon. I found an actor named David Gautreaux to play the part. He was a nice young man, a nice actor, and all of that would have worked. Though there was still considerable concern over how much box office we would have without Spock. But we proceeded.

DAVID GAUTREAUX (actor, "Xon")

I personally was never a fan. I never watched the show. I bought a television two weeks after I was signed for the role, because I was given an advance large enough to actually do something like that. Studying the episodes I got what I thought was a firm grasp of what makes a proper Vulcan. One of my big inspirations came from the *In Thy Image* script, where Xon is described as smelling rather strongly, having just beamed aboard from a meditative monastery in the Gobi Desert.

I actually went on a meditative trek and fasted for ten days. I allowed my hair to grow long, I started researching to be a Vulcan with no emotion. For an actor, that's death. I was looking at it from an actor's point of view, which is how do you appear as having no emotion without looking like a piece of wood? I went to several acting coaches. Jeff Corey [Leonard Nimoy's former acting coach and a guest star on the original series] is the one who gave me the key of how I could actively play the pure pursuit of logic as being my primary action. Then I felt I needed a physical equivalent, and I followed the teachings of Bruce Lee, who taught about dealing with emotion and a freedom from emotions that allowed you to live in a nonviolent world. That's really what he was all about, despite the impression he gave.

I was looking forward to playing Xon. His actions were tremendous. His strength without size, and the aspect of playing a full Vulcan. When I say that, I mean somebody who had a larger presence than, say, Spock's father, who was [also] a full Vulcan. By presence I mean a more involved presence on the show and in the running of the ship. It was a very exciting premise to be playing. But to me, it was a potentially good gig that didn't work out.

ROBERT GOODWIN

Bob also cast Persis Khambatta in the role of Ilia, despite the fact that Michael Eisner said, "There will be no bald-headed woman in this show." He thought it was an unattractive look and would turn people off. So we did a screen test with a bunch of ladies in bald-head caps and Persis, for some reason, looks great with no hair. The rest of them didn't look so gorgeous, but she was still pretty. Eisner took one look at the test and said okay. He didn't even call me personally. He just sent the word out that it was all right.

PERSIS KHAMBATTA (actress, "Ilia")

I was told that the girl, Ilia, was supposed to be bald, so I went and bought a bald cap from a drugstore for a dollar. I walked in to see Gene Roddenberry and I was wearing this cap—I wasn't even wearing it perfectly, just enough so he could have an idea of how I looked without hair. I said to him, "I'm sure you're going to test girls for this part. Would you give *me* a chance?" I'm good in front of a camera, but if I have to do a cold reading . . . well, a lot of actors can just take a script and start reading and acting immediately. I feel more confident having a screen test done, because then I'm more prepared for it. Also, the director can see how I look, because my personality changes a lot on camera.

Gene did give me a screen test. I felt very excited when I was told that of all the girls, I was the one who got it. I always loved *Star Trek*. I watched it in London and thought it was a fantastic show, it had a lot of class. But I'll tell you, I was even *more* pleased when they decided to make it into a feature film instead of a TV series.

HAROLD LIVINGSTON

December came along and my contract was coming up. Before they could fire me, I quit. We had too many problems there. If I do a poor job, I'll tell you it's bad and I'll welcome help. I'm certainly not infallible. None of us are. But Roddenberry would never admit that he wrote a bad line or couldn't write.

ROBERT L. COLLINS

Roddenberry had a purist approach. This was his *life*. *Star Trek* and Roddenberry are synonymous. He would continually say, "This is not *Star Trek*." One could argue that it may not be *Star Trek*, but it's good. And at the same time you had to realize that on a human level, on a personal level, that he was all wrapped up in it. His whole way of defining himself was involved with the series and with this project. We all wanted to help him realize his ambition, and we wanted to make a good picture, too. Paramount was kind of holding a gun to his head, saying that they were going to do it, and then that they weren't going to do it. That tension, I think, flowed through all of us. I'm not sorry about calling people assholes if I think they are, but I liked Roddenberry and I always felt sympathetic toward him and the project.

HAROLD LIVINGSTON

Gene's made an industry of *Star Trek* and he's done nothing else. Everything else he's done—the few other things—are just shameful to watch. It's a disgrace. Gene's values lay in his knowledge, his experience . . . if he had just imparted that and let the professionals do their job, you'd have had a picture.

The film was in preproduction and they had gone back to basically what I wrote, with Collins as a writer, restoring much of what he left out, but little of Gene's.

ROBERT L. COLLINS

Somewhere around that time we were talking about special effects. *Close Encounters of the Third Kind* was just about to open, and the word around town was that it was spectacular. So Roddenberry and I went down to the Pacific Theatre and sat down for what I think was a noon performance. We came out and were both pretty blown away by *Close Encounters*. I turned to him and said, "There goes our low-budget special effects." After *Star Wars* and *Close Encounters,* you couldn't do those kinds of special effects anymore. That means a whole new thinking and a whole reorganization of the production and concepts. They needed a great deal more money and time, and there were only a few people who could do the effects.

We spoke to John Dykstra and Robert Abel. Abel is an irritating asshole, but he came on board and decided that he would make it into a Robert Abel Production. His budget, which had been one or two million dollars, suddenly jumped between seven and ten million dollars. The budget kept rising and Paramount was getting more nervous. In the meantime, we were all sitting around trying to think of the number of Trekkies in the United States and the dollar admission that would result from the film. It was a little like McCarthy trying to figure out how many communists were in the State Department. Everybody had a different number every day.

As plans for a movie version of *In Thy Image* continued to move forward, and the scope of the film continued to grow, it was becoming obvious that what was conceived as a small, low-budget film was going to be anything but. Eventually this would result in Robert Wise coming aboard as director, who in turn would insist that Leonard Nimoy reprise his role of Spock for the movie.

ROBERT L. COLLINS

We were preparing to make this picture, but the writing was on the wall. I was a television director who had not done a feature film at that time. It was evident that they were going to hire somebody who was used to working with big-budget special effects. Paramount wasn't brave about such things, so I called up Jeff Katzenberg and said, "You're going to replace me, right?" He said, "No, Bob, never. Take my word for it, Bob. Trust me."

Then my agent, who at that time handled Robert Wise, called me and said, "Look we've got an offer for Robert Wise to replace you on the picture." Apparently Paramount couldn't remember that we both had the same agent, so I called up Jeff again and said, "Look, are you going to replace me?" He said, "Absolutely not. Never. You're absolutely staying with the project." I pointed out that Robert Wise and I had the same agent, so he said, "If Robert Wise doesn't do it, then you are absolutely going to do it." I kind of laughed about that for a while. I knew it would happen sooner or later. They wanted to get somebody in place before they fired me. So they got Wise, and the first step was to redecorate my office.

ALAN DEAN FOSTER

Obviously the real reason the *Star Trek* film finally got the go-ahead was because of *Star Wars* and *Close Encounters*. After that, and this is supposition on my part, everybody started running around like crazy. I think that after being told, "Yes, we're doing a series; no, we're doing a movie; *yes,* we're doing a movie," everybody hears money. Everyone ran around trying to find something so that they could get started *right away* with budgeting and casting. Unfortunately, once it became a big-budget movie, I didn't get so much as a phone call or an invitation to come down to the set.

DAVID GAUTREAUX

I was doing a play at the time, trying not to think that I was going to be playing an alien for the rest of my life. Then I spoke to Gene Roddenberry and said, "What's the story? Did you see that Leonard Nimoy is coming back to play his character? What's going to happen to Xon?" He said, "Oh, Xon is very much a part of the family and you're very much a part of our family." I responded, "Gene, don't allow a character of this magnitude to simply carry Mr. Spock's suitcases on board the ship and then say, 'I'll be in my quarters if anybody needs me.' Give him what I've put into him and what you've put into him. If he's not going to be more a part of it and more noble than that, let's eliminate him." They continued with the idea of Xon for quite a while.

HAROLD LIVINGSTON

After I left, they hired me on *Fantasy Island* as a producer. They'd already shot five or six episodes in Burbank and everybody hated it. The producer was a kid named Michael Fisher. Everybody hated him. So ABC had me come on, there was even a whole story in *TV Guide* at the time about bringing me in to save it. So they bring me in, but the idea is not to tell Michael Fisher because I'm in Beverly Hills at the 20th Century–Fox lot and Michael is in Burbank. So what do I care? I start to develop thirteen scripts and I even rewrote one of his. So mine are not ready to be filmed yet and they've got to go on with his because of the schedule.

And the first show goes on and it's a fucking runaway hit! It's a fluke. Second week goes on to bigger numbers. I drive into my office on the lot and my parking spot is blanked out. I go up to my office and my office is empty, the secretary is gone, all my possessions, cigars, boxes, are on the fucking pavement. So I go in and Aaron [Spelling] ducks me. I finally corner him about two days later and he says, "These things happen. I'll make it up to you. What do you want?" I said, "You have a show called *Vega$* that hasn't sold yet. If it sells I want it." He said, "You got it." I said, "Call my agent right now, in front of me." Calls my agent and Aaron says, "If I sell *Vega$*, Harold is the producer. Harold gets the show."

So I still have a contract and every Thursday afternoon at two o'clock the doorbell rings and there's Aaron's chauffeur who hands me an envelope with a five-thousand-dollar check for the four or five weeks that are left on my contract. Anyway, it's a good thing for *Vega$* that I went back to *Star Trek* when Roddenberry called, because I'd have changed the whole goddamn thing.

JON POVILL

It was [Jeffrey] Katzenberg who courted and brought in Wise, though if you ask [Robert Wise's wife] Millie Wise, she will readily tell you that Jeff threw Bob under the bus pretty much as soon as the project was "done"—quotation marks appropriate considering that we released what was essentially a rough cut of *Star Trek: The Motion Picture*. In point of fact, as I was under contract as story editor, I continued working with writers and bringing in commissioned scripts until my contract ran out, even though we were told that they were going to feature sometime in the middle of my story-editor tenure.

ROBERT GOODWIN

When they went with Robert Wise as director, Gene and I were never really informed of what the steps of the deal were. It turns out that Robert Wise is used to getting directing *and* producing credit. Apparently he would not accept a producer, so Gene Roddenberry was moved to executive producer and I was asked by Gene and the studio if I would stay on as associate producer. But I didn't want to spend a *minute* of my life doing that. I was an associate producer ten years earlier, and it was taking a step backward, especially facing two years of production. I came to work one day and they had taken my name off the door. My stuff was packed in boxes in the hall and the janitor told me I had to be off the lot in twenty minutes.

JON POVILL

For me personally, I had very mixed feelings about it becoming a movie. I was the story editor of *Star Trek: Phase II* and my shows and my credit were gone. They weren't going to be made. I was kept on as production coordinator as we went to the Robert Collins version, which was a low-budget feature. At the same time, when Robert Wise came in, that generated fresh enthusiasm for sure. There was nobody involved who *didn't* think that this was the big time.

SLOW MOTION

"I NEED YOU . . . BADLY."

The transition of *Phase II* to what would become *Star Trek: The Motion Picture* was fraught with changes. For starters, although the "In Thy Image" teleplay would still serve as the basis for the film's story line, writer Harold Livingston was gone and replaced by Dennis Lynton Clark. Production designer Joe Jennings and consultant Walter "Matt" Jeffries (who still had a full-time gig on *Little House on the Prairie*) were replaced by Harold Michelson; costume designer William Ware Theiss saw his responsibilities taken over by Robert Fletcher; story editor Jon Povill became associate producer; and Robert Collins was replaced by legendary director Robert Wise in the center seat, who in turn ensured that Leonard Nimoy would reprise the role of Spock, thus making David Gautreaux's Xon superfluous. At control of it all—or so he thought—was Gene Roddenberry.

GERALD ISENBERG (producer, *Star Trek: Planet of the Titans*)

Michael Eisner and I were very close until the *Star Trek* event. I dropped out after *Planet of the Titans* had been canceled and they were doing *Phase II*. But when I realized they were making a movie, I went back to him and said, "You know, Mike, I have a contract that says if the movie is to be produced, I am the producer," and he said, "No, you passed." My response was, "No, Mike, I passed on a TV series, I didn't pass on the movie." He said, "No, you're out and you can't be involved." It wasn't as though I wanted to be involved, it was that I had a piece of the action. I got myself out of Paramount and took my TV company away. That's how we settled it.

GENE RODDENBERRY (producer, *Star Trek: The Motion Picture*)

Paramount turned me down a couple of times for a movie, then finally they said, "Write a script and we'll give you an office on the lot and think about it." They were not that serious about the movie when we first started it. I think they had in mind a two- to three-million-dollar picture. *Star Wars* woke them up to the fact that these things I'd been telling them for a number of years were true: There was an audience of millions of people out there who are interested in "message literature."

They wanted something that was good, staple Americana—like *Grease* or *Saturday Night Fever*. They wanted something they could understand and deal with. So after they read my script and turned it down, they called in—over the period of a year—maybe fifteen writers. And none of them did any better, because all these writers were trying to give them science fiction, and that's the last thing they really wanted.

DAVID GERROLD (author, *The Martian Child*)

Studio executives are maligned by everyone who works for them. If a studio makes fifteen hit pictures in a year, who gets the credit? The directors, the actors, the executive producers of the picture, but the studio executive who said, "I'll buy this picture, I'll finance it," he's just lucky enough to be sitting there when they brought the project in? I have to tell you, I've spent a lot of time with studio executives, and they can tell the difference between a good story and a bad story. They get excited when they work with exciting people. You don't get to be the head of a studio by accident, and the ones I've met are not stupid men. Admittedly there have been some stupid men as studio executives who can make mistakes, but twenty years at Paramount? Down the line they're doing all these great pictures like *The Godfather* films, *Saturday Night Fever* . . . and they can't get *Star Trek* on the boards? Give me a break.

GENE RODDENBERRY

I would have had the same problems at any other studio, and, indeed, science-fiction writers have all had the same experience. George Lucas fought the same fight. He had the good fortune to have a hit motion picture behind him, and he could say, "I'm sorry, this is the way we'll do it," and make it stand. I could do that on a television show; I could not do that on what was, essentially, a first science-fiction motion picture. I had several pictures behind me, but I never had any hits.

JON POVILL (associate producer, *Star Trek: The Motion Picture*)

Everyone on the show was pretty much thrilled at the prospect of working with Robert Wise. His presence brought an entirely new feeling of stature to the production. We felt like the everlasting cloud of doubt over the project had finally lifted and now it was really going to happen. And that proved true almost entirely thanks to Bob, who held the picture together through a constant stream of crises. He got a ton of blame for the way the picture turned out, but I feel rather strongly that if not for him, there would have been no further incarnations of *Trek*. If Bob had failed, I think Paramount would have given up. Maybe they'd have gone back to the notion of doing a series, but they sure as hell wouldn't have thrown any more money at a feature. It's always bothered me that, through the years, Bob wound up with none of the credit and all of the blame for the issues with *The Motion Picture*.

RICHARD TAYLOR (designer, Robert Abel & Associates)

Robert Wise was a kind of strange choice for director. He'd done *Run Silent, Run Deep* but wasn't really a science-fiction buff. He'd rather do *Sound of Music*. He was older and he would sit there on sets and drift off and then have a masseuse keeping him awake. I don't think he was ever very enthusiastic at all about directing this movie, and he was wrangled into it and made good money doing it. He was not passionate about it. It was a job.

DAREN DOCHTERMAN
(visual effects supervisor, *Star Trek: The Motion Picture*–Director's Edition)

I think that's a little unfair. Robert Wise is a very quiet man. Very level-toned in his reactions to things, because that was just his nature. All of the guys at Abel were extremely excited to be working on *Star Trek*. They were jumping all over the place to please everybody and show them all the neat stuff they were doing. Bob Wise was, like, "That's great, let's see if that works. You guys carry on." That could have come across as lack of enthusiasm, but he had so much other stuff to deal with. He had to balance the crew, the actors who hadn't worked with each other in ten years, the writer who was almost killing the producer. All of that stuff he had to deal with. Honestly, the Abel guys were not very conducive to speedy shooting onstage. The necessities were very taxing on him. They needed to shoot the wormhole sequence two or three times with different cameras and different film stocks, just to have stuff.

ROBERT WISE (director, *Star Trek: The Motion Picture*)

I have always been intrigued by science fiction, even though I have only done two other films in the genre, and I thought it was time that I did a science-fiction picture that took place in space. Both of my other ones were earthbound. In *The Day the Earth Stood Still,* we had a visitor from outer space coming *to* Earth in a spaceship, so that really intrigued me more than anything else. From the beginning I liked the idea of doing *Star Trek*. It was really the fascination and the desire to do a film that dealt with the experience of being in space.

SUSAN SACKETT (assistant to Gene Roddenberry)

Robert Wise is a very serious man and there was not much levity on the set. He had a very tough job to do, because this was a big reunion and it had a lot of things built into it of necessity because it *was* a reunion picture. Things were tough for Robert Wise and, in all fairness to him, that would probably be why his was a more serious production.

ROBERT WISE

I knew of the TV series, but I had not become a Trekkie when the TV series had first come out and I had only seen one or two segments, which I thought were all right, but I didn't get hooked on it. After the president of Paramount asked me if I would be interested in considering directing the movie, I said, "Well, I just don't know. I'll have to read the script, of course, and I would have to see several more of the TV segments." I had to get familiar with what it was and what had caused it to become so immensely popular. So that's what happened: I read the script and I saw about a dozen episodes of the series so I could become familiar with it, and make my own judgment.

The other thing is that when I read the script, Spock wasn't a part of it. I have three Trekkies in my own family. My wife, Millicent, read the script, and she was outraged when she discovered that Mr. Spock was no longer among the crew. "Why?" she asked. "Because," I said, "Leonard Nimoy was doing the play *Equus* on Broadway when the last version was written." Millicent said, rather emphatically, "With no Spock, there can be no *Star Trek,*" and she was just as emphatically backed up by my stepdaughter, Pamela, and her husband, Robert. Their vehemence impressed and shook me. I went to Paramount and repeated their words:

"With no Spock, there can be no *Star Trek*." So the studio enticed Nimoy back into the fold with a considerable amount of money.

WILLIAM SHATNER (actor, "James T. Kirk")

Leonard had a beef and it's a legitimate one. It's about the merchandising and it's something that irked me as well. Our faces appear on products all over the country, all over the world, and we've not really been compensated fairly for it. Leonard was walking in London, England. He stopped to look at a billboard. The billboard's divided into three sections. The first section is Leonard's face with the ears—Spock—the ears are drooping. The second section of the billboard has Leonard, with the drooping ears, holding a tankard of ale. The third section has an empty tankard of ale and Leonard's face, with pointed ears straight up in the air. So Leonard and I had this battle, with whoever licenses *Star Trek*, for a long time. So Leonard goes back to the studio and says, "There's a demeaning billboard of me out there. Did you guys okay it?" So he goes to his lawyer and tries to sue. But at that point, Paramount wanted Leonard, and Leonard wanted fair recompense. It was only reasonable that Paramount meet his demands.

EDDIE EGAN (publicity department, Paramount Pictures)

There was a lot of bad blood between Roddenberry and Paramount because of the vagaries of his merchandising contract through Lincoln Enterprises. Paramount got no split from that, but they were obligated to turn over any film trims and so forth, and that persisted into the movies for a while until someone put an end to it. From what I was told, the contract was so vague for the TV series that it said he could use discards from the series, meaning anything that was thrown away; call sheets, pieces of sets, unused film that was going to be destroyed—which were dailies or alternate takes—and he had the absolute right to them. I think Desilu wrote that contract and at that point there was no foresight to realize that those things could be valuable.

Gene held Paramount to that for years and years and years, which also spun into the bad blood between Paramount and Nimoy and Shatner about their share or royalties, because they had no share in any of those things that Lincoln sold. That was a *big* part of Nimoy's settlement with Paramount before he agreed to star in the movie. And then because he and Shatner had favored-nation clauses, Shatner got cut into that also.

GENE RODDENBERRY

They started off wanting to blithely recast. And until six months before we actually began shooting, they were still trying to get Kirk killed off in the first act. "At the very least, Gene, you can promote him to admiral and bring in a new star," they said. I refused to do this, because I think William Shatner is an extraordinarily fine actor. There was also a whole comedy of errors with Leonard Nimoy, because, at one time, the studio decided that the only way they wanted to do it was as a two-hour movie special and pilot of a new *Trek* TV series. Leonard Nimoy refused because of Broadway commitments and the time and energy required by a series.

I felt very much the same way. A legend grew that we threw Nimoy out of the show; that was not true. He did not want to do a television show. Nimoy and Spock are very important to *Star Trek,* but none of us was absolutely essential. There are writers and producers around who can do what I do—just as there are good actors around who could do another kind of Mr. Spock or Captain Kirk. *Star Trek* would still have been *Star Trek.* I'm glad we didn't have to, but I would never hold up a production because any one of us was not able to do it. That wouldn't be fair to the others.

LEONARD NIMOY (actor, "Mr. Spock")

We've had a long and complicated relationship, Paramount and myself. We had a lot of details to work out. There have been periods of time when the *Star Trek* project was moving forward and I was not available. I went off to do *Equus* on Broadway. During that period of time, the concept changed to a TV series. It was difficult then to get together because there was a question of availability. When the project turned around and I was available again, we started talking immediately. It has been complicated; it has been time-consuming. But there was never a question of reluctance to be involved in *Star Trek* on my part. I've always felt totally comfortable about being identified with *Star Trek,* and being identified with the Spock character. It has exploded my life in a very positive way. The Spock character has always been a part of my life. I have never tried in any way to reject that. I'm very proud of the fact that I'm associated with the character.

JON POVILL

Here's what the problem was between Gene and Robert Wise: Paramount told Gene that he still had creative control, so he had no reason but to be thrilled this was all happening. But they also told Robert Wise that *he* had creative control and neglected to tell Wise that Gene had creative control. It was not a good working situation.

HAROLD LIVINGSTON (writer, *Star Trek: The Motion Picture*)

Gene was supposed to have limited creative control, but he made Bob Wise's life miserable. But Wise was smart enough not to get into any arguments with him. Instead, he indulged and pacified him. He believed—and rightly, I'm sure—that anything else would have been totally nonproductive. I'm the only one unwise—pun intended—for that. But Wise had a picture to make and he had to keep the peace.

ROBERT WISE

Working with Gene was comparatively easy. Of course, as much as producers and directors are separate entities, you always have little conflicts at times, but by and large, it was fine. When I came on after being asked to direct the film, I said, "What about Mr. Roddenberry? Because it's his baby," and they said, "Well, you'll have to work it out." So Gene and I talked at some length about how we could work together, how he and I saw the whole thing. We came to reach a working agreement about halfway in our positions, and I think we functioned pretty well on that level.

GENE RODDENBERRY

There were a lot of places we disagreed, but in a friendly, professional way. My taste for costumes was a little different than his, but in the end I went with his taste because he was the man responsible for creating the whole visual image. If it had been more than just a question of taste, if I had thought the costumes violated *Star Trek* format, then we would have probably had a very serious fight. But we didn't, because it was just a question of taste. There are some places where we wanted to do something, I can't remember an example right now, and

I would say, "Bob, the *Star Trek* format has always been this. I don't want to lock you into format, but let's not change unless we have some value that makes the change worthwhile."

DAVID C. FEIN (producer, *Star Trek: The Motion Picture–Director's Edition*)

This is my understanding: The project was already overcontrolled by Gene before Bob ever got there. The studio already had a lot of issues with Gene's absolute control and absolute power over the entire project—and all projects in regards to *Star Trek*—and this was a big deal, of course. Here's this guy who absolutely wants to tell great stories—I don't necessarily disagree with Gene being as protective or even as influential as he wanted to be. He's had some great successes with all of this. But the studio wanted a *movie,* and they wanted a movie that could be done on budget and on time without the chaos that was potentially there. One of the executives at Paramount proposed the idea of bringing on Robert Wise to direct the film. You see, Gene's favorite film of all time is *The Day the Earth Stood Still,* and what could you say to Gene to get him to be somewhat under control or somewhat cooperative? You needed to get someone that *Gene* respected. Somebody who would lead *Gene* to say, "Here's somebody who could potentially do a better job than me *or* at least I would love to collaborate with, but I would trust them." That's how Bob came on board. I think it was, "How can we control Roddenberry in making a collaborative, fantastic movie?" Gene was at the top of his game, he was *Star Trek,* so what do you do? You get his idol.

JON POVILL

I think there's some truth in that. I know Gene certainly did have a lot of respect for Bob Wise, at least in the early going. It became less so the more dissension there was on what to do. When Bob overruled him and the studio stood with Bob, that was a problem.

ROBERT WISE

When I came on the project, they already had the original team of special-effects men, Robert Abel and Associates, at work, and a number of the sets were already done, but there is one area that I did have influence on: I upgraded the sets considerably from what they had originally built. What you saw in the film is not at all what I came on to.

JOSEPH R. JENNINGS (production designer, *Star Trek: Phase II*)

I was involved with the feature for a time, but when Mr. Wise came aboard, I felt that he really didn't want anybody who had been involved with the proposed television series. As a result, most of them disappeared along with me. The sets had proceeded to such a degree that they insisted on including my name on the credits. When the second feature was being made, I was brought back.

The sets we had designed for *Phase II* were a great deal more sophisticated in their mechanics than the ones on the original series had been. The reason for doing so was that the bridge of the *Enterprise* was designed to go into series, so we were designing to be all things to all people. As a result, all of the devices were practical and they worked off proximity switches. This was not for one specific show. What you're being asked to do is design a set that will function for three years of shows, so we were being a great deal more sophisticated than perhaps we would have been were it laid out to be a feature picture in which there were a certain given set of actions that had to be performed on that set. Then you only build those things that operate properly. When you talk about going to series, you don't know down the line what you're going to need.

GENE RODDENBERRY

Changes within the *Enterprise* came from outside artists who would bring them to Bob and me for our approval. It was a very involved process. Bob and I began chatting before we had our first sketch. You know, "Make sure it looks like this, and that . . ." We inherited a bridge that had been designed for a TV show, and I said, "Bob, I don't want to stick you with something we designed for TV, which is a totally different type of image. I think that now you should bring in your own designer and revise it."

RICHARD H. KLINE
(director of photography, *Star Trek: The Motion Picture*)

Robert Wise, Harold Michelson, and I, along with a production sketch artist and several other talented concept individuals, had to constantly put our heads together and try to plan ahead. There was hardly a day that we didn't meet during lunch to discuss what we were going to be doing after lunch. It always seemed to be "right up to airtime." That is the sort of pressure we were under in trying to get the project completed properly and on time, in trying to shoot the most sophisticated of all science-fiction films without sufficient preplanning. Our main problems stemmed from not having Doug Trumbull and company aboard earlier, plus the fact that the story was being written as we went along—which made it most difficult to plan ahead.

HAROLD MICHELSON
(production designer, *Star Trek: The Motion Picture*)

We had what we thought were some really outlandish ideas of the way things would be three hundred years from now. Then I sent out these ideas to the Jet Propulsion Laboratory and our ideas seemed old-fashioned. I had to do whatever I could to make it look like something more impressive than just a TV show. The version that appeared on television utilized small sets, and much of the action was played against blank walls. This was due to time and budget restrictions, but it was acceptable on the small canvas of the television tube. However, we were making a big picture for wide-screen presentation, so I had to try to open it up and create an illusion of a tremendous amount of space. This is the reason Bob Wise asked for the huge recreation area in which four or five hundred people appear. It was there to show the audience that this ship was really loaded with people.

RICHARD TAYLOR

When I first walked through the sets I kept thinking, "Haven't these people seen *2001*? Haven't they seen *Star Wars*?" Because both of those movies had phenomenal designs, and as you well know, they both still hold up. Those space suits and the design of the *Discovery* were so beautifully done and well researched and based on real technologies.

Now, it wasn't our job to design the sets, but the sets and all the continuity of the film had to fit together, and there were parts of the *Enterprise* model that had to match up to the sets. The engine room, the bridge, the recreation room. And seeing out the windows to the nacelles and all those kind of things had to have a continuity. What I wanted to do initially was to bring as much new technology to the design of all this as possible. I had been to the Lawrence Livermore lab, seeing things they were doing there. I had been reading voraciously about how space structures could be made or would be made in the future. And I wanted to apply as much of that as possible.

HAROLD MICHELSON

When we came on the job, a bridge had been built for what at one time was planned as another TV series. When the decision was made in favor of a big-budget, theatrical movie, everything had to be done over. The bridge had been built in a number of sections, which could be moved in or out according to the scene being filmed.

RICHARD TAYLOR

I looked at the sets that existed and they were just really not the quality that they needed to be. I won't say they were laughable, but the quarters of the *Enterprise* looked to me like something from an army base. And, of course, one of the things I had to look at were the models being built. The *Enterprise* was not at all built with the look or the technology it needed to be for models using motion control and for multiple passes to be made on. This model that was being built was roughly three-and-a-half feet to four feet long. I looked at that model and it just wouldn't work. When you're shooting models and you want them to look real on camera, they're called miniatures, but they're not, they're actually quite big. The *Enterprise* we built was eight feet long.

RONALD D. MOORE
(supervising producer, *Star Trek: The Next Generation*)

The *Enterprise* in *The Motion Picture* is the best of all the designs. It's sleek and beautiful and everything is in proportion. It moves really well, it photographs like a dream, and it's an incredibly detailed model. That's a fantastic version of the *Enterprise*. The original is the original, and it will always be a brilliant original creative design, but the movie version takes it to the next level in a way that subsequent iterations of the *Enterprise* did not do. The subsequent ones all feel like they're trying to reach for something that they never quite grasp, but the *Motion Picture* version gets there and it's a brilliant design.

RICHARD TAYLOR

To do close-ups of things and to have scale, you have to make the model bigger so you can get detail on the surface and the camera can get close to that. Small models you can never get close to and have detail, and they look like toys. So their model just wouldn't work. And then the sets themselves, including the bridge, looked like they were from the fifties. I won't criticize anybody for how those designs happened, because I will tell you that Gene Roddenberry had his thumb on a lot of things, and I was very frustrated working with him because he had some constraints that he felt had to be. And they defied logic many times.

HAROLD MICHELSON

Richard Kline likes to film within a set, so the sections of the bridge were virtually welded together. As a result, the seams wouldn't show and it would look solid. The engine room is greatly expanded. Mr. Wise wanted a feeling of tremendous power, but not with the coloring of fire as we would get today. So we went to different shades of blue going to white. The vertical core, now two and a half stories high, and the horizontal part of the engine, appearing to go off into infinity, were all newly designed and made of Plexiglas. To make room for the horizontal section, we broke through the end of the set and, using forced perspective, gave the exaggerated impression of its length. In the filming, small people, midgets, were used as crew members at the far end, continuing the perspective. What we did was break out from a small set into a lot of size.

RICHARD TAYLOR

The other part of the design things with the *Enterprise* had to do with the bridge. And we had to do all these effects on the viewscreen. One of the things that drove me crazy about the original show was that here are these people off in the distant future, yet when they get in any emergency situation they are all falling around on the bridge, grabbing on to stuff. It's like, what the fuck happened to seat belts? I mean, we have seat belts now and this was in 1979. Why were these people so stupid in the future that every emergency they were falling all around the bridge? So I went to Roddenberry and I said, "Can we design seats that have a way of holding them in the seat?" And he finally agreed, so I designed the chairs that folded up over laps.

The other thing that I wanted to do on the bridge that I had seen at Lawrence Livermore was that tactile screens were the way the future was going to be, and not 1950s-era toggle switches and buttons. One of the cool things about a tactile screen is the animations and the things could happen on there. You can touch it and it can configure itself and that could be so visually cool. Roddenberry absolutely rejected that. He said, "No, I want switches, I want buttons, I want stuff that people touch and click and all of that." To me those were decisions just dating the thing before you even got started.

ROBERT WISE

I insisted on changing the costumes as soon as I came in on the project. The originals looked like pajamas or something. Too much like comic books.

ROBERT FLETCHER
(costume designer, *Star Trek: The Motion Picture*)

The basic uniform was the most difficult to design, because it had to bear some reference to the original clothes and yet be entirely different. It had to look like the future, but not be so extravagant that it drew attention to itself. That was one thing Robert Wise did not want to happen. He wanted the clothes simply to be there, to be accepted, to look logical—to seem very real. I found that the most difficult part. It's much easier to do an extravagant and flamboyant costume for some alien prince, something you can really get your teeth into, than trying to tread very delicately on eggshells and not offend the original Trekkers.

WALTER KOENIG (actor, "Pavel Chekov")

Personally, I thought they were terrific. A real improvement over the pj's we wore on the series—except that they were uncomfortable. I was impressed. One button was worth more than an entire costume in the old days.

ROBERT FLETCHER

Another thing I changed was the basic color concept. The original *Star Trek* was brightly colored, but a lot of that came about because color TV had been recently invented and all the networks wanted as much color as they could get for their money, right away. Robert Wise and I felt that the brilliant color was not very realistic, that it seemed distracting. Also, military organizations have the tendency to keep things more utilitarian, and this will probably continue in the future.

I found Gene Roddenberry great fun to work with. He very definitely said what he liked and didn't like. . . . It was give-and-take; he was not inflexible. If I had a good reason for something, he'd listen. Sometimes, though, I didn't understand what he meant and it was difficult for him to read a sketch, so I was careful to show as many samples as I could so that he saw the thing in the flesh, as it were.

Obviously when it came to "surface" details, things went fairly smoothly, but if anything threatened—it did on more than one occasion—to shake *Star Trek: The Motion Picture* to its core, it was the battle for the proper screenplay and the war waged over the film's visual effects. In both cases, the situation stemmed from the fact that the script and the effects house (Robert Abel & Associates) had been designed to launch *Phase II* and *not* serve as the basis of a multimillion-dollar feature film.

When *Star Trek: The Motion Picture* was officially announced by Paramount on March 28, 1978, via press conference, Susan Sackett wrote of the script in her Star Trek Report column in *Starlog*: "Dennis Lynton Clark is doing the final rewrite and polish of the script, which was written by Harold Livingston and Gene Roddenberry, based on a story by Alan Dean Foster and Gene Roddenberry. Dennis recently wrote the screenplay for United Artists' *Comes a Horseman*, from his own novel."

DENNIS LYNTON CLARK (writer, *Comes a Horseman*)

The whole situation was very frustrating. Gene Roddenberry's a very nice man, but he became very strange about *Star Trek*; it was like his child. The problem with Gene is that his heart was never in the right place at the right time. It's a good heart, but he puts it aside at the wrong times. I was the subject of an awful practical joke, and it was right at the beginning of our relationship, so it set things off badly. I really don't know how to describe him. He's a nice man . . . unless you give him some power. That practical joke was the beginning of the end. I got pissed off, Gene got pissed off, and the only mediator was Bob Wise, who looked at me and said, "I'm going to have to fire you, aren't I?" And I said, "Yes."

ROBERT WISE

I had as much influence on the script as I possibly could. It was one of those situations where we started with an incomplete script—we knew the story, of course, but the actual final parts of the script were being worked on constantly as we were shooting. When we actually started early on in 1978, we only had the first act of the script written. From there on the second and third act we were changing and rewriting. I had some influence on the first act as it went, I tried to have as much as I could on the rest of the film, but it is a very sloppy way to make a film by any means.

GENE RODDENBERRY

We took some losses because of the decision to shoot the TV script, but not because the studio was foolish. Costs were mounting up. They had to keep this actor on and that stage ready . . . so the studio didn't have the option to say, "Take three months and then take another start at it." They felt they just couldn't do it from the viewpoint of sound management and economics. These are the kinds of decisions those people must face and it's very easy for an artist to say, "Well, I won't sell out to you." But it's not that simple. They have their problems, too, these people over in the front office. Do they do idiotic things? Yes, of course they do. So do we, at our typewriters, in front of cameras—although we prefer to think everything we do is golden.

WALTER KOENIG

I was rather in awe of Robert Wise. We started the picture with only two-thirds of a finished screenplay, though. You cannot back yourself into a corner like that. The whole idea behind screenwriting is rewriting and we didn't have the luxury of rewriting because we were writing with the camera and reshooting was enormously expensive. So we started out with a story about an antagonistic, omnipotent being that was this great threat, and somewhere in the middle of the story we decided it's not really that at all. It's this awe-inspiring entity that's trying to achieve another level of consciousness. What happens to the conflict? We didn't have a tension-filled conflict, we had people with wide eyes marveling at the enormity and strangeness of this thing. It's great for a travelogue, but it's not great for good storytelling and it failed in that regard.

DENNIS LYNTON CLARK

I guess I was involved with the project for about three months, two of which were spent hiding out from Nimoy and Shatner, because they didn't want me to talk with them. I'd have to leave my office when they were on the lot, because actors want to tell you, "This is how I perceive the character," and Gene didn't want their input. He didn't want me to have their input. He didn't even like Bob Wise's input.

WILLIAM SHATNER

Our area is pure science fiction. *Star Wars* was a science-fiction cartoon. Great science fiction is an illumination of the human condition in a future environment under different terms. We always had a quality of believability going for us as well as a certain chemistry. I felt a tremendous obligation not to let down the reputation of the old series while we were filming the movie.

JOSHUA CULP (assistant to Dennis Lynton Clark)

Dennis cranked out twenty or twenty-five pages, taking the really kind of limp-wristed opening that the movie has and injecting it with some great stuff. Including some wonderful scenes of Spock on Vulcan talking to one of the high priestesses about his double nature and how to deal with it all. They had the big press conference with all of the actors and Paramount brass, Robert Wise and Gene and everybody else. Once that had happened, *the next day* Roddenberry came into Dennis's office with, like, thirty pages of notes on the first twenty-five pages of new screenplay. This continued for the next several weeks until Roddenberry had stalled the rewrite process to where Bob Wise had to shrug his shoulders and say, "I guess we're going with Roddenberry's script, because, clearly, we're not going to get a new script in time to do the work that's necessary to prep it." A week or so later, Dennis was cut loose and we went off to work at Fox.

HAROLD LIVINGSTON

On a Saturday night, I get a call at ten o'clock at night. I pick up the phone. I knew it was Roddenberry. "Hello! How are you?" he asked. I answered, "What the fuck do you want?" He says, "Listen, I got a problem." I said, "I know you have a problem. So what do you want from me?" He said, "I want you to read a script." I said, "Whose script? Yours? I won't read it." "No, this is Dennis Clark's." Not ten minutes later the doorbell rings and there is a messenger with the script. Gene asked me to read it and get back to him no matter what time that night.

I read the script. My script, rewritten a number of times. Total shit. So I call him up and I said, "Forget it." He said, "Listen, will you meet me and Bob Wise tomorrow morning?" So I agree. It's the first time ever I met Bob Wise, the revered director. My first words to him were, "Mr. Wise, you better take a gun and shoot yourself." Which went over good. And Gene, of course, laughed. The upshot of that is they hired me back—so now I got him by the balls. I go back to work for ten thousand dollars a week and I'm rewriting my own script.

SUSAN SACKETT

What people don't understand is television does not always translate into feature-length motion pictures. This was one of the first TV shows to become a motion picture. There were so many attempts at the story that had started out as the beginning of what was going to be one of many TV episodes, and then they chose this particular story and everybody had a finger in the pie and it grew. What we ended up with was pretty good considering everybody had input. It was story by committee, although Gene took it and finalized it. It probably suffered from that.

HAROLD LIVINGSTON

Nimoy was a tremendous help to me. He used to come to my house every night and we would have to fix what Gene did, because Gene would rewrite it and give it to the production people. Nimoy had good character sense. Shatner did, too. But I didn't work as closely with Shatner as I did with Leonard because he lived nearby. And he knew characterization because he was more *Star Trek* than I was. He helped me in that respect.

LEONARD NIMOY

One of the things that *Star Trek* fans always enjoyed a lot about the series was the humor. There was always something tongue-in-cheek if not flat-out comedy. There was always some wry look, a line, an eyebrow raised, something that let them in on the joke. On *Star Trek I* it was forbidden. I mean it was *forbidden*! It was decided that we were doing a very serious motion picture here, we would not do funny stuff.

At the end, in fact it was the last day of filming, we were shooting the tag scene on the bridge. The adventure is over. The world has been saved. Everybody is safe. Kirk had brought together this crew after a hiatus for this one special mission. He has taken McCoy out of retirement, called Spock off Vulcan. Now it is time to take everybody back. He says to McCoy, "I can have you back on Earth in two days." McCoy says, "Now that I'm here, I might as well stay." Then he says to Spock, "I suppose you want to go back to Vulcan." Spock's line, as written, was "My business there is finished." Final rehearsal before the take, Kirk says, "I can have you back on Earth . . ." McCoy says, "No, I'll stay here . . ." and he says, "I suppose you'll want to go back to Vulcan." And I said, "If Dr. McCoy is to remain on board, then my presence here will be essential." Everybody roared—which I knew they would. But then I saw the command group gather. They really huddled. Bob Wise came to me and he said, "Seems inappropriate to be doing humor at this point." I said, "I offer it to you. I can't make you take it." They wouldn't let me do it. They were really adamant about it. That picture had a very classy look, but it was not a lot of fun—either to do or to watch.

HAROLD LIVINGSTON

I had an understanding with young Mr. Katzenberg and Mr. Wise and Gene that I would do it as long as Gene didn't write. I didn't want Gene to put pen to paper. You want me to write it? *I* will write it. *I'll* do all the rewriting you want, but *I* will do it. I had a certain style I wanted to do the script in and I had directions I wanted the characters to explore.

The first thing that happened was that I rewrote X number of pages and they were to be pouched to Eisner and Katzenberg in Paris. Eisner called up and said, "What kind of shit is this?" I said, "What are you talking about?" "This script you sent me?" "It's a good script. I didn't send it without Bob's approval." So I went to Bob Wise, and we find out that Gene's secretary got the script, put it aside, and sent *Gene's* script to Eisner. *That's* the kind of shit that went on. Gene would be very remorseful and contrite: "I was just trying to help." I said, "Listen, Gene, I'm not going to do this if you're going to keep this up." Well, I quit three times. I resigned. I'm talking about ten thousand dollars a week.

WALTER KOENIG

We didn't have a finished screenplay and know exactly where we were going with it. And then halfway through the picture the clause on Bill and Leonard's contracts kicked in that they had dialogue or story approval if the picture went beyond so many weeks. So those meetings in the morning between Gene Roddenberry, Livingston and Jon Povill and Jeffrey Katzenberg and Bill and Leonard and Bob Wise were seven people deciding what they were going to shoot that day, and many with vested interests that it would be shot a certain way.

JON POVILL

Probably Nimoy and Shatner had been given certain latitude in respect to their own situation. Nimoy had a certain amount of control of what and how Spock was going to be portrayed. There were a lot of different controls out there and, not surprisingly, that resulted in a lot of dissension. It was not that anybody was trying to steer the project wrong. Yes, Shatner's always trying to do the best thing for Shatner, but by and large everybody was trying to do the best that they could for the project. It's just that it was being pulled in a lot of different directions.

HAROLD LIVINGSTON

As we began shooting, we would get to a point where I would send in pages and then Gene would send in different pages and Wise would get two different versions. Sometimes I would write it and put my initials on them and Gene would put "G.R., 4PM" under mine, as though that's what should count and my pages should be ignored. This was the way the picture was made. For the third time I quit, I said, "Screw it, nothing is worth this." Gene has a brilliant story mind for this kind of thing, but he's a bad writer. He's clumsy.

JON POVILL

The dueling drafts! Harold at four, Gene at five. And I had pages in there as well. I swear, my blood pressure went up forty points, essentially because part of my job was trying to find common ground between Gene and Harold, and try to mediate their drafts. And *that* was what killed my relationship with Roddenberry, because I was supporting Harold far more than I was supporting him.

That was very definite, and because of it I became a traitor in Gene's eyes, and our relationship collapsed. It was still cordial, but it was never actually confronted because Gene never really confronted anything. He was passive-aggressive. But it was never the same after that. Even if I had sided with Harold a total of 50 percent of the time, that still would not have been enough for Gene. Gene would have needed, like, 90 to 95 percent, and that just wasn't going to happen. I was doing the best I could for what was best for the project. That's what I always do and it's bitten me in my ass my entire career. To some extent, the people that Gene considered "interlopers" were trying to save him from himself, and to some extent they weren't. There were things that Harold wanted to throw out—I can't remember what—that were good or probably would have been good had they made it in.

Bob was looking to make the project as good as it could be. He was out for what was best for the project. Bob was more than happy to support the 20 percent of Gene's ideas that were good. More than happy to. He actually would *look* for things. He would say to me, "Is there a way to make this work?" That was something he *couldn't* say to Harold, because Harold would say, "No! It's just fucking shit." So I would be tasked with finding a way to make something Gene did acceptable to Harold. Bob was not in competition with Gene at all. Gene was in competition with *everybody*. Look, the movie had enough problems as it was. Gene's ideas would have made it worse.

HAROLD LIVINGSTON

I get a call from Jeff Katzenberg to come to the office at seven p.m. He has to go out for a phone call. His secretary comes in and says, "Can I get you a drink?" It's seven p.m. and I always have a drink, so I said, "Yeah, I'll have a shot of gin." She walks out and locks the door. I'm locked in! Twenty minutes later Katzenberg comes back, and I'm whacked out of my head, and I make a deal with him to come back for more money, and I also got a fifty-thousand-dollar script commitment out of him.

They started to shoot the film and Gene just kept rewriting. Driving everybody nuts. Somehow we finished the movie. Gene got the last word anyway.

GENE RODDENBERRY

During the same period I was novelizing the script into a *Star Trek* novel. So I've had sort of the unusual experience of watching us cut scenes and finding myself, later on, sitting at the typewriter and writing the scene, and having the opportunity to see and study what it is there that you get with a camera that you've got to do with words in a novel and what are the differences. Now, do the two compare? For me, it was like a college course in cinematography and writing.

HAROLD LIVINGSTON

What he did was he had made a deal with Pocket Books to novelize my screenplay for four hundred grand. And boy, did he enjoy telling me *that*!

One addition that Roddenberry undeniably made to the screenplay was the notion that to ultimately stop the returning, marauding space probe—identifying itself as V'ger, and revealed to be the ancient NASA probe *Voyager 6*—it releases all of its accumulated data. In later drafts, the data release would be into Commander Will Decker before he and Ilia—who has been killed and replaced by a robot probe in her image—transcend this dimension. Livingston's original version had the probe merely recognizing humanity's positive qualities and departing the galaxy.

GENE RODDENBERRY

The script started off a bit simpler, because it had been written as a two-hour television program. It got more and more complex as it got to be a bigger and bigger movie, and we started adding things on to make use of the wide-screen, big-vision, like the wing-walk, where they go out on top of the *Enterprise* saucer section. I put that in. I put the climax of the show inside V'ger, where the original script did not.

HAROLD LIVINGSTON

Back on *Phase II*, Robert Goodwin theorized that I just pissed away the ending, because I was so disgusted with the situation. I think the truth is that I couldn't come up with an ending. I just couldn't do it. The problem was that we had an antagonist so omnipotent that to defeat it, or even communicate with it, or have any kind of relationship with it, made the concept of the story false. How the hell do we deal with this? On what level? Everything pretty much worked in the story until we got to the ending. We tried all kinds of approaches, including aesthetic, theological, and philosophical. We didn't know what to do with the ending.

JON POVILL

We knew we had to have a big special-effects ending. The problem of what was going to happen at the end and why it was going to happen was one that plagued the script from the very start. Then Gene came up with the idea of the machine dumping its data into Decker, with a light show of all the information it had accumulated. We were going to get all this amazing, incomprehensible stuff that V'ger had accumulated in its travels across the universe, and of course, nobody could come up with these images, so that didn't work. It was pretty much my contribution to say that the reason for what was happening was that this thing needed to go on to the next plane of existence. That it was transcending dimensions and going on to the next. It then became logical that the machine would need that human element to combine with. It was the only thing that could have made sense.

Harold was *not* enthusiastic about this idea, but he accepted it because there was no choice in the matter as we were writing as we shot. To the "whole capture the creator, join the creator thing," he said, "what the fuck are you talking about?" But the idea was in advance of the singularity that now people are talking about for real in terms of the time when it will be possible to capture human consciousness in a computer, keeping a person's thoughts, memories, and ideas and going forward forever and expanding upon it. In the computer setting, the mind can think in infinite dimensions. This is now a possibility, and I was there, sort of anticipating it, which is something I'm kind of proud of.

GENE RODDENBERRY

Right down to the last day of filming, I would get strange looks from people who would say, "That fellow over there is the one who thinks a machine really can be alive." As if I invented that thought, rather than it being something that very serious scientists have talked about and speculated about for years. Paramount was so convinced that the things I was talking about were such total nonsense that it was worth some money to hire an expert to back up their belief that it was nonsense. That expert was Isaac Asimov, and of course he *didn't* back up their beliefs. The funny thing is, I've been an Asimov fan for more years than I care to think about, and I learned many of my ideas from *him*.

JON POVILL

Throughout we were trying to figure out what was it that made *Star Trek* special. How to identify the key elements of *Star Trek* that made it unique, and how do we translate those for the big screen? A lot of it is the intimacy of the Kirk-Spock-McCoy relationship, and the intimacy of that on the small screen. But you don't get that on the big screen. Are people in love with space? Are they in love with the concepts that the best *Star Trek* episodes dealt with, the philosophies, the ideals that it embraced? What made *Star Trek Star Trek*? There was great dissension about how to bring that to the screen. Everybody had different ideas. I felt that we had to do something philosophically special, and Gene was in accord with that. That was one area that we agreed upon. Harold not so much. Harold didn't give a shit about that. Harold gave a shit about the action and the drama. He wasn't crazy about the time that had to be spent reintroducing everybody, because from his perspective it slowed things down.

ROBERT WISE

After I had made the film, I learned that the story line was similar to two of the old episodes, "The Changeling" and "The Doomsday Machine." I was in New York after the opening of the movie in Washington, DC, and my wife was with a friend in Bloomingdale's where they had a big display of *Star Trek* merchandise. There was a young girl there who turned to my wife and said, "Why didn't they do a fresh story?" That was the first time I heard of that problem.

GENE RODDENBERRY

After having done seventy-nine episodes covering a fairly wide field, it would have been hard to do anything and not have it bear some resemblances. I think the film appeared to resemble certain episodes more at the end, because many of the things that made the script different were, bit by bit, sliced out of the movie. They were the "talky" things. The personal stories were excised from the script or the shooting schedule. Then it became more and more like things we had done before.

JON POVILL

Through it all, Bob Wise was doing a balancing act. Bob had so many problems in so many directions between the physical demands of shooting the thing, the need for pages—because there were days we would go to set without them—and the insane personality differences. The demands of Shatner and Nimoy, who were coming in with their own ideas. Roddenberry coming in with his ideas. Harold coming in with his ideas. Me coming in with my ideas. If this was an elephant by committee, it was Bob who was trying to piece the thing together. A lot of strong personalities and a lot of very different opinions. And on top of all of *that,* he had the special-effects people saying, "We can do this, we can do this, we can do this, and we can do this. It's going to look great . . . but we can't deliver anything yet. *However,* here's the drawing of what it's *going* to be. . . . We just need more floppy drives," or something.

Another pitfall involving the production of *Star Trek: The Motion Picture* was that it had been "blind-booked" into theaters for December 7, 1979. This meant that theaters guaranteed a minimum cash payment—in this case a total of about thirty-five million dollars—provided it made that release date, sight unseen. In other words, as far as Paramount was concerned, absolutely *nothing* could delay its release . . . though the film's special-effects debacle was the one thing that could have imperiled the studio being able to release the film on time.

GERALD ISENBERG

The whole production got away from them. They hired a guy named Bob Abel to do the special effects. I knew Bob and he was a codirector of a movie I'd made on fifties rock and roll. He was a documentary and commercial director at the time and now, seven years later, he's sold himself as a special-effects guy, so they invested another five million dollars in him and had *nothing.* It was a complete waste, it was a nightmare, and they were now locked in to a release date and there was nothing they could do.

ROBERT WISE

On *Star Trek* I had so much to deal with which was not even done yet. Scenes in which my actors had to play and react to that screen. All that came in months and months later. The best I ever had for them to react to was a projection of a sketch or a picture of what the effects men were planning to achieve. That's all I had for them. I had to remind them of what was going on in terms of the action, to describe the best I could from the script and my own ideas of the sketch what they were supposed to be looking at. It takes some very professional actors to respond to something like that, and that made it very difficult—in fact, it was perhaps the most difficult part of the film. And then we had, of course, the big problem of having to change the special-effects people after a year.

RICHARD TAYLOR

Bob Abel had produced some feature-film documentaries like *Mad Dogs & Englishmen* and the documentary *Making of the President 1968*. But as far as a dramatic theatrical film, it was the first piece that the studio worked on. And of course, this was all pre-CG. So the studio was noted for its graphics and it had opened the Pandora's box for a whole new form of advertising. Very extreme visual stuff, very psychedelic. When we got involved, Paramount was pretty well down the trail on creating a television feature of *Star Trek*. And they had built sets to a particular point. There was an *Enterprise* model that was being built and a dry dock, a V'ger, and some other things. As a knee-jerk reaction to the success of *Star Wars*, they decided to turn it into a theatrical feature.

And somewhere along the line, they knew that it was time to relook at the whole thing and to bring a contemporary visual-effects company in to try and upgrade the whole visual aspect of the film. I don't think that they really analyzed the Abel studio in terms of Did we have a model shop? Did we have a matte-painting department or any of that kind of stuff?

SUSAN SACKETT

The production itself wasn't as rushed as the special effects were rushed, and that was because of the screwup by Robert Abel. When suddenly we were given a date for this movie to premiere in theaters, and told it must be ready because they went out and presold the movie and taken blind bids for December 7, we had to have special effects and we had almost none.

RICHARD TAYLOR

It wasn't in Bob Abel's nature to say "I fucked this up," but he really did over-extend us and overpromised. He really went into these meetings and would kind of take over. Bob Abel was a talented man and he really knew talent and how to hire it. He was a glib, rapping, Jewish salesman. He had a film background from UCLA and had directed some documentaries, some good ones. But he just would go in and dominate a meeting. I remember during the meetings thinking, Jesus, Bob, shut up. You're not directing this movie. But he would make commitments for us to do something and then turn around and say, "Okay, Richard, go get her done."

ROBERT WISE

I want simply to say that they were very creative people and they had excellent ideas, but the big concern that we had was whether they would be able to execute all of the effects in time so the film would be ready for its release date of December 7, which was absolutely imperative. That was what made us decide to change. It wasn't lack of creativeness or abilities or anything like that. They were very good, had very good ideas, but I don't think they were equipped yet to execute fast enough such a big amount of very sophisticated effects. That was a giant picture in terms of effects and work involved.

DEBORAH ARAKELIAN (assistant to Harve Bennett and Robert Sallin)

They showed thirty seconds of footage to Bob Wise, and one of the producers told me it was the only time he saw Wise look angry. He walked out of the screening. It was a potato on the motion-control device, because the *Enterprise* had not been built yet.

JON POVILL

I didn't see Bob go into that screening, but saw him shortly after he came out and he was angrier than I'd ever seen him. This was a man with seemingly endless patience—certainly not a man prone to flying into rages—but he was *fuming*. Said he wanted Abel and his company off the picture immediately and never wanted to see the SOB again.

Abel had been working on the film for longer than Bob had, and this was the first time he'd shown any test footage. After stalling and stalling and stalling for months. I never saw the footage, but Bob clearly thought it was absolute crap. Abel had been hired off the strength of a famous and visually groundbreaking commercial he'd done for Levi's jeans. But we later learned that the commercial, though beautiful, was very late and very over budget. He kept showing us amazing conceptual drawings that would have been great, except he actually had no clue how to deliver them. It would have been a trial-and-error process that might have worked eventually or might not—but we sure as hell would have had no chance whatsoever of opening on December 7 if he'd stayed on.

JOSEPH R. JENNINGS

On *Phase II,* I had objected strenuously to the hiring of Abel and company, because I felt they were incapable of doing the job. Paramount spent a great deal of money on them and wound up with nothing. They were very good salesmen. That's it. And their record was plain to be seen. They had been doing commercials, all of which had gone radically over budget. They had one, a Levi's commercial, which everybody was all hopped up about. And he came on with a presentation you wouldn't believe. Mr. Wise was very attracted to young people with new ideas. I was about his age. I was not the age of Abel and company, and we certainly did not see eye to eye. That you can write in great big bold letters.

I had one or two illustrators part time, and with the money that Paramount was giving Abel, they had five or six of them, all of whom were turning out very finished airbrushed illustrations of circumstances that really had nothing to do with the script but were very impressive. I feel that the creative people were definitely suckered in by that, because they thought they were getting something that no one had ever heard of—very art deco. And I said, "Who the hell wants an art deco spaceship?" Yet it apparently all looked very attractive. As I say, they sold very well. When they got the chance, all they did was continue selling. It was a very costly error.

SUSAN SACKETT

In a very short time, Doug Trumbull and his crew were hired. They did a lot of beautiful special effects, some totally superfluous, and all of them were included because Paramount said we bought and paid for them, so we are going to put them in the film. It became a big special-effects and light show, and a lot of that should have been trimmed. We would have done that had we had the time. The long ride around the *Enterprise* looks really nice, but doesn't do much to advance the story. But on the other hand, some people love that. They think the *Enterprise* is the star of the show. Shatner would have you believe differently.

RALPH WINTER (postproduction supervisor, *Star Trek II*)

By July, Abel had only delivered one sixteen-millimeter high-speed blowup of the wormhole. He was trying to pioneer with his very smart team a new level of visual effects and he couldn't deliver. In that sense, *Star Trek V* was exactly parallel to that. That's why Doug Trumbull took over. Barry Diller said to him, "It doesn't matter what you spend. We already presold this movie to theaters. You have to deliver this thing. Spend whatever it takes." A lot of people made their careers and built companies based on *Star Trek*. You could track the credits of people in *Star Trek: The Motion Picture* for the next twenty years. They were all in the effects business of every major motion picture from there on out. So it was groundbreaking in what they did in six months. But there was a price to be paid.

EDDIE EGAN

At Paramount, there was absolute panic and fear of lawsuits. It was one of the broadest releases of all time at that point and they had extracted very, very strict terms from the exhibitors for the privilege of playing the movie. There were many people who thought there would be no movie to deliver based on what happened with the visual effects. It also presented practical problems for advertising and publicity. There was no film to show. There were no materials to cut TV spots from that featured special effects until very late. Later, there would be a lot of vendors put on to cut TV spots on a wing and a prayer, with slugs in them that said, "This shot will show *Enterprise* moving left to right toward camera." Those were *very* worrisome days.

RICHARD TAYLOR

The original budget that we had to do the effects for the movie was twelve million dollars, and we had a good plan going. We started down that trail and would be designing shots and things and they kept changing the script. Every time you change the script, we had to reboard it and refigure out stuff. We hadn't shot any scenes for the film yet, because the fucking script kept changing. So we were just beginning to start principal photography on the models, and because they kept changing the script, our budget started going up. It was fourteen and then it got to like sixteen and then they said, "Hold it. You don't know what you're doing and we want to bring in Doug Trumbull," who had done *Close Encounters* and has made science fiction. "We want him to take an objective look at this and see if he thinks you can really finish it."

ANDREW PROBERT (concept designer/production illustrator, *Star Trek: The Motion Picture*)

I started on the project with Abel and then went through the painful process of changeover to Trumbull. Trumbull took me on as one of several people that were pulled through that, so in a way I feel kind of lucky by that and certainly complimented by it. Initially when the studio brought Abel on to the film, they were very excited by the possibilities that could happen by using Abel for the special effects, because Bob had done a lot of really nice things up to that point, not to mention some nice things since, so everyone was very optimistic. Bob's main concern in doing *Trek*'s effects was to give the audience something that they'd never seen before, and consequently, this entailed a lot of research and development, which ran the budget way over what he had expected.

Obviously when you're doing research and development work, there's really no useable footage because most of it deals with testing and wedging—which is testing light exposure. And Paramount sort of set up an ultimatum that if there wasn't any workable footage by a certain date, Abel would be taken off the project. We scrambled to get something going, but it just wasn't there in time, so there was a big blowup between Robert Wise and Bob Abel. Then they just turned to someone who was more or less within their sphere of influence, and that was Trumbull, and he indicated that he could "save" the picture for them.

RICHARD TAYLOR

While we were building these models, Trumbull came over several times and I could see he was lusting on these things. He was like, "Holy fuck, those models are really good. I didn't have anything to do with them." And so when it came for the objective review of what we were doing, there was no objectivity at all. It was like he basically said, "No, they aren't going to be able to get this done. The only way it's going to get done is if I do it, and I'll do it if you'll let me direct this movie *Brainstorm* after." So he threw that into the pot. And he came in and took over and a bunch of my people got taken by him from Abel's. Then he realized he couldn't get all this shit done either, so he recruited Apogee with John Dykstra and gave them a percentage of the work. And time was running out, so all of the sudden people are working golden time. And triple golden time. It cost forty million dollars in the end. Frankly, I didn't believe it when they told us we were off the picture. I had about a hundred and some people working for me one day and the next day I don't have anybody working for me.

I was actually in the camera room shooting a shot when they came in and said, "Richard, we've got to talk to you." And I said, "What?" and they said, "You're not on the movie anymore." I said, "What?" And they said, "Trumbull is taking over the picture and we're off the show." And I said, "I don't believe it. I'm going to keep shooting." And I kept shooting until they finally came in and unplugged the camera and said, "No, it's over. It's all fucking over." I left Abel's shortly after that, because I'd worked there from '73 to '79 and I'd helped create this studio. I thought we had worked our ass off to this point and we had done some great stuff and we were on track and he kept dragging us into more stuff.

JON POVILL

If we had six months longer to finish the effects the way they could have been done, if we'd had good special-effects personnel from the beginning instead of having to start over in January or February of '79, it would have been a very different movie. It still wouldn't have been good, but it would have been vastly better.

ROBERT WISE

Extra time would have made a difference, and I think that both Doug and John would admit that. By saying this, I don't want to imply that I don't think they did a fantastic job. The two of them did, and their people did a fantastic amount of excellent work to get the picture ready by the date, especially considering the fact that they had started behind schedule. I can't give them enough credit or praise for the job they did. However, given more time, let's say another three or four months, I think they would both agree that there are areas which could have been improved or done slightly differently.

One aspect of the film that is an indisputable triumph is composer Jerry Goldsmith's Oscar-nominated soundtrack (for the record, it lost–incomprehensibly–

to Georges Delerue's score for *A Little Romance*) which helped define what *Star Trek* music was for the next generation, literally and figuratively.

JERRY GOLDSMITH (composer, *Star Trek: The Motion Picture*)

The problem was I didn't have a theme. We recorded thirty minutes of music and everybody says, "Wow, that's wonderful." A couple days later I got a call from Bob Wise and he said, "I want to talk to you." He came over and said it wasn't working, because there's no theme. So once I got my ego under control, I agreed that he was absolutely right! So for two weeks I sweated that one out, and the rest is history: the *Star Trek* theme was born.

LUKAS KENDALL (editor, *Film Score Monthly*)

The best score of the movie series still has to be Jerry Goldsmith's for *The Motion Picture*. It's a magnificent achievement—modern, timeless, and unforgettable, with the definitive theme for the franchise. The movie, for all its faults, is still a towering piece of cinema, and the score a major component. But it was chaos to create: Goldsmith couldn't write without a finished film, and they were feeding him scenes and VFX sequences piecemeal. They'd book the 20th Century–Fox scoring stage not knowing whether they'd have music to record; sometimes they had a ninety-eight-piece orchestra sitting there with nothing to do, so they'd record umpteen takes of the main title.

JERRY GOLDSMITH

If it wasn't for Jeffrey Katzenberg, it would have never gotten done. He just wouldn't take no for an answer, and he was really like a high-school coach. He pushed everybody and got 'em going, and gave us pats on the back and cheered us on. He was fabulous. And I said after that, "Boy, this kid's going to go a long way," and I was right on that. In hindsight it was a lot of fun, but the actual doing of it wasn't so much fun.

The drama of the behind-the-scenes production of *Star Trek: The Motion Picture* was so all-encompassing that it can sometimes be forgotten that the entire cast from the original series was reunited and attempting to capture what had so successfully worked before. Additionally, Persis Khambatta, cast as Ilia in *Phase II*, was brought over to *Star Trek: The Motion Picture,* with Stephen Collins joining the production as Commander Will Decker.

ROBERT WISE

When Paramount held the press conference announcing the film, they set up a large table with Roddenberry, all the cast, etc. When my turn came to speak, I said, "You know, I'm the alien here," because I was the only one who hardly knew anything of *Star Trek.* They all knew more than I did. But it worked very well. They're all very good actors, very professional. I found all of them, and particularly Bill and Leonard, to be professional and very good actors.

WALTER KOENIG

A highlight for me was the first day, when I was at my console and Nichelle was at hers and George was at his, and Bill, the captain, walked onto the bridge for the first time, and I said, "Kep-tin." We all jumped up and ran over to him. I got such a high, such a rush at that moment that it took all my self-control not to embrace him. It was such a lovely moment. I *should* have embraced him.

WILLIAM SHATNER

It was a strange feeling, full of complex, even conflicting emotions. Ten years in my life suddenly had been swept away just as though they never had existed. I knew it was 1979, but it seemed like 1969 was just yesterday. Time seemingly stood still since I had last taken my place on the bridge of the U.S.S. *Enterprise* and uttered those now familiar words, "Captain's log, stardate . . ." I felt exhilarated, gratified, nostalgic. At the same time, there was a tinge of disbelief and a bit of concern. I guess each of those feelings was traceable to the fact that all of us had waited so long for this to happen. It was difficult, after so many false starts over a number of years, to realize *Star Trek* was really back.

DeFOREST KELLEY (actor, "Dr. Leonard 'Bones' McCoy")

The whole thing has been remarkable, an incredible experience. From the beginning. When we were all brought together again, for the first time in ten years, it was hard to realize it was really happening. Yet we also had that strange feeling that the last decade had never existed. The family was just picking up right where it left off.

LEONARD NIMOY

I was looking forward to reprising the character, because I certainly wouldn't want either one of two things to happen—anyone else playing it, or *Star Trek* happening without me.

JAMES DOOHAN (actor, "Montgomery 'Scotty' Scott")

The only thing I can remember thinking at that time—because to me, work was work, and I had to work to make a living—all I could think of when they were going to start a movie again was, "Thank God, maybe we'll make a living out of this show!" Because it was ten years later and we knew what the fans thought. I went to 250 universities and received standing ovations all the time.

GEORGE TAKEI (actor, "Hikaru Sulu")

The characters were all good friends and compatriots, and the context was of course *Star Trek*, so there was the feeling of coming home, but there was also that feeling of excitement and of scariness as well. Here we had this distinguished, legendary director, Robert Wise, so there was that sense of moving into another stratosphere in one's career progression. Then it wasn't really going home, because there was a whole different feel about that show. The costumes were different; the feel of the set, even though the geometric configuration was still the same, the tone, the color, the steeliness, and the monochromatic look was totally different. There was also this electricity in the air that there was a lot of money, and the buzz was that this was the most expensive movie up to that time. So it was a little bit of going home again, but more than that, it was a new and heady as well as an intimidating and awe-inspiring progression in terms of career and the project.

WALTER KOENIG

Standing on the set for that first shot where Kirk comes in and George [Takei] and Nichelle [Nichols] and I rush up to him and when we were setting up the lighting for that shot I finally believed we were making this movie. I was just caught up in a wonderful sense of euphoria, it's one of the highlight moments of my involvement with *Star Trek*. The sense of yes, we are doing this, how neat, how unusual . . . how extraordinary.

> Eric Harrison, a friend of Robert Wise's, shared his unguarded thoughts about the tenor of the set with his friend actress Katharine Hepburn in a letter he sent to the beloved actress at the time. Harrison mused, "I gave your regards to R. Wise. He was thrilled and hopes when you come out here that you will visit. I think it would do a lot for his morale. The studio belongs to the oil company Gulf & Western and *Star Trek* is the first film with their own money so they constantly pace the set plus the fact that the technical problems are enormous. One whole week's film has to be reshot because of a bug in the camera. So what was to finish the 21st of October is now 23rd of December. When I gave your regards to Wise, the first wardrobe lady was there and she did *Rooster Cogburn* with you."

WILLIAM SHATNER

By the time we completed five months of filming—we used to do a TV show in one week—I felt we had achieved a galactic jump from our past efforts. What impressed me most, even more than the enhanced physical scope of its sets, costumes, and special effects, was the way the story had been developed. Captain Kirk has meant so much to me, been such an influence on my life as well as my career.

PERSIS KHAMBATTA (actress, "Ilia")

I was so nervous on my first day, I couldn't even remember my lines. I had to create a character and wasn't sure what a Deltan was, exactly. On the second day of shooting I realized that I had to talk to Gene. I said to him, "Gene, you have to tell me what a Deltan is like." So he gave me four pages of synopsis, which I think he gave to all the actors, even Leonard Nimoy. I read about the character and I really liked her. In some ways she is like me. She comes from a more spiritual world, beyond the material, where people count. Where you read people's minds through the senses. It was something I felt very close to.

Unfortunately the script didn't give me ways to express those things in the film. But some of those ideas must have gotten through, because so many people have commented on the sensuality that Ilia had, even though it couldn't be expressed after she becomes a probe. One can't express a probe being sensual. The woman's basic expressions are in the eyes and mouth, and I think I tried to show this in the scenes with Stephen Collins. You see, I am very much like a Deltan in some ways. Ilia is into people and the beauty of everything.

RICHARD H. KLINE

One of the two new major cast members was Persis Khambatta, a very striking woman who had to shave her head completely to play the role. That might sound easy enough, but I must say that it was rather difficult to retain a visual continuity because, just like a man with his beard, she would develop a "five o'clock shadow" on her head. Also, as a result of the constant shaving of her head day after day, she would develop a rash, and a very clever type of makeup had to be applied constantly in order to hide it.

RICHARD TAYLOR

One of the most difficult things that I had to do on the whole film—that was mind-blowingly difficult—is that freaking glowing thing on Ilia's neck. You couldn't track it digitally like today, it had to be done practically. She had a shaved head, no hair to hide any wires or anything, and it's got to glow. So what it was was a prop that we designed, and we had multiples of these things that fit on her neck, and there were two tiny tungsten wires, like a hair, and they went around the back to a battery pack that was behind her. You would get like two takes of a shot before you had to change the whole thing out.

RICHARD H. KLINE

In terms of story point, it was supposed to be a sensor light, a direct feed to what was controlling her. It was about the size of a nickel and twice as thick, and we would have to stick it onto her throat in the cavity above the chest and then run two wires around to her back where there was a battery. That poor girl was taped and untaped more times than a Rams linebacker is before and after games during their entire career. She would stand for hours while we applied these various devices to her.

PERSIS KHAMBATTA

One of the highlights of the film for me was working with Robert Wise. I learned to trust him. He understood that I was a newcomer and that I had a role that wasn't easy. It was a difficult part for me. Once I became a probe, I couldn't blink and that jewel in my neck burned me. They had to put a switch up my arm so I could turn it off. I would try not to switch it off until the lines were complete, because I didn't want to spoil a good scene. Robert Wise was so patient. If the light in the jewel didn't work, he would have to wait three or four hours to reshoot the scene. It was a delicate little device.

RICHARD TAYLOR

If I was directing the movie, I'd say, "Look, she has the thing but then it turns itself off and falls away and it goes under her skin—some way she doesn't have to wear this the whole time." Because to make that thing on her neck glow was slowing the production down like crazy, and they're, like, "Taylor, have you got that fucking thing working?" And I'm like, "Fuck me! Who came up with this idea?"

WALTER KOENIG

Persis had a very refreshing narcissism. She was very candid about it. She thought she looked beautiful and she was the first to mention it. That was okay, she *did* look great.

DOUG DREXLER
(special effects makeup, *Star Trek: The Next Generation*)

When we snuck on the lot during production, my friend and I were coming around the corner, and she walked right by us with that real short white dress, with these amazing legs, and she just looked at us and smiled and said, "Hi, boys." We almost melted; she looked *so* beautiful.

HAROLD LIVINGSTON

The only thing I remember about her is why the hell did they shave her head? What a stupid thing to do! That was Roddenberry's idea.

STEPHEN COLLINS (actor, "Will Decker")

When I was auditioning, I asked them if they could send me a script and they said they couldn't. "We can't let it out of the studio." They took me to Paramount and ushered me into a sort of cell where I was allowed to read the script. It was like one of those scenes in *All the President's Men* where they say, "Okay, you can look at that, but only for half an hour and we'll be watching."

I was completely unfamiliar with *Star Trek*. Not out of antipathy, but just because I had somehow missed it. I was not among the devoted, but I had heard it was going to be a big movie. I was just curious about it as I would be about anything that comes to my attention. I liked Gene Roddenberry so much immediately. He's a wonderful combination of being remarkably articulate and well-spoken and yet he has the kind of innocence of a three-year-old. He's just like talking to a big kid.

Gene did not work closely on *Star Trek: The Motion Picture*, although he did work very hard on it. There was a difficult political situation where I felt that Gene was being kept outside the reach of the film. There was a feeling like, "Okay, now we're making a movie and the people who made the TV show can only help us so much." Gene was professional about it. He was absolutely wonderful to work with, but he didn't have final say on many things. Television is an executive producer's medium, but on a film it's the director's medium, and Bob Wise was really calling the shots. Gene was around most of the time, but things were taken out of his hands.

HAROLD LIVINGSTON

It was really dumb of Collins to say that Gene wasn't involved enough. He was involved *too* much and *that* was the problem.

STEPHEN COLLINS

What I didn't know when I signed on for the movie was that Bill Shatner and Leonard Nimoy had script approval. They had the power to bend the story however they wanted. The story had to end with Decker merging with Ilia, but the original scenario was much more centered on Decker. I'm not saying that it weakened the final product—there were other reasons for that—but it weakened my role in it considerably. Decker was not very well-rounded and became sort of two-dimensional and uninteresting.

HAROLD LIVINGSTON

That stuff about Nimoy and Shatner having script control is totally inaccurate. As for Mr. Collins, I know that I went out of my way to make him comfortable. I asked for his suggestions concerning his part, because it was his big break and I liked him. He forgets, I suppose, that he made a point of telling people how helpful I was to him and how much he appreciated me for it. So I don't know where he gets off making those remarks. Either his memory fails him or he finds it expedient for his career to sound off in that thoughtless manner.

> At the center of the story of the film were significant arcs for Kirk and Spock. Kirk, who feels he is disappearing into a Starfleet desk job, is desperate to get back in a command seat, and so obsessed with doing so that he makes some glaring mistakes upon retaking command. Spock—who, when we meet him early on, is back on his home world of Vulcan—is attempting to purge himself of the remnants of human emotions within. Sensing V'ger, and the belief that it holds the key to his metaphysical search, he rejoins the *Enterprise* crew and, over the course of the story, actually learns to *embrace* his human half. Both are significant character stories, but focusing on those characters—and the interactions that were a hallmark of the original television series—was difficult given the nature of V'ger and the film's focus on visual effects.

DeFOREST KELLEY

I was worried when I saw the script, because the characterizations were not there, and the relationships were not there. I was disturbed, and so were Bill and Leonard. We had to put up a great fight. I think anyone will tell you that if the actors hadn't fought like hell to reestablish those relationships, they never would have been there. We would have had a special-effects war. So there was a great deal of difficulty with the script, which was finally resolved to a certain extent. I still don't think there's enough of the interpersonal relationships in there, and I regret that some of them were lost. But Paramount didn't believe that the characters were as important to the public as they really were, and we couldn't tell them.

There was a scene where Spock, McCoy, and Kirk meet to discuss Spock's strange behavior. To me, that was the closest thing to a real *Star Trek* confrontation that there was in the picture. Here the three of us came together, Spock comes in to talk about his problems and what's going to happen to him, and I have the line, "Well, you're lucky we just happen to be going your way." The three of us were actually very natural; that's where we should be, and what we should be doing. It was somewhat like going back in time.

LEONARD NIMOY

That was a tough time. It was complicated, it was somewhat schizophrenic for a while, and it was not an easy jump back into Spock's skin. Particularly because there were writing issues. The script that I read for the movie did not even contain the Spock character, so it was a case of them describing to me what Spock would be doing in the next draft of the script. That took a little time, and a little fine-tuning to finally get it to fruition. I was never totally satisfied with that movie.

JON POVILL

In truth, part of the blame for this goes to Harold, because he didn't really know the characters. The interaction between the characters was, I think, more rigid than it had been in the series. Harold's military background and military perspective was such that it was more clipped and military and less personal than it had been in the show. I think that that rests on Harold.

ROBERT WISE

It wasn't as if somebody sat down at the beginning and said, "Listen, we want to get a lot more special effects." It was not a deliberate move to shift the emphasis from one area to another. That was really because of the story. That was the script, or the story we had to tell, and we didn't try to put more special effects in it. I didn't try. None of us tried. We had people reacting to things that were happening on the screen, so we had to show these things. So if there is a valid criticism coming from those Trekkies who really love these characters with all their heart, there still wasn't anything we could do about it. We would have had to have a totally different story.

LEONARD NIMOY

Star Trek I—which filmed for six months—was really a trial for the actors, because we were not very much in it at all. We were, much of the time, looking off camera at things that would later be done by Doug Trumbull or his crew. We were looking in wonderment and awe and saying things like, "What do you think it is?" "I don't know" "What do you think it is going to do next?" "I don't know!" Very exciting stuff.

GENE RODDENBERRY

This is the first time a television show ever became a major motion picture, and Robert Wise did a remarkable job in adaptation from one medium to another. Many people don't seem to be aware that they're two entirely different mediums. You strive for different values in television. It's a more intimate medium, where you can get into multiple characters and character conflict that can be very exciting. With motion pictures the trend has been to make it a sensory experience with stereo sound and bigger screens. Television cannot create that illusion, so it goes for other things. It intellectualizes rather than sensorizes the product. And a major motion picture spectacle doesn't lend itself easily to Mr. Spock's cute little remarks with Captain Kirk. The conversion of a two-hour television show into a movie was much more difficult than anyone could've believed.

And the difficulties regarding the script continued right to the last moment, when a battle erupted between Livingston and Roddenberry over credit, with Alan Dean Foster caught in the cross fire.

HAROLD LIVINGSTON

The writing credits for the film proposed to the Writers Guild by Paramount was "screenplay by Harold Livingston and story by Alan Dean Foster." They left Roddenberry out, so he protested. He's the one who launched the protest. I *knew* he couldn't win an arbitration, because it wasn't his script. Anything he'd done was tossed out, or most of it. In any case, I blackjacked Foster into splitting the story credit with Gene. He agreed to do it and Gene wouldn't accept it. On that basis, I said, "Okay, Gene, screw you. We'll go to arbitration." When I said that, he withdrew and he withdrew in a funk. He was *mad*.

GENE RODDENBERRY

It was my policy all through *Star Trek*: If a writer felt he wanted credit and wanted it badly enough to have a Guild action on it, I'd withdraw.

HAROLD LIVINGSTON

I said to Gene, "If you felt you deserved credit, then you have a system for determining this. Why didn't you use it?" He said, "I don't want to lower myself to that." At that point, I guess, he decided to withdraw and assume this injured pose. But he would have lost this arbitration, because he didn't write any script. All he did was rewrite, patch up, fool around, and screw everything up.

JON POVILL

Gene didn't deserve coscreenplay credit. The credit arbitration procedure is that they heavily favor the writer of the first draft, and Harold wrote the first draft. Unless you drastically change something, you're not going to get credit.

ALAN DEAN FOSTER

The first thing they did was try to deny me screen credit. When the credits came out to be filed with the Guild, they read, "screenplay by Gene Roddenberry and Harold Livingston, story by Gene Roddenberry." I'm a very low-key guy. I'm a handshake-is-my-bond kind of guy. I called my agent and said, "What's going on?" And she said, "Oh, that's nothing." "What do you mean, that's nothing?" "Nobody's mad at you or anything, that's just the business." I said, "Well, it's not *my* business." My agent then suggested I file for solo story credit. I said, "Sure," because I did 98 percent of the writing on the treatment.

HAROLD LIVINGSTON

I told Foster, "Just because Roddenberry is being a son of a bitch doesn't mean that you have to be one, too."

ALAN DEAN FOSTER

I thought about it and said, "You're right." I called and said, "Look, all I'm interested in here is having it read the way it read on the earlier script, which is 'story by Alan Dean Foster and Gene Roddenberry,'" because it was, as I freely admit, based on his one-page idea. I then get this very strange letter back saying that Gene Roddenberry is off in La Costa someplace recuperating, he's very tired, very busy, and he really doesn't have time for this. I just laughed. Is this real life or kindergarten? I just threw up my hands and said, "Fine, whatever," and that's why I have sole story credit on the movie.

JON POVILL

I had miscalculated tremendously by not going for a story credit on the film. Harold was telling me that I absolutely should, but I was trying to salvage my relationship with Gene by *not* going for it. I felt badly for Gene that he had originally wanted coscreenplay credit with Harold, and Harold assured him that he would fight him to the death on it. So Gene was in for story credit and Harold said that was okay. I didn't want to apply for story credit and have any chance of fucking up that credit for Gene. Then, of course, he took his name off of it. That would have been *a lot* of residuals over the years.

ALAN DEAN FOSTER

By then I'd worked with Gene Roddenberry and George Lucas [on *Star Wars* novels]. In a nutshell, Roddenberry was standard Hollywood and George Lucas was anti-Hollywood. I never got the feeling from George that he particularly cared whether he received any great critical acclaim or even if he made a lot of money. I got the feeling that *Star Wars* was based on something he loved seeing as a kid and that's what he wanted to make and he hoped he could make it so he could see it on the screen. I don't think he cared about the fame or the money.

Dealing with Lucas was like dealing with the quiet kid in the back of the class who hardly ever speaks up. Gene was, like, "I'M *STAR TREK*!"

On December 6, 1979, one day before its official debut, the forty-four-million-dollar *Star Trek: The Motion Picture* had its world premiere in Washington, DC, at the K-B MacArthur Theater, followed by a black-tie reception at the National Air and Space Museum. There had been no previews and, as a result, Wise, who began his career as the editor on Orson Welles's *Citizen Kane*, considered the film's release version nothing more than a "rough cut." The following day, the vast majority of critics would attack the film for its—according to many—listless pacing and overreliance on visual effects over character interactions.

EDDIE EGAN

I was sent along with many other people from the New York and L.A. offices of Paramount to Washington, DC. One of my duties there was to ride in a limo to pick up Robert Wise and his wife at the airport and to bring them to a hotel and get them settled in for the premiere the next night. He actually got off the plane with two cans of film under his arm.

He was a very kind man, but I could tell he was troubled and frustrated and just exhausted from the process. I was with him the next day when he did a round of interviews and then went with him and his wife to the premiere and stayed with them at the party afterwards.

WALTER KOENIG

Gene had just seen the cut and it was literally still wet. We were flying to Washington, DC, and I asked, "What do you think of the picture?" He answered, "It's a good picture." It was a death knell. As soon as he said that, I knew it wasn't going to work. He didn't put it down, he didn't denigrate it, but I heard it in his voice. I absolutely knew. Then you hope against hope that it's going to be good, and you see the limousines and the red carpets and the spotlights. Then you see those first five minutes with the music and you see V'ger and the destruction it causes. I got very excited, but shortly thereafter I began to become aware of time, that time was passing. That I wasn't involved in the picture. I was sitting in the audience and my heart sank.

HAROLD LIVINGSTON

At the premiere, Roddenberry got up onstage and thanked Bob Wise and virtually everybody, but never once mentioned my name. Bill Shatner got up and said, "Listen, let's not forget Harold Livingston, who wrote this fine picture," which got me a nice round of applause. It was a very nice and big thing of him to do.

DOUG DREXLER

I remember Roddenberry and Harold Livingston at the premiere sitting together very quietly. Roddenberry was sweating. He literally was sweating. He looked very uncomfortable and knew that he had a problem. The print, I had overheard somebody say, was flown in wet. The movie was never really finished.

SUSAN SACKETT

The only thing I remember from the premiere in Washington was a little display case that had actual moon rocks in it and being fascinated by them. It was everybody's dream come true to come to a premiere and be treated like royalty.

EDDIE EGAN

My most vivid memory of the night of the premiere was when the picture ended, Leonard Nimoy went down the aisle to Todd Ramsay, the editor, and said, "I need to speak to you," in a very certain tone that he was unhappy about something. I found out later from my dealings with Leonard that he was unhappy that the scene where Spock cried, which was put back in for the director's edition, had been taken out of the movie. That was what had really ticked him off that night, because all of them were seeing the movie for the first time, including the director.

I had never heard of—and certainly never in my experience later have I ever known of—a film to hold press screenings at a theater that was commercially showing the movie on the same evening of the day it opened. That wasn't to hide the picture from bad reviews—no one had seen it to know whether it would get good or bad reviews. It was a practical thing.

DOUG DREXLER

Jerry Goldsmith was sitting right behind me. His wife coughed all the way through the movie. We went to the Air and Space Museum for the big party afterward, which was the entire bottom floor of the museum. And they had a full orchestra with the music. It was a big deal. I remember coming out and hearing women going, "That was just perfectly awful." And the dry-dock sequence in particular, if you weren't a fan. But to me, it's one of the greatest moments in science fiction ever. When reviews started coming in, they were pretty much chopping it up. And it was hurting me. It was as if it was my own child. I remember how upset I was. Joel Siegel reviewed it on ABC. He was a *Star Trek* fan, but I remember his review wasn't that kind, although it was diplomatic compared to some of the others. Then he said, "But the *Enterprise* . . . it was made for the big screen." I'll never forget it as long as I live. I'm getting chills thinking about it. *It was made for the big screen.* And it really was.

RONALD D. MOORE

I thought it was a beautiful film, and at the time I was struck by the message of the movie, and it felt very much in keeping with the show. I did sort of feel at the end that this was a retelling of "The Changeling," but I was very excited. When I saw generally it was getting negative reviews, I was very defensive of the movie for quite a while. In fact I wrote a letter to *Trek* magazine and they printed it. It was the first and only letter I'd ever written to a publication and they actually printed it and it was me defending the film. Many years later when I was working on *Next Generation,* Eric Stillwell brought in a copy of that *Trek* magazine to embarrass me in front of the entire writing staff.

MANNY COTO (executive producer, *Star Trek: Enterprise*)

I was one of those guys who was in denial. I was running around saying it was great. It wasn't until *Star Trek II* came around that I realized I didn't much like the first one, but we were so excited about it, we couldn't leave it. We were fanatical, and we convinced ourselves that it wasn't as bad as it really was.

DAVID A. GOODMAN (co-executive producer, *Futurama*)

I saw it in White Plains, New York, at a theater near where I grew up. The audience was really into it. They cheered every time a cast member showed up onscreen. Spock first and then Shatner and then whenever you'd see everyone else on the bridge. You didn't hear the dialogue for a lot of the movie because there was so much cheering going on. Showing the *Enterprise* in dry dock was just this incredible experience, because I'd been watching reruns so many times, seeing the same special effects over and over again, so the idea that the *Enterprise* responded when Kirk said "Take us out" was such a crazy, exciting moment. As a *Star Trek* fan, that was the most amazing moment of *Star Trek: The Motion Picture* for me.

MANNY COTO

I sympathize with the guys who went to go see *The Phantom Menace* and convinced themselves that it wasn't as bad as it was. *Phantom Menace* is worse, I would argue, than *Star Trek* ever was, but we were kind of in denial. There were some beautiful shots of the *Enterprise* and we got to see some Klingons, so it wasn't a total disaster, but in large part it was pretty boring.

CHRIS GORE (founder, *Film Threat* magazine)

Why does Kirk's Starfleet uniform make him look suspiciously like a dentist? And what's the deal with Kirk's obsession with Vulcans? He wants a green-blooded science officer badly: "I'd still like a Vulcan there if possible." Kirk sounds like a bachelor with a fetish for blondes. And like Godzilla's affection for Tokyo, the *Enterprise* is, of course, the only ship in range of . . . whatever.

DAVID A. GOODMAN

They made a stiffer, more *2001*-type of science fiction, which I don't think is what *Star Trek* was. Obviously, *The Wrath of Khan* ended up being closer at least in spirit—to me—to the original *Star Trek* and not just because it was a sequel to the original show. It was more colorful, the costumes and the characters; there was more humor. Also, I saw *Star Trek: The Motion Picture* so many times that by the time *Wrath of Khan* came out, I could identify all the stock footage they used.

SCOTT MANTZ (film critic, *Access Hollywood*)

A lot of people were disappointed when the movie came out because it was boring, there wasn't enough action, and the characters were not the same characters that people were familiar with from the original series. I was not one of those people. I liked it the first time I saw it, because of the scope of the film and seeing the *Enterprise* on the big screen with all the detail. The special effects were cool. What really struck me about the movie was the music. Jerry Goldsmith's score was and still is one of my favorite music scores of all time.

WALTER KOENIG

What *Star Trek I* had was a true science-fiction story. It was innovative storytelling as far as it went. This was not simply a story that we pulled from a horse opera and made into a science-fiction movie. It was indigenous to the genre . . . and it should have been since it was borrowed from other *Star Trek* stories.

EDDIE EGAN

It was not the emotional, character-driven, serious, funny, interplay-between-the-characters that people know and we know to be the heart of what makes *Star Trek* work, but it had elegance and an intellectual concept that can stand right up there with the best science fiction movies ever produced.

CHRIS GORE

I saw the film in 1979 with my dad, who was also a huge *Trek* fan. We would watch the original series together and discuss episodes in detail. The first *Star Trek* movie was what got me reading magazines like *Starlog, Fantastic Films,* and *Cinefantastique.* I sought out any shred of information about the upcoming *Star Trek* movie. This was before the Internet, when a trip to the corner store was for buying comics and movie mags. From the opening overture, I was transported to another time in a familiar galaxy with an optimistic view of the future. Much has been discussed about the flaws of *The Motion Picture,* but it has actually aged the best of the old *Star Trek* films. Try watching *Star Trek III* without cringing multiple times.

JAMES DOOHAN

It got boring getting to V'ger. Who wants to see a bunch of clouds, which aren't terribly interesting after the first thirty seconds anyway?

DAVID GERROLD

The fans had come off this two-year high with *Star Wars,* and the audience wanted more *Star Wars,* but there wasn't any more. So they went to see *Star Trek* and they were hungering for more, so *Star Trek* benefitted from the *Star Wars* phenomenon. They went and they saw it over and over again, but it was embarrassing to watch the fans because they were all apologists for this picture: "Well, it's not that bad. It's a different kind of *Star Trek.*" Instead of really just acknowledging that it was a bad movie, they tried to explain that it was wonderful and you were an idiot for not understanding it. It was wonderful to watch them fuck their minds over to explain away a bad movie. The truth was that there was this movie that they wanted to love and they were so disappointed, but they wouldn't dare say that they were disappointed.

BRYAN FULLER (executive producer, *American Gods*)

It's a really interesting, very rich film. Most people dismiss it as dull, but I think they're not paying attention. *Khan* is much more rock and roll. It is much more of a cowboy picture. It has such drive and momentum. There's no chance to stop and pontificate, which *Star Trek: The Motion Picture* allowed the audience to do. But I think during that time a lot of them had their eyes roll in boredom, but not me.

I understand it's a colder, more intellectual film, particularly when you compare it to *The Wrath of Khan,* which was "let's Moby Dick this son of a bitch." Whereas *The Motion Picture* was filled with a lot of ideas and the notion of bringing *Star Trek* into a Kubrickian universe where we can explore intellectual ideas.

ROD RODDENBERRY (son of Gene Roddenberry)

Bob Justman said my father wasn't a great writer, he was a great *rewriter*. That doesn't bother me too much, because I think I might believe that. Not that he was a bad writer, but the stories that my father put his weight behind were often slow. *The Motion Picture* is an example. Now, you may love it and I have respect for it and I appreciate what it is, but it's slow-moving. I'll use the word *thoughtful*. It's more about ideas and less about action. I'm not sure my father should have done the movies. It was his show, if he'd done them all like *The Motion Picture,* they'd be more *Star Trek,* but would they have been good movies? Would they have made the money they made? I don't know.

WALTER KOENIG

There are myriad reasons for the lack of success, including setting a release date for the picture in advance. According to Gene, he fought that, because it really did back him into a corner and made the picture that much more expensive. They had to go on double time, golden time, and at one point they were shooting around the clock in postproduction. So I guess it was a cursed project from the start.

GENE RODDENBERRY

Rushing costs money in this business. When there are only two or three people in the world who can do a certain optical and only one is available, you're not in a good bargaining position. But these are the kinds of problems that are dealt with in the real world of picture-making, which are very seldom talked about in fan magazines, or are understood by those who make dramatic comments or criticism.

RALPH WINTER

We watched the movie as reference on *Star Trek II*. It came to the end of the movie and I got the squawk box from the projectionist, and he goes, "I'm really sorry. I made a mistake. I left out one of the reels." And I go, "No worries." Twenty minutes of the movie we missed, and no one noticed.

HAROLD LIVINGSTON

I was upset with the film. It just wasn't what I wanted. I can't honestly say this wasn't my fault, because in the end I took the rap for it anyway. But if I do a poor job, I'll tell you it's bad.

ROBERT WISE

Do I like the film? That's awfully hard to answer. Often we directors generally like our latest film best . . . I like it. I don't think it's everything I hoped it'd be and certainly I had no idea it was going to cost the tremendous amount of money it cost. None of us did. I am sure Paramount would not have gotten into it had they realized at the beginning it was going to cost that much.

EDDIE EGAN

No one at Paramount was happy about the way the film came together, because of the ugly dynamic between Roddenberry and the studio, and the script problems and the actors all getting involved with the script. Too many cooks in the kitchen *always* leads to disaster, and that was a big part of the problem.

I also rememember Nimoy saying to me years later that he was very fond of Bob Wise, but he got an uneasy feeling the first time he met him. He said when he went to his house, the house was very severe . . . it wasn't homey at all. It was very antiseptic, cold and orderly. He said it gave him pause. He had great affection for him though and thought that he and many other people would have lost their shit or had a nervous breakdown making that movie under those conditions and he apparently never showed it to anyone on the set.

GENE RODDENBERRY

My attitude on the movie is this: While the film failed in a number of areas where I would have liked it to have succeeded, it was a successful adaptation of the television story to the screen. We could have done more—and we could have done a lot less—but we did what we could under the time, conditions, and circumstances, and the fact that God double-crossed us by making us fallible. The film has some failures . . . it also has some remarkable successes in it. I think, considering the way it all happened, we came out with a remarkably good film, and I'm very pleased to have been a part of it. It could have been better—*yes*! I don't ever expect to make a film where I don't look back and say to myself, "Ah, I'd like to change this and this."

ALAN DEAN FOSTER

When I was submitting stories to *Phase II* and everything was all hunky-dory and chatty, one day Gene put his arm around me—he was a tall guy—and he said, "You remind me of me when I was your age." That's an exact quote. I thought, "I'm nothing like you, what are you talking about?" He said, "I'm going to teach you everything I know." At that point I'd written something like twenty books and I thought, "That's very nice, but I don't think there's that much you can teach me." I kept quiet, because he was being nice. But *Star Trek* was the worst experience I ever had. Nobody had ever tried to do to me what they tried to do. But that's just the way it is, apparently. They put you in the shark cage, you learn how to fight with the other sharks, or you go back in the goldfish bowl. I belonged in the goldfish bowl. My wife and I picked up and moved to Arizona.

In the end, Gene *did* teach me quite a lot about the business, although I don't think that's what he originally had in mind.

NICHOLAS MEYER (director, *Star Trek II: The Wrath of Khan*)

I had a conversation once with Barry Diller, who said that a really sickening moment for him was being in New York and seeing lines around the block for the first *Star Trek* movie, and knowing that it wasn't everything that it could be. And I do not knock the first movie. Robert Wise has forgotten more about filmmaking than I'll ever know, and somebody had to go boldly and try this. You learn from other people, you build on the efforts and the mistakes or the successes of other people. So I am not a person who says, "Oh well, this is a perfectly shitty film." I'm just grateful that it was there. But for Barry, he said, "Gee, people really want to see this stuff and we're going to make money off it despite the fact that it was a runaway production and we spent forty-five million dollars. We're going to make another one of these and we're going to do it until we get it right."

ROBERT WISE

This was the first film that I did where I *didn't* have time for it. Normally we would see a picture and go back and have time to work on it a little bit more. But we didn't have any time. I saw it all completely together on Monday before it premiered in Washington on Thursday. One of the reservations I have about the film is that I didn't have the time to fine-tune it.

> In the end, Wise would get that opportunity to fine-tune *Star Trek: The Motion Picture,* in the form of the film's director's edition, which was released on DVD on November 1, 2001. Prior to that, however, in its initial television debut on the *ABC Sunday Night Movie,* a number of scenes were added that provided some of the character moments fans felt were missing from the theatrical version.
>
> The reedited director's edition, which featured Wise's preferred cut of the film along with new computer-generated visual effects, was overseen by Wise himself along with the Robert Wise Productions team of Dave Fein, Michael Matessino, and Daren Dochterman.

SUSAN SACKETT

No one contacted us about the ABC version. It just showed up that way on the tube and on video. We were not consulted, but very pleased over it. We had no idea how it happened or why it happened. This was all the footage Mr. Roddenberry had written a memo about in 1979 when the film was being cut. We went into one of the rough cuts and he wrote about a twenty-page memo saying he would like to see this and could you add this, trim this, put this line in. Someone got a hold of that memo of what he would like to have put in the film. Had they listened to him in the first place, it would have been in the film, and this is what they used as the basis for their reedit for television. Everything that was done was what he had requested in this memo.

WALTER KOENIG

I don't trust my own feelings sometimes. Everybody seems to think that that extra footage helped the film, and when I saw it I didn't really see that. Maybe because I don't have the objectivity. In the reediting they added a scene of mine after I get burned and Ilia heals my burns, but when you have just a few scenes to begin with, it seems like I had more involvement than it might otherwise.

DAVID GERROLD

[The ABC, VHS, and laserdisc version of] *Star Trek: The Special Edition* is seventeen minutes longer, but it feels seventeen minutes shorter because of that character stuff that was added in. It's a difficult picture to sit through. The first half of the picture is quite good, but the problem is that the cut is wrong. They left in the special-effects sequences that should have been much shorter, and Robert Wise intended them to be much shorter, and they cut out little pieces of character that said the story was about Kirk and Spock. The reason that *Star Trek: The Motion Picture* made so much money had nothing to do with the story. It had everything to do with Kirk, Spock, and McCoy.

DAVID C. FEIN

I would go so far as to say as much as *Star Wars* was a success and was a massive change to the industry, *Star Trek: The Motion Picture* was a massive hit to Bob's life and Bob's career. There was so much attention being spent on this, and there were so many people who were looking for someone to blame. Bob is such a gentleman that no matter who is technically at fault, he was the captain of the ship. It was his project to do. It was his responsibility in the end. It was the only project that didn't go smoothly in his career. And to not only not go smoothly, but to become the tremendous problem that it was, and have so much riding on it and the studio needing it so much, it was difficult. If you really look at his career, he didn't do many other films after that. And he had been on a roll.

DAREN DOCHTERMAN

We contacted Mr. Wise and brought up the question of whether he'd like to talk about *Star Trek: The Motion Picture.* He had never talked about it previously, because he was so upset with the way he was treated by the studio, the way it all came out and the fact he never had preview screenings. It was just a bad experience for him, and, of course, after the movie came out the actors started bad-mouthing it, especially when *Wrath of Khan* was released. "This is more like it, the *Star Trek* that we wanted." C'mon, they didn't know. So we approached Mr. Wise. At this point the special editions of the *Star Wars* movies had come out and done really well. This gave us an angle to say, "If you could have those missing weeks from your postproduction schedule, Mr. Wise, what would you have done?" So he started to think. We scheduled a screening of the original movie at the Directors Guild, just for him and us. We sat him down, showed him the movie, and he started to open up a little bit. I guess a lot of memories came back to him because he hadn't watched it in eighteen years. He hadn't seen it since the Washington, DC, premiere on December 6, 1979. He started to open up about it and said, "You know, maybe we could at least give it a final cut."

DAVID C. FEIN

Not only was it tough at the time, but for us to have to take years of knowing him before he would even talk about the movie was *very* emotional. It was *very* personal for him. I can't tell you how important it is in my life to know that this brilliant man didn't have to go to his grave with such huge, unfinished business. Admittedly the business won't be finished until the director's edition is issued on Blu-ray.

DAREN DOCHTERMAN

We got a hold of the original files he had donated to the USC cinema school. Boxes and boxes of his original files from that time, including a complete book of storyboards, his shooting script, and all sorts of notes. Notes from Gene Roddenberry, Harold Livingston, and his notes in his script. That was a huge amount of information, and we started to see the storyboards of effects shots they planned to do but never got around to. There just wasn't any time. We started to pick some moments that could have been made better by that extended post-production schedule. I did some Photoshop comps, did some screen grabs to show him things we were thinking about attempting. He said, "Wow, I think we can actually do this. Let's get a message out to Sherry Lansing at Paramount and see if she'll go along with it." And that's what we did: he drafted up a letter and sent it to Sherry Lansing. After several months they said, "Get a budget together," and that's how it started.

DAVID C. FEIN

The truth of the matter is that Bob's legacy is the director's edition. *That's* the movie that—as close as possible to what we had; we couldn't shoot anything new—was the movie that he wants people to look at as Bob Wise's *Star Trek* film.

DAREN DOCHTERMAN

When he saw the film, he was smiling ear to ear. He loved it and he was so glad that he had a chance to go back. This was a very heartfelt moment when he said, "This is the only one I didn't get to finish." That just about brought us to tears; what a great feeling to help him achieve that.

JON POVILL

I wish the making of the movie had been a happy experience for him. I remember that when we were in production on the film, every day Bob would have lunch in his office and have *one* glass of vodka, pretty much straight up. Certainly not to excess. Just one to steel himself for the rest of the day. The overall frame of it was: "Thirty-five years, I've never experienced anything like this. *Just un-fucking-believable.*" He just could not believe how dysfunctional this production was.

HAROLD LIVINGSTON

Part of my contract says Paramount has got to give me an extra fifty thousand bucks when the movie goes into profits. Still negative. It's grossed around five hundred million dollars.

KHAN GAME

"I REPROGRAMMED THE SIMULATION SO THAT
IT WAS POSSIBLE TO SAVE THE SHIP."

Star Trek: The Motion Picture, despite largely scathing reviews, grossed an astounding $11,926,421 its opening weekend on 857 screens, eventually topping $139,000,000 worldwide. Shortly thereafter Gene Roddenberry began work on a treatment for a sequel.

"We know a little bit more about how to use *Trek* in motion pictures," said Roddenberry at the time. "The second run in anything is easier. If you've ever played golf, the second try you can always sink the putt. It's the first shot at the hole . . . The sequel story is much more intra-crew, intra-character. It has many more of the difficult decisions that Kirk always had in the TV episodes, decisions about morality and ideals. It's good *Star Trek.* It would have made a good three-parter on the TV show—if I'd had the money to do it."

Stung by criticism of the first film, Roddenberry was intent on revisiting elements of *Star Trek* that had proved so popular in the past: time travel, the Klingons, and Sarek and Amanda, Spock's parents. In his sixty-page treatment dated May 21, 1980, Roddenberry proposes an outrageous story, presaging the similarly themed *Next Generation* film *First Contact,* in which the *Enterprise,* returning home to Earth, encounters bodies floating in space, some are naked, others are in space suits. Discovering a survivor, they realize history has been changed by the Klingons and the Federation eradicated. Only those who have traveled at warp speed are immune to the changes in the time line.

Starfleet doesn't exist and the Earth is now inhabited by a vicious race of protohumans. The *Enterprise* conceals itself behind the moon with the arrival of the vicious Klingons, who have used the Guardian of Forever from "The City on the Edge of Forever" to change time. While visiting the former site of Starfleet Headquarters, Amanda is brutally raped and Sarek sacrifices his life to save Kirk and Spock from the Klingons in the hopes they can reverse the changes to the time line. The *Enterprise* returns to the Guardian planet and follows the Klingons back in time, despite an attempt by the Klingons to block the time gate, to shield a small Klingon scout ship that returned to 1960s Earth. The *Enterprise* manages to make it through, but is damaged and crashes in northern Canada, where a U-2 spy plane mistakes it for an alien ship. As a result, JFK cancels his trip to Dallas and is *not* assassinated, prompting a visit to the Oval Office by James T. Kirk himself, who comes face-to-face with the then president.

Ultimately, the *Enterprise* is able to repair the time line and return to the twenty-third century, leaving behind a very much alive President Kennedy but with the addition of a newfound wife for McCoy as a result of their interference in Earth's past.

HARVE BENNETT
(executive producer, *Star Trek II: The Wrath of Khan*)

Gene opposed every one of the *Star Trek* films on the grounds that they were not good *Trek*. He now takes credit for having been the spiritual father of the best one, *Star Trek IV*, because he had told us to do a time-travel story. The fact is we had rejected a time-travel story about coming back to try and stop the assassination of Jack Kennedy, and that story, for good reason, was thrown out years before because it, like going to see God in *Star Trek V*, was a story with an impossible preconclusion. You knew that even Kirk couldn't stop that, and if he did, how would we explain that now? And why is Jackie married to Onassis? And on and on, and we said, "No, we don't want to do that story." He flooded everybody with reprints of that thing, which he had written, God knows when, and he fought tooth and nail right down to the $110 million domestic gross, and he said, "Well, I told them to do time travel in the first place."

SUSAN SACKETT (assistant to Gene Roddenberry)

The proposal was written as a separate story back in about 1980, right after *Star Trek: The Motion Picture* was released. Basically, the studio was a bit leery of having Gene as a producer on the next *Star Trek* because they had to find a scapegoat for their failure to hold back costs on the first movie, and it was outright their fault. They ran ten million dollars over budget insisting we stick with Robert Abel and Associates when they failed to produce anything for us. Some people at the studio felt that they would rather not be involved with that producer, they wanted to bring in somebody else rather than Gene Roddenberry, which is basically what they did.

The story itself had to do with going back in time through the time gate, they are tracked by the Klingons, who go back in time, and they follow them there and they try to rescue the Earth. Somebody thought it had something to do with they had to kill Kennedy, which was not true. It happened around that time in history. As with Edith Keeler, they had to allow history to unfold the way it was meant to unfold, and that was the involvement with the Kennedy thing. I really don't know why they didn't do it. It was a damn good story.

SCOTT MANTZ (film critic, *Access Hollywood*)

After the Klingons go back in time to ruin humanity's future, the *Enterprise* goes back to stop that from happening. But they make things worse by accidentally revealing themselves to Earth's inhabitants, and the problems keep snowballing from there.

The biggest snowball is that the *Enterprise* has materialized in November of 1963, just days before President Kennedy's assassination in Dallas, and in effect prevented this turning point of the twentieth century. So now the *Enterprise* will have to go back in time again even further, but not before Kirk has a heated exchange with Kennedy, who is then beamed aboard the ship.

While there is certainly a cool factor in seeing Kirk encounter another U.S. President after Lincoln in "The Savage Curtain," there's no power to the punch at the end the way "City on the Edge of Forever" had, and it ends up being a pointless, emotionally uninvolving voyage.

RONALD D. MOORE (writer, *Star Trek: First Contact*)

There were persistent rumors that *Star Trek II* was going to be a time-travel story about going back to the Kennedy assassination, and Spock was going to be the shooter on the grassy knoll for some reason. There were fans whom were up in arms and writing these really angry letters, "If Spock is the shooter on the grassy knoll, I will never watch again."

EDDIE EGAN (unit publicist, *Star Trek II: The Wrath of Khan*)

There was a version written which was more or less the ending of "The City on the Edge of Forever," but instead of Kirk suddenly stopping McCoy from grabbing Joan Collins's character, something happened in Dealey Plaza and some aberration in time was causing things *not* to occur correctly. Spock appeared behind the fence and fired the shot and everything returns to normal. Of course, the attitude of the studio was mostly just horror; that you can't make a movie like that. Their thoughts about Gene were "It's just in bad taste and we don't like you, anyway, so go away."

SCOTT MANTZ

Boy, what a mess. Paramount was wise to toss it to the side in favor of the greatest *Trek* movie of them all, *The Wrath of Khan*. Interesting that while *Wrath* served as a sequel to one of the most popular original-series *Trek* episodes of all time, so did GR's treatment. In this case, it was a sequel of sorts to the *Citizen Kane* of *Star Trek* episodes, "The City on the Edge of Forever."

And just like "City," the script dealt with Kirk and Spock going back in time to restore the future. As a result, the story seems awfully redundant of "City," despite all the bells and whistles that a big-budget feature could provide.

HARVE BENNETT

Gene is frequently a historical revisionist, and he uses a phrase that is difficult for anybody else to refute: "That is not *Star Trek*." When a man of his eminence and his position says that, especially in my early days, I didn't want to go against the church. But the fact of the matter is he uses that phrase whenever he chooses to. It makes no sense. He fought the character of Saavik savagely, saying you couldn't intermarry Vulcans and Romulans, that it was not possible. It had never been done, and he would cite everybody from Arthur C. Clarke to Isaac Asimov, who he would always run to and they would always say, "Yes, Gene, you're right." I am not a science-fiction writer. I just tell good yarns. You get into a situation where you say, "I'm not Heinlein, I'm not Clarke." I'm just a pop artist trying to tell a story here.

When I signed on, the phrase that was in my mind, and that I've used a lot, is that the franchise was a beached whale and it was my task to resurrect it, to give it CPR and to return to the central thing that had made people so loyal to the series for decades.

RICHARD ARNOLD (*Star Trek* archivist)

Harve said that *Star Trek* was a beached whale, one that he had rescued and breathed new life into. That really hurt Gene. When Gene said at one point during a disagreement, "over my dead body!," Harve had said that that was fine with him. Gene did his best to try to work things out with Harve where and when he could, but Harve made it very difficult for him. Gene did his best not to be a thorn in Harve's side, but at times found that he had to.

DAVID GERROLD (writer, "The Trouble with Tribbles")

After *Star Trek: The Motion Picture,* the studio looked at what the picture earned and said, "If we had brought this picture in for nine million dollars, we would have made *a lot* of money. We have the sets standing, the actors will be available to us. If we could do inexpensive *Star Trek* movies . . ." So they call in Harve Bennett and said, "We're going to have you do a *Star Trek* movie for TV. If it turns out well, we'll release it theatrically."

After *Star Trek: The Motion Picture,* Gene had no clout. It was a critical disaster and for a while it looked like it was going to be a financial disaster. I don't know what the details were, but essentially they looked at the box-office results and said, "Take Gene out of the saddle." They kicked him upstairs and said, "Gene, you will be executive consultant. We'll give you an office and we'll have you approve all of the scripts, but your creative control over *Star Trek* is over because we can't afford you." They were probably a lot more tactful than that, but that's what they did.

EDDIE EGAN

There were some people there who had been on the TV side of things, the Desilu side, which became part of Paramount, and people who had known Gene back then who would roll their eyes anytime his name came up. The reason, and this has been well established, is he was a pain in the ass on the series and was quick to take credit but was rarely around for the hard work. There was a lot of that in evidence apparently during the making of the first movie. Certainly I observed that given his reduced role on the three sequels I worked on. He just wasn't a producer in the sense that a picture of that size and inherent value needed.

HARVE BENNETT

Any time a guy loses a command and is still hanging around, it's difficult. The fact of the matter was that Gene had already done that during the series; in the third year he had left to do other things. In this instance it began on *Star Trek: The Motion Picture,* where he was superseded and overruled many times during the final stages when the studio took over the massively rising budget, and the problems with the special effects and so forth.

DAVID GERROLD

The only success he's ever had in his entire life was *Star Trek*, and he likes being the Great Bird of the Galaxy. He believes his own publicity. He's a legend in his own mind.

EDDIE EGAN

When you talked to Roddenberry, he always kind of looked at you with his head cocked, like he was waiting for you to say something wrong or to piss him off. He's just one of those guys whose mind had an area that was completely brilliant, but the larger part of his mind was his personality and an insecurity that just got in the way all the time. It limited his ability to enjoy his success and feel recognized for the brilliant things he did, and the good things he did for people. His insecurities and his inability to focus seemed, to me, to be his biggest challenge.

GENE RODDENBERRY
(executive consultant, *Star Trek II: The Wrath of Khan*)

My contract gives me the total right to produce and write all motion pictures. But I did *Star Trek* seventy-nine times. I just can't be a creature of *Star Trek* all my life. I wanted to see bright, new people come in and put a good stamp on it and add certain differences. As the consultant, they sent me everything from the first story idea to the final draft of the motion picture. I also saw dailies and rough cuts and all of that. I made my comments to them. I told them the only time I would say "No, stop, I refuse to put my name on it" is if they should break any of the very basic things about *Star Trek*. Affection for all life-forms or if they should land on a planet and start zapping creatures there because they're different. I certainly wouldn't insist on taking my name off or breaking the contract merely because they don't have quite the uniform I like or merely because they want to crash the *Enterprise*. If you're going to have good people, you've got to give good people some latitude to do it their way.

EDDIE EGAN

When you're the creator of the show or the writer of the original concept, you have to be consulted and engaged on a certain level. There are no parameters for that engagement, but when the second movie started, Paramount made it very clear to him that they were declaring the parameters. He would be shown the scripts, he could review dailies, he could comment on a cut, but it was Paramount's final and absolute decision whether or not to cooperate or ignore.

He definitely had weird things written into his contract on the movies. I remember seeing an abstract of his rights once, and someone had actually thought of a clause that said the intensity of the musical fanfare, under Roddenberry's on-screen credit, could be no less than that of the musical fanfare when Shatner's name was on the screen. I don't know if that was actually carried through, but he thought of that, and had it papered [into his contract].

HARVE BENNETT

I came to Paramount with no anticipation of doing feature pictures at all. I was here to do television. But the second week I got a call from [studio president] Barry Diller, who used to be my assistant at ABC, and Michael Eisner, who used to be a counterpart of mine at ABC in New York, and running the entire operation was the great immigrant, Charlie Bludhorn, who built Gulf & Western and bought Paramount. Barry calls me in and says, "Will you come to a meeting in my office?"

They asked me what I thought of *Star Trek: The Motion Picture.* I said it was boring. Bludhorn turned to Eisner and Diller and said, "Aha! By you guys bald is sexy." To me he said, "Do you think you can make a better movie than that?" I said, "Yeah, I could." He said, "For less than forty-five fucking million dollars?" "Oh," I said, "where I come from I can make a lot of movies for that."

DEBORAH ARAKELIAN (assistant to Harve Bennett and Robert Sallin)

Star Trek I had been a financial drain on the studio and a drain on the actors, who were none too pleased at the end of it. It just went on forever and it cost a lot of money, so Paramount said, "We'll make another *Star Trek,* but it has to be on a television budget and a television schedule." And that was the mandate that was given to Harve and, ultimately, to Bob Sallin, who was the line producer. Bob Sallin staffed it with people that knew how to work on schedule and on budget. It was brought in as promised, and the amazing thing was that it was the antithesis of the *Star Trek: The Motion Picture* situation. Everybody had fun.

Harve Bennett's involvement in *Star Trek* first began in 1980, when he was brought over to Paramount to produce for their television division. Born Harve Bennett Fischman, Bennett was a child genius who was one of the original radio and TV *Quiz Kids*. His successful television producing career included stewarding *The Mod Squad* and later The *Six Million Dollar Man* and *The Bionic Woman*. He had previously served as a network executive at CBS and, later, ABC, where among the numerous shows he oversaw was *The Long Hunt of April Savage,* starring Robert Lansing, which Gene Roddenberry had produced for Sam Rolfe. During the production, Roddenberry and Bennett sparred heavily, and Roddenberry had him thrown off the set. Bennett, however, would eventually have his "wrath."

In 1980, after a recent series of wildly over-budget Hollywood films, including *Apocalypse Now, Star Trek: The Motion Picture,* and *Heaven's Gate* (the latter decimating United Artists), Paramount knew they had to produce the next *Star Trek* film on a substantially lower budget. Chairman Charles Bludhorn, along with Barry Diller and Michael Eisner, realized the best way to do this was to hire an experienced television producer. Some early rumors had the low-budget *Star Trek II* pegged as being a movie-for-television then known as *The Omega Factor*.

HARVE BENNETT

Someone conceived the idea of giving this kind of film to the people whose background and training was essentially in the more cost-conscious area of television. They chose wisely, because they picked good storytellers and not just people who make pictures for controlled budgets. However, it was never seriously a television project. The minute the script began shaping up, it was clear to all that we had something terrific.

GARY NARDINO (president of production, Paramount Pictures)

When I was assigned the responsibility to do *STII* because of the bad economic situation they had on *TMP,* I invited Harve, who I had already brought in to the studio to do *Star Trek*. You went from a $44 million *Star Trek* movie to the one they assigned me to supervise that we did for $13 million and it made almost as much money as the first one. We delivered a good movie in that genre as well as good finance. It was done under the production auspices of television. That transition from *STII* to *STIII* was how I became executive producer of *Star Trek III* and I went on from there and did comedies and Harve kept on doing *Star Trek*.

GERALD FINNERMAN (director of photography, *Star Trek*)

Harve Bennett called me and he said he didn't realize I had done the show. I was under contract to Columbia for a few years and had done a lot of projects for Harve including *From Here to Eternity,* the miniseries that he was nominated for an Emmy for. He said that he had not realized that I had done *Star Trek* until he had read the book *The Making of Star Trek,* and we talked about the possibility of me doing *Star Trek,* but at that time they didn't know whether it was going to be a feature or television and I didn't want to do television.

DEBORAH ARAKELIAN

I was working in the administration building, and the guy who would ultimately be the executive producer of *Star Trek II,* Harve Bennett, is seeing my boss on a regular basis because he's working with her. He's sitting outside her office and he says, "My girlfriend really wants me to do *Star Trek II,* the studio has asked me to do it, and I don't speak *Star Trek.*" I said, "Well, I do." We started talking about it and he started showing me some story ideas, and the next thing I know, I'm the first person hired to be on *Star Trek II.* I was the assistant to the producers, Harve and to Bob Sallin. I took a gigantic cut in pay. I knew I had to do this. I always looked at my time at Paramount as grad school. I ultimately spent seven years there, and the last two years were working on *Star Trek.* I had the time of my life working on *Star Trek II.* There was just a surprise around every corner and I had a blast.

HARVE BENNETT

The main thing that rang false about the first film was that the characters had gone twenty years and hadn't aged, which, to my way of thinking, was totally unbelievable. I felt a major element in future films would be to have the characters age and to focus on what they were going through as people as they did so. At one point, I even sat down with Shatner and told him point-blank that there was a real danger in having a middle-aged Kirk running around like a thirty-year-old.

I am the same age as Shatner, and was going through my own time of change. I wouldn't have dared try to look like I was twenty-five, and I was aware of how silly Bill looked radiating this gauzy look. Even Leonard had too much makeup—

he had Lillian Gish lips [in *The Motion Picture*]. I decided *Star Trek II* was going to be gritty, about people and how they cope with aging.

ROBERT SALLIN (producer, *Star Trek II: The Wrath of Khan*)

Before I joined Harve on the project, I sent him a lengthy memo. I had studied *Star Trek* I and I pinpointed a lot of the fundamental weaknesses of the first film. First and foremost, I felt it was too much a special-effects picture and that the humanity of *Star Trek* just wasn't there. Let the special effects support it, as any effect should support basic storytelling, not be driven by the effects, which so many science-fiction films are. I felt that the look of the picture from a design point of view had been all wrong, the lighting was too flat and uninteresting.

HARVE BENNETT

What I saw that I liked about *Star Trek* were the relationships between the three men, and the sense of male bonding and family and the ethics, the morality—though there are times and episodes, and I can't trace who is responsible, when *Trek* was as kinky a show as ever came down the pike. They had Kirk play an entire episode as a woman.

ROBERT SALLIN

I made a very strong point about one thing. I said, "Let's not attack this as though it's another film project or another television project. I want to interview every member of the crew. I want to make sure that these guys are not only mentally competent, but I want an attitude here. I want an attitude that we're all in this together." As corny as it sounds, I wanted to make sure we had a great time making this film.

MICHAEL MINOR (art director, *Star Trek II: The Wrath of Khan*)

Harve wanted something uplifting, something that would be as fundamental in the twenty-third century as the discovery of recombinant DNA is in our time. Then something just came to me and I said, "Terraforming." Harve asked, "What's that?" and I told him it was the altering of existing planets to conditions which are compatible to human life. I suggested a plot, just making it up in my head while talking on the phone. The Federation had developed a way of engineering the planetary evolution of a body in space on such a rapid scale that instead of eons you have events taking place in months or years. You pick a dead world or an inhospitable gas planet, and you change its genetic matrix or code, thereby speeding up time. This, of course, is also a terrible weapon. Suppose you trained it on a planet filled with people and speeded up its evolution. You could destroy the planet and every life-form on it. Harve liked the idea a lot. At the story conference the next day, he came over, hugged me and said, "You saved *Star Trek*!"

ROBERT SALLIN

I applied some old commercial-production techniques. I storyboarded everything. I had a chart made which listed, by scene, every special effect and optical effect, and I timed each one. I designed and supervised all the special effects. Mike Minor, our art director, sat up here in my office and did the storyboards. Then I held meetings with four or five optical-effects companies, and some of those meetings ran over three hours. I gave them thorough information, so that when the movie was finished, the amount of deviation from the plan was very slight. On this film it was more like I was codirecting as well as producing, *and* I was the visual-effects supervisor.

In the first movie there were quite a few problems with special effects. Because I knew how to handle and manage production, I was left very much alone by the studio. They were all a little intimidated by what had gone on previously, and the idea of special effects escalating the way they did on *Star Trek* I was a major fear and concern. This time we came in so close to budget that you couldn't go out for a decent lunch on the difference.

MICHAEL MINOR

I laid out four different features in storyboard. Literally different plots, different characters, different events, different effects. I put in maybe four hundred man-hours before we settled on what we used to get bids for the effects.

When he first got involved, Bennett had written a one-page story concept titled "War of the Generations," which was presented to Paramount executive Gary Nardino in November 1980. A month later, it was expanded into an outline and then a script by Jack Sowards, which in turn would be continuously rewritten by him and Bennett. "The War of the Generations" involves Admiral Kirk taking command of the *Enterprise* to rescue a lost love from a rebellion on a distant Federation planet. In the process, Kirk is captured by the leader of the rebels, revealed as his own son, who sentences him to death. Before Kirk can be killed, the shadowy hand behind the rebellion is revealed: Khan Noonian Singh and his band of eugenically bred superhumans on Ceti Alpha V. Khan's true intent is to capture a Federation starship (shades of *STV*) and conquer the United Federation of Planets (ironically, this is similar to an early unrealized concept for *Star Trek Beyond*, the latest in the Bad Robot produced film series, where Khan would have manipulated the Klingons into conquering Earth). In the end, Kirk and his son join forces to defeat Khan, leaving them in the coda to "together, boldly go where no man has gone before."

HARVE BENNETT

After considering other writers, I found out that Jack Sowards, a great movie-of-the-week writer, was a *Star Trek* fan. We talked and he clearly knew more about *Star Trek* than I did, so I hired him. Jack and I went to work, and I say we went to work because the process is like this: you talk, and you rap, and the responsibility is that the writer records, in whatever fashion he chooses, the fruits of the give-and-take of this process. His task is then to go and make it become a script.

JACK B. SOWARDS (writer, *Star Trek II: The Wrath of Khan*)

For me, I think the biggest problem is that I started working on the show in December 1980. I met Harve at his house and he had a page of a story worked out. It was a good idea. In other words, somebody gives you a good idea and you say, "Oh, hell, you do this, you do this," and it just sets you off. April 11, 1981, was the Writers Guild strike deadline and we were always working against that deadline. When you're doing a feature, three months is not a long time, so we were always working under that deadline. As a matter of fact, on April 10, I handed in the final draft of my script. That was one of the downsides. We knew that the writers were going to go on strike and I couldn't write beyond that point.

HARVE BENNETT

What we started with was, "Who is the heavy? Who is the black hat? We won't make this picture unless there *is* a black-hat heavy." You know the solution the writers and producers came up with: Khan.

"Space Seed" kept haunting me. I thought it was fabulous. I had seen Ricardo Montalban when I was a little boy, while visiting a soundstage at MGM, and he was doing his first dance with Cyd Charisse. I was there to interview him as a *Quiz Kid* reporter. He always fascinated me. And "Space Seed" spoke to me. I called Ricardo, who was in the midst of shooting *Fantasy Island*. We had lunch and he was charming. "You write *theeese* for me!" he said in that wonderful accent.

JACK B. SOWARDS

I thought "Space Seed" was wonderful. Ricardo Montalban is a classically trained actor. Anybody who can deliver those lines has got to be. Most actors in town would mumble them, but the man knows just how far to go. If you've watched *Fantasy Island* or his movies, there's a smoothness. In this, he was something totally different and he knew just where to go with it without going over the edge. He *is* Khan. He brings that sort of macho arrogance to it, and you believe this is a genetically engineered man who is stronger, smarter, and brighter. A hero is nothing without a villain. If you overcome a slug and a snail, you haven't done anything. If you overcome something like Khan, a hero is defined.

NICHOLAS MEYER (director, *Star Trek II: The Wrath of Khan*)

The story that I was told about the death of Spock was that Leonard, having been disenchanted with the first motion picture, wasn't eager to do any more *Star Trek* and that as a way of enticing him or exciting his interest was Harve Bennett promising him a great death scene. That's all I know. I have to say at this point I have no memory after all these years of any of these five other scripts of *Star Trek II*. I remember two things: I think one script had people singing "Happy Birthday" to Spock in Vulcan. And I remember that there was a simulator sequence in one of the scripts. I don't remember how Spock died in anything. He probably always died somewhere near the end. My idea was to have him die in the first scene.

LEONARD NIMOY (actor, "Mr. Spock")

There have been times when I've been concerned about the future of my career, because of the identification with the character. But I never had a confrontation with the studio in which I've said I would never play the part again. My only concern with *Star Trek* has been that if we're going to do it, we do it well. I don't want to just do a rip-off *Star Trek* title just because people will pay to see it. If it's going to be good, I wanted to be there. I'd hate like hell to see a great *Star Trek* movie hit the screen and not be in it. I'd feel very jealous. [At the time] I really was adamant that I would not work on *Star Trek II* because I had been so frustrated with the other and I was feeling very negative about the whole thing.

JACK B. SOWARDS

When Harve and I had our first meeting, Harve said, "Look, Nimoy has refused to do it." I said, "You want Nimoy to do it?" He said, "Yeah," and I told him to dial Nimoy's number. He picked up the phone, dialed the number, and said, "What do I say?" I said, "You say, 'Leonard, how would you like to play your death scene?'" And Leonard's comeback was, "Where does it come in the picture?" Harve looked at me and said, "Where does it come in the picture?" And I said, "Right up front. Right in the very beginning." A minute or two later Harve hung up and said, "Leonard will do it." Of course when we wrote it, it came in the very beginning. But every time we wrote a little bit more, we moved it back and we moved it back and we moved it back until it came at the end.

HARVE BENNETT

Spock is the most important character. I've always thought that. Remember *The Man from U.N.C.L.E.*, in which the real star was David McCallum, but Robert Vaughn was the star and matinee idol? Bill is the centerpiece, but the thing that makes it work is this extraordinary oddball who makes the show unpredictable. Agreeing on Spock's death was the beginning of an evolution that got so convoluted that its resemblance to the final film is, of course, a process.

LEONARD NIMOY

[Harve] caught me completely by surprise with that one. The more I thought about it, the more I thought, "Well, maybe that's the honest thing to do. Finish it properly rather than turn your back on it." So, eventually, we agreed Spock would die. There was a lot of controversy over whose idea it was and why. It was even said that it was the only way I would do it and that it was in my contract that Spock would die! It got to be a messy situation.

When Harve and I started to explore the idea, I thought back to the first season of *Star Trek*, when the Spock character had taken root and been widely accepted. The whole concept of his lack of emotionality, his control of emotions, was a very interesting and important part of the character. Dorothy Fontana, who was a writer on the series, came to me on the set one day and said, "I'm going to write a love story for Spock." I told her she couldn't do it, because it would destroy the character, destroy the whole mystique about whether or not he's emotional. The whole story we'd been telling was that he was completely in control of his emotions. She said, "I have an idea that might work, and I'm going to try it." She did, and wrote "This Side of Paradise," a beautiful episode in which Spock fell in love. At the end of it, there was a bittersweet parting and it was all over. And he had gone through this fantastic experience.

With Jack Sowards officially on board, Bennett's initial outline was expanded into a full treatment dated December 18, 1980. In the story, the Federation has ceased colonization of new worlds and Starfleet is solely tasked with protecting and developing the territories within its existing realm. On one such world, the society's youth is being coaxed to rebellion by a mysterious "Teacher." Aboard the *Enterprise*, Spock is killed at the very beginning of the film attempting to shutdown a damaged warp engine. After Spock's meaningless death, Kirk comes aboard the *Enterprise* and upon examining Spock's personal logs realizes that Spock was attempting to reengage with his emotions after his encounter with V'ger in *TMP*.

Shortly thereafter, the *Enterprise* encounters a refugee ship with Diana, an old flame of Kirk's with whom he had a son, unbeknownst to Kirk but known to McCoy. Kirk arrives on the rebellious planet, encountering his son, and is blamed for the carnage, only to discover the mysterious Teacher's identity: Khan, who is able to marshal massive psychic abilities to manifest illusions, much like the Talosians in "The Cage," around Kirk and David.

In his next version, Sowards introduced the character of Janet Wallace from the *TOS* episode "The Deadly Years" (a former Kirk love interest whose son David Wallace would be an antagonist in this version) as well as the first mention of Saavik, the male Vulcan first officer aboard the *Enterprise*. It is also the first time that Commander Terrell is introduced as is the *Reliant*, which attacks the *Enter-*

prise. The Omega weapons system, which would later become the Genesis Device, is also introduced here as the object of Khan's obsession.

In February of 1981, Sowards elaborated on his previous outline and turned in a first draft of what was now entitled "The Omega System," in which Kirk is a vice admiral and Uhura is his assistant. While Khan remains the villain, his wife, Marla McGivers, introduced in the *TOS* episode "Space Seed," is still very much alive. By April of 1981, Sowards's new rewrite was now entitled "The Genesis Project." Janet Wallace is gone, replaced by Carol Baxter and her son, David. In this draft, Spock makes it midway through the picture before his death. Khan and Marla McGivers were the only ones who survived being stranded on Ceti Alpha V, but Khan is still able to project images into people's minds.

That evolving screenplay had several significant elements that would ultimately make it into the final draft: first, it was a sequel to the original-series episode "Space Seed," in which Khan has escaped from Ceti Alpha V and is seeking vengeance against Kirk. Additionally, the story would feature the death of Spock.

The screenplay would also deal with a midlife crisis for Kirk as he attempts to recapture the man he once was, while simultaneously being reunited with former love Carol Marcus and meeting his son, David, for the first time. All of this would be played out against the backdrop of the the Genesis Device, created for terraforming but which has the power to destroy worlds if used for more sinister purposes.

ROBERT SALLIN

Kirk goes through a great deal of introspection and reflection on his life. In a sense, he's having a midlife crisis. Throughout the film we exposed and plumbed the interpersonal relationships that were established back on the series.

JACK B. SOWARDS

The only thing we had to do with the characters was let them age. They're a good set of characters you can move anywhere, and these actors are so good. They're so used to working with each other and they have such a rapport. It's almost as if they can read each other's minds. They know when the cue's coming and how to play it, and it's a pleasure to work with people like that.

Work on the screenplay continued over the next several months, though no one seemed to be entirely satisfied. By July of 1981, an attempt at finding fresh blood led Bennett to original-series writers David Gerrold, Theodore Sturgeon, and Samuel A. Peeples, the latter of whom wrote an outline and eventually a screenplay that pretty much utilized all of the existing elements of the scripts written by Sowards and Bennett with the *exception* of Khan. Instead, he introduced the aliens Sojin and Moray.

HARVE BENNETT

Sam Peeples had done outstanding work in other areas when I was at ABC. He had done two pilots that I had been involved with, and I thought he could write robustly. I brought him in, he read the script, and I said, "Sam, you know more about *Star Trek* than I do. I want you to fix this." He said, "I know just what to do." The result was his script.

Entitled *Worlds That Never Were*, submitted in July 1981, and eschewing the characters of Khan and McGivers for his new antagonists, Peeples's script also has Spock, not unlike Obi-Wan Kenobi, reaching out from beyond the grave to talk to Kirk and McCoy, imparting crucial information that saves the day. Shortly thereafter, a script was developed, dated August 24, 1981, entitled *The New Star Trek,* consisting of a pastiche of ideas from the various outlines (with the first mention of Saavik as female and half-Romulan) that preceded it, including the aforementioned scene in which the crew sings happy birthday to Spock in Vulcan.

DEBORAH ARAKELIAN

It was a no-win scenario for whoever walked in there. They actually had me reading SF writers and suggesting some of the best SF writers in the business. It was a dream job: I was being paid to sit there and read for a while. But Harve went to a couple of previous *Star Trek* writers and it didn't work.

HARVE BENNETT

Star Trek writers came in with supreme egos. I had worked with many of them before and found them, like most science-fiction writers, very unyielding to comment. Harlan [Ellison] was in a class by himself. He gave me an outline on *The Mod Squad* that would have cost twenty million dollars to produce. When I asked him to think reasonably, he responded as if I were questioning Allah. I worked with D. C. Fontana on *Six Million Dollar Man* and had a similar experience. I said, "Hey, we're not doing Chekhov here."

ROBERT SALLIN

Neither the Jack Sowards or Samuel Peeples script worked. It felt like television. It felt like a long television episode, and I didn't believe that the underlying humanity and the relationships between the people were very strong. There was a lot of intergalactic weirdness in the scripts which I felt was defeating.

SAMUEL A. PEEPLES (writer, "Where No Man Has Gone Before")

I didn't like the basic premise. My personal objection to the original version was simply that it was cast too much in the mold of the 1967 *Star Trek* episodes. When Gene Roddenberry and I first discussed his project, long before the first pilot script was written, I was much taken by Gene's imaginatively pragmatic approach. Extrapolation was the key to the visual reality he sought after. But somehow, along the way, pragmatism became dogma and only what had been used before was acceptable. This, I believe, is the major fault of *Star Trek: The Motion Picture*. It is far too easy to be influenced by the traditions *Star Trek* has initiated. Tradition and déjà vu and nostalgia cannot be major influences in the new *Star Trek*. It is common sense to use the basics that have proven so right, but it is also common sense to open our minds to the very expansive creativity that brought *Star Trek* to us in the first place.

It's for this reason I didn't hesitate to break old barriers, try new themes, ideas, dialogue, and characterizations. *Star Trek* had grown and expanded its horizons. The "heavies" in this version is a good example. They are not representations of "evil" or "good." They were, perhaps, the first totally alien concepts used in *Star Trek*—one more departure from traditional themes—beings from another cosmos. Their universe is not ours; their motivations are hidden from us. But within the projected limitations of their own environment, they are logical and normal.

In the end, though, I was never actually given an assignment and *never* asked for one. I wasn't happy with what I wrote and neither was the producer, so it just died.

DEBORAH ARAKELIAN

Then Harve took a swing at it, but it didn't work. He sweated bullets over it. He worked on it. But Harve was a TV executive first and foremost. Then he became a producer. This was a job for a pure writer, in my not so humble opinion. It's not slamming Harve. This was just not his forte. I'll tell you how he did it, he hired the right people. He may not consider that his greatest talent. But frankly his greatest talent was assembling the right team on *Star Trek II*. *Star Trek III* was not as successful because they replaced a lot of the people.

ROBERT SALLIN

I had a lot of sleepless nights about the process. I knew this script just didn't feel right. It didn't feel right as a *Star Trek* picture, and at its core it didn't feel right as anything good. I was getting pressure from the studio: "We're going to be filming such and such a date," and we just didn't have anything that made any sense. I just thought it would look like a Saturday-morning television show if we did something like this. It had no stature, no quality, no uniqueness to it.

DEBORAH ARAKELIAN

Harve is not a natural-born writer, but he wanted to write the screenplay. Not a good idea.

ROBERT SALLIN

Jack was a much more solid writer and made huge contributions to the script. But even then, Harve was always rewriting Sowards. He used to throw all of these versions of the script into what he called the arbitration box. I knew nothing about this kind of thing. What that was, to a certain point, was that Harve eventually took that to the Writers Guild and submitted it in an attempt to receive the sole writing credit. This is true. They rejected him. That was not too cool.

DEBORAH ARAKELIAN

So, between Harve writing it and before that some writers that were hired that couldn't deliver, they had gone through their story money and there was none left. The studio was not going to shoot the final draft that Harve turned in. It was awful. He's not a great writer, but when you're that close to *Star Trek* you really want to put your fingerprints on it as much as possible. I don't question his desire to do that, but Nicky Meyer is a real writer.

JUDY BURNS (writer, "The Tholian Web")

Harve Bennett, who had hired me several times to do *The Six Million Dollar Man*, called me and asked if I wanted to rewrite the Jack Sowards script for *The Wrath of Khan*. I read it, gave him all of my suggestions, and said, "You're really into this and love it so much, why don't you rewrite it yourself?" He said, "Maybe I will," and that's what he did. I could kick myself now that I didn't rewrite it, because almost everything I suggested to Harve was used in the rewrite.

Since Leonard Nimoy wanted Spock to die, I said to Harve, "You mustn't kill Spock in such a fashion that he can't be brought back." It was such a final idea originally that it was impossible to bring him back. He also died in such a way that there was no emotional impact on the viewers, and I said what they were missing in that script was the relationship between Spock and Kirk, which was so critical and which ultimately ended up in the scene between the two of them as Spock is dying. Originally, that scene didn't exist. Those were specifically my notes, all five pages of which had to do with character, because Harve had never done *Star Trek* before. Thank God he found Nicholas Meyer, a very good character person.

DEBORAH ARAKELIAN

Bob Sallin came in, looked at me, and mind you, I've just taken a huge cut in salary to do this. I'm practically living on friends' sofas. And he says, "I've got bad news. We're going to be out of a job in a week because the studio is not going to shoot Harve's script and they're not going to give us any more money for development."

ROBERT SALLIN

I had put together a list of about thirty or forty directors, and I was almost universally turned down. Nobody wanted to touch *Star Trek*, nobody wanted to do a sequel, no one wanted to do science fiction or anything with special effects. I was dumbstruck. One day my secretary suggested Nick Meyer.

DEBORAH ARAKELIAN

I said to Bob Sallin, "The development executive on this is Karen Moore. Karen Moore is very good friends with Nicholas Meyer. Nicholas Meyer has directed one movie, he's a fledgling director but I know he's a really good writer. What if you hire him as a director and he quietly rewrites the script?" Now, ultimately, Nicky did not quietly rewrite it, but Bob thought that was a good idea and he didn't have any others at the time.

NICHOLAS MEYER

There was a movie that I wanted to make and tried to make for fifteen years, based on a book by a Canadian author named Robertson Davies called *Fifth Business*. I didn't want to do anything else. I wound up doing *Time After Time,* and people said if you do this and it's a hit, then they'll let you do *Fifth Business.* So *Time After Time* was a hit, but it wasn't a big enough hit, and they weren't going to let me do this because at that time no one had heard of or was interested in Robertson Davies.

DEBORAH ARAKELIAN

When Bob Sallin came back to the office at the end of whatever meeting that he took in the administration building and he looked at me and he said, "I've got some bad news for you. We're going to be out of a job in a week," *that's* when panic became the mother of invention and I strongly suggested they look at hiring Nicky and then he took that idea back and it flew. He had nothing to lose, and they sold that idea and they hired Nick to direct it and, of course, Nick obviously rewrote the entire script and wrote a great script. Bob had had a long history in the commercial business and had worked with all of the best cinematographers. And the concept was to surround Nick with the best. And to be there to prop him up, and it worked.

NICHOLAS MEYER

I was sitting in my house in Laurel Canyon just vegetating. I had a childhood friend who was now an executive at Paramount. She'd come on board with Louis Malle for *Pretty Baby* and had done such a good job for him that the studio hired her. It was a Sunday, and my recollection is that we were flipping burgers on a grill, and my friend Tony Bill was there, and Karen said, "What are you doing?" And I said, "I'm waiting." And she said, "If you want to learn how to direct, in my opinion, you ought to direct and not just sit up here holding your breath because you're not getting your way. Maybe what you ought to do is go down and meet Harve Bennett because he is going to make the next *Star Trek* movie and I think you guys would get along."

I said, "*Star Trek*? Is that the one with the guy with the pointy ears?" And she said, "You're such a snob. Just meet the man, why don't you?" And if this had been my mother talking I probably wouldn't have gone but, for whatever reason, she got through to me, and so I went to see Harve on the Paramount lot. As I recall, he cracked open a couple of beers and we sat there and we had a long conversation about it.

ROBERT SALLIN

I went to see Nick, had an interesting conversation, and then brought Harve over. I admired Nick's writing, but I wasn't keen on his directorial ability. But I did like the way he wrote and his sense of story was fabulous. So I took Harve over and we had a long meeting. Afterward, Harve turned to me and said, "You know, if we go with him, he's going to be trouble." I said, "What do you mean? He's great." Well, Harve perceived something which I didn't, which was that [Meyer] has a very substantial ego. He's a very intelligent guy and not without talent. I pushed and I said, "I think we really have to do this, because we don't have anyone who is even remotely interested in doing this." The long and short of it is that we did it, and when Nick read the various versions of things that Harve was struggling with, he realized that the thing simply didn't work. It was his uncredited rewrite that we actually shot. He gets, as far as I'm concerned, all the credit. He really did a masterful job of taking these disparate parts and brought them together into something that was cogent, made sense, and was an entertainment.

NICHOLAS MEYER

Harve showed me the first movie and some episodes, and I remember thinking that it all pleasantly reminded me of something I always liked. It took me a while to remember and it was probably in the middle of the night I woke up thinking, "Oh yes, you used to love those C. S. Forester books about Captain Hornblower."

And I said, "This is Hornblower in outer space," and that's when everything really clicked into place.

HARVE BENNETT

I think—and this is where Nick and I part ways with Gene—that *Star Trek* is a naval show; always was and always will be.

NICHOLAS MEYER

Roddenberry definitely averred or opined that *Star Trek* was not a naval operation, not a military operation, it was a sort of a Coast Guard, is how he put it. And I thought watching these episodes that that didn't seem to be the case. This was definitely a form of gunboat diplomacy, in which the Federation was a yardstick of correctness. Would we weep for Hamlet if we didn't know what the fuck he was on about? We understand perfectly, that's why we keep doing it. Would we suck in our breath, awestruck at the sight of the Michelangelo *David* if we didn't understand the idealized human form? It's all the same. And it doesn't seem, aside from certain technological advancements, the world has substantially changed. People are still making fists and cutting off each other's heads. And, in that sense, my version of *Star Trek* was a gloomier, darker version. But the people were still the same people. They were just having to confront a less optimistic reality.

HARVE BENNETT

When I saw *The Seven-Per-Cent Solution,* I was so impressed with the screenplay that I went out and read the book, and I was even more impressed with the book. Nick read my rewrite of Sowards and Peeples and said, "This has promise. What if . . ."

NICHOLAS MEYER

Harve said he was going to send me draft five of the script, and I woke up one day and said, "What happened to that script?" It never showed up. I called Harve and he was sort of embarrassed and said, "I can't send it to you. I don't like it. It's not good. And it's 178 pages." I said send it anyway and he sent it. I didn't know what I was reading and I said, "Well, what about draft four?" And he said, "It's just five different attempts to get a different *Star Trek* movie." So I said to send them all. This van shows up and there were all these scripts and even though I read very slowly, I read all these different scripts—and along the way a dim idea had begun to percolate through me. Philosophically, I said that I was simply going to take these characters more seriously and more literally than anyone has ever taken them before.

DEBORAH ARAKELIAN

Nick was hired. And Nick didn't even know it came from me to the extent that he bought a washer and dryer for Karen Moore's house to thank her.

NICHOLAS MEYER

I sat down with Harve Bennett and his producing partner Robert Sallin, they'd been at UCLA together, with a yellow legal pad which is never very far away from me, and said, "Why don't we make a list of all the things that we like in these five drafts? A major plot, a minor plot, a sequence, a scene, a character, a line of dialogue, it doesn't matter. Then I'll try to fashion a new screenplay that accommodates as many of these things as possible." They didn't seem to like my idea and I said, "What's wrong with what I just said?" They started telling me this whole thing about ILM, the special-effects house, needs a script in twelve days or they can't get delivery of the visual effects in time for the release of the movie. And I said, "What release?" because it was only the second movie I'd ever been involved with as a filmmaker. And I thought, "Holy cow, they'd already booked this thing into theaters." Twelve days? I don't know why I wound up saying, "I think I can do this in twelve days, but we've got to get going, guys."

They still weren't happy and I said, "Well, now what's the problem?" And they said, "The problem is we couldn't even make your deal in twelve days," and that's when I made my fatal error of forgoing money and credit on the writing of it because I just thought, "If we don't get going on this now, then there's no movie."

ROBERT SALLIN

It is, in all candor, Nick's uncredited rewrite that is on the screen. Contrary to what the critics may say, Harve made contributions, I made contributions, but it was Nick's final version that we used. Nick never took credit for it, and he told me his agent said he was crazy.

NICHOLAS MEYER

I don't remember what happened in those twelve days; I must have gone into some kind of alternate state of being, because I really don't remember anything except that my back was killing me at the end of it because I was bent over a Smith Corona portable electric.

DEBORAH ARAKELIAN

Some writers are particularly good, and for me it was a joy watching Nick fix this thing on the fly, because it was like an advanced college class on screenwriting. It was screenwriting 303. It wasn't 101. It was brilliant watching him strip away the stuff that just was unnecessary and get to the basic through line, telling a good story simply and making it a tight, clean script. The way I learned to write, right down to the word, if there's no reason for it, don't put it in. It's got to serve a purpose. And a lot of that I learned from watching Nicky work. And believe me, Nicky and I are not exactly friends, but he is a *real* writer. He has technique and he's got chops, and he knows what to do and how to fix a script.

NICHOLAS MEYER

Screenwriting, for me anyway, always amounts to a form of short-order cooking. I thrive on that kind of front burner, walking into the propeller, you've got to do it, so do it. There's a certain adrenaline by-product that, if you're lucky, infects the actual end result. I've taken long periods of time to write scripts and they've come out well, but certainly in the case of the second *Star Trek* movie, that working under the gun, as it were, was good for it.

To some degree, the same is true of *IV* and probably *VI*. Movies didn't always take so long to get made; they just used to happen faster. Nowadays they do draft after draft after draft of things and the life gets squeezed out of them, the spontaneity gets squeezed out of them, the intuition gets squeezed out of them. The advantage I had in writing those scripts is that there wasn't time to be second-guessed by a bunch of executives or people saying, "Well, what if we did *this*?" and everybody sticking in their oar. It just worked out that you had to kind of go with your gut and go, go, go . . . or there wasn't going to be any movie.

HARVE BENNETT

Star Trek has enormous snob appeal. It purports to be a program for the bright. If you watched *Trek* it was like going to a Mensa meeting. If you compare the shows of the sixties, as to intentions and content, a *Star Trek* alongside a *Starsky and Hutch* or *Bonanza,* you have something that aspired to as high as TV would allow it to go. It was smart.

NICHOLAS MEYER

I'm not terribly interested in space. But I was interested in real ships—*Run Silent, Run Deep,* frigates blasting each other. I wanted the characters to look like sailors, not like they were wearing pajamas. I wanted the *Enterprise* to be reminiscent of a tin can. These are not comfortable places, so let's rip up the carpet, put in more instrumentation, electronic bosun's whistles and ship's bells. I did what I could to echo a nautical frame of reference.

GEORGE TAKEI (actor, "Hikaru Sulu")

When I first got the script and saw the kind of participation Sulu had, I saw that he wasn't much more than a talking prop. There was no character there, and I decided that I just couldn't go back under those conditions. My heart just wouldn't be in it. I told this to Harve Bennett and Nick Meyer and they understood, but the script was already written and there wasn't much that they could do with it at that point . . . Harve understood the problems and had a few scenes added that bolstered my part a little, but I was still unhappy. Filming was due to begin soon and a decision had to be made. So they made certain promises and I was on the set the first day of filming without even a contract. The first shots included me on the simulation bridge, so I was locked in. Unfortunately, when the film came out, some of the little scenes, which would have added to my character, ended up on the cutting-room floor.

DeFOREST KELLEY (actor, "Dr. Leonard 'Bones' McCoy)

At first I turned it down. I strongly disliked the earlier script that had been handed to me. I felt it was a busy story and didn't work, so I had a big conversation with Harve Bennett. He was upset. I said I would rather *not* be in it, because the role was not meaningful, and the script was just *not* a good *Star Trek* script. He said, "What do you think we should do?" "I think you should hire a writer who has written for *Star Trek* before and rewrite it!" He looked at me funny and said, "Well, who would you hire?" I said, "Gee, Harve, I don't know, I'm not in that line of work."

DEBORAH ARAKELIAN

It was a dysfunctional family reunion. De is such a gentlemen who couldn't care less. What a lovely human being. De tended a garden; he carried a picture of his shih tzu in his wallet. He pulls out the picture of his dog like he was pulling out a picture of his kid. He was a sweet man. De was just above it all; you couldn't say or do anything that would shake him. The only time I saw him a little on edge was when we were doing ADR [additional dialogue recording], because De was a little older than the rest of them. He felt that his voice wasn't strong enough, so he really got into ADR and pumped everything up beautifully. He had that big career in westerns and stuff before *Star Trek* began. He was on another level. He appreciated *Star Trek* but it didn't define him.

WILLIAM SHATNER

I was nervous about it. Especially after the first film. The success of your performance, essentially, rests in the words. Everything rises and falls on the script. When a script is good, it takes a heroic effort to ruin it. As this script developed, I swung wildly from awful lows to exalted highs. I began to realize that the movie might be good.

DEBORAH ARAKELIAN

John Belushi was on the set one day studying Shatner. He did a brilliant Shatner imitation on *Saturday Night Live*. He was perfecting it. He was just sitting there watching Shatner. I said to the associate producer, "Don't let him go because The Blues Brothers just played the wrap party for *Laverne & Shirley* and I wanted to get them for our wrap party," so I dropped everything and ran over, and Belushi had gone. They let him go and that night he died.

NICHOLAS MEYER

I have always thought, to the extent that I've had any clear thoughts about *Star Trek,* that it was something that for one reason or another never quite fulfilled its promise. Either because in terms of a TV show, they couldn't afford the sets or the effects, or because in the first movie they dropped the ball somewhere. This was an opportunity to make something right that had never quite been on the nose before. The more specific you get, the better. It was not necessary for me to see Admiral Kirk go to the bathroom, but I said why couldn't he read a book?

At which point I grabbed the first book off my shelf, which was *A Tale of Two Cities,* and for some reason or another, I just stuck with that, which was interesting because it's the one book that everybody knows the first and the last line to. That became the bracket of the movie and also somehow became the theme of the movie. Leonard and Shatner got excited, because they always felt in some way that they had the Sydney Carton–Charles Darnay relationship going on between them. That's very specific, and from the book we got the glasses, which was specific, too . . . and real! From all of that came age. Interestingly enough, *Star Trek II* is not very much about science fiction, the Genesis Planet aside. Its themes are entirely earthbound—death, aging, friendship.

DeFOREST KELLEY

I feel that Meyer brought it to life and really made it a kind of *Star Trek* script. When he sent me that draft, I said, "That's more like it," and I went with it.

WALTER KOENIG (actor, "Pavel Chekov")

I never wanted to be teased by the prospects of another film. I remember reading the script and thinking this can't be true, this is so nice for my character. It came out of the blue for me. I had no reason to believe that they were going to elaborate on what I had done in the past. I kept holding my breath when I was reading it and thereafter, wondering whether or not it was all going to come apart somehow.

NICHOLAS MEYER

When Bill Shatner first read the screenplay that I had written for *Star Trek II,* he thought it was a disaster, and we had this meeting. I was so upset that I just kept jumping up to go pee. I didn't know whether it was the humiliation or rage or what. And Bill said, "Are you okay?" And I said, "Oh yeah, indigestion." It *wasn't* indigestion.

When he finally left, I was just crestfallen and thought, "This is never going to happen." And Harve sat there and said, "Well, yeah, but what he really said was only *this.*" And he broke it down into these bite-sized pieces. And when I stopped panicking and realized the value and the insight and the precision of what Harve had isolated, I thought "Oh." I went home, and twelve hours later I'd turned the thing around again and Bill was happy. He just wanted to be the first guy through the door.

In my relations with Harve, he was always the mentor and I was always the kid, which I thought suited us both. I said this to Harve at the time that he didn't give himself enough credit sometimes for being Harve Bennett. There was a kind of insecurity or inferiority thing going on as opposed to the rather thoughtful and well-read and diligent person that he was. And very, very smart. He was one of those kids that went on the radio because he was a kid genius.

RALPH WINTER (postproduction supervisor, *Star Trek II: The Wrath of Khan*)

Harve was very calm about all that stuff. That was the statesman in him. He was able to manage all those emotions and everything else very well. A lot of the stuff that I learned from him is you need a calm presence on the set to give the crew and everyone else confidence that not only you know what the hell you're doing, but that the ship is heading in the right direction.

WILLIAM SHATNER

Nick Meyer had written a script and we were in love with the script and impressed by his creative ability. So even though it was only the second picture he had directed, we felt that his imagination should be given full flower. And so here he was. He had written the script, but he hadn't directed very much. Whatever help we could give him was offered and he would accept it or not accept it, depending on whether he thought we were correct.

NICHOLAS MEYER

In the case of the cast, they had a lot of ideas about how their characters behaved or spoke. But I never viewed them in an adversarial capacity once Bill decided that he loved the script. There were times when they would get bent out of shape over something, but it was all over the course of a day's work. I remember having a close-up of Nichelle Nichols at the end of the day and she said that's not fair, because no one looks their best at the end of a day. It was only my second movie, so I wasn't thinking in those terms. I remember Leonard didn't like the set of his cabin on the *Enterprise.* And you know what? He was right. In that sense, it was a totally professional series of exchanges. I was treated with respect and they liked me more than not. And I think what they really liked was the script. Because they liked the script and I had written it, they were inclined to give me the benefit of the doubt.

DEBORAH ARAKELIAN

Try telling him what to do. I dare you. Nicky is Nicky. He is larger than life. His persona is much larger than Bill's. Nobody can tell Nicky what to do. Bill could have tried, but he would have failed miserably. And why mess with it? They were getting a great product. Only a total freaking moron would say you need to rewrite that scene because there is not enough of me in it. I saw none of that going on.

ROBERT SALLIN

I watched dailies. Remember the scene in the container on the sand planet where Khan and his followers are living? Khan delivers this fabulous speech and there are all of these cutaways to reactions. I looked at it and realized that Nick shot it with the wrong screen direction. I was livid. I went to the set and found out a couple of people had warned him about it and he ignored them. I went to Nick, controlling myself, and said, "All of that stuff you shot of the reactions is going to have to be reshot." He said, "Why?" and I explained it to him. He said, "I'm not doing a picture about screen directions." How do you like that? We reshot it. That was the kind of thing I was dealing with a lot.

Remember when they open the picture with the training exercise? The exercise fails and Shatner comes through the door with the light behind him. My feeling was that his arrival has to be like the Second Coming. I had a discussion with Nick about how to do it, and I said, "You must put the light directly in line with the lens so that the figure of Shatner blocks it and is surrounded by the fingers of light and smoke and it all comes out equally." I go up to San Rafael with ILM, I come back, and Shatner's off to one side and it looks terrible. Again, I went to Nick and said, "That shot doesn't work." "Why? Why?" "Because you didn't do what I suggested and it doesn't work. It's not appropriate for this key moment. Here's how it has to be." I explained to him again what had to be done and he said, "That's fine. I'm going to get credit for it anyway."

WILLIAM SHATNER

By the time we were ready to shoot, I knew *Wrath of Khan* would be great. We had ILM for the effects, so the movie couldn't *look* bad. We also had a very human *Star Trek*-ian script. It was a wonderful working experience. It was as if the years between this film and the old show never existed.

At one point, production was rocked by public outcry following media announcements that in *Star Trek II*, Leonard Nimoy's Mr. Spock was going to die. The shocking thing is that the leak came from an inside source.

ROBERT SALLIN

The studio did not generate any of the rumors about Spock's death. People have assumed that when this movie was conceived the first thing the studio did was to run out and create the rumors that Spock was going to die, to get the Trekkies excited and generate publicity. I know that the position of the studio brass was that they would just assume nobody said anything. Early drafts of the script were stolen and made their way into the hands of fans, and that fueled the furor.

DEBORAH ARAKELIAN

Gene Roddenberry was none too happy we were going to kill off Spock. He didn't hide that. The big shocker for everybody was toward the end of principal production Leonard coming back and saying, "You know, I had such a good time with this I'd be willing to do one more." That was where they decided to add a scene to give them an avenue into *Star Trek III*. Nicky Meyer had no problem splattering green blood all over the place when it came to killing Spock. There was an attempt by Harve to keep everything under wraps. We did not want this leaking out, but it did leak out.

SUSAN SACKETT

Some things Gene fought for and did not get and would very much like to have had. In the second movie, for example, he fought very desperately against any attempt to kill the Spock character, and he was overruled.

DEBORAH ARAKELIAN

There were only like six or seven copies of the story outline that were circulated and only two people who needed to know. Harve came to me and said, "I need you to devise a way that if somebody leaks this we might be able to track it back to the person who leaked it." It was a typo. Everybody had a distinct typo. Literally it was like a period snuck into each page. That's what I did.

Harve said, "Don't tell me what you do, just do it." So I did. I sort of embedded my own little special code. At the time, we were using typewriters, but this rudimentary code actually worked because at one point it was leaked, it was published, and instead of retyping the text it was just photographically put out there in one of the rags. And so Harve came in and plunked a newspaper in front of me and he said, "Okay, track it!" And I could. I went back to his office. I said, "Here's the legend. Here's whose copy this was. Now what are you going to do about it?" It was Gene's.

Gene never knew anything about this. I never told him. I can say with 100 percent certainty that it was Gene's copy that was leaked. There was nothing Harve could do about it because it was Gene's copy.

JOEL ENGEL (author, *Gene Roddenberry: The Myth & Man Behind Star Trek*)

Gene Roddenberry's treachery caught Harve by surprise, given that Harve thought he had GR's approval and imprimatur. It didn't occur to him that GR might leak a plot point to undermine Harve's work. And it's telling that GR couldn't imagine Spock's rebirth. My recollection is that they didn't have a working relationship, since there was nothing for GR to do but sit there like Jabba the Hutt and have the scripts and rough cuts brought to him for his amusement. Roddenberry was indulged to stop him from unleashing the dogs of war, the fans.

HARVE BENNETT

In those days fanzines were the equivalent of the Internet. They're still out there, but in those days there were like a hundred thousand subscribers to such publications, and after the first outline of *Star Trek II* was distributed within Paramount, within two weeks every fanzine was crying, "They're going to kill Spock!" That was followed by a massive write-in campaign. I think they sent a hundred thousand letters saying don't kill Spock, and put a terrible crimp in the most difficult problem I had, which was convincing Leonard Nimoy to get back into the ears. Leonard wanted nothing to do with the next feature, having had a bad experience on *The Motion Picture*. So I had convinced him by telling him he was going to get the greatest death since *Psycho*—the genius Hitchcock kills the largest star in the picture a third of the way through, and no one could believe it. Suddenly it was no longer a Janet Leigh vehicle.

Anyway, I said, "That's what we're going to do to you; no one will know and they will be scared shitless." He said, "Ooh, I like that," and his actor side said, "That is a great death scene, and I'm through with it. I'm not Spock." But now we're confronted with the world knowing we're going to kill him, so that ended that surprise. I then had to *really* convince Leonard that we could make it work, and told him how. By that time, though, Leonard had regained his enthusiasm, reading with Bill, and he'd met some of the cast again and there was a certain warmth that was reentering the whole franchise. He said, "You fix it that way and I'm aboard," so that ended that problem. But I will forever know who ratted us out and he did it again, by the way, when we destroyed the *Enterprise* in *Star Trek III*.

I was so frustrated with *that*, I said, "The hell with it," and two weeks before *Star Trek III* was released, the promo department said, "Oh, you've got to see our trailers; our trailers are so terrific for *Star Trek III*." In the trailer they proclaim it as the "final voyage of the starship *Enterprise*." The first thing, "BOOM!" and the ship blows up ten seconds into the trailer. The *Enterprise* is blowing up before your eyes. So that ended *that* surprise, but these are the vicissitudes of doing it in the Hollywood system.

NICHOLAS MEYER

We were sitting in one of those little screening rooms at Paramount looking at test footage of something. I was sitting behind Harve and we were all still mumbling about getting letters and flak about killing Spock. And the simulator scene in my script had already been written and I had started off the movie with it. But without the death of Spock. So I said, "We kill him in the simulator right at the beginning." And Harve whirled around and he went, "That is brilliant!"

DEBORAH ARAKELIAN

Starting out with the *Kobayashi Maru* was great because it threw all of the really hard-core people off. It was just a publicity thing. They were not *really* killing Spock. After the simulator scene, Kirk saw Spock and asked, "Aren't you dead?"

HARVE BENNETT

Moving Spock's death to the end of the film made it stronger, and if I thought Gene knew what he was doing, and knew the long-range results, I would honor him fully. But it was accidental. It did, however, let us set up the nobility of the real death.

EDDIE EGAN

The letters and phone calls that came in from people were more outraged at the idea of Spock's death than they were happy that Paramount was making another movie. They always sort of considered Paramount to be this monolithic evil corporation that didn't care about *Star Trek* at all. I would say to these people, some of whom I became very friendly with over time, "You have to understand, they're making another movie. If they hated *Star Trek*, they wouldn't make another movie. They barely made a dollar on the last one." That became part of my job. It was like holding the virtual hands of these people over the phone and just responding to letters and talking to fans, as well as these sorts of normal customary duties of publicity.

WALTER KOENIG

Harve Bennett had given me a copy of the script and asked me to do a Trekkie run [for accuracy to series canon] based on some comments I had made on an earlier draft where they had Spock dying in the first act, and I said this was absolutely unconscionable; this is the climax of your story. He's not one of these guys in the red shirts. I guess he was reasonably impressed with that, because he then asked me to do a Trekkie run and there was some dialogue about Khan saying, "Mr. Chekov, I remember the face"—which he couldn't possibly have since I wasn't on the series when he did that episode. I was faced with the ethical dilemma of mentioning it to Bennett or letting it go. I chose survival as opposed to ethics and I didn't mention it and, in fact, Ricardo didn't even know it. He didn't know that he hadn't met me before.

NICHOLAS MEYER

Montalban had the longest credits of anybody, and if you watch him at his best in certain movies, he's a fantastic actor. He was the only one who couldn't come to rehearsals. We rehearsed the movie around my dining room table and he was doing *Fantasy Island*. So I didn't really know him. I had lunch with him and that was it. And you know, directors always want to know one thing about the actor: Is he crazy? How crazy? Am I going to live or do I have to pull the boat over the mountain? Ricardo was a very courteous, very polite, very well-bred gentlemen.

He came to the set the first day ready to work and in full makeup. We had this whole six-page monologue about who he is and why he's so pissed off at Kirk at having been marooned on this planet. I thought, "Let's try to film it in one shot. Let the camera sort of dance around him and let him work up a head of steam." A head of steam is what he worked up, all right, because when we first were doing it, he was screaming and bellowing. This is only the second movie I've ever directed, this guy's got more credits than I've got inches in height, and I thought, "What to do, what to do?"

While they're lighting I asked him into his trailer and to have a little conversation. I remember saying, "You know, Laurence Olivier said that an actor should never show an audience his top because once you show your top, they know you've got no place else to go." And he said, "Ah, I see, you're going to direct me. That's good. I need directing, I don't know what I'm doing up there." And then he proceeded to regale me with some choice Mervyn LeRoy stories. "Ricardo, Lana, make it a good scene!" That wasn't very helpful to him.

RICARDO MONTALBAN

When I started to articulate the words of Khan for myself, I sounded like Mr. Roarke and I was very concerned about it. Then I asked Harve Bennett to send me a tape of the old show that I did. I ran it two or three times. When I first saw it, I didn't even remember what I did. On the third viewing, a strange thing happened to me and I started reliving the moment, and the mental process that I had arrived at, at that time began to work in me and I associated myself with that character more and more.

Now this character presented a different problem. The original character was in total control of the situation. Guided simply by his overriding ambition. The new character, however, was now obsessed. He was a man obsessed with vengeance for the death of his wife, for which he blamed Kirk. If he was bigger than life before, I felt he really had to become bigger than life almost to the point of becoming ludicrous to be effective. If I didn't play it fully and totally obsessed with this, then I think the character would be little and insignificant and uninteresting. The danger was in going overboard. I had to be, if not deranged, then very close to it. I had to find a tone of really going right to the razor's edge before the character becomes a caricature.

NICHOLAS MEYER

I remember saying apropos of Khan, "You know, the thing about a crazy person is that a crazy person doesn't have to raise their voice because you just never know what they're going to do . . . *next!*" And I sort of lashed out with my arm around his neck and then he understood, he got it. And then it was just a question of endless fine-tuning. He would look at me before every take or after every take and go, "Too much, too little?" It was like driving a Maserati, you just didn't have to do much to get the response.

WALTER KOENIG

Working with him was a pure delight. He was always there for your close-up. I remember Nick saying something to him about his performance needing fine-tuning, and I thought, "Oh shit, here it comes." Instead he says, "Ah, you're right." It was beautiful. That's the way every theatrical experience should be and with us, unfortunately, it wasn't.

Wrath of Khan was a delight from start to finish and one of the greatest delights was working with Ricardo Montalban and Paul Winfield [who played Terrell, captain of the starship *Reliant*], and not being on the *Enterprise* having to be judged by our leading man, not having scenes reblocked by our leading man, which I found very oppressive. I'm working with actors who give as well as take. Totally professional.

ROBERT SALLIN

Leonard and Bill have been doing this forever and they know these characters. It's not that they weren't delivering performances, because they were. But then Ricardo comes on to the set. We had him for ten days, and the first shot was a master shot that ran almost ten minutes; a full reel of film. Man, he was phenomenal. Just a delight. So after that day, suddenly everybody sharpened up a lot, because he was so good. He had raised the bar.

RALPH WINTER

In *The Wrath of Khan* there was never an on-camera scene in the same room with Ricardo Montalban and Bill Shatner. It was all on viewscreens. It was all ship-to-ship and there was never any face-to-face encounter. You can't do that today.

NICHOLAS MEYER

They should have met. Mary, Queen of Scots, and Elizabeth the First never met and playwrights have been putting them together ever since.

JACK B. SOWARDS

Kirk and Khan may not have met in the film, but they did in my script. You bet your ass. In my script, Khan was more of a mystic than Attila the Hun. I invested Khan with certain powers. He could make you see things which didn't actually exist. It was a battle of wills, which Kirk ultimately wins when Khan realizes he cannot control his mind. Nobody wins the fight and it ends up as a fight in space with the ships. It was a twelve-page fight that they simply took out and threw away. The fight would have required a lot of special effects, because it was really a mind attack by Khan on Kirk and Kirk's being able to resist it. He would take it to different places. They would be on a shore somewhere, fighting with whips. They would be in a stone room of a castle. When you got into the whole thing, it was a very expensive process, so I can understand their dropping it. But not the face-to-face confrontation. I could never understand that.

RICARDO MONTALBAN

I don't think this was a drawback. Actually, that was an element that was interesting. It was difficult as an actor, but that separation of the two ships gave it a really poignant touch to the scenes. The fact that being so strong, there was such pressure knowing that he *can't* get his hands on Kirk. I didn't mind that. I minded as an actor. I wish William Shatner and I had somehow been able to respond to each other at the time. The actual situation, though, I thought was a plus. We left the audience wanting them to get together and we don't.

Beyond Ricardo Montalban, perhaps the greatest standout was the first starring role for now veteran actress Kirstie Alley, who portrayed the half-Vulcan, half-Romulan Lt. Saavik in *The Wrath of Khan*. "I liked the *Star Trek* TV series," Alley related at the time. "In fact, I've been rehearsing Spock for some years now. I would pretend that I was his daughter. Every week, every episode, I'd sit there thinking, 'I should play Spock's daughter.' I mean, I could arch my eyebrows as good as Leonard Nimoy. Whenever I'd watch the show, I'd write dialogue for myself so I could actually take part in the story. When Leonard said a line, I'd respond. So when I was told about the part, I was very excited. I went in there and acted like Spock. Then Nick Meyer said, 'Boy, you have him down. Did you know that?'"

ROBERT SALLIN

I thought Kirstie Alley was a really nice young lady, but I became concerned as I saw her working on the set with Shatner and Nimoy. I went to the honchos and said, "You have a brand-new actress here. Shatner and Nimoy are going to chew her up and spit her out." Back in the days of the television series, Shatner used to take other people's dialogue and make it his. Leonard and Shatner are really top-level actors, really good actors, and she was just beginning.

I didn't want her to get buried, so I suggested that we get her an acting coach to work on the rough spots or just someone she could talk to, because Nick was not that kind of guy. He couldn't provide that kind of support for an actor. So I pushed it. I took her to lunch and as gently as I could made the suggestion. She said, "Oh, sure, that would be helpful." She was really nice about it. We hired a really good guy who was with her for two or three weeks and it helped her settle in and deal with the process.

EDDIE EGAN

On the film there were the usual tensions with the newcomers, like Kirstie Alley. By the nature of being new, there's attention that's focused on the character or their story line and that means there's attention taken away from one of the original cast member's story line. I remember them all being very cordial. Not Bill so much, because Bill is Bill. But Kirstie persevered. She had a rough go the first few weeks. People were not pleased with her performance. There was talk that they were going to have her voice replaced for the entire movie. They actually didn't do that, but they did have her rerecord most of her role in looping just to get some infliections that weren't present in the production audio.

DEBORAH ARAKELIAN

My greatest regret is that I couldn't find a way to steal Khan's necklace. I thought that was the best piece that had ever been created. I don't know where it ended up, but if you ever find it I want it. The uniforms were particularly nice. [Wardrobe supervisor] Agnes Henry had done such a tremendous job on the uniforms, and as such the pins were disappearing left, right, and center, which was driving up their budget.

They started stitching them onto the outfits so it was more difficult to steal and that didn't work. I started getting phone calls from the administration building asking us to liberate pins for certain people. So I would call the stage and they would steal a pin here and there and it would go to the administration building. Finally, I started bitching to Leonard. I said, "You know what, I've stolen a pin for every goddamn person in this place. I got nothing." So Leonard stole a pin for me and now I have a pin that was officially stolen by Nimoy.

NICHOLAS MEYER

The studio didn't interfere at all because there just wasn't time. I had, on the one hand, Harve Bennett. I also had Austen Jewell, who was the production manager. The things that happened I didn't know about until later. Robert Sallin tried to have me fired. He didn't like the way the movie looked. My job was ultimately saved by Michael Eisner.

ROBERT SALLIN

I'm not proud of myself for this, but it really was a result of never having produced a major picture on a major lot before. We were three days into shooting and we were a week behind. I didn't know what to do. I called Harve, who was in London doing *A Woman Called Golda*. He had nothing to do with the running of *Khan* at all, except the script. I finally had a meeting with Michael Eisner and told him I thought we were going to have to replace the director and he said, "We can't fire him, because no one will want to work at Paramount." I was a director and there was no way I would be a week behind in two or three days. Especially on a film like this one that had so many conditions placed on it because of what happened with the first movie. I just felt that pressure all the time. Needless to say, this didn't rocket me to the top of Nick's best buddy list. But I had always tried to just help him; I wanted to get that picture to be the best picture that could be made, and certainly a terrific *Star Trek* experience. That was my focus. The rest of the stuff was how you got there.

RALPH WINTER

I remember the ending of the movie when we previewed it; the first ending where Spock dies was a downer. It was depressing, and I remember being in Gary Nardino's office with all the executives. It was Eisner, Katzenberg, Diller, a bunch of people there, and really, that's where the idea came from for the final shot that was added on the Genesis Planet, actually Golden Gate Park, of discovering the casket and raising the possibility that Spock could return. That ending is what shaped the movie, and when we shot that and previewed it, it made all the difference. It gave you a hopeful ending and it led to another movie.

EDDIE EGAN

That door was not open in the original script. He was gone. But as [Nimoy] worked on the picture and began to enjoy himself and feel like they were getting back in the groove, he used that to his advantage. He said, "If I go this way and we agree that there's a possibility that Spock will come back, I'm going to ask for something." Obviously that was directing the third movie.

> The events of *The Wrath of Khan* culminate with Spock's attempt to save the *Enterprise* from destruction, and in the process he is exposed to a lethal dose of radiation. Spock's selfless decision results in the character's poignant passing. There is, however, an enigmatic moment offered an instant earlier where he uses a Vulcan nerve pinch to render McCoy unconscious, places his hand on the doctor's face, and utters the ambiguous word "Remember."

LEONARD NIMOY

I found myself being moved by the scene very early, at about the point where Kirk says to Scott something about you have to get us out of here in three minutes or we're all dead. You see Spock hear that and react. I'm already feeling emotional about what's coming. I really came within a hairbreadth of walking off the lot rather than playing the scene. The day we were going to shoot it, I was very edgy about it and scared of it. Scared of playing it, almost looking for an excuse not to, finding something to pick an argument about. It was a very tense time. And I *still* feel that way seeing it. It's a moving scene and I'm pleased with it in the context of the film. I'm glad we did it. I think we did it well. I think we did it honestly and sincerely.

NICHOLAS MEYER

The question in my mind was not whether Spock died, but whether he died *well*. His death needed some organic relationship to the rest of the movie, and a plausible connection to whatever else was going on. If we did that, I don't think anyone would question it. On the other hand, if the movie suddenly turned around a corner on two wheels and "we fulfill Nimoy's contract by bumping off his character which he has grown tired of playing," if indeed that was the scenario, which I have never heard, that wouldn't be so good. That rumor that we were going to have more than one ending, that we were going to let the audience decide . . . that was all bullshit. Art is not made by committee . . . and it's not made by voting.

SUSAN SACKETT

I don't know if that ending with a suggestion of hope is a cop-out, but it's something that Gene fought for badly. He did not want to see his character killed off without having any hope. Having his molecules blasted all over the universe would have made it very difficult for him to ever return as that character. Gene created that character and he did not create the demise of that character, and he wanted it so that there would be some way to recall that character when needed, and that was the reason for the open-endedness.

NICHOLAS MEYER

The scenes which were the most difficult, or at least the most wrenching to do, were the death of Spock [sequences]. Everybody stood around the stage in tears, which was very surprising to me because I was not that experienced as a movie director and I was amazed at how moved they were. The next day at the dailies, same thing. Everybody cried. I come from the "less is more" school of thinking. You can have somebody point to something and say "Look at that!" and you don't have to cut to what he is pointing to. In fact, you can raise considerable tension by *not* showing the audience what the character sees.

For example, once Spock enters the reactor room I deliberately didn't cut back to him for a long time. After hearing "You can't go in there, you can't go . . ." you gotta be wondering, "What's happening to him?" You want to see what's going on there. It's a matter of choice, of taste. I would rather underplay and let the audience's imagination rise to meet something halfway. From what I've seen of the series, I tend to think they overacted or showed too much. My attitude has changed perceptibly. I don't know whether it was the actors themselves or the characters, but I finally thought, when I was watching the death scene and I realized that *I* was choking up, I thought, well, we have now transcended the subject matter. This is no longer simply about a man with pointy ears . . . which is how I felt because I didn't know it that well.

HARVE BENNETT

We went to the mat only when I said that as keeper of the franchise, I have to give people an ambiguous hope. Nick said, "No, the opera is over, the fat lady has sung, and Carmen is dead." I think he was wrong. There wouldn't have been a *Star Trek III* or *IV,* which were pretty good pictures. Spock was a secret weapon. He is the pivot, the true uniqueness of the show.

WILLIAM SHATNER

I don't know whether the *Star Trek* series could have gone on without Spock. It certainly would have been different and probably not as good. The Spock–Kirk interrelationship is really the key to so much for the way the stories are told.

HARVE BENNETT

I'm the guy who brought the Bionic Woman back to life after she was dead, dead, dead, so I'm an old hand at how you can change course if everybody wants you to. In fact, it would be fair to say that no matter how big the stories of *Star Trek,* the fact remains it is still a series. It is a continuing adventure with the same characters and has the matrix and nature of a television series, which is that the characters have to keep coming back and you have to keep making them fresh by exploring new avenues of their lives. That's the tough part of making series-oriented material.

ROBERT SALLIN

One of the major conflicts Nick and I had in the making of the picture was the whole idea of planting the seed that Spock might come back. It was not in the original script, that idea of going back to the planet. Nick hated the idea, but the studio wanted it because they were getting so much flak about killing Spock.

NICHOLAS MEYER

I fought very hard to make him dead, and the shots that imply a resurrection—
the vision of the casket on the Genesis Planet—were done over my dead body,
with my enormous objection. I objected so strenuously, and went to such lengths,
that a producer on the film referred to me as morally bankrupt. He said, "You'd
walk over your mother to get this the way you wanted," and I said, "You know, I
think you're right. I don't believe you can bring a dead person back to life." Having seen *Star Trek III,* I still don't believe it. But okay, he's back, Leonard is back
and since it's Leonard, I'm happy.

HARVE BENNETT

The last weeks of *Star Trek II* were frenetic because of an organized campaign:
Don't Kill Spock! And the studio panicked that this would affect the box office.
Nick Meyer was steadfastly going to walk off the picture. He said that we said we
would kill him, so we're going to kill him. Leonard was getting threatening
letters. This was a serious thing, and I felt that the compromise we had to make
was that we made an ambiguity out of the ending by saying, "There are always
possibilities."

RONALD D. MOORE

It totally choked me up. I was there with my high-school sweetheart and we got
out and I was very quiet, and I was crying and she was, too, and we couldn't believe it had happened. We couldn't believe they'd done it, and it was beautifully
done, and I kind of knew they were probably going to bring him back but at that
point I didn't want them to. When they announced the title of the third one, I
was kind of disappointed. I love the character, but I just felt like it was taking
something away from this experience that I'd just had, that had touched me and
moved me really deeply, because I loved the characters and I loved him and I
loved Kirk. I felt the pain of that loss and what that meant, it really affected me,
and then in the very next movie they were going to wipe it away. I felt like it was
taking something from me rather than giving something back. It was a cheat,
and one of the things I thought when I saw *Wrath of Khan* originally was how
bold it was *not* to cheat, how bold it was to actually kill one of these characters
and to make it stick and not have them wave a magic wand like they did on the
TV series and have Bones or someone come back at the end. So I was really kind

of bummed that they weren't going to stick with it and keep going and deal with the consequences in the *Star Trek* universe.

WILLIAM SHATNER

Bringing back somebody from the dead loses validity. I think that as a dramatic device a time warp does the same thing for me. To go back in time is to rob you of the essential jeopardy. It should be life and death and if it's death, it should be death.

NICHOLAS MEYER

The only other run-ins I had with the studio were over the title. The title of the movie was *The Undiscovered Country*. And they wanted to change it to *The Vengeance of Khan*. I knew that wasn't going to work because George Lucas was doing a movie at the time called *Revenge of the Jedi*. And we wound up where we wound up.

GENE RODDENBERRY

It was an exciting picture. I had many problems with it, though. They were very lucky they had the actor they did in Ricardo Montalban to play Khan since it was not a well-written part. "I will chase you through the moons of Jupiter" and so on. In the hands of almost any other actor, it would have gotten snickers from the audience. Montalban saved their ass. Khan was not written as that exciting a character, he was rather flimsy. The Khan in the TV episode was a much deeper and better character than the movie Khan, except that Montalban pulled it off.

HARVE BENNETT

Gene is a remarkable visionary and a very bad supervisor of other writers. He alienated some really creative people who were doing their very best to make his show a hit. That's the summation of what my perspective is. I had very little to do with him in the movies, because I was fortunate enough to have a mandate from Paramount to not pay any attention to him, which is easier said than done because he is a master manipulator of a loyal and large following. It's like the Bolshevik party. It isn't that there were so many of them, it's that they were so smart and so vociferous.

In a September 29, 1981, memo to Bennett, Roddenberry expressed a bit of frustration over the situation between them: "You have never requested nor even made it possible for me to act in any way as 'Executive Consultant' on this movie. Or even as 'Infrequent Advisor.' You did not ask my comments on the story . . . neither did you ask for my comments on the writer selected; we never discussed director other than your calling me the day before his name was announced. Although I may have sometimes wondered if you could not have profited from at least some of my experience, I am neither embarrassed [nor] annoyed over the way you clearly preferred for it to be. You are the man running the *Star Trek II* movie and I accept your right to run it your way."

While he felt that certain criticisms of the script were "fairly unimportant," there was a concern that certain philosophical tenets of *Star Trek* be maintained, particularly where it came to celebrating the differences between species rather than seeing them as a detriment. "If *Star Trek* slides into becoming just a routine 'space battle show' (an SF form which the critics now consider 'tiresome'), then I have no doubt but that *Star Trek* will slide downhill rapidly. In this case, I am doubly concerned because I have an interest in this property remaining valuable. However, there are some areas of script comment which I consider the most important of all—examples of these are things like *Star Trek*'s avoiding the use of violence in story solutions, maintaining the importance of the Prime Directive, continuing our reminders that to be different does not mean that something is ugly or to think differently does not mean that someone is necessarily wrong. It seems to me that there is something very decent and very necessary in saying such things to people, especially today."

DEBORAH ARAKELIAN

The studio would only do it on their terms. Gene was between a rock and a hard spot. Either he does it according to their liking, which is to take the check, and smile, and be a friendly consultant, or it doesn't get done. So I think Gene made the right decision. It was not easy for him. Couldn't have been tougher. He handled it well. As well as he possibly could. Harve kept Gene in the loop as much as possible. Gene's office was just a stone's throw away from ours. We didn't see a lot of him once the movie was shooting.

HARVE BENNETT

One thing about Roddenberry: as he aged, he somehow became disassociated with the very thing he wanted the show to be. For example, his concept was nautical, the officers are addressed as "mister," a naval tradition. There's a captain, tactical officer, gunnery officer, all that stuff. Engineering is below, and he, in his words, described *Star Trek* as Horatio Hornblower in space. Okay. Makes enormous sense. And Kirk is Hornblower. Now we start, and from the first outline in addition to the leakage, he whined and complained that we were making a militaristic show. It was frustrating. The studio promised, "We'll handle him, don't worry about Gene, we'll handle him." Ha! I would call occasionally and I would say, "Hey, you guys said . . ." and they'd say, "You're doing fine. See you later!" So it *did* fall on me to respond to his long, haranguing memos. Once in a while he'd pop in an idea, in a long haranguing memo, and we'd use it. And we'd thank him for it. But essentially he was our opponent in so many ways.

RALPH WINTER

It was clear from people like Leonard and Bill Shatner, when they dedicated the Gene Roddenberry building, that they were going to talk about people like Harve Bennett and Gene Coon, who have made this thing successful. There were so many times when there were problems and someone didn't know how we would get by, and it would fall on Harve to solve it. Harve is absolutely the unheralded guy to save the series of films.

NICHOLAS MEYER

The history of human endeavor has frequently [been] comprised of certain institutions which are based on two archetypes. There's a guy who comes along and, with a certain kind of messianic fortitude and charisma, conjures up a universe out of nothing, hot air, if you'll pardon the expression. He makes it happen. Usually, he never stays around to run it.

The task is always turned over to a can-do type who is distinctly lacking in messianic qualities, but is a very good organizer. Jesus Christ presumably founded the Christian faith. But it seems like it was either Peter or Paul who got the thing rolling as a business. *Star Trek* would not have existed without Roddenberry. There's no question about that. I have no wish in any shape or form to detract from the magnitude of his accomplishments, but I also think that nothing can stay the same forever. For things to grow, there have to be these Joshua types, of which I suppose I am one, who pick up the burden and carry it. Maybe we carry it clumsily . . . or in the wrong direction . . . but we fucking carry it.

RALPH WINTER

Gene kept sabotaging us. It was too bad. I remember a fight on the second movie; Nick wanted David Marcus to wear a sweater over his shoulder, wrapped in the fashion of the time. Backward over his neck. Roddenberry hated that. Nick also had a "No Smoking" sign on the bridge of the *Enterprise*. And he and Roddenberry went round and round about no smoking because, Roddenberry said, "No one is going to smoke in the twenty-third century." And Nick said, "People have been smoking for hundreds of years and they will for hundreds of years." And they were at it on the set. They were arguing and yelling, it was bizarre. But that was part of Gene's view of the future and utopia and what he believed.

GENE RODDENBERRY

I also objected to other little things. Remember when the eel came out of Chekov's ear? What did Kirk do? He had a look of disgust on his face and grabbed his phaser and went "zap." Now, how dare he destroy a life-form that had never been seen before! It needs studying. They had him act like an old woman trampling on a tarantula. Now that's not the Kirk we built up for three years. So many of those fine little things in the episodes, hundreds of them, are what gave *Star Trek* its quality. Unfortunately, they began doing those things incorrectly in that movie. There was also a great deal of violence. But yet, it was exciting—exciting photographically. I'm grateful that it did what it did.

DEBORAH ARAKELIAN

Gene did have the most interesting group of friends that showed up at the set. Buzz Aldrin was a trip. Unfortunately he showed up on a day when they were throwing fireballs on *Star Trek II* and the fire marshal had the set closed down. He didn't understand why he couldn't go to set. I said, "Fire marshals have it closed. Come back tomorrow." And he literally said, *"Don't you know who I am?"* So, I started laughing and said, "You'll burn up like the next one." But Gene was always in contact with people at JPL. He really had a sense of staying in touch with scientists and keeping apprised of that stuff and so we would have people like Aldrin show up that were guests of Gene's.

For *Star Trek II,* the film's diminished budget made it impossible to rehire composer Jerry Goldsmith (an Academy Award nominee for *Star Trek: The Motion Picture*). Instead, Meyer and Sallin took a chance on a relative newcomer, James Horner, whose films at the time largely consisted of low-budget sci-fi for horror-meister Roger Corman, including *Humanoids from the Deep* and *Battle Beyond the Stars.*

ROBERT SALLIN

I went to Joel Sill, who was the music person at the studio. I said, "Joel, I'd like to listen to some tapes. What I don't want is musical wallpaper. I want someone who's young, who is eager for this, and somebody who is technically accomplished. I don't want that stuff I hear on television." He gave me twenty-five or thirty tapes that I took home and listened to every single one. There were some big names there, too, by the way. I heard this one and I came back and said, "This is my guy." He smiled and said, "I'm so glad. I've been trying to get him in here for years." His name was James Horner.

JAMES HORNER (composer, *Star Trek II: The Wrath of Khan*)

I felt it was very important musically to bring the audience back to ground zero, as it were. There are certain givens: the *Enterprise* is a given, Kirk is a given, Spock is a given, Uhura is a given, and the fanfare theme, that theme is a given. I felt I was fighting an instinct not to use it, and I thought it would be very interesting to use it. I talked it over with Harve [Bennett] and we all agreed it would be good to use it. I remember when audiences first heard the music and heard the whole buildup in the main titles, and they went crazy. They were cheering. I chose to use it in a very haunting way when Spock dies. I just wanted "Spock's Theme" and the *Star Trek* theme and all my themes to be playing simultaneously there. That was a very emotional section.

ALEXANDER COURAGE (composer, *Star Trek*)

James Horner has used it here and there, pieces of the fanfare and all that, because he was told to. It's that simple. I know a lot of people around town and I go into the store and they know I have written it and they say, "Are they going to use your theme in the picture?" I say, "Well, I guess so," and they say, "They'd better!" So that's generally the way it seems to have worked.

JAMES HORNER

When I was asked to do *Star Trek II,* I made a promise to Harve Bennett. He asked me to do number three, if and when it was made. I made that promise to him and it was a promise I kept. I have mixed feelings about doing large orchestral scores. It's great for the ego, but artistically, it's not that fulfilling. As soon as you try and bend the producer and try to get him to take some chances, they get very nervous because it's so expensive. The recording session for *Star Trek* was upward of four hundred thousand dollars when you had a ninety-piece orchestra for six days.

JOE KRAEMER (composer, *Mission: Impossible–Rogue Nation*)

I'd also heard Elmer Bernstein was first hired to score *Trek II,* but left after he saw a rough cut, and it was at this point Horner was brought on board. Horner certainly capitalized on the opportunity—I think his score for *II* is the high point of his career.

LUKAS KENDALL (editor, *Film Score Monthly*)

Want some real trivia? Two major film composers have made cameos in *Star Trek.* James Horner is a crewman holding a vacuum cleaner in *Star Trek II.* And in the original series, Basil Poledouris is a security guard ("Obsession"), Klingon ("Errand of Mercy"), and Nazi soldier ("Patterns of Force"). Basil was a film student at USC and he and his friends used to be Hollywood extras.

NICHOLAS MEYER

When it came time to do the DVD version of the movie or the television version or whatever it is, the studio loses all interest in it and you get to do what you want. I had a movie that worked really well by this time, and the public and critical reception of the movie had already established that, so the question was, do I really want to do a so-called director's cut, and the answer was no.

But I did have a couple of issues where they had made a mistake. It was battles that I had lost at the time. And one of them was the whole notion that Scotty's nephew was killed in the engine room explosion and that's why he's so flipped out. And I just put it back in. But there weren't a lot of those. There weren't enough of them to say this is the director's cut. I just thought that's a gyp, trying to get people to spend more money to buy it again.

GENE RODDENBERRY

Scotty stands there . . . he holds the body of Midshipman Preston. Why has he come to the bridge instead of taking the injured man to sick bay? Starship personnel, even distraught uncles, should react at least as logically as twentieth-century sailors.

While production on the film went relatively smoothly, the relationship between old college friends Robert Sallin and Harve Bennett was becoming more acrimonious, much of it stemming from the fact that Sallin was being credited as producer while Bennett had the title executive producer. On television, executive producers were considered a show's guiding force, but on film, it's a far less prestigious title usually reserved for financiers, line producers, and executives and not the actual filmmakers.

ROBERT SALLIN

Harve was incensed that I was credited as producer, and I said, "That's because I'm producing. That's what you hired me for and that's the job I'm doing." His idea was that everybody worked for him and he was the guiding genius behind this film, and he just wasn't.

After production wrapped, I was called up to a meeting with Gary Nardino and he said, "We'd like you to stay on and produce more *Star Trek* pictures." I said, "What about Harve?" and they said, "We want him doing television." Precise words. I wanted to think about it, but I came back and said, "I can't. No matter how much of a disagreement I have with Harve, I cannot do that to someone who gave me this opportunity." So I walked away. In retrospect, I think it was a mistake. When you're on a major lot in Hollywood, it's quite a power base. Again, I didn't understand how the game was played. I thought it was all about making films. It's about making deals.

The film opened on June 4, 1982, and was an immediate smash. In response, the studio's president of distribution, Frank Mancuso, sent a Western Union telegram to the principals to congratulate them on their success: "This weekend *ST: TWK* set motion picture history. *ST 2* grossed $14,347,221 in 1,621 theatres, making it the biggest 3 day opening in motion picture history. I wanted to share this information with you and thank you for all your cooperation which allowed us to make history together."

MANNY COTO (executive producer, *Star Trek: Enterprise*)

I totally loved *Khan,* but I was skeptical at first. When I heard it was going to be Ricardo Montalban returning as Khan, I was like, "Really? From *Fantasy Island*?" It was kind of a joke. But of course, that immediately faded away the minute he appeared on-screen. It was one of the greatest introductions of all time.

DEBORAH ARAKELIAN

You piss off any given fan of any given show, they will scream, rant, and rave, but they *won't* boycott it. They'll go see it because they can't believe you're actually doing it. When I was sitting in the first showing in Westwood and Leonard's chair goes empty, oh my God. There was a woman in the back who went, "Oh my God, they're doing it! They're doing it." They are screaming at the screen. It was beautiful. It was fabulous. It was great.

WALTER KOENIG

If you can point to one single element that makes this film successful, it is the presence of a formidable, worthy antagonist. You can't have conflict unless you have something to butt up against. V'ger was more like something you were in awe of. Ricardo Montalban, on the other hand, did a wonderful job with the character of Khan. Not only is he a presence in terms of villainy, but he's also a character of depth. Even when you hate him, you feel a certain sympathy toward him. That, to me, is extraordinary. Nick Meyer was quoted as saying that he wanted to direct Montalban in *King Lear* and I can believe it.

LEONARD NIMOY

In doing [*Star Trek: The Motion Picture*], somebody, somewhere decided that if we're going to do a motion picture, it must be different than what we did on TV, so we must now start to work out the differences. We'll change the color of the bridge, the wardrobe, the attitudes of the characters. It seemed to me that somebody was watching *2001* a lot, and getting into a cerebral, futuristic trip rather than an adventure romp, which is what *Star Trek* is built on. Maybe it's because they felt that people would not pay to see in the theater what they had seen on TV, that they would want something different. My opinion is that if we can do the best *Star Trek* episode ever done, well produced and well acted, and put it on the big screen, it will work. What happened on *Star Trek II* is that our perspective of what *Star Trek* is really supposed to be has been verified. The audience has said, "Yes, that's right."

GEORGE TAKEI

In *The Wrath of Khan* we have genuine drama because of the confrontation of two strong, cunning, inventive adversaries who are driven to an inevitable collision. You know that they are not going to avoid each other, that there is going to be some dramatic confrontation. Ricardo Montalban is an awesomely well-suited adversary for Kirk.

DeFOREST KELLEY

In my mind, there's no comparison [between the first two films]. It's not easy to convince the studio that, as successful as *Star Trek* was, the fans nevertheless had a deep feeling about the characters, and that you can't ignore it. In my opinion, that was the mistake that was made with the first film, ignoring the relationships that were so popular in the TV series.

JAMES DOOHAN

To me, this movie is *Star Trek* the way it should be. The first one was just some grandiose idea that somebody had. There is gorgeous action going on at all times. The characters all have some great things to say. It's a beautiful blend of all of the good things that were in all of the good shows that we had in the series.

EDDIE EGAN

It was a very interesting experience working on that film in terms of just knowing these people personally that I had seen on the screen for so many years. *And* seeing Paramount itself just being so buoyant about it. Moviemaking is hard work and a lot of it is boring, but there was a lot of camaraderie on the set and everyone just seemed to have a sense that what they were doing could result in something really meaningful in terms of the legacy of *Star Trek* and, more optimistically, for the future of *Star Trek*.

ROBERT SALLIN

For all of the problems we had with Nick, he was a first-rate writer. It was his pulling together the dangling components. He shaped it, he did the whole thing in like ten or twelve days. He just took it and did it and I praise him for it. If we hadn't stumbled onto him, I don't know what we would have done.

NICHOLAS MEYER

A lot of people said *Star Trek II* was such a terrific movie and had a lot of unkind things to say about *Star Trek I,* but I don't think they realize that *Star Trek II* wouldn't have been so good if someone hadn't gone boldly where no one had gone before and showed us, in effect, what not to do when it was really important. It's damn hard work to make those movies and I'm not going to look down my nose at any of them.

IN SEARCH OF

"THE WORD IS NO. . . . I AM THEREFORE GOING ANYWAY."

Whereas, given its cost, a sequel to *Star Trek: The Motion Picture* was questionable for some time after its release, there was no such hesitation in the aftermath of *The Wrath of Khan*. A critical and commercial success that was far more profitable than its predecessor due to its significantly lower budget, Paramount gave Harve Bennett the green light for a third film the day after it opened.

But somewhere around that time—and in recognition of the success and power of the Khan character—an unrealized prequel, and heretofore unknown spin-off, was briefly put into development.

EDDIE EGAN (unit publicist, *Star Trek III: The Search for Spock*)

A spin-off was being pursued and a script was written. It was called *Star Trek: Prison Planet*, and it was to deal with what happened after the *Botany Bay* crashed on Ceti Alpha V, and before the *Reliant* got there in *The Wrath of Khan*. It was completely designed as a vehicle for Ricardo Montalban, and it was supervised by Harve. But then the decision was made to focus exclusively on *Star Trek III* instead.

By September 16, 1982, Bennett turned in his initial story line for the film, titled *Return to Genesis*. Although differing quite markedly from the film that would ultimately result from it (Romulans as villains instead of Klingons, Saavik confessing her love for Kirk, Sulu masterminding the stealing of the *Enterprise* to save Spock while Kirk was under house arrest, Spock being discovered as a primitive Neanderthal on the Genesis Planet), there were elements that would remain until the end (Kirk scuttling his starship to take out the enemy, the stealing of the *Enterprise* to mount a rescue mission of Spock on Genesis, with now Kirk instead of Sulu leading the effort). The rapidly aging Spock mirroring the unstable planet (an idea originally suggested by Gene Roddenberry's secretary, Susan Sackett), the return of Spock's *katra* from McCoy's mind to his body via a Vulcan ceremony, Saavik and David on the Genesis Planet, and the Klingon Kruge are all elements which would be introduced later.

EDDIE EGAN

There was a version of the story that had a very prominent role for Spock's brother, who somehow ended up on the *Enterprise* and is part of the voyage back to Vulcan to bring Spock's body back. That was eventually dropped, but I don't know whether that actually led later to the character of Sybok in *Star Trek V,* but he was certainly a big part of the script in the earliest versions.

HARVE BENNETT
(producer-writer, *Star Trek III: The Search for Spock*)

I had to make a story out of the following "givens." One, there is a casket on a planet that has been created by the reformation of life forces, and life has been created from death. Two, "There are always possibilities." Three, before he died, Spock said, "Remember." Remember what? The puzzle was solved so easily that I think seventeen other people could have written the script to *Star Trek III.*

If you end a film with a Genesis Device that can, in one *poof* create life where there was lifelessness, you have created an enormous story device that cannot be ignored. Now, the fans would be justified in saying, "Well, why not just create a planet as a plot solution?" Or, "What would happen if the Klingons got hold of this? They wouldn't use it to make a planet, they would destroy a planet."

Therefore, the final puzzle solving was the denial of the validity of the Genesis Device. That was—as "the Lord giveth, the Lord taketh away"—necessary or we would have expanded the borders of *Star Trek,* even subliminally, that it would have had the same impact the A-bomb had on the twentieth century, so as to make conventional things no longer viable. That's fine, but who needs to restructure *Star Trek* on that basis?

WILLIAM SHATNER (actor, "James T. Kirk")

An accident happened on *Star Trek II.* Maybe it wasn't an accident if you don't believe in accidents. But it was really very strange. We were getting ready to do the death scene of Spock. This wasn't scripted, but Leonard put his hand on De-Forest's head and he was looking for something mysterious to do. For some reason, in this last scene, Leonard said, "Remember." It was very mysterious. It was meaningful to somebody in *Star Trek,* but we didn't know what it meant. And that was the end. Spock was dead and the question was, Will there be a *Star*

Trek III and how could you do it without Spock? But that was a whole other question. As far as everyone was concerned at that time, Spock was dead.

HARVE BENNETT

It would have been very easy to say at the conclusion of *Star Trek II* that all the things we had done to modify that film's ending to be ambiguous about the death of Spock were carefully designed and that the plot for *Star Trek III* was already in my mind. Not true. All of that, like most decisions I have ever made, are done in a flurry of intuition and sometimes pressure of time.

LEONARD NIMOY
(actor/director, *Star Trek III: The Search for Spock*)

It was obvious that there was some kind of ticking clock going on in McCoy's mind that might be explored later. What is McCoy carrying around in his head that he may not even know about consciously yet that may spring to life later and be a factor in the new movie? Could you imagine what would happen if Kirk had any reason whatsoever, if he were given reason to believe or hope there might be a way to get Spock back? To save him or help him? He would be obsessed, wouldn't he?

HARVE BENNETT

Somewhere along the line I read a fan poem in one of the hundreds of fan magazines about *Star Trek*. It was first-person Kirk. It said, "I left you there. Why did I do that? I must come back to you, my friend." I thought, "That's it!" I suddenly had a thrust. It got a lot easier from that point.

Behind the scenes, there were a number of changes between films. Producer Robert Sallin, following his falling-out with Bennett, departed. Ralph Winter, a producer working for the studio in postproduction who had been enormously helpful on the previous film, joined the team as associate producer, and Harve Bennett chose to serve as both sole writer and producer of the film.

RALPH WINTER
(associate producer, *Star Trek III: The Search For Spock*)

I was working on the second movie as an executive. I worked for Paramount in postproduction. Because I had familiarity with computer graphics and computer science from my years at Caltech, I was attracted to it and no one else cared about it. What happened was I helped Harve Bennett with some other projects, cutting trailers for him, doing some work on the side. Sallin was the producer, Harve was the executive producer on *Star Trek II*, and we created a relationship, and he said, "Why don't you leave Paramount and come work for me because I've got *Star Trek*, I've got *The Powers of Matthew Star* and *A Woman Called Golda*." So I went and joined Harve's staff and I was the associate producer on *Star Trek III*.

DEBORAH ARAKELIAN (assistant to Harve Bennett and Bob Sallin)

I really didn't enjoy working with Ralph Winter the way I enjoyed working with Bob Sallin. I was much less invested. Sallin and Harve had a huge falling-out which was kind of painful to watch. When the movie started, there was only four of us in the office. It was like a suite of offices, and Bob and Harve were constantly going back and forth. It was great in the beginning, but somewhere toward the end those doors closed and did not reopen. It was extremely uncomfortable. It certainly wasn't because Bob wasn't doing a great job—he did a *spectacular* job. It is hard for me to imagine a friendship of that many years coming to an end like that.

SUSAN SACKETT (assistant to Gene Roddenberry)

Harve did a lot of things that annoyed Gene, so I wasn't crazy about that because I didn't want to see him hurting Gene, but I thought he was very good at what he did. He knew how to get things done, but I never trusted him too much. He finally gave me credit for the Genesis revival of Spock, where he begins to regenerate after he's dead on the Genesis Planet and comes back to life as an infant, which was my idea.

The primary inducement for convincing Leonard Nimoy to reprise his role as Spock in *The Wrath of Khan* was the death of his character in the film. The question for the next entry was whether the actor would be willing to reprise the character yet again. His answer, naturally enough, would become the catalyst for the third film—driven home by the fact that director Nicholas Meyer would *not* be returning to the franchise at that juncture.

NICHOLAS MEYER (director, *Star Trek II: The Wrath of Khan*)

I didn't know how to do resurrections. I thought Spock should be dead. And I thought it'd be unfair to the fans—like we were fucking with them.

DEBORAH ARAKELIAN

The notion of the third one became very real when Leonard came into the office one day and said, "I had such a good time on this, let's do another one." And it's like, "But you're dead . . ."

LEONARD NIMOY

When Spock died in the end of *Star Trek II* and the studio started talking about a resurrection—for lack of a better word—they called me and asked if there was anything I would like to do at the studio, adding, "We would like you to be involved in the making of *Star Trek III*." Meaning that they wanted me to act in the picture. I said I wanted to direct. The reaction was very good. They put me through the coals later to test my commitment and sincerity. I felt that it was time I stopped fooling around with directing and really got serious about it.

DAVID GERROLD (writer, "The Trouble with Tribbles")

Leonard had wanted off *Trek*. He did not want to do *Star Trek II*, did not want to do the first film. It wasn't just a negotiating ploy. He truly wanted to put Spock behind him. He finally got smart and said, "I can't put Spock behind me, so I will use Spock to elevate my career elsewhere." Leonard Nimoy is no dummy.

LEONARD NIMOY

I had been directing for a very long time, I started directing theater in the fifties and films in the seventies. I didn't pursue it simply because I was having too good a time as an actor. I had wanted to direct *Star Trek* from the time we started doing the series. Bill Shatner and I both did. We were not allowed to. It's just as simple as that. We were refused the opportunity. But the idea of directing is something I had been dealing with for some time, although not prominently.

While Nimoy was directing plays in the early sixties, Gene Roddenberry secured him a set visit to *The Man from U.N.C.L.E.* to audit the directing of the series. MGM executive David Victor offered prophetically in a letter at the time, "I hope someday he will be a very successful director." In fact, had *Star Trek* survived to a fourth season, it's likely Nimoy would have helmed an episode, following in the footsteps of his costar William Shatner who was going to direct a third-season episode, "The Joy Machine," when the network order was truncated. Subsequently, Nimoy did direct several episodes of episodic television, including episodes of *Night Gallery*, *T.J. Hooker*, and *The Powers of Matthew Star*.

LEONARD NIMOY

For many years my concern had been to try to build a career outside of *Star Trek* so that it wasn't that single straight line of only *Trek*-oriented work. So there was nothing for us to discuss. I said to Gary Nardino—I was being arrogant—with all due respect to Bob Wise, who directed the first picture, a top-notch film-maker; and all due respect to Nick Meyer, an extremely talented writer-director who directed *Trek II*, I know more about *Star Trek* than either of them and I said I could direct *Star Trek III* successfully. When I first presented the idea of my directing to Paramount, the response was very good—but there were certain trepidations. We had to talk them through.

My position during those discussions was: "I don't want you to perceive me as a problem. I don't want you to think I'm an actor trying to build a directing career on the strength of my leverage. I want you to see me as the *solution* to your problem. You need a director, and I know this material. I will bring you a movie that will satisfy the *Star Trek* audience." I didn't want to take the posture with the studio of "You want me to act in *Star Trek III*? Then *I'm* the director, period."

WILLIAM SHATNER

I would surmise that when Leonard was able to leverage his desire to direct against the very natural desire to grow and expand his horizons as an artist, that he wanted to direct the film. So he was able to use the leverage of them wanting him to do Spock with his desire to direct. I would think that those men who finally agreed made some kind of deal that if he wanted to direct, he had to come back at least for the fourth *Star Trek*.

RALPH WINTER

We selected Leonard because he was very familiar with the material, obviously, and had been in front of the camera for many years. He'd directed a *T.J. Hooker* and some *Night Gallery* episodes at Universal, and had directed on the stage. And it was bound to spark interest at the box office, getting one of the cast of the family of *Star Trek* to be involved creatively in putting the show together. We thought that would be an advantage. I think it was. It turned out very nicely and Leonard knows about Vulcans and mysticism and everything that is involved with that culture on film.

Leonard knew about that and wanted to bring to life a lot of the things that had been glossed over or never really developed before. For a long time he wanted to participate in creating and putting that vision on film. Plus we were seeing it through his eyes for the first time after all these years of playing that character, and working and interacting with those other characters.

DAVID GERROLD

He is a good director and a good actor. He is good at what he's good at. He's not Dustin Hoffman or Spencer Tracy, he's Leonard Nimoy. Then again, John Wayne was John Wayne.

LEONARD NIMOY

We worked out what I felt was a constructive approach. Basically, I told them, "Promote from within." Michael Eisner [then Paramount president] got very excited about it and said, "Great idea! Leonard Nimoy directs *The Search for Spock*!" It went downhill from there. At one point they said, "No, we're not going to do it." Harve and I kept operating on the assumption that it was going to work out and kept talking story ideas. In April of '83, I started my prep on the picture, reported on the lot, and immediately went to work with Harve.

HARVE BENNETT

On *Star Trek III* I said, "Look, it's got to be faster and more efficient than the writing of *Star Trek II*." So I was the sole writer on *Star Trek III*, which was the easiest writing job I ever had. The reason for that is that since it was so direct a continuation of *Star Trek II*, the outline was already in place. I knew exactly what I had to do and I did it in six weeks. One of the virtues of having grown up in TV as both a producer and writer is that you're forced to function at a rapid tempo. You don't have time to overthink. And I recognized that it's the greatest lesson I could have learned.

I see people in the feature business agonizing over treasured scenes and treasured words, stuff that makes no sense to shoot. It is the stuff of which colossal disasters come. No one wants to part with a vision. Well, in TV you don't have time for those extravagances, you're much more into committee thinking. Now, these things bear negative connotations in our society, but the good side of real collaboration between trained professionals is that no one steps on anyone else— there is a tremendous give and take of ideas in a rapidly changing situation. And when you hit something that's working, everyone senses it, puts their differences aside, and goes on to the next problem.

For instance, I had written the *Star Trek III* script for Romulans. But Leonard felt that the Klingons were more exciting, more theatrical. I went back to some TV episodes and I realized he was quite right. A sampling of mail also indicated that the fans wanted to see Klingons. So I rewrote my script and "Klingonized" the characters.

The most extraordinary thing about Leonard was his functioning for me as editor. He would read my drafts. Now, you don't get compliments from Leonard. He's very Vulcan. Very tied in. His passion is contained. He said, "This is very promising." I had to adjust to that, because I'm an enthusiast. But in the course of his method, he challenged me and when I couldn't get what he was trying to say, he'd say, "Let me write a draft." And he's a good writer. There are pounds of stuff in the screenplay that are pure Leonard.

WILLIAM SHATNER

Leonard and I are the dearest of old friends. We had shared a mutual struggle with management in various stages, whether it was a script, a thought, a concept, or a dressing room and asked each other what we thought. We'd have a plan! Whenever we were to deal with management, we'd plan it out together. Now, suddenly, my "brother" was saying, "Well, you should do this and I think you should do that." There was an awkward period of time for me, although I don't think for Leonard, when I felt more alone in anything I might have objected to. From my point of view, it was more awkward in the beginning than with either of the other two directors. But that slowly erased itself.

EDDIE EGAN

There was definitely a different dynamic on *Star Trek III*, because two peers were at the helm. It was very much a Shatner vehicle and it was directed by Nimoy. As a result, those two were thick as thieves. I think *there's* a place where the cast might have felt a little isolated from their colleagues, because of that dynamic being so front and center on both the production side as well as the acting side.

HARVE BENNETT

When the draft of the piece was finished and Leonard and I were both very happy with it, we sent it to Bill. He called and said, "I'd like to have a meeting." So we came over on a Sunday morning to Bill's house. Bill said, "Are you happy with this script?" I said, "Yeah, we like it a lot." Leonard said, "Promising. Very promising." Bill said, "Well, I just can't do it." The complaint was that there wasn't enough of him in the material. That he was standing by, that he wasn't leading. We said, "Let's talk about it." There was merit in much of what he said.

STEVE MEERSON (cowriter, *Star Trek IV: The Voyage Home*)

The approach we were told to take on *Star Trek IV* is that Kirk really had to be the one to lead everyone. Not necessarily that he had to actually have the idea to do something, but it had to *appear* as if he had the idea. We were told Bill had to be the leader at all times.

HARVE BENNETT

You have to understand, it's not quite as selfish as it seems. This is their career. It's like a quarterback saying, "Who's going to be blocking for me?" The actor says, "How am I going to come off? Are they going to like me? Are they going to love me so that I can make the next picture?" Being a star over a long period of time is a nerve-racking affair. So that's where his trust was, and we had neglected to protect our star.

The compromises that came out of that were funny. Bill said, "I think I should be in the scene where Bones talks to Spock." We said no. "You see, that's a very lovely scene and I should be there. Why am I not there?" We said, "It feels like one of those moments when two guys are joined together and Bones has not really had his moment." On that one he said, "Why don't we shoot it both ways?" Then he said, "Now Bones gets to go up there with the priestess, don't you think I should be up there and do something that makes it all happen?" We said no. He said, "Well, maybe that's too much." I said, "Bill, I'll tell you what you are. You are a quarterback who wants to call the play, run back, throw the pass, catch the pass, score the touchdown, and lead the cheers." He hugged me and said, "You're right. I can't help it."

Bill is a Shakespearean actor. It shows in everything. He has to wind up to draw a gun. And Bill has, in candor, a great talent and a great ego. Did you notice the last scene as the cast is surrounding Spock? Who remembers where Kirk is? By himself. He knew where his light is. This is not a fault. It's the way he is. He's a matinee idol in the traditional, historical sense of that word.

DENNY MARTIN FLINN (cowriter, *Star Trek VI: The Undiscovered Country*)

In *All About Eve* there's a marvelous line where Hugh Marlowe says, "It's about time the piano realizes it has not written the concerto." You deal with star actors in every film and every television show.

WALTER KOENIG (actor, "Pavel Chekov")

Initially, I was apprehensive with *Star Trek III*. I didn't know what to expect, Leonard's not the most effusive guy. He is by nature a little bit on the distant side and he never established a real rapport with us. Perhaps with Bill, but not with the supporting actors. He was always present and a delight, but I didn't know whether he would try and interpret our roles, and that's a concern I always have when an actor is directing.

He didn't do any of that, he primarily directed by omission. He only spoke about your performance if he didn't think it was going well. If you did it well, he'd just say "Cut, print." That was it. He said very little to me either through the course of *III* or *IV*, because I guess he thought I was okay. I saw him get angry once because somebody had done something that was kind of a caricature and he said, "Don't do that." That was the only time I ever saw him express any emotion.

LEONARD NIMOY

I must be really naïve about this. I was surprised that there was so much interest and so much concern about that. The interests and concerns are valid. I just didn't perceive the potential problems or friction that other people perceive. My fellow actors were concerned about it before we started doing the picture. I simply took it as fact that I had their best interests at heart. That I would know their characters well, and I certainly knew their potential well and would try to explore it. That was one of the things I argued in that period of time when I was asking for the job.

HARVE BENNETT

Do you have any idea, can you project in your minds, the sibling rivalries, the little passions, the petty jealousies that no one ever talks about? I'm not talking scandal gossip. I'm talking about the day-to-day grist of living in a family. "Well, he had the close-up yesterday, I think I'll have the close-up today." It's deadly if someone can't come in and make everybody pull in the same direction.

Leonard handled the *Star Trek* family in the most elegant way. He never raised his voice. He got the best out of them and I will tell you: they had fun. There was more fun on *Star Trek III* on the stage than I had witnessed at all on *II*, which was much more strained. And even I thought he got things out of Bill that were vulnerable, that were Shatner letting down his operatic style.

LEONARD NIMOY

I discussed it later, after the fact, with some of the cast, and they admitted to me that they had been concerned. I think the concern grew out of a potential competitiveness. I discovered that there was more of a sense of competition between actors than I have ever been aware of. That's a strange thing to say. I'm an actor, have been in television and films since 1950. This was the first time that I had it really enunciated to me that some of the actors in the cast were concerned that my competitiveness would be a detriment. We got over that very quickly. Generally they saw that I was well prepared, that I was well intended where they were concerned, and they were given the opportunity to develop and have some fun in their performances.

JAMES DOOHAN (actor, "Montgomery 'Scotty' Scott")

Nicholas Meyer was so in love with *Star Trek* and was such a terribly good director. He's one of the best directors we ever had, but the best we ever had was Leonard Nimoy. The beautiful thing about Leonard is that when he directed the third movie, he tended to talk an awful lot, but he was still terrific. When he directed *IV,* he hardly talked at all. In other words, I can picture him going home at the end of the day and saying to himself, "Oh boy, I sure talked an awful lot directing that movie, I'm going to shut up when it comes to number four!"

GENE RODDENBERRY
(executive consultant, *Star Trek III: The Search for Spock*)

I'm delighted Leonard Nimoy directed. I was hesitant at first about him doing *Star Trek III*, because I thought he didn't have the broad background of experience. But then I began to think, "Well, he does know the show, this way you don't have to break a new director in." It worked out well.

> Among Roddenberry's continuing concerns—he was still serving as executive consultant—was the film's screenplay, which had been sent to him. In a seven-page memo, dated June 3, 1983, Roddenberry cogently addresses the many flaws he found in Bennett's script. Among the concerns he delineates are Saavik acting out of character, an emphasis on drunkenness, the lack of viability for the massive space dock, the "twentieth-century concept" of the *Enterprise* being considered obsolete, the automation of the starship that does not necessitate the use of a large crew, and the idea that the Genesis Planet is off-limits, feeling it "comes off like political foolishness seen in our twentieth century now."
>
> But his biggest concerns were over the MacGuffin used to resurrect Spock. "Suggest that the entire 'regrowth' of Spock needs some careful reexamination. For one thing, it does not seem at all reasonable that young Spock's mind would be a 'void.' One could get oneself easily painted into a corner by stuff like this and probably deserves more care and more careful explanation than the usual story situation . . . What does Spock mean to the Vulcan race? These comments and this scene are really very difficult to understand since *Star Trek* has always played Spock as a half-breed Vulcan, sometimes barely tolerated by pure Vulcans. The fact he may be quite famous in Starfleet for his rare ability does not make him a revered figure on his own planet. Yes, the temples and the thousands of extras and the torchlight parades make for interesting photography, but do we really want to risk this if it comes off unbelievable or even amusing to some?" He concludes with a criticism of the finale. "Is the fact that Spock now recognizes Kirk a sufficient ending to a major motion picture?"

HARVE BENNETT

A great motion picture has a very similar last scene. It was almost, beat for beat, the last scene in *The Miracle Worker* by William Gibson. It is the moment in which, after the entire play, little Helen Keller is at the well with her teacher and she begins to get some understanding, and finally with her hand on his face she says, "Water." And the teacher says, "Yes!"

The studio notes at the same time, dated June 8, 1983, reflect a desire to give Uhura a greater piece of the action, noting, "Film could use a few active femme characters, and Uhura is a beloved regular" as well as asking that there be some mention of Carol Marcus. "Need to reveal what she's doing now. Wouldn't there be some mention of her by David or Kirk upon their son's death?" Harve Bennett's terse response: "No." The studio also suggests that Kirk's infamous "I have had enough of you" to Kruge as he pushes him into the lava pit be changed to "This is for David," and evoke the tone of Indiana Jones versus the "sword-wielding attacker" in *Raiders of the Lost Ark*. This note was ignored as well.

In Gene Roddenberry's last memo on the final draft script, dated August 1, 1983, he doesn't mince words. "If shot without revisions, this draft would create some fairly serious problems for me and, in my opinion, also for Paramount as regards the continuing viability of the *Star Trek* property. The problems I see have mainly to do with script items contrary to what has been established and proven successful in the *Trek* format." He dismisses as hokey Scotty's foiling of the *Excelsior*'s pursuit by removing a chip from their transwarp drive. "This could come across as unbelievable, even laughable. When are we going to stop portraying Kirk's beloved Starfleet as a 'Pirates of Penzance' admiralty? It flies directly into the face of an optimistic future, one of the format's most powerful elements according to every study and poll made of *Star Trek*."

Roddenberry was also particularly concerned with what he refers to as "Vulcan immortality" and the notion that Kirk, Spock's "blood brother," would not be aware of the situation; as well as the idea of Spock's mindless body being brought to Vulcan to have his *katra* restored to him. "I can't imagine," Roddenberry muses, "there have been many planet Genesis effects around before, certainly even fewer of them involving a Vulcan, and this can hardly avoid being a very special thing. But the feeling one gets from the script now is 'Hey, here's another Genesis effect victim and his mindless body, so let's climb to the temple on old Mount Whassit again."

He takes Leonard Nimoy's potential staging of the final scene to task as well. "A principal concern with the scenes as presently written lies in what the audience and critics may make of Leonard Nimoy directing Leonard Nimoy's cocreation in scenes that read, at least, like a DeMille creation."

RALPH WINTER

Gene was very involved in consulting with Harve on the story and during the production. But Harve Bennett is the one who was developing the story and producing it. He certainly developed this whole idea from its very inception, and it didn't hurt to keep it on track, getting his blessing and all that.

GENE RODDENBERRY

Being an executive consultant is really what I want to be. Basically, my contract gives me about the same no matter what I do now. I guess after so many years you get certain privileges. I'd say the main difference is that they listened to me a little more carefully than on the last movie. I think Paramount came around to decide that, well, maybe it wasn't just a big mistake—maybe there *was* some thought behind it all.

DEBORAH ARAKELIAN

Gene and Harve were a lot alike except for the fact that Gene had created something that Harve never created that's his and it will always be his. Harve produced *Six Million Dollar Man* and *Bionic Woman* and participated in one of the largest lawsuits known to ABC over royalties. Harve was not an easy man. He's not a simple man. He's very complex, but in terms of why *II* worked and *III* didn't, you have to go to the script first and foremost. Everybody that's got a half of a brain cell knows that there's a huge difference between the scripts in *Star Trek II* and *Star Trek III*.

WILLIAM SHATNER

They did *TMP* and it was not successful. It was only because of Paramount's belief that there must be some box office somewhere that they hired Harve Bennett who again set the tone of the way the subsequent movies were going to go. Gene was again in the background, offering advice, but not interested in the creative process.

DAVID GERROLD

Harve Bennett knew what he was doing. He did these nice, crisp little movies that are doing like a hundred million dollars each, which is something that Gene Roddenberry has never been able to do. We get into meetings for *Star Trek: The Next Generation,* and in the first six weeks, Gene is saying, "I don't want anyone telling Harve Bennett anything." We ran into Harve Bennett at the ceremony for George [Takei's] star and, of course, we're all being polite, but I'm watching Gene, and Gene is shining Harve on. "Yes, we're having great fun, we're going to make it work." Harve gets up and leaves and Gene looks at me and says, "See how I handled him?" And I'm thinking, "Jesus, what a scumbag." At that time, it's like watching these two guys dancing around each other like they're in competition, which is so stupid. Harve Bennett didn't want to be an enemy. Gene turned him into an enemy.

WALTER KOENIG

Harve wanted to remold the show in his own image. He's obviously a bright man and has a good sense of which stories work. I don't think he liked working in Roddenberry's shadow. He resented him. Harve had a tendency to talk about us to other people. George [Takei] came back and would recount what Harve had said about me. And he [Bennett] spoke to me about other actors on the show.

EDDIE EGAN

There was some friction between Harve and Leonard on *III,* which I never really understood. I believe it was Harve feeling a little sensitive to not getting enough attention for being the person who was the architect of the rebirth of *Star Trek.* In the second movie, people were just glad that it was back and the crew was acting like they expected them to act. Then the news on the third one was that Leonard Nimoy is directing, it's in good hands. So I think Harve just felt a little left out of being the focus of attention. He was also the hammer that had to lay down the law about how long they could go on shooting days and whether they could ever go outside anywhere; all of the budgetary things fell to him to impart to Leonard.

I think he also told Leonard a few times that certain scenes were not staged well and they had some disagreements about that. By the way, the advice was good and once Leonard got over the interference part of it, he was okay. Overall, though, there did seem to be some element of a different dynamic between them.

Although the regular cast was present for *Star Trek III,* Kirstie Alley, who had played and made quite the impression as the half-Vulcan, half-Romulan Lt. Saavik, decided not to reprise the role for a variety of reasons, resulting in her being replaced by Robin Curtis. Alley explained to *Starlog* magazine at the time, "I thought [Robin Curtis] was at a real disadvantage playing a role someone else established, especially with *Star Trek,* which has an enormous following. I think she did a fine job. I have no problem with what she was doing except that, when I saw the film, I said, "She isn't Saavik, *I* am!'"

Also MIA was Bibi Besch as Carol Marcus, who was simply written out. Merritt Butrick was back as David, but in Bennett's tale the Genesis Device was not quite as nobly created as first perceived (using highly unstable protomatter in its matrix), and in Bennett's view David needs to be punished for his hubris, the character ultimately perishing at the hands of the Klingons on the Genesis Planet, after he and Saavik have discovered the rapidly aging Spock.

One final "character" to get the axe was the *Enterprise* itself. In a shocking and moving moment, Kirk orders the self-destruction of the starship to save his crew (who have beamed down to the surface of the Genesis Planet) to stop a large contingent of marauding Klingons.

An addition to the cast was actor Christopher Lloyd (*Taxi, Back to the Future*) as the Klingon Kruge, who wants to retrieve the Genesis Device to bring back to the Empire.

SUSAN SACKETT

Kirstie Alley was caught between a rock and a hard place. I think her agent and Paramount screwed up in trying to close the deal for her and they didn't come to terms. I don't think it was her fault. That's showbiz.

DEBORAH ARAKELIAN

There is that amazing thing where Kirstie's breast size seems to change radically in the movie. I don't know if you have noticed that. Take a very close look at the elevator scene and then look at the rest of the movie. She's wearing a tunic. It is impossible to miss. Poor Agnes Henry had to remake the uniform. If it is not a weight thing, what could it possibly be? I didn't feel them, but all I know is that those puppies grew tremendously from the elevator scene to the rest of the movie. She left for a period of time ostensibly because there had been a death in the family. And they redid the production schedule to accommodate her absence from the set. When she came back, let's just say a lot of reconstruction work had to be done on her uniform.

HARVE BENNETT

Our big problem came with the lady who played Saavik. She wanted as much as Bill Shatner. We thought it was funny at first. There was no movement in negotiation. We thought that Saavik's part in this was wonderful. We didn't want to cut it out. We decided to recast the character and keep the part. How did we fare in putting Robin Curtis in where Kirstie Alley had gone before? About even.

ROBIN CURTIS (actress, "Saavik")

There was not a word mentioned to me of her. I don't think it had anything to do with bad feelings or being an outcast or anything like that. I think that it was the most professional and healthy approach to the whole situation. This was Leonard Nimoy's baby. Being a beginner, given that this was my first film, I just left myself totally in Leonard's hands. I never got a sense I was following in someone else's footsteps, which was lovely. I'm so different physically from her that I think that in itself is kind of riveting. They didn't try to copy. They didn't try to mimic.

HARVE BENNETT

Curiously enough, no one said a thing. Part of it is probably that Alley had a different quality. The character's latent sexuality was very appealing and indicated that there was something under that that might be Romulan. Robin is almost pure Vulcan. And Leonard directing was much more inclined to Vulcanize her rather than try to dig for the Romulan, which wasn't really applicable here.

ROBIN CURTIS

I did want to keep things fairly separate between myself and Kirstie Alley, and as it turned out, each and every one of the people involved in *Star Trek III* were wonderful. Leonard set an example that everyone followed, and that is to say I was never made to feel like I had to fill someone else's shoes. Never for a moment was I made to feel like that, and I think that was really Leonard's healthy approach to the whole thing.

DEBORAH ARAKELIAN

Robin Curtis was just a really delightful person. Very sweet in a really miserable situation of having to reprise that role so quickly after somebody else had created it. It was a nasty position to be in.

HARVE BENNETT

Carol Marcus was the fifth member of a four-man relay team. She was the extraneous character. She was in the story outline. I thought it might be fun to have her relating to David and have something going with Saavik.

But then protomatter came up. Then something happened: Did Carol know? If Carol knows about protomatter, everything about David making a mistake doesn't wash. Then it's not David's ambition, it's mother and son in some kind of Oedipal whim to cheat the world together. And they don't tell Kirk, which is very out of character. Also, then I would have had to kill them both. Writer's problem. Answer: Don't get Carol involved. Get her out of this issue. David doing it without his mother's knowledge enriches it for me. And his father certainly doesn't know.

If you think it's tough answering that, think of how it was when I tried to explain it to Bibi Besch. She was deeply upset. She cried. She thought it was a rejection of her talent. She thought she must have done something wrong. But I got a lovely letter from Bibi after the picture opened. It said, "I've seen the picture. Now I understand. You were right. I hope you can find a place for me in one of the other films."

WILLIAM SHATNER

I thought the loss of David Marcus and the *Enterprise* were very clever devices used to create drama in a situation. The problem is that, in a continuing series of movies where the characters appear through all the films, we have to raise some jeopardy. But everybody knows the characters are not going to die.

HARVE BENNETT

I confess to being old-fashioned. There is in my vision such a thing as ultimate retribution. The reason David dies, structurally, is because he's messed with

Mother Nature. He allowed himself to bend the rules at the wrong time, in the wrong place. He's there on that planet for only that reason. The whole story dates back to David putting protomatter in the matrix. The death of Spock—everything—rests on his shoulders if you want to blame him for it.

Also, we did not feel that the character of David was a viable character upon which to build further stories. We didn't set out to kill him. We didn't even set out to use him, but when I got to the crisis and came up with the idea, "I'm going to kill one of them," it became obvious which one I would have to kill, because it was the one I didn't need. I had no idea what the future of Saavik might be.

Clearly, I couldn't kill Spock a second time or the picture would be over and David was extraneous then. It was like the [Decker] character in the first movie: it was a good try and it is very interesting to see the number of tries to bring "new blood" into "the family." Kirk changed the computer on the *Kobayashi Maru* scenario before *Star Trek II*. His son says to him, "You've cheated." His father says, "I changed the rules." Well, it turns out that the kettle was calling the pot black. David says it at a time when he knows he's changed the rules.

LEONARD NIMOY

As a director, I'm probably somewhere in between Bob Wise and Nicholas Meyer. Not as precise as Bob, not as imaginative or rough-edged as Nick. I think the major difference, and for me the most important difference, is my attitude toward the story and the actors. Wise and Meyer are looking for a different kind of final product than I am.

HARVE BENNETT

I'll tell you, what was a great directorial achievement by Leonard was getting emotion over David's death out of Shatner, because he wanted to play it more stylistically. It's the only scene I remember where Leonard said, "Clear the bridge." Literally, he said, "Will everybody please leave? I want to talk to Bill." I never asked him what he said to Bill. It was very personal. It was director talk to actor.

LEONARD NIMOY

On the day of shooting that scene, he and I got ourselves off into a corner and discussed it slowly in a relaxed atmosphere and privately. What I said to him was this: "You have to decide how far you want to go with this. How far you want to take this reaction. My opinion is that you can go pretty far and get away with it, maybe strip off some of the veneer of the admiral, the hero, always in charge, always on top of the situation, and show us a vulnerable person." He took it further, frankly, than I expected him to. And it was scary.

I mean, how many space epics do you see where your hero, on receiving news, stumbles back and falls on the person's own ship? You don't see that a lot. It was a scary thing for all of us hoping that it would be perceived as a very touching moment. Some little kid breaks into laughter in the audience and you're dead. We did several takes and used the one where we really thought Bill lost control and stumbled and fell. It looked accidental, not a performance. I'm very moved by it. In my opinion, it is some of the best work he has ever done. It looked as though he had received a physical jolt, as if somebody had hit him with the information. He looks deeply hurt. Some of the most personal and vulnerable work I've ever seen done in the role of Kirk.

WALTER KOENIG

I went to school with Chris Lloyd. We used to be best buddies, it could have been a trip. It wasn't. He was very much into his character, which was good, but he was not very approachable as a consequence, and the rapport we had had as kids in a playhouse was not there for me. I always want to go home again and I guess you can't.

EDDIE EGAN

I think he just felt very out of place. There were whole parts in the movie where he didn't interact with any of them until the end except with Robin Curtis and Merritt Butrick. No one likes wearing that kind of makeup in that kind of heat for that many hours a day. It was a very quick job. He didn't work that long. The movie was also shot at an extremely quick pace.

DEBORAH ARAKELIAN

Chris Lloyd stayed to himself. He would sit there in full makeup with his little wire glasses on reading the trades. I wish I had a picture of it, it was pretty funny to look at. He had almost no interaction with anyone. Came in and did his job, such a professional. I used to go to the *Taxi* stage and watch him work and he was so amazingly funny. Probably my second favorite show to watch film next to *Mork & Mindy*. You never saw the good stuff. They couldn't air that stuff. They would shoot way into the mornings.

HARVE BENNETT

The death of the *Enterprise* caused serious ripples. The death of David did not. That's backward for me. "How could you destroy the *Enterprise*?" is a burden I take full responsibility for. I will justify it to the end and once again I think I have been playing fair.

RICHARD ARNOLD (*Star Trek* archivist)

Harve showed no respect for Gene and what he had created. When it came to destroying the *Enterprise*, Gene felt that it was like killing off one of the characters. As a pilot during WWII, Gene felt that "she" deserved better. Harve said that he felt more like a helicopter pilot during the Korean War . . . if you crashed your helicopter, you could always get another one. This very different approach to "equipment" was only one aspect of their difficult relationship, one that had a history that went back to 1965, when Gene had Harve thrown off of the set of his pilot *The Long Hunt of April Savage*.

KEN RALSTON
(visual effects supervisor, *Star Trek III: The Search for Spock*)

It was something I always wanted to do. I hate that ship. I've said that a hundred times, but it's true. I think it's ugly—the most silly-looking thing. The model itself is murder to work with. I would hope that the idea actually originated with me on *Trek II*. I talked to Harve Bennett about doing that to the ship—blowing it up. I'd like to take some credit, at least, for blowing it up—for physically doing it. Watching that thing go was one of my favorite parts.

RALPH WINTER

I remember that the conventional wisdom is you can't kill Spock and the answer is you can, if you do it well. And the same thing is you can't kill the *Enterprise* when you can—*if* you do it well. It was that zigzag storytelling structural thing that both of them understood very well. The way *Star Trek* is opera in space

HARVE BENNETT

My choice was a humanistic choice. It began as a writer's problem. Usually it happens when you reach a sticky point. I had a whole justification for it. Oliver Hazard Perry of the U.S. Navy scuttled the *Niagara* at the Battle of Lake Erie and won the battle as a result. He was rowed on a rowboat to another ship and took command. Perry happens to be one of James T. Kirk's great heroes. Actually, there is a model of the *Niagara* in Kirk's quarters for those who love *Star Trek* trivia. So the scuttling of the ship to achieve the greater good is a tactic. Also, with the death of his son and the hopelessness of the situation, it seemed like the right solution.

GENE RODDENBERRY

I felt it wasn't really that necessary. I would have rather seen the saucer blow up, at the end of the picture we could have had a new saucer come down and reunite the two. Symbolic of the end of the story. They preferred to do it the other way.

SCOTT MANTZ (film critic, *Access Hollywood*)

I remember being almost as upset watching the *Enterprise* blow up as when Spock died. The destruct sequence, which goes back to "Let That Be Your Last Battlefield," was a nice touch of continuity. But when the bridge blows up and you see the words "U.S.S. *Enterprise* and NCC-1701" disintegrate, it was heartbreaking. It doesn't just blow up like a big burst of sun. It blows up in pieces and the *Enterprise* disintegrates, which is really spectacular.

KEN RALSTON

It was a full miniature blown up. Then we had to pull a matte off that and put some stars in because it was just shot against black. We weren't about to destroy the $150,000 model. I was tempted though—tempted many times to take a mallet to it. Next we cut to the famous number being eaten away and the explosions going off. Bill George devised a light Styrofoam that he laid over this incredible grid work—something he came up with in twenty minutes or so. It looked great. There is also a stock explosion from *The Empire Strikes Back* in there, too. It comes out from underneath the dish to make the explosion seem a little more cohesive and not so much of an effect.

WILLIAM SHATNER

Two elements that were expendable, David and the *Enterprise,* were killed off because nothing else *could* be killed off. In fact, the real problem is, what else can we kill? We're looking around for people to die!

DeFOREST KELLEY (actor, "Dr. Leonard 'Bones' McCoy")

When I read that in the script, I couldn't believe it. You know, I thought, "My God, the *Enterprise* is a bigger star than any of us. If they're shooting this guy out of the script, they can shoot anybody out."

HARVE BENNETT

There are two elements in the making of a story, whether it's on film or not. Suspense and surprise. You're either hoping a character will do something or he does something that you didn't expect. The sure knowledge of the audience saying, "Oh, no, they're not going to do that," and the sheer surprise of saying, "Oh, yes we are!" There are many other moments in the film which were intended to be one or the other. The death of David is one clear example of surprise, because you're playing off the clichés of the expected. One of the joys of motion-picture writing as opposed to television is that you have full use of those two ranges. In television the surprise is limited and suspense is limited to the fact that the episode must end with the hero surviving.

WALTER KOENIG

I felt it was too similar to *Star Trek II* in terms of the major conflict. The bad guys wanted the bomb and we are trying to keep them away from it. It lacked a soul and a real emotional center, and it was not as good a story as *Star Trek II*. The one thing that was the saving grace of the picture was the destruction of the *Enterprise*.

As with every film, *Star Trek III: The Search for Spock* encompassed a wide range of production challenges, many of which were met and others that were . . . attempted. Like its predecessors, the film was shot on soundstages rather than on location.

LEONARD NIMOY

The shooting began on August 15, 1983. It was forty-nine days of shooting during which the biggest problem I had was lack of sleep. I went to bed at nine o'clock or nine-thirty, set the alarm for five o'clock or five-thirty, and would be up at three o'clock, the head going with ideas. I was just so supercharged and wired. It was a constant tiredness of the best kind.

HARVE BENNETT

Nimoy is three yards and a cloud of dust. Fundamental. Here's the camera— shoot a movie. Willy Wyler shot like that. It works when the actors are working well, and the *Trek* family adored Leonard.

CHARLES CORRELL
(director of photography, *Star Trek III: The Search for Spock*)

Originally, when we were in preproduction on this picture, I was opposed to doing all the interiors inside on stages. Unless you really work hard and are able to control everything, things can take on a kind of phony look. I thought that we should go to the island of Kauai to do the Genesis Planet. The other shots that concerned me were of Vulcan. My original feelings were that I wanted to take those scenes out to Red Rock Canyon just above the Mojave and really shoot at sunrise. In the early days of *Star Trek* everything they did was inside on stages.

Most of *Trek* I and II were also done on stages. The producer, Harve Bennett, and the director, Leonard Nimoy, decided to stay with that format. Most every film shot today is done on locations. It isn't often that you get to do a whole show where they use massive stages and huge sets. The Genesis Planet was on Stage 15 at Paramount—probably one of the largest stages in Hollywood. Because it had to literally collapse in places during the earthquake, it was built sixteen feet off the floor. The main part of the floor was rigged so that rocks would shoot up out of the ground. They were on catapults. Trees were rigged to fall and start fires. The ground would belch. It was massive, and Bob Dawson, our special-effects supervisor, did a great job. He must have had twenty or thirty people on the set the days we shot the planet destruction.

KEN RALSTON

One thing that is tough about *Trek* movies—some of the shots are so long, almost endless. Not at all like *Star Wars* where everything is ten frames long and you can get away with murder on some shots. *Trek* shots hang on for a long time and the mistakes show up a lot more. You have to take a little more care with the effects aspect of it.

CHARLES CORRELL

I took a look at a lot of the old shows that were shot by Gerald Finnerman, and I noticed that they created a science-fiction feeling in those days by incorporating a great deal of color. Sometimes there was a purple feeling in places or they would use a red gel or blue or orange. They utilized the color and that gave the shows a real sci-fi touch. Then I looked at the two features that preceded this one. They both had their own flavors, but I thought that there was something about the original show that wasn't in either of these features. That touch of color or the overuse of color is what is missing.

LEONARD NIMOY

There is no question in directing yourself that you need help. [Harve Bennett, William Shatner, director of photography Charles Correll, and others] are people off camera I've come to trust. I cannot emphasize enough that you don't make these pictures alone. You sure need an awful lot of talented support. In some cases, there is simply the fact that there are things going on behind you that you cannot see as an actor.

The biggest problem I had, and this is really silly, but it happens that it was the scene in the sick bay of the Bird of Prey. Spock is unconscious and McCoy is talking to him. Now, not only am I in the scene but I have to play the scene with my eyes closed. So I can't even look to see if the actor I am playing the scene with is looking anything like I think he should look. It drove De Kelley crazy. He swears that I was trying to direct him with the movement and flutter of my eyelids. It was very difficult. In a sense, I was very pleased and relieved that the design of the story allowed me to do a minimal amount of performing.

HARVE BENNETT

Next time you see the film, there is a scene during the stealing [of] the *Enterprise* sequence when civilian clothes are seen for the first time. The first time you see Chekov, well, we didn't see his costume objectively next to Kirk's macho jacket and Bones's marvelous pants. But all of a sudden we see Chekov onstage and he has this great Little Lord Fauntleroy white collar. We got by it without reshooting the day with a series of clever cheats. We got a new collar, picked up close-ups on the black turtleneck for the rest of the picture. But he still has it in the master shot. Bob Fletcher, our costume designer, did Bones from his Georgia background, Kirk from his admiration of naval flyers and stuff like that. This was supposed to be Chekov's admiration—get this—of the poet Pushkin. Now that's a fine hobby for a Russian space person to have, but Pushkin is always drawn in his great Byronic collar from that period and it looks darn silly. So that one shot with the collar still exists.

WALTER KOENIG

That little pink suit [I was wearing] was interesting because I thought it was kind of ridiculous looking. Robert Fletcher patterned it after some Russian artist who dressed that way. We had shot some footage with it and Michael Eisner looked at the dailies and said he didn't like it and Leonard came up to me and said, "We're going to take you out of the costume." I said, "Thank God," and he said, "Why didn't you say something?" I was a little bit irritated, thinking, "Why the hell didn't I say anything?" It was because I was so into this mind-set that I was just the hired help and had no input. It never occurred to me that I might say, "I don't like this" and that's probably my fault.

JAMES HORNER (composer, *Star Trek III: The Search for Spock*)

I was involved with Harve just about every day, as I was with Leonard. He had a lot of input into the score. Leonard and I met on several occasions and had multiple conversations. The things he said he liked best about *Star Trek* was the

romantic, beautiful music; the sensitive stuff in *Star Trek II,* not the big, bombastic stuff, and this is exactly the stuff in *Star Trek II* that I liked the best. So the
whole score for *Star Trek III* is exactly that. It was much more romantic and
much more wistful and sweeping than *Star Trek II* was.

Star Trek III is a sensitivity epic. It was much more of a character film. There
are a lot of action sequences in it that are wonderful. My score for *Star Trek III* is
so much better than *Star Trek II.* It's just so much more elegant. It's a completely
different type of film and the whole mood the score portrays is one of searching
and emotionalism as opposed to the rather heroic, bombastic *Star Trek II.*

Obviously the film is called *The Search for Spock,* so I used Spock's theme
somewhat. I used the theme of the *Enterprise* and Kirk's theme. That's the thing,
when you have a film that's an ongoing series and you have the same characters.
You are basically committed. That was something I was aware of when I was
writing *Star Trek II.* I was writing in the view that I will have to reuse themes in
Star Trek III.

DEBORAH ARAKELIAN

The best thing about *III* was Dame Judith Anderson as a Vulcan priestess. Everybody loved Dame Judy and that was the second time I met her. I first met her
when I was a college student and she was doing *Hamlet.* It was a very obscure
thing and she toured the college circuit and was magnificent. Years later they cast
her in this and what a damn treat. There's actually a photograph of me sitting
in her chair on the set because the back of the chair said, "High Priestess." It was
the perfect place for me to park my keister.

LEONARD NIMOY

In the editing process, specifically, the most interesting challenge was how to tell
the story and in what sequence. Having seen it on the screen in its rough-cut
form, we all came to the conclusion that there was something about the juxtapo-
sition, scene to scene, idea to idea, character to character; it wasn't quite in its
proper order. The jigsaw puzzle hadn't quite fallen into place. Gradually we
worked our way toward it and discovered what the picture turned out to be. The
flow just didn't want to come to life until we repositioned certain of the opening
scenes. For example, what we came to call the caper, which was the gathering of
the samurai to steal the *Enterprise.* In its original form, it was scattered in pieces
through the first third of the film and they were all wonderful, fun pieces. But

somehow, when you cut away from each of the happenings, it was always as though the fun was being interrupted. When you get back to it, you have to get geared up to have fun again. And suddenly that little piece would be over and you were being interrupted and taken away from the story again.

The one major reconstruction that took place in editing was to put much, if not all, that caper together as a piece so that once we start with the idea of Bill Shatner walking up and saying, "The answer is no, I am therefore going anyway," it starts.

Production was temporarily halted when a fire swept through several sound-stages on the Paramount lot, damaging part of the Genesis cave soundstage, but it was quickly extinguished. The press latched onto a story in which William Shatner, brandishing a hose, helped douse the fire. Director of photography Charles Correll mused at the time that he wished the stage *had* burnt down so they could have shot the scenes on location in Hawaii instead, as he had lobbied for, rather than a soundstage.

DEBORAH ARAKELIAN

It wasn't a joy to shoot. Right down to the fire on the set. There were a couple of fires at Paramount that seemed convenient. At Paramount, it's old timber. Very flammable. There was a Western Street at one point and then there was a fire and then there was no Western Street. There was a point in time when there were two or three fires back to back. And the one that was threatening our stage was the second or third fire. The *Angie* stage went up right after the wrap party. One fire threatened one of the *Star Trek* sets, which was pretty frightening. The firemen were great because Paramount is such a tinderbox they were there in a heartbeat. If that fire had taken out that stage, that would have been a very expensive blow to *Star Trek III*. There were news cameras around and at one point I'm watching TV and there's Shatner in the midst of the firemen. I think he actually was holding a water hose.

RALPH WINTER

Stage 15 burned on that movie. Shatner was there on the news and helped put it out. It wasn't staged, but Bill was not helping with the garden hose. It was a very hot fire and it burned right to the ground. Years of lead paint, which was toxic.

SUSAN SACKETT

It had no effect at all upon the filming of *Star Trek III*. It turned into a nice [piece of] publicity for William Shatner, who was shown, fire hose in hand, saving Paramount single-handedly.

EDDIE EGAN

I don't think a fire department would let an actor wearing a polyester uniform man a hose during a major fire.

> While not the critical darling that *Wrath of Khan* had been, *The Search for Spock* had a comparable box-office gross, much to the delight of the studio. Outside of the destruction of the *Enterprise,* the fans were certainly pleased—though perhaps not as pleased as most of the participants.

WALTER KOENIG

After *III*, I was looking forward to working with Leonard Nimoy on *IV* and that turned out to be a very nice experience as well.

LEONARD NIMOY

I wasn't making a personal statement. The major theme in this film is about friendship. What should a person do to help a friend? How deeply should a friendship commitment go? What price should people be willing to pay? And what sacrifice, what obstacles, will these people endure? That's the emotion line of the film. For me, that's its reason for existence.

HARVE BENNETT

For me, this movie is about honor and friendship and decency and values higher than the complex value system we have inherited since the atomic age. It's a return to innocence.

DeFOREST KELLEY

I enjoyed watching *Star Trek III* more than I did *Star Trek II*. This one comes closer to the TV series than the others. I have had full confidence that Leonard could direct *Star Trek,* or for that matter, anything he wanted to had he been given the opportunity. Leonard is the kind of director who will accept input from you because he knows that we know and feel certain things about our characters.

DAVID GERROLD

Star Trek III is a dreadful movie. There's no story there. It's still a wonderful picture because the characters are so wonderful, the scenes are so wonderful, and it's crisply directed. You don't care how bad the story is. You go and look at the first three films, and the stories are all silly, and the pictures are all wonderful because the characters are good.

DAVID A. GOODMAN (consulting producer, *Star Trek: Enterprise*)

Nimoy's direction is very amateur and TV-ish and he doesn't really create a world. But on the flipside of it, you have three ships in that movie that have been in all the incarnations of *Star Trek*. It's a testimony to Industrial Light and Magic that the work they did on that is so amazing: the Bird of Prey, the *Excelsior,* and the science vessel. The work that was done on a low budget was so good that lesser people have relied on that work for years—which says something about the level of work that was going on. I thought Christopher Lloyd didn't feel like a Klingon to me and I loved that his dog is terrible, but I've *still* watched it dozens of times.

DEBORAH ARAKELIAN

Leonard's a good director. I think he did a better job outside of *Star Trek* than in. He did a *really* good job directing *Three Men and A Baby*.

EDDIE EGAN

It looks more like a TV movie than the first film did, which was just a result of Paramount trying to squeeze as much as they could out of this thing that was printing money for them. It certainly suffers from budget restrictions, whereas Nicholas Meyer found ways to work around that.

If you look at *Star Trek II*, they were very smart about how they did things, minus a few places like the Genesis Cave and that horrendous effect when you finally see it. That was redone at the last moment when the head of Paramount saw it and refused to let the picture be released that way.

FRED DEKKER (consulting producer, *Star Trek: Enterprise*)

The plotting, the mission, the character work, it felt very much like a continuation of *The Wrath of Khan*, which is a movie where I feel like every decision was the right one. *Search for Spock* was emotionally and tonally and storywise just a continuation of it, so I ate it up with a spoon. I've also come to the conclusion that *Star Trek II* doesn't work as well if you haven't spent hundreds of man-hours with these characters like I have. Eventually, I want to show it to my wife, to my kids, to my grandson. But unless you've spent a lot of time with Spock being Spock, his death is probably not going to have a huge impact on you. If you have, it's devastating as much as it is with any human.

LEONARD NIMOY

On *Star Trek III*, I felt that film was really about camaraderie. It was about commitment to friendship and loyalty amongst a band of people. During the course of the designing and framing of it, I kept saying to Charlie Correll, who filmed it, that I wanted it operatic. I wanted fire, storms, great passions. This is not just about life, it's about commitment, personal need, and demands. Richard Schickel in *Time* magazine said, among other things, that was the first space opera really worthy of the name. I was so happy to see that, because I had really been talking Wagner—Sturm und Drang.

SCOTT MANTZ

The best moment for me in *Wrath of Khan* outside of the action and Spock's death is when David goes into Kirk's quarters and Kirk says, "I poured myself a drink, would you like one?" And David's voice is shaking and he goes, "I'm proud to be your son." He hugs him. It's a great moment. Or the scene when they're on Regula and Kirk goes, "How am I feeling? Old." What happened? The problem with *Star Trek II* to *Star Trek III* is at the end of *Star Trek II*, Kirk is rejuvenated. He feels young. The beginning of *Star Trek III,* he's depressed again. It's so somber for the first twenty or thirty minutes until they steal the *Enterprise*, which was fun. It's the best scene in the movie.

DAVID A. GOODMAN

Stealing the *Enterprise* is one of my favorite sequences in any of the movies. I wish it actually was longer. That's a movie in and of itself.

RONALD D. MOORE (writer, *Star Trek: First Contact*)

I liked that they were advancing the story and characters in what became a trilogy, which is really unique in a movie franchise property. They had really taken the characters on a journey and moved them forward and changed them. It broke my heart that they destroyed the *Enterprise* . . . that was almost as hard as Spock's death. Because I was still connected to the idea that it was the original ship, which had been overhauled and it was still the five-year-mission ship. That meant a lot to me, so when it was destroyed, it was a great loss. Part of my childhood went with it. They get it back, but it was never the same. That ship was gone. There were other ships called *Enterprise,* but the emotional connection that it was the original ship was missing after that.

RALPH WINTER

We tried to make sure there was actually meaning and value in what the story and journey was about. That was important, particularly to Harve, who was our caretaker and anchor in all things *Star Trek*. We also did this in *III* with the creation of the Klingon language. It was actually a friend of Harve's, Marc Okrand, who was doing subtitles for ABC. He was doing the live closed-caption stuff. We instructed him on how to develop that Klingon language and he went on to do *The Klingon Dictionary.* They quote all that made-up language now on *The Big Bang Theory.* It all started with Marc Okrand and Harve Bennett.

LEONARD NIMOY

I have been around a long time. I have been on soundstages since 1950. But I never dreamed I would find myself directing a twenty-two- or twenty-four-million-dollar big physical picture . . . and feeling totally comfortable, not awed by it at all. None of it scares me, I've seen it all done before or I know a way can be found to do it if you get the right people.

DEBORAH ARAKELIAN

Star Trek III was not fun. It left a really bad taste in your mouth. You can feel when things are going well. When you're on the set and there's an electricity in the air. There wasn't that. The only time that people perked up was when Dame Judy was around—and she only worked like two days. I was not glad when *Star Trek II* wrapped. I felt a sense of loss. I was glad after *Star Trek III* wrapped. I couldn't wait to get the fuck out of there.

A WHALE OF A TALE

"THERE BE WHALES HERE."

Until the release of J. J. Abrams's 2009 reimagining, *The Voyage Home* was the most successful *Star Trek* film of them all. With little violence and humor that harkened back to classic episodes like "The Trouble with Tribbles" and "A Piece of the Action," *Star Trek IV* brought with it an eco-friendly message at its heart and a cautionary warning about endangered species—in this case, the imperiled humpback whale. Additionally, its fish-out-of-water-story of twenty-third-century characters stuck in the San Francisco of 1986 was an irresistible premise that its filmmakers milked to the fullest. Although dismissed by some die-hard fans as too whimsical and slight to be considered among *Star Trek*'s greatest adventures, there's little doubt that the success of *Star Trek IV* would ensure that the franchise would continue to live long and prosper for many years to come.

EDDIE EGAN (unit publicist, *Star Trek IV: The Voyage Home*)

The difference from the studio perspective on this film was that it was a full-fledged movie again with a movie budget, supervised by the movie group. Everyone was just incredibly excited about the potential of the story and the fact that it could take place outdoors on real locations for a legitimate reason.

I think the studio realized that they had imposed limitations on the films in terms of how they looked and recognized what the audience expects to see in a movie theater. Just the fact they were able to use different kinds of lenses made a big difference in how the movie looks, plus they could use cranes and dollies and things like that that they weren't able to use on the previous two movies. At that point, the studio was convinced that this could be a continuing series of films and it was given first-class treatment.

LEONARD NIMOY (actor/director, *Star Trek IV: The Voyage Home*)

I was asked to do *Star Trek IV* before *Star Trek III* even opened. I had had some constraints on *Star Trek III*. I was told flat out that they wanted my vision on this one. "This is a Leonard Nimoy film." That being the case, Harve and I were asked to develop a concept. I went off to Europe to work on *The Sun Also Rises*. While I was there, I also wrote a seven- or eight-page outline of what I thought the film could be about. Harve came over and we collaborated on the material . . . it went in as the very first concept.

HARVE BENNETT (cowriter/producer, *Star Trek IV: The Voyage Home*)

In moving through the trilogy, I confess that every one of the major tricks I learned in television, I used. Here are the three tricks of the trilogy: *Star Trek II*, in television we call that the "bottle show." The "bottle show" in television takes place in an elevator that's hopefully trapped between two floors. Or it takes place in a mine shaft where people are desperately coming to try to save you and you have to stay down there and talk a lot. Sixty-five percent of the film was on the *Enterprise* bridge in one incarnation or another. It was also the *Reliant* bridge, and that is an incomparable savings in terms of time, dollars, and moves. We'd shoot a scene, move the people out, repaint it, and it would now be the *Reliant*.

Star Trek III was the classic television, "the leading actor loses his memory" show. I did that on *Mod Squad, Six Million Dollar Man, Bionic Woman*. You usually do it when your leading actor is exhausted or needs a rest. He's in a coma-like state. In *Star Trek III*, we had a man who was directing the movie, and who had never directed a feature before, and we felt that to act and so forth would kill him. We had our choice of how to utilize that asset and what we did was we spent most of our money building one great set, the Genesis Planet, and the story became "let's find him while he directs." For *Star Trek IV* we decided to use local location. We had to add some size to the picture, so what do we do? We go out. How do you go out in the twenty-third century? You come to the *twentieth* century.

LEONARD NIMOY

We decided early on that we wanted to do a time-travel story. When I say "we," I'm talking about Harve Bennett and I. We were asked by the studio to come up with a story, and our very first conversation was about doing time travel, which we both agreed was a good idea. We also felt that we should lighten up. The picture should be fun in comparison to the previous three.

STEVE MEERSON (cowriter, *Star Trek IV: The Voyage Home*)

We sat in a room with Leonard and Harve. Leonard told us that he wanted to do a departure, although they weren't sure what they wanted to do.

LEONARD NIMOY

When we started out to do this picture, I went to three universities—the University of California, Santa Cruz; Harvard; and MIT—to talk to three different professors who are physicists, scientists, and futurists. I spent several hours talking to them about their immediate concerns for the future of the planet. We talked about their ideas for potential contact with extraterrestrials. What it might be like. Where it might come from. How it might come. How we would deal with it. The philosophy of it. And the immediate impact on the sociology of the planet, the religions of the planet. I had some great times.

PETER KRIKES (cowriter, *Star Trek IV: The Voyage Home*)

They wanted to do a film sort of based on "The City on the Edge of Forever." Leonard started talking about plankton, cells, that cells become plankton, that things eat plankton, and then whales entered the conversation. We said, "Why not make it as simple as the whale and the whale song?" That was our idea, though that's not to say Leonard hadn't done research on whales, because he had.

LEONARD NIMOY

I was also in touch with Edward O. Wilson. In his book *Biophilia*, he tells us we could be losing as many as ten thousand species off this planet per year—many of them having gone unrecorded. We won't even have known what they were and they will be gone. He touches on the concept of a keystone species. If you set up a house of cards you may be able to pull away one card successfully . . . and another card successfully. But at some point you are going to get a card that is a keystone card. When that one is pulled away, the whole thing will collapse.

The same might be true of species: a planetary imbalance might be caused by the destruction or loss of just one. Our tendency is to say, "Here's this pressure group pestering us—but things aren't really bad yet. Let's pay attention to the things we really have to." But when the ozone question or the species question or whatever gets really bad, we'll turn to scientists and say, "Okay, here's the money, God damn it. Fix it!"

They, at some point, may have to come back and say, "It's too late. We cannot do that anymore, there was a time when we might have . . ." There is a fantasy that if we did have a holocaust kind of war on this planet, those who are left could eventually rebuild the planet. It's simply not true. They could never again reach the technical accomplishments that we have reached.

STEVE MEERSON

Leonard had mountains of information on various things. We were hired in February of 1985 and between that time and May or June, Peter and I did several outlines of what eventually became the story. Harve and Leonard took our outline and went through it step by step with the studio executives, and we got the go-ahead to start writing.

LEONARD NIMOY

What we set out to do, frankly, was very dangerous. I was trying to service a lot of masters. I wanted to continue and wrap up some threads that were left over from *Star Trek III*. At the same time I wanted to make an entirely different kind of film. Those ideas seemed in opposition to each other, but I think we pulled it off.

RALPH WINTER (executive producer, *Star Trek IV: The Voyage Home*)

It was Leonard's idea about saving the whales as opposed to, as he famously said, "trying to save the snail darter." Saving whales made it a bigger movie.

LEONARD NIMOY

At the same, I wanted to make a film that would be accessible and enjoyable to people who had not seen *Star Trek III* in order to enjoy this picture. I also wanted to make it accessible to people who don't go to *Star Trek* movies. I wanted to make it a movie-movie. It starts out like a *Star Trek* movie and then makes a left turn. It is intentionally very different. I felt very strongly about the fact that *II* and *III* were really two of a kind. They both were played with black-hat heavies. *We are the good guys and they are the bad guys and we have to beat them.* I really wanted to make a change in that.

SUSAN SACKETT (assistant to Gene Roddenberry)

I didn't know Leonard that well, but one day I was chatting with his secretary in the outer office and he says, "What kind of questions do you think Spock should try to solve in a puzzle in the movie?" and I said, "Ask him to disprove God." He didn't run with it.

LEONARD NIMOY

The first movie had no comedy at all. The second film had a little. The third film had a little. But there we were dealing with a lot of serious drama. There was a lot of life and death going on. I just felt it was time to lighten up and have some fun. That meant that if we were going to do time travel, the best thing we could do was come back to contemporary Earth, where we could have some fun with our people. They would more or less be a fish out of water on the streets.

WILLIAM SHATNER (actor, "James T. Kirk")

We discovered something in *Star Trek IV* that we hadn't pinpointed in any of the other movies and it just shows how the obvious can escape you. There is a texture to the best *Star Trek* hours that verges on tongue-in-cheek, but isn't. There's a line we all have to walk that is reality. It's as though the characters within the play have a great deal of joy about themselves, a joy of living. The energy, that joie de vivre about the characters seems to be tongue-in-cheek but isn't, because you play it with the reality that you would in a kitchen-sink drama written for today's life.

LEONARD NIMOY

We were talking about the idea that if alien intelligence was trying to contact us, it would probably take quite a long time for us to know what it is saying, and for us to communicate with it. I became intrigued with the idea that there was some lack of communication that was causing the problem. [I was] aware that humpback whales sing this unusual kind of song, which we don't understand but which obviously means something to them. It's quite a complex structure, and that's very interesting.

We don't know, and we may never know, what the communication is all about, so suppose that something in the twenty-third century is trying to communicate with them and they're gone. That's how it all happened, and it's a hell of a lot more interesting and challenging, cinematically, to come back to the twentieth century to pick up a pair of whales than it is to pick up a plant or insect.

HARVE BENNETT

We went through every writer we could think of. We finally found Steve Meerson and Peter Krikes, whose work was highly regarded. Nothing came of it. Some of that, in fairness to them, was because we had saddled them with what appeared to be a male character that we thought was going to be Eddie Murphy at one time.

STEVE MEERSON

Eddie Murphy was going to play a college professor who taught English, but a professor who we probably all had in the sixties or seventies, who's a little bit wacky and believes in extraterrestrials. Every Wednesday, he would open up his class to a discussion and the room would light up with conversation.

HARVE BENNETT

Now, the meeting with Eddie Murphy was a little bizarre. He had a separate meeting with Leonard. Leonard said, "He's a little strange in a room." So he came in with two guys, good-looking guys, and they were all in black leather. [We] told Eddie this story and he thought about it for a while and he said, "It's good. Let me see a script," and walked out. We sat there and thought, "Wouldn't it be terrific to have Eddie in this movie?"

Later, the studio started getting very anxious for a very good reason. Here you have a franchise called *Star Trek* and it performs in a certain wonderful way. Here you have a franchise called Eddie Murphy and it performs in an even bigger way. Why not take them together and form one franchise? Bad economics, because you are probably diminishing by compositing. So the studio was resistant to it, but Eddie has a certain amount of clout, and he said that he hadn't decided whether he wanted to do it or not, and so much of the development of the story was with the very distinct possibility that Eddie Murphy was in it.

PETER KRIKES

He would play whale songs, and it was the whale songs he played in the classroom that the ship locked on to. That was in the first draft we wrote, but the second draft was different. After you write a first draft of anything, once the director, the cast, and the producers come aboard, *everything* changes, and not necessarily for the better. But the tone was pretty much a reflection of what was in the movie. For example, there was a scene where the Eddie Murphy character was trying to convince the Catherine Hicks character that aliens do exist on Earth. In the first draft, Hicks was a newswoman and there was a marine biologist as well. Gillian Taylor was ultimately a marriage of about three characters. Murphy believed in aliens and saw them beam into his classroom.

STEVE MEERSON

It was the boy who cried wolf. No one would ever believe him, so he took it upon himself to follow the crew, and in one scene, he lifted a phaser from Kirk, took it back to the newswoman and said, "See, they really *do* exist." And she says, "What's this?" and casts the gun aside, accidentally activating it. The phaser lands on the floor and her cat jumps off the couch. We follow her to her bedroom and she goes to sleep. The cat keeps phasing things out of the apartment by hitting the phaser, and when she wakes up, she sees that all the furniture is gone.

EDDIE MURPHY (actor, comedian)

I'm a Trekkie. I've always loved *Star Trek* and have wanted to do one of the films. I wanted to be in *Star Trek* and that's where they got the idea of coming back in time to Earth in 1986.

PETER KRIKES

We were given two instructions: keep Eddie Murphy in mind for the guest star, and make sure that the character of Admiral Kirk is the driving force behind every aspect of the story.

STEVE MEERSON

The approach we were told to take is that Kirk really had to be the one to lead everyone. Not necessarily that he had to actually have the idea to do something, but it had to *appear* as if he had the idea. I think the perfect example in the movie is when Spock goes into the belly of the Bird of the Prey to use the computers and learns that the alien probe is emitting the sound of whale songs. It's *Kirk* who has the idea to go back through time, although Spock is the one who plants the suggestion in Kirk's mind. Kirk verbalizes it, and that's the way it had to be played. We were told Bill had to be the leader at all times. In that scene, if you're reading it, you say, "It's Spock's idea," but on film Spock's discovery that it's humpback whales is not as important as Kirk's idea of going to get them.

PETER KRIKES

Visually, the scene between Spock and his father at the end is another example. You kind of ask, "Why is Kirk standing there listening to this?" He has to be a part of *everything*.

STEVE MEERSON

I know a lot of the cast wasn't happy about Eddie Murphy possibly being cast. I think all of those guys became terrified that Eddie would blow them off the screen. They also got a lot of negative mail from the fans.

HARVE BENNETT

When Eddie Murphy fell out, we had to readjust the script. But by then it had turned to paste. It just didn't work. Essentially we didn't have a script we felt good about or one that was even submittable to the studio.

STEVE MEERSON

Actually, every beat of the film's first, second, and third acts is *exactly* the same as our script. The *only* thing that changed slightly was that our Eddie Murphy character and the marine biologist were combined.

EDDIE MURPHY

The script was developed, but we eventually dropped the idea. *Golden Child* came along and I decided to do that film instead, because I thought it would be better for my career. In retrospect, I think I might have been better off doing *Star Trek IV*.

PETER KRIKES

If you look at our script and the movie you saw, basically everything is still there, like Eddie Murphy going to meet the aliens in the park to bring them gifts, and he runs into the invisible ship . . . which is what Catherine Hicks did when she ran into the park to find Kirk. The structure really is exactly the same.

Also, she grabbed Kirk's waist and is beamed aboard the Bird of Prey with him. In the script, Murphy says good-bye to Kirk who starts to beam out, then grabs him by the ankles and is transported aboard. He goes back to the twenty-third century and salutes Kirk when they get the *Enterprise-A*. You know when Spock nerve-pinches the guy on the bus? In our draft, that took place in an underground subway system.

You can't imagine the frustration of them trying to take all the credit for something that was completely blocked out for them. Plus, they removed a lot of the emotional qualities that we thought it would have.

PETER KRIKES

There was a scene with Kirk on the bridge of the Bird of Prey. They cut out five lines where Kirk says to Saavik, "Have you told him yet?" And she says, "No. I'm taking a maternity leave."

STEVE MEERSON

That's why she's standing with Amanda when the Bird of Prey leaves. Because Amanda *knows* Saavik is carrying Spock's kid. All they did was cut out five lines of dialogue, and you lost that whole thing.

PETER KRIKES

One of the things we had in our earlier drafts that they took out was what happened when they first went through time. Instead of the horrible time sequence that looks like Russian science fiction, we had them using the slingshot effect around Jupiter and Mars. Also, when they first appeared in the twentieth century, they were in a fog, and as they lowered, the monitors picked up all of the cheering and applause. As they come out of the fog, they find themselves over a Super Bowl game and everybody thinks it's a halftime show. Then, they cloak and disappear.

STEVE MEERSON

I like our ending better. Our sequence of events was similar. After the shuttle has picked them up and Earth is saved, we cut to this little chamber where they're waiting to stand trial. They discuss whether or not they would do everything the same if they could . . . and they say they would. We cut away to Spock and Sarek, who have that same talk that they had in the movie. It was originally much more bonding, but they removed about half a page of dialogue, which changed things quite a bit.

PETER KRIKES

Basically, Sarek was saying, "You're half human and I'll never understand that, but I accept you."

STEVE MEERSON

Everyone is confused, saying to the pilot, "Where are you taking us?" That's when the pod rises and you see the new *Enterprise-A*. It would have been much more emotional, instead of saying "You've been exonerated for this, this, and this," you could have done it in three sentences, and with everyone cheering, screaming, and yelling, it would have been an emotional high. Harve likes bookends, which is why the film begins with a trial and ends with a trial. That was always a point of contention between the three of us, that you didn't need to do that sequence again because it would be understood why. You could just take them to the ship so that everyone would be on a high, rather than waiting for it to happen. Structurally, I think they made a mistake.

PETER KRIKES

They also took out a scene we wrote which dealt with the people's mortality and age.

STEVE MEERSON

My favorite scene we wrote was between Bones and Scotty, where they talk about the fact that they're getting too old to be doing this. I personally think they [De-Forest Kelley and James Doohan] would have loved to play it. It was two guys sitting on a park bench in Union Square, completely out of time and space, saying, "We're really getting too old. If we ever do make it back, maybe we ought to give it all up and retire." Then, they both decided that they'll *never* retire, because there's more to life than sitting on your duff.

HARVE BENNETT

I remember saying, "Well, I know it's corny, but it would be better if the marine biologist was a woman. Kirk hasn't had a woman to play to, which he does so wonderfully. The whole series is the woman of the week. Remember that whale special we saw where the girl was bidding adieu to the whale who had to leave Marineland because the female was pregnant, and they could not keep them, and they had to send them back to the sea, and she was bereft? *That's* the lady." Leonard thought it was great. So now we're getting down to where we've got a movie to make and whole new script to write. That's when we were fortunate enough to find that Nicholas Meyer was available.

NICHOLAS MEYER (cowriter, *Star Trek IV: The Voyage Home*)

The other script, which I never read, involved Eddie Murphy. I got this call from [Paramount executives] Dawn Steel and Ned Tanen who said, "We have a situation, we're going to start this movie and we just threw out the script and we need your help and it's your friends." I remember going to meet with Harve and Leonard and saying, "What is it?" And Leonard said something like, "It's something nice." And then they told me the story. And very quickly I could see how it broke down into the bookends in outer space before the journey. And then there's the middle part on Earth. Harve said, "You write the middle part on Earth and I'll write the other parts."

DONALD PETERMAN
(director of photography, *Star Trek IV: The Voyage Home*)

Star Trek always was filmed mostly on a stage before, and they could never use long lenses because it's impossible to get back far enough. On this one, because we shot in San Francisco, we tried to make it a little different by using really long lenses as much as we could. We tried to stay away from all the cliché places. We used the bridge, because that's part of establishing the story, and when we shot downtown we showed part of the Transamerica Building, but we didn't go to Fisherman's Wharf, we stayed around the gritty parts of the city.

Leonard was all dressed in his robes and with his ears on, behind the camera directing the cast—and then he'd step into the scene. It's okay when Robert Redford does it, because he looks like a normal guy, but when you have a guy with long pointed ears, it's different. The most interesting thing about it is that we finally got the *Star Trek* stars out on location.

NICHOLAS MEYER

When I realized they went to San Francisco, I also thought, "Well, hey, I've done this movie before with *Time After Time*. Couldn't they go someplace else?" I suggested Paris. And for whatever reason, they said no, they couldn't go to Paris. Maybe the whales wouldn't fit in the Seine.

LEONARD NIMOY

We were off the soundstages for the first time. The first three pictures were almost exclusively on the soundstages. In *Star Trek I*, we were off the soundstage for a couple of days, on *Star Trek III* we were off for a couple of nights for the Vulcan exterior scenes. To get off the soundstages on this one was very invigorating. It gave a lot more energy to me and the cast of the picture. I had a little bit more time. I shot *Star Trek III* in forty-nine days, and on this one I had fifty-three. Actually, I had fifty-seven—and I came in four days early.

RALPH WINTER

Being on the street in San Francisco with Leonard, the famous five corners place, and a couple of others where we had a camera hidden in a van where Chekov was asking innocent bystanders as they came where the nuclear "wessels" are was hilarious when we were shooting it. We had fun doing it.

DONALD PETERMAN

We also shot in San Diego for a while on the U.S.S. *Ranger,* the same aircraft carrier that was used in *Top Gun*.

RALPH WINTER

It was real-world environments that you hadn't seen, and time travel allowed us to do that. Nick had done *Time After Time* and so he was particularly sensitive about what you can and can't do.

We did some other local locations in L.A. with the transparent aluminum factory and the Apple computer. I wrote that joke for Harve and Leonard. When Scotty picks up the mouse and speaks into it, I said this would be hilarious. They didn't really understand it, so I wrote a little of that scene. We couldn't get Apple to play ball with us and donate some computers, but we ended up using the Apple computer anyway. It felt right, the perfect fish out of water from the twenty-third century coming back and not understanding what computers could do. We shot some of the stuff on the ground in Golden Gate Park, which was Will Rogers State Park in Santa Monica.

EDDIE EGAN

It was a week and a half or so in San Francisco, and things became very tense there between Leonard and Harve. I don't actually know what precipitated it, but the last month of the production was not a particularly happy time for Leonard. There were things going on in his personal life that were distracting him, and just the size of the production was a little hard for him to wrap his head around sometimes. I don't know the details, but I *do* know that at one point Leonard banned Harve from the set.

RALPH WINTER

We also did a lot of old-fashioned effects. For the finale, when they've returned to the future and crashed in the bay, we opened up the water tank at Paramount to do the storm—which had not been used in decades. We cleared out that parking lot, we swept it, washed it down, and Michael Lantieri, who was brought on to be the special-effects guy who had worked at Imagineering at Disney, developed a track below the water and it would have a hump on it and a tail. He found a twenty- by forty-foot-deep hole in the tank that had never been used. It had been filled up with sand. He was poking around with an iron bar and the bar went through and there's a very thin asphalt cap on it. When we dug it out, we realized Paramount built that tank in the twenties or thirties and it had tie-downs and everything, so we used that for building sets.

When Bill goes down underwater to free the whales, that's really Bill doing a lot of that stuff. We built those sets dry and then we filled them with water. The tank hadn't been used in years. We had to call Jimmy the plumber out of retirement, because nobody knew how to turn on the pump. It held over a million gallons of water which had to be filtered, heated, and disinfected. In April of '86, when we were shooting, it was warm outside, so it became the studio swimming pool during lunch hour. The water was only three or four feet deep but a lot people came out and ate their lunch with their feet in the water. We used giant jet fans and fire hoses, smoke machines to create all that fog and put the cast out there in wet suits and hosed them down and created that storm sequence right there. Very old-fashioned filmmaking.

DONALD PETERMAN

We had another unit in Hawaii, right off Maui, photographing live whales. There's a man and his wife there who have a license to allow photography of humpback whales. You have to have a license to get your boat close to them because of the possibility you're going to ram into one of them or scare them. So we cut above the water and got these shots.

RALPH WINTER

It was the first *Star Trek* movie to really get out on location. We spent more than the third movie, we spent twenty-one million dollars, so we had a bigger budget for some of the things that made it feel large. For instance, we spent over a million dollars on the whales. With particular cetacean experts who knew how whales move, what they look like, what the skin texture was. ILM did such a good job on those whales, those whales went on tour for a year or more around the world to museums because the expertise, the art, and science of what they had done was very good. We had a guy who did the basic research for that and he'd been a leading research guy. He just applied the same kind of discipline to this.

One of the reasons we think that it really didn't win visual-effects awards is people didn't really understand how good it was. We did do some live photography of whales out in the Pacific. We gave Mark Ferrari and his wife, Debbie, a sixteen-millimeter camera and sent him out into the Pacific because he was a researcher, and the federal law says you can't get within a thousand yards of a humpback whale. It's against federal guidelines. So Mark knew that, but with the zoom lens they were able to capture some breaching whales where they come out nose first and then they fall on their back and make that big splash. So there's three shots in the movie of real humpback whales doing that. And that's what Leonard wanted.

The remainder of all the whale work in the movie is done in a pool in northern California where they turned off the filter and turned off the pump and put in a very fine dirt that gives it a little more texture. It makes it feel more like you're in the ocean. Sometimes movies do a bad job of the water being too clear. This wasn't too clear. The whales were sort of like windup bathtub toys. Slowing that down, overcranking the camera, gave it a majestic quality, and all of these shots were done in a pool.

We had some federal game-reserve person who came to the studio, and they wanted to screen the movie because they heard there was some violation of the thousand-yard rule. We had a screening and the guy during some of the pool shots said, "I know that is in Hawaii, I know where he shot this." I shut down the screening. I said, "You're wrong. That's in a pool in northern California. If you can't tell that from the real stuff we can't trust that you know what you're talking about." That really added size and scale to that movie that the previous movies didn't have, and it was effects in the real world. It wasn't space effects. That was a big difference that helped contribute to the success of that movie.

NICHOLAS MEYER

It was fun in a weird way. This may be my fanciful recollection, but I don't think I felt a great deal of pressure. The easiest thing for me to do is write dialogue, which is not always what movies are about but, in this case, it was such a no-brainer. It was a comedy and I don't get to write a lot of comedies.

HARVE BENNETT

Nick and I had written the final script of *Star Trek II* in ten days. This one we wrote in about twenty, and it was very simple to do it that way because I took act one and act three and Nick took act two. Now, if you think about that in structural terms, I got us into the dilemma and into time travel, he carried us through San Francisco, and I got us back. That was like breathing for me, because it's pure *Star Trek*. Then we swapped pages and I rewrote him a little bit and he rewrote me a little bit and we put it all together and had a script.

Nick always said, "You know the problem with this script is you've got five endings." And he was right, we *did* have five endings. He said, "Why don't you have the whales save the Earth and let that be the end of the picture?" "No," I said, "that's the end of the picture for the hoped-for extended audience who's never seen *Star Trek* before. But for people who have seen *Star Trek* before, we have a trilogy to complete. So, we've got to get them back, get them off the hook, and give them the *Enterprise* back so that when we finish this picture, we have brought the franchise back to square one and it can go anywhere it wants to go. That's only fair. Besides, that's what the fans want." So that's what we did. We kept every ending.

NICHOLAS MEYER

In my version of the script originally, when they all leave to go back, she [Gillian] didn't leave. She said if anyone's going to make sure this kind of disaster doesn't happen, somebody's going to have to stay behind, which I still think is the "righter" ending. The end in the movie detracts from the importance of people in the present taking responsibility for the ecology and preventing problems of the future by doing something about them today, rather than catering to the fantasy desires of being able to be transported ahead in time to the near-utopian future society of the *Star Trek* era.

RALPH WINTER

We had a great time. The punk on the bus, Kirk Thatcher, was Leonard's assistant, and Leonard gives him the nerve pinch to quiet him down and the bus cheers. We had a hilarious time with that. And then the so-called music coming out of the boom box was our sound-effects designer Mark Mangini and Kirk Thatcher. The two of them composed this song called "I Hate You" and the name of their group was Edge of Etiquette. We had a lot of fun on the side doing all that stuff.

CATHERINE HICKS (actress, "Dr. Gillian Taylor")

I'm really proud of *Star Trek IV*, and that's coming from a non-*Trek* fan. I must have been on another channel as a kid. I've started watching the show since and I'm getting a crush on Spock. But while we were shooting, I deliberately didn't rent the movies, because I thought I would use my total ignorance of Gillian's character. She doesn't know what's going on either.

DeFOREST KELLEY (actor, "Dr. Leonard 'Bones' McCoy")

I have always felt from the very beginning that the core of *Star Trek* was the family. It was always this group of people who were working in this bizarre-type world together. That's what made the show successful. One of the greatest mistakes in the first motion picture was that they neglected the people.

CATHERINE HICKS

I loved her line "I have no one here," before she jumps into the transporter beam. I don't know why, it just touches me. It's poignant and sad. At the time I didn't know it, but seeing the film I realized that was my favorite line. My favorite moment, even though I'm not playing it, is when William Shatner as Kirk quotes D. H. Lawrence. Something comes across the ages. It's such a surprise that this man knows that—it makes us kindred spirits for one second.

WALTER KOENIG (actor, "Pavel Chekov")

I loved the script. I read it in Harve Bennett's office and I chuckled and I said this is wonderful, and it was the only time that I really felt confident that I knew what I was talking about. I didn't see how it could miss. What great fun. It seemed to have everything for mass entertainment approval. For the first time, I felt my dialogue was indigenous to character and only Chekov could say those lines; they were written for him. We had a big crossover audience which accounts for the $109 million domestic that we did. It had wonderful comedy moments, and the scene between Bill and Leonard and Catherine Hicks in the truck is classic. It's spontaneously done even though it may have been shot four or five times—the anachronisms of being three hundred years out of time just worked beautifully as far as I was concerned.

DAVID A. GOODMAN
(executive producer, *Family Guy*)

The cast is at the top of their game in that movie, they've never been better. Especially Shatner and Nimoy, so that's really what you're enjoying. The comedy still works for me, and there's a moment where Spock mind-melds with the whale. You buy that he's actually talking to a whale and the whale understands. That's also the magic of *Star Trek,* you believe in it, you believe in him and it works. It's those little details that make the movie stand above the others in a lot of ways.

LUKAS KENDALL (editor, *Film Score Monthly*)

The most unusual *Star Trek* movie score is Leonard Rosenman's for *Star Trek IV*; Rosenman and Nimoy were good friends. I remember, as a kid, thinking, "Why is there Christmas music in *Star Trek*?" But it captures the spirit of the movie—that was the first time that *Star Trek* was acknowledged as meaningful American pop culture, not just some goofy TV show. It remains the last *Star Trek* score to be nominated for an Oscar.

JOE KRAEMER (composer, *Mission Impossible: Rogue Nation*)

I love the *Star Trek IV* score. I think it is a worthy heir to the music written for many of the original series' lighter episodes, such as "Shore Leave" and "The Trouble with Tribbles." From the opening trumpet statement of Courage's fanfare, to the militaristic main theme, to the quasi-baroque B-theme for the whales, with its contrapuntal descending lines, I find the score inventive, and most important, fun! It's pretty much the only *Trek* feature-film score you can honestly say is fun. I love the Russian theme for Chekov's escape from the navy ship *Enterprise,* and the jaunty romp for the sequence where they break out of the hospital. I also find the use of Courage's theme on the reveal of the *Enterprise-A* at the end one of the best quotes of the original music in the film series. Even the somewhat dated use of the eighties jazz-fusion band Yellowjackets for the Market Street sequence in San Francisco has its charms.

SCOTT MANTZ (film critic, *Access Hollywood*)

The only thing I don't like about *Star Trek IV* is Leonard Rosenman's score. It's too bad they couldn't have James Horner back to complete the trilogy. It's too fantastical. I don't have anything from that score on my iPod.

JOE KRAEMER

It's very much the redheaded stepchild of the film scores, and I've never been able to figure out why. The score for *IV* is almost completely devoid of the dark galactic musical explorations of Goldsmith's contributions, the obsessive intensity of Horner's scores, or the overwhelming sense of dread in Eidelman's score for *VI*.

Instead, Rosenman constructed a more traditional score that pays homage to the series' sixties TV roots with its stacked brass pyramids and delightful woodwind melodies—compare Chekov's Russian music in this film to Finnegan's Irish music in "Shore Leave."

PETER KRIKES

The experience was a real roller coaster for us, but it was the most successful in the series. *That's* a wonderful feeling.

STEVE MEERSON

We were both delighted that we were a part of something that will go on forever, and I also think it said some things that needed to be said. There are some important messages there, and being allowed to have that forum was very exciting. It's hard for me to say this, but it was worth all the aggravation.

RALPH WINTER

The movies endure. I've spoken to elementary schools about what I do and when they read off some of the credits, the kids get excited about *The Voyage Home*. It reminds me that those kids weren't even thought of when we made the movie, and yet they can still enjoy what the movie is about today. It's the lasting effect of what we do as storytellers.

LEONARD NIMOY

The feeling on the first film was that we had to do a "motion picture." Nick Meyer brought a jauntiness back to it. I tried in *Star Trek III* to do a dignified job of resurrection, and do it with a sense of mysticism, a sense of wonder and, above all, to really capture the loyalty of these people for each other; their willingness to sacrifice themselves and their careers for the purpose of helping Spock. Having done that, I really wanted to have a good time. Somebody had been constantly dying in the films, and this time I said, "Nobody's going to die. I don't want anybody hitting anybody" or any of that stuff. If anybody was going to be injured, it was going to be accidental. I insisted that there be no bad guy. We had done two pictures in a row with black-hat heavies, and I didn't want a bad guy anywhere. Circumstances would be the problem. Lack of awareness, lack of concern. Ignorance would be the problem. Not a person. With this one we've really gone full circle and come home, which is why, in a sense, we called it *The Voyage Home*. We're saying, "Enjoy yourself, have a good time, and don't mind us as we drop off a few ideas along the way."

GOD COMPLEX

"WHAT DOES GOD NEED WITH A STARSHIP?"

Given the box-office success of *Star Trek IV: The Voyage Home,* anticipation was high for its June 9, 1989, follow-up. With William Shatner availing himself of the so-called favored-nations clause in his Paramount deal—guaranteeing him anything Leonard Nimoy contractually gets and vice versa—he was ready to take the helm of the newest voyage of the *Enterprise* as director. Additionally, he tasked himself (as was his contractual right) to develop the story line for the film alongside producer Harve Bennett.

Unfortunately, despite the lofty aspirations of everyone involved, *Star Trek V* was reviled by fans and greeted by critical brickbats upon its release, much of it attributable to the subpar visual effects provided by Associates & Ferren, along with studio-mandated humor to "lighten up" the rather dour proceedings in the hopes of duplicating *Star Trek IV*'s incredible box-office success.

With a lackluster domestic gross of only $52,210,000, *The Final Frontier*'s title almost proved prophetic for the future of the original motion-picture franchise.

RALPH WINTER (executive producer, *Star Trek V: The Final Frontier*)

All the years working on the *Star Trek* movies were terrific. It was very enjoyable and good people. We had fun. We had challenges like any movies, but it was sort of can't-do-anything-wrong years. But *Star Trek V* almost killed the franchise. There were so many problems with that movie. It just didn't resonate with the audience and Larry Luckinbill, who played Sybok, is a great actor, but it all came off a little too operatic and a little too interior. There wasn't a bad guy to battle who seemed to be as strong. It seemed to be a remake of a TV show, and the audience responded that way.

HARVE BENNETT (producer, *Star Trek V: The Final Frontier*)

I would say the *Star Trek* trilogy probably stands because of its centering on the life, death, and resurrection of Spock. This film is continuous only in the sense of time. What we are trying to do in each picture is explore other angles and other undiscovered depths of these very legendary and familiar characters. And that's not too easy, because you reach a point where you say, "How much more can we explore these people?" But remember, these people are also aging, which they did not do in the series. So as they age, they are revealing more and more of their back- and foreground stories. That's where the challenge is for me: to try to keep mining these relationships.

Star Trek V also has with it an imperative of going back to deep space. *Star Trek II, III,* and *IV* were all, to some extent, manageable in terms of budget, shooting time, and scope. With *Star Trek V* we came to the space imperative and we had some very, very difficult appetites: planetary and construction appetites, things you have to show and places you have to go, and an alien here and there. All these things make the cost and complexity of the film more difficult.

DAVID LOUGHERY (writer, *Star Trek V: The Final Frontier*)

Something I've noticed in all sequels, and it's true of the Bond films, certainly. Each time you make another movie, they get more and more abstract. The situation gets kind of broader and stranger and sort of out of control a little bit, because, basically, you've done the thing so many times that you've always got to try and do something a little bit more the next time. This is always a problem with sequels in that they get bigger and the themes increase and get larger, too, and you get farther and farther away from the truly basic appeal of the films, which are the characters that we've fallen in love with. If you can do a great drama that just takes place between these characters in one room, the audience wouldn't give a shit. They'd love it. They're not really that interested in the spaceship effects, but we keep trying to get bigger and bigger. You know, "Let's go visit God" and all these gigantic things.

WILLIAM SHATNER (actor/director, *Star Trek V: The Final Frontier*)

I took the TV evangelist persona and created a holy man who thought God had spoken to him. He believed God had told him, "I need many followers, and I need a vehicle to spread my word through the universe." The vehicle he needed became a starship, which the holy man would captain when it came to rescue some hostages he had taken. Finally the *Enterprise* arrives at the planet where God supposedly resides, in the center of the universe. Kirk, Spock, McCoy, and the holy man are beamed down to the planet. It's like drawings of Dante's inferno, like a flaming hell. When God appears, he seems like God . . . but gradually, in a conversation between God and the holy man, Kirk perceives that something is wrong and begins to challenge God. God gets angrier and angrier and begins to show his true colors, which are those of the Devil. So essentially that was my story: that man conceives of God in his own image, but those images change from generation to generation, therefore he appears in all these different guises as man-made gods. But in essence, if the Devil exists, God exists by inference. This is the lesson that the *Star Trek* group learns. The lesson being that God is within our hearts, not something we conjure up, invent, and worship.

DAVID LOUGHERY

Paramount liked Bill's outline, but they thought it was a little too dark. After the success of *Star Trek IV*, they wanted to make sure that we retained as much humor and fun as possible, because they felt that was one of the reasons for the big success of that film. They wanted us to inject a spirit of fun and adventure into the story. They just wanted a balance between the darker elements and some of the lighter stuff. Everybody felt they'd had their romp and now they were getting a little more serious again, but let's keep that spark alive.

WALTER KOENIG (actor, "Pavel Chekov")

I think when comedy comes out of story it can be enormously affecting and successful. When it's a sidebar or artificially transplanted onto your story, then it's not as successful. What happened with *Star Trek V* is that we had comedy that either had nothing to do with the story—like the campfire scenes—or it somehow diffused the dramatic moments, like the climax of the story when Kirk is saying "What does God need with a starship?" In *Star Trek IV*, it was the perfect marriage.

DAVID LOUGHERY

One particular change that resulted was in the character of the holy man, Sybok. Originally he was a very messianic, possessed kind of figure who was willing to trample anyone who got in his way, but he began to remind us too much of Khan and we had to take him in a different direction. It would have been easy to write Sybok as a black-hat, but that was, again, too much like Khan.

HARVE BENNETT

The problem with *Star Trek V* was to take a talented and wonderful man, Bill Shatner, and try and dissuade him from doing the story he wanted to do. I had not wanted to do *Star Trek V*. I was told Bill was going to direct it, and I said fine, and then Bill had story approval, which I said was a terrible situation—especially once I heard the story he wanted to do.

RALPH WINTER

Star Trek V was not a good movie. After the success of *IV*, we were all sort of smoking our own publicity shots and thought everything was going to work out just fine. From a variety of things, the production, the visual effects were horrible and Bill was committed to direct because he agreed to let Leonard direct *IV*. But Leonard had that gene and Bill didn't. And Bill hasn't gone on to do much else in directing. It's a different skill set. And it wasn't bad. Bill was very enjoyable to work with; we had a lot of fun. I laughed more on the production of that movie than anything I've worked on. But ultimately it just wasn't good storytelling. It was too interior. It actually, in some ways if you think about it, was kind of a remake of the first movie. But we were blinded and didn't see all of that ourselves.

EDDIE EGAN (unit publicist, *Star Trek IV: The Voyage Home*)

I don't think he was the guy who should have been at the helm of that movie and the way he works affected every aspect of it. But, look, we've all been in work environments where there are people in a work dynamic that everyone sort of just skirts around and doesn't want to deal with. Then you finally give up dealing because of that, and the best thing to do as a boss is to remove that person from the mix, because it's ruining the dynamic of the larger group. Here, you had a guy—and I'm not saying negative or positive about him—who had that kind of dynamic. He's argumentative and has a very, very healthy ego, and an ego fueled by watching his costar reap the benefits of directing the previous two movies. Unfortunately I just think he wasn't as collaborative as Leonard is by nature. I think Bill is more of a seat of the pants kind of guy. He's not going to take time to think about things. He's just going to show up that day and say, "Let's try this," and a lot of *Star Trek V* feels that way.

WILLIAM SHATNER

What the final result was, was the final result. I have certain regrets, but I feel in total that a lot of the vision was there. I made one major compromise at the beginning, which was mitigating the original idea of the *Enterprise* searching for God. The enormous thrust of the idea was eviscerated and that was my first compromise. It seemed that was a necessary one due to the fact everybody was very apprehensive about the obvious problem. I thought [the film] was flawed. I didn't manage my resources as well as I could have, and I didn't get the help in managing my resources I could have. I thought it was a meaningful *attempt* at a story and it was a meaningful play. It carried a sense of importance about it.

DAVID LOUGHERY

It became one of those three-week skull sessions where Harve, Bill, and I sat in a room and came up with a story line that Paramount approved, and then I went ahead and wrote the screenplay, which went through many, many rewrites, as these things often do.

The idea of God and the Devil was reflected in the script's earlier drafts. Those drafts were much cleaner and more comprehensible in terms of the idea that you think you're going to Heaven, but you turn out to have found Hell. We weren't literally saying Heaven and Hell, but we were suggesting the idea that it was, like, "Wait a minute, is this God or the Devil?" without saying specifically that it's either, but instead is an alien entity that has tapped into our perceptions about where they're going.

We wanted to challenge the audience's imagination and expectations when they realized that this is what Sybok's divine mission was. We really wanted the audience to stir around, look at each other, and say, "Are they serious? Can they possibly mean that we're going to see God?" Because, for me, *Star Trek* is the only arena in which you might actually try to do that. *Star Trek* has always been big enough to encompass almost any kind of concept, so we thought when we dropped the bomb and said, "Oh, by the way, we're going to see God," it would be something the audience would be excited about and say, "Gee, maybe they will . . . who knows?" We did, however, run into some problems, one with Gene Roddenberry.

GENE RODDENBERRY
(executive consultant, *Star Trek V: The Final Frontier*)

I would have not done it that way. I suggested the idea that saved it in a small way—let what they find be a powerful alien who thought it was God. Originally, the alien *was* God, a very bad idea. No one person made it terrible, and no one wanted it to be terrible.

DAVID LOUGHERY

Maybe when Gene wrote *The God Thing* back in the 1970s he turned around and figured that it didn't work, and it wouldn't work the way we were doing it either. I just don't know. We managed to pull off something that is able to tread the line.

WILLIAM SHATNER

Gene did come down strongly against the story and set up circumstances that were negative and unfortunate. There's nothing wrong with a good story about the search for the meaning of life. That's basic to any great storytelling, no matter what form it takes, whether it's the Bible or a myth or a fairy tale. I was hoping to be able to accomplish that with *Star Trek V.*

DAVID LOUGHERY

I don't think it was too controversial and I don't think anyone was too radically upset by what we did, although it seems to me that *Star Trek* was always meeting God in some way or another. The idea permeated many of the old episodes, and it certainly played a part in the first movie.

HARVE BENNETT

If the logline in *TV Guide* does not interest you, then it's a pretty good indication that the premise of the story is not interesting. The logline of *Star Trek V* is "Tonight on *Star Trek*, the crew goes to find God." If you saw that in an episode of anything, you'd say "That's a hoot, isn't it?" No one is going to find God, because that's like finding the fountain of youth, which was, incidentally, Shatner's backup story.

DAVID LOUGHERY

Beyond the whole God concept, I was also thinking of the Kirk, Spock, and McCoy relationship. One of the things that occurred to me is that if you look at *Star Trek,* you see these three men who are in middle age and their lives have been spent in space. They're not married, they don't have families, so their relationship is with each other. They represent a family to each other, maybe without always acknowledging it. That, to me, was the most attractive thing, saying "What is family?" If it's not three people who care about each other, I don't know what it is.

The only scene that I can think of that never changed at all, and it was one of the first scenes I wrote, was that campfire sequence. I know there are a lot of people who were kind of upset by that scene, but I love it. It was pure character, and I think that's why I wanted to do *Star Trek* in the first place.

The evolving screenplay became the story of the Vulcan Sybok abducting representatives from the Federation as well as the Klingon and Romulan empires, and using them as bait to lure a starship. Naturally that starship is the *Enterprise,* which Sybok (who improbably turns out to be Spock's half brother), utilizing great prowess in Vulcan mind control, gains command of. By freeing crew members from their greatest personal pain, he is able to recruit his army of followers. Even Spock and McCoy are swayed to his side, leaving Kirk to take on Sybok alone.

The last was a plot point that didn't sit well with either Leonard Nimoy or DeForest Kelley, who not only felt their characters wouldn't betray Kirk, but that their "greatest pains" (in Spock's case, his half-human, half-Vulcan heritage; and in McCoy's, performing an act of euthanasia on his slowly dying father) were ill-conceived.

DAVID LOUGHERY

One of the smart things we did early on was bring Leonard and De in to go over the script, because we wanted their input. These guys have lived with these characters, at that time, for more than twenty years and have very strong opinions on what their characters would and wouldn't do. There were problems with this, too, however. As originally conceived, only Kirk held out against Sybok, which gives you more of a one-man-stands-alone kind of thing, betrayed by his best friends. Leonard and De objected and it was changed. Suddenly there were three guys against Sybok. When you start doing that kind of stuff, bit by bit you remove and dilute the real strength of the original vision and finally you end up with a bit of a mishmash. It would have been great for Kirk to have squared off against Spock in some way. But you find the script beginning to accommodate the needs of the actors, who know their characters and say, "Spock wouldn't do that." It's kind of indefensible. You don't really have an argument that can turn them around on something like that.

DeFOREST KELLEY

When the scene was first presented to me, it was a little harsher. Once we smoothed it out, I still knew it was going to be a difficult scene to do, and I felt if it didn't come off exactly right, we could be in trouble.

WILLIAM SHATNER

After De read the script, he didn't want to do the scene. So I took him to lunch and tried to convince him it would work. I said, "De, this is the best scene you've had to play in a long time." He's such a wonderful actor, and I really felt he hadn't had a chance recently to show what he was capable of doing. Finally, after much talking, I convinced him to do it.

DeFOREST KELLEY

I don't know whether the public realizes it or not, but a character that people have watched for so many years was being stripped in front of them of a very private and secretive situation that took place in his life. That moment of McCoy's privacy in *Star Trek V* would have been divulged to Kirk before anyone. His opening line, "Oh my God, don't do this to me," meant so many things: he knew that it was happening to him there, in front of these people. Plus the fact that he had to relive it again was tough.

WILLIAM SHATNER

His one stipulation was that we add an explanation of why McCoy committed the euthanasia. We added a short bit of dialogue where Sybok asks, "Why did you do it?" and McCoy answers, "To preserve his dignity." With these new lines, De felt that McCoy's motivations were clearer and more understandable.

DeFOREST KELLEY

The more I looked at it and studied the scene, the more important it became to me, because it's a topic that goes on today. I thought it would be interesting to lay it out in the presence of a motion-picture audience and let them decide within themselves what is right or wrong.

Along with the challenges inherent in realizing the flawed screenplay were myriad production problems, including the originally conceived finale. In that sequence, a horde of gargoyles are released on "God's" planet and attack the landing party. Captain Kirk must also confront a giant rock man, a concept successfully realized many years later in Galaxy Quest to more comedic effect. As a result of budgetary issues, all these elements were excised from the final film.

WILLIAM SHATNER

I didn't have the sense to hoard my money for the grand finale. I was very busy spending wonderful dollars fighting for effects in the opening. I'm not that much of a neophyte not to know that you need a good opening, but I hurt my finale by not having enough money. Nothing I could do to the studio would make them say, "Here's another three million dollars for more gargoyles and special effects," which it needed.

DAVID LOUGHERY

When the torpedo came down and explodes the hole, it's like the bottle is uncapped and the imps spill out, free, and chase our characters back to the shuttle. That was our original concept. A movie, especially a movie like this one, goes through so many transformations from original story to final film. Because of all the hands involved in the making of these movies, it sometimes starts to take on a committee atmosphere to moviemaking. Things don't turn out exactly the way you originally wanted them to, but there are reasons for that.

WILLIAM SHATNER

I was required to reduce the budget, and I kept slicing away at the ending. I didn't realize until we got there how much of the ending I had lost and what a disservice I had done to the film. That was lesson number one.

RALPH WINTER

We never ran out of money. We ran out of good ideas and good execution. What we thought with the rock creature was just completely silly and we bagged it. It became obvious that it was just silly and it would have been more expensive. On some of these movies, the third act doesn't get developed at the same pace.

DAVID LOUGHERY

We certainly wish we could have hung on to some of the concept. That sequence got lost when it became financially impossible for us to create the gargoyle creatures. You're always sorry to see those things go, because your imagination is one thing and the budget is something else. In various places, we had to make certain cuts and rearrangements based on how much we could afford.

HARVE BENNETT

Basically, I was called in to control Bill's appetites. They were extravagant because he didn't know anything. He had spent all those years in front of the camera, and believed because he had directed *T.J. Hooker* and Leonard had done it, he could too. Bill would come in and present a concept and he thought he was discovering the wheel. It's funny how first-time directors try to be pioneers in the craft.

WILLIAM SHATNER

It's like youth. I wish I were able to say it was because of my youth. A first-time director knows no boundaries, and it's not knowing them that you shatter them. Rather than accepting the status quo, I tried to break boundaries and make the camera do things that it wasn't supposed to, not because I didn't know how, but I thought that by standing firm and being as adamant as possible it would happen. But there came a point where I had to compromise. I was rushing around trying to save what I thought was my movie, but I had spent days and weeks with Harve telling him the story and him telling me his version of the story and the script, and we worked in a very close and intimate way. It got to the point where we were talking about the death and birth of people close to us, and there were times where tears passed between us in the intimacy of his office. These moments are part of *Star Trek V* for me. If anybody else is doing another trip, that's their problem.

ANDREW LASZLO
(director of photography, *Star Trek V: The Final Frontier*)

Working with Bill was a great incentive, because, frankly, when an outsider directs a *Star Trek* movie, I don't think it measures up. If they had called me and said, "We'd like you to shoot this film and it'll be directed by so-and-so famous director," the attraction would have been a great deal less. The reason I was attracted by the aspect of Bill directing the film is that he has *been Star Trek,* he *is Star Trek.* You remove him from the scene and there is no *Star Trek.* Who understands *Star Trek* better from the point of view of its special audience than the person who is *Star Trek*? I also wanted to do it because it was part of a very famous and well-known series, and having done a couple of those before, such as *First Blood* and *Poltergeist II,* I wanted to get another one under my belt.

WILLIAM SHATNER

Technically, it went well, I thought. We hired a lot of different people. We went to New York and got other special-effects people. So we experimented and I had to learn a great deal, not only about film but the politics of film.

ANDREW LASZLO

We were both under different kinds of pressure having to do with the tightness of the schedule and different ways of doing things. And this sometimes pitted us against each other. I understood that Bill was under tremendous pressure, this being his first big movie, especially since he hoped to match the success of Leonard Nimoy. Sometimes these pressures resulted in creative differences, but we managed to do the film not in spite of them, but because of them. It was a great experience and somehow, as we went through it together, we became good friends.

WALTER KOENIG

I read the script in Harve's office and I was trying to be diplomatic, because we had already had problems in terms of discussing story, and I told him, "Don't you think coming back and doing the campfire scene at the end is sort of gilding the lily?" He said, "Yes, I do, but he wants to shoot it that way and in the editing, we'll pull it way back." That didn't happen, but that's what he said to me.

HARVE BENNETT

It was a passive premise. The chore became to make the trip as interesting as possible, and to that extent we succeeded. The film was real good until the moment when the inevitable truth poked its head out and said, "Hey, this isn't God," and everyone said, "We knew that all the time, but we were having a good time up until then."

LEONARD NIMOY (actor, "Mr. Spock")

Bill worked very, very hard and he directed it as well and as capably as any of our other films. He was not riding on a good script. If you're not riding on a good script, you're the person people point fingers at. And he was responsible. It was his story. I've had that experience. I did a movie for Paramount [*Funny About Love*] that didn't work at all. I wasn't successful with the script.

DAVID LOUGHERY

In retrospect, you look back from the distance of a number of years, and I've always felt—it was always in the back of my head—that one of the problems is that it's a reactive story rather that an active one. What I mean by that is that our guys are kind of required to stand by and be dragged along on somebody else's quest. In this case, Sybok's. It's sort of *his* quest and *his* passion, and Kirk, Spock, McCoy, and the rest of the crew are dragged along almost as though they were a supporting cast to this guy. If it had been Kirk who suddenly had this vision of God and hijacked his own ship and turned against the Federation, *then* you've got this much more active, passionate kind of story.

LEONARD NIMOY

I complained. I said, "I think you've got some problems here," and the message I got back is "We know what we've got and we know what we want to do." Having sent in my notes, once they got them it's not my place to say "You must do the following." Once the tank starts rolling, it's tough to stop it. It's very interesting. You cannot draw a rule and say "It must be done this way." Sometimes things bubble together and sometimes they don't, even though you've got very well-paid and professional people doing the job. Sometimes it works and sometimes it doesn't and that's why some pictures succeed and some pictures fail.

WALTER KOENIG

I didn't initially feel the project was doomed. Bill's a bright man. He understands the camera very well. I don't think he has as good a story sense as he does of camera and how to direct. I never said I felt the picture failed because of his direction. It failed because of the story concept. I don't think it was well thought out. We had the same problem we had on *Star Trek: The Motion Picture*. We had an antagonist who changes, who goes through a metamorphosis, and suddenly the guy that we've been booing and hissing is one of us and we introduce a whole other character to be an antagonist at the end of the story without building to this and without ever having a sense of learning to fear and to hate the evil entity.

JAMES DOOHAN (actor, "Montgomery 'Scotty' Scott")

All we needed, and all of us say this, was a good script. Unfortunately, we didn't have one in *V,* and even that made pretty darn good money for an ordinary movie. It was just a very bad script and a lot of things were badly done. He was not up to the task, there's no doubt about that, and one of Bill's problems is that Bill thinks of Bill whereas with Leonard, he thinks of the show and he thinks of himself second.

WILLIAM SHATNER

Yes, the cast loved Leonard, and why not? He's a very lovable person. I don't know why, a couple of people of the cast—and they've never said it to my face—didn't enjoy making the film with me.

WALTER KOENIG

What it speaks to is that the supporting cast doesn't have the influence with the executives in the front office that the big three do. Originally, Leonard and De-Forest's characters fell sway [to Sybok's mind control] and Kirk was the only one that didn't and they objected rightly, but the rest of us weren't in a position to object. In my case, the onus was pretty much off of me because you didn't see me convert and the consequences of the conversion. I abhorred the idea because it was really a religious conversion the way it was originally written, which was particularly objectionable. The holier-than-thou sort of stuff was almost a Moonies kind of thing.

EDDIE EGAN

I think these actors have told these stories so many times that they actually believe they happened. Is Bill a larger-than-life actor with an ego? Absolutely. Are the others? Absolutely. But they're *not* the hero of this story. No one would ever construct a story that is equal part Kirk, Spock, McCoy, or Scotty. It wouldn't work. You wouldn't know who to focus on. They were brilliant actors playing supporting roles, and it's not something I think they ever acclimated themselves to in the structure of the movies as opposed to how they are hailed and received and applauded at conventions. People take little Shatner bits and exaggerate them. He was a guy with a job. He just wasn't as gregarious as the others and Leonard was more gregarious than he was, because Leonard is just more curious about people and he likes conversations. But I really think that a lot of the situation is telling a story so much that you now believe it, and it's like the Brian Williams effect. Every time you tell it, you add a layer to it until it implodes.

So the idea that they should be equal is nuts. I mean, even DeForest Kelley, the nicest man on Earth who could have taken some issue with not being a true trinity, knew his place and knew what his character was. And that character was designed and welcomed as the voice between the hot head and the logical one. He was happy to be that voice.

RALPH WINTER

We were one of the few who have actually been able to shoot anything inside of Yosemite. That's a national treasure. They were terrific. We left it better than we found it and they were happy with us. We got some spectacular footage. The second-unit director who did all the climbing footage up El Capitan is the father of the lead singer of Maroon 5. I remember him giving me a tape of his son's band.

ANDREW LASZLO

We went to great expense and a lot of difficulty to visit various locations, including Yosemite National Park and Trona Pinnacles. The opening sequence, a variation on the long-lens shot of Omar Sharif riding his camel toward camera in *Lawrence of Arabia,* as well as some of the later sequences, were shot in the California desert where we built an entire little town that was supposedly on this hostile, arid planet. We actually landed the shuttlecraft by suspending it from a huge construction crane. Not only does it land on the sand dunes, but a second later the rear hatch opens and out pop a bunch of marines who jump over the camera, followed by the crew of the *Enterprise.* We did that in a single shot. Everything becomes very difficult when you work in the sand—vehicles can't move, especially those that can transport and then lift a very large eight-thousand-pound object.

HARVE BENNETT

We did some reshooting. We did do a day and a half that Bill directed to tie certain things together, compared to hundreds of other movies that go out and shoot five weeks and millions of dollars. You're speaking about a day and a half of pickup shots. There was an absence of understanding with the Klingons. There was no understanding about why the guy [Klaa] apologizes to Kirk. That was necessary because of the evolution of the Klingon relationship in *The Next Generation*.

DAVID LOUGHERY

One of the things that was cut out of the movie is that the reason Captain Klaa was so passionate about chasing down Kirk was that he not only wanted that feather in his cap, but because there was still a bounty on Kirk's head. That was a thematic thing that would have joined into the next movie. Then they had this ridiculous reshoot that was done without me in which Kirk comes aboard the *Enterprise*. In the original script he walks in on the Bird of Prey, the chair turns, and here's Spock. They have this embrace—"Please, Captain, not in front of the Klingons"—and there's a big laugh. But they went back and shot this bit where Klaa is forced to step out and say, "I apologize." Their thinking there, I guess, is that he had gone off on his own after Kirk. That was something that bugged me. The only thing I do get out of it that's really pleasurable is that during that reshoot, which was two or three months afterward, in the close-up of Bill his face looks about ten pounds fatter than in the previous shot. So there's a little bit of revenge there, although I don't blame Bill for that. Or anybody, really. It's just one of those situations where they felt they had to plug a hole.

WILLIAM SHATNER

Having done a quick course with Joseph Campbell, I've realized the magic of *Star Trek* is to provide a mythology that this culture doesn't have. As he pointed out, mythology relates man to his environment and tries to explain some inexplicable dilemmas and the dichotomies that face us. Because of the construction of our culture, we don't have time for that because all of us are busy solving these problems with science. I think mythology is best served by an individual, along with his hearty band of brothers, as was done so many times, so well by the Greeks.

Not since the Robert Abel debacle on *Star Trek: The Motion Picture* had visual effects proved to be such a detriment to one of the features. For *Star Trek II, III,* and *IV,* the studio relied on the safe choice of George Lucas's Industrial Light & Magic. For *Star Trek V,* the producers turned to East Coast–based Associates & Ferren to create the film's elaborate visuals. But unlike on the 1979 film—when the studio fired Abel and replaced him with Douglas Trumbull and John Dykstra's Apogee, who created some of the most stunning visual effects of all time—Paramount had no appetite this time for incurring any cost overruns, and as a result accepted the largely amateurish special effects. After *Star Trek V,* ILM was again hired for every *Star Trek* movie up until *Nemesis,* on which they were replaced by Digital Domain.

RALPH WINTER

I took a lot of personal hits about that and I feel a tremendous sense of responsibility and it hurts. At the time, I made the decision on what I felt would be best for the picture. It was not a capricious decision. It was based on testing we all did. There were a number of people involved in that decision, but I was leading the process. I felt like we were going to get something better and, in the beginning, we did . . . but it didn't work out that way.

BRAN FERREN (visual effects supervisor, Associates & Ferren)

There was a lot of time wasted on this film. Ultimately, every model we received from Paramount had to be completely refurbished prior to shooting. We had to have Greg Jein build some new ones while we created five planet landscapes and moons as well. One entire side of the *Enterprise* model was spray-painted matte gray, destroying the meticulous original paint job. We had to go in and fix it before we could shoot it, which took two painters and assistant about six weeks to do.

WILLIAM SHATNER

We had problems that we might not have had if we had different personnel. I followed other people's leads because I did not have firsthand knowledge of these things, but I was in on the decision so I make no excuse for that. It's an instance where my lack of experience showed.

RALPH WINTER

We were high on the success of *IV*. We thought we could no wrong. David Loughery, the writer, had done a lot of good movies. It was all within the construct of what Bill and Harve wanted to do. And Leonard was a part of that. But we almost killed the franchise. My part in killing it almost was the digital effects. I was reacting against the high costs of ILM, and so we went with another company. Bran Ferren sold us on a lot of cool technology at the time. He's a brilliant man. Ultimately, he was a mile wide in terms of his ability and intelligence, but the follow-through and infrastructure of actually delivering fell apart. And so, in the crush of trying to get that work done, he just didn't have the infrastructure to make it happen. All of his film had to go through one machine to get all the work out and we couldn't do it in time, so he had to compromise. The effects on that movie are dreadful. ILM knows how to deliver. The chance we took to save money and get fresh ideas is just too difficult to do on a franchise big-budget movie. It almost ended my career and the franchise. I took a lot of heat for it. You know: "How could you let this happen?"

HARVE BENNETT

That's peripheral. You should have seen ILM's tests for God. They were silly. We went with the creative judgment that Bran had a more vigorous attack to help us sell the illusions, and it was a picture, as discussed, that needed fancy footwork. In addition to that, it is only correct to note that by the time we were ready to start, ILM was overcrowded. We would have been the fourth or fifth major picture, and we would have received at their hands, not withstanding our relationships, the D team instead of the A team. That was an important consideration. All the people we had worked with [before] were booked.

KENNY MYERS
(makeup effects supervisor, *Star Trek V: The Final Frontier*)

How do you make God? When they said we had to make God, I went crazy! Our first question was whether to go for that classic Jesus look, or for an alien look. The first thing Bill suggested was to think of the audience—a lot of baby boomers—and their ideas of God. We decided we needed something people could immediately identify with, so we chose Charlton Heston's Moses combined with God as depicted on the Sistine Chapel ceiling as the look that would sell most people. It's that long flowing white-haired look combined with that very fatherly, smooth talker that just makes you feel comfortable.

BRAN FERREN

A project like *Star Trek* allowed us to fuse a lot of different technologies together simultaneously—integration of transportable data files from computer graphic systems to electron microscopes to optical printers—that actually worked rather well on a project like this. It's the only way we could have done it all in three months. Still, it was a fun project to do. But it would've been nice to have had a year.

WALTER KOENIG

No matter what my differences are with Bill, each time he has said he would do one of these films, no matter how outrageous the discrepancies in salaries are, I breathe a sigh of relief and say thank you, because I know the pictures *wouldn't* be made unless he was there and he knows they wouldn't be made, and that's why he's so difficult sometimes.

RALPH WINTER

I had a great time with Bill. He was terrific and a lot of fun. I enjoyed it a lot.

DAVID A. GOODMAN (coexecutive producer, *Futurama*)

Almost every line of dialogue is a cliché: "They don't make them like they used to; the right tool for the right job; I know this ship like the back of my hand." It's terrible writing.

JAMES DOOHAN

The only reason that I agreed to it was they had spent two hundred thousand dollars on that set. I can tell you for certain that it took at least thirty-five takes for me to build up to that scene where I knock myself out. I'm usually called "one-take Doohan," but I was not happy, and nobody was happy with Bill.

WALTER KOENIG

My main concern was [whether] Bill was going to manipulate us and to reinterpret our characters. In fact, he was quoted in *Starlog* as saying he's had things he wanted to change in our characters for years and this is our opportunity. A more pretentious comment I couldn't believe, and I was very upset about that, and I was angry, and I told George and Nichelle and Jimmy if at any point he picks on any of us, I'm walking off the set. I will not stand for that, he cannot do that to us. I had heard stories about him from *T.J. Hooker* when he directed, and even when he didn't direct, how he had caused grief for other people, and that's what I was anticipating.

I had underestimated Bill again . . . he was so cordial and so generous with his approbation that it became almost a gag. I would say, "Yessir, Captain," and he would say, "Walt, wonderful, wonderful!" He was very affirming and very supportive. I knew the part would be small, he's talked about how the big three is what carried the TV series and that he wanted to do an episode of the series on a bigger level. So I knew the part was going to be very small, but as it is I still had more to do on *Star Trek V* than I did on *Star Trek VI*. I only worked eight days on the picture, so I didn't have any time to develop an animosity, and the way he dealt with us was very pleasant.

SCOTT MANTZ (film critic, *Access Hollywood*)

I saw *Star Trek V* on the day it came out. I went to the GCC Northeast Philadelphia where I grew up and felt like I had seen the "Spock's Brain" of *Star Trek* movies. What the hell was that? It was embarrassing. "Row, row, row your boat." The special effects were awful. "Jim, please, not in front of the Klingons." I mean, c'mon, it was bad. I walked out of that movie with my phaser between my legs. Just embarrassed. I cannot watch *Star Trek V*. It is unwatchable to me . . . like *Generations, Insurrection,* and *Nemesis.*

DAVID A. GOODMAN

McCoy is watching Kirk on El Capitan in the beginning of the movie, and he's got twentieth-century binoculars, and Kirk is tiny and falls off the mountain. McCoy starts running and he gets there immediately. There are a couple of good action scenes in the beginning, but in general, the casting is terrible. I liked the idea of Nimbus III. I've always liked those things in *Star Trek* where we're shown that not everything works out great. And the ending is terrible. I know the plans had him being chased by rock monsters, but the ending doesn't seem to make any sense.

I'm also not a religious person, but it takes the cheap way out saying God "is right here, the human heart." It's like you're just going to dismiss thousands of years of human religion with *that*? Either explore it and say something or just stay away from it—but I still watched it *way* too many times.

RONALD D. MOORE
(supervising producer, *Star Trek: The Next Generation*)

It seemed cheap on the screen technically. It didn't look like it was made as well as the other movies; the visual effects were terrible. The story was just not compelling and it felt silly at some points. It was indulging silliness—not humor, but just silliness. I just didn't think it worked. The "row, row, row your boat" scene is nice and it's sweet and sentimental, though it's turning up the saccharine level pretty high, but you could deal with it. If everything else in the movie had worked, it would have been regarded as just a sweet wonderful little scene in a good movie, but as it is, it set the tone that they were going to a weird silly place.

HARVE BENNETT

The appetite for *Star Trek* movies was seriously impacted by the success of *Next Generation*, not destroyed, just kind of subdivided, and the feeding frenzy we experienced on *Star Trek II, III*, and *IV* did not exist on *V*, even if it had been a better movie.

RALPH WINTER

If you develop a story that says "We're going to look for God," right away you might be disappointed because what you find may not be what you think you should find. So that's very tough story material to grab a hold of.

RONALD D. MOORE

When I was doing an interview for the Shatner documentary on *The Next Generation,* David Gerrold was there and was saying to Shatner as I walked in the door that "What does God need with a starship?" is one of the great Kirk lines . . . and it's one of the greatest lines in cinema. I just remember thinking, "You've got to be fucking kidding me. Really?" I didn't buy that line at all. He said it and I went, "Really?" It felt like they'd strained to get to this point where he can say this line.

WILLIAM SHATNER

It took me a while to take another look at *Star Trek V.* In the end, I think I learned a great deal directing a multimillion-dollar picture like that. It was an enormous responsibility to be in control of that much money, and I realized that I hadn't spent the money wisely in allowing for a big finale. I'd blown it in the first half and had nothing in the second.

DENNY MARTIN FLINN
(writer, *Star Trek VI: The Undiscovered Country*)

Part of working on sequels is adding to something that already exists, and what exists works real well, so don't fuck it up. That's a tremendous responsibility. With *Star Trek* I, the studio said, "If it hadn't cost us forty-five million dollars, we would have made more money." It bombed critically too, and it was Harve Bennett who came along and got back to what had driven the episodes, which is a bit of action-adventure with a strong guest star. *One* was a bore and *V* also suffers terribly from something that is a dangerous formula to film. If you spend two hours telling people "Wait until you see what's around this corner," you had better have something around that corner to show them, whether it's a monster or a concept of God or whatever the hell it is. They were big letdowns.

RALPH WINTER

Three or four weeks after we finished shooting, Bill goes, "I'm done. I've cut the movie together and I'm done." I looked at Harve and we just shook our heads, because you need time in the cutting room to retell the story and shape it. But there is no way you can do it in a three-week period. That's the first indication that we were in trouble. We needed more time and more work and we had to figure it out. And then you have to take a chance of putting your baby out there ahead of time to a crowd and seeing what they say. That's always hard.

WILLIAM SHATNER

Directing film is a wild adventure for anyone equipped to do it. I made compromises on *Star Trek V* thinking I had to do that, that's the nature of the business. But the line where you do not compromise I couldn't tread because of a number of factors, not the least of which is my own nature. I got to learn when it's time to stand and when it's time to turn. That, really, for a knowledgeable person in the business is a more important lesson than where the camera is and how to play a scene and what your establishing shot is. Those mechanics of making a film no longer become a point of discussion, it's automatic, it's there creatively. I had the most joyful time of my life directing *Star Trek V*.

RALPH WINTER

Recently, I noticed the front page of *The New York Times* showcased some guys that are free-climbing El Capitan with no ropes. I tweeted Bill Shatner, saying, "Check out the front page of *The New York Times*. I think you did this in the future."

UP THE ACADEMY

"I AM A GRADUATE OF STARFLEET ACADEMY;
I KNOW MANY THINGS."

After the box-office implosion of *Star Trek V,* producer Harve Bennett sold Paramount on a plan to reboot the franchise with a prequel film, *The Academy Years,* that would show how Kirk, Spock, and McCoy first met at Starfleet Academy—a film that he would direct. In many ways anticipating J. J. Abrams's reinvention, *The Academy Years* would have starred a new cast replacing the pricey original ensemble. William Shatner and Leonard Nimoy would have reprised their roles in bookends designed to introduce and end the film. At the time, the announcement was greeted by much antipathy on the part of creator Gene Roddenberry and the fans as well as the original cast, which feared losing a lucrative gig. Its ultimate cancellation marked an acrimonious end to the Harve Bennett era of *Star Trek.*

DAVID LOUGHERY (writer, *The Academy Years*)

Every time they went to make one of these *Star Trek* movies, the producers and the studio always ran into the same problem in getting the original cast together. The reasons for that are money, power, creative differences, ego, health, unavailability . . . all of those things.

RALPH WINTER (producer, *Star Trek VI: The Undiscovered Country*)

I had pitched Harve an idea, *The Academy Years,* at his daughter's bat mitzvah. I remember saying to him we shouldn't make *Star Trek V.* We should make *Star Trek V, VI,* and *VII.* We've just demonstrated with *Star Trek III* that we can do a young Spock. We should see how these guys meet the first time. And build something that would be a reboot of this with younger characters to pick up with when these older characters don't want to do this as much. He loved the idea. We followed up on it. We got the studio excited about it. David Loughery wrote a script and it was terrific. It was set in Huntsville, Alabama. It was the training ground for Starfleet Academy. It was young Kirk and Bones and Spock, who was the first off-worlder to attend. The three of them become friends and they're all the extremes that were presented in the TV series. Spock is überlogical, Kirk is the ladies man and always out there, and Bones is trying to be a medical student.

HARVE BENNETT (producer, *Star Trek V: The Final Frontier*)

A proposal was made to me that we could do *Star Trek* in the beginning, which was Ralph Winter's idea. Let's do them at the academy. That picture seems to have worked in a variety of incarnations including *Top Gun*.

DAVID LOUGHERY

Harve always had this ace up his sleeve, which was if we can't get everybody together for one of the *Star Trek* movies, we should do a prequel.

HARVE BENNETT

I suggested we develop a series of films to be another franchise, another tentpole that we could open. We could do a prequel and find out how Kirk and Spock met at Starfleet Academy. When we were doing *Star Trek V,* we got the studio to approve work on the script. It is an excellent story, but it has been misperceived. It's a great story finding out about this young cocky character on a farm who goes to flight school and meets up with the first alien that comes from Vulcan and how they meet the other characters. It would have been a gift for the fans on the twenty-fifth anniversary.

DAVID LOUGHERY

When I heard about the idea, I thought it was terrific. Not from the point of view of recasting, but from the point of view of storytelling, because I worked so closely with these characters on *Star Trek V* that the idea of doing an origin story—where you show them as young cadets and kids—was tremendously exciting. What it was, was a real coming-of-age story. In outline form, it was the story of Kirk and Spock meeting for the first time as cadets here on Earth. We've got a young Jim Kirk, who's kind of cocky and wild. He's not exactly what you might think starship-captain material might be. He's like one of these kids who would rather fly hot planes and chase girls. Spock is this brilliant, arrogant, aloofto-the-point-of-obnoxiousness genius. It's the mask he's hiding behind to cover his own conflicting human emotions. He's an outcast, he left Vulcan in shame against his father's wishes, and like all adolescents, he's trying to find a place to fit in, but he keeps screwing it up.

Over the course of this story, which is one year at Starfleet Academy, Kirk and Spock are sort of put to the test and they begin as rivals and end up as friends and comrades who learn that they have to combine their talents for the first time to defeat a deadly enemy. In the final scene, where they say good-bye at graduation and go their separate ways, we're able to see the legends that these two boys are going to grow up to become.

HARVE BENNETT

We did the best we could on *V* and when it was over, I went to see [studio president] Ned Tanen, who was the last of the decisive people at Paramount before the bean counters took over, and he said, "Well, are we going to do another one?" I said it was time to do the prequel, and he said, "Do it." It was later that everybody else asked for long meetings. Our model, or mock-up, was *Santa Fe Trail*, a Warner Bros. movie made in 1940 about John Brown's raid on Harpers Ferry. We gave Kirk a genuine love affair with an eighteen-year-old, her first. The girl dies heroically. Kirk, insane with grief, performs his first heroic act against all odds. And Spock saves the day in a struggle with racist overtones, getting the medal of honor. The prequel story ends over the grave of his lost love, giving some insight into why Kirk never falls in love again for the rest of the *Star Trek* series. At the end of the film, while the older Kirk is contemplating her passing, Spock beams down and asks him if he's going into teaching or back to the ship. They have a sentimental exchange and Bill says, "Beam me up."

DAVID LOUGHERY

We felt that there was a powerful story there, one that the audience would be interested in. We're always interested in young Indiana Jones and young Sherlock Holmes, and how they started and come to be who they are. This was sort of the way to explain Kirk and Spock and where they came from.

HARVE BENNETT

We had a better movie and we had a film that would have allowed them to make the same *Star Trek VI* eighteen months later.

WALTER KOENIG (actor, "Pavel Chekov")

I think there was a fat chance of that happening. I can't read Harve's mind, but if *The Academy Years* had done well, they would have gone on with that group. If it hadn't, they probably would have abandoned the whole project.

HARVE BENNETT

It meant a lot to me because I came out of UCLA film school wanting to be a director and other winds blew me to other ports. It was a desire of mine to direct, and it was accepted by the studio and, the fact is, part of the deal was for us to do a *Star Trek VI*, with the original cast after *The Academy Years*.

DAVID LOUGHERY

Harve *really* wanted to do it. He wasn't really interested in producing anymore.

GENE RODDENBERRY (creator, *Star Trek*)

I didn't like it. Who was going to cast the new Kirk and Spock? I could have done so if I thought it was a good idea, but it didn't fit in with the rest of *Trek*. It wasn't good. Some of it was like *Police Academy*. You could hardly do this without the magic of a group of characters tailored for *Star Trek*, which this was not.

RALPH WINTER

Gene just stomped his foot and threatened the studio to not support the movie or endorse it. And they needed his endorsement for the core fans. They listened to that. But he didn't have any veto power.

DAVID LOUGHERY

We were really caught off guard and surprised by the fans who reacted so negatively to the idea of this movie. Somehow they conceived it as a sort of spoof or a takeoff. That's where we got off on the wrong foot. The fans had misinformation, which may have been put out there by people for their own reasons. Certainly if we were going to make a movie like that, it meant that Walter and whoever wouldn't get that job a year or two down the line that they had come to expect. I don't know if that's the case, but I do know that the misinformation released had people convinced that we were going to do a cross between *Police Academy* and *The Jetsons*. But I think it's traditional that the fans have objected. Harve's always been smart enough to double-cross them. Give them what they've objected to, but surprise them with something that makes it good and works out.

JAMES DOOHAN (actor, "Montgomery 'Scotty' Scott")

I was impressed with Harve when he first came in and did *Star Trek II* and *III*, but I think he got a little greedy. He wanted things his own way. He wanted to take over *Star Trek* for himself. He obviously did not realize the strength of the old cast. The whole thing would have been starting out as if from scratch. I think it was [Paramount CEO Frank] Mancuso who didn't realize we were not going to be in it. When he found out, [he] said good-bye, Harve.

HARVE BENNETT

There was pressure from a lot of people not to do this. I don't think there was any question that the self-interest of the supporting cast was not served by it. And if I was George Takei, I would do exactly what he did, and if I were Jimmy Doohan, I would be a really unhappy man. The only one I'm really furious at though is Jimmy Doohan. He said I was fired and I can't abide lies. I was offered one and a half million dollars to do *Star Trek VI* and said, "Thanks, I don't wish to do that. I want to do *The Academy*."

WILLIAM SHATNER (actor, "James T. Kirk")

Harve was striving to find an answer for the studio's question: "Are these guys too old to continue?" So he tried to find a solution as a storywriter and he must have said here's a way of going. Apparently everybody agreed, but at some point they shut him down after preparing this production for a year, and he got very upset about it and left. I wasn't too clued in on the politics of what was happening. I had heard about the prequel and was considering my options, but it was never approved and we didn't know whether or not there would be another *Star Trek* until the last second.

HARVE BENNETT

My last words to Frank Mancuso before he was asked to leave [by the then recently installed head of Paramount, Stanley Jaffe] was if it was a question of anyone's concerns about my directing, I'd back off on that. They then offered me *Star Trek VI* and gave me a pay-or-play commitment to direct and produce *The Academy Years* afterward. My position was, and I think it was correct, that they would pay me to do *VI* and make the movie which would have been a real big, fat check for me and never make *The Academy Years*. To be paid off because the movie I might have done, which is being done by others, would close the franchise was not my intention. I had a life, it's not like I hadn't done anything else before *Star Trek*. The *Star Trek* curse is something that the poor supporting cast has to live with, but I don't.

RALPH WINTER

The Academy Years may have looked like a mistake, but look at the franchise as a whole. We had a successful series of feature films, then a new television series, and with the [original] film series ending, it made sense to start a new series of films. You could have opened a whole new frontier. When *Star Trek: The Next Generation* came out, the people said, "This will never work, how can we have a new captain? It will never equal Kirk and Spock." But they achieved their own success. It could have been the same with a prequel cast.

HARVE BENNETT

The Academy Years, like *Star Trek IV,* would have reached beyond the cult. It would have interested people who had never seen a *Star Trek* film which did not exclude the regulars, but it simply said, "If you don't understand what it's all about, come see how it all began."

GLEN C. OLIVER (film critic, *Ain't It Cool News*)

Colored by more than a few shades of *Top Gun*, the screenplay was filled with tremendous moments of warmth and heart—and focused heavily on its characters' journeys toward understanding themselves individually, and recognizing their potential as a group. It is as character-centric as *The Wrath of Khan* or *The Search For Spock*, and features the same unapologetic devotion to exploring the human condition demonstrated by those titles. Despite a few misplaced, miscalculated attempts at humor, there's a lot of truth in Loughery's work in *The Academy Years*—touchingly, surprisingly, admirably so at times. This would've been a very nice and affecting origin story when factored into the broader framework of the franchise, and that it didn't make it to screens remans highly regrettable.

DAVID LOUGHERY

I had an overall deal at Paramount and I thought that if I wrote it while we working on *Star Trek V,* it would be a great way to kind of balance my time, because we were shooting one *Star Trek* and working on the possibility of another one. It was never seen as a way to replace the original cast. Harve had always described it as a lucky strike extra. A special kind of present. And also, we realized that if things went along as planned, we could get it out for 1991 and the twenty-fifth anniversary as sort of a special gift to the fans, a look back. There was no reason why one couldn't continue to make *Star Trek* films with the original cast. It was just something that we thought could be done separately and as a bonus.

I would say I wrote three drafts over a period of about a year and a half. The first draft, the studio loved it. We thought, "Great! This is fantastic." They wanted a few minor changes, but we were really excited. But then, gradually, the studio kind of became reluctant in terms of setting a start date, and also, by that time, I think *Star Trek V* had come out and been a little bit of a disappointment and they were wondering whether they wanted to make *any* kind of another *Star Trek* movie at one point. Also, there were changes in the Paramount administration and a couple of the people who had really been supporters of the prequel left. Then I guess the studio started to think that they could squeeze one more *Star Trek* with the original cast.

RALPH WINTER

Harve was an elder statesman. He was a gentleman and he taught me a great deal about how I produce movies today. He was a writer-producer that comes out of that television tradition. He left all the production things to me. He didn't care about that as much as he cared about what the story is about and how is it going to be clear to the audience. If anything, he was *too* nice. But unfortunately we disagreed at the end of *Star Trek V*. He wanted to do the picture that we had developed, but ultimately Frank Mancuso wanted to mark the twenty-fifth anniversary. And so he wanted a movie with the original cast and Harve wanted a movie with a young cast. He drew a line in the sand and didn't participate in *Star Trek VI*. But that script, Paramount owned it, and then J. J. took off with it and updated a lot of stuff in the first movie that is clearly, if not an homage, a redevelopment of that script.

In the opening scene of the screenplay we developed were cornfields and a mailbox that is flapping back and forth in the wind and it says, "Kirk" on the mailbox. It sits on that for a moment, and then you hear something in the distance, and coming right at camera is a crop duster. A futuristic crop duster. And this young kid is at the wheel of it trying to fly it like a fighter jet. And he crashes it into the farm and burns it down. That's the opening of the *Star Trek* screenplay. We felt like we had something worthwhile and Harve put his job on the line. That's how much he believed in it.

HARVE BENNETT

It's forever marketable, because it deals with Spock and Kirk at seventeen, eighteen. It deals with the origin of prejudice against Vulcans, the invention of warp speed, the origins of the show. We were not only right there on this, but we were ready to cast it. I wanted Ethan Hawke to play Kirk—he hadn't even done *Dead Poets Society* yet. And I said, "I want John Cusack to play young Spock." He was then in his early twenties, but could have played teenaged, but they didn't see it. Martin Davis at Paramount said, "We can't do a picture without the real Kirk and Spock," so I put in something in the beginning in which the real Kirk and Spock appeared and told the story, then we flash-forwarded to them at the end. But that wasn't enough. They said the audience would be frustrated. I disagreed. They said they needed something for the twenty-fifth anniversary and it had to be something else. My term was up and I said, "Get somebody else." To this day, it's hard for me to talk about, because not only would it have been the biggest grosser of all, but it would have spawned yet another franchise.

THE FINAL ROUNDUP

"ONLY NIXON COULD GO TO CHINA."

With studio president Frank Mancuso passing on *The Academy Years*, it was full speed ahead for *Star Trek VI*, an anticipated swan song for the original cast with plans to pass the baton to *The Next Generation* in the next film. Unfortunately for the studio, the twenty-fifth anniversary was rapidly approaching and there was no script, no director, and no producer after Harve Bennett walked away from what would have been a lucrative gig. Paramount quickly enlisted star Leonard Nimoy as the film's executive producer and he, in turn, recruited writer-director Nicholas Meyer into the fold to deliver a film on a highly accelerated production schedule.

DENNY MARTIN FLINN
(cowriter, *Star Trek VI: The Undiscovered Country*)

Frank Mancuso had called Leonard into his office and said, "Leonard, help me make this film." At that point, Leonard was the producer, writer, the director, the star, and it was up to him to discharge those duties or pass them on to other people. Mancuso apparently knew he could trust him to get the whole thing going and to get it going quickly. That had something to do with *Star Trek V*. Let's face it, nobody wanted to have anything to do with anybody who had anything to do with *V*, except as necessary. I don't think *Star Trek V* was entirely Shatner's fault by any means. Moviemaking is a very collaborative business, but no one was happy with it.

WALTER KOENIG (actor, "Pavel Chekov")

I was supposed to come in and pitch Frank Mancuso my idea for *Star Trek VI* [*"In Flanders Fields"*]. I ended up submitting it on paper. I had three of the characters dying in the story. I thought we were all done. Certainly after *Star Trek I*, I thought we were done.

MARK ROSENTHAL
(cowriter, *Star Trek VI: The Undiscovered Country*)

We—Larry Konner and myself—were under contract at Paramount, and the feeling was that they were not going to do another *Star Trek* movie. The guys were getting old and *Star Trek V* was a disappointment. There was a bad taste in everyone's mouth and no one wanted to go out like that. They knew the twenty-fifth anniversary was coming up, and we were approached by the vice president of production, Teddy Zee, who called us up and said, "Frank Mancuso has spoken to Leonard. Leonard was still upset because of the last one and he was floating out the idea of one last adventure." He asked us what we thought about it. The reality was that I am a Trekkie and my partner is incredibly non-science-fiction oriented. We were kind of a yin-yang, but we liked that idea, because Larry would provide good balance.

RALPH WINTER (producer, *Star Trek VI: The Undiscovered Country*)

Bill had a good time directing *Star Trek V* and we stumbled. I'm sure Bill feels hurt by the results of that, but he's a big guy. He knows what happened and he's got his head held high and he's fine.

WILLIAM SHATNER (actor, "James T. Kirk")

I felt a sense of loss that I couldn't be the problem solver. I would have loved to have been immersed in those very same problems and bring to bear what I had learned on the previous film. But on the other hand there was a sense of tremendous relief, as I was only too aware of the pressures on Nick Meyer both from a production point of view and a political view from the studio, and as time would get short, the anxiety that was involved in trying to get it done on time. I was very sensitized to the things he needed to accomplish.

MARK ROSENTHAL

Our initial response was that we should do something where *The Next Generation* has to come back in time and work with the classic cast. The poster would be Patrick Stewart, William Shatner, Leonard Nimoy, and Brent Spiner. That would have easily been a hundred-million-dollar film. Feelers were put out on that and there were some very strong *negative* responses. The TV department was totally against it. The TV series was doing extremely well, and everyone was afraid that the old guys' egos would get involved and they would say that it was a sign of a lack of confidence that they could carry the film. So that was the end of that.

LEONARD NIMOY
(actor/producer, *Star Trek VI: The Undiscovered Country*)

The Berlin Wall had come down. The Russian government was in severe distress. Communism was falling apart. These changes were creating a new order in our world. I thought there would be a kind of dialogue, a new thinking of these relationships. Realizing that over the twenty-five-year history of *Star Trek* the Klingons have been the constant foe of the Federation, much like the Russians and Communists were to democracy, I wondered how we could translate these contemporary world affairs in an adventure with the Klingons. I thought it would be ideal since the Klingons were a parallel for the Communist bloc, the "Evil Empire." It just made sense to do that story.

MARK ROSENTHAL

The main thing we were concerned with was that we had never really gotten details about the Klingon Empire. There was a whole question of whether we should go to the actual home planet. What happened was that they felt in terms of budget, re-creating the entire planet would be impossible, so it became this prison concept. The original idea was to go to the actual capital city. I still think this was a better idea, but you can see how this process happens.

The first *Star Trek* had a horrendous budget and it was a bad movie. Paramount began to realize that the Europeans did not grow up with *Star Trek*, so there's a very small market for it. The studio always feels that they have to make their money in a domestic situation, which for a big-budget special-effects movie is tough. When you write, you try to come up with stories that take place in one ship, because that's pretty cheap to do. When you start talking about sets and locations, the budget gets very high. Leonard decided that he didn't want to direct this movie. We knew that Nick was interested. He was negotiating an overall deal with Paramount and we were pretty much left alone and began writing.

NICHOLAS MEYER
(cowriter/director, *Star Trek VI: The Undiscovered Country*)

I had just had a terrible experience making a movie, *Company Business*, in which I had my nuts handed to me. It was ghastly. And so the idea of climbing back on a horse, *any horse,* was really important and I thought I probably couldn't have a friendlier horse than the *Star Trek* horse. I had absolutely no idea what a *Star Trek* movie would be. I never do. I never get many ideas, and the ideas I get, most of the time stink.

I was on Cape Cod with my family where I go every summer for a couple of weeks, and Leonard, who hails from Boston, flew to Provincetown for the day. And it was a very pleasant day. We walked up and down the beach and he said, "I have an idea for another *Star Trek* movie." And he said, "You know the Klingons have always been our stand-in for the Russians." And I'm thinking, "Did I know that?" It seemed obvious the moment he said it. And he said, "The wall is coming down, and what if the wall came down in outer space? Who am I if I have no enemy to define me?" And all he needed to do was prime the pump. Leonard went back to California and I thought, "Okay, we're off and running." And then he called me and said, "This is very strange but they hired two other guys."

MARK ROSENTHAL

The wonderful thing about *Star Trek* was that it was always sort of an allegory of the United States and the Soviet Union. We had two meetings with Leonard and Teddy [Zee], where we said the film should be about a peace with the Klingons and that it would be a nice parallel to reality. We were always arguing politics, so we thought this would be an opportunity to get some allegory in there. In other words, if it had been a movie like the first one, about a satellite coming back, we would not have done it. I think *Star Trek* works best when it's an allegory.

NICHOLAS MEYER

I still was the director on the project and it was really strange. And then I got a call from one of the executives, John Goldwyn, who said, and I quote, "The boys are having a little trouble getting started." And I said, "What do you mean they're having a little trouble getting started? Send them to London, because that's where I live and I'll talk them through it." Which may not have been the right thing. I probably should have touched base with Leonard to see what he thought, but I don't know what I thought I was doing. Probably not very smart.

One of these gents showed up in London, stayed a couple of days with a yellow legal pad on his lap. Back in those days it wasn't an ice planet, it was a sand planet. [Studio executive] David Kirkpatrick said, "I'm tired of sand." And we later changed it to ice. And then they weren't happy with that script, and finally I was being brought back to write it. In the meantime, my wonderful assistant and sometimes screenwriter Denny had fallen gravely ill. I decided that I would cowrite it with him; it would give him a reason to get through radiation and all that other stuff. I could tap into all his wonderful stuff and he'd make some money. At this point, Paramount was not in a position to say anything but yes. They didn't know who he was. It didn't matter.

DENNY MARTIN FLINN

Nick was involved with *Company Business* in London and wasn't going to be able to write the screenplay in time to get the film into production for the release date that would coincide with the twenty-fifth anniversary. So he told Paramount that the only way he could do it is if he could cowrite the script with me, and that's how it came about. He was kind enough to trust me, and while he was in London we communicated via computer. When we turned in our first draft, the studio green-lighted it.

MARK ROSENTHAL

Leonard at one point went to see Nick, after we had had all our meetings. What he did was present our story to Nick. I know Nick honestly believed that the story came from Leonard, but that was after three months' work. We know Nick's a writer. We weren't naïve about it. We knew he would rewrite whatever we did, but we didn't expect them to try and freeze us out.

NICHOLAS MEYER

Leonard said to me, "Let's make a movie about the wall coming down in outer space." His statement just spoke to me. What I wanted to do with it was to widen the world of *Star Trek* before closing out the series. The thing I've learned from these movies is that your only chance of succeeding is not to repeat yourself, not to try the same exact thing. I didn't want to go mano a mano because I had done that with *II,* and I didn't want to make a comedy because I felt *IV* was the most broadly comedic of any of them. So I thought, "I want to make an ensemble piece and I want it to be a political thriller."

WILLIAM SHATNER

It was a very good idea. It's a classic *Star Trek* idea in that the important issue of the day is incorporated in the story of *Star Trek,* and by doing so—and because we put it into the future—we're able to comment on it as though it has nothing to do with today, yet it makes a commentary.

MARK ROSENTHAL

At one point we had a discussion about using Chernobyl, and that really opened the floodgates. Then we began to look at specific events. Everyone was paranoid that someone is going to try and sabotage the peace between the Soviet Union and the United States. Why not have the same thing occur between the Klingons and the Federation? It all kind of led to the idea of assassination. What if Gorbachev was assassinated and the blame fell on Kirk? That was really the key.

NICHOLAS MEYER

Star Trek in many ways tends to reflect what's going on in the real world. At its best, *Star Trek* appears to function as pop metaphor, taking current events and issues—ecology, war, and racism, for example—and objectifying them for us to contemplate in a science-fiction setting. The world it presents may make no sense as either science or fiction, but it is well and truly sufficient for laying out human questions. Removed from our immediate neighborhoods, it is refreshing and even intriguing to consider Earth matters from the distance of a few light-years. Like the best science fiction, *Star Trek* does not show us other worlds so meaningfully as it shows us our own—for better or for worse, in sickness and health. In truth, *Star Trek* doesn't even pretend to show us other worlds, only humanity refracted in what is supposed to be a high-tech mirror.

DENNY MARTIN FLINN

When *Star Trek* relies on science fiction, it's a big failure. Maybe that's part of why nobody likes *Star Trek I* and *V* very much. Gene Roddenberry originally called *Star Trek* "*Wagon Train* to the stars," because westerns served the purpose in our society of being morality tales about good guys versus bad guys and, in many cases, in those thousands of westerns it was irrelevant that the setting was the old West. What was important and great in a movie like *Shane,* for instance, was the story of the individual in society, and *Star Trek* is best when it's a morality play. That's what Gene called the original episodes, so when Leonard came up with the idea that the Klingons could stand in for the Russians and we could deal with the end of the Cold War, we were home free in terms of fundamentals that we knew worked.

MARK ROSENTHAL

I can tell you that from April to August of that year we developed the story and the screenplay, and suddenly we were pushed off. It's funny, too, because Larry and I are a couple of lefties and anyone who knows us knows we wrote the story.

NICHOLAS MEYER

The studio had a whole bunch of notes and suggestions which I unwisely did not pass on to Leonard, because I told myself, "Let him make up his own mind without the promptings of the studio." But he was very pissed off and he thought I was duplicitous. Maybe I was. I think I just wanted him to not have their notes and just do his notes. We ironed it out and eventually that's how the script was written. I never saw what the other gents had done. I'm so susceptible, so easily influenced that, as in the case of *Star Trek VI,* I knew if I saw it I'd never shake it out of my skull.

MARK ROSENTHAL

One of the things that Nick changed in the movie is there's this relationship between Spock and Valeris. We said, "Look, Spock was already killed in one movie, so we can't do that. If this is going to be the last movie, let's do something really shocking. Let's break the mold a little bit." In fact, I remember in the first meeting with Leonard, we sat and watched the Robert Bly tape about old warriors.

Bly is an American poet who started the men's groups that go out into the woods. His position is that there are no positive male guardian figures, and one of his theories is that the old warrior in tribal society has to teach the young warriors how to do things.

We kind of watched that tape and said, "These guys are old warriors now, let's really make it that they're at the end of their career." I very much wanted to have Kirk fall in love with Saavik, a Vulcan, so that they would produce a people who would be like Spock, who himself had a human mother and a Vulcan father. I thought it would be a wonderful way to bring the characters and their relationships to a close. Obviously they changed that to Spock falling in love. Frankly, I don't feel it's as satisfying.

RALPH WINTER

Nick is real smart. He's such a good writer. He's really committed to his work and he works very hard and pushed everybody and the envelope. Leading the troops, he challenged everyone to put out their best, and we had a good time doing it. He's terrific and he does things that seem a little unorthodox. He brings a class and sophistication to the material that is great.

MARK ROSENTHAL

We had done a couple of things which they kind of simplified. Instead of Kirk just going to the Klingons, he was arrested by Sulu and turned over to them, which was a very dramatic moment for Sulu. We also wanted to do this thing where while he was in prison, some of the characters they had met over the twenty-five years would be there, which we felt really would have tied up the entire series.

We also discussed the fact that the Klingons are this aggressive race. Originally, they supposedly had this reptilian background. In regards to this whole thing about Kirk and his search to uncover the conspiracy behind the assassination, we come upon more primitive Klingon tribes who had an almost religious representation for the Klingons. They would be much more primitive and violent. We were going to do a whole thing on the anthropology of the Klingons, but all of that was dropped because it would have been too expensive.

The other thing that we did, which Nick changed, was if you look at the second movie which he directed, he dropped in all of those references from *Moby-Dick* and *A Tale of Two Cities,* but this whole thing with Shakespeare in *Star Trek VI* . . . I think it got carried away. What we did was we had a literary reference from a wonderful poem called "The Idle King," and it was about Ulysses and the end of his life, where he and his crew are very old and they decide to go off on one last voyage, and it was very clearly a voyage to death. You know, old men rowing the boat again. So we had this bit where Kirk mentions it to Spock. Then Kirk is turned over to Sulu who turns him over to the Klingons, only it turns out that the president of the Federation arranged it all secretly so Kirk *let* himself get arrested. Ours had a little more twists and turns. We had this thing where Kirk at the beginning is talking to Spock about the Trojan horse, and the way they get him out is they let the Klingons capture the *Enterprise,* which they seem to have abandoned. But they've stowed away, like Ulysses and the Trojan horse, and that's how they free Kirk. So we had different literary references. I think that ours was a lot more textured. All of the beats of the story were worked out in the script. Then Nick came in with Denny. There was a lot of budgetary simplification.

NICHOLAS MEYER

Frank Mancuso and [Paramount chairman] Martin Davis took me to lunch when I was living in London, at Claridges, and proposed a sixth *Star Trek* movie that Leonard was going to executive-produce for a budget of thirty million dollars and I said okay. When I arrived in America, I walked into a meeting with [president of the Motion Picture Group] David Kirkpatrick and [Paramount Pictures president of production] Gary Lucchesi and they said, "Now, we're talking twenty-five million dollars." I said, "In London, Frank said thirty and that's what I agreed to."

I knew what had happened in the interim, which was that the feature division had just had flop after flop after flop, and they were forty-million-dollar movie flops. They were running scared, but I did the math for them. I said, "Look, here's the problem: you have fourteen million dollars above the line [for cast, directors, producers fees, and screenwriters] in this movie just for starters. You have four and half million dollars in special effects, and these are all the numbers from *Star Trek V.* You have two and half million in post, whatever it was. And I'm willing to live with all of that at *thirty,* but don't ask me to make *Star Trek VI* for less than *Star Trek V,* because the money isn't there. Where's the movie going to be? I added it up and you have two million dollars left to make the movie!" And they said, "Would you excuse us for just a minute?"

They walked into another room leaving [producer] Steve Jaffe, Ralph Winter,

Leonard, and me sitting in Lucchesi's office. They came back in and said twenty-seven million, and I said, "You're confused. I'm not negotiating with you. I'm just giving you information. This can't happen." They accused me of not being a team player and I responded, "Oh, please. Don't give me the not-team-player thing. I'm going to go to Frank Mancuso and I'm going to lay out these numbers and let him make up his own mind what we're doing here." Which is what I did. I went to Frank and I laid it all out in black and white and I showed him the [budget] top sheet for every *Star Trek* movie starting with the 1979 one, which I think was forty-five million dollars. And I think *Star Trek II* was eleven million dollars. And each one after that was 41 percent more expensive than its predecessor. I said the only exceptions to this are *II*, which was made for 25 percent of *I*, and *VI* which I'll make for the same price as *V*, but I can't make it for less and here's why. He was very courteous; he heard me out. I left and he canceled the movie.

STEVEN-CHARLES JAFFE
(producer, *Star Trek VI: The Undiscovered Country*)

We were at a budgetary impasse and everyone resigned themselves to the fact that it was not going to happen. I went home and was very, very upset about it, because this meant a lot to me for personal and professional reasons. I just couldn't go to sleep. I grew up watching *Star Trek* on television, and doing this movie was a private honor. A lot of us took pay cuts and people say, "You took a pay cut on *Star Trek*—that's Hollywood, not personal." It meant a lot to us and the more we got involved with it, the more we were emotionally involved. I'm very happy to say I had a big part in making sure the movie got made. It was all teamwork.

NICHOLAS MEYER

What saved it was a phone call from Stanley Jaffe [the new head of the studio, no relation to Steven-Charles Jaffe] while I was throwing things in a box to leave my office and wondering what I was going to do about the rent on the house and stuff. He said, "I hear you got problems." "Well, I need five million dollars." And he said, "You got it." And that was the end of that.

RALPH WINTER

Bill and Leonard made concessions to get this picture made because they wanted to make it. We all did. Everyone made concessions, and frankly, Nick and Steven and I deferred a significant portion of our salaries to get this picture made, because we believed the story was worthwhile.

NICHOLAS MEYER

I told them it would take fifty-five days. They said, "You have fifty-one," and I yelled and screamed and they finally gave me fifty-three . . . and I came in at fifty-five.

WALTER KOENIG

They deferred part of their salaries. That's not the same as taking points. This was guaranteed, I hasten to add. The sixth movie was: "Let's cash in on the twenty-fifth anniversary; maybe there's still some tread left on the tire." But it's true the studios were backing down from big-budget films. Paramount had just gotten burned with *Godfather III*.

NICHOLAS MEYER

I remember at one point when we were filming the peace conference in the film; by this time everybody knew that the film was pretty damn good. John Goldwyn, who was the executive on the film, was looking at some of the chairs that we were using in this meeting and he just shook his head and said, "We should have given you the money."

LEONARD NIMOY

I'm a Roddenberry disciple. He was very much involved. I went to him for regular meetings on this script. Every time we had a draft, I met with him and we discussed it. He was very intrigued with the idea that we would be exploring the relationship with the Klingons. He was concerned in this particular story about the prejudice question, and it *is* an interesting issue. Sometimes when you show people showing a prejudice, even though your intention is to show that they're wrong, there are going to be people who identify with them.

NICHOLAS MEYER

Without seeing himself in relation to Roddenberry as the heir or the keeper of the flame, Leonard knew how these movies worked, he knew the shape of the bottle. He was very protective of that. At one point, Kim Cattrall had posed for some still photographs on the set of the bridge of the *Enterprise* and they were racy photographs. She was just having fun. And he said no. He killed all of those. That was not going to be.

RALPH WINTER

I screened the movie *Star Trek VI* for Gene Roddenberry about a week or two before he died. He's a character. He had a great idea and he executed the great idea, but he couldn't follow through and he was not a people person. He was cantankerous and he had some kind of weird deal that if he found a problem with any of the scripts, they had to pay him to fix it. So he always had problems. He had to accept it. If he didn't, they had to pay him to fix it and change it. And so he was always employed. His wife was down in the cutting room taking short ends of film prints and cutting them up and selling them for a dollar apiece. It was an odd group. But he loved the last movie. He watched it in a wheelchair covered with a blanket. He was cold and he was clearly on his way out. He had a great idea and he sponsored a great franchise.

SUSAN SACKETT (assistant to Gene Roddenberry)

The man was two days away from death when he saw *Star Trek VI*. They propped him up in a chair. He didn't have a clue what was going on. I don't think he had anything in his head at that point.

NICHOLAS MEYER

I cannot at this time remember whether I knew that he was ill or not. But regardless, even if he'd been in the peak of health, it would hardly have excused the somewhat impatient and high-handed way I was dealing with him. It's interest-ing, I had quite forgotten that we'd had run-ins over the screenplay of *Star Trek II* as well. I didn't recollect any of that until I was shown evidence of our correspondence. The *Star Trek* conception is a bottle, and into that bottle you can pour different vintages, but you're not allowed to change the shape of the bottle. And I think that the way I see it, rightly or wrongly, is that I was sort of obeying those rules. Maybe the brew that I had put in there was a stronger brew . . . or stranger, but it still fit into the bottle.

LEONARD NIMOY

Here you've got a couple of guys saying, "What do you think of the smell? Only the top-of-the-line models can talk." Gene was concerned about that stuff. He [Roddenberry] said, "I don't feel good about *Enterprise* crew talking that way." We pointed out these are bad people who are racists and who turn out to be assassins. "I'm just uncomfortable with a couple of guys walking around in Fed-eration uniforms talking that way about another race." And I understood it. It's a danger. By and large, he was quite taken with the idea of a Klingon détente. It was his idea to put a Klingon in the Federation on *The Next Generation* and this was the beginning of that link.

NICHOLAS MEYER

Very famously William Gillette asked Arthur Conan Doyle if he wanted Sher-lock Holmes to be put on the stage, and Arthur Conan Doyle said, "Sure." There was a famous exchange of telegrams between Gillette and Doyle. "May I marry Holmes?" and Doyle cabled back, "You may marry him or murder him or do what you like with him." Doyle always had very ambivalent feelings about Holmes, whom he had tried to kill off at least twice. Roddenberry was arguably much more protective and controlling about the world, the universe that he had created. And I think I was content to keep these characters as I found them. Kirk the bold adventurer, Spock the logical one, Bones the bleeding-heart lib-eral, and so forth. But where we differed was in our ongoing view of the human condition. Gene Roddenberry believed, or said he believed, in the perfectibility of man.

DENNY MARTIN FLINN

The first thing I did was sit down and in two days watch all the films and some of the episodes. Since I wasn't a Trekkie, nothing was risky for me. There was an attitude on my part that if somebody in the first draft says Klingons don't eat with their left hand, they eat with their right, I'll just change it. That gave me a certain amount of freedom. I didn't worship those characters, so I was able to see them in a rather fresh light. The same was true with Nick, who, having done *II* and *IV*, knew a great deal more about it than me, but nevertheless is not constrained. He's willing to add to the lore.

WILLIAM SHATNER

In the script there's a wonderful line, "In space, all warriors are cold warriors." Both sides have come to define themselves by their antagonism. "What will I be without my enemy?" The best *Star Trek* stories have their genesis in real life.

DAVID A. GOODMAN (coexecutive producer, *Futurama*)

Star Trek VI did something that *Star Trek* always did, which was to say something about something currently going on, but in space. It's a movie that still holds up because, as opposed to *Star Trek V*, which is terribly cast, *Star Trek VI* is brilliantly cast. And I loved that Brock Peters, who was a good guy in *Star Trek IV*, turns out to be one of the conspirators. I saw *Star Trek VI* eleven times in the theater; there was something very satisfying about it.

DENNY MARTIN FLINN

There are three kinds of people in the universe of *Star Trek VI*. The people who wanted peace, the people who did not want peace for their own self-interest, and then there were people like Kirk, who had lived a certain way for twenty-five years vis-à-vis the Klingons, but were intelligent enough to say, What does the future have to offer? Maybe this isn't wrong. We were lucky to be able to see Kirk as a man who, if he was rigid at all, at least recognized his own rigidity. And, of course, it allowed us to create a character that in essence was a spokesman for the uncertainties and the whole idea of the undiscovered country. The future, being scary, got nailed down because we had a character that could say that.

NICHOLAS MEYER

The heroic thing about Kirk and the rest of the crew is their effort to acknowledge, to confront, and ultimately try to overcome their prejudice. If a man leaps into a raging torrent to save a drowning child, he performs a heroic act. If the same man leaps into the same pond to save the same child, and does so with a ball and chain attached to his leg, he must be accounted not less heroic, but more heroic for overcoming a handicap. That's what heroism and drama is about. Kirk is more of a hero for being a human being and not less because he's superhuman, which I never believed.

WILLIAM SHATNER

The portrayal of Kirk attempts to show a man who has spent a lifetime imbued with the idea that his mission in life is to subdue, subvert, and make the enemy submit to his nation's or his Federation's view. That's his whole training and that is the military training. He learns differently, and that is the classic dilemma that *Star Trek* has sought to present in its most successful shows.

LEONARD NIMOY

Spock experienced prejudice growing up half Vulcan and half human. In *Star Trek VI,* Spock becomes an emissary against prejudice and discovers, during the course of the story, his own prejudices.

NICHOLAS MEYER

Leonard is a highly intelligent, highly professional guy who's been around, who knows this business back and forth in ways that I certainly didn't at the time, and I would say even now he's several classes ahead of me. As the executive producer, he was certainly my boss, and the movie was his conception. It started off as his idea. There are certain people that you always sort of put a foot wrong with in some way . . . and I think I frequently put my foot wrong with Leonard.

I don't know if he brought out the worst in me or I brought out the worst in myself. But I think I exasperated him. Sometimes justifiably and maybe sometimes not. When we were editing the movie, he took the last reel home with an editor and played with it and then brought it back, and I did not realize that as far as he was concerned, this was final cut. I thought this was his pass at it and I would take a pass at it. And he was very angry that I had played with it. And in that case, I didn't think that was my fault. I don't think I understood and I probably would have argued about it and said, "Can we talk about this?" But it never even occurred to me. But there were other sections where I was clearly out of line and he took umbrage.

LEONARD NIMOY

Nick Meyer is a gadfly. Nick loves to speak in headlines. I remember one day we were talking about opera and he declared, "*Carmen* is the greatest opera ever written!" He was saying it as if he wrote it. There is something that attributes to him in that statement. That it is his perception, and therefore it's his baby. There is something possessive about it in the pronouncement. He's a great PR man. Of course, that's what he was before he wrote novels and screenplays.

NICHOLAS MEYER

During one of these movies, and I can't remember which one it was, I somewhat grandiosely said, "Well, they don't have any right to criticize me. I am the man who saved *Star Trek*." And Leonard said, "Oh, you? You alone?" And I felt stupid the moment I'd said it. It was like I was listening to my own PR. I thought, "You sound like a jerk."

RALPH WINTER

We went away from the visual effects on *Star Trek V* because we thought we were going to get something new and different from another guy, which didn't happen. We went back to what we know is proven, and stuff that ILM did was spectacular. We were the benefactors of technology for *T2*. The look of the picture, the cameraman, the set dresser, the designer—everything about this film was trying to stretch and be something the other films weren't. I was a key member of *Star Trek V,* and when someone talks about it, it hurts.

DENNY MARTIN FLINN

The budget caused us to lose several sequences which would have been very beneficial to the film. When you're in preproduction, sometimes what you substitute is better, so who's really to ever know? But my original vision of the film, which certainly would have been twice as much money, was an epic action-adventure, and it became a kind of detective story action-adventure. The word *epic* would not be considered applicable. Money always impacts on art.

Much like films such as *The Dirty Dozen* and *The Magnificent Seven,* the film would have opened with the recruitment of its protagonists, in this case by an enigmatic Federation envoy. After the teaser sequence in which the Klingon moon Praxis is destroyed and Sulu, who has been promoted to captain of the *Excelsior,* informs the Federation, the retired crew of the *Enterprise* would have been gathered together for one final mission. In the unfilmed sequence, the envoy with a mysterious glowing hand was to arrive first at Kirk's home during a rainy and foggy San Francisco evening while Kirk is making love to Carol Marcus, with whom he has apparently reconciled. "This sailor is in port for good," promises Kirk. "Take a good look at my retirement pay if you don't believe me. I can hardly afford to cross the street." But when there's a knock at the door, Kirk is stunned to find he's been called back to active duty. As Kirk leaves, Carol pleads, "But he's retired . . . you're retired!"—losing Kirk once again to a mission.

Getting into a flying car with the alien, Kirk is propelled through the skyline of San Francisco to where they find McCoy inebriated at an upscale medical dinner where the doctors are lamenting about a patient who actually had the audacity to request a house call, much to McCoy's utter disdain. Kirk is surprised to find that Sulu is registered as "still active" and Spock's status is mysteriously "classified."

The next stop is a hangar bay where Professor Montgomery Scott is lecturing a group of college students about Klingon technology in front of the Bird of Prey, fished out of the harbor from *Star Trek IV,* while a bored Chekov is found at a chess club losing to an alien. As they leave, Kirk warns Chekov about his opponent, "Never play chess with a full Betazoid," leaving Chekov to reply, "I vas robbed." Meanwhile, Uhura is recruited at a Federation radio station where she hosts a talk show. All of them gather at Starfleet Command for a briefing.

NICHOLAS MEYER

I loved [the roundup] and didn't want to lose it, but we just couldn't afford it. The movie was made under a very, very tight budget. The thing that *II* and *VI* have in common is that they're the only two in the series that cost less than their predecessors. I run a very tight ship. We wouldn't have gotten the movie made otherwise.

DENNY MARTIN FLINN

What I had done originally was to give every one of the seven principal actors an entrance. The scenes demonstrated who those people were and what they did when they weren't on the *Enterprise*. They were either retired or rotated to R & R, and it added some humanity and humor to the characters. I called it the roundup. It would have been a very effective sequence and we held on to it until the very last minute, but Paramount was saying, "We're going to discontinue pre-production unless you cut another million dollars out of the budget." We just had to drop fifteen pages. Maybe what I'm thinking of would have been rambling and slow and dropped in editing anyway, but there was a kind of *The Over-the-Hill Gang Rides Again* attitude.

NICHOLAS MEYER

I don't think the studio was willing to spend that kind of money. They were very disappointed with the revenues of *Star Trek V*, which was a very expensive movie. I don't think it lost money, but I don't think it made the kind of money they wanted.

DENNY MARTIN FLINN

Money always impacts art. Our budget was low for a science-fiction film. But it's hard to call *Star Trek* science fiction. We weren't trying to do *Terminator, Star Wars*, or *2001*, so maybe *Star Trek* is better off when it comes more from drama and less from the invention of more scenes with aliens and things. In fact, I found that because *Star Trek* grows out of a television series, there has always been an attitude of low budget; here's an alien planet and there's a foam rubber rock, and there's a red cyclorama in the background. The fans have not only put up with that but embraced it. It's as if they're saying, "We don't need your high-tech jazz to tell a morality play." Maybe it's smarter to do *Star Trek* with a smaller budget and force writers and directors not to rely on fancy pyrotechnics.

For the scenes on the ice planet, Rura Penthe, Steven-Charles Jaffe, also the film's second unit director, headed to Alaska for three days of filming to supplement the stagebound shots of the Klingon penal colony.

STEVEN CHARLES-JAFFE

It was two and a half days of very intense second unit work on a glacier, which normally would have taken a week and a half to two weeks to shoot. We were getting up at four in the morning, driving an hour, and flying an hour in a helicopter. It was ten degrees and we had one stunt man in about three and a half hours of very heavy makeup. We had a crew of thirty people and four helicopters. It was a real challenge.

NICHOLAS MEYER

Every director in the world would say, "I could've used more [money]," and I'm no exception. I didn't have it and that's the real world. You have to play the game. People may say how come we didn't do this or that, but that's nitpicking.

Long before he donned a Bajoran uniform aboard *Deep Space Nine* as Odo, actor Rene Auberjonois played the treacherous Colonel West, an Oliver North analogue, who is in league with the other conspirators, including *Star Trek IV's* Admiral Cartwright, once again played by *To Kill a Mockingbird's* Brock Peters.

RENE AUBERJONOIS (actor, "Odo," *Star Trek: Deep Space Nine*)

I almost wasn't in *Star Trek VI*, because the character was almost entirely cut out. I did it because Nick Meyer is a personal friend and asked me to. I was in Scotland hiking with my wife and rushed back to get the makeup all done. I've played a lot of different kind of parts and I usually play villains and I love them. I remember when my son was much younger and I was doing *Richard III* at the same time I was doing *Benson* and he asked, "Why do you always play the bad guy?" and I said, "It's because they're usually the best part to play."

NICHOLAS MEYER

When we were making *Star Trek VI* there was so much fighting in the executive offices. Frank Mancuso had been running the studio, Sid Ganis was head of production, and then Frank Mancuso left, Sid Ganis left, David Kirkpatrick left, and it was just like a musical chairs. Nobody was minding the store, so, we were left alone to make that movie. I think that a lot of times they are simply penny wise and pound foolish. They were always looking to cut the wrong corner, and the same thing with the budget for that whole movie. Where I had proved with geometric logic and hard numbers that every *Star Trek* movie, with the exception of *II,* cost 41 percent more than its predecessor, and I was proposing to do *VI* for the same price as *V,* two years later, they were still going to chop four or five million dollars out of it. It was silly.

I remember that when the movie was over and we were in the cutting room, the coup happened in the Soviet Union. Gorbachev disappeared and nobody knew if he was alive or dead. And I blush to say that we thought, "Oh, this is so cool for the movie." We really didn't waste a thought, certainly not that first day, on what had happened to this poor man. And I remember John Goldwyn calling and saying, "How soon can we get the movie out?" I said, "We're waiting for three hundred special-effects shots, I don't think we can get it out right away." There's a certain tunnel vision.

WALTER KOENIG

I was absolutely fucking miserable from day one on *Star Trek VI*. It was so disappointing to me . . . and I didn't even have Harve Bennett to blame anymore. Ralph Winter is a charming, delightful, and considerate man, and I had considered Nick a booster of mine because he had written the best stuff in *Star Trek IV* as well as directing *Star Trek II,* but I found this script to be so totally devoid of any individuality for the supporting characters. It was as if you could literally have taken one long speech and taken a scissor to it, cut it into pieces, and handed it to us.

For me, it was not a wrap-up at all. I thought, at last some recognition, some attention had to be paid to the supporting characters, and given their moment. There were no first-person personal pronouns; none of us ever said "I." It was always "Keptain, there is a ship out there," not "Keptain, I see a ship out there and I'm worried about this." We were there as expository vehicles, and that alone, and that was really painful. My sense of ego and identity just cried out for some opportunity to express character, and it was just not available.

RALPH WINTER

I remember on *Star Trek VI* I had an idea that we should do a press conference to promote the movie on the bridge of the *Enterprise* and we should do it with all of the cast. Leonard kind of pushed that off and said, "Do you want Jimmy Doohan to make up stuff about the engineer? And what the engineer thinks about *Star Trek*? Because what Jimmy Doohan does is from a script. You don't want Jimmy Doohan writing that stuff." It's one thing to let Leonard and Bill do that who had more of a public presence, but with the rest of them, it could have been a disaster. I always thought that would have been a cool idea if we could have pulled it off, but the studio was afraid that if it wasn't scripted, they were not sure what they were going to say, so it didn't get very far.

WALTER KOENIG

I had written pages of notes before we started shooting and gave them to Ralph, who thought they were all very germane. It was not to subvert the story, but to make the words the character had on-screen at that time significant. Ralph told me he gave them all to Nick, who never acknowledged them, so every time we did a scene, I was angry. I became angry at the other actors. I didn't blow up or scream and carry on, but I was in a state of constant agitation. I wanted this to be what the other actors apparently felt that it was, which was a wrap-up in a way that made it feel that we had grown as characters and the audience had an opportunity to really experience who we were. Ultimately, what I decided is there is a huge irony about *Star Trek*. It was always a show about the future, and the supporting characters were hopelessly immersed in the past. We never grew, we were the same characters we were on the television series, and we never had a chance to develop, to go into the future with the stories and the *Enterprise*. We were forever stuck back in the sixties in terms of the lack of dimension of the characters and the studio perspective on who we were as actors and characters.

RALPH WINTER

Jack Palance was an early choice for Gorkon, the Klingon chancellor, although David Warner did a great job for us. He's a good actor and he fit the role so we brought him back.

NICHOLAS MEYER

Chang [the Klingon general] is not Khan. Khan is a very specific individual, and they're not the same. You want an antagonist worthy of somebody's steel and you want to throw people curveballs if you can.

It's the only time other than [for] the *Star Trek* cast that I ever knowingly wrote for one actor, because I had this CD of Christopher Plummer doing the excerpts from *Henry V.* And I so fell in love with this that I thought, "I'm going to write a character based on the guy who's doing these excerpts and then I can just get him to recite Shakespeare for me whenever I want." I said to Mary Jo Slater, my indefatigable casting director, "Mary Jo, do not come back without Chris Plummer or I can't make this movie."

DENNY MARTIN FLINN

The person I had in mind for the changeling was as different as night and day from Iman. I had Sigourney Weaver in mind, but I'm not sure that we didn't come up with a better choice. I just saw the character as a big, ballsy, space pirate; a female version of the dark side of Han Solo.

RALPH WINTER

Nick wanted to go with actors who were going to make a contribution and really wanted to work with us. That's what attracted us to Kim Cattrall, Rosanna DeSoto, and Kurtwood Smith and, in other places, we went for a specific look, and also a good actor, Iman.

HARVE BENNETT (producer, *Star Trek V: The Final Frontier*)

The only serious problem that I would have never allowed if I were king was that, for the first time in the *Star Trek* movies, they violated the rules of some of the characters. They did not behave in character, and the reason for that is Nick always wanted to do that and I was always there to say no. I would have never had Spock do some of the things he did in that movie, and I would have never allowed Shatner to be in drag and fight with himself and to do all that stuff, because those things in the series did not appeal to me because it was like, "Look at me, I'm Bill Shatner."

The final thing, and Nick surprised me on this, is that in *Star Trek II* we got away with quoting *Moby-Dick* and *A Tale of Two Cities* because it worked and Nick had a blinding vision that this was like *Moby-Dick* and the whole picture became a metaphor. And it was a very good metaphor. But Christopher Plummer plumbing the depths of Shakespeare and coming up with "to be or not to be" because he ran out of other quotes, came to me like a punching bag and that pulled me out of the picture.

WALTER KOENIG

The thing I can say about *Star Trek VI* that it has going for it that none of the other films had is the preponderance of quality guest performers. We have some really strong people. Kim was wonderful; there's a mind-meld scene that's the first time a mind meld is really sexy. It's very sensual.

KIM CATTRALL (actress, *Star Trek VI: The Undiscovered Country*)

I took the name Valeris from the Greek god Eros, the god of strife. And we dropped the vowel because it sounded more Vulcan. I felt it was very much my own. I don't think she's like the other women in *Star Trek*. In the sixties, they were mostly beautiful women in great-looking, tight outfits with fabulous makeup and hairdos, more set decoration than real motivators in the mechanics of the plot.

NICHOLAS MEYER

I met a lot of pretty girls. It was amazing. There were some beautiful women who came out for it. But Kim was the only one who got the Vulcan-ness of it. The straight-faced "You must be very proud," [and] "I don't believe so, sir."

STEVEN-CHARLES JAFFE

It's not easy to play a Vulcan. There are a lot of people who did readings where either there was nothing there with absolutely no emotion, or there was too much. Kim was exquisite, because she had the proper balance of not showing emotion but also being very alive. You knew there was this very smart person worthy of being opposite Leonard Nimoy as Spock.

NICHOLAS MEYER

Leonard always told me that he never played a man with no emotions, but a man who always was holding his emotions in check.

KIM CATTRALL

I wanted a very definitive Vulcan woman. I was a warrior. I wanted a bold look to make it very different from what had come before. I came in to Nick after everything was settled and I said I want to have traces of Leonard, so I dyed my hair black and had it done very sixties and shaved my sideburns, because I felt my ears would look much stronger. I was a revolutionary and I wanted my appearance to reflect that. The great thing about the hairdo was the way I could just put it over my ear so you wouldn't be able to see the ears. Then I could sort of surreptitiously put it behind my ear and that was really fun. I've kept all my ears. It's a wonderful memory of having done the movie.

DENNY MARTIN FLINN

There was a desire to get Kirstie Alley to play Saavik. When that looked like it was going to be impractical, we couldn't stand around waiting for a decision—maybe the money was too much—for whatever reason. We reached a point where Kirstie Alley could not be counted on to do the film and we said, let's forget it. Let's create another character, which led to some nice changes.

KIM CATTRALL

I told Nick I really wanted to wear a skirt, like Uhura, since I have great legs. He said, "Kim, if I put you in a skirt, people will be looking at your legs." And I said, "So?" The uniforms are nice, but they were made in 1982 for someone else. I really wanted a new uniform, but when they fitted me for a costume they told me they couldn't get any more material. I didn't want to sweat in someone's old jacket. I had to completely reshape it so I'd look like a woman. I wasn't into hiding things at that point in my life. I feel good about the way I look and as a woman I enjoy feeling sexy. I think in science fiction, women should look great . . . and so should men. That's why people go to the movies.

NICHOLAS MEYER

The history of *Star Trek* is like *Rashomon*. I'll give you an example. Leonard Nimoy gave an interview where he claims one of the times he got most upset with me was when we were filming the confession scene where Spock is mind-melding with Valeris to ferret out the traitors. It's a very emotionally intense scene. And he said that I showed up on set that day dressed as Sherlock Holmes, which was very distracting and trivialized the moment. In fact, I've never dressed up as Sherlock Holmes . . . ever. I was, however, dressed in a suit and tie that day since I was going to the symphony. So it definitely was a case of our memories playing tricks on us.

KIM CATTRALL

My first scene was in sick bay. We did one of the last scenes first and it was like some wonderful fantasy. I would look over at Chekov and say, "Am I dreaming or is this true?" It's like being caught between fantasy TV land as a kid and the reality of being a working actress—this is my character, this is my job. At the first rehearsal the cast comes up to you, and these people whom you've watched since you were seven or eight on television welcome you aboard. You can't help but feel part of this unique legacy and family.

RALPH WINTER

We did some fun things in that movie with weightlessness and floating blood and all that stuff. But ultimately the story is not that good guy–bad guy classic movie like *Wrath of Khan* was. It was a bit more intellectual.

LUKAS KENDALL (editor, *Film Score Monthly*)

The musical miracle of the movies is that twice Nicholas Meyer had no money for a name composer and picked an entry-level twentysomething—James Horner (*Star Trek II*) and Cliff Eidelman (*Star Trek VI*)—and both worked out brilliantly. As great as Goldsmith's first *Star Trek* score is, personally I like *Star Trek II* even better, with Horner's nautical sweep and heartfelt take on Spock. That's as good as film scoring gets. At the scoring sessions, Meyer, an avid classical music buff, recognized Horner pilfering from Prokofiev's "Battle on the Ice" from *Alexander Nevsky* in "Battle in the Mutara Nebula." He pulled him aside and asked, "What is this?" Horner sheepishly admitted, "I'm young, I haven't outgrown my influences."

NICHOLAS MEYER

I would work with Cliff Eidelman again in a heartbeat—he supplied that rather extraordinary score. It was a blessing in disguise. Art thrives on restrictions. It's when you can't simply throw money at something you can get very clever and very creative. The whole idea is that any art should leave something to the imagination. That's where the viewer comes in; those horses tug that plow when they meet your eye. Oscar Wilde said that all art is useless, unless you impute significance to it. So I think that being unable to simply write a check to Jerry Goldsmith and have him do the heavy lifting made us do more heavy lifting. Or finding James Horner and stuff like that was good stuff. And ultimately enriched the series. It was another vintage to add to the brew.

LUKAS KENDALL

Eidelman's score for *Star Trek VI* is interesting for making the "villain" music the main theme and the heroic theme secondary; usually it's the opposite. Meyer wanted that score to be an adaptation of Holst's *The Planets*, but the rights were too expensive. Today, they'd be free—it's public domain.

CLIFF EIDELMAN (composer, *Star Trek VI: The Undiscovered Country*)

My Klingon theme is very different. I gave the Klingons more of an ominous theme and made it the main title. It's violently different from Holst, but the pulse is there to create a menacing idea. It gave me a theme for the opening.

When Kirk takes control one last time and as he looks out into the stars, he has that spark again. . . . one last time. And there's an unresolved note, because it's very important that he doesn't trust the Klingons. He doesn't want to go on this trip even though the spark is there that overtook him.

The film culminates with the final log of the Starship *Enterprise-A*. But in the version on screen, it's the cast, not the characters, signing off, which proved a disappointment to some.

CLIFF EIDELMAN

They reversed the order of the names so Shatner's is last, like an opera. It's a minute of signing off, which is real emotional.

DENNY MARTIN FLINN

My original script read that the signatures were James T. Kirk, Mr. Spock, etc. What we were doing was offering them a chance to sign the final log. I thought that would be rather touching, especially since it was the last film [with the original cast]. But it got changed to the actors instead of the characters and I personally disliked it very, very much. One of the actors who is executive produer who shall go unnamed, liked it. I suppose he'd rather see his own name than his character's name up on the screen. I thought no one gives a fuck about Leonard Nimoy and William Shatner and those people in any substantive *Star Trek* sense. Those people are Mr. Spock and Kirk and Dr. McCoy. I didn't see any point to the actors signing their name.

RALPH WINTER

There was a sense that this was it, that we were not going to make any more, so there was that bittersweet thing. Harve wasn't a part of that. It's the last movie for the original cast. We were clawing at the end of that genre of film about space battles with these great galleons in space, the Horatio Hornblowers, fighting. But it seemed clear to me that we weren't going to be able to compete with the fast moving TIE fighters of *Star Wars* and the need for bigger action. The action in *Star Trek* in television was mostly contrived. We would need to seriously reinvent it. That's why I wanted to go back and do the 1950s Republic serial view of the future with *The Academy Years*, because I felt that had more marketability than to just keep going in the same direction.

WILLIAM SHATNER

In *STVI* we took the legacy that Gene and Harve left us, and very successfully continued making a film that Nick, who has been a leading part of the continuation of *Trek*, had written and directed. And there are also the rest of us who have had our input, because if we didn't know something by now about *Star Trek*, we ought to be put away.

LEONARD NIMOY

I remember a story I heard about Gregory Peck and his early days. He met John Wayne for the first time. He told Wayne, who was an established star, that he had just finished making a movie. Wayne said, "Is it a good one?" And Peck said, "Yeah." Wayne said, "That's good. It takes two good ones out of five to keep the bicycle turning." I thought that was a very apt remark to make. You make two good films out of every five and you will spin. If you make less than that, chances are you get to the point of diminishing returns. You start to lose your opportunities. The offers don't come so readily. My sense of the *Star Trek* movies we made was that we did at least two out of every five good ones. We kept that thing spinning.

To Be Continued . . .

COMING THIS FALL
THE FIFTY-YEAR MISSION:
THE NEXT 25 YEARS
From The Next Generation to J. J. Abrams

ACKNOWLEDGMENTS

The authors would like to profusely thank everyone who graciously took the time over the years to be interviewed by us, in some cases multiple times for many, many hours. In addition, we're deeply indebted to David E. Williams, Sheldon Teitelbaum, Steven A. Simak, Joe Nazarro, Jeff Bond, James Van Hise, Karen E. Willson, John Kenneth Muir, Randy and Jean-Marc Lofficier, Tony Timpone, Dan Madsen, Steve Kriozere, Scott Arthur, and Jennifer Howard at the Archive of American Television, who were willing to share their own original material to help supplement this volume, where necessary.

In almost all cases, material is taken from original interviews conducted by the authors over the last three decades, with the exception of the aforementioned additional material as well as comments excerpted from public appearances at press conferences and/or conventions, along with original memo excerpts.

In addition, special thanks to our research assistants, without whose help we would probably be publishing this book for the sixtieth anniversary: our indispensable senior research assistant, Jordan Rubio, as well as Jacob DuBoise, Marie Lombardi, Derek Hedbany, and New York University professor Andrew Goldman, for his gracious assistance; as well as the enormously helpful staff of the UCLA Library Special Collections. Thanks for the use of the room.

The authors would also like to thank Stephen Pizzello of *American Cinematographer* magazine, for his contributions to this volume. Thanks also go to our friend Mark Gottwald, former publisher of *Cinefantastique* magazine, as well as to current publisher, Joe Sena.

No book on *Star Trek* would be complete without acknowledging the inestimable contributions to the genre by the late Frederick S. Clarke, creator of *Cinefantastique,* without whom none of this would have been possible. Fred was a mentor and an inspiration and—along with Kerry O'Quinn, founder of *Starlog*—is a legendary pioneer in the field of erudite sci-fi television journalism long before the world had ever heard of the Internet.

We would be remiss not to thank our patron saint, editor Brendan Deneen, his intrepid assistant, Nicole Sohl, and our publisher, the terrific Thomas Dunne. Our gratitude as well to our agent, Laurie Fox, at the Linda Chester Agency, for all her boundless enthusiasm throughout the process. Also, special thanks to our excellent copy editor, MaryAnn Johanson, without whose tireless efforts this book would be incomprehensible. Also a tip of the fedora to the brilliant Seth MacFarlane, for his contribution of this book's foreword. (Anyone who would cast *Flash Gordon*'s Sam Jones and feature "All Time High" from *Octopussy* in a movie is okay in our book.)

And, of course, our most profound thanks to the late, great visionaries Gene Roddenberry and Gene L. Coon, without whom we would not still be talking about (and watching) *Star Trek* five decades later.

We would also be remiss not to mention the thoughtful, supportive, and immensely talented Michael Piller, who left this world way too soon, as well as the late Robert H. Justman, Harve Bennett, and the incomparable Leonard Nimoy, who could've lived and prospered a little longer.

And last, but certainly not least, William Ware Theiss, for those amazing costumes that will forever be seared into our brains . . . until they are stolen by Imorg, at least.

ABOUT THE AUTHORS

MARK A. ALTMAN has been hailed as "the world's foremost Trekspert" by the *Los Angeles Times,* and has covered *Star Trek* for over a decade as a journalist writing for such publications as *The Boston Globe, Cinefantastique, Sci-Fi Universe,* and *Geek,* for which he was a founding publisher and editorial consultant. Altman also wrote numerous issues of the *Star Trek* comic book for DC and Malibu Comics.

Altman is probably best known to rabid *Star Trek* fans as the writer and producer of the beloved love letter to *Star Trek,* the award-winning cult classic *Free Enterprise,* starring William Shatner and Eric McCormack, the 1999 feature film about two dysfunctional *Star Trek* fans who meet their idol and find out he's more screwed up than they are. Altman was honored with the Writer's Guild of America Award for Best New Writer at the AFI Film Festival, among numerous other awards bestowed on the film.

Subsequently, Altman has been a writer-producer on such TV series as TNT's *Agent X,* ABC's *Castle,* and USA Network's *Necessary Roughness,* as well as the executive producer of HBO's *Femme Fatales,* which *Entertainment Weekly* called "a badass-chick anthology series" and the *Huffington Post* hailed as "pulpy fun."

In addition, Altman produced the big-budget film adaptation of the best-selling videogame *DOA: Dead or Alive,* as well as James Gunn's superhero spoof *The Specials* and the *House of the Dead* movies, based on the videogame series from Sega.

Altman has spoken at NYU Tisch School of the Arts and at numerous industry events and conventions, including the ShowBiz Expo and the *Variety*/Final Draft screenwriters panel at the Cannes Film Festival. He was a juror at the prestigious Sitges Film Festival in Barcelona, Spain, and has been a frequent guest and panelist at Comic-Con, held annually in San Diego, California, and a two-time juror for the Comic-Con Film Festival. He is also a 2014 graduate of the WGA showrunners' program and is a member of the Television Academy.

Altman lives in Beverly Hills, California, with his wife, Naomi; children, Ella and Isaac; three cats named Ripley, Giles, and Willow; and one tribble, which is hardly any trouble at all.

EDWARD GROSS is a veteran entertainment journalist who has been on the editorial staff of a wide variety of magazines, among them *Geek, Cinescape, SFX, Starlog, Cinefantastique, Movie Magic, Life Story,* and *SciFiNow.* He is the author of such nonfiction books as *Above & Below: The Unofficial 25th Anniversary Beauty and the Beast Companion, X-Files Confidential, Planet of the Apes Revisited, Superhero Confidential: Volume I,* and *Voices from Krypton.*

Gross lives in New York with his wife, Eileen; their sons, Teddy, Dennis, and Kevin; and a lovable mutt named Chloe.

To contact the authors with comments, questions, or requests for author appearances, please send an e-mail to us at: 50yearmissionbook@gmail.com.

Follow us on Twitter at:
@50yearmission
@markaaltman
@edgross